Reader's Digest
Great Biographies

CAPTAIN BLIGH AND MR. CHRISTIAN
by Richard Hough

It was a tragedy of truly classic proportions, the mutiny aboard His Majesty's ship *Bounty*, in 1789.

In this re-creation of those events—sometimes moving, sometimes shocking—distinguished naval historian Richard Hough sheds new light on the character of Captain Bligh and on the ultimate fate of the mutineers. Hough's search for the truth led him first to the Pacific Islands where the story all began. It also led, eventually, to the dark recesses of the heart, where he found that jealousy, pride, and envy had sown the seeds of the disaster.

Bligh turned to Christian and asked, "Do you consider this treatment a proper return for all the friendship I have given you in the past?"

Christian was visibly upset and uncertain how to answer. What was there to say? Their relationship, once so deep and passionate, had been shattered. In the words Christian spoke he showed again how deeply disturbed he was. "That—Captain Bligh—that is the thing—I am in hell—I am in hell!"

—from Captain Bligh and Mr. Christian

Reader's Digest

GREAT
BIOGRAPHIES

Reader's
Digest

GREAT
BIOGRAPHIES

selected
and
condensed by
the editors
of
Reader's
Digest

The Reader's Digest Association, Inc.
Pleasantville, New York
Cape Town, Hong Kong, London, Montreal, Sydney

The credits and acknowledgments that appear on pages 606–608
are hereby made part of this copyright page.

Library of Congress Cataloging-in-Publication Data
(Revised for vol. 5-12)
Reader's digest great biographies.

Contents: v. 1. The Spirit of Saint Louis/by Charles A. Lindbergh. Florence
Nightingale/by Cecil Woodham-Smith. Edison/by Matthew Josephson. Hans Christian
Andersen/by Rumer Godden—[etc.]—v. 11. Captain Bligh and Mr. Christian/by
Richard Hough. The agony and the ecstasy/by Irving Stone. The life and work of
Sigmund Freud/by Ernest Jones. Good night, sweet prince/by Gene Fowler—
v. 12. St. Francis of Assisi/by E. M. Almedingen. Napoleon/by Emil Ludwig.
Act one/by Moss Hart. My early life/by Winston S. Churchill.
 1. Biography—Collected works. I. Reader's Digest Association.
 II. Reader's digest. III. Great biographies.
 CT101.R42   1987   920'.02   86-29816
 ISBN 0-89577-259-0 (v.1)   ISBN 0-89577-303-1 (v.11)

Contents

CAPTAIN BLIGH
AND
MR. CHRISTIAN

A condensation of the book by
RICHARD HOUGH

•

Title painting by David Blossom
Illustrated by Chris Mayger

Their conflicting destinies
were charted not by honor,
but by the mysterious passions
of the human heart

The mutiny aboard the *Bounty*—it was the most celebrated event in the annals of maritime history. At the center of it, the complex young Mr. Christian and the irascible Captain Bligh. Their fateful confrontation, and its terrible aftermath, has all the power of a great novel; yet the story is true, the characters are real, and their ordeal is history.

Prologue

"THE PEOPLE ARE RIPE FOR ANYTHING"

A FEW MINUTES before 4:00 a.m. on April 28, 1789, Midshipman George Stewart felt his way down the main hatchway of His Majesty's Armed Vessel *Bounty*. The ship was creaking gently, like the bones of a tired old man, as Stewart went below to rouse his friend Fletcher Christian, now acting lieutenant. There had been little wind, and the air on the lower deck was humid and rank with the smell of sweat, damp timber, soiled clothes and old cooking.

Christian, who was to have the next watch, occupied a berth a few steps forward from the ladder, on the starboard side, behind a canvas screen. A lantern hung there, and when the screen was lifted Christian could just make out Stewart's silhouette. Stewart, at twenty-three, was a year younger than Christian—shorter and leaner, too. They had been together for more than nineteen months.

Christian did not need to be awakened. If he had slept at all since he had climbed into his hammock, it was only fitfully. On the previous evening, in desperation, he had lashed the two masts lying in the ship's launch to some planks to make a crude raft. He intended to desert ship here in the middle of the Pacific and paddle to one of the Friendly Islands, through which the *Bounty* was sailing.

It was a suicidal plan. Only three days earlier a party from the *Bounty* had been molested while collecting water on one of the Friendly Islands. A man coming ashore alone, without the awe-inspiring presence of a great ship anchored close by, was likely to meet a violent end. Yet Christian had determined to go through with his plan, and had risked divulging it to several others, including Stewart. He had even managed to stow provisions and articles for trading in preparation for his escape.

Stewart leaned over Christian's hammock to call him to his watch and found, as he related later, that his friend was "much out of order." He begged him to abandon his plan, knowing that conditions on board the *Bounty* without the second-in-command would become intolerable for all. Christian, a master's mate, provided both a release for their captain's uncertain temper and a link between the officers and the restless crew. With "the people" (as the enlisted men were called) Fletcher Christian was popular.

"When you go, Christian," Stewart pleaded quietly, "the people are ripe for anything."

Christian was in no condition to evaluate the implications of this information. When Stewart left, he pulled himself up the ladder through the main hatchway and came on deck. There was a light swell and a faint breath of wind from the east, hardly enough to fill the sails. The new moon had long since set and it was still dark. However, an active volcano on an island less than thirty miles away intermittently lighted the sky.

During the first few minutes of his watch another midshipman appeared. Christian recognized Edward Young at once by his walk and burly build. He was tough, ruthless, and a close friend. He, too, had heard of Christian's plan to desert ship and was as anxious as Stewart had been that he should not carry it out, though for different reasons.

Young *wanted* a mutiny and had to be certain of Christian's support, since his good relations with the lower deck were a priceless asset in a rebellion. So he quietly repeated Stewart's information that the men were "ripe for anything." But Young went further, and his plan was simple. While everyone was asleep below, he and Christian should seize the ship. There was no need for bloodshed, though they would need control of the arms chests. The captain and his clerk, John Samuel, and midshipmen Hayward and Hallett would be seized and cast adrift in the ship's small cutter. They had a better chance (though they did not deserve it) of reaching an island than Christian would in his makeshift raft. Leaving Christian with these fearful thoughts to contemplate, Ned Young went below.

The next step was Christian's. But he remained inactive for some time, struggling between the temptation to desert and the infinitely more fearful yet intoxicating temptation to incite mutiny.

Two of his friends had now independently told him of the mutinous state of some of the people, and he had seen evidence of it himself, for they were always ready to confide in him. They only awaited a leader. Not only was he the only man on board who could prevent a mutiny, he was also the only one who could successfully lead one. But Christian understood the price of mutiny. At worst, disgrace for his family, and death at the end of a rope for him. At best, fear and guilt for the rest of his life, since the man who must be deposed, cast adrift, almost certainly to die, was one to whom Christian owed his advancement to acting lieutenant and whom he had loved and admired—his captain, William Bligh.

Chapter One

"A FATAL TURN TO THE AFFAIR"

IN APRIL 1789 Lieutenant Bligh, captain of the *Bounty*, was thirty-four years old. He came of good yeoman stock. The Blighs were minor landowners in Devonshire; some went to sea, others, like William's father, Francis, into the civil service. William's own career was never in doubt. He would go to sea. His home city, Plymouth, had been on the threshold of great nautical events for centuries, and when William Bligh was a boy of thirteen, James Cook in the *Endeavour* cleared Plymouth Sound on the first of his three great voyages to the Pacific.

Francis Bligh took a great deal of trouble over his only son's education. By the time the boy was fifteen he had a good knowledge of science and mathematics, could express himself well and drew with clarity and imagination. He first went to sea at sixteen as an able seaman. Knowing that he had to show both a good record and exceptional skills if he was to win promotion—he lacked the patronage of anyone influential—he decided to specialize in navigation, hydrography and cartography. He had his warrant as a midshipman within six months, and his passing certificate for that rank before he was twenty-one.

Then in 1775 there occurred a series of events that would later bring together William Bligh and Fletcher Christian. Bligh was on board a small and (as he described it) "very leaky" sloop, HMS *Ranger*. The American Revolution had just broken out, and the *Ranger* was given the chore of searching suspect ships for contraband in the Irish Sea. She spent much of her time in the port of Douglas in the Isle of Man owing to her unseaworthy condition. During one of these long periods of shore leave, Bligh met the Betham family, and fell in love with their daughter, Elizabeth.

The Bethams were influential, rich, and accomplished in the arts and commerce. When Bligh first met Elizabeth Betham, he found her intelligent and understanding. She was not especially beautiful, but she had charm and liveliness. Elizabeth liked the crisp, clever, self-confident young midshipman, with his definite ideas and determined ambition, and before the *Ranger* left Douglas for the last time early in 1776 the young couple had "come to an understanding."

Elizabeth and William knew that it would be a long time before they met again. News of Bligh's exceptional skill as a navigator and hydrographer had reached the ears of James Cook himself, and on March 20, 1776, Bligh had received his appointment as sailing master on HMS *Resolution*. He would sail with the world's most famous explorer, who was soon to embark on his third great voyage.

The main purpose of this expedition was to discover (no matter how many had failed before) a northwest passage from Europe to India through America. The British government had now offered a £20,000 reward for the first man to find a way. James Cook was determined to be that man. He spent a year in the South Pacific and planned to make his attempt to find the passage eastward from the Pacific instead of westward from the Atlantic.

As sailing master, William Bligh was Cook's right-hand man. He also became directly involved in the subsequent events that led to Cook's death.

IT WAS JANUARY 1779 when Cook had reluctantly brought his two vessels, *Resolution* and *Discovery*, south from Alaska after a valiant but unsuccessful struggle to find a way through the ice. He planned to winter in the Sandwich Islands while he prepared for a second attempt. On January 16 he made out a small indentation in the coast of Hawaii, and as usual, the sailing master was sent to reconnoiter in the *Resolution*'s pinnace.

Bligh explored the bay with his usual care, taking soundings and drawing a rough chart. It was called Karakakooa Bay, he learned, and was some three miles across at its entrance, with two villages, Kowrowa on the western shore and Kakooa in the center. That night Cook wrote in his journal: "Mr. Bligh returned and reported that he had found a bay in which was good anchorage and fresh water tolerable easy to come at. Into this bay I resolved to go to re-fit the ships and supply ourselves with every refreshment the place could afford." It is the last entry contributed by Cook.

When the Englishmen took their vessels into Karakakooa Bay, every native who could find room in a canoe came paddling as fast as he could toward the two sloops. They clung to the gunwales of the ships' boats, climbed up the sides of the *Resolution* and *Discovery*, packing the decks, the masts and yards so tight that the *Discovery* began to list from their weight.

There did not appear to be any menace in them, though they purloined everything removable in the usual Polynesian manner. Yet nowhere in the islands—though the sailors had experienced everything from warm hospitality to downright hostility—had there been such a feeling of tension and emotionalism. The

Karakakooans seemed to be on the edge of a nervous breakdown.

During the weeks that followed, relations between the excitable natives and their exasperated guests became increasingly difficult. Yet repairs were effected and Cook's ships stocked with vast quantities of foodstuffs. Outwardly, harmony was maintained between the leaders of both sides. Then, on February 14, when the *Resolution* was anchored less than half a mile from the northwest shore of the bay, the captain received the ominous news that the *Discovery's* large cutter had been stolen during the night.

Cook was furious. He determined to go ashore at once with a party of marines and bring the native chief back to his ship as hostage. He had used this method of retrieving items stolen by islanders before with unfailing success. He gave orders also for a boat from each ship, one of them commanded by William Bligh and the other by Lieutenant Rickman, Bligh's junior by several years, to patrol the entrance to the bay. They were to prevent any of the natives from escaping. Nothing was said about opening fire if the need arose; Cook detested violence and avoided it whenever possible.

There was no good landing place for a boat at Kowrowa, and Cook had to use a rocky promontory as a jetty. He clambered out onto the slippery rocks and made for the village, with Lieutenant Phillips, the marines officer, following with his men. They found Chief Terreeoboo in his hut. The fat old man appeared bewildered by the early call, and Cook was soon convinced that he knew nothing of the theft of the cutter. When the captain invited him on board his ship, the chief readily agreed to come, and they began to walk toward the shore.

At about this time there was heard the distant sound of musket fire from the bay. Immediately all signs of friendliness and respect from the natives dissolved, and they began arming themselves with stones and spears.

It was clear that they suspected Cook's designs on their king. Accordingly Terreeoboo was permitted to remain, and when the natives saw that he was safe they allowed the marines to return to the shore without him.

At this delicate moment, with Cook and Phillips some thirty yards from the shore, the mob's fury was suddenly reenergized by news brought by runner of slaughter out in the bay. Bligh had fired at one large canoe which had attempted to escape.

Stones now began to fly about the beleaguered party. A young warrior lunged at Phillips with his dagger. Phillips deflected the blow. Another came at him from behind. Phillips turned, discharged a ball and killed him instantly.

The screaming mob closed about Cook. The marines on the shore fired one volley, and then a second. The front ranks of the natives were decimated. But the rest came on, running over the bodies, and the marines were overwhelmed. As they struggled in the shallow water their brains were beaten out against the rocks.

Cook had already been knocked down by one stone. Beside him Phillips had drawn his sword and was seen holding back the mob for several seconds. Then, as Cook rose, he was rushed and stabbed from behind. When he fell a second time the nearest warriors pounced on his body in a frenzy of eagerness to share in the glory of the assassination.

Phillips could do no more. Still using his sword to great effect, he retreated across the rocks, dived into the water and swam to the boat. Too late the *Resolution*'s guns roared. The smoke drifted across the bay as if to salute the death of the great navigator, a death that everyone agreed to be the direct result of Bligh's impetuous firing on the canoe—an action, according to a fellow officer, which had given "a fatal turn to the affair."

As soon as he had navigated the *Resolution* back to England, Bligh made his way to the Isle of Man. There he married Elizabeth Betham on February 4, 1781. She, like her husband, was twenty-six years old. She was clever and talented, and her support in the troubled years ahead was unswerving. The marriage also secured him a wide range of connections, all powerful and potentially valuable.

For the next two years England was still at war. Within ten days of his marriage Bligh was appointed master of the captured

French frigate *Belle Poule*, in which he saw action for the first time at the bloody but indecisive engagement at the Dogger Bank. Then, as a junior lieutenant, he took part in the relief of Gibraltar. He reached England again on November 14, 1782, just in time for the birth of his first daughter, Harriet Maria.

For nearly five years he did not have another naval appointment, and half pay was a mere two shillings a day, hardly enough for a growing family. Bligh settled down with Elizabeth and their baby in their modest home in Douglas, and began inquiries among his wife's relatives for work.

Elizabeth's mother's uncle, Duncan Campbell, was a prominent West Indian merchant and shipowner. He quickly showed his confidence in Bligh by appointing him to command one of his merchantmen, and later to be his agent at Port of Lucea, Jamaica, for several months. Now well paid, Bligh brought his family to London. While he was bringing shiploads of sugar and rum across the Atlantic, Elizabeth gave birth to two more daughters.

Then, in the late summer of 1785, Bligh received a request from old family friends of Elizabeth's for a berth for Midshipman Fletcher Christian on Campbell's fine new ship, the *Britannia*. Aware that to sail under William Bligh would provide priceless experience, Christian also wrote to him direct. "Wages are no object: I only wish to learn my profession, and if you would permit me to mess with the gentlemen, I will readily enter your ship as a foremaster, until there is a vacancy among the officers. . . ."

That seemed to Bligh to be the right spirit, and he responded that Christian would be welcome on these terms.

There was no strong maritime tradition in the Christian family, yet at eighteen Fletcher made the surprising decision to join the navy. He took readily and happily to life at sea, to the privations as well as to the boisterous company and to the delights of new places and peoples. He got on well. His good education, his lively mind and manner, ensured that. In 1784, as a twenty-year-old midshipman on the homeward passage from his first voyage to the Far East, he was given a watch in HMS

Eurydice. This was unusual for a young man with only two years' service.

The next year he sailed with Bligh on the *Britannia.* He was five feet eight inches tall, dark-haired, handsome, strong and well built. He was also—fatally—as emotional, passionate and mercurial as Bligh himself.

For most of the time Christian was a lively and amusing companion but he was also subject to moods of depression. These bleak periods did not usually last for long and his resilient spirit soon would reassert itself. Ashore, he was the first to attract the women. They loved the combination of his swash-buckling self-confidence and his seeming vulnerability.

During his second voyage on the *Britannia* he was promoted from gunner to second mate. This and other special favors aroused resentment in Edward Lamb, the mate of the *Britannia.* Seven years later, when Bligh was under fierce attack, Lamb wrote to Bligh: "When we got to sea I saw your partiality for the young man. I gave him every advice and information in my power, though he went about every point of duty with a degree of indifference that to me was truly unpleasant; but you were blind to his faults and had him to dine and sup every other day in the cabin, and treated him like a brother in giving him every information."

By now Bligh's success in the service of his benefactor, Duncan Campbell, had attracted the attention of many people. The most important of these was Sir Joseph Banks, scientist and explorer, naturalist and visionary, a man of great wealth and influence who had sailed with Cook on his first Pacific voyage and was now president of the Royal Society.

Like Campbell, Banks had substantial financial interests in the West Indies, and for more than a decade the cost of feeding the slaves working on the sugar plantations there had been a constant worry. The main problem was that most of their food had to be imported from North America.

As long before as 1775 the Society for West India Merchants had offered to underwrite the expense of importing a cheap food-yielding plant into the "West India Colonies"; and in its turn the Royal Society offered its prestigious gold medal to the first person who succeeeded in conveying "six plants . . . in a growing state." The plant that the merchants and the Royal Society were chiefly interested in was the breadfruit, a prolific, tough, doughy plant that grew readily all over Polynesia. It could be made into a durable paste, for use during the few months that it was not in season; and from the fiber beneath its bark a useful cloth could be made.

A contemporary historian wrote: "If a man plants ten of them in his lifetime, which he may do in about an hour, he will completely fulfil his duty to his own and future generations as the native of our less temperate climate can do by ploughing in the cold winter, and reaping in the summer's heat."

Early in 1787 Banks and Lord Sydney, one of King George III's principal secretaries of state, began discussions on the transport of some breadfruit plants from Polynesia to the British West Indies. Formal authority for the voyage was given in May 1787.

The vessel was to proceed by way of Cape Horn to Tahiti for the collection of upward of one thousand breadfruits, thence to the West Indies. Time was short if the worst Cape Horn weather, which began around April, was to be avoided, and urgent consideration was given by Banks and Lord Sydney to the choice of vessel, of master to command her, and of a botanist to supervise the horticultural aspects of the voyage.

The selection of botanist was no problem. David Nelson was Banks's man. Quiet, unassuming and diligent, he had sailed with Cook on his last voyage, had successfully collected plants and seeds and knew how to look after them at sea. He had already been to Tahiti and even had a fair smattering of the language. When the call came, he gladly gathered together his plant presses and drying papers, his wooden boxes and casks. For his assistant he chose twenty-five-year-old William Brown from Kew.

Banks had no doubts about the choice of commander either, and Bligh heard the first official news of his appointment on August 5. It was the greatest honor that could have been paid to the thirty-three-year-old lieutenant. He wrote to

Banks: "I have heard the flattering news of your great goodness to me, intending to honour me with the command of the vessel which you propose to go to the South Seas, for which, after offering you my most grateful thanks, I can only assure you I shall endeavour, and I hope succeed, in deserving such a trust."

Bligh's vessel had been chosen in his absence. She was the *Bethia,* a three-masted merchantman built two and a half years earlier, ninety-one feet long overall on the upper deck, handsomely ornamented with a figurehead of a woman dressed in a riding habit.

Modifications to the *Bethia* for her unusual new function were put in hand without delay. "The difficulty of carrying plants by sea is very great," Banks emphasized. "A small sprinkling of salt water or of the salt dew which fills the air even in a moderate gale will inevitably destroy them if not immediately washed off with fresh water. It is necessary therefore that the cabin be appropriated to the sole purpose of making a kind of greenhouse . . . and that in case of cold weather . . . a stove be provided by which it may be kept in a temperature equal to that of the inter-tropical countries."

The whole of the lower deck from a point midway between the main and mizzen masts and the stern, normally the most comfortable area in a ship, was sacrificed to the greenhouse, with rows of pots to accommodate over one thousand plants. This meant overcrowding, on a voyage that was certain to last nearly two years, for the ship's complement of no fewer than forty-seven. There could also be no accommodation for Royal Marines, either for punitive measures ashore or to give edge to the captain's authority on board. The ship's commander would have to fend for himself.

Honored and flattered as he was at this appointment, Bligh was from the beginning alarmed that he was to have no marines on such a long and hazardous voyage, nor any commissioned officer to share his responsibilities and support him.

During September the *Bethia,* now more appropriately named the *Bounty,* was fitted out. Provisions for the voyage

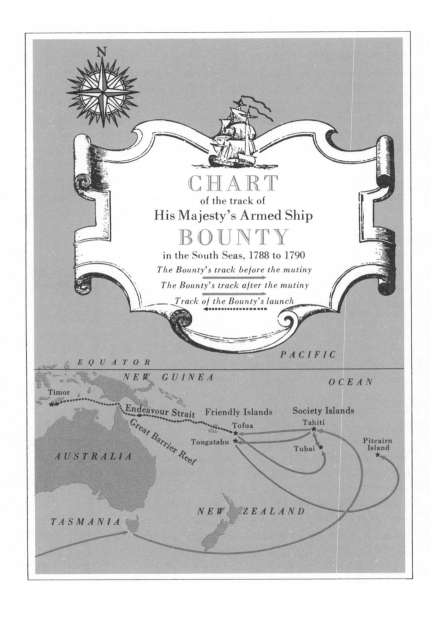

N

CHART
of the track of
His Majesty's Armed Ship
BOUNTY
in the South Seas, 1788 to 1790
The Bounty's track before the mutiny
The Bounty's track after the mutiny
Track of the Bounty's launch

PACIFIC

EQUATOR

NEW GUINEA

OCEAN

Timor

Endeavour Strait   Friendly Islands   Society Islands

Great Barrier Reef   Tofua   Tahiti

Tongatabu   Tubai   Pitcairn
Island

AUSTRALIA

TASMANIA   NEW ZEALAND

consisted largely of the basic—and notorious—ship biscuit, tough and weevil-ridden; salt pork and beef in casks; dried peas; grog (rum), beer and wine. In addition there were supplies of the marvelous new portable soup. This concoction was regarded as an acceptable substitute for fresh vegetables, and therefore antiscorbutic. It was made by boiling vegetables until finally the remaining juice solidified, and in that state, it was supposed to last forever. The carpenters had also built four cages on the forecastle for a dozen hens, some pigs and half a dozen sheep.

The *Bounty*'s mission was regarded primarily as a trading one. Accordingly, to buy 1000 breadfruit plants Bligh obtained no fewer than 2800 steel blades of various kinds, 1000 knives with wooden handles and sheaths, several thousand nails, 48 saws, and numerous hatchets, gimlets, rasps and files—all beloved by the Polynesians and worth a king's ransom in local currency, though a mere £125 in England. Those old favorites, mirrors and colored beads, were included, along with six dozen coarse shirts for special presents. In addition there were one hundred gold ducats for more sophisticated trading places, like Batavia or Java, for the replacement of lost plants en route—if any could be found—and for purchasing provisions.

Besides this provisioning, Bligh's most important task was the selection of his officers and men. Except for the gardener and his assistant, all were selected by Bligh personally. One of the first chosen was fourteen-year-old Peter Heywood, son of a close friend of the Betham family, a lively boy whom everyone liked. When Elizabeth's father wrote recommending this "ingenious lad," Bligh willingly complied.

Elizabeth herself had already staked a claim for John Hallett, brother of an old friend. And the Bethams also asked Bligh to include Tom Hayward.

Then there was Edward Young, a saturnine young man, reputed to have West Indian blood in his veins, whose mother could trace her lineage back to Queen Mary Stuart. Bligh had once been entertained by his family in the Orkneys, and thought Edward "had the look of a stout able seaman."

These, then, were the midshipmen, all young, all enthusiastic for the adventure that lay ahead, all seemingly able.

Bligh also knew, either personally or by reputation, most of the warrant and petty officers—William Peckover, for instance, the gunner, who had sailed on all three of Cook's Pacific voyages, and the quartermaster, John Norton. John Fryer, the *Bounty*'s master, was unknown to him, but he came with a good reference, and Bligh told Banks that he was confident that he was a good man.

The surgeon, Dr. Thomas Huggan, was grossly overweight and appeared to be a very steady drinker. However, "the doctor has a good character," Bligh wrote cheerfully to Banks.

There was no shortage of enlisted men to choose from, and Bligh believed that when he had sorted through all the candidates he had chosen well. The captain was insistent on having a musician in the ship's company, both to cheer the men and to provide the music for dancing. He knew how slack the men could become on a long voyage, especially when the trade winds blew steadily day after day and there was little to do. There was some difficulty in finding a fiddler prepared to face the rigors of a two years' long circumnavigation, and in the end he had to make do with Michael Byrn, who was nearly blind.

Fletcher Christian's master-pupil relationship with Bligh had developed into something deeper. Now twenty-two years old, a first-class navigator and promoted to master's mate, he was one of the first to know that he would be sailing to the South Seas.

The only officer holding the king's commission was Bligh. Christian and the other midshipmen—really apprentice officers— were classed as enlisted men (and could therefore be flogged) but messed separately and had other privileges.

Bligh received his orders to take the *Bounty* from London to Spithead on October 15, and sent his family ahead of him so that he could spend his last days with them at Portsmouth.

It was a terrible passage down the Channel. Nevertheless the captain found little to complain about. The men worked well together, and Bligh thought that he would soon "have them all in very good order." His final sailing orders were needlessly delayed until November 24. By then the weather had changed for the worse, and when at last he did make sail into the Channel he was beaten back again. His only consolation was that he was able to spend a little time longer with "my dear little family." It was not until two days before Christmas that a fair east wind blew, and he was able to set sail.

Chapter Two
"THE COMPLETEST SHIP THAT EVER SWAM"

BLIGH'S ORDERS WERE to sail from England to Tahiti, a distance of over twelve thousand miles, stopping only at the Canary Islands. He was to arrive in Tahiti in late March or April 1788, when the breadfruit would be ripe for transplanting. This timing was already in jeopardy, as rounding the Horn would now require a great deal of luck as well as good seamanship. Yet Banks considered that it was worth taking the risks, as it would mean getting cheap food for the plantation slaves a year earlier.

For the twenty days of their passage to the Canaries the men learned one another's ways, the habits and weaknesses of their officers, and above all watched their commander, on whose discretion their well-being and their lives were going to depend, perhaps for several years. There were things about him that were already causing a measure of uneasiness—the uncertain nature of his temper in particular. They were all used to bad language. There was nothing shocking about that. But Bligh never seemed to stop, even when he was talking conversationally. They had never heard anything like it before.

THEY SIGHTED THE Canaries in cloudy, heavy weather on the morning of January 5. Twenty-four hours later the *Bounty* moored off Santa Cruz de Tenerife, a neat, trim little Spanish town, all church spires and straight roads flanked by low houses.

It took four days of hard work to take on board fresh provisions and water. Bligh complained at the high prices of everything, but with no other port on his route, he had to pay out. As it was unlikely that there would be another chance of writing home, Bligh left behind at Santa Cruz reports to be taken by the next ship bound for England saying all was well. Only the surgeon gave cause for complaint. Fat Dr. Huggan lurched about the ship, forever swinging a bottle. The *Bounty* herself was "the completest ship I believe that ever swam, and she really looks like one fit to encounter any difficulties."

Once clear of Tenerife, Bligh called together the ship's company and read an announcement. Its terms have a direct bearing on much of what happened later. "We are proceeding to Otaheite [Tahiti] without stopping and by way of Cape Horn. But because of the delays in England the season is now far spent and we may be defeated in our efforts to reach the South Sea by this short route. But I am determined to try. If I fail in the attempt I shall put about to the Cape of Good Hope and proceed by the easterly route to the Society Islands. In either event, it is necessary to be careful of our provisions, especially our biscuit. I shall therefore now reduce the allowance to two-thirds, all other provisions remaining at full rations."

The ship's company was to be put on three watches. This meant that the men would work four hours on watch and eight off, instead of four hours on and four off. The men were also told that the evenings would be laid aside for their amusement and dancing. As to the watch keepers, the master and gunner would be in charge of watches as before. For the third watch, Mr. Christian would be in command.

What an oddly uneven announcement this was! On the one hand it showed caution, care and consideration for the men. The common crew—"the people"—were generally treated as slaves. Cook, however, was of a new enlightened school of commanders which recognized that the survival of the ship's company during a long voyage depended on the health and well-being of each man. Bligh had witnessed Cook's success, and his own concern for a rigid economy of victuals, a careful regard to a balanced diet, and compulsory dancing and games in the evenings made good sense.

On the other hand, Christian was no better qualified to be the officer of the third watch than the other master's mate, Will

Elphinstone, or Midshipman Tom Hayward. Bligh's choice showed the same favoritism as he had shown in the *Britannia,* where it had led to resentment. Already Christian was being invited to Bligh's cabin in the evenings, and soon after this he was shot up to the rank of acting lieutenant and into the position of second-in-command, over the head of Fryer—the master to whom he had been mate.

Only midshipmen Hayward and Hallett, and Bligh's dour clerk, John Samuel, disapproved. Fryer himself showed no resentment at the time; yet he certainly felt the injury, and his relations with Bligh became increasingly touchy, until the two were scarcely on speaking terms.

It took the *Bounty* more than four weeks to reach the Equator—some seventy-five miles a day—through fair but humid weather. Though the ship was aired whenever possible and washed down below with vinegar, everything was quickly covered with a fine white mold.

According to Bligh's log, and the journal he published later, those first weeks were happy. On the crossing of the line there was much dancing, hilarity and tipsiness. Three bottles of rum were shared out, and each man had half a pint of wine as well. But had there been troubles, it would hardly have been in Bligh's interest to recount them. James Morrison, the bo'sun's mate, in *his* journal, wrote of discontent within a few days of leaving Santa Cruz. First there was the matter of the missing cheese. Bligh ordered a cask to be opened in front of the ship's company, as was the custom, to prevent any suspicion of malpractice. Two cheeses were missing. "They have been stolen," Bligh declared angrily.

"This cask has been opened before, sir," said the cooper, Henry Hillbrant, daringly. "It was opened by the order of Mr. Samuel at Spithead and the cheeses were sent to your lodgings."

Bligh turned on Hillbrant. "I'll give you a damned good flogging if you say any more of this." Then to the ship's company: "The allowance of cheese for the officers as well as the people will be stopped until this deficiency is made good."

The matter of the missing cheeses was followed some three

weeks later by the pumpkin affair. With the temperature in the eighties, pumpkins Bligh had bought at Santa Cruz began to go bad. To avoid waste and consume them quickly, Bligh ordered Samuel to issue them instead of biscuit, one pound of pumpkin for two pounds of biscuit. The men refused with one voice.

When Bligh heard of this near-mutinous protest, "he came up in a violent passion," declared Morrison, "and called all hands."

"You damned infernal scoundrels!" Bligh shouted at them. "I'll make you eat grass or anything you can catch before I have done with you!"

THE VOYAGE CONTINUED with fair winds from the Equator until the *Bounty* had the first taste of Horn weather nearly six weeks later. During this leg, slackness and dirt were Bligh's first enemies. The men scrubbed themselves down daily, and every afternoon they combined exercise with hygiene by pouring water down one pump to the bilge and pumping it up again with the second pump. The captain was satisfied only when the water coming up was pure as the water poured down. Bligh equated a sick man with personal failure, and he recorded with satisfaction that the *Bounty* survived the tropics with no serious sickness.

The first southern gale struck the *Bounty* at the entrance of the Strait of Magellan, but the wind died quickly, and two nights later, in bright moonlight, the mountains of Tierra del Fuego, the first land they had seen since the Canaries, emerged in the southeast. Bligh ordered a sheep to be killed to celebrate. "It gave them a pleasant meal," he recorded.

James Morrison told this story differently, too. The sheep, he said, had died of starvation, and they had to throw most of it overboard. Moreover, it was a substitute for the day's ration of meat, not a supplement.

On March 24 Bligh noticed the sky "very much streaked and appearance of wind." But the ship's long ordeal did not begin in earnest until the night of March 28. A westerly gale brought strong, slanting rain, and the seas often broke over the deck— "it exceeds any I have seen," Bligh noted in his log. He knew what he was up against, and his respect for the power of the elements was as massive as his determination to prevail. His weapons were his ship and his men, and he nursed them both devotedly.

Day after day, as he tacked and wore, gaining a few miles in a few days and losing them all and more in a few hours; as he took his observations lashed to the mast, watched every change of the weather from hail and snowstorms to squalls and brief periods of moderating gales; ordered the sails furled, or reefed, or set according to the constant changes in direction and strength of the wind—all this time, sodden, half frozen and weary himself, his first thoughts were for the welfare of his ship and men.

This was William Bligh at his best, gladly agreeing to the men's request for unwatered grog to keep out the cold, deputing two men from each watch to supervise the only fire below to dry out the clothes and the hammocks of the others, ordering hot soup for all and hot breakfasts of boiled wheat and sugar, and a pint of decoction of ground malt once a day.

The *Bounty* and her company both reacted stoutly, and for two weeks of this battering the ship showed few signs of the strain she was undergoing. Then "she begins to be a little leaky," Bligh noted flatly, and ordered the men to the pumps every hour. He gave attention to his men by sacrificing his cabin at night, which allowed more room between decks and "rendered those happy who had not dry beds to sleep in."

By the middle of April, Bligh was beginning to lose hope. Because of the sails' weight and stiffness from snow and ice, the weakened men found it well-nigh impossible to haul them up and furl them. When they came down from the yards they were unable to speak and scarcely able to stand still. Still, no ship's company could have been more loyal, determined and tenacious.

On April 13 Bligh wrote: "It is now three weeks since we came round Staten Land, a time we have spent with much fatigue and almost constant bad weather. Few ships could have gone through it as we have done, but I cannot expect my men and officers to bear it much longer."

Eight days later, with nine men out of action, the *Bounty* badly leaking and no sign of the weather easing, Bligh knew that he had been defeated. Just before five in the afternoon he called all hands aft and told them that he was going to put over the helm and bear away for Africa. "You have endured much and I congratulate and thank you all." The whole crew—until that moment close to despair—spontaneously burst into three cheers for their commander.

Bligh had proved himself an unsurpassed captain in a time of adversity. To have survived those weeks of Horn weather without the loss of a man, or a spar or even a yard of canvas, was a stunning achievement.

The *Bounty* made good speed across the South Atlantic, running at up to nine knots with a strong westerly wind. But the weather remained consistently foul and it was not until they were almost in sight of Table Mountain that it at last eased. On May 24 the *Bounty* came to anchor in False Bay, Cape of Good Hope. It was the crew's first sight of other human beings in eighty-six days.

The *Bounty* remained at Cape Town for thirty-eight days. The ship was in poor shape after her Cape Horn battering. The carpenter and his crew had a lot of repairing to do, and every day the boats plied between the shore and the ship, bringing a mass of miscellaneous stores. These included apple-tree saplings and all sorts of seeds for Nelson, the botanist, to plant on Pacific islands.

Although it was midwinter in Cape Town, rainy and cool, the crew thrived on the diet of fruit and vegetables, fresh meat and real bread instead of ship biscuit. Bligh noted with approval the neatness and cleanliness of the town, but deplored the condition and treatment of the slaves. "One could not fail," he wrote, "to reproach the owners of a want of decency and compassion in not relieving such a degree of wretchedness."

At four o'clock in the afternoon on July 1 the *Bounty* weighed anchor. Ahead lay the longest leg of the voyage, across the Indian Ocean for well over six thousand miles to Tasmania, which was still thought to be the southern tip of Australia.

It seems almost miraculous today that after forty-nine days a navigator equipped only with suspect charts, a compass, a chronometer, nautical tables and a sextant, could make accurate landfall not just on a coast but on a particular rock—the Mewstone off Tasmania. But then Bligh was a peerless navigator, and on August 19, he worked the *Bounty* carefully—noting every detail for future navigators—into Adventure Bay.

Christian took a party ashore for wood, others took casks in the launch to fill with water, some of the men fished and Christian succeeded in shooting a few birds for the pot. Although they were curious about the natives, the islanders always retreated silently inland before they could be approached with gifts. David Nelson collected soil and specimens, and planted some fruit trees, vegetables and seeds in a clearing. (In afteryears Bligh claimed to be the progenitor of Tasmania's apple industry.) On September 4 they set out on the last leg of their journey to Tahiti.

At sea the first major trouble with one of his officers occurred, significantly, on the day with "the wind as steady as a trade," the temperature at a mellow sixty degrees Fahrenheit and the weather fair. On the morning of October 9 there were clerical formalities to be carried out—monthly expense books to be signed both by the commander and the master. Bligh examined the books, signed and sent them to Fryer for his signature. But Fryer, a petulant, uneasy man who had made no trouble when passed over for promotion, now would not add his signature unless Bligh himself signed a certificate confirming Fryer's own good behavior during the passage: something for the record in case of trouble later.

Bligh was livid and turned up all hands. Then, with Fryer at his side, he read aloud the Articles of War, with all their hints of dire retribution. His clerk, Samuel, produced the books and Bligh held them out to Fryer. "Now sign them books," Bligh ordered.

Fryer took the pen, and in a voice so loud that none would miss his words, he said, "I sign in obedience to your orders, but this may be canceled hereafter." And he did so. According to Morrison this was only one of several rows between commander and master before they reached Tahiti.

Bligh's relations with Surgeon Huggan also were going from bad to worse. One of his able seamen, James Valentine, had been taken ill in Adventure Bay, and in accordance with usual practice had been bled from the arm by Huggan, who neglected to look after it properly. The arm became inflamed, and Valentine retired to his hammock. The captain visited him and found him in a very poor condition. A few days later Valentine died.

Bligh was very put out, because he had hoped to complete his voyage without a casualty—an impressive confirmation of his quality as a commander. But as the *Bounty* sailed into the tropics and the temperature and humidity rose daily, more men were taken ill. Huggan said it was scurvy. Bligh was outraged. Only inferior commanders, with dirty ships and dirty men eating a poor diet, experienced this dread disease among their crew. Bligh examined the men with care. "It appeared to be nothing more than the prickly heat," he wrote in his log.

Nevertheless, more fell ill, and Bligh became very worried. He asked for the full sick list from Huggan and was astonished to discover that only one name appeared on it. Huggan was obviously unable to carry out even the simplest duties. The captain ordered the sick men off all salt provisions and gave them flour and a daily dose of essence of malt instead.

Under Bligh's care the health of the men improved as Huggan's condition grew worse. On October 24 Bligh discovered that his surgeon had been lying on his bunk in an alcoholic stupor for four days. Disgusted, he ordered his cabin to be cleaned out and his stock of liquor removed and hidden. Huggan was later seen lurching about the ship searching for his bottles. He failed in his quest and eventually returned, thwarted, to his cabin.

Two days later the doctor's condition had so improved that Bligh felt that he was capable of carrying out one last important duty before they landed. Cook had been accused of allowing his men to spread venereal disease among the innocent natives. "To free us from any ill-founded suppositions," Bligh ordered every officer and man to report to Huggan for venereal inspection.

That night Bligh wrote with satisfaction: "Every person is totally free from the venereal complaint."

Early on the evening of October 25, 1788, dead on course as always, Bligh sighted the towering green volcanic peaks of Tahiti. The sky was clear, a favorable and gentle trade wind fanned them, the temperature was seventy-eight degrees. It was ten months since they had left England, and they had sailed more than 27,000 nautical miles.

The *Bounty* drew close to the island during the night, and by the following morning they could make out deep valleys, thick, rich forests, coconut palms along the sandy shoreline and groves of breadfruit trees. Here and there they could pick out natives' huts arranged in small groups. It truly appeared the paradise on earth of which they had all heard such extravagant accounts.

THE *BOUNTY'S* WELCOME was characteristically Polynesian. As Bligh worked the ship through a break in Tahiti's reef and into the clear calm of Matavai Bay, hundreds of long canoes came out from the shore. In them were the most attractive people the crew of the *Bounty* had seen on all their voyage. Tall young women held armfuls of fruit. Their hair, woven with hibiscus flowers, fell to their shoulders and half across their breasts. Their skin was a rich olive in color, their eyes were as black as their hair.

Tahitian men and girls swarmed from the canoes up the sides of the *Bounty,* cluttering the upper decks. They climbed the rigging, scuttled down the ladders, chattering, laughing, shrieking, insatiably curious. "Where is the great Cook?" they asked. (They pronounced it Toot.)

Bligh had warned his men that they must not refer to the assassination, since Captain Cook had already become a legend to the Tahitians. "Here is the son of Cook," David Nelson told them in their own tongue, pointing to Bligh.

Soon they were busily trading, and the minor chieftains exchanged gifts of hogs and fruit for hatchets and mirrors. The coconut harvest was at its peak and the crew all drank deeply of the restorative milk as they bartered and made their choice of

the girls who showed off their bodies with uninhibited enthusiasm.

At this stage there was little thieving, to Bligh's surprise and relief. When one native was caught stealing, a chief flew into a rage and drove the culprit overboard into the sea. Then, as the sun went down, the native men were ordered ashore. Only chosen girls, sometimes two to a man, were allowed to remain, sharing hammocks or lying with their lovers on deck through the hot night.

After the discomforts, the harsh discipline, the celibacy of the past ten months, there now began a long, lazy period of self-indulgence that wrought great changes in the crew. The *Bounty* began to look like a small village, with the womenfolk settling in comfortably, stowing the hammocks at dawn, folding the bedding, fetching and preparing the food, gossiping among themselves and making love to their men.

The person most changed by this new life was Bligh himself. From October 26, 1788, to April 4, 1789, Bligh became the benevolent autocrat of northern Tahiti, the honored viceroy of King George III, instead of the stern commander of a ship at sea. Bligh had watched at close quarters how Cook time and again had succeeded in acquiring the affection and respect of the Polynesians with firmness and kindness. Bligh had learned his lessons well—above all he remembered the results of his own fatal impetuosity at Karakakooa Bay.

David Nelson had given Bligh lessons in Tahitian on the passage out, and from the moment when the *Bounty* dropped anchor in Matavai Bay the captain set about "cultivating a friendship with the natives." First he sought out the one man on whom would depend the success of his whole breadfruit enterprise. This was Teina, the ruler of this area of northern Tahiti, a fine, sturdy figure of a man, six feet four inches tall, a stern authoritarian among his people. It is clear that he became deeply attached to Bligh, and not only for what he could cadge from him. He was saddened as well as chastened when Bligh was angry with him and transparently delighted when he was reinstated in his esteem.

Teina's wife, Queen Itea, was an equally formidable figure, a veritable giantess. Bligh described her as "a very resolute woman, of a large make, and has great bodily strength." They had four children under six years; the eldest boy, in accordance with local custom, was made nominal king at birth. Teina would reign as regent until his son became a man.

Bligh, a sentimental man with those who showed him affection, returned the friendship of the muscular ruler and his massive wife with ardor. The two men would talk for hours on end about Polynesian and English manners and customs, and especially about life in the royal palaces in England. Teina could not hear enough about King George III.

Bligh, however, was horrified by some of the Polynesian sexual practices—what he called "numerous sensual and beastly acts of gratification"—and to hear that the queen shared her bed equally with her husband and his servant. Clearly promiscuity was also accepted as normal within families, and brothers freely slept with each other's wives. Outside the family it was something different, and while Bligh was at Matavai there were cases of knifing for infidelity outside the family.

But not for one day did Bligh forget the main purpose of his visit to Tahiti. The first thing he had to do, after establishing cordial relations with Teina, was to raise the subject of breadfruit tactfully. On a warm rainy day in November they sheltered in a hut and Bligh talked to the regent. "You have many good friends in England," he said, "including King George. When ships come again to Tahiti they will bring more presents for you."

Teina, "much pleased and satisfied," urged Bligh to stay at Matavai. "Do not go to the other islands. I will gladly send any presents King George might prefer—hogs, plantain, bananas, coconuts, breadfruit—"

"Breadfruit is a very good idea," said the captain. "King George will like that." And so the matter was concluded. The minor chiefs were informed by Teina that King George was to be presented with as many breadfruit saplings as the ship could carry, and the following day Bligh went ashore with Nelson and his assistant, Brown, to locate the most suitable place for a nursery garden.

They found it at Point Venus, the northern extremity of the Tahitian coastline, where one of Tahiti's biggest rivers meets the sea. David Nelson chose a spot close to this river for his garden. Full-grown breadfruit trees rose there to become two-hundred-year-old memorials to this determined gardener! From that time until the *Bounty*'s departure the area was forbidden to the natives. To reinforce security Bligh made Christian commander of a shore-based establishment. Peter Heywood, Peckover, the gunner, and four armed men provided the defense force.

So, once again, Christian had been given a situation of comfort and privilege, and he settled down happily to a life of indolence. Like all the *Bounty*'s men, he had many girls to choose from and for a time lived a promiscuous life. Then he found a real *taio,* the daughter of a chief, called Mauatua, whom he renamed Isabella. In the eyes of the men of the *Bounty* all the Tahitian girls were beautiful, but there was something especially radiant about Isabella. Christian also acquired, as many of them did, a male *taio*—a servant and friend.

The *Bounty*'s enlisted men were allowed ashore on leave two at a time and were free to do as they liked so long as they adhered to Bligh's rules of conduct, which adjured them "to study to gain the good will and esteem of the natives." There was not in fact very much to do ashore, and since officers and men alike admired the tattooing with which all the natives adorned themselves, the *Bounty*'s company, almost without exception, were tattooed to pass the time. And they soon vied with one another for the most elaborate design.

On shore or on shipboard, on watch or off, the demands made on most of the men were very light. One or two were kept busy. Peckover, for example, was responsible for trading; and Bligh encouraged the armorer and the carpenters to meet the natives' needs. The natives brought to them the precious iron tools and toys which they had acquired from Cook, now in need of repair. It all helped good relations.

From Morrison's and Bligh's journals we can visualize the scene on a December evening, with the *Bounty* anchored a mere hundred yards from the beach. Bligh would be ashore with

Nelson, and most of the *Bounty*'s company would be on deck, lying about with their *taios,* chatting or fishing with lines over the side. Earlier the women had prepared food in the galley below—fish, pork, breadfruit, plantains, bananas and other fruit. Now the air was still, the bay calm, the temperature in the lower eighties.

On one side the mountains rose dark against the starlit sky, toward the open sea the breaking rollers on the reef cast a white line separating the lagoon from the Pacific. The natives, as usual, were out fishing, each canoe and the sea about it illuminated by a splash of yellow light from a burning reed bundle.

As always, the beating of the surf on the reef was the predominating sound. The other sound that was with them day and night, however calm the lagoon, was the creaking of the *Bounty*'s timbers. Byrn struck up a tune on his fiddle; the women chatted among themselves and later drifted off with their men.

Even now, however, Bligh's command was a lonely one. If he had wanted a female *taio,* it would not have conformed to his dignified status to take one. He kept himself occupied with study of the Tahitian people. He entertained Teina, his wife and their large family, and kept anxious watch over the progress of the breadfruit plants. Indeed, On December 5 the whole transplantation, and even the *Bounty* herself, was placed in jeopardy when a tropical storm struck Tahiti.

That afternoon the seas broke over the reefs, converting Matavai Bay from tranquil lagoon into boiling caldron, "threatening us with instant destruction." The rain came down in torrents, and Bligh had to draw on all his skill to ride out the storm.

Ashore, the river burst its banks, and Nelson and Brown struggled to save their breadfruit by digging a trench to divert the floodwater. Mercifully the rain eased off later in the day, the river subsided, and in the end few plants were damaged.

Matavai Bay was clearly no ideal anchorage. Bligh found a better one six miles west of Point Venus at Oparre. There he discovered a little bay of sufficient depth, better protected from the sea and the trade winds. Over Christmas the encampment on Point Venus was dismantled, and over seven hundred potted breadfruit plants were transported in the ship to Oparre.

The young breadfruit plants flourished in their new garden, as did the seeds of the mutiny. It was on the brief voyage to Oparre that the extent of the decline in spirit and efficiency among the ship's company became evident. As the *Bounty* entered the bay, her forepart ran firmly aground. Using both the bower and kedge anchors, Bligh was finally able to have the ship drawn from the reef and refloated. But the two anchors and their cables became fouled, and it took more than twenty-four hours to free them.

Bligh was exasperated with his officers. The men whom he had chosen with such care now became victims of his foul tongue and fitful temper. "If I had any officers to supersede them," he wrote, "or was able to do without them, considering them as common seamen, they should no longer occupy their respective stations."

Fletcher Christian suffered most. Bligh saw him less frequently now that Christian lived ashore with Isabella, and so meetings—not always private—only occurred as a result of Bligh's displeasure at some actual or imagined failure in the acting lieutenant's duties.

Things were no better among the seamen. The frequency of floggings began to rise steeply—for insolence, disobedience and neglect of duty. Huggan had continued to drink himself senseless every day since their arrival and died on the evening of December 10. But one of the last duties he had been able to perform was checking "the venereal list." Eighteen officers and men had to apply to the surgeon for a venereal cure; and, incidentally, be fined. The spread of venereal disease in the crew led Bligh to the conclusion—since confirmed—that gonorrhea was rife among the Tahitians long before the arrival of the Europeans.

Worse trouble was to come. Between midnight and 2:00 a.m. on January 5, able seamen Muspratt and Millward, and Charles Churchill, the master-at-arms, stole a complete arms chest, climbed into the small cutter and deserted ship. This was not difficult as Hayward, mate of the watch, was asleep as usual. The theft was discovered when the watch was relieved at 4:00 a.m. Bligh was not informed until half an hour later. He ordered Hayward confined below in irons, and the hunt began at dawn. When the men were recaptured the ship's company was mustered, and Bligh read out the Articles of War. He publicly rebuked Hayward, and then ordered twelve lashes for Churchill and two dozen each for the others. The three men were confined in irons until February 4, when they were brought up and the punishment was repeated.

The *Bounty* was becoming a slack ship. On January 17 Bligh had ordered the sail room to be cleared and the sails taken on shore to air. Among them, rotten and mildewed, were unused spare sails which had previously been reported in good order. So his officers were liars and slackers. "Scarcely any neglect of duty can equal the criminality of this."

As the *Bounty*'s long stay in Tahiti drew to a close with the strengthening of the breadfruit plants, the final breakdown in order and discipline approached, and the other Bligh—the fair-weather commander—began to emerge more clearly. His first failing was lack of imagination. For more than five months, amid the seductive delights of one of the most beautiful islands in the world, he left his men to the supervision of his officers and cursed them when he discovered they had failed him. But they were failing a commander who himself had failed the severest test: to lead when things seem to be going smoothly.

ON FEBRUARY 27 Bligh wrote that "the plants are in a very fine state and Mr. Nelson thinks they will be perfectly established in the pots in the course of a month." In the early days of March he began to give serious attention to the state of the ship.

The last days at Oparre were chaotic, crowded and moving. There was chanting and dancing, eating and drinking and love-making, all on a glorious scale. For the women it was considered a triumph to conceive a half-European child, and they were as open in their appetites as in their sentiments, lamenting the imminent severance of long friendships.

Somehow, amid what Bligh described as "a vast excess of grief," the delicate task of ferrying over one thousand breadfruit plants to the ship was completed without a casualty. Below decks aft the *Bounty* took on the appearance of a floating conservatory.

On the evening of April 3 the crew said a last farewell to their *taios,* and the canoes paddled slowly away with many cries of sadness. Only Teina, his sister and brother and the queen, were allowed to remain on board as a special privilege, grateful for one more evening with Bligh.

"May God bless and protect you for ever and ever," were Teina's last words as he went over the side to his waiting canoe. He had with him Bligh's last and highly prized presents—two muskets, two pistols and four thousand rounds of ammunition. This once obscure regent of a part of northern Tahiti was now the richest and most powerful ruler in the whole of the Pacific.

The crew lined the side of the *Bounty* and gave Teina and his relatives three cheers in Royal Navy style. At 6:30 a.m. on April 4 anchors were weighed and the *Bounty* set sail on a west northwest course. The three weeks' long passage of the *Bounty* from the tranquil waters of Tahiti to Tofua was most curious. Bligh's uneven temper, his parsimony, his relentless demands for perfection, his lack of self-control, his weakness for publicly humiliating his officers—all show that he was at the end of his tether.

The *Bounty* needed an iron hand. Every crew member had been affected by the relaxed time ashore. But the pressure should have been applied evenly and with justice, not with abuse, empty threats and histrionics followed by a sudden return to familiarity as if nothing had happened. "Which of the young gentlemen will dine with me tonight? Mr. Christian . . . ?"

Christian's own agonized summary of his state of mind during these weeks was that he was in hell. "Whatever fault was found," reported one witness later, "Mr. Christian was sure to bear the brunt of the captain's anger."

But why? It could be explained easily if we knew—but we never shall for sure—that Bligh and Christian had a homosexual relationship going back to their first voyages together, when the

Britannia's mate had seen Bligh's "partiality for the young man." In the navy of that time, intimate friendships were often made on the long, lonely voyages. So long as they were not damaging to discipline they were accepted as a normal part of shipboard life. As for Bligh and Christian, all we know for certain is that Bligh's friendship with him was both intimate and long lasting, and that at Tahiti, when Christian shared his bed with a particularly beautiful young woman, it was broken. Was the renewal of their relationship in the confined quarters of the *Bounty* especially hard for Christian to bear? Certainly, from his behavior, it seems that Bligh was experiencing jealousy.

IN SPITE OF the long-drawn-out and emotional farewell, there were few regrets among the men at leaving Tahiti. Only a handful of them had developed "strong connections" with the native girls—perhaps only Christian and a few able seamen had remained with the same girl for most of the time. For the rest, "everybody seemed in high spirits," according to Morrison. They talked of home, predicted the length of their passage and calculated the wages that would be owed to them.

At first it seemed good to be on the move again, but the hard work, slim rations and the irascibility of their commander soon changed all this. Bligh had reinstituted his daily inspection for cleanliness. Most of the men were found wanting and had their grog stopped. On April 12 a seaman was given twelve lashes for neglect of duty. On another day during exercises Bligh and Christian fell out about some real or supposed failure. The captain cursed him roundly in front of the crew. Christian responded mildly. "Sir, your abuse is so bad that I cannot do my duty with any pleasure." Bligh then berated him again.

There was to be one stop for wood and water before the ship made for the notorious Endeavour Strait, north of New Holland, as Australia was then known. This was to be at Nomuka in the Friendly Islands some 1800 miles west of Tahiti. Bligh sighted the outlying islands on April 22. Although he claimed to know Nomuka well, he had difficulties in finding the most convenient and safe anchorage. When he went ashore he gave the chiefs presents generously and was dissatisfied with the *quid pro quo*—a number of coconuts, of which the *Bounty* already had sufficient.

The next morning, a nasty dark day of spitting rain, Christian went ashore with eleven men carrying casks for the collection of water from a pond a quarter mile inland. Will Elphinstone took four men with axes and saws for felling and cutting up timber. Christian's orders from Bligh were curious. He was to take arms ashore but they were to be left in the boat because he said they would be "much safer on shore without them."

Christian met with trouble the moment he landed, and the natives harassed his men all the way through the woods to the pond. Under conditions of great danger, with the natives "poising their clubs or spears with a menacing look," Christian managed to bring off two boatloads of filled casks. He returned to the *Bounty* with the second boatload and reported to his captain that he was having great difficulty carrying out his duties.

"You damned cowardly rascal!" shouted Bligh. "Are you afraid of a set of natives while you have arms to defend yourselves?"

"But the arms are of no use while your orders prevent them from being used," Christian replied.

Bligh did not change the order, and Christian continued with his duty. When the captain later sent Fryer ashore in the large cutter with a reinforcing party, merry hell was going on at the beach. Soon children were in the water all around the cutter, climbing on the oars, trying to get over the gunwale, shrieking and laughing, half in fun, half in hysteria. One of the sailors, fearful that the cutter would drift on shore, threw out the grapnel. Quick as a flash, some children cut the small anchor's rope and made off with it. Still, amid this pandemonium, Christian managed to hoist the remaining casks aboard the launch and get away without injury.

Bligh was beside himself with fury when he heard of the loss of a grapnel. "God damn your blood," he shouted at Christian, "why did you not fire—you an officer?"

At last the *Bounty* slowly moved out to sea. Little progress was made in the light winds. Bligh was not seen on deck next morning, and the *Bounty* was at peace.

The captain remained below until noon, when he emerged from the hatchway and made his way along the deck to his own personal pile of coconuts bartered from the natives. Suddenly he swung around to call for the master. "Mr. Fryer," he said accusingly, "don't you think these coconuts have shrunk since last night?"

Fryer looked at them carefully. "Sir, they are not so high as they were," he admitted, "but I think the pile may have been flattened by the men walking over them during the night." This could well have been the case but, convinced that he was the victim of a robbery, Bligh ordered every coconut stowed below brought on deck. Everyone had traded for a supply, and it was some time before the men stood beside their individual piles as if on inspection parade, some bewildered, some angry, all apprehensive at this fresh demonstration of their captain's eccentric behavior.

Christian bore the brunt of Bligh's attack. "Damn your blood, you have stolen my coconuts," Bligh addressed him.

"I was thirsty," Christian answered, at once confessing to his crime. "I took one only, and I am sure no one touched another."

"You lie, you scoundrel." He shook his fist in Christian's face. "You must have stolen half of them."

Then he turned from Christian and confronted the rest of his officers and men, shrieking and waving his fists. "There never was such a set of damned thieving rascals under any man's command before. . . . I suppose you will steal my yams next. But I'll sweat you for it, you rascals. I'll make half of you jump overboard before you get through Endeavour Strait."

He turned to his clerk, standing at his side, and in a loud voice so that all could hear, said, "Mr. Samuel, stop these villains' grog and give them but half a pound of yams tomorrow. The officers' coconuts will be stowed aft, and no one will touch them." At that, he turned abruptly away and went down to his cabin.

In the eyes of the officers Bligh was committing robbery not only of their coconuts but of their grog and the food to which they were entitled. No wonder, as Morrison observed, "the officers then got together and were heard to murmur much at their treatment."

But Bligh had not yet finished with Christian. That afternoon Bligh came on deck again. When he spotted Christian he re-opened his attack, calling him a thief and a scoundrel. When Christian managed to get away from his tormentor, he came forward, tears coursing down his cheeks. In spite of all he had suffered, it was the first time any of the men had seen him brought to this condition.

"What is the matter, Mr. Christian?" asked William Purcell, the ship's carpenter and one of the few warrant officers.

"Can you ask me, and hear the treatment I receive?"

"Am I not as badly treated as you?" Purcell suggested. There was a measure of truth in this. Purcell had been one of Bligh's most long-suffering victims.

"You have something to protect you," Christian said, referring to Purcell's privileges as a warrant officer. "But if I should speak to him as you do, he would probably break me, turn me before the mast, and perhaps flog me. If he did," he continued in a desperate voice, "it would be the death of us both, for I am sure I should take him in my arms and jump overboard with him."

Others overheard, and as the evening advanced, rumors circulated through the hot oppressive night that the second-in-command was contemplating desertion. There was real concern among many of the crew. They were genuinely fond of Christian, who was easy on discipline, made them laugh and helped to make life endurable. What would it be like without him?

There was not a man on board who expected soft treatment at sea. Many had suffered under harder men than Bligh and served in ships where flogging took place much more frequently than on the *Bounty*. Neither did flogging in itself create disaffection. It was one of the accepted unpleasant aspects of life at sea, like weevils in the bread or a squall off a lee shore.

The restlessness now stirring stemmed from two causes: the widespread resentment at the recent injustices and real fear for the future. The notorious dangers of Endeavour Strait, to which Bligh frequently referred—its shoals, its hidden coral reefs, its rocks and islets—all stoked the fires of anxiety in the men's minds. It was a hazardous passage. Under a commander who seemed to have lost control of his senses, the prospect was fearful.

As the light faded a volcanic eruption on the island of Tofua—they had seen its smoke as far distant as Nomuka and it had never since been out of sight—brightened into a flickering flaming torch that lit up the surrounding sea.

Christian was in his berth going through his possessions when he received a message that the captain desired his company at supper. An invitation to supper was not unusual after a row, but was surprising after today's events. In any case, Christian was completing arrangements that would result in his never seeing Bligh face to face again. "Tell Mr. Bligh that I am indisposed, and give him my compliments."

Having failed with Christian, Bligh sent to the "young gentlemen's" mess. Would any of them care to sup with their captain? Only Tom Hayward accepted, and as he left, his fellow midshipmen booed him. The captain's supper invitation was not his only peace overture of the evening. During Fryer's first night watch Bligh came up on deck and began chatting cordially.

Fryer commented conversationally, "There is a fair breeze springing up, sir, and we had a new moon earlier. That bodes well for our arrival off the coast of New Holland."

"Yes, Mr. Fryer," Bligh answered. "It will be lucky for us to arrive on that coast with a good moon."

Bligh then gave instructions for the night and returned to his cabin, from which he was to emerge a prisoner six hours later.

Chapter Three

"CONSIDER WHAT YOU ARE ABOUT, MR. CHRISTIAN"

So IT WAS THAT at 5:00 a.m. on April 28, 1789, Fletcher Christian reached his agonizing decision to lead a mutiny rather than desert ship. He went forward to approach Matthew Quintal and Isaac Martin, two able seamen of his watch whom he judged to be riper for rebellion than anyone else. Quintal was a stocky, violent man of twenty-one; Martin, the only American in the crew, was nine years older, tall, lean and tough. Christian told them he intended to take the ship—"but there is to be no murder." Already by that step he was fatally committed, incitement to mutiny being a capital offense. He asked for their support and for their opinion on who would join them. Quintal showed immediate enthusiasm, Martin was less certain but at length agreed. That made four mutineers, counting Ned Young. How many more?

They could certainly count on Charles Churchill, one of the toughest men in the *Bounty*. Despite the price he had paid in January for deserting, he was a near-certain ally. Then there were Quintal's friend Will McKoy, Matt Thompson, a hardy veteran of forty, Alex Smith, Jack Williams. They had all shown disruptive intentions in the past and were among those flogged for insolence or disobedience. That would make nine.

There was a figure standing at the stern. They could just make out his silhouette against the first gray light now stealing over the horizon—Charles Norman, the carpenter's mate, an odd fellow at the best of times. He was staring at the sea. Not quite right in the head, not a reliable ally.

Christian decided to ignore him. Instead he sent Quintal below to raise those they had selected, while he took aside in turn the other men in his watch whom he thought he could trust.

The first act in the conspiracy ran smoothly. Quintal disappeared quietly down the forward main hatchway. He roused the chosen men, whispering, "Christian is seizing the ship. Are you with us?" Each man rolled from his hammock and climbed up on deck, at first numbed, then excited at the prospect. By good chance one of these men had the keys to the arms chests. Fryer as master would normally have kept them, but, weary of being disturbed by men on watch who would often take a fancy to shooting a bird or a shark, he had recently handed them over. But for Fryer's slackness there could never have been a mutiny.

It was at this point that Christian made an alarming discovery:

two of the four men they intended to seize were asleep on top of the arms chests—John Hallett below, Tom Hayward up on deck.

The situation was restored by Christian's decisiveness. He went below and brusquely roused Hallett, ordering him up on deck to attend to his duties. As soon as he had gone, Christian opened the chest and ordered Thompson to stand guard over it and to hand out arms. Christian himself took no half measures, arming himself fully, in the style of a pirate, with musket, fixed bayonet, a pistol, a box of cartridges and a cutlass.

Up on deck again, he discovered that Hayward had risen and disappeared. (In fact he had been shaken awake by Charles Norman, who wanted to show him a shark—a common enough sight in these waters.)

The first crisis had been overcome. It was 5:15 a.m. The sun would rise in an hour and a half. By then the ship would be in Christian's hands. It was astonishing that the mutiny could gather so many followers without the knowledge of a single nonparticipant. On deck Christian already had Quintal, Martin, Churchill, McKoy, Thomas Burkitt and Williams—all seamen with either a cutlass, or a brace of pistols, or a musket with a fixed bayonet.

Able seamen John Sumner, Alex Smith and Henry Hillbrant appeared from the hatchway, all equipped with arms handed out by Thompson, who followed them on deck. There was still no sign of Ned Young.

Midshipman Hallett had disappeared. Hayward was still out of sight at the stern, watching the white trail of the shark with Norman, and remained unaware of what was going on until he turned at the sound of men approaching him. Christian was in the lead, a wild sight with his long dark brown hair falling loose to his shoulders.

Hayward walked bravely forward to meet him. "What is the cause of this act?" he demanded of his senior officer.

"Hold your tongue," Christian told him curtly.

Christian deputed Martin as armed guard over Hayward and also over Hallett, who had now reappeared and was standing, helpless and terrified, by the side of the older midshipman.

With control of the upper deck established, Christian led a party down the ladder to the after cockpit. Bligh's cabin door was ajar and he was asleep on his bunk. Fryer, his cabin opposite, had his door closed. Christian, followed by four others, stepped into the six by seven foot cabin. There it would have been hard to raise, let alone aim, their muskets. Bligh was roughly awakened and instantly pulled from his bunk.

"What's the matter? What's the matter?" he demanded.

"Hold your tongue, sir," Christian told him.

Suddenly the full danger and horror of the situation struck the captain and he called out at the top of his voice, "Murder!" over and over again.

His cries were heard from one end of the *Bounty* to the other. The ship's company responded instantly, and in different ways. Some imagined they were being attacked by native canoes, and raced up on deck to repel boarders. Others thought one of their number had gone berserk. For some minutes the *Bounty* was in a state of confusion and uproar. Men running up the ladders collided with those coming down, shouting news of the mutiny. One or two hotheads threw in their lot with the rebels and were given arms. But most stayed neutral, warily watching the tide of events.

Bligh could not understand why no one came to his aid. He felt sure that only a handful of men were concerned in this mutiny. What of Fryer, the ship's master, for instance?

John Fryer had been asleep when Sumner and Quintal burst into his cabin. He attempted to rise, but was held down and was "so flurried and surprised" (he said in court later) that he forgot all about the pistols he always kept in his cabin.

"You are a prisoner," he was told. "Hold your tongue, sir, or you are a dead man." There was no doubt that they meant it.

Fryer lay still, listening to the sounds of tumult. Through the glass panel of his door he could see figures struggling up the ladder, among them his captain, dressed only in his shirt and nightcap, hands bound behind his back. The tail of Bligh's shirt had been caught in the knot, exposing his buttocks.

"What are you doing with the captain?" he said.

"Damn his eyes!" said Sumner. "Put him into a boat and let him see if he can live on three-quarters of a pound of yams a day."

"Into the boat? What boat?"

"The small cutter," answered both Sumner and Quintal.

"Good God! The small cutter's bottom is almost eaten out with the worms."

"Damn his eyes! The boat is too good for him." And the two mutineers divulged the rest of the plan. With Bligh were to go John Samuel, Hallett and Hayward. Fryer now asked to be allowed up on deck to speak to Captain Bligh. Shouted messages passed between the master's cabin and the upper deck. Christian, rightly judging that the master would be another disruptive influence in an already dangerously confused situation, said no at first, then relented. Sumner and Quintal escorted Fryer up the ladder.

At the moment when Fryer appeared on the upper deck the sun, deep red and larger than life, heaved itself out of the eastern seas. The scene it lit was even more chaotic than anyone below could have imagined. Everybody was making a noise, either cursing, jeering or just shouting, for the reassurance it gave them.

Bligh was the central figure on this crowded stage, shouting the loudest, threatening and demanding to be released, as full of violent spirit as ever. He stood abaft the mizzenmast; Christian held the end of the cord that tied his hands, his guards had muskets cocked and aimed at him. "I dare you to fire at me!" he shouted at them, and they lowered the barrels and uncocked them. It was a small but notable victory.

Standing near Bligh and Christian on the quarterdeck were the hard-core mutineers Churchill, Quintal, McKoy, Martin and Burkitt. Forward on the forecastle deck some ten men were at the booms assisting in hoisting out the cutter.

"Mr. Christian, consider what you are about," Fryer said, appalled by the scene.

"Hold your tongue, sir. *Mămōō!*" *Mămōō*—silence—was one of their most frequently used Tahitian expressions.

Fryer persisted, raising his voice. "Mr. Christian, let Mr. Bligh go down to his cabin and I have no doubt that we will all be friends again in a very short time."

Christian said, "Hold your tongue! Not another word or you are a dead man. You know, Mr. Fryer, that I have been in hell for weeks past."

Christian's eyes were "flaming with revenge," as Morrison described later. But Fryer did not retreat. For the first time that anyone could remember, he showed real courage. He begged Christian at least to give the captain a chance of getting ashore, and reminded him of the state of the small cutter.

"No, that boat is good enough," Christian answered.

Fryer edged closer to his captain and, speaking softly, suggested that he should stay on board in the hope of retaking the ship.

Bligh replied with a bellow as loud as before, "By all means stay, Mr. Fryer. Isaac Martin is a friend," he said, indicating the American, who was standing aft among the hen coops and who had earlier given Bligh a glance which he had mistakenly interpreted as friendly. Then Bligh began to shout hysterically, "Knock Christian down! Knock Christian down!"

No one moved. Christian ordered Quintal and Sumner to take Mr. Fryer back to his cabin and they quickly led the master away. At the hatchway Fryer spoke to James Morrison, eager to learn of any who were not committed mutineers. "I hope you had no hand in this business?"

Morrison answered that he knew nothing about it. "If that's the case," Fryer said quietly, "be on your guard, there may be an opportunity of recovering the ship."

Morrison's reply was unencouraging. "Go down to your cabin, sir, it is too late for that."

On deck Christian still held the line that tied Bligh's wrists; in his other hand he held a bayonet. Whenever Bligh started to shout at them, McKoy, Churchill and Christian repeated the word *mămōō* and threatened to run him through or blow his brains out. For a time it seemed as if the mutiny was nothing more than an excuse for exchanging obscenities. At length Bligh appeared to be running out of words and stood with a furious expression on his face, licking his parched lips. One of his guards stepped forward and fed him a newly peeled pomelo. Soon Bligh's voice regained its full force.

Christian caught sight of John Smith, Bligh's servant and cook, and ordered him below for bottles of rum from the captain's cabin to serve out to all the crew under arms. "And also bring up the captain's clothes," he added.

Before Smith carried out his bidding he untucked his master's shirttail from the knot binding his wrists, making him a more decent figure. Then he went below and returned with Bligh's trousers and jacket, and a tray of glasses, tin mugs and bottles of rum.

There was a lull in the uproar as Smith helped his captain on with his trousers and put the jacket over his shoulders. Then he took up the tray and served the mutineers. His task completed, he went below.

On deck the drinking continued. Every man with a musket also had a mug or glass of potent navy grog in his hand. Bligh watched hopefully. Much more of this and the mutiny might turn into a drunken orgy, which could have one of two results: a quick end for him, or the chance of a counterattack. Bligh looked from one familiar face to another. Some were blackly hostile, others uncertain, some hid their fear. There were surely more than enough who would follow him, but the mutineers did not relax their guard.

At 7:00 a.m., one and a half hours after Bligh had been dragged from his cabin, the small cutter was at last got into the water. It at once began to sink. One might as well throw Bligh and his cronies straight into the water as into that boat. Also it now became clear that it was no longer a matter of casting adrift the captain and three others. At least twenty of the crew, including William Cole, the bo'sun, and William Purcell, the carpenter—both valuable men—were loyal to Bligh and determined to leave the ship with him. Christian had seriously miscalculated. If he kept behind by force those who wanted to leave, there would be the constant threat of a countermutiny. Reluctantly he ordered the large cutter to be lowered into the water, but there was scarcely room even in this.

"You must give us the launch, Christian," Cole demanded.

Purcell, too, spoke in an agonized voice. "Mr. Christian, I want to see my native country. Let us have the launch and do not make a sacrifice of us."

Young chose this moment to appear from hiding with a musket and fixed bayonet. He resolved Christian's dilemma by indicating assent to Cole's demand.

"Hoist out the launch, Mr. Cole," said Christian.

The launch was twenty-three feet long, and six feet nine inches in breadth. It could be rowed, and two masts could be stepped. There were six seats for the oarsmen and a five-foot seat along each side in the stern. Fifteen men would be its normal maximum capacity. As soon as it was in the water, the men who had chosen to follow Bligh hastened to collect their possessions and any supplies they could lay their hands on. Purcell demanded his tool chest. Christian at first refused, and then yielded to Purcell's pleas.

Some of the men were already in the boat, receiving and stowing their gear with frantic speed. At every additional item the launch rode lower in the water. Christian was trying to stem the flow of goods, waving his bayonet, threatening and calling out, "Carry nothing away!" No one took much notice. Morrison (though no one was certain which side he was on) had dropped a towline and grapnel into the launch; and Cole went up onto the quarterdeck after a compass, despite the armed opposition.

When Quintal saw the bo'sun trying to get the compass from the binnacle he exclaimed, "I'll be damned if you have it! What do you want with a compass with the land in sight?"

Cole protested boldly. "Quintal, it is very hard you'll not let us have a compass when there are nine more in the storeroom." Burkitt was the only man near, ferocious and armed to the teeth. To Cole's surprise he spoke up for him. "Quintal," he said, "let Mr. Cole have it." Cole hastened away with the precious compass.

Bligh's clerk was economical in collecting his personal possessions, just a few shirts and stockings in a pillowcase. He was more concerned with his master's box of surveys, his timekeeper, log and journals. Churchill intercepted him and seized all but the last two. To Bligh's vehement protests he replied savagely, "Damn your eyes, you are well off to get what you have!"

Amid this tumult two men remained outside the mainstream of the mutiny. Incredibly, the shark was still attracting the attention of Charles Norman, who remained leaning over the stern rail as if nothing had happened. The blind fiddler, Michael Byrn, sat in the rejected large cutter, crying in fear and bewilderment.

By eight o'clock several loyalists already on board the launch were attempting to create order. On the quarterdeck Christian was still beside Bligh, as he had been now for almost three hours. His agony of mind was reflected so clearly in his dark face that even the most frightened men remembered it long after. Several of those present, including Bligh himself, considered that he might take his own life at any moment.

Christian turned to midshipmen Hayward and Hallett. "You are to go into the launch now," he said. Bligh's wrists were then untied, and he was hustled toward the gangway. He appeared utterly exhausted. Christian said, "Come, Captain Bligh, your officers and men are now in the boat and you must go with them."

Bligh looked earnestly into Christian's eyes. "Consider what you are about, Mr. Christian," he said. "For God's sake, drop it. I'll give my bond never to think of it again if you'll desist." Christian made no reply. "I have a wife and four children," Bligh pleaded.

"It is too late. I have been in hell."

"It is not too late," said Bligh.

"No, Captain Bligh, if you had any honor, things would not have come to this, and if you had had any regard for your wife and your family you should have thought of them before and not behaved so much like a villain."

Amid the growing impatience of mutineers and loyalists alike, they continued their dialogue. For a second it seemed that there was a chance of Christian weakening. Then Ned Young appeared, musket in hand. He seemed to emerge from nowhere whenever events reached a critical point. Bligh looked at him accusingly. "This is a serious affair, Mr. Young," he warned.

"Yes, sir," said Young, "it is a serious matter to be starved. I hope this day you get a belly full."

Christian, energized by the presence of Young, made some quick decisions. He saw that he could not work the ship in any sort of emergency with the men left to him. He wanted no troublemakers, but he did want skilled men. He called Joseph Coleman, the armorer, and McIntosh and Norman of the carpenter's crew to come back from the boat, but not the carpenter himself.

Bligh, seeing that the launch would not survive a day with so many on board, added his own voice, suddenly reassuring and hearty. "You can't all go in the boat, my lads. Some of you must stay in the ship. Never fear, my lads, I'll do you justice if ever I reach England." The three men climbed up the gangway. Fryer for his part was trying to persuade Christian not to put him in the boat, claiming that the mutineers would need him to sail the ship.

"We can do very well without you, Mr. Fryer," said Christian.

Bligh broke in, this time in contradiction: "You are to remain on board the *Bounty*, Mr. Fryer."

Nobody seemed to want the ship's master. But Christian had the last word, backed by a threatening cutlass. "By God, sir, go into the boat or I'll run you through."

That left only Bligh. He turned to Christian and asked, "Do you consider this treatment a proper return for all the friendship I have given you in the past?"

Christian was visibly upset and uncertain how to answer. What was there to say? Their relationship, once so deep and so passionate, had been shattered. In the words Christian spoke he showed again how deeply disturbed he was. "That—Captain Bligh—that is the thing—I am in hell—I am in hell!"

Bligh walked down the gangway in dignified silence and stepped unaided into the launch, where a place had been cleared for him in the stern. He was followed a few moments later by one of the mutineers carrying Christian's own sextant and nautical tables.

Christian said, "There, Captain Bligh, this is sufficient for every purpose. You know the sextant to be a good one." They were the last words he spoke to his captain.

"Mr. Christian, send me down some muskets, for God's sake," Bligh cried out.

The mutineers had been momentarily subdued during the captain's disembarkation, but on hearing this demand the wilder elements gave vent again to curses and threats. Churchill, however, did lower four cutlasses at the end of a line.

Cole gave orders to cast off. As they drifted astern last messages were called from the *Bounty*'s quarterdeck. Charles Norman, his shark now forgotten, was in tears, as were several others. "I wish I could go with you to see my wife and family," he cried. "Remember me to them."

The launch rubbed along the *Bounty*'s hull, slipping by degrees toward the stern quarter. It was nearly ten o'clock, the sun already very hot. What little wind there had been earlier had died, and the sea was gently undulating. Bligh and Cole got the men to the oars and the gap between the two ships began to widen. They could faintly hear Christian's voice calling for the topgallant sails to be loosed aboard the *Bounty*. It was like eavesdropping on a world they would know no more.

If the sea remained calm, the nineteen loyalists, including the captain, had a good chance of making Tofua, the volcanic island which had offered them such pretty lights the night before. But after Tofua? The nearest European settlement was thousands of miles away; their launch was no longer than four men stretched out; the distance between gunwale and the water less than the length of a man's hand; and they had food and drink for no longer than one week.

Chapter Four

"PUT UP THE HELM, MR. FRYER"

As the *Bounty* bore away slowly to the northwest, Cole and Fryer created some sort of order in the launch. Bligh sat silently in the stern contemplating their situation. As always, he was filled with the comforting knowledge that he had done

Chris Mayger 72

no wrong, that he was a victim of villainy and circumstances beyond his control. Clearly, as he wrote in his log shortly after, Christian and his fellow pirates had never intended to leave Tahiti, with "its allurements of dissipation."

Typically, however, even as he was consoling himself that he was innocent, Bligh was preparing to recoup his fortunes. First he must make his way to England, then he must clear his name, regain the favors of his patron, exact revenge on those who had injured him and complete the breadfruit mission. Nothing less than this would satisfy him.

Through the hot afternoon, with six men at the oars, the launch made slow progress toward the steep black volcanic cliffs of Tofua. It was already dark when they finally drew near the shore. Hearing the rollers beating on the rocks, Bligh decided to stand off through the night and keep two men at the oars. To warm and give his men cheer, Bligh served them all half a pint of grog, about one third of their total supplies. It was the last generous ration of any kind they were to enjoy for seven weeks.

The island was an inhospitable place five miles long and four miles wide. The present eruption of its volcano was a mild one, more like a slow leak in the earth's crust. In the morning Bligh took the launch along the coast and discovered a small cove. But the men who waded ashore found only some fresh water. That afternoon they worked the launch south till they spotted some coconut trees high on the cliff tops. A small party got ashore through the surf, climbed the cliffs and collected twenty coconuts. That night they each had a coconut and made themselves as comfortable as they could in the boat.

Next morning Bligh led another shore party in the hope of collecting provisions. After issuing a morsel of bread and a teaspoon of rum to every man, he scrambled over the side, taking two cutlasses and his precious log.

This time the party found lengths of vine hanging down the cliffs, clearly provided to assist climbers. It was their first proof that the island was inhabited. Bligh led the way boldly to the cliff top, and later discovered a cave at the head of the cove, where they spent the night.

The following morning some friendly natives appeared, and the sailors exchanged buttons torn from their jackets for plantains and breadfruit. Bligh explained that their ship had been wrecked and that they were the only survivors. The natives showed no signs of either joy or sympathy. Toward evening, Bligh wrote in his log in the cave, "I saw with peculiar pleasure that we had increased our stock of provisions, and that at sundown the natives left us."

Now confident that this island might supply them with the provisions they would need to survive the long open boat voyage he was planning—of which his men still knew nothing—Bligh sent parties inland to trade. More canoes, some from other islands, began to appear, and gradually the first familiar signs of hostility began to creep into the conversation. Out of the corner of his eye Bligh saw a party of natives moving toward the line securing the launch to the shore. They seized the line and attempted to drag it ashore. Bligh recognized the need for immediate action. His only weapons were the two cutlasses, and his men were outnumbered by more than ten to one.

Bligh rushed at one of the chiefs, holding his cutlass over him and demanding that his men should let go of the line. The chief gave the required order, and the natives retreated.

By noon the situation on the beach had formed a familiar pattern. Trading continued, but it seemed now more like a ritual prelude to violence. In the early part of the afternoon the signs of hostility increased. A strong and threatening body of natives lined the shore, ostentatiously separating Bligh and his party from their launch. With superb insouciance, Bligh settled down in the cave to write up his log so that the world might know one day how he had died. When he had finished, he gave the book to Peckover. "Get it to the boat if you can," he told him, "and tell Mr. Fryer to keep her well in on the beach when he sees us breaking out."

Peckover walked boldly down the beach, pushing his way through the crowd, the book under his arm. He broke through, waded out to the launch and delivered the message and the log.

Several chiefs now came up to Bligh's cave. "Will you not stay the night?" asked one.

"No, I always sleep in my boat," answered Bligh. "But in the morning let us do more trading."

"You will not sleep on shore," said another. It was a statement which suggested he would not leave it either. "We will kill you!"

Bligh seized one of their number by the arm, holding his cutlass in his other hand as a sign that he would strike if an attack were made. Then he led his party down from the cave, across the beach "in a silent kind of horror," as he described it.

It was a repetition of that nightmare scene in Karakakooa Bay just ten years earlier. Between his party and the launch were two hundred warriors. Bligh walked straight toward them as if they were urchins at a street corner. Something in his demeanor served to hold back the massed natives until the last of his men had scrambled safely into the launch. Then the chief in Bligh's grip broke free. At once another chief raised his hand as an order for an all-out attack. Bligh saw this signal and ran into the sea, struggling through the waves toward the launch.

Bligh's courage inspired his men. Not one panicked. Six were at the oars, ready to row as soon as their captain was on board. The *Bounty*'s hefty quartermaster chose this moment to match his captain's gallantry and leaped into the surf to tackle the oncoming natives singlehanded. In a second he was hurled to the ground and beaten to death with stones. The natives struggled for possession of his trousers as he died.

Fryer helped to haul his captain into the launch. The stones were flying thick and fast, many of them wounding the men. Other natives had waded into the surf, some seizing the stern. Bligh slashed at the natives' arms until they released their grip.

The fleeing launch was still no match for the natives who pursued them out of the cove. Again and again their canoes closed on it; they released salvos of stones like broadsides. "Come back for the man you have left behind!" they taunted.

Bligh realized that soon his men would all be stunned or dead, and the launch overwhelmed. "Throw over your clothes!" he ordered. It was like throwing raw meat to a pack of wolves. At once the natives dived into the water, struggling to be the first to reach these prizes. Now using sail, the launch put on speed, and with darkness falling and the sea rising, the Tofuan coastline faded into the distance.

The horrible death of the quartermaster proved a blessing to his shipmates, for John Norton had been the weight of two men. His absence meant five percent more food for every man, five percent more room in the packed little craft.

It was almost dark, the sea was choppy, and they were taking in water as they began tacking south into the rising wind. Bligh told his crew they were heading for Tongatabu, an island he had visited with Cook. Here, he said, they were sure of acquiring all they needed. Mr. Cole, the bo'sun, said, "Sir, I would rather trust to Providence and live even on an ounce of bread a day than to go to Tongatabu, for I believe the natives would take everything we have, then cut us to pieces."

There was a murmur of agreement. Then Peckover spoke up. "Could we not make Timor, sir?" The gunner's suggestion found instant and excited response from the men because they knew there was a long-established Dutch settlement on the island. It was as if in a few days they would be walking up the quay at Kupang to a warm welcome.

Bligh recognized the dangers in this euphoric mood, and warned them of what lay ahead. In a twenty-three-foot open launch they would face storms and the danger of shipwreck. They had not a single map. They might die insane from the heat and from thirst. The food would be rationed severely. They had on board one hundred and fifty pounds of biscuit in bags, some of it already spoiled by seawater, twenty pounds of pork, a few coconuts and breadfruit, the last moldy. For drink, they had twenty-eight gallons of water, five quarts of rum and three bottles of wine. That was all.

"Well, my lads, can you live on two ounces of bread and a gill of water a day?"

There was a chorus of agreement. Bligh was still not satisfied and asked each individually if he was prepared to face stringent rations. "Aye, sir!" "Aye!" There was not a voice of dissent.

"Then in God's name put up the helm, Mr. Fryer."

The launch swung around and scudded before the wind at a fine pace. "Let us give thanks for our miraculous preservation," Bligh began the prayers that night. "Oh Lord, we have faith that you will continue to offer us your gracious support."

THE SKILL, COURAGE and endurance of the launch's crew were put to severe test within hours of their decision. By the middle of the next morning they were being driven before a full easterly gale. For the next two days they constantly had to bail for their lives. Even during their worst sufferings, Bligh continued to plot their progress, taking readings at noon whenever the sun could be seen. When the sea was rough the only way he could do this was by standing in the center of the boat, steadied by a man on each side. He continued to record all the new land he discovered, including twenty-three of the Fiji Islands.

On the evening of May 6 the launch passed close inshore of several of these attractive islands. The men could see clearly the streams pouring down the cliffs from the mountains while they eked out their ration of stale water, and ate their two ounces of moldy bread within full sight of plantains, yams and bananas. It was hard to bear, but there were no protests. The islands were obviously inhabited, and in their weak condition and without firearms, the risks of being seized were too great.

On the following day rain came down, heavily and continuously. By spreading a sail they were able to collect thirty-four gallons in one night, and this probably saved their lives. As Bligh wrote, "I consider the general run of cloudy and wet weather to be a providential blessing to us. Hot weather would have caused us to have died raving mad with thirst."

As the launch continued on its westerly course, through recurrent gales and downpours of tropical rain, the men weakened day by day. Bligh resorted to a variety of makeshift methods to preserve their health and spirit. He had them make a patchwork Union Jack out of a bundle of old signal flags which had been thrown into the boat. He encouraged them to throw out fishing lines, which were a subject of endless speculation, though they never brought a fish on board. In the evenings he would lead his men in songs, rousing the weak or reluctant until all were singing, the brave sound reaching far out over the lonely surrounding sea.

An elaborate ritual grew up around the simple process of consuming a few ounces of food each day. Bligh himself always broke his bread in small pieces and mixed it with his water ration in a coconut shell, "taking care never to take but a piece at a time so that I am as long at dinner as at a more plentiful meal!"

After twenty-one days at sea he discovered that there was enough bread on the present allowance for only another twenty-nine days. Already all the men were showing signs of weakness. "Our appearances were horrible," wrote Bligh, "and I could look no way but I caught the eye of some one in distress." He hardened his heart. That evening he told his men there would have to be a fifty percent cut in their basic food. He wrote in his log that it had been "like robbing them of life."

As a token that Providence might finally favor them, boobies and noddy terns were sighted, a sure sign that land was not too far distant. At noon the next day one of the men caught a noddy in his hand and killed it. Bligh, who described this noddy as the size of a small pigeon, divided it—entrails, bones and all—into eighteen parts. In accordance with naval tradition, one man stood with his back to the launch's company while another pointed in turn to the spread-out parts, calling, "Who shall have this?" The first man answered each time with a name until all the bird had gone.

Exactly one month after he had been cast adrift with no more than a sextant, an old quadrant and a book of tables, Bligh caught his first glimpse of Australia and brought the launch to within sight of the Great Barrier Reef.

The only European who had sailed and charted these waters was Cook. He had only just escaped destruction on the 1500-mile-long reef, but he had reported gaps through which a ship could enter into the island-studded calm water beyond. To penetrate this reef in a launch, manned by a crew in the last stages of weakness, was hazardous indeed. One touch of that razor-sharp coral, and their boat would be torn to splinters.

The next day it was Fryer who spotted a possible gap. At first it looked too narrow. Then as they ventured nearer it seemed to open before their eyes. With the wind behind them, and assisted by a fast current, the launch shot through into the calm waters beyond.

Late in the afternoon Bligh ran in to a fine sandy beach on an island which he named Restoration Island: both for the anniversary on this day of the restoration to the throne of King Charles II in 1660, and to commemorate their own salvation. When the moment came for the crew to step ashore, many of them could scarcely make their way through the water and onto the beach. Cramped for so long, starved almost to death, they were, remarked Fryer, "like so many drunken men."

At Restoration Island the men's speedy recovery was matched by the rapidity with which they reverted to their old ways. Within twenty-four hours, when their bellies had been filled with berries and oysters, the grumblers began to grumble, the slackers to slack, and Bligh himself to hector and nag, curse and threaten.

On the second day Bligh ordered his men off to search for oysters and settled down in the shade to write up his log. It was a repetition of the situation in Tahiti, with Bligh absenting himself from his men, appearing only occasionally and then to upbraid them. By now everyone was in a bad temper, for besides the reaction to their ordeal, most were suffering from stomach pains from the unaccustomed food. Also they were anxious again for their safety. Natives in great numbers had been sighted on the mainland, waving their spears threateningly.

That evening they embarked again to search for another temporary home. At Sunday Island, named for the day of the week they landed, matters got worse and there was almost another mutiny. Again the dispute was over food. Bligh sent out foraging parties in different directions about the island, then claimed that all the food gathered was in his charge. Purcell resisted this hotly. Bligh cursed him and said, "If I had not brought you here you would all have perished."

"Yes, sir," Purcell replied sarcastically. "If it had not been for you, we should not have been here."

This was too much for Bligh, who seized his cutlass, sliced the air above Purcell's head and ordered him to fetch another cutlass to defend himself.

Fryer now stepped between the men. "No fighting here," he told them.

Bligh turned on Fryer. "If, sir, you interfere with me in the course of my duty, you will certainly be the first person I shall put to death." This silenced the master. Bligh ordered the parties away again on a further search, and they obeyed reluctantly. The risk of rebellion was ended. Bligh ordered a small fire that night, but Fryer made one of his own, which got out of hand. For fear the natives would attack, Bligh then ordered the launch to sail the next morning.

Once they were again at sea a remarkable change came over the men. Although they were back on rations little better than before—just a few dried oysters or clams to add to their bread allowance—for a time everyone was full of confidence and good spirits. The grumbling ceased and Bligh again became undisputed commander.

Just before dawn on June 3 they reached the feared straits north of Australia. As they would need daylight to negotiate the hazards of uncharted reefs and unpredictable currents, it was not until noon that Bligh ordered the helm to be put over. The route he took was the narrow, dangerous channel—separating Prince of Wales Island from the continent—known as Endeavour Strait. But Bligh safely negotiated shoal water, rocks, sand banks and reefs, like the peerless navigator he was.

By evening they were free from the worst dangers, and open sea lay ahead. It had a tonic effect on all hands. This bright optimism, however, was short-lived. The strength they had gained from their few sustaining meals among the islands did not last long. After only four days the men became lethargic and slept much of the time. They had to be awakened for their bite of food.

On June 10 Bligh considered that more than half of them were showing signs of "an approaching end to their distresses." However, he did not yield an ounce on the rations, though there still remained enough for another fifteen days and there were already signs of land ahead. Strict economy had become his obsession.

By the following day everyone was at the last extremity. Never had their prospects seemed lower. Bligh looked at their swollen legs, their "hollow and ghastly countenances," observed their extreme weakness, and wondered what had come over them. Cole regarded his captain and observed, "I really think, sir, that you look worse than anyone in the boat."

This brought Bligh back to reality. He laughed and returned him "a better compliment."

Yet, though Bligh might appear as bad as anyone, he was the only one who still remained confident that the boat would reach its destination. At noon he calculated that they were less than one hundred miles from Timor. When he passed this information to his men they showed "a universal joy and satisfaction."

The island was finally sighted soon after 3:00 a.m. on June 12. Even the weakest among them rose from the bottom of the launch and broke into hoarse cheers of relief; then, led by Bligh, they knelt down in prayers of thankfulness for their deliverance.

Chapter Five

"A GREAT ROCK"

AT MIDDAY ON April 28, 1789, the *Bounty* was a ship without a commander, its company stunned by the sudden breakdown in law and order. Only Christian had his wits about him. Haunted though he was by the last sight of the packed, wallowing launch, he knew that these men, the guilty and the nonguilty, were his responsibility. Still, he was not going to propose himself in command. Others must do it. They did so, eagerly and unanimously.

Christian now acted briskly. If they were to survive, there must be discipline again. He ordered the midshipman George Stewart, a nonmutineer and a severe taskmaster, to command the second watch. Then, just as he had made the appointment of the *Bounty*'s new captain a democratic decision, so he consulted his men about their long-term plans.

"Where will you sail to now, lads? Remember that if the launch reaches a port there will be an immediate search for us. And they will look for us anyway later when the ship does not return."

"Carry us wherever you think proper, sir," one man spoke, and there appeared to be general agreement with him. Tahiti, the mutineers knew, was out of the question as a permanent home. It would be the first place that any searching vessel would make for. They needed a remote island, and Christian told his men that he had chosen Tubai, some three hundred miles south of Tahiti, noted but not landed on by Cook. It was far from the likely route of any traffic of searching vessels, and had a single harbor with difficult access. Cook had written of the natives that "their countenances express some degree of natural ferocity"; but they could hardly be worse than those on the Friendly Islands.

Everything was made shipshape on board for the long voyage east. The piles of fruit which had covered the decks under Bligh's regime were tidied up. All but a few of the breadfruit plants were hurled into the sea. Christian then moved into Bligh's cabin, and with a complement of only twenty-five they all enjoyed less cramped conditions. However, discipline was no less severe than under Bligh, but no one was inclined "to dispute the superiority of Mr. Christian."

Tubai was sighted a month after the mutiny, a typical volcanic Polynesian island some five miles long. Dozens of canoes were launched from the beach and soon the *Bounty*'s decks were thick with natives, scrounging and thieving for all they were worth. Christian had difficulty getting rid of them without violence, and it was obvious that they would be back in greater strength.

The next morning's assault was executed with cunning. First eighteen nubile young women, the pick of the Tubaian girls, came out to the ship. All were well versed in seduction, and while they were busy at work, the main attack came. Fifty canoes, all manned by warriors with spears, approached, and the baying of conch shells filled the bay with an insane, threatening chorus. Christian ordered the *Bounty*'s four-pounders to be fired into the packed canoes at point-blank range. The result was devastating. A dozen died in the attack, many more were wounded, and the rest—men and girls—screamed and fled.

Christian named their anchorage Bloody Bay. Later he went ashore with an armed escort to survey the island. In spite of the catastrophic start, he remained convinced that he could dominate these people. The land was ripe for cultivation, and in the unlikely event that a searching ship might arrive there, it would be an easy place to defend. It would make an ideal settlement, but first they needed livestock, women, and native men to serve them. All these were unavailable.

"We lacked women, and remembering Tahiti, where all of us had made intimate friendships, we decided to return there, so that we could each obtain one." So wrote the mutineer Alex Smith, who now revealed that this was an assumed name, and reverted to his own name, John Adams. The *Bounty* sailed back again to Matavai Bay on June 7, 1789.

There was enormous excitement among the natives on Tahiti when the *Bounty* was sighted, and Christian watched the canoes coming out to meet them with complete equanimity. He had an ingenious story ready, built on Bligh's earlier tale that Cook was still alive.

They had met Captain Cook, Christian told the chiefs, and Captain Bligh had gone on board with some of his men, taking with them the ship's launch and all but a few of his plants. Cook and Bligh had then sailed off together to a settlement in New Holland which Cook had been sent to establish by order of the king. As soon as possible, Christian continued glibly, Bligh would come back to Tahiti with more gifts for his old friends.

All this was believable to the Matavaians, and when Christian told them that their beloved Cook would like food, livestock and native helpers for this new settlement, they all fell to with a will. Soon the *Bounty* began to look like Noah's ark—460 live hogs, fifty goats, chickens, a bull and cow originally left at Tahiti by Cook, and for good measure some dogs and cats. The crew had less success recruiting natives, who showed a disappointing reluctance to leave their families. Finally only Jenny, Mary, Sarah and Isabella, who still regarded themselves as the wives of Adams, McKoy, Quintal and Christian, agreed to remain on board, together with seventeen men and boys and one young girl. But at the last minute seven more women were tricked into sailing with the ship.

By now Christian had realized the cardinal mistake he had made in not disposing of his nonmutineers. They knew all his plans and no matter how many promises they made, nor how good their intentions, if they were allowed to remain at Tahiti, the news that the *Bounty* had gone to Tubai would leak out sooner or later. The only way to avoid this risk had been to prohibit shore leave to all the ship's company and forbid them, under the threat of the most savage punishment, from talking to the natives about their plans. Like it or not, they must now all stick together.

The *Bounty* sailed out of Matavai Bay on June 16, 1789, and anchored off Tubai a week later. Conforming to colonizing practice, Christian led his mixed party ashore and started work on a fort without further delay. It was to be a magnificent affair, nearly one hundred yards square, with earthen walls eighteen feet thick at the base, surrounded by a twenty-foot-deep moat, and entered by a drawbridge. On each corner one of the *Bounty*'s four-pounders was to be mounted, and the ship's swivel guns were to be placed along the walls. Within this fort they would be secure from both native uprisings and attack from the sea. Above it, even while it was under construction, the Union Jack flew bravely.

A halt to the promising start of this new settlement was brought about by two forces, one from within, one from without. The Tubaians, submissive after their earlier bloody defeat, became increasingly anxious. They watched the moat being dug, and told one another that they were to be exterminated and this was to be their mass grave. But the more serious source of conflict stemmed from the colonists' continuing shortage of women. The men became increasingly reckless in their efforts to persuade some of the local girls to join them, and several times on these hunting expeditions they were ambushed, stripped of their clothes and beaten.

Like any good colonial governor, Christian tried to conciliate the chiefs, but violence was inevitable. Woundings, abductions and killings culminated in a minor colonial war—muskets against spears—in which sixty-six natives were killed. The Englishmen suffered only two injuries, but Christian's brave plans were shattered. He gathered his men about him for a discussion of their future. Sixteen out of twenty-five voted to return to Tahiti.

Christian accepted the decision gracefully. "Gentlemen," he said, "I will carry you wherever you please. I desire no one to stay with me. But I have one favour to request—that you will grant me the ship, tie the foresail and give me a few gallons of water, and leave me to run before the wind, and I shall land upon the first island the ships drives. After what I have done I can not remain at Tahiti. I will live nowhere where I may be apprehended and brought home to be a disgrace to my family."

This speech, its emotional overtones, its frankness, were all typical of the man. His great enterprise had failed; they did not need him any longer. But his old friend Young spoke up. "We shall never leave you, Mr. Christian!" Other voices joined his. "We will never leave you!" Eight in all.

The men put their plans into immediate effect. Everything that had been brought ashore was taken back to the *Bounty*. Christian also had Brown collect some of the finest fruit plants he could find and stow them in the great cabin. Then on September 18 all embarked, together with some local natives who had linked their fortunes so closely with the white men that they feared for their future on the island. The *Bounty* put to sea.

Christian never knew how close to discovery they had been at Tubai. A month before they left the island, the brig *Mercury* had passed within two miles of Tubai at night and had observed only the lights on shore. In daylight she could not have failed to spot the *Bounty*. Nor did he know that Bligh had now reached Timor safely and had already dispatched reports of the mutiny, with a detailed description of every one of those who had remained on board the *Bounty* so that "the pirates" might be identified and apprehended.

THE *BOUNTY* ARRIVED off Tahiti for the third and last time on September 22, 1789. There had been no further disagreement among the crew. Christian was to have the ship and the eight hard-core mutineers who had agreed to stick with him: Young, Mills, Quintal, McKoy, Adams and Williams, the American Isaac Martin and William Brown, the assistant gardener from Kew. With the help of two Tubaian natives, who had sworn everlasting loyalty, and some more men they hoped to persuade to accompany them from Tahiti, Christian reckoned that he could work the *Bounty* safely. Isabella, Mary, Jenny and Sarah would of course remain with their *taios*. The other men would find their own women.

Midshipmen Stewart and Heywood, Byrn, Coleman, Norman and McIntosh, who had taken no part in the mutiny, felt safe enough to set up home at Matavai. Here they would remain until they could take passage on board a passing vessel, or were picked up by a searching British ship. Besides these six men, ten others preferred to risk discovery at Tahiti.

Christian went ashore with the first of the Tahiti party. He was anxious to be away quickly. He was filled with unease, trusting neither his companions nor the Matavai chiefs, who must now soon learn the truth about Bligh and the mutiny, either from his shipmates or the natives who had been abducted to Tubai earlier and were now returning to their homes.

The news that met him on shore only increased his anxiety. A great ship like the *Bounty* had only recently left. The ship's master, Captain John Henry Cox, had been puzzled by Teina's tale of the *Bounty* returning under a new captain and leaving again loaded with livestock for a place where Captain Cook had built a new settlement. Captain Cox had explained to Teina that

Cook had been dead for years, and to prove it had presented him with a dramatic picture of the assassination. The chief was furious at the deception that had been perpetrated on him. Christian had wanted to fill some of his casks with water, but now he thought that even this was too risky.

The last picture the world had of Fletcher Christian for more than eighteen years was of him standing on the black volcanic sandy beach of Matavai Bay, the cutter drawn up ready to take him to the *Bounty* anchored a half mile out. He was in earnest discussion with Stewart and young Heywood, giving them both hope and warning. A ship would certainly come.

"When it does, give yourselves up at once," Christian told them. "Do not attempt to hide. You are both innocent. No harm can come to you, for you took no part in the mutiny."

Then he took Peter Heywood aside and asked him to deliver messages to his own family. Christian recapitulated in detail the events connected with "that unfortunate disaster" as he wanted his family to know them: "Tom Hayward was asleep, John Hallett not yet on duty, and it was then that the idea of taking the ship first entered my head. I alone was responsible for this act." He was determined that no one else should be implicated. It was his mutiny, his alone.

ALMOST EVERYONE BELIEVED that the *Bounty* would remain at anchor for two more days to take on wood and water, and that evening there were numbers of natives on board, supping and drinking with the remaining mutineers. When darkness fell and while the festivities continued below in the forecastle, Christian and Young silently cut the anchor cables, hoisted sail and stood out past the reef. It was the only way they could be sure of having enough women this time. Without them Christian knew that their settlement, wherever it might be, was doomed before it began.

Next morning Christian and Young took stock of their spoils. In all they had eighteen women, only four of whom were on board of their own free will, and six men. Two of the men were the Tubaians, the other four were victims of Christian's trick. All were regarded by the Englishmen as menservants—slaves, really—to help with the heavy work. All passed muster for this role. Unfortunately the same could not be said for all the women. These included six who, although somehow included in the evening's festivities, were past their best childbearing years. Later next day, when the *Bounty* was passing the neighboring island of Mooréa and a canoe put out from that island, Christian had the six surplus women "who were rather ancient" taken off. The other kidnapped women watched them leave the ship with envy—if only they too were old and fat!

Christian now conducted the important business of pairing off the women, the white men being given a range of choice. Only one of the natives was given a wife of his own.

That accomplished, the *Bounty* continued before the wind through the Cook Islands searching for a spot that met their needs. The island must be remote, harborless and uninhabited. The last requirement was the most important. An inhabited island meant not only possible trouble at the hands of the Polynesians, but also communications. The word of a white settlement would travel at the speed of the natives' great ocean-sailing, twin-hulled canoes. At one island after another it was the same story. They would approach, examining it through the glass to judge its coastline and interior, draw near it with caution and expectation; then they would spot dark figures on the beach, and canoes putting out; and Christian would order the helm put over and they would run out to sea again.

Gradually Christian's naturally cheerful nature, scarred by guilt, turned dour. There was now no gaiety on board the *Bounty*. With tempers fraying, the ship continued its restless voyage until she left the waters of eastern Polynesia far behind and was back among the Friendly Islands.

Here Christian was forced to anchor, collect water, barter for food and make a final decision about their future. The trading was conducted peacefully, and at the end of two days Christian had made up his mind. He had already studied Bligh's charts, and among books he had consulted was a volume of Hawkesworth's *Voyages*. On page 561 he read of Carteret's voyage:

We continued our course westward till the evening of 2d July [1767], when we discovered land to the northward of us. Upon approaching it the next day, it appeared like a great rock rising out of the sea: it was not more than five miles in circumference, and seemed to be uninhabited; it was, however, covered with trees . . . it having been discovered by a young gentleman, son to Major Pitcairn of the marines . . . we called it Pitcairn's Island.

This sounded highly promising to Christian. Its only drawback, as far as he could calculate, was that it was so distant—almost three thousand miles east, and against the trades all the way. Young and the others agreed that they should make the attempt, and on November 15 the *Bounty* made sail and headed southeast.

Two discouraging months passed before the "great rock" at last broke the horizon ahead of the *Bounty*'s bows. Carteret had been two miles out in his reckoning, but there was no mistaking it—the silhouette matched exactly the careful engraving in Hawkesworth's book. The date was January 15, 1790. Nine months after the mutiny Christian had found the home for which he had searched for so long.

There was no sign of life, only seabirds wheeling about the cliffs. The island was thickly wooded, two miles long by perhaps one mile wide. The land rose precipitously on the southern and western sides, and with only a few breaks in the cliffs along the northeastern coastline as well. There was little level ground, but the gentler slopes on the eastern side of the island offered the prospect of farming.

Three days later, when the wind slackened enough for Christian to bring the *Bounty* closer inshore, the large cutter was hoisted out. Christian and three others, with three natives, rowed across what was to become known as Bounty Bay, were picked up by a rolling breaker and hurled onto a beach—no more than a dozen yards wide—at the base of a steep cliff.

They struggled up the cliff three hundred feet to a ridge. Christian was soon satisfied that the beauty of the place was peerless, the soil rich, the fruit abundant, the climate benign.

Here, on this level strip of land above the beach, their dwellings built behind the thick banyans would be invisible from the sea.

On the following day the *Bounty* was brought in closer to shore, and the ship's company, together with the livestock, were ferried onto the narrow beach. There was much to be done just to tide them over—a sailcloth was rigged for a roof the first nights, and they built open fires to cook their meals, but they survived all this stoically. In their new element, after four months of wandering, cheerfulness and relief predominated. Above all, Christian himself was a happy man again. One of the men told of his "joyful expression such as we had not seen on him for a long time past."

Chapter Six

"PANDORA'S BOX"

On HIS ARRIVAL at Kupang in Timor, Bligh dined in the house of the second-in-command of this Dutch settlement, the governor being indisposed. He left the table as soon as it was polite to do so, and retired to his room. Above food and drink, it was peace that he wanted. Here, alone for the first time since the night of the mutiny, utterly weary in mind and body, he lay down to rest and give thanks to Almighty God, "Who had given us power to support and bear such heavy calamities, and had enabled me at last to be the means of saving eighteen lives." As soon as he had rested he wrote to his wife, ending with blessings to "the little stranger"—the infant who had been born after he left England. In fact there were twin girls, making five in all so far. Later, Bligh prepared a complete account of all his troubles for Sir Joseph Banks. He knew well that if he was to survive at all in the navy, it could only be with the support of his patron. In the accompanying letter he wrote: "In this, you will find, sir, the misfortunes of a man, who pledges his honour to you, which could not be foreseen or guarded against, whose conduct will bear the test of the minutest enquiry, and who only regrets that you should see him so unsuccessful."

As to the rest of the survivors, all at first seemed to recover wonderfully under the care of the Dutch settlers, and Bligh was given a large house for himself and his shipmates. It would be pleasant to report that this was a happy establishment, but from the time the *Bounty*'s survivors recovered their strength until Bligh at last got away from them, their life together was filled with petty squabbles.

To Bligh's troubles was added the sudden loss of his friend, David Nelson. This ever-enthusiastic gardener caught a chill, and he died of "an inflammatory fever" a few days later.

Since a ship was not expected at Kupang for some time, Bligh determined to go to Batavia, where there were more frequent ships returning to Europe. He therefore bought, with money he could raise on the strength of his rank, a schooner which he named HMS *Resource.* It was only eleven feet longer than the launch, but it was properly decked and a good deal more comfortable.

The *Resource* got away from Kupang on August 20, towing the *Bounty*'s launch and escorted by two armed native boats for protection in the pirate-infested waters. This last voyage of the *Bounty*'s survivors was one of incessant grumbling, misery and contention, but they arrived without serious incident at Batavia some four months later. The last days together of the *Bounty*'s survivors were no happier than the previous weeks. The monsoon had arrived, the climate was wretchedly uncomfortable and unhealthy. Bligh caught a bad dose of malaria, and four others died of it.

The next ship for Europe would sail in two weeks, and Bligh learned that there were accommodations on board for only three. He reserved these for himself, his clerk and his servant. Meanwhile, the others reasonably asked, how were they to keep themselves until they, too, could get home?

Bligh was the only person who could help them, but Thomas Ledward, acting surgeon since Huggan's death and hitherto a stout supporter of his captain, wrote home to his uncle: "The captain denied me, as well as the rest of the gentlemen who had not agents, any money unless I would give him my power of attorney and also my will, in which I was to bequeath to him all my property, this he called by the proper name of security. . . . In case of my death I hope this matter will be clearly pointed out to my relations."

Ledward at length obtained a berth in the *Welfare,* which did not live up to its name and was lost en route with all hands.

BLIGH FINALLY LANDED at Portsmouth on March 14, 1790. He hastened to London, presented himself at the Admiralty, and word of the mutiny then spread quickly. The *Gentleman's Magazine* echoed the general feeling that "the distresses he has undergone entitle him to every reward. In navigating his little skiff through so dangerous a sea, his seamanship appears as matchless as the undertaking seems beyond the verge of probability."

King George received Bligh and he was entertained at a series of adulatory banquets. At the Royalty Theatre a "fact told in action" spectacular entitled *The Pirates!* drew great crowds. It included a Tahitian dance, and "An exact Representation of the Seizure of Captain BLIGH in the cabin of the *Bounty,* by the pirates." His account of his misfortunes, sent to Sir Joseph Banks, had had the desired effect. Sir Joseph was already busily engaged in persuading the lords commissioners to prepare another breadfruit expedition—again to be commanded by Bligh. And as further proof of his confidence in his protégé, Banks saw to it that the House of Assembly in Jamaica granted Bligh a gratuity of five hundred guineas in appreciation of his efforts.

United with his beloved Betsy and his girls at Lambeth, Bligh spent much of the summer of 1790 writing up his narrative, based on the log he had retained through all his adventures. It was an instant success, and everyone accepted that Bligh was a victim of a plot and was in no way to blame. In October a token courtmartial found that "the *Bounty* was forcibly seized by the said Fletcher Christian, and Lieutenant Bligh is honourably acquitted of responsibility for the loss of his ship."

Events seemed at last to be flowing in Bligh's favor. The promotion he had sought for so long came to him rapidly, first to commander and a few weeks later to post captain. His family life was joyous and serene. A sixth child—yet another daughter—was born on February 21, 1791.

And a twenty-four-gun frigate, the *Pandora,* had been dispatched to the Pacific to search for the *Bounty* and her mutineers. She carried a strong party of marines, and Tom Hayward and John Hallett among the officers. Their eagerness to settle accounts with Christian and their familiarity with Tahiti and with the ways—as well as the looks—of their old shipmates, were reckoned to be priceless assets in the search. The commander of the *Pandora* was a truly ferocious martinet (beside whom, it was said, Bligh was a lamb), one Captain Edward Edwards, forty-eight years old, survivor of a mutiny of his own which he had put down with consummate ruthlessness.

Finally Banks's efforts to get away a second breadfruit expedition proved successful. This time Bligh took no chances. He insisted on two ships, a brand new West Indiaman, the *Providence,* and a supporting brig, the *Assistant.* He took endless pains over his officers, too, choosing only those with the best records. In addition he had on board a lieutenant of marines, two corporals, a drummer and fifteen marine privates.

On August 3, with the blessings of the king, his patron and the whole nation, "Breadfruit Bligh" (as he had come to be nicknamed—by some affectionately, by others ironically) sailed again for Tahiti. There must be no more trouble. He knew that he would not be forgiven a second time.

THE FIRST NEWS Captain Edwards heard when he arrived at Tahiti on March 23, 1791, was that the *Bounty* had sailed away, its destination a secret, six months earlier. On board had been Fletcher Christian and eight mutineers.

Of the sixteen members of the *Bounty*'s company who had settled on Tahiti, two (Churchill and Thompson) were dead. The intention of most of the remainder was to give themselves up without delay as a demonstration of their innocence.

Their eagerness was so great that it became something of a race to reach the English man-of-war. The winner was the armorer, Coleman. Even before the *Pandora* had dropped anchor, Coleman was in the water swimming out. Peter Heywood was next. He found a canoe and paddled eagerly out and climbed aboard. He was met on the quarterdeck by Lieutenant Larkin, the ship's first lieutenant.

"I suppose you know my story, sir?" Heywood began. Receiving no answer, he went on, "I belong to the *Bounty*."

Larkin again made no comment. The young men, under armed guard, were taken below to the captain's cabin.

Hearing that his old friend Tom Hayward had miraculously survived and was on board, Heywood asked eagerly for him, "supposing he might prove the assertions of our innocence." But Heywood's hopes were soon dashed, for Hayward "received us very coolly, and pretended ignorance of our affairs!"

His old messmate's failure to support him was a savage blow. Then "appearances being so much against us," Heywood later recounted, "we were ordered to be put in irons, and looked upon,—oh infernal words!—as *piratical villains*." It had become horribly clear that Edwards intended to treat them all as guilty of mutiny until they had been proved innocent.

On the following day, Edwards dispatched Tom Hayward to round up the handful of mutineers who had decided to make a stand in the mountains. His men had a hard time of it among the steep gorges and dense forests, but a good intelligence service was on their side. The natives quickly forgot old loyalties and guided them toward the runaways' hideout. When finally discovered and surrounded, the mutineers decided they had no alternative but to put down their arms. Their hands were bound behind their backs and they were sent down to the boat under a strong guard. Thus was the *Bounty*'s crew on Tahiti apprehended.

THE *PANDORA* REMAINED anchored at Matavai for five weeks, while Edwards did his utmost to extract from Teina and his chiefs information about the likely whereabouts of the *Bounty*.

The captain was unsuccessful in this. Christian had told no one of his destination for the good reason that he had not known it himself.

On the *Pandora's* quarterdeck a cell was built for "the pirates." It was entered by a scuttle in its roof and ventilated by two nine-inch-square scuttles. Inside, each of the fourteen prisoners had his legs in irons, his wrists handcuffed. One of them described how these were secured: "The first lieutenant in trying the handcuffs, took the method of setting his foot against our breasts and hauling the handcuffs over our hands with all his might, some of which took the skin off with them, and all that could be hauled off by this means were reduced and fitted so close that there was no possibility of turning the hand."

"Pandora's Box" was the name the prisoners gave this black cell. "The heat of the place when it was calm," wrote Peter Heywood, "was so intense that the sweat frequently ran in streams to the scuppers, and produced maggots in a short time. . . . These troublesome neighbours and the two necessary tubs which were constantly kept in the place helped to render our situation truly disagreeable."

While they were in Matavai Bay they were at first allowed to see their *taios* and their children, conversation being conducted through the vents. Stewart's marriage had been romantic and blissfully happy. Years later a missionary to Tahiti was told of its ending. "A beautiful little girl had been the fruit of their union, and was at the breast when the *Pandora* arrived. The interview was so affecting and afflicting that the officers on board were overwhelmed with anguish, and Stewart himself, unable to bear the heartrending scene, begged that she might not be admitted again on board. She was separated from him by violence and conveyed on shore in a state of despair and grief too big for utterance." Stewart's Peggy died of a broken heart two months later.

The prisoners remained in Pandora's Box for four months longer, while the *Pandora* sailed from island to island in the Pacific, searching for Christian and the *Bounty*. By the middle of

August, Edwards had to admit defeat and set course west for the long passage home.

Edwards was no navigator. He was, in short, as incompetent as he was wickedly cruel. He approached the Great Barrier Reef at a point where there are few breaks, and the result was that the *Pandora* was wrecked.

As she filled, preparations were made on deck for abandoning ship. Meanwhile the prisoners, tumbled together in one corner of Pandora's Box, became increasingly anxious. In desperation they at last broke their leg irons, to give themselves at least some chance of swimming if the hatch was ever unlocked so that they could escape.

This is how Morrison described what happened next: "As soon as Captain Edwards was informed that we had broke our irons he ordered us to be handcuffed and leg-ironed again with all the irons that could be mustered, though we begged for mercy."

Later Coleman, Norman and McIntosh, whom Bligh had named as being forcibly detained on board the *Bounty*, were released to work at the pumps. Byrn also was released. The rest could only resort to prayer, until in the last panic-stricken minutes when the captain had already abandoned ship (he was by no means the last to leave), the master-at-arms dropped them the key to their irons. There was one moment of heroism in this dismal episode. At the very last, a Will Moulter, the bo'sun's mate, risked his life by pausing to unbolt the scuttle. The prisoners who had been able to release their irons fought their way out through the narrow gap and plunged into the sea. But four were still manacled and they went down in the ship—John Sumner, Dick Skinner, Henry Hillbrant and Peggy's beloved George Stewart.

During their period of recovery on a nearby island, the prisoners were kept apart from the others, firmly tied and deliberately deprived of any shade from the tropical sun. On the long journey that ensued they were kept bound hand and foot in the bottom of the open boats. Kupang was reached on September 17, and they were placed at once in prison, in stocks. A week later when the Dutch surgeon made a routine visit, the stench and filth were so awful that he refused to enter until the place had been cleaned out by slaves.

This ill-treatment continued all the way back to the Cape of Good Hope, where Edwards transferred them to the man-of-war HMS *Gorgon.* It says much for their physical and mental resilience that any survived. The worst of their ordeal was now over. They were treated humanely on the *Gorgon*, and their condition had much improved by the time they reached Spithead. There they were removed to HMS *Hector,* to await their court-martial. According to Morrison, "we were treated in a manner that renders the humanity of her captain and officers much honour, and had beds given us and every indulgence that our circumstances would admit or allowed."

MEANWHILE, ON PITCAIRN, Christian's first favorable impressions had been confirmed. Rolling land accounted for about a third of the island's 1200 acres. The island's plentiful timber was ideal for building and for making canoes. The seas were rich in red snapper, mackerel, gray mullet and lobster. The red colluvial soil produced fine vegetables and fruit, and many brilliantly colored flowers like hibiscus and bougainvillea.

Besides all these rich advantages Pitcairn enjoyed a mellower climate than Tahiti. Some eighty inches of rainfall a year were spread out evenly; and the temperature in winter rarely fell below sixty-five, or in summer rose above eighty degrees.

Christian remained in command for the first week. He had no intention of taking on the responsibility of governing the island, but everyone recognized the need for a strong organizing hand until they became settled. After that they would see. Isabella made herself responsible for the women's affairs.

By midday on January 23, 1790, the work of unloading the *Bounty* was finished. The ship herself had been stripped of her masts and spars, her stocks of cord and rope, the cabin fittings, the ladders and companionways, the rails and the decks. Never again would the settlers have the opportunity of acquiring ready-sawed and matured timbers on this scale, nor—of almost greater importance—the nails that secured them.

Now the men stood about on the forecastle deck, drinking mugs of rum from the last barrel still on board. Quintal and McKoy, notorious for their tippling, had been at it all through the morning as they worked.

Christian appeared from below, stripped to the waist, and, like the other mutineers, almost as brown as the natives. "Well, lads," he asked, "are we to run her ashore now?" There was much talk, and feelings were not unanimous.

One or two favored keeping the *Bounty* at anchor for a while longer; others were for destroying her at once—before minds could change, before perhaps the natives might form a conspiracy to sail away with the women. The middle course was to run her on shore where she could later be dismantled.

None of them saw Quintal disappear below. Suddenly they heard above the sound of the pounding surf cries of alarm from the women on the shore. Christian looked around; there was smoke rising from the main hatch, increasing in volume every moment and he could hear the dread crackling sound of fire.

Everyone ran aft, but they were helpless. The fire was growing fast, whipped up by the onshore wind. All buckets, even the pumps, had been sent ashore the previous day.

"It's no good, lads, into the cutter," Christian shouted. Only then did Quintal appear aft, a lurching figure, drunk as a lord, a sly expression on his face.

"Where have you been, you scoundrel?" shouted Christian.

"Best be done with her," Quintal answered, "or the Indians would have had her." And, as the roar of a sudden new gust of flame sounded behind him like an explosion, he was over the side before any of them.

Even down on the water they could feel the heat, as the flames shot half as high as the masts had once stood. Christian steered the cutter toward the beach, riding in high on a wave. The women waded out to meet the boat, clutching at the gunwale, all wailing in a chorus of grief, some tearing their hair and beating their fists against their temples.

With the coming of darkness the spectacular but melancholy scene caused many of the white mutineers as well as the natives to cry in chorus with the women. Voluntary exiles the white men may have been, but the end of the *Bounty* was like the slamming of a prison door; while for the conscripted natives and most of the women it was the end of any hope of returning to their Tahitian homes.

By midnight the *Bounty* was burned to the water. Only one or two of her ribs still rose, scarlet and curving, above her corpse. These remained flaming a while longer like torch-lights above a ceremonial funeral carriage, before they collapsed with a hiss into the waters of the bay that was to bear her name forever.

No one seems to have thought of punishing Quintal for burning the *Bounty*. McKoy believed that his friend had done the right thing. The opinion of the others, led by Christian, was that this was no time to fall out among themselves. Besides, there was too much to do. It would be easy enough to survive here like animals; but if they were to create a civilized community there must be order, and this required a lot of hard work.

The first and most difficult task was to drag their stores to the small plateau above the bay, where they intended to build their dwellings. Ropes and pulleys were used, and by the end of February all but the heaviest lengths of timber had been hauled up the three-hundred-foot cliff.

Christian had surveyed the island, and he put it to the other white men that the land in the center, with its shallow valleys and good natural drainage, should be divided into nine equal parts, each a private estate for one of them. Here they would grow their own crops, sharing between them the services of the six native men. The arrangement was agreed to without fuss. Some men were better off than others, but the merits and the demerits worked out fairly evenly. On an island so richly endowed it seemed unnecessary to quarrel about small advantages.

For what now happened at Pitcairn we have to rely on Jenny's reminiscences nearly thirty years later, the stories handed down to the children and grandchildren of the original settlers, notably Quintal's son Arthur, John Adams's accounts given to several visitors before he died, and traditional legends—sometimes unexpectedly fresh—which were to be heard on the island well into this century.

There is a good deal of disparity between the recorded times of events but a surprising unanimity on what happened and in what order. There is no reason to doubt that the main outline of the story of life—and death—on Pitcairn is true.

During these first months they were all too busy to give much thought to the confined nature of their environment, or to the potentially dangerous injustices of their community. Home-making is an absorbing occupation, and there was no time for brooding. The families built their houses in clearings chopped out from the trees on the plateau, using as material both timbers salvaged from the *Bounty*'s wreck and trees they felled on the sites. The standard pattern was two rooms, one above the other, the lower raised a foot or two off the ground, the upper reached by a ladder. The pitched roof was covered with thickly-matted palm leaves, and along the sides ran a wooden gutter to catch the rain, which was fed into one of the *Bounty*'s casks. Advice was proferred from family to family, but no rules were laid down. All that Christian insisted on was that the houses must be invisible from the sea, and a long line of banyan trees was left on the seaward side of the community like a permanently drawn curtain.

By the middle of the year—it was winter but the drop in temperature was scarcely discernible—the village was beginning to assume an orderly aspect. Jack Williams, who had often acted as armorer's mate to Coleman, had set up the forge; and the new farmer-sailors had begun to clear their land and plant yam and sweet-potato seeds, and sugarcane, banana and plantain plants, which they had brought from Tahiti and Tubai.

The chickens scratched about the village, and the evocative sound of the cock crowing provided the white men with a morning reminder of home. But the hens were not willing

layers in this climate, and it was this failure to provide eggs that led to the community's first tragedy. Seabirds nested thickly on the cliff faces, so the women went out daily to collect their eggs. In October, Jack Williams's wife slipped and fell to her death. It was their first loss—but by no means the last on these dangerous cliffs—and Williams took it hard.

A few days later Isabella gave birth to the first native-born Pitcairner. She and Christian named him Thursday October Christian. Then one woman of the three shared by the Tubaians fell ill with a growth on her neck and died within a few weeks. So now the six natives had only two women between them.

Still, by the end of 1790 the community had settled into a routine. The women did the cooking and housework, washed the clothes and made new ones from the *Bounty's* sails. When they wanted meat the white men went out and shot hogs which ran wild like the other livestock they'd brought from Tahiti. The native men lived at peace with one another, and relations were good with most of the white men.

Quintal and McKoy—whose violence was uncontrollable when they were drunk, and bad enough when they were sober— had little to do with the others. Jack Williams, Pitcairn's only widower, was unhappy and increasingly resentful. He kept himself occupied at his forge, mending and making tools, converting cutlasses into billhooks and keeping an edge on the axes.

The other mutineers formed two main groups. In one were Adams and Young, who had adjoining gardens and houses and lived closely with the natives; they were judged by the others to exchange wives freely with each other and the native men. In the second group were Christian, Martin, Mills and Brown.

Fletcher Christian's friendship with Ned Young had died a slow death since the mutiny. The growth of Christian's regret and remorse was matched by his feeling of resentment toward the man who had incited him, until he began to believe, with some reason, that the tragedy would never have occurred but for the malevolent intervention of this dark intriguer. For his part Ned Young, a highly educated and articulate young man, felt he was being treated shabbily and detested Christian's piousness and moodiness. It was not he who had acted violently. His motive in suggesting that they should rid themselves of their tyrannical commander was to relieve his friend of the burden hanging from his neck—to show him the way out of his private hell. In Young's eyes it was Christian's decision alone which had started the mutiny.

The women now began to show signs of restlessness. Even those who had come of their own free will felt an acute longing for the wider spaces, the gossip and familiar faces of Tahiti. Once the community was established, Christian allowed his authority as leader to diminish. He would disappear for long periods, and would sit in the cave—known later as Christian's Cave—high above the cliffs, staring out to sea. He always went armed with a musket, perhaps to blow out his own brains, or perhaps in fear of what was about to happen.

During the next eighteen months the decline in the spirit of the Pitcairn community continued, although several more children were born. Then, some time in the middle of 1792 Jack Williams, deciding that he had had enough of celibacy, confronted Christian and the other white men. Surly and defiant, he told them that he intended to take by force one of the natives' wives. Christian was outraged. "They have but two women for six. This can only lead to violence," he said.

"Then I shall take the cutter and seek a woman elsewhere," Williams said. "I would rather be captured and taken back to England in irons than remain on this island any longer."

Christian and the others suddenly realized that Williams was in a strong bargaining position. He was the only man who could handle a forge. Without him they would be condemned to a primitive existence. Christian spoke quietly to the others, then turned to him. "Who is it you will have?"

Williams, truculent in his moment of triumph, spoke sharply. "Nancy or Mareva. Either will do."

"We shall draw, then," said Christian decisively. He said to Brown, "Will, take two sticks, one short one for Nancy and one long one for Mareva."

Brown presented his two fists, the ends of the sticks projecting above his thumbs. Williams drew out the shorter of the two.

NANCY AND HER native man, Talaloo, were eating their evening meal when they saw Christian leading the eight white men, armed with muskets, toward their house.

"Nancy, you are to live with Jack Williams," said Christian. "He has been without a woman for too long."

Nancy had long wanted to leave Talaloo for the lonely white man. Like Mareva she felt of a lower caste than the other women with their white-skinned men. She nodded and went willingly with her new mate.

The next day all the community went about their business in the normal way, except that the white men carried their pistols in their belts and tended to keep together more than usual. Talaloo had left his house and was hiding at the west end of the island, the natives reported. Brown and Christian, whose gardens adjoined at the west end of the village, talked apprehensively of what might now happen. If it came to civil war, only Menalee, who regarded himself as Christian's *taio,* might remain loyal. The muscular Tetaheite and his friend Oho, both from Tubai, had long since turned surly and distant. Timoa and Nehow—from Tahiti—went about their daily duties silently and inscrutably.

Nothing happened for several days. There was still no sign of Talaloo. Then one evening at the very end of September, when the women were together preparing food for their men, Isabella overheard Nancy singing a Tahitian song quietly, as if to herself. It was a simple, extemporized song such as the natives often sang, but Isabella picked out this warning: "Why do the men sharpen their axes? To cut off the white men's heads."

She slipped away and hastened to her husband with the message. Christian acted instantly. Loading his musket, he hurried to the house where the native men always gathered in the evenings and burst in on them. They were all there except Menalee. Talaloo had come back, no doubt to organize the massacre. As further confirmation of Nancy's warning, there were axes lying about.

There was pandemonium in the little room, and in the confusion Talaloo, followed by Timoa, fled toward the entrance. Christian pulled the trigger at point-blank range, but the musket misfired. Then he, too, fled.

He reached his house without injury. Later Menalee told him that the natives had indeed conspired to attack the white men as they lay asleep, that their hate was boundless, and that Talaloo and Timoa had fled into the hills. Oho had also fled, armed with an axe and swearing vengeance.

Three days of armed truce passed, during which there was no communication between the white men and the native men except through Menalee. On the fourth day Timoa and Talaloo, armed with axes, surprised the women fishing from the rocks of Bounty Bay, seized Nancy and disappeared.

When the white men heard of this kidnapping, they decided that only with the death of Talaloo could there be peace again on Pitcairn. Menalee was given the role of agent provocateur. He was to pretend that he had changed sides. Isabella would cook three puddings. One would be poisoned. Menalee, armed with a concealed pistol, must go up into the hills with these puddings and seek out Nancy and the two Tahitians.

"You must say to them, 'I have brought you food to sustain you,' " Christian instructed his *taio* carefully. "Then you must say, 'Soon we will rise and kill all the white men.' Then you must give Timoa and Nancy each a pudding, and the third pudding to Talaloo. If he does not die, you must shoot him."

The next evening Menalee returned with Timoa and Nancy. Timoa told Christian and Brown what had happened. "Menalee brought three puddings, and he said they were for us as we must be hungry. He told us that all the natives, the men and the women, would rise up against the white men. But I knew that this was not true and that Menalee had been sent by you. Menalee made Talaloo take one of the puddings."

Nancy said, "But Talaloo would not eat his pudding. He threw it in the bushes and ate mine instead. Menalee asked,

'Why do you throw away your good pudding?' But Talaloo did not answer."

"So Talaloo still lives?" said Christian.

"Mămōō, mămōō, master," said Menalee impatiently. "This is not the end of the story. Next I pulled out my pistol and held it to the back of Talaloo's head and pulled the trigger. But there was only a little sound, not a big sound. It did not fire. Talaloo turned and saw the pistol in my hand. He looked at me with fear in his eyes and ran into the forest. I ran after him."

"He ran fast," broke in Nancy.

"I ran like the wind," Menalee cried proudly. "I caught him and together we rolled on the ground striking at each other. Talaloo was calling to his wife for help."

"Talaloo did not know how much I hated him," said Nancy. "I took up a stone and beat at my husband's head."

"We beat his head until he was dead," boasted Menalee.

"This is only the first killing," Christian said to Brown. "The blood will flow fast on Pitcairn now."

IT WAS A QUIET evening and for once there was no wind. The seabirds were silent, the tall palms along the cliffs stood upright and still. One of the babies was crying somewhere, but otherwise the village was quiet. Nancy had slipped back to Williams's house. The smoke from the cooking rose straight up into the darkening sky as Christian and Brown, Mills, Martin, Williams, Quintal and McKoy talked together softly in Christian's house.

"We must sleep with our muskets loaded," said Brown, "and we must trust no one. Not even one another. Do not trust me. And certainly not Ned Young. He is too much with the natives."

"We should have killed them all long ago," muttered Quintal.

"We have been soft with them," added McKoy. "Kill Oho now. He is out there somewhere still. That one is a plotter."

There was a strong feeling that Oho must go. He was their greatest danger. Perhaps Tetaheite, too. But certainly Oho.

"Send Menalee again," Martin suggested. "He is a good

killer." Someone else added tartly, "He needs a woman with him to help."

At length it was agreed that Christian should send his *taio* out on the hunt again the following day. If he succeeded, they would trust him in future. If he failed, he would be shot as a traitor.

On the next morning, Christian carried out the plan as agreed except that he sent Timoa, too, as support. The two men found Oho alone, hungry and frightened. They pretended to commiserate with him, pledging revenge on the white men. Then at a moment when Oho's back was turned Menalee drew out his pistol and killed him with one shot in the head.

AFTER THIS SECOND murder it seemed that the natives had been cowed into submission. But even after six months without further bloodshed, trust was not reestablished—neither between natives and white men, nor among the men of the same race. Young and Adams took no part in their old shipmates' affairs, while Christian, Brown, Mills and Martin were increasingly watchful of the natives—even of Menalee.

McKoy and Quintal were more or less drunk all the time now. They had reached the end of their share of the *Bounty*'s wine and spirits, but McKoy, who had once worked in a whisky distillery, succeeded in making a brew from the root of the ti plant which grew freely everywhere on the island. It was even more potent than navy rum.

The women now despised their fellow countrymen and—except for Isabella, who remained loyal to the end and was expecting a third child—had also lost respect for the white men. These were no longer the mysterious white-skinned masters who had once so strongly attracted them with their fine clothes, their possessions, their ardent passions. The white men rarely washed. Their clothes had long since worn out and they dressed like the natives, with no more than a belted skirt about the waist and a hat to keep off the sun. They, too, went barefoot, and their manners had become increasingly brutish.

Plotting began again in September 1793. This time the natives succeeded in keeping the plot a secret. Menalee was not included, except as a possible victim. This time they would have firearms. Musketry did not come easily to them, but Young and Adams had instructed them how to shoot birds and hogs.

On the morning of September 20 the white men were out in the fields. Menalee was helping Mills. The other native men, too, began the day by working on the plantations. Then, one by one, the three of them—Tetaheite, Nehow and Timoa—stole away and made for the village. Unnoticed by the women, each succeeded in stealing a musket and ammunition.

The natives crept up first on Jack Williams, the man who had started all the trouble. He was repairing his fence where some dogs had got through. They shot him in the back of the head as he was leaning over to secure a post, and he died instantly.

Among those who heard the shot was Isaac Martin. Assuming that Brown or Mills was out hunting, he called across the valley to Christian, who was invisible but within earshot, "Well done! We'll have a feast today."

Next, the natives saw Mills and Menalee working together. Tetaheite decided to split this potentially dangerous combination. "We have shot a great hog," he called to Mills. "We need Menalee to help us carry it."

Mills released Menalee from his work, and Menalee strode off toward Williams's garden. He was almost on top of the body before he saw it. Then he saw the three natives.

Menalee turned as if to run away. But Tetaheite, who was as strong as two men, held him and whispered threateningly, *"Mămōō!* Be with us or you will die. All the white men are to die!"

By unhappy chance, Menalee's own *taio* was to be the next victim. Knowing that to sound a warning would lead to instant death, Menalee remained in agonized silence as they crept up behind Christian, who was digging yams.

Tetaheite fired into the back of Christian's head, carrying out the execution with speed and skill. Christian died almost instantly. But as he lay on the newly tilled soil, he called out—not very loudly, not in a tone of agony or anger—but simply, "Oh, dear!"

Two white men heard Christian's death cry, for McKoy had come into Mills's plantation to ask him something. Now alarmed by this second shot and the sound of the voice that had followed it, McKoy said to Mills, "That was surely some person dying?"

"I think it was only Isabella calling her children to dinner," Mills replied.

A moment later Menalee appeared in the clearing. He was panting as if he had run far, and he spoke in a tense voice. "Your house is being robbed by Tetaheite and Nehow. Go there quickly!"

McKoy, now acutely alarmed, ran down the valley. Before he reached his house a third shot rang out. It came from inside, and the ball whistled past his head. So Menalee had tricked him. All four natives had risen in revolt.

McKoy ran back up the hill. He was a fast runner in spite of his drinking and easily outpaced the heavier Tahitians. He made first for the spot where he believed Christian to be working. Instead he found his corpse; the blood from his head wound soaked the soil. Another shot sounded, scarcely a hundred yards away. Menalee had acquired a pistol and had run up to Mills as if to warn him of the danger. Mills, unsuspecting, had gone to meet him and was shot in the face at point-blank range.

Now McKoy ran to give the news of Christian's death to Isabella. Shortly after Christian had left for his work, she had gone into labor. When McKoy burst into her house, she was already giving birth to her third child, with Nancy as midwife.

Menalee had now run amok. He saw McKoy leave Christian's house and guessed that he would make next for the house of his friend Quintal. He ran through the trees to get there first, picking up a large stone on the way since he did not know how to reload the pistol.

McKoy and Menalee reached Quintal's house together. McKoy yelled, "Mat, get to the woods with your musket!"

When Quintal came out he saw the two men struggling on the ground beside his pigsty, and McKoy was proving the stronger of the two. As Quintal raced to help him, he saw McKoy lift Menalee up bodily and hurl him over the fence into the sty among the pigs, where he lay still. Quintal grabbed another musket for McKoy and told his wife, Sarah, to warn the other white men; they then made off into the hills to await the outcome of this day of murder.

ISAAC MARTIN HAD heard the shots and shouts but he had heard no word of warning. So when he saw three armed natives coming across his land, he awaited their arrival, unsuspecting—he knew Young and Adams were in the habit of lending the natives muskets. Tetaheite and the others came straight up to him. They were laughing and put the barrels of the muskets to Martin's belly as if this were a practical joke; they loved practical jokes.

"Do you know what we have been doing this morning?" Tetaheite asked. "We have been doing the same as shooting hogs"—and two of the natives pulled the triggers together.

There were two clicks. Martin joined in their laughter. It was like old times. They had often laughed together at simple jokes.

Tetaheite and Nehow recocked their muskets and, still laughing, again pulled the triggers. This time both muskets fired. By some miracle the shots did not kill Martin. Clutching his stomach, he ran off, not to his own house, but to Brown's. He got there before his pursuers, and collapsed on the floor.

Menalee was the first native to arrive. As he burst in he seized one of the *Bounty*'s sledgehammers from a hook on the wall and beat out Martin's brains as he lay on the floor. He turned next to Brown, who was frantically trying to load his musket. Brown then burst past him, racing for the entrance, dodging past Nehow and Tetaheite.

Then an odd thing happened. Timoa was outside, musket reloaded and raised. For some reason Timoa had taken a fancy to Brown—or perhaps it was only sudden pity. No one would ever know. But as Brown dashed past, Timoa said in English, "Fall when I fire."

Brown ran, and when he was a dozen yards from his house he heard a shot and at once fell to the ground, feigning death. This did not satisfy Menalee. He ran up to Brown, striking him a terrible blow on the head.

Brown rose to a sitting position, calling out for mercy. "If you are going to kill me, let me see my wife first," he begged.

Menalee first allowed him to go, but then snatched a musket from Nehow, and shot Brown dead.

FIVE WHITE MEN WERE already dead. But the natives could no longer hope to finish their business as stealthily as they had begun it. Down in the village pandemonium had broken out. Calls of warning and shouts for help reached as far as the hills and echoed back from the forests. There was no telling now who was killing whom, where the next shot might be fired or who might die.

Jack Adams, who was working in his field, heard Sarah Quintal call out to warn him of the danger. He put down his tools and made for Brown's house. He saw no bodies. But the four natives were standing about the entrance, leaning on the butts of their muskets as they had often seen the white men do. Adams regarded them all as his friends and was not put out by the sight of the four muskets.

"What is the matter?" he called out.

They all turned together, threateningly, raising their muskets at the same time. Adams did not linger. He ran off into the forest, making for his own house. He was hastily filling a bag with some yams when all four natives burst in. Menalee fired across the room as Adams struggled to escape through the window. The ball struck him in the back of his shoulder and passed out through his neck, sending him tumbling to the ground outside.

Menalee raced around the house and hurled himself onto the wounded man, beating him again and again with the butt of the musket. Tetaheite was the next to arrive. His musket was still loaded and he held it to Adams's body and pulled the trigger. But again it misfired.

Adams was a strong man and there was plenty of life in him yet. He struggled to his feet and ran fast inland, leaving a trail of blood but easily outstripping his pursuers.

Timoa got nearest to Adams in the race and he called out to him to stop. "It's all right," he shouted.

At a safe distance and from a safe height above the natives, Adams paused. He needed to stanch the flow of blood. He turned back and looked down at them.

"Why is it all right?" he called to them. "You want to kill me."

"No," replied Timoa. "We do not want to kill you. We forgot that Mr. Young told us to leave you alive for his companion."

Adams considered his situation carefully. He badly needed attention to his wound. If they were determined to kill him, they would get him in the end. There was little to lose by putting his trust in them, for what it was worth. So, holding some palm leaves to his neck, Adams walked slowly back to the four natives, and together they made their way, as if by a prearranged plan, to Christian's house.

Here an orgy of grief was taking place. Isabella lay on her bed nursing her new child, a baby girl. Young sat in a chair Christian had made, as though it were the throne to which he had succeeded. No one present realized that this one white man, around whom they were gathered, had brought about this massacre; that he had briefed and incited the four native men, just as he had earlier spurred on Christian to take the *Bounty*. As before, he had absented himself discreetly while the cruel deeds were done.

Into this crowded little house Jack Adams was led, pale from the effects of his wounds, bewildered by the size of the gathering, shocked and in pain. "Why did you do it?" Adams asked, talking quickly in English so that the women would not understand.

"They would do it one day themselves. This island is like Tofua, always erupting. Soon it would have gone up in a great explosion. It is better to control an explosion as I have done."

Young was quite calm about it. Now there would be no

shortage of women. He had already planned to have Isabella as a second wife. He had always admired her looks. He would have Nancy, too, making three in all—a small harem.

Although Young would wait a few days before putting these plans into effect, he spoke now of Adams's likely choice, thinking it might cheer him. Quintal and McKoy were not yet dead, but what of their handsome wives, Sarah and Mary?

SARAH SUCCEEDED IN rejoining Quintal in the hills. There he and McKoy built themselves a shelter in a good tactical position and awaited the inevitable attack by the four natives. It was not long coming.

The natives' attack was a brief and abortive business. They fired a few shots without effect, and when the fire was returned fled back to the village, where they were severely rebuked by Young for lack of courage.

The wave of violence ran its course, bringing new jealousies in its backwash. Only one week after the massacre, in the evening when the natives were gathered in the center of the village, Menalee became jealous of the attention Timoa was showing one of the women and took up a musket and shot him dead. Tetaheite and Nehow then attacked Menalee, who fled from the village with his musket.

Menalee made his way to the hideout Quintal and McKoy had built. They seized their weapons and were about to fire at him.

"I have come to be your *taio*," he called out. "Do not kill me."

"Put your musket down on the ground," Quintal ordered. "Then you may come to us."

Keeping the native covered with his musket, Quintal told Sarah, "Go to the village. Ask Mr. Young why Menalee has come to us."

Sarah returned later with a letter from Ned Young. It told how Menalee had killed Timoa, and recommended that they should kill him if they valued their lives. He himself intended to arrange for the death of Nehow and Tetaheite.

Menalee's was an easy execution. McKoy shot him in the back with his own musket. But now McKoy and Quintal believed that Young might have laid a trap for them in the village, so they remained clear of it.

Three days passed. Then Young's wife, Susan, appeared from the village with a message that the two natives were dead and they could come back to Young.

When they asked for proof, they did not have long to wait. Susan returned with a bag; inside it were the severed heads of Tetaheite and Nehow.

"You see they are dead," she told them triumphantly.

So McKoy, Quintal and Sarah returned to the village with Susan, believing that their troubles were at last over.

NOW THAT THE NUMBER of men had been reduced to four, only the original wives remained all the time in the same house. The others moved from bed to bed as their fancy, and the men's fancies, took them. But with peace and security and the end of the racial struggle, the women soon became restless again. In April 1794 Jenny told Young that the women were going to build their own boat, and to ram home her point she began dismantling the timbers of one of the houses. Young and Adams discussed this new challenge to their authority with some anxiety and decided to humor the women. A boat of sorts was completed, and on August 13, 1794, it was launched in Bounty Bay. "According to expectation she upset," noted Ned Young dryly in his journal.

In one last desperate attempt to get away, the women conspired to murder the white men and leave in the *Bounty*'s cutter. The plot was disclosed in time by one of their number, but the men went through another period of fear and suspicion before they were satisfied that they were out of danger. Time was the best cure for the women's restlessness—time and the community's fecundity. By early 1795 the population had so increased that even Jenny could see that they could never all pack into the cutter with their children, even if they did succeed in killing the remaining white men.

Even without violence at the hands of the women, tragedy on this unhappy island struck again and again. In 1796 McKoy's body was discovered at the foot of the cliffs below Christian's Cave. He had evidently bound his own hands and feet, tied a weight about his neck and leaped to his death.

The death of McKoy had a fearful effect on Quintal. He drank as heavily as ever and led a life separated from the rest, with his wife, Sarah, whom he beat mercilessly. One day in 1799 Sarah, too, was found dead at the bottom of the cliffs. Quintal said that she had gone searching for birds' eggs. He demanded Jenny in her place, threatening Jack Adams and Ned Young with instant death if she was not handed over.

The two men realized that Quintal had lost his reason—as McKoy had, from the raw alcohol he brewed from ti roots, so they battered in his head while he lay in his house in a stupor.

THE FINAL MURDER on Pitcairn had a profound reforming effect on Young and Adams. First they forbade all alcohol. Then they suddenly gave themselves to the Christian faith with the zeal of evangelical missionaries. Shame for their past misdeeds must have been one reason for this conversion. But there was another. Young had been unwell for some time. He was losing weight, had long suffered from asthma and now knew he was dying.

Jack Adams, brought up among London's docks, was scarcely literate. Knowing that Ned Young would soon be dead, leaving him the father of this flock of women and children, he took reading lessons from his companion every day, so that he would be able to officiate at divine service and lead their hymn singing after Ned was gone. Consequently, when Young finally died in 1800, Adams rose to his responsibilities splendidly. He was warmly supported by the women and the older children, to whom, at the age of thirty-three, he was already like an aged prophet, their undisputed temporal and spiritual leader. The community remained at peace, soothed by prayer and the new spirit of love.

FOR YEARS THE OUTSIDE world remained ignorant of all this. The women grew fatter and middle-aged, and their children began to cast about for wives. In 1807, Thursday October Christian, now a man, surprised everybody by asking McKoy's widow, Mary, to marry him, and in 1808 she gave birth to a child, her fifth, nearly twenty years after her first on Tahiti.

In the same year a sail was sighted.

Captain Mayhew Folger of the sailing ship *Topaz* of Boston, Massachusetts, was one of the first sealers ever to pursue his prey in the southern Pacific. On September 28, in acute need of water and fresh provisions, he dropped anchor in Bounty Bay. Within half an hour an outrigger canoe had come alongside, and Folger could look down from the bows of his vessel to see three young men waving their paddles above their heads. To his astonishment the tallest of the three canoeists called out in English, "Where do you come from?"

"Come on board, we will not harm you," Folger replied.

The young men climbed up to the deck and stared about the ship in wonder. All three were tall and muscular, and dusky rather than brown-skinned, with full lips and wide-set black eyes.

"What is the name of this island?" Folger asked.

"Peetcairn, sir."

"Were you born here, are you English?"

"Yes, we are English," the eldest answered, and then asked, "Are you English?"

"No, we are American."

The young men seemed to be relieved at this.

Like his companions, the tallest youth wore a cloth around his waist with a knife stuck into the belt. He also wore a straw hat decorated with cocks' feathers. Now he introduced himself as Thursday October Christian, the others as his brother Charles, and James Young. "We were born here. But not our mothers and fathers. They came here a long time ago in a ship as big as this."

"Where are your mothers and fathers?"

"Our fathers are dead. They died long ago. I am the oldest man," said Thursday proudly. "Except for Mr. Adams, of course."

"Who is Mr. Adams?"

"He is a very old man. He teaches us about God. He would like to see you if you are not English."

Folger went ashore with them and was led up a steep cliff track. There were children everywhere, all light-skinned, who spoke an odd dialect in which he could recognize English words. Then he saw older women standing outside their houses, fat and dark and handsome, pure Polynesian, smiling and waving shyly.

Folger was brought at last to a middle-aged man sitting outside his house with two women beside him. He was pure European, a stout and stooping figure, with long gray hair falling over his shoulders. His features were fine, with a long nose and steady brown eyes. There was a pale, wrinkled scar on one side of his neck. His shoulders, chest and legs were covered with tattoos.

The man rose and extended his hand in greeting when Folger approached. "I hear you are from our old English colonies in America. My name is John Adams. We are glad to welcome you to our island."

On that day Adams related to the American the story of the *Bounty* and her men since she had last been seen sailing out of Matavai Bay nineteen years before, from the early days of earnest endeavor, through the decadence of the mid-1790s, to the death by murder or suicide of all but two of the male community. Then he spoke proudly of their conversion to the word of God. "We are happy today. May God preserve us as we are."

Later Adams learned with amazement and relief that Bligh and many of his men had survived to return to England, and that those who had chosen to remain on Tahiti had been brought back to a court-martial. Some had been hanged, Folger remembered, but he could not remember their names or how many.

Folger then reembarked, taking casks of water and as much fresh food of all kinds as his long boat could carry. "We will return to you in eight months," were his last words to Adams.

The consequences of this sealer's chance call at Pitcairn were

surprisingly slight. The *Topaz* never returned, and life continued its uneventful course. Folger had, however, corrected the
calendar for Adams: in Christian's long search about the southern Pacific he had failed to allow for the *Bounty*'s crossing the
date line, so ever since, they had lived one day behind, holding
the Sabbath on a Saturday. This was now corrected, and Christian's first-born son, Thursday October, changed his name to
Friday.

The story of the fate of the *Bounty* mutineers was not heard in
England for another five years. Folger's sealing voyage was a
long one, and the War of 1812 cut off most communications
between England and the United States. When at last a letter
from Folger arrived at the Admiralty in 1813, the lords commissioners were too busy with more important things to be bothered with some doubtful tale about a long-forgotten mutiny.

Among the Admiralty's problems at this time was the
American frigate *Essex*, which had been seizing British whal-
ing ships off the coasts of South America. Two frigates were
sent from England to destroy her. En route to Valparaiso, they
sighted Pitcairn.

The arrival in 1814 of two warships flying the British flag
caused consternation on the island. The women and older children had long known that their leader was a hunted man. They
also knew that it was only his authority that held their community together.

Friday Christian and one of Ned Young's boys went out in a
canoe to greet the ships' commanders. Thus the sons of two
mutinous midshipmen faced the Royal Navy's authority for
the first time, determined to protect the last of their fathers'
shipmates.

They need not have worried. The officers were kindly men
who harbored no vengeful feelings about the remote event in
the Royal Navy's history. One of them wrote of Friday October:
"A tall fine young man, about 6 feet high, dark black hair, a
countenance extremely open and interesting." He found
Young, too, "a very fine youth."

After being assured that the Royal Navy intended no harm,

Christian and Young took the two commanders ashore. They talked at length to the man who long ago had held Captain Bligh at bayonet point in his cabin. His piety and the Christian simplicity of the life he had created on the little island convinced them that it would be "an act of great cruelty and inhumanity" to arrest him and take him home to inevitable court-martial and execution. So they left him there, with the Royal Navy's blessing.

Jenny, above all the women, longed to return to Tahiti and her family. She got her way in the end, too. But not until 1817. In that year the American ship *Sultan* called at Pitcairn, and she persuaded the commander to take her on board.

By the time she reached her home the first Christian missionaries were at work on Tahiti, and to one of these she gave her first account of the events since she had left the island in 1789. It was published in the Sydney *Gazette* on July 17, 1819.

Ten years later "Reckless Jack" Adams, as he had once been known, died, deeply mourned by his wife and mistresses, children and grandchildren. He remained the most honored figure in Pitcairn's history. His grave—set alone among orange, lemon and banana trees, close to his original home—was tended with special care and always decorated with flowers. The example of his piety had saved Pitcairn when it was so nearly too late.

Chapter Seven

"THE WORST OF SERPENTS"

THE COURT-MARTIAL THAT assembled on board HMS *Duke* in Portsmouth harbor to try the ten officers and men of the *Bounty* was a great British *cause célèbre* of the autumn of 1792. Those who stood trial were Midshipman Peter Heywood, armorer Joseph Coleman, bos'un's mate James Morrison, carpenter's mate Charles Norman and his assistant, Tom McIntosh, and five able seamen—Tom Ellison, Tom Burkitt, John Millward, Will Muspratt and blind Michael Byrn. Under the presidency of Lord Hood, eleven Royal Navy captains sat in judgment on the prisoners.

At that time Bligh himself was at the other end of the world. He had arrived at Tahiti in April, and was soon away again with his supply of breadfruit plants—twice as many as before. He would land with them in the West Indies in January 1793, to general acclaim and a reward of one thousand guineas.

However, when later he wrote with seeming truth that, "This voyage has terminated with success," he was sadly unaware of two bitter and ironic consequences. The first was that when his breadfruits matured and fruited, the slaves would not eat them. The second was that while he was away, many influences in England were at work against him in the matter of the court-martial. His absence reduced the power of the prosecution; it was held to be a travesty of justice that the court-martial should sit at all without the chief prosecuting witness. And both the Heywood and Christian families had powerful connections and could destroy the good name of Bligh, who lacked such support.

The Heywoods were a large family, and Peter Heywood was the apple of the family's eye. His father had died just two months before Bligh had returned to England in 1790, and when his grief-stricken mother wrote anxiously to Bligh asking for news of her son, he had replied:

Madam:
I received your letter this day, and feel for you very much, being perfectly sensible of the extreme distress you must suffer from the conduct of your son Peter. *His baseness is beyond all description,* but I hope you will endeavour to prevent the loss of him, heavy as the misfortune is, from afflicting you too severely. I imagine he is, with the rest of the mutineers, returned to Otaheite.

I am, Madam,
Wm. Bligh

Certain that Peter could never have committed the crime of which Bligh accused him, Mrs. Heywood wrote to all her friends and relatives with naval connections. Peter's uncle, Commodore Thomas Pasley, was in Portsmouth when the prisoners arrived in 1792, and he took the trouble to seek out Fryer,

Cole, Purcell and Peckover, all of whom confirmed Heywood's innocence. He also closely interrogated the young man himself and was able to reassure his family that he was confident that Peter had played no active part in the mutiny; and he arranged for him to get the best possible legal advice.

This was not a time of soft justice in England, least of all to mutineers and pirates, but as stories of Bligh's behavior before the mutiny spread, people began to think that there was more to the notorious case than met the eye. Also, Captain Edwards's treatment of the prisoners had become widely known and tended to bring public sentiment around in favor of Heywood and the others and against Bligh.

The trial began on September 12, 1792. From the outset it was evident that Coleman, Norman and McIntosh would be acquitted, since Bligh had left behind the statement that they were forcibly detained. It was also pretty clear that four of the seamen who had been seen bearing arms during the mutiny— Ellison, Burkitt, Millward and Muspratt—had little hope of escaping the gallows. The interest in the trial, apart from the usual morbid fascination, lay therefore mainly in the fate of Heywood and Morrison, especially Heywood.

On the morning of September 18 Lord Hood announced the court's verdict—"that the charges have been proved against the said Peter Heywood, James Morrison, Thomas Ellison, Thomas Burkitt, John Millward and William Muspratt, and I do adjudge you and each of you to suffer death by being hanged by the neck." He went on to "humbly and most earnestly recommend the said Peter Heywood and James Morrison to His Majesty's royal mercy." The rest went free.

The Heywood family were thus condemned to another period of agonizing doubt, but all was well, both for Heywood and Morrison. A free pardon was sent two weeks later. On Commodore Pasley's recommendation Lord Hood himself offered to take Heywood on his flagship, *Victory*.

To acquit, and at once to reinstate, an officer who had been one of Bligh's chief targets was a public rebuke to the absent captain, and everyone recognized it as such.

Morrison, too, had no difficulty in finding a ship. Of the four mutineers condemned to death, Will Muspratt eventually won his freedom on a legal technicality; and so, of the twenty-five who remained behind in the *Bounty* only three met the common fate of every mutineer.

THE EIGHTEEN MONTHS' long period between William Bligh's return from Jamaica and his next employment in the Royal Navy was one of anxiety and unhappiness for him. As soon as the court-martial was over, fierce contention had broken out among the families involved; and the Heywoods and Christians relentlessly set about the destruction of Bligh's reputation. Especially damaging was the publication by Fletcher's brother, Edward Christian, of the minutes of the court-martial, with a long, cleverly written appendix of his own. Although Britain was now at war with France, and his contemporaries were gaining distinction in battles and adding to their fortunes with prize money, Bligh was kept on half pay, an embittered and penurious officer with few people except his loyal wife prepared to support him.

His chance came at last, when the controversy was dying down, in April 1795. He was appointed to the command of the *Calcutta,* which was ordered to join the fleet of Admiral Adam Duncan in the North Sea, blockading the Dutch fleet.

In the following January he was given the command of the much larger *Director.* Dull blockade duties occupied the *Director*'s company for many months. In March 1797 Bligh was aware of a dangerous spirit running through the ship. Six men refused or neglected their duties. Bligh served out lashes to them all, and to five more a few days later. The running of the ship became more and more difficult, and Bligh soon realized that this was no passing restlessness. He took the *Director* to Sheerness, and there, at 9:00 a.m. on May 19, 1797, he was for the second time ordered off his ship by mutineers.

This time Bligh was in good company. For the whole command of the Royal Navy at Nore had risen up against their officers, demanding improved pay and conditions. Bligh took an active and responsible part in the closing stages of this "Mutiny of the Nore."

By this time Bligh was nearing the end of his active service in the Royal Navy. His reputation as a navigator and hydrographer, as naturalist and scientist, was untarnished. He was now a Fellow of the Royal Society and had been presented with its gold medal. His family life remained blissfully happy, and there was no more loving and anxious father. Yet his professional life was rarely free from discord, and Betsy seemed to be forever involved in defense of his reputation.

In 1804 there was yet another court-martial. At this time Bligh was commander of the *Warrior*. He had a good deal of trouble with his second lieutenant, John Frazier. Then Frazier had an accident. He fell between casks loaded in a launch and claimed afterward that he was unable to keep his watch. Bligh, considering him a malingerer, had him charged with "contumacy and disobedience." On the surgeon's evidence, Frazier was acquitted. The lieutenant wasted no time in pushing home his advantage and reported that Bligh "publicly on the quarter deck . . . did grossly insult and ill treat me . . . by calling me rascal, scoundrel and shaking his fist in my face and that . . . he behaved towards me and other commissioned, warrant and petty officers in the said ship in a tyrannical and oppressive and unofficerlike behaviour."

When the news of this accusation reached the Admiralty, it was decided to court-martial Bligh in turn. The *Warrior* court-martial, as it came to be called, was the last inglorious event in Bligh's naval career. This was no public *cause célèbre,* but the outcome was humiliating. His officers might, as Bligh complained, "turn out to be the worst of serpents," but the court-martial's considered opinion was that "the charges are in part proved, and we do therefore adjudge Captain William Bligh to be reprimanded and to be admonished to be in future more correct in his language."

Bligh was restored to his command and wrote without delay to Banks, complaining about everything—the court-martial, the findings and his officers. "Instances of my doing good," remarked Bligh to his patron, "and rendering service are numerous since my youth to this moment. I defy the world to produce one act of malevolence or injustice."

Once again the powerful hand of Sir Joseph Banks offered him a new and seemingly golden opportunity to end for the time being his long period of misfortune. Banks's offer was the governorship of New South Wales, with a salary of £2000 a year, and a pension of £1000 a year. It was an opportunity that Bligh could not pass by. The one serious drawback was that he would have to leave behind his beloved Betsy and his children. As he explained sadly to Banks in his reply, her nerves had so suffered on account of her husband's troubles that she could not possibly undertake such a long sea voyage. "The sound of a gun or thunder" was unbearable to her, and even when Bligh's ship was in port she could remain on board only a few hours.

In February 1806 he bade his wife and five of his daughters farewell. His daughter Mary accompanied him. She had married a naval officer, John Putland, who had agreed to act as Bligh's lieutenant during his governorship of the colony.

Bligh found conditions in New South Wales far worse than he could have dreamed possible—a corrupt, violent, drunken and immoral community, controlled by a ruthless military junta, the New South Wales Corps. The settlers, the farmers and the convicts, with few exceptions, had all succumbed to alcoholism. Women sold their bodies, men their land and their stock, for rum. The officers of the corps saw that they got it—at a price.

The governor, Bligh discovered to his chagrin, was regarded as no more than a cipher. He fought valiantly but unskillfully against this gangster regime, but he was quite out of his depth in this world of chicanery and corruption.

Here, in this remote outpost, without the support of law, military strength or influential friends, Bligh was more helpless than he had ever been in the past. There was no Betsy, no Banks, to support him. His daughter could do nothing, his son-in-law was dying of consumption. The small company of friends he had made when he had first arrived soon dissolved.

On January 26, 1808, there was a military coup. Major George Johnston, the corrupt commanding officer of the New South Wales Corps, went to arrest Bligh in Government House. The manner of his arrest is the most controversial event in the notorious Rum Rebellion. All that is known for sure is that he took a lot of finding and that he was eventually discovered in a back room underneath a featherbed, wearing his naval uniform and a gold medal he had earned in battle. Was it cowardice that sent him there, or did he hope that the soldiers might eventually look for him elsewhere, thus enabling him to escape?

Bligh, as so often before, is his own stoutest defender: "For twenty-one years I have been a Post-Captain, and have been engaged in services of danger, not falling within the ordinary duties of my profession. . . . Was it for me then to sully my reputation and to disgrace the medal I wear by shrinking from death, which I had braved in every shape?"

After suffering numerous humiliations and vicissitudes, Bligh sailed from New South Wales on April 27, 1810, and arrived in London six months later.

After this ordeal, the last of so many, Bligh applied for promotion to flag rank. His request was granted. He never hoisted his flag, never went to sea again, but at least he could retire from his turbulent public career as William Bligh, rear admiral of the Blue, who had fought alongside Nelson and was one of the greatest navigators and explorers of his day. Bligh's devoted and dedicated wife fell ill, and she died in 1812. Bligh died in December 1817, some twenty-four years after the man who was once his close friend and who became his greatest enemy.

Epilogue

"A CRIME OF SO BLACK A NATURE"

THE SOLUTION TO THE mystery of the *Bounty* mutiny lies somewhere in the passage between Tahiti and Tofua. To understand what may have happened it is necessary to look far back at a little considered side of life in the Royal Navy.

The moral standards in the Royal Navy had never been lower than they were at the end of the eighteenth century. To reduce the dangers of "indecent conduct" the navy encouraged natives abroad—as well as wives at home—to come on board whenever the ship was in port. No one can say whether, on balance, these tactics were successful, but the reports of courts-martial reveal numerous cases of "gross indecency." For every case brought to court, there were certainly many hundreds which went unpunished.

Those who attempted to bring about moral reform in the navy had no doubt that the encouragement of prostitution on shipboard actually encouraged "indecent conduct" at sea too. One pamphleteer angrily demanded, "What can be more *unnatural,* more contrary to all the feelings of our common nature, than the open, undisguised, unblushing, promiscuous concubinage, which now takes place on board His Majesty's ships of war?"

From many such protests we can judge how widespread "intimate friendships" were in the navy at that time. The ship's commander, with his own cabin and the privilege of privacy, and with special responsibilities such as Bligh had for the "young gentlemen" on his voyages, was in a special position to enjoy such relationships.

Bligh's friendship with Christian, as we have seen, was most intimate and long-lasting. This was their third voyage together, and it is clear that Christian was singled out for special favors in the *Britannia* and later in the *Bounty.* He had the key to Bligh's liquor store and when standing watch would often send down one of the men to fetch him a tot. He is reported as having had supper with Bligh every other night.

There were disputes between the commander and his protégé before they reached Tahiti, but they were few and not very violent. At Tahiti the close relationship was broken. Christian lived with a native woman, while Bligh, with Cook as an example, lived an abstemious life.

Let us look back to early April, 1789. Bligh is angry at the state of the ship and the slackness of officers and men. If he had been experiencing jealousy, which is extremely likely, then his first target for vengeance would obviously be Christian. And it is at this time—according to all accounts—that Fletcher Christian's ordeal began.

The days between Matavai Bay and Tofua reveal a commander who was at the end of his tether, behaved violently and irrationally, showed extreme possessiveness and a truly fearsome venom toward his officers, and toward Christian in particular. After refusing to spend the evening with Bligh for the last time, Christian, in a deeply disturbed state of mind, determined on a step so dangerous that it amounted to suicide. He was foiled, was offered an alternative course of action which at any other time he would not have contemplated—and which he almost instantly regretted. "It is too late," was his *cri de coeur* to Bligh. "I have been in hell."

If it seems odd that in the heat of the court-martial and its aftermath no one made an accusation of "indecent conduct" against Bligh, there are three possible explanations. The first is that no one knew for sure. The second, that it might implicate others. The third, that it was an especially dangerous accusation to make against a commanding officer.

In any case, I believe that the solution of the *Bounty* mystery lies somewhere in this forbidden darkness.

Bligh and Christian were both highly strung. Bligh's qualities and weaknesses as a leader are now clear to us: an unsurpassed foul-weather commander who revealed his lack of self-confidence only when the going was good; courageous, dutiful, a superb seaman and navigator, but fretful, impatient and seriously lacking in imagination. Shrewd people who met him for the first time would see the short, stout figure with wide-set mariner's legs, small, bright, angry blue eyes set against a wax-pale complexion, and would think, There is a difficult man! Christian, on the other hand, exposed shamelessly his insatiable appetite for affection, and Bligh, who pretended to himself that he was above such things, fell under the spell of Christian's charm and liveliness.

Bligh promoted this weak, moody, temperamental and sentimental young man above his ability. Where Bligh had moments of magnificence as a leader, Christian had none. Just as he destroyed the community of the *Bounty* with an explosion ignited by pent-up despair, so he later brought about the destruction of the community he had founded on Pitcairn by a failure to rise to the responsibilities of leadership. There was just not enough fiber in him to endure the harsh treatment and the humiliation he suffered under Bligh.

Was all this enough to drive Fletcher Christian to mutiny? Not at first perhaps. Knowing him as we do, we are not surprised that he preferred to slide out of his crisis. It needed a Ned Young—the *Bounty*'s Iago—to put steel into Christian's resolve, and to bring about the most celebrated mutiny of all time.

THE
AGONY
AND THE
ECSTASY

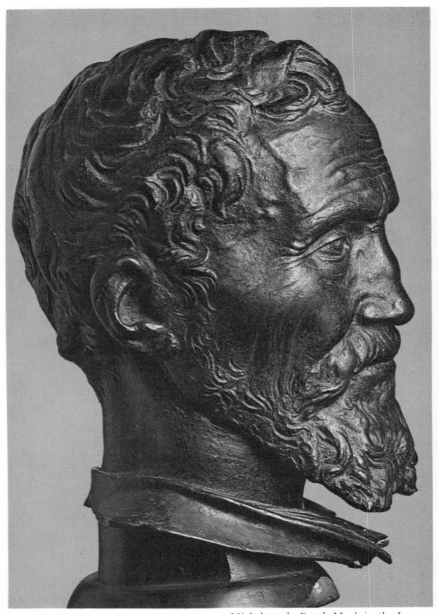

Michelangelo Death Mask in the Louvre

A condensation of

THE
AGONY
AND THE
ECSTASY

the biographical novel of

MICHELANGELO

BY

IRVING
STONE

Illustrations by Giorgio De Gaspari
Chapter decorations by James Alexander

Into the strife and brilliance of fifteenth-century Florence was born one of the greatest geniuses the world has ever known. His name was Michelangelo Buonarroti.

His was a dazzling period—a time of political unrest and religious upheaval, of artistic rivalry and court intrigue—and Michelangelo was at the center of it all. A stubborn idealist, seldom at peace with himself, Michelangelo was a master not only of painting but of architecture, science, and above all of sculpture—a man whose consuming love, overriding all other passions, was for the gleaming stone and for what he could wrest from it.

BOOK ONE

The Studio

E SAT BEFORE the mirror of his second-floor bedroom, overlooking the Via dell' Anguillara in Florence, sketching his own lean cheeks with their high bone ridges, the flat broad forehead, the dark curling hair, the amber-colored eyes wide-set but heavy lidded.

"My head is out of rule," thought the thirteen-year-old, "with my forehead overweighing my mouth and chin. Someone should have used a plumb line."

He shifted his wiry body lightly so as not to waken his four brothers. With rapid strokes of the crayon he began redrafting his features, broadening the cheeks, making the lips fuller. "It's too bad a face can't be redrawn before it's delivered to the client," he thought.

Notes of a bird's song came fluting through the big window: that would be his friend Granacci. He hid his drawing paper under his bed and went noiselessly down the circular stairs to the street.

Francesco Granacci was a tall nineteen-year-old, with hay-colored hair and alert blue eyes. For a year he had been providing Michelangelo with drawing materials and prints borrowed surreptitiously from the studio of the painter Ghirlandaio, where he was apprenticed.

"You're really coming with me this time?" Granacci asked.

"It's my birthday present to myself."

"Good. And remember what I told you about Domenico Ghirlandaio. He likes his apprentices to be humble."

They crossed the Square of the Old Market, where fresh beeves hung on pulleys in front of the butchers' stalls. Michelangelo stopped to gaze at Donatello's St. Mark standing in a tall niche of the church Or San Michele. "Sculpture is the greatest art!" he exclaimed with emotion.

"Stop gaping," said Granacci, "there's business to be done."

Together they entered the Ghirlandaio studio. It was a large high-ceilinged room with a pungent smell of paint and charcoal. In the center was a plank table around which half a dozen sleepy young apprentices crouched on stools. In a corner a man was grinding colors in a mortar, while along the walls were stacked plans and sketches for frescoes the Tornabuoni family had commissioned for the choir of the church of Santa Maria Novella.

On a raised platform sat a man of about forty, his wide-topped desk the only ordered spot in the studio, with its neat rows of pens, brushes, sketchbooks, its implements hanging on hooks.

Granacci stopped below his master's desk. "Signor Ghirlandaio, this is Michelangelo, about whom I told you."

Michelangelo felt himself being spitted by a pair of eyes reputed to be able to see more than those of any other artist in Italy. The boy too used his eyes, drawing in his mind the artist sitting above him, the sensitive face with its full lips, prominent cheekbones, long black hair, the long supple fingers.

"Who is your father?" demanded Ghirlandaio.

"Lodovico di Lionardo Buonarroti-Simoni."

"I have heard the name. How old are you?"

"Thirteen."

"We start at ten. Where have you been these three years?"

"Wasting my time at school, studying Latin and Greek."

A twitching at the corner of Ghirlandaio's lips showed that he liked the answer. "Can you draw?"

"I have the capacity to learn."

"He has a good hand. I've seen his drawings on the walls of his father's house," Granacci said.

"Ah, a muralist," quipped Ghirlandaio.

Michelangelo took Ghirlandaio seriously.

"I've never tried color. It's not my trade."

"Whatever else you may lack, it isn't modesty. Very well, suppose you sketch for me. What will it be?"

Michelangelo's eyes traveled over the workshop, swallowing impressions the way country youths break bunches of grapes in their mouths at autumn wine festivals. "Why not the studio?"

Ghirlandaio gave a short laugh. "Granacci, give Buonarroti paper and charcoal."

Michelangelo sat down on a bench to sketch. His eye and hand were good working partners, and for the first time since entering the studio his breathing was normal. Soon he felt someone leaning over his shoulder. "I'm not finished," he said.

"It is enough." Ghirlandaio studied the paper. "Granacci was right. You have a strong fist."

Michelangelo held his hand in front of him.

"It is a stonecutter's hand," he replied proudly.

"We do not use stonecutters here. I'll start you as an apprentice, but you must pay me six florins for the first year."

"I can pay you nothing."

Ghirlandaio looked at him sharply. "The Buonarroti are not poor. Since your father wants you apprenticed . . . "

"My father beats me every time I mention painting."

"Will he not beat you if you tell him I have accepted you?"

"My defense will be the fact that you will pay him six florins the first year, eight the second, and ten the third."

"But that's unheard of!"

"Otherwise I cannot come to work for you."

The apprentices made no pretense of working while they watched this scene. The boy stood his ground respectfully, gazing straight at Ghirlandaio as though to say: "I will be worth it to you." The artist felt a grudging admiration. He said, "Bring your father in."

At the door, Granacci threw an arm affectionately about the boy's shoulder. "You broke every rule. But you got in!"

WALKING PAST THE stone house of the poet Dante and the church of the Badia was for Michelangelo like walking through a gallery: for the Tuscan treats stone with the tenderness that a lover reserves for his sweetheart. From the time of their Etruscan ancestors the people of this region had been quarrying stone from the mountains, hauling it by oxen to their land, cutting, edging, shaping and building it into houses and palaces, churches and loggias, forts and walls. From childhood the Tuscans knew the feel and smell of stone; for fifteen hundred years their ancestors had worked the native *pietra serena*—serene stone—building a city of such breathtaking beauty that every Florentine vowed: "Never shall I live out of sight of the Duomo!"—Florence's domed cathedral.

Arriving home, he went through the side entrance of the Buonarroti house into the family kitchen. Lucrezia, his stepmother, was making *torta*. The chickens had been fried in oil, ground into sausage with onions, parsley, eggs and saffron. Ham and pork had been made into ravioli with cheese, flour, clove and ginger, and laid with the chicken sausage between layers of dates and almonds. The dish was being covered with pastry before being placed in the hot embers to bake.

"Good morning, *madre mia*."

"Ah, Michelangelo. I have something special for you today: a salad that sings in the mouth."

Each morning Lucrezia rose at four to reach the market just as the farmers arrived through the cobbled streets, their carts filled with fresh produce, eggs, cheese and meat. She selected only the very best figs, peaches, beans, peas; so Michelangelo and his four brothers called her *Il Migliore*, The Best.

She was a docile creature—else why would so young a woman marry a forty-three-year-old widower with five sons, a brother and sister-in-law and a mother to cook for?—but in the kitchen she was a lioness in the tradition of Marzocco, Florence's heraldic lion. Michelangelo, in the bedroom next to his parents' room, often heard their predawn debates while his stepmother dressed for marketing.

"Every day you want a bale of herring, a thousand oranges."

"Lodovico, you are one who would keep money in the purse and hunger in the belly."

"Hunger! No Buonarroti has missed his dinner in three hundred years."

Now Michelangelo walked through the family room with the oak bench facing the fireplace, the six-foot bellows propped against the stone, the wall chairs with leather backs and leather seats. The next room was his father's study; here Lodovico sat cramped over his parchment account books. For years his sole activity had been a concentration on how to retain the remnants of the Buonarroti fortune, which had shrunk to a ten-acre farm in Settignano and a house with a disputed title.

Lodovico heard his son come in and looked up. He sported a luxurious mustache which flowed into his beard, cut square four inches below his chin. His hair was streaked with gray; across the forehead were four deep lines; his brown eyes were melancholy. He was a cautious man who locked the door with three keys.

"Good morning, *messer padre.*"

Lodovico sighed. "I was born too late. One hundred years ago the Buonarroti vines were tied with sausages."

He knew to the last florin how much each Buonarroti generation had owned of land, houses, business, gold. The family records were the Old Testament of his life. "We are noble burghers," he would tell his sons. "Our family is as old as the Medici."

When the powerful pro-Church party, the Guelphs, rose to power in Florence, the Buonarroti family had also risen rapidly: Buonarroti had been mayors and members of the city council.

The last official recognition of the family had taken place fourteen years before, in 1474, when Lodovico himself had been appointed *podestà,* or visiting mayor, for two hamlets high in the Apennines.

As he stood in the recessed window, letting the thin sun warm his shoulders, the boy's mind went back to their house in Settignano, overlooking the valley of the Arno, when his mother had been alive. Then there had been love and laughter; but when his mother died, his father retreated in despair to his study, while his Aunt Cassandra took over the care of the household. Michelangelo was lonely and unwanted except by his grandmother, Monna Alessandra, and the Topolinos—a stonecutter's family across the valley. The stonecutter's wife, Monna Margherita, had suckled him as a baby.

Even after his father had remarried and the family had moved to Florence, he fled at every opportunity to the Topolinos. In their yard he would set to work cutting the *pietra serena* from the neighboring quarry into beveled building stones for a new Florentine palace, working out his unhappiness in the precision blows the stonecutter and his sons had taught him.

Michelangelo pulled himself back from his memories. "Father, I have just come from Ghirlandaio's studio. He has agreed to sign me as an apprentice."

Lodovico rose to a commanding position over the boy. This inexplicable desire of his son to become an artisan could be the final push that would topple the Buonarroti into the social abyss.

"Michelangelo, I sent you to an expensive school so you could do well in the Wool Guild and someday become a rich merchant. That was how most of the great Florentine fortunes started, even the Medici's. Do you think that I will let you waste your life as a painter, bring disgrace to the family name? For three hundred years no Buonarroti has fallen so low as to work with his hands."

"That is true. We have been usurers," the boy said.

"We belong to the Money Changers Guild, one of the most respectable in Florence. Moneylending is an honorable profession."

Michelangelo sought refuge in humor. "Have you seen Uncle

Francesco grab his coins and fold up his counter outside Or San Michele when it starts to rain? No one ever worked faster with his hands."

At the mention of his name Uncle Francesco came running into the room. He said in a hoarse voice: "Michelangelo, what perverse pleasure can you derive from injuring the Buonarroti?"

The boy was furious. "I have as much pride in our name as anyone. Why can't I learn to do work that all Florence will be proud of, as they are of Donatello's sculptures and Ghirlandaio's frescoes?"

Lodovico put his hand on the boy's shoulder, calling him "Michelagnolo," his pet name. This was his favorite of the five sons, the one for whom he had the highest hopes. "Michelagnolo, Donatello began as an artisan and ended as an artisan. So will Ghirlandaio."

"Art is like washing an ass's head with lye," observed Francesco, for the Tuscan's wisdom is a web of proverbs; "you lose both the effort and the lye."

"Bleed me of art, and there won't be enough liquid left in me to spit," cried Michelangelo.

"I'll teach you to be vulgar," Lodovico shouted.

He started raining blows on the boy. Michelangelo lowered his head like a beast in a storm, murmuring his grandmother's proverb: "*Pazienza!* No man is born into the world whose work is not born with him."

From the corner of his eye he saw his enormously fat Aunt Cassandra in the doorway, heard her booming voice join in. Then, suddenly, all words and blows stopped, for his grandmother had entered the room. She was a retiring woman who exercised her matriarchy only in moments of family crisis. Lodovico slumped into his chair. "Never let me hear again about being apprenticed to artists," he said.

Monna Alessandra said to her son, "What difference does it make whether he joins the Wool Guild and twists wool or the Apothecaries and mixes paints? You won't leave enough money to set up five geese, let alone sons. All five must look to their living; let Michelangelo go into a studio as he wishes."

"I intend to be apprenticed to Ghirlandaio, Father. You must sign the papers. I'll do well by us all."

"We have not a scudo to pay for any apprenticeship."

Michelangelo said gently: "There is no need for money, *padre*. Ghirlandaio has agreed to pay *you* for my apprenticeship. He thinks I have a strong fist."

Lodovico crossed himself. He said: "Truly I have conquered myself in more battles than a saint!"

GHIRLANDAIO HAD THE most bustling, successful studio in Italy. He and his brothers, also painters, had been trained by their father, an expert goldsmith who was known for a wreath called a *ghirlanda,* which many fashionable Florentine women wore in their hair.

Michelangelo found the studio teeming with activity but good-natured. Mainardi, who was in charge of the apprentices, took him in tow. "The purpose of painting," he explained, "is to be decorative, to bring stories to life, to make people happy; yes, even with pictures of the saints being martyred. Remember that, Michelangelo, and you will become a successful painter."

There was no formal method of teaching at Ghirlandaio's studio. Its philosophy was expressed in a plaque nailed to the wall:

> *The most perfect guide is nature. Continue*
> *without fail to draw something every day.*

Michelangelo had to learn from whatever task each man had at hand. Ghirlandaio created the overall design of the frescoes for the Tornabuoni choir. He also did the more conspicuous panels and those containing important portraits. Major portions of the other panels were painted by Mainardi, Benedetto, Granacci and Bugiardini, the most experienced apprentices; the youngest ones practiced on the lunettes, which were hard to see.

Two weeks flew by and the magic day of Michelangelo's contract signing and first pay dawned. He felt he had done little to earn his two gold florins: picking up paints at the chemist's, screening sand and washing it in a barrel with a running hose.

Awakening while it was still dark, he climbed over his young brother Buonarroto, dressed and went to the workshop. Ghirlandaio's good morning was short. He had been working on a study of St. John Baptizing the Neophyte and was upset because he could not clarify his concept of Jesus. Michelangelo watched with apprehension: would he forget what day it was? When the others came in, Granacci saw his friend's expression. He went to Ghirlandaio's brother David, who was paymaster, and murmured in his ear. David reached into the leather purse hooked onto his belt and handed Michelangelo two florins and a contract book. Michelangelo signed his name beside the first payment, then wrote the date: *April 16, 1488.* Joy raced through him as he anticipated the moment when he would hand the florins to his father. Then he was aware of an enthusiastic hubbub among the apprentices and the voice of Jacopo, imp son of a baker.

"It's agreed; we draw from memory that gnome figure on the alley wall behind the *bottega.* The one who draws the most accurate reproduction wins and pays for dinner. Cieco, Baldinelli, Granacci, Bugiardini, Tedesco, are you ready?"

Michelangelo felt a dull pain in his chest; he was being left out again. His had been a lonely childhood; he had had no intimate friend except Granacci. Often he had been excluded from games. Why? Because he had been small and sickly? Because there was not enough laughter in him? He desperately wanted to be included in this young group.

Jacopo was calling out: "Time limit—ten minutes."

"Why can't I compete, Jacopo?" Michelangelo cried.

Jacopo scowled. "You couldn't possibly win, so there would be no chance of your paying."

"Please let me try, too. You'll see; I won't do too badly."

"All right," Jacopo agreed finally. "Now, everyone ready?"

Excitedly, Michelangelo picked up charcoal and paper and began outlining the gnarled figure he had seen on the alley wall.

"Time limit!" cried Jacopo. "Line up your drawings on the table."

Michelangelo put his in line and Jacopo stared at it astonished. "I can't believe it. Look! Michelangelo has won!"

There were cries of congratulation. He glowed with pride. He was the newest apprentice, yet he had won the right to buy everyone dinner. . . . *Buy everyone dinner!* His heart sank. There were seven of them. . . . Two liters of wine, soup, veal, fruit! A sizable hole in one of his gold pieces.

On the way to an inn, with the others rushing ahead laughing among themselves, something bothered him. He fell in step beside Granacci. "I was gulled, wasn't I?"

"Yes. It's part of the initiation. If you had known, would you have made yourself draw badly?"

Michelangelo grinned sheepishly. "They couldn't lose!"

THE NEXT DAY he watched Ghirlandaio complete an oil portrait of Giovanna Tornabuoni, painted as a separate commission. "Oil painting is for women," Ghirlandaio said sarcastically. "But I can use this figure in the fresco. Never try to invent human beings, Michelangelo; paint only those whom you have drawn from life."

It seemed to Michelangelo that the skilled apprentice Benedetto, who never worked freehand, paid more attention to the mathematical squares on the paper before him than to the character of the person portrayed. He told Michelangelo: "The face is divided in three parts: first, hair and forehead; then the nose; then the chin and mouth. Now take the proportions of a man—I omit women because not one of them is perfectly proportioned. The arm with the hand extends to the middle of the thigh. The length of a man is eight faces; it is equal to his width with the arms extended."

Michelangelo tried drawing to this geometric plan, but the restriction was a coffin into which he could squeeze only dead bodies.

From Jacopo he received not technical instructions but news of the city. Nothing nefarious was hidden from Jacopo. Daily, he made the rounds of the inns, the wine- and barbershops, the quarters of the prostitutes, the groups of old men sitting on stone benches before the palaces, for they were the best purveyors of scandal.

Ghirlandaio had a copy of Cennini's treatise on painting; although Jacopo could not read a word, he was pretending to read passages he had memorized: *"As an artist your life should always be regulated as if you were studying theology, philosophy, or any other science, eating and drinking temperately to save your hand. One thing will render your hand so unsteady that it will tremble and flutter more than leaves shaken by the wind, and this is frequenting too much the company of women."* Jacopo threw back his head and laughed. "Now you know why I don't paint more: I don't want the Ghirlandaio frescoes to tremble and flutter like leaves in the wind!"

One night, Michelangelo and Granacci walked through the Piazza della Signoria, the square before the Signoria where the city council met. A large crowd was gathered. On the balcony of the palace an ambassador from the Turkish sultan, garbed in a turban and flowing robes, was presenting a giraffe to the council. Michelangelo wished he could sketch the scene. He complained to Granacci that he felt like a chessboard, with alternating black and white squares of information and ignorance.

Next day he returned to the studio early. He had decided that he must study the drawings of his master. Under Ghirlandaio's desk he found a bundle labeled "Slaughter of the Innocents," took it to the table and spread out the studies for the fresco. They had simplicity and authority. He began copying them and had made a half dozen sketches when he heard Ghirlandaio behind him: "Who gave you permission to pry into that bundle?"

Michelangelo put down his charcoal, frightened.

"I want to learn. The quicker I learn, the more I can help."

The intensity in the boy's eyes banished Ghirlandaio's anger. He took Michelangelo to his desk, handed him a blunt-nibbed pen and picked up another for himself. "Here's how I use a pen: circles for the eyes, angular tips for a nose, like this; a short nib to render a mouth and score the underlip."

Michelangelo followed the older man with quick movements of the hand. With a few rapid strokes Ghirlandaio could achieve a lyrical flow of body lines and at the same time give the figures individuality. A look of rapture came over Michelangelo's face. He asked if they might sometimes draw from nude models.

"Why should you learn to draw the nude when we must always paint the figure draped?" demanded Ghirlandaio. "No one has worked in nudes since the pagan Greeks. We have to paint for Christians. Besides, human bodies are ugly. Painting should be charming, refreshing. I like to draw figures walking delicately under their gowns. . . ."

"And I would like to draw them the way God made Adam."

GHIRLANDAIO'S PANEL OF THE birth of St. John was finally ready to be transferred to Santa Maria Novella. Everyone bustled about, collecting charts, sketches, brushes and other equipment. All was loaded on a small cart behind an even smaller donkey, and off went the entire studio with Ghirlandaio at its head and Michelangelo driving the cart.

He pulled the donkey up in front of the church, entered the bronze doors and stood breathing the cool, incense-heavy air. The church stretched before him, more than three hundred feet long; he walked slowly up the main aisle, savoring every step. It was like a journey through Italian art: Giotto, Masaccio, Brunelleschi, Ghiberti; and then the magnificent Rucellai chapel, built by his own mother's family two centuries before.

He had never gone into the chapel, for he was not allowed even to mention the Rucellai name at home: after his mother's death the Rucellai had cut off all communication, not caring what happened to her sons. But now he was going to work in Santa Maria Novella; had he not earned the right to enter the chapel?

He walked up the stairs, slowly. Once inside the chapel with its Cimabue Madonna, he fell to his knees; this was the chapel where his mother and his mother's mother had worshiped. Tears flooded his eyes. Prayers sprang to his lips unbidden. Was he praying to the Madonna or to his mother?

He rose and left the chapel, thinking of the contrast between his two families. The Rucellai had built this chapel at the same time that the Buonarroti had come into their wealth. But the Buonarroti had never commissioned a chapel. They had always been hard men with a florin, willing to invest only in houses and land. Michelangelo had never seen a painting or a sculpture in a Buonarroti house, though they had lived for three hundred years in the most creative city in the world, where even modest homes had religious works that had come down through the generations. The Buonarroti were not only stingy, they were enemies of art; they despised the men who created it.

A shout from Bugiardini on the scaffolding called him. Bugiardini was plastering the area to be painted that day, and Ghirlandaio had already outlined some figures. Michelangelo watched as he mixed mineral earth colors in little jars of water, and commenced painting. He had to work swiftly before the plaster dried; if he had failed to gauge accurately how much he could do that day, the remaining dry plaster would have to be cut away the following morning, leaving a seam. Michelangelo sprinkled the area with water just ahead of Ghirlandaio's flying brush.

The climax of the panel was reached when Ghirlandaio painted the exquisite young Giovanna Tornabuoni, robed in rich silks and jewels, gazing straight ahead and not in the least interested in Elisabeth in her high-backed bed, or John, suckling at the breast of another Tornabuoni beauty. Two old Tornabuoni aunts appeared as visitors to Elisabeth.

When the plaster began to dry, the burnt lime recovered its carbonic acid from the air, fixing the colors. The pigments remained on the surface of the plaster in a crystalline coating of carbonate of lime. The panel now had a metallic luster which would protect the colors from heat, cold or moisture. The amazing fact was that each day's segment was drying slowly to the very colors Ghirlandaio had created in his studio.

Standing before the brilliant panel, the boy realized that this was not the birth of John to the modest family of Elisabeth and Zacharias; it was a social gathering in the home of a merchant prince, devoid of religious spirit. Florence was Ghirlandaio's religion. He spent his life painting its people, its palaces, its streets and pageants. And what an eye he had! Nothing escaped him. Since no one would commission him to paint Florence he had made Florence Jerusalem, and all the Biblical people modern Florentines.

Michelangelo walked out of the church feeling depressed. The forms were superb; but where was the substance? He too wanted to learn to set down what he saw; but what he felt about what he saw would always be more important.

He drifted over to the Duomo, where the apprentices with other young men of the city gathered on the cool marble steps to view the passing pageant. Every day in Florence was a fair. The girls were blond, slender, erect; they wore colorful head coverings, high-necked gowns with pleated full skirts, their breasts outlined in filmier fabric. The older men were in somber cloaks, but wealthy young men wore their long hose with each leg dyed differently and patterned according to the family coat of arms.

Jacopo, sitting on top of a Roman sarcophagus, kept up a running commentary on the passing girls, seeking out the ones to whom he awarded his highest accolade: "Ah, how mattressable."

Michelangelo went to Jacopo's side and ran his hand over the funeral procession of men and horses on the sarcophagus. "Feel how these marble figures are still alive and breathing!"

His voice carried such exultation that his friends turned to stare at him. His secret—his hunger to carve—had burst into the open. He said, "God was the first sculptor; He made the first figure: man. And when He wanted to give His Commandments, what material did He use? Stone. Look at all us painters lolling on the Duomo steps. How many sculptors are left in Florence?" His eyes glowed in the fading light as he told them why there were no more sculptors: the strength needed to use hammer and chisel exhausted mind and body, in contrast to the brushes, pens and charcoal which the painters used so lightly.

Jacopo hooted, and Granacci answered his young friend: "If fatigue is the criterion of art, then the quarryman is nobler than the sculptor, the blacksmith greater than the goldsmith."

"But you do agree," Michelangelo said, "that art is noble in the degree to which it represents the truth? Sculpture is closer to true form, for the figure emerges on all four sides. It takes a thousand times more accuracy of judgment and vision."

Jacopo jumped down from his perch. "Sculpture is a bore. What can they make? A man, a woman, a lion, a horse. Then all over again. Monotonous. But the painter can portray the whole universe: sun, moon and stars, mountains, trees and rivers. The sculptors have all perished of boredom."

Tears of frustration welled in Michelangelo's eyes. "Painting is perishable: a fire in the chapel or too much cold, and the paint begins to fade, crack. But stone is eternal! Look at this Roman marble sarcophagus; as clear and strong as the day it was carved. . . ."

Mainardi raised his arm for attention. "Michelangelo," he said gently, "has it ever occurred to you that the reason there are no sculptors left is because of the cost of marble and bronze? Paint is cheap, commissions are abundant. Who would provide you with stone or support you while you practiced on it?"

Michelangelo could not answer. Without another word he walked away from the Duomo.

THAT NIGHT HE rolled and tossed. Buonarroto, who shared his bed, was placid in sleep. In the other bed slept the good and evil of the Buonarroti sons: Lionardo, who yearned to be a saint; and Giovansimone, lazy and rude, who had once set fire to Lucrezia's kitchen because she had disciplined him. Sigismondo, the youngest, slept in a trundle at the foot of Michelangelo's bed.

The room was hot. Michelangelo sprang out of bed, dressed and left the house. He walked through the city to a country road and made his way toward his old home in Settignano. When dawn flashed hot and bright, he paused on the Settignano hillside to watch the round hills of Tuscany emerge from sleep. He cared little about the poppies and cypresses that so moved painters: he loved the Arno valley because it was a sculptured landscape. God was the supreme carver.

He climbed the road into the hills, between walls standing as much as thirteen feet high, and built to last a hundred generations. Stone was the dominant factor: with it the Tuscan built his houses, enclosed his fields, terraced his slopes. Nature had been bountiful with stone; every hill was an undeveloped quarry.

As Michelangelo walked through the tiny settlement toward the Buonarroti villa he passed stoneyards used by the greatest Florentine sculptors. None of them was active now. Donatello had died twenty-two years ago and Bertoldo, the heir to his vast knowledge and workshop, was ill. Andrea and Giovanni della Robbia had abandoned stone sculpture for enameled terra-cotta reliefs. The Pollaiuolo brothers had moved to Rome. Yes, sculpture was dead. He had been born too late. Sick at heart, Michelangelo moved on.

THE BUONARROTI VILLA stood on a five-acre farm, leased to strangers on a long-term agreement. The house of *pietra serena* was beautiful in its austere lines, with broad porches overlooking the valley. He could remember his mother kissing him good night in his big corner room looking out across the fields.

Now he scampered down the hill between wheat and ripening grapes, and climbed the opposite ridge to the Topolino stoneyard. He paused when he came in sight of it. This was the picture which meant home and security for him: the father working with iron chisels to round a fluted column, the youngest son beveling a set of steps, one of the older two carving a window frame, the other graining a door panel; the grandfather polishing a column on a pumice wheelstone. Behind them were three arches, and under the arches scurrying chickens, ducks, pigs.

In the boy's mind there was no difference between a *scalpellino* and a *scultore,* a stonecutter and a sculptor, for the *scalpellini* were fine craftsmen. Every stone of the Florentine palaces was cut, beveled, given a textured surface as if it were a piece of sculpture. So proud were all Florentines of their simplest paving blocks that they bragged of the wretch who, being jostled in the cart that was taking him to the Palazzo della Signoria for hanging, cried out: "What idiots were these, who cut such clumsy blocks?"

The father heard Michelangelo's footsteps.

"*Buon dì,* Michelangelo. *Come va?* How goes it?"

"*Non c'è male.* Not bad. And you?"

"*Non c'è male.*"

The boys called out with welcoming warmth, and Michelangelo said, "*Salve,* good health, Bruno. *Salve,* Gilberto. *Salve,* Enrico."

A *scalpellino*'s words are few and simple, matching the single blow of the hammer. When he chips at the stone, he does not speak at all: one, two, three, four, five, six, seven: no word from the lips, only the rhythm of the moving hand with the chisel. Then he speaks, in the period of pause: one, two, three, four. The sentence must fit the rest count of four, or it remains unsaid.

The sons were given hammers and chisels at the age of six, and by ten were working full time. There was no marriage outside the stone ring, and no outsider could find work at the quarry. Between the arches hung an oblong piece of *pietra serena* with examples of the classic treatments of the stone: herringbone, punchhole, rustic, crosshatch, linear, bevel, centered right angle, receding step: the first alphabet Michelangelo had studied.

Topolino spoke. "You're apprenticed to Ghirlandaio?"

"Yes."

"You do not like it?"

"Not greatly."

"Who does somebody else's trade makes soup in a basket," said the old grandfather.

"We could use a cutter." This was from Bruno.

Michelangelo looked to the father. "*Davvero?* It is true? You will take me as apprentice?"

"With stone you're no apprentice. You earn a share."

His heart leaped. Everyone chipped in silence. The father had just offered him a portion of the food that went into the family belly. "My father would not permit me. . . . But can I cut now?"

The grandfather replied: "Every little bit helps."

Michelangelo sat before a roughed-out column, a hammer in one hand, a chisel in the other. He had a natural skill; under his blows the *pietra serena* cut like cake. Contact with the stone made him feel that the world was right again.

The *pietra serena* they were working was an alive blue-gray. It was durable yet manageable. The Topolinos had taught him to seek the natural form of the stone; never to grow angry or unsympathetic toward the material: "Stone works with you. It reveals itself. But you must strike it right. Each stone has its own character. It must be understood. Remember, stone gives itself to skill and to love."

The stone was master; not the mason. If a mason beat his stone as an ignorant farmer might beat his beasts, the warm breathing material became dull; died under his hand. To sympathy, it yielded: it grew luminous and sparkling. Stone was mystic: it had to be covered at night because it would crack if the full moon got on it. Stone was called by the stonecutters after the most precious of foods: *carne,* meat.

Monna Margherita, a formless woman who worked the animals and fields as well as the stove and tub, came out of the house and stood listening. Of her Lodovico had said bitterly, when Michelangelo wished to work with his hands: "A child sent out to nurse will take on the condition of the woman who feeds him."

She had suckled him with her own son for two years, and the day her breast ran dry she put both boys on wine. Water was for bathing before Mass.

Michelangelo kissed her on both cheeks.

"*Pazienza, figlio mio,*" she counseled. "Ghirlandaio is a good master. Who has an art, has always a part."

The father rose. "I must go to the quarry. Come help load."

They rode on the high seat behind two beautiful white oxen. In the fields the olive pickers worked on ladders made of slender tree stalks. Baskets were tied around their waists with rope. They held the branches with their left hands, stripping the little black olives with a milking movement of the right.

As they rounded a bend, Michelangelo saw the quarry with its blue and gray *serena* and iron-stained streaks. High on the cliff several men were using a *scribbus*—a point—to mark out a block to be quarried. He could see the point marks outlining blocks throughout the formation.

The work area where the blocks fell after they were loosed was shimmering with dust. Topolino inspected the newly quarried stone: "That one has knots. Too much iron in this. This one will be hollow." Until finally: "Ah! Here is a beautiful piece of meat."

Michelangelo planted his legs wide before the block and swung his weight from the hips; Topolino tipped it up with an iron bar. Between them, they moved it over the boulders to open ground; then, with the help of the quarrymen, the block was fulcrumed up into the cart.

Michelangelo wiped the sweat from his face and bade Topolino good-by. *"A domani,"* replied Topolino, flicking the lines for the oxen to move off.

Until tomorrow, Michelangelo thought, "tomorrow" being the next time I take my place with the family, be it a week or a year. He made his way down the mountain, feeling fifteen feet tall.

HAVING TAKEN A DAY off without permission, Michelangelo was at the studio early. Ghirlandaio had been there all night, drawing by candlelight. He was unshaven, his beard blue in the flickering light. He rose, raised his hands and shook his fingers up and down loosely, as though trying to shed his troubles. The boy came to him and gazed down at dozens of irresolute sketches of the Christ whom John was to baptize. The figures were slight to the point of delicacy. "I'm intimidated by the subject," Ghirlandaio growled.

For a week Michelangelo himself tried to draw a Christ. Finally he set down a figure with powerful shoulders, robust thighs, big solid feet: a man who could split a block of *pietra serena* with one blow of the hammer. Ghirlandaio was shocked when Michelangelo showed it to him. "Florence wouldn't accept a working-class Christ," he said.

Michelangelo smiled. "Christ was a carpenter."

A few days later the studio was buzzing. Ghirlandaio had completed his Christ and was blowing it up to full size to transfer to the fresco. When Michelangelo saw the finished figure he stood stunned: it was *his* Christ; but Ghirlandaio apparently had forgotten the boy's drawing.

The following week the studio again moved *en masse* to Santa Maria Novella to start a fresco of the Death of the Virgin. Michelangelo stood beneath the painters' scaffolding, unnoticed, then walked down the long center nave toward the sunlight. He turned to take a final look at the scaffolding rising tier upon tier in front of the stained-glass windows; at the artists, tiny figures before their work; at the sacks of plaster and sand, the plank table of painting materials. He pulled a wooden bench in place, took drawing paper and charcoal out of his shirt and began drawing the scene before him. After a while he felt someone staring holes through him from behind, and turned to find Ghirlandaio.

Ghirlandaio whispered hoarsely, "There are some things you know more about than I do, and I have been working for thirty years! Come to the studio early tomorrow. Perhaps we can make things more interesting for you."

Next morning Ghirlandaio had Granacci put him to work on a rock wall at the back of the studio yard. "Your plaster has to be sound," Granacci told Michelangelo. "If it crumbles your fresco goes with it. Check for saltpeter; it eats up your paint. Your lime should be old. I'll show you how to use a trowel to get a smooth surface. Plaster has to be beaten with the least possible amount of water, to the consistency of butter."

"Granacci, I want to draw with a pen, not a trowel!"

Granacci replied sharply: "An artist has to be master of the grubbiest detail of his craft."

When the mixture was right he handed Michelangelo a flexible trowel with which to apply the plaster. Michelangelo soon had the feel of it. When the plaster had dried sufficiently Granacci held up an old studio cartoon—a full-sized drawing to be transferred to a fresco. Michelangelo used an ivory pointing stick to punch holes through the cartoon, outlining several figures on the plaster; then he filled the holes with charcoal. When Granacci removed the cartoon, the boy took red ocher and drew a connecting outline between these dots. When this had dried, he dusted off the remaining charcoal with a feather. There was now the outline for a picture.

Mainardi came into the studio and forcibly turned Michelangelo to him. "Remember that fresh plaster changes its consistency. In the morning you have to keep your colors liquid so that you don't choke up its pores. Toward sundown the plaster will absorb less. But before you can apply any colors you must learn how to grind them."

The colors came from the apothecary in walnut-sized pieces of pigment. A piece of porphyry stone and a porphyry pestle were used to grind. No paint on a Ghirlandaio panel was ground for less than two hours.

Ghirlandaio had entered the studio.

"Hold on," he exclaimed. "Michelangelo, if you want a real mineral black, use this black chalk; if you want a slag black, mix in a little mineral green."

"What's the good of teaching him about colors," Granacci exclaimed, "if he doesn't know how to make his own brushes? Look, Michelangelo, these hog bristles are taken from white pigs; be sure they're domestic. Use a pound of bristles—"

Michelangelo threw his arms up in mock despair. "Help! You're crowding my three years of apprenticeship into one morning!"

IT WAS AUTUMN before he was ready to create his first fresco, from drawings he had made for the Death of the Virgin. He and Granacci climbed the scaffolding loaded with buckets of plaster and water; brushes, mixing spoons, cartoons and colored sketches. Michelangelo laid a modest area of *intonaco,* then held the cartoon of a bearded apostle to the wall. When it was outlined, he mixed his paints and picked up a finely pointed brush. He paused and turned to Granacci with big eyes.

"I can't be of any more help to you, Michelangelo," Granacci said. "The rest is between you and God. *Buona fortuna.*"

He scrambled down the scaffolding.

Michelangelo was alone at the top of the choir. For a moment he was dizzy: how vastly hollow and empty the church looked from here! In his nostrils was the dampness of the fresh plaster and the pungency of paint. He took a little *terra verde* and began to shade the darkest parts of the face: under the chin, the nose, the lips. . . .

By the third day everyone knew he was not following the rules. He was drawing nude figures, then draping them with robes—the reverse of the usual practice of suggesting a man's bones by the folds of a cloak. Ghirlandaio made no effort to correct him.

His two figures were a distinct picture by themselves, located in the bottom corner of the panel. The rest of the lunette was crowded with more than twenty figures surrounding the Virgin's bier. It was difficult to find Mary.

When Michelangelo came down from the scaffold the last time, everybody contributed a few scudi to buy wine. Jacopo raised the first toast: "To our new comrade. You've stolen the fresco."

Late that afternoon Ghirlandaio called him aside.

"They are saying I am jealous of you. It is true. Oh, not of those two figures, they're immature and crude. But I am jealous of what will ultimately be your ability to draw."

THE VALLEY OF THE Arno had the worst winter weather in Italy. The skies were leaden, the cold bit at the flesh. Ghirlandaio's studio had but one fireplace. Here the men sat at a semicircular table facing the flames, their backs cold but their fingers getting enough heat to let them work. Santa Maria Novella was even worse. Drafts rattled the scaffolding; the apprentices painted in a high wind.

By March, warmer skies were powdered with a touch of blue. One day Granacci burst into the studio. "Come with me," he said to Michelangelo. "I have something to show you."

In a moment they were in the street. Granacci took Michelangelo to a gate opposite the cathedral and opened it. Michelangelo entered and stood confounded. He was in an enormous garden; at the end of a path were a pool, a fountain, and a marble statue of a boy removing a thorn from his foot. On the wide porch of a casino a group of young men were chiseling stone. In front of the garden walls were loggias displaying marble busts of Roman emperors; cypress-lined paths curved through lawns as big as meadows.

Michelangelo stuttered: "Wh—what . . . is this place?"

"A sculpture garden, my friend," said Granacci. "Lorenzo de' Medici, *Il Magnifico,* has started a school here. He had Bertoldo carried here on a litter from the hospital, and told him he must restore Florence to its days of greatness in sculpture. Bertoldo got off the litter and promised Lorenzo that the era of Donatello would be re-created. That's Bertoldo over there. I met him once."

They walked over to the casino. Half a dozen men from fifteen to thirty years old were working at tables. Bertoldo, so slight as to seem all spirit and no body, wore a turban. He was instructing two boys in roughing a piece of marble. Since he was busy, Granacci led Michelangelo on through the casino, which displayed Lorenzo's collection of cameos, coins and medals, and examples from all the artists who had worked for the Medici family, a trove that staggered the boy.

"Who are the apprentices?" Michelangelo asked as they walked home. "How did they get in?"

"Lorenzo and Bertoldo chose them."

"And I have more than two years left at Ghirlandaio's. *Mamma mia,* I have destroyed myself!"

"*Pazienza!*" consoled Granacci. "You are not an old man yet."

"Patience!" exploded Michelangelo. "Granacci, I've got to get in! Now! I don't want to be a painter. I want to be a marble carver. How can I get admitted?"

"I don't know."

Tears of frustration came to Michelangelo's eyes. "Oh, Granacci, have you ever wanted anything so hard you couldn't bear it?"

"No. Everything has always been there."

"How fortunate you are."

Granacci gazed at the naked longing on his friend's face. "Perhaps."

BOOK TWO

The Sculpture Garden

 HE WAS DRAWN TO the sculpture garden as though the ancient statues were magnets. Sometimes he did not know that his feet were carrying him there. He would find himself inside the gate, lurking in the shadows. He did not venture to the casino where Bertoldo and the apprentices were working. He just stood motionless, hunger in his eyes.

Long into the night, he thought of it. "There must be a way. Two whole years with Ghirlandaio! How will I endure it?"

One day, just a year after Michelangelo's apprenticeship, he came into the studio to find it crackling with tension. Ghirlandaio was sitting at his desk, his scowl black.

"Il Magnifico has summoned me and asked if I would like to send my two best apprentices to his new school," he said.

Michelangelo stood riveted to the studio floor.

"No, I would not like to send my two best apprentices!" cried Ghirlandaio. "To have my workshop raided! But who dares say no to *Il Magnifico?* You, Buonarroti. You would like to go?"

"I have been hanging around that garden like a starved dog in front of a butcher stall," pleaded Michelangelo.

"Basta! Enough! Granacci, you and Buonarroti are released from your apprenticeship. Now back to work, all of you!"

Joy drenched Michelangelo like a warm rain. He went to Ghirlandaio's desk. He wanted to thank him; but how do you thank a man for letting you abandon him?

Ghirlandaio saw the conflict on the boy's face. He spoke softly. "You were right, Buonarroti: fresco is not your trade. That last figure you did looks as if it were carved out of rock. You have talent as a draftsman; perhaps you can transfer it to stone. But never forget that Domenico Ghirlandaio was your first master."

That evening Michelangelo and Granacci went into the family room where his father sat hunched over the angular corner desk.

"Father, there is news. Granacci and I are leaving Ghirlandaio's, to study sculpture in the Medici garden."

"Michelangelo a sculptor!" Lodovico raised anguished arms. "A sculptor is only a laborer, like a woodchopper. How large is your wage?"

"I don't know. I didn't ask."

"You didn't ask!" sneered Lodovico. "Do you think we can support you forever in your follies?"

Granacci said, "I asked. No pay. Just instruction."

Lodovico collapsed heavily onto a hard leather chair, tears coming to his eyes.

Detachedly Michelangelo thought: "We Florentines have no real sentiment, yet we cry so easily." He put a hand on his father's shoulder. "Father, give me a chance."

Lodovico said, "I will never give my consent." He rose and left the room.

"You must seize this opportunity anyway," said Granacci.

THE MEDICI SCULPTURE GARDEN was unlike Ghirlandaio's rushing workshop. On the warm April day when Michelangelo began his apprenticeship, the feel of the garden was: "Take your time. We have only one mission here: to teach. You have only to grow. *Calma!* Prepare yourself for a lifetime of sculpturing."

Bertoldo, with his snow-white hair and pale-blue eyes, was the inheritor of all the knowledge of the Golden Age of Florentine sculpture. He loved only two things as well as sculpture: laughter and cooking. He had written a cookbook, and his humor was as spicy as his chicken *alla diavola*.

He linked his thin arms through those of the new apprentices.

"Not all skill is communicable," he explained. "Donatello made me his heir, but he could never make me his peer. We all are as God made us. I will show you everything Donatello taught me; how much you absorb depends on your capacity. And now to work."

Michelangelo thought, "Just let them put a hammer and *subbia* in my hands and they will see the chips fly!" But Bertoldo had no intention of putting these tools into the hands of a beginner. He assigned Michelangelo a drawing desk on the portico beside a seventeen-year-old apprentice called Torrigiani, a handsome, blond, green-eyed young man, who soon became Michelangelo's closest companion among the apprentices. He was audacious and quarrelsome, but he gave Michelangelo a quick, warm friendship.

When Michelangelo asked whether Granacci did not think Torrigiani fascinating, Granacci replied guardedly: "I have known him all my life. Before you make a friend, eat a peck of salt with him."

He had been in the garden for a week when Lorenzo de' Medici entered with a young girl. For the first time Michelangelo saw the man who, without official title, ruled Florence and had made her wealthy not only in trade but in art, literature, scholarship. Forty years old, Lorenzo had a roughhewn face that appeared to have been carved out of mountain rock; a jutting jaw, a turned-up nose, large dark eyes and a mass of dark hair. He was just over medium height, with a sturdy physique which he kept in condition by hard riding and hawking.

He was an omnivorous reader of Greek and Latin, a poet and the builder of Europe's first public library, for which he had assembled ten thousand manuscripts and books. He was acknowledged to be the greatest of all patrons of literature and art, and his art collection was open to all artists and students. He provided villas for scholars on the slope of Fiesole, and here the leaders of his "Plato Academy," Pico della Mirandola, Poliziano, Ficino and Landino, helped create a new intellectual life.

Lorenzo, though the richest man in the world, had an open, lovable nature, and a total lack of arrogance. He walked the streets of Florence unattended, speaking to all citizens as an equal, exercising absolute authority in matters of policy, yet governing Florence with such good judgment, courtesy and dignity that people who might otherwise be enemies worked together harmoniously.

This was the man who stood a few feet from Michelangelo, talking affectionately to Bertoldo about some antique sculptures that had just arrived from Asia Minor: for sculpture was as important to Lorenzo as his fleets of ships, his chain of banks, his millions of florins' worth of trade each year in wool, oil, wine, perfume, flavorings and silks.

Lorenzo stopped to chat with the apprentices, and Michelangelo turned his gaze to the girl walking beside him. She was a pale, slight thing, younger than himself; as Lorenzo passed his table Michelangelo's eyes met hers. He stopped in his work. She stopped in her walk. He could not take his gaze from her piquant face. Michelangelo felt an awakening between them, a quickened breath. For a moment he thought she was going to speak to him. But Lorenzo put his arm about her tiny waist, and they strolled out into the piazza.

Michelangelo turned to Torrigiani.

"Who was that girl?"

"Contessina. *Il Magnifico's* daughter. The last one left in the palace."

LODOVICO HAD NEVER given his consent to Michelangelo's entering the garden and declined to acknowledge it. Michelangelo's family saw little of him anyway, for he left at dawn, came home at twelve to eat, and loitered on his way home in the evening so they would be in bed and there would be only his grandmother waiting in the kitchen to give him a light supper. Theirs was an abiding love.

At the garden he plunged into drawing. Models came from every quarter of Florence: scholars in black velvet; bull-necked soldiers; swashbuckling toughs; peasants; monks; nobles in red and white silk hemmed with pearls; chubby children to serve as models for cupids.

Michelangelo grumbled at Bertoldo's criticism of a torso he had drawn: "How can we draw only from the outside? All we see is what pushes against the skin. If we could follow the inside of a body: the bone, muscle . . . "

"Doctors are allowed to dissect one body, one day a year, in front of the city council," Bertoldo said. "Other than this it is the worst crime in Florence. Put it out of your mind."

"My mouth, yes; my mind, no. I'll never sculpture accurately until I can see how a human body works."

"Not even the Greeks dissected, and they were a pagan people. Must you be better than Phidias?"

"Better, no. Different, yes."

He began staying late in the garden, unknown to anyone, picking up tools and working the scraps of stone lying about: yellowish-white travertine from Rome, dark-green marble from Prato, reddish-yellow marble from Siena. His greatest joy came when someone left behind a fragment of pure white Carrara, a rare and costly stone. He began to experiment with the point, the toothed and flat chisels, working surface textures on the marble. It was the finest hour of the day for him, alone in the garden, with only the statues for company.

Inevitably he was caught; but by the last person he would have expected. Contessina de' Medici came to the garden nearly every day now, if not with Lorenzo, then with the scholarly Ficino or Pico della Mirandola. She spoke to the other apprentices, whom she had known a long time; but no one introduced Michelangelo. Still, he knew instantly when she entered the gate. Always she stopped at Torrigiani's table, and he could hear her laughter as Torrigiani amused her. She never looked at Michelangelo.

When she left he felt emotionally exhausted. Fourteen-year-old Michelangelo could not understand this. He knew no girls; he cared nothing for girls. Why was it painful when he saw Contessina laughing with Torrigiani? What could she mean to him, this princess of the noble Medici blood? He wished she would stay away, leave him in peace. . . . It was a long time, deep into the summer, before he realized that he was jealous of Torrigiani.

And he was appalled.

And now she had discovered him in the garden after the others had left. She was with her young brother Giovanni, a fat boy with a cast in his eye, who, in the manner of that corrupt time, had already been given many church offices, and was about to become a cardinal. They were accompanied by their cousin Giulio, the illegitimate son of Lorenzo's beloved brother Giuliano who had been stabbed to death in the Duomo by conspirators against the Medici.

As the two boys inspected the garden, Contessina spoke to Michelangelo for the first time.

"*Buona sera,* Michelangelo."

"*Buona sera,* Contessina." He was carving a piece of *pietra serena.* He did not stop working on it.

"The stone has a smell."

"Of freshly picked figs."

"And this?" She pointed to a piece of marble on the bench beside him. "Does it smell of freshly picked plums?"

"No, it has hardly any. Smell for yourself."

She crinkled her nose, laughing at him. He began raining blows with the chisel that sent the chips flying.

"Doesn't such furious work exhaust you? It would me."

He knew of her frailty, the consumption that had taken her mother and sister within the past year. Lorenzo was so devoted to her, they said, because she was not long for this world.

"No, no, cutting stone does not take strength out of you, it puts it back in. When you work this white marble it comes alive under your hands."

"Under *your* hands, Michelangelo. Will you finish that design on the *pietra serena* for me? I like it."

She stood still, above him, as he crouched over the stone. When he came to a hard spot he looked around for a water bucket, saw none, and spat precisely on the area he wanted to soften.

Amused, she asked, "What do you do when you run dry?"

He blushed. "No good stonecutter ever ran out of spit."

WITH THE FIRST INTENSE heat in the garden came the first casualty: a young apprentice called Soggi. His enthusiasm withered like the meadow grass. "A butcher on the Ponte Vecchio is

looking for help," he said. "The chisel, it's just like a knife. . . . "
So moonfaced Bugiardini, from Ghirlandaio's studio, took his
place.

Granacci also found he could not work with stone, and Lorenzo asked him to become manager of the garden. He enjoyed
this, spending his days making sure that the proper stone, iron
or bronze arrived, setting up contests for the apprentices. He
also painted. Michelangelo was angry when Lorenzo pressed
Granacci into service to design banners and arches for a
pageant.

"Granacci, how can you stand here singing happily, painting
decorations that will be thrown out the day after the pageant?"

"But not everything has to be profound and eternal. Pageants
and parties give people pleasure, and pleasure is as important as
food or drink—or art."

"You . . . you . . . Florentine!"

MICHELANGELO WAS UNHAPPY at home. Lodovico had managed
to learn how much other apprentices were receiving in prize
money, awards and commissions. "But you?" he demanded one
day. "Not one scudo after eight months. Why the others and not
you?"

"I don't know."

"Lorenzo has never noticed you?"

"Never."

"Does Bertoldo praise your work?"

"No. Though I draw better than the others."

"If you are to be a sculptor, why don't you do sculpture?"

"Bertoldo says I'm not ready."

"But the others sculpture. That means that you have less
ability than they."

"That will be proved when I get my hands on stone."

"When will that be?"

"I don't know."

"You are almost fifteen. Are you to earn nothing forever?"
Lodovico cried. "I should beat you with a stick. When will you
get some sense in your head?" He slumped into a chair. "Lio-

nardo is studying to become a monk. Whoever heard of a Buonarroti a monk? You want to become an artist. Whoever heard of a Buonarroti an artist? Giovansimone is become a street rowdy. Whoever heard of a Buonarroti as a *malandrino?* Sigismondo cannot learn his letters. Whoever heard of an illiterate Buonarroti? I don't know what a man has sons for!"

Michelangelo put a finger lightly on his father's shoulder. "Trust me, Father. I am not looking for wool on an ass."

BERTOLDO WAS PUSHING him hard, never pleased, crying: "No, no, you can do it better! Again!" Making him draw models from a ladder above, the floor beneath, obliging him to come in on a holiday to create a theme that would embrace all the figures he had sketched during the week. Walking home with Granacci at night, Michelangelo cried in anguish: "Why am I the only one who cannot enter competitions or work on commissions? Or even visit the palace and see the art works? You're the manager now. Speak to Bertoldo. Help me!"

"When Bertoldo considers you ready for contests, he'll say so."

There was something else he was unhappy about: with the wet weather, Lorenzo had forbidden Contessina to leave the palace. Now that she no longer came, the garden seemed empty, the days long.

In his loneliness he turned to Torrigiani, and they became inseparable. When Bertoldo saw a drawing of Michelangelo's in which he imitated Torrigiani, he tore it into shreds. "Walk with a cripple for a year and at the end you will limp!" he said.

FINALLY, BERTOLDO REALIZED that Michelangelo had reached the bounds of patience. One day he put an arm as brittle as an autumn leaf about the boy's shoulder and said: "And so—on to sculpture!"

Sweat poured out on Michelangelo's forehead. His heart pounded.

"Now what is sculpture?" demanded Bertoldo. "It is the art of removing all that is superfluous from the material under treatment, to reduce it, with hammer and chisel, to the form in the artist's mind. Or one may make successive additions, as in modeling in clay or wax."

Michelangelo shook his head. "Not for me. I want to work as the Greeks did, carving straight from the marble."

"A noble ambition. But first you must learn to model in clay and wax."

Bertoldo showed him how to make an armature, using sticks of wood or iron wires. Once the framework was up, Michelangelo started applying the warm wax to see how close he could come to creating a three-dimensional figure from a two-dimensional drawing.

"It must be perfect, not only from the front but from every angle," said Bertoldo. "Which means that every piece has to be sculptured not once but three hundred and sixty times, because at each change of degree it becomes a different piece."

Michelangelo was fascinated. After he had massed his wax on the frame, he worked it with tools of iron and bone, refined it with his strong fingers. The results had raw power.

"But no grace," Bertoldo said. "And not the slightest facial resemblance to the model."

"The devil with portraiture. I never will like it."

"Never is longer at your age than mine. When you're hungry and the Duke of Milan asks you to do his portrait . . . "

Michelangelo glowered. "I don't get that hungry."

Spring was coming; Lodovico now insisted that Michelangelo leave the garden in April if he could not earn some money. He asked Bertoldo's permission to copy in stone some of the clay figures he had been modeling.

"No, my son," said Bertoldo, "you are not ready."

"The others are; I am not?"

"You have much to learn. *Pazienza.* God shapes the back to the burden."

MICHELANGELO STILL HAD NOT been invited to the palace; and when Lorenzo invited even Bugiardini, he felt his own exclusion implied rejection. Then, one March day, Bertoldo said: "There's a newly discovered Faun just arrived at the palace.

Pagan Greek, fifth century B.C. You must see it. Come along."

The Medici palace was large enough to house a numerous family, the government of a republic, a world-wide business, and a center for artists and scholars. Yet it was austere, with a majestic simplicity.

They went through a massive gate into the square courtyard where Michelangelo saw two of the great sculptures of the city: the Davids of Donatello and of Verrocchio. He rushed with a cry of joy to touch them before following Bertoldo into the palace. As they went from room to room his head began to spin: no good Italian artist was unrepresented. Marbles and paintings were in every hallway, salon, office, bedroom. Finally, they reached Lorenzo's study. His desk was set beneath shelves full of treasures: jewels, cameos, small marble bas-reliefs. "Over there is the new Faun," Bertoldo said. "I will leave you to study it."

Michelangelo went close to the Faun and looked into its gleaming, wicked eyes. The long beard was stained as though with wine spilled in merriment. It seemed so intensely alive that Michelangelo threw back his head and laughed. Then he took drawing paper and crayon from inside his shirt, and sketched the antique, time-battered Faun as he imagined it would have appeared when the Greek sculptor carved it two thousand years before.

A faint perfume came to his nostrils. He whirled abruptly.

Many weeks had passed since he had seen her. She was such a slight little body! "Michelangelo . . . "

How could there be so much joy from this mere pronouncing of a name? "Contessina! I did not dare hope I would see you. Bertoldo brought me to see the Faun."

"Father won't let me come with him to the garden until spring. You do not think I will die of consumption?"

"You will live to bear many sons." Color flooded her cheeks. "I have not offended you?" he asked apologetically.

She shook her head. "They told me you were blunt." She moved closer to him. "When I am near you I feel strong. Why?"

"When I am near you I feel confused. Why?"

She laughed, a gay, light sound. "I miss the garden."

"The garden misses you."

"I should not have thought it noticed."

"It noticed."

She turned from the intensity in his voice. "Your work goes well?"

"*Non c'è male.*"

"You're not very communicative."

"I do not aspire to be a talker."

"Then you should mask your eyes. They say things that please me."

He felt exposed, humiliated for showing emotion. He picked up his sketching paper. "I must work now."

Anger flared into her eyes. "One does not dismiss a Medici," she said. Then a tiny smile moved in. She put out her small hand, fragile as a bird in his rough paw. "*Addio,* Michelangelo. Work well."

That night he was sleepless. In his mind was the picture of a small piece of marble, lying in the grass in the rear of the sculpture garden. It was exactly the right size for a Faun like the one in Lorenzo's study—but his own! . . . At dawn he went to the garden, found the marble block, and carried it to the rear of the casino. He knew he had no right to touch it, for that was disobeying Bertoldo, who thought he was not ready for stone. Well, he was on his way out anyway if his father had his way.

His hands caressed the stone, searched out its contours. For him it was a living, breathing substance. "Why," he asked himself, trembling, "do I feel this way?" Not until this moment with his hands tenderly on the milky-white marble, had he come fully alive. This was what he must be: a white-marble sculptor, nothing more, nothing less. He picked up Torrigiani's tools, placed his chisel on the block, struck the first blow with his hammer. He, the marble, the hammer and chisel were one.

THE FAUN WAS completed. For three nights he had worked behind the casino; for three days he had hidden it beneath a wool cloth. Now he carried it to his workbench. He was willing for Bertoldo to see it: his own sensual, gloating Faun. He was polishing it when Lorenzo came down the walk.

"Ah, my Faun," he said. "But you left out his beard."

"The sculptor is not a copyist. He must create something new from something old."

"And where does the new come from?"

"From where all art comes. Inside himself."

He saw a flicker in Lorenzo's eye.

"Your Faun is old, but you left him all his teeth," he said.

When he left, Michelangelo took up his chisel and went to work on the Faun's mouth. Lorenzo returned to the garden the next day. He stopped in front of the workbench. "Your Faun has matured twenty years in a day." Lorenzo seemed pleased. "I see you have removed an upper tooth. And two lower ones in the other corner."

"For balance."

"It was perceptive of you to rework the entire mouth." Lorenzo stared at him for a moment. Then he said, "I'm pleased."

The next morning a scarlet-coated page appeared and Bertoldo called out: "Michelangelo, you are wanted at the palace."

Was he to be sent home for stealing that block of marble? He looked at Bertoldo, but the old man's expression told him nothing. He followed the page to *Il Magnifico*'s library, where he was seated behind his desk.

Lorenzo said, "How old are you, Michelangelo?"

"Fifteen."

Lorenzo opened his desk and took out a parchment folio. From it he spread out dozens of drawings. Michelangelo could not believe what he saw. "But . . . those are mine!"

"Just so. We have put many obstacles in your path, Michelangelo. Bertoldo has given harsh criticism and little praise or promise of reward. We knew you were gifted but did not know your character. If you had left us for praise or money . . . "

There was a silence in the beautiful room: Michelangelo could not speak. Lorenzo came around to the boy's side. "Michelangelo, you have the makings of a sculptor. Bertoldo and I are convinced that you could become heir to Ghiberti, Donatello. I would like you to live in the palace as a member of my family. From now on you need concern yourself only with sculpture."

"I like best to work in marble."

Lorenzo chuckled. "No thanks, no expression of pleasure at coming to live in the palace of a Medici! Only your feeling for marble. Will you bring your father to me?"

"Tomorrow."

IN THE PALACE, standing before Lorenzo, the son found the father humble, pathetic. And he felt sorry for him.

"Buonarroti, I would like Michelangelo to live in the palace, and become a sculptor. Everything will be provided for him."

"*Magnifico messere,* I cannot deny you," replied Lodovico, bowing deeply. "All of us are at the pleasure of Your Magnificence."

"Is there anything in Florence I can do for you yourself?"

"There is a place open in the customhouse—"

"The customhouse! I had expected you would ask something grander. But you may have the place." He turned back to Michelangelo. A warm smile lighted the dark, homely face. "It is sixty years since my grandfather Cosimo took Donatello into his house to execute his great bronze David."

BOOK THREE

The Palace

AT THE PALACE, a page escorted him up to an apartment above the central courtyard. Bertoldo opened the door. "Welcome, Michelangelo, to my home. *Il Magnifico* thinks I have so little time left he wants me to teach you in my sleep!"

Michelangelo saw two wooden beds, each with a coffer at its foot, in the wings of an L-shaped, tapestry-hung room. Bertoldo's leather-bound cookbook, and models of some of his sculptures were displayed in a cupboard in the corner. "Your sculptures are beautiful by candlelight," Michelangelo said.

"Poliziano says, 'Bertoldo is not a sculptor of miniatures, he is a miniature sculptor.' Isn't it a bit pathetic that from your pillow you can see my whole lifetime of work?"

"But sculpture isn't measured by how many pounds it weighs."

"Mine is a modest contribution: talent is cheap. Dedication is expensive: it will cost you your life."

"What else is life for?"

"Alas, I thought it was for many things: falconry, good food, pretty girls. You know the Florentine adage, 'Life is to be enjoyed.' But a sculptor must create a *body of work*—enough to permeate the whole world."

Next day the palace tailor brought Michelangelo a new outfit. He stood before the mirror surveying himself. It was amazing how much more attractive he looked in the crimson *berretto,* violet cloak, golden shirt and stockings. And he himself had changed: he was taller, and he had put on weight.

In his absorption, he did not see Bertoldo enter.

"You fancy yourself in that raiment? It is for feast days only. Put on this blouse and tunic."

Michelangelo sighed. "Ah well, put not an embroidered crupper on a plow horse."

THAT EVENING THEY made their way to the dining hall, where a U-shaped table seated sixty people. Contessina put her hand on the chair next to hers, inviting him to join her. The table was set with square, gold-trimmed crystal, silver plates with the Florentine lily inlaid in gold. The palace orchestra was playing in a shell-shaped niche. He watched the colorful array of diners: Lorenzo's daughter Lucrezia and her husband, Jacopo Salviati; two cardinals from Spain; reigning families from Bologna, Ferrara, Arezzo; scholars from Paris and Berlin; members of the Signoria, or city council, of Florence; merchants from Athens, Peking, Alexandria, London. Piero de' Medici, oldest son of Lorenzo, and his elegantly gowned wife, Alfonsina, of a noble Roman family, came in late and had to sit at the foot of the table. Michelangelo saw that they were offended.

"Piero and Alfonsina don't approve of all this republicanism," Contessina whispered. "They think we should hold court, with only Medici allowed at the head of the table."

Giovanni, Lorenzo's second son, and his cousin Giulio entered. Giovanni, the churchman, was tall and corpulent, with a heavy face; Giulio, dark, handsome and saturnine. His eyes slashed through the assemblage, missing nothing that could be useful to him.

The servingmen passed heavy silver trays of fish. A young man in a multicolored shirt picked up a small fish, put it to his mouth, then to his ear as though talking to it, and after a moment burst into tears. Michelangelo looked in perplexity at Contessina.

"Jacquo, the palace buffoon," she said.

"Why are you crying, Jacquo?" asked Lorenzo.

"My father was drowned years ago. I asked this little fish whether he ever saw him anywhere. He said he was too young to have met him and suggested that I ask the bigger fish on the platter."

Michelangelo was too surprised at finding a buffoon at Lorenzo's table to smile. Contessina, who had been watching him, asked, "Don't you like to laugh?"

"I am unpracticed. No one laughs in my house."

"You are what my French tutor calls *un homme sérieux*. My father is a serious man too. Still, he enjoys all this noise and talk and fun."

The servants brought in suckling pigs, roasted on a spit, with rosemary in their mouths. An improviser upon the lute entertained by singing the news and gossip of the week, accompanied by satiric comments in verse.

Later, as the guests promenaded, Contessina slipped her arm through Michelangelo's. "Do you know what it means to be a friend?" she asked.

"Granacci has tried to teach me."

"Everyone is a friend to the Medici," she said quietly, "and no one."

THE FOLLOWING MORNING Bertoldo took him to the marble blocks in the sculpture garden. "I am not a great sculptor," he said. "But with you perhaps I can become a great teacher.

Remember that the figure you carve must run with the block: to see how the veins run, pour water on it."

Then Bertoldo told him about air bubbles, spots in the marble which become hollow after weathering. They cannot be seen from the outside, and one must learn to know when they are inside.

"Here is a punch. It is a tool to remove stone. Here are an *ugnetto* and a *scalpello* to shape it." Bertoldo showed him how to tear out large pieces of marble with rhythmical strokes, making circular lines around the block; how to work all parts simultaneously, balancing relationships.

The workshop was also a combination forge, carpenter's and blacksmith's shop. Granacci had bought rods of Swedish iron so that Michelangelo could make himself a set of nine chisels; for "the man who does not make his own tools does not make his own sculpture."

The next morning Michelangelo rose quietly in the dark in order to be in the garden at dawn. The first rays of the sun revealed the truth about marble, making it almost translucent; all veins, faults, hollows were mercilessly exposed.

He went from block to block, tapping with his hammer. The solid blocks gave out a bell-like sound, the defective ones a dull thud. One small weather-beaten piece had developed a tough skin. With hammer and chisel he cut down to the pure milky substance below. To learn the direction of the veins, he held his hammer tightly and fractured off the high corners. He liked what he saw; took a piece of charcoal and drew the head of an old man on the marble. Then he pulled up a bench, straddled the block, gripping it with both knees, picked up hammer and chisel. Tensions within him fell away with each falling chip. Stone filled him out, made him whole. His arm grew lighter and stronger with the passing of the hours, as he wholly possessed the stone. It was the act of love, creating the living work of art; for Michelangelo it was the supreme sensation.

When Bertoldo came in and saw him at work, he cried out, "No, no, that's the wrong technique. Stop!"

Michelangelo did not hear him. Bertoldo shook his head in amused despair. "As well try to keep Vesuvius from erupting."

LORENZO'S "PLATO ACADEMY" was the intellectual heart of Europe: a university and a printing press which proposed to turn Florence into a second Athens. Michelangelo met the Plato group at supper in Lorenzo's study where fruit, cheese and bread were served from a food lift in the wall. Ficino, Landino, Poliziano and Pico della Mirandola were the outstanding brains of Italy. Michelangelo heard their case against the churchmen of that time. Much of the clergy had become immoral in personal conduct and lax in clerical practice. The outstanding exception was the Augustinian Order at Santo Spirito, living in flawless self-discipline under a man Michelangelo knew, the vigorous Prior Bichiellini.

Pico della Mirandola, youngest of the group, said, "I think I have an answer to this problem. There is a Dominican monk in Ferrara called Savonarola. His ambition is to purify the Church. I've heard him preach. He shakes the ribs of the cathedral."

"If he would work with us . . . " said Lorenzo.

"Your Excellency might request his transfer to Florence?"

"I'll attend to it."

The scholars next turned their attention to Michelangelo, recommending books he should read, offering to teach him Greek and Latin. Certain he could learn neither, he was relieved when they went on to other subjects. The most important idea he gleaned from the swift, learned talk was that religion and knowledge could exist side by side, enriching each other. This little group of men was attempting to create a new philosophy under the banner of a word Michelangelo had never heard before: *Humanism*. Gradually he gathered what Humanism meant: *We are giving the world back to man, and man back to himself. Without a free, vigorous mind, man is but an animal. We return to him his arts, literature and sciences, his independence to think and feel. He must not be bound to religious dogma like an unthinking slave.*

Later he said to Bertoldo, "They made me feel stupid."

"They can give you heroic themes to ponder." Then, to console the tired youth, Bertoldo said, "But they cannot carve marble, and that is a language as eloquent as any."

PALM SUNDAY WAS A warm spring day. On his washstand he found three gold florins which Bertoldo said would be left for him each week by Lorenzo's secretary. He could not resist the temptation of showing off to his family. On his bed he laid out another new outfit: embroidered blouse, surcoat with silver buckles, wine-colored stockings.

On the street he met Torrigiani, who stopped and seized his arm. "I want to talk to you. Alone."

"Why alone? We have no secrets."

"We shared confidences, until you moved into the palace."

There was no mistaking the envy behind Torrigiani's outburst. Michelangelo spoke gently, hoping to placate him.

"But you live in your own palace, Torrigiani."

"Yes, and I don't have to play cheap tricks like knocking out a faun's teeth to ingratiate myself with the Medici."

"You sound jealous."

"Of what! Of an insufferable, solemn prig, setting down charcoal lines with his grimy hands?"

"But good charcoal lines," protested Michelangelo.

Torrigiani went purple in the face. "Are you implying that mine are not?"

"Why do you always bring a discussion back to yourself? You're not the center of the universe."

"I was to you, until your head got swollen."

Michelangelo stared at him in amazement. "You were never the center of my universe."

He turned and ran down the street.

His new clothes were not a success. His father felt hurt, as though the finery was a reproach to him. He gazed at the gold florins without comment, but Lucrezia bussed him happily on both cheeks. "Now tell me! Do the palace cooks use zedoary? What of their famous sole cooked with banana strips and pine nuts?"

"Forgive me, *madre mia,* I don't know."

She shook her head in despair.

Then the rest of the family assembled and wanted to hear the news. "How do the Medici treat you?" Lodovico said. *"Il Magnifico?"*

"Well."

"Piero?"

"He is arrogant; it is his nature."

"Giovanni, the cardinal-to-be?"

"He treats all alike. As though each meeting were the first."

Lodovico said: "Piero's attitude will prevail: you are in the palace as a humble workman." He eyed the three gold coins Michelangelo had placed on the desk before him. "What are they? A gift? A wage?"

"Bertoldo said it was a weekly allowance."

His Uncle Francesco could not contain his delight. "Splendid! We can rent a stall. Michelangelo, you will be a partner."

"No!" Lodovico's face was red. "We are not the poor."

"This is not charity." Michelangelo was indignant. "I work from light to dark."

"A gift is a whim. Next week there may be nothing!"

The three florins were more than Lodovico would earn in months at the customs: Michelangelo realized that he had seemed to be bragging. With his head on his chest, Lodovico went on, "Think how many millions of florins the Medici must have if they can give a fifteen-year-old student three of them each week." Then, with a quick movement, he swept them into the top drawer of his desk.

"Art is a vice," Lionardo announced pontifically.

"But, Lionardo, our churches are filled with art!" Michelangelo said.

"We have been led astray by the devil. A church is not a fair; people must go to pray, not to see a play painted on the walls."

Lodovico exclaimed: "Now I have two fanatics on my hands."

He left the room, followed by the whole family except for Lionardo and Monna Alessandra. Michelangelo too wanted to leave; the day had been a disappointment. But Lionardo would not let him go. He moved into an attack on Lorenzo and the Plato Academy as pagans, enemies of the church.

"I have heard no irreverence," Michelangelo said placatingly. "Lorenzo is a reformer; he wants to cleanse the Church."

"Cleanse! Only a toady like yourself would be unable to see that Lorenzo is a debauched man and a tyrant."

Before Michelangelo could reply, Monna Alessandra said, "He has kept Florence from civil war! For years we destroyed each other, family against family, neighborhood against neighborhood, with blood flowing in the streets. Now, because of the Medici, we are a unified people."

Lionardo refused to answer his grandmother. "Michelangelo, this is my farewell to you. I leave tonight, to join Savonarola in San Marco."

"Then Savonarola has arrived? Lorenzo invited him."

"A Medici lie! Why should Lorenzo summon him, when Savonarola intends to destroy the Medici? I leave this house as Savonarola left his family in Ferrara: with only a shirt on my back. I shall pray for you in my cell until there is no skin left on my knees."

ONE DAY THE FOLLOWING week, a groom knocked on the door of his apartment.

"His Excellency, Piero de' Medici, commands Michelangelo Buonarroti to present himself in His Excellency's anteroom."

Michelangelo thought, "How different from his father, who asks if it would give me pleasure to join him . . . "

He followed the groom to Piero's anteroom. Piero's wife, Alfonsina, in gray damask embroidered with jewels, was sitting on a purple throne chair. Piero pretended he had not heard Michelangelo enter. His back to his guest, he was studying a bone tabernacle decorated with painted stories of Christ. Finally he turned and said: "Michelangelo, I wish my wife's portrait sculptured in marble."

"Thank you, Excellency," replied Michelangelo, "but I cannot carve portraits. The likeness would never satisfy you."

"Michelangelo, I *order* you to carve my wife in marble!"

Alfonsina spoke for the first time. "Please discuss this in your own room."

Angrily Piero opened a door and stalked through, Michelangelo following. Looking at Piero's statues and paintings, he exclaimed: "Your Excellency has superb taste in the arts!"

"When I want your opinion I shall ask for it. Meanwhile, explain why you think you are better than our other hirelings."

Michelangelo forced himself to reply politely. "I am a sculptor, resident in this palace at your father's request."

"We have a hundred tradesmen dependent upon us. What they are told to do, they do. You will commence tomorrow morning. And see that the statue of Her Excellency is beautiful."

"Not even the greatest sculptor could do that."

Piero's eyes flashed. "You . . . peasant! Pack your rags and go!"

Michelangelo went to his room and began collecting his things. There was a knock and Contessina entered with her nurse. "I hear you have refused to carve Alfonsina's portrait," she said.

"I refused."

"Would you refuse if my father asked you to do his portrait?" Michelangelo was silent. Refuse Lorenzo, for whom he felt so deep an affection? "Would you refuse," she went on, "if *I* asked?"

He was trapped. "But Piero did not ask me. He ordered me."

Then Lorenzo came into the room, his eyes snapping. "I will not have this happen in my house," he said. "I asked your father to cede you to me. I am responsible for you."

Michelangelo's eyes blazed. "I have no apologies to offer."

"I am not asking for apologies. You came here as one of the family. No one may order you out of your own home."

Michelangelo's knees went weak.

Lorenzo spoke more gently. "But you, too, have much to learn. . . . Do not rush back here every time you are offended, and start packing your possessions. That is not loyal to me."

Michelangelo was trying to hold back the tears. "I owe His Excellency an apology. I was unkind about his wife."

"He owes you one."

Contessina lagged behind to whisper: "Make it up with Piero. He can cause a lot of trouble."

HE HAD WORKED ENOUGH now to try a theme. He remembered the Madonnas of the Rucellai chapel in Santa Maria Novella and felt again his love for his mother, his sense of loss, his hunger for her love. With Lorenzo he made a tour of the palace to examine many Medici Madonnas. In Lorenzo's bedroom they stood before Botticelli's Madonna of the Magnificat.

Michelangelo was silent. When he thought of his mother he saw her as a beautiful young woman, as the young woman in the painting was beautiful; yet it was a different beauty, coming from within. Not a woman desirable to all men, as was Botticelli's; but one who would love a son and be loved by him. He said: "I feel close to the Madonna. She is the only image I have of my mother. Now I must search out what I'm trying to say about her."

He went into the poorer parts of town where the women worked on the sidewalks before their houses, weaving cane chair seats or wine-bottle covers, their babes on their laps. He watched the farmers' wives around Settignano who gave no second thought to his drawing them while they bathed or suckled their young. He was not looking for portraiture, but for the spirit of motherhood.

Sketching, he mused about the character and fate of Mary. The Annunciation was a favorite theme of Florentine painters; but in all the paintings he remembered, the Archangel Gabriel's message seemed to come to Mary as a complete surprise, as if she had been given no choice. But could that be? Could so important a task have been forced on Mary without her knowledge or consent? Since God must have loved Mary above all women to choose her, must He not have told her His plan, related every step of the way from Bethlehem to Calvary? And in His wisdom and mercy have allowed her the opportunity to reject it?

He decided that he would carve Mary at the agonizing moment of decision, while suckling her infant, when, knowing all that was to come, she must determine the future. Now that he understood what he was about, at last he was able to draw. Mary must be heroic in stature, a woman with the inner force and intelligence for decision. He reviewed the hundreds of sketches he had made in the past months: in figure, Mary could be a composite of these strong Tuscan mothers. But how did one portray her face? His memory of his own mother had a dream-like quality.

He put the drawings aside. To conceive this piece of sculpture he must know the marble from which it would draw its sustenance. With Granacci he set out to visit the stone shops of the city; but they failed to turn up the Carrara block for which he was searching. "Let's try the Settignano yards," he said.

In a yard there, he saw a piece that captivated him at once. It was of modest size, but gleaming white. He tested it for cracks, flaws, bubbles, stains. "This is the one, Granacci," he cried with glee. "It will hold my Madonna and Child. But I'll have to see it by the first rays of sunlight."

"If you think I'm going to stay here until dawn . . . "

"No, no, you settle the price. Then I'll borrow a horse from the Topolinos for you and you can go home at once."

He slept at the Topolinos' and was standing over his marble when the fingers of dawn came over the hills. The block had no flaw, no discoloration; the crystals flickered brilliantly on its surface.

The word "marble" came from a Greek word meaning "shining stone." How his block glistened as he set it up on his wooden bench! He had lived with it for several months now, come to understand its nature. He knew every layer, every crystal.

He picked up his hammer and *subbia* and began cutting with the *colpo vivo,* the live blow, his passage handled in one "Go!" He was not working from his drawings or clay models; they had all been put away. He was carving from the images in his mind.

He was at work in his shed when he received a visit from Giovanni de' Medici, the fifteen-year-old near-cardinal. Though he was totally unblessed with looks, his expression was intelligent and alert. With him was his cousin Giulio; handsome, trouble-loving, and cold and hard as a corpse. Recognized as a Medici by Lorenzo, but despised by Piero because he was illegitimate, Giulio had made a place for himself by attaching himself to fat, good-natured Giovanni, providing his pleasures and doing his work.

"I came to invite you to join my hunt," said Giovanni.

Michelangelo had heard about the hunt. Hunters, horsemen and grooms had been sent to the mountains which abounded with hares, stags and wild boar, and an area had been enclosed by sailcloth. Peasants kept the game from breaching the cloth fence.

"Forgive me," Michelangelo said, "I am in the marble, and cannot leave."

Giovanni looked crestfallen. "How very odd. You want only to work? You have no room for diversion?"

"For me, marble has the excitement of the hunt."

"You would really prefer your work to my hunt?"

"Since you give me a choice, yes."

Giovanni and Giulio moved off without a further word.

Michelangelo returned to his carving, the incident going out of his mind. But that evening Contessina whispered to him: "Giovanni's hunt is his supreme effort of the year. For a few hours he is the head of the family; even my father defers to him. If you reject his hunt you reject Giovanni. He is so kind; why should you want to hurt him?"

"I don't want to hurt him, Contessina. It's just that I want to carve all day, every day, until I am finished."

She cried, "You've already made an enemy of Piero! Must you do the same to Giovanni?"

He could think of nothing to answer.

ON THE LEFT of his design was a flight of stone steps. Mary was seated in profile on a bench to the right, the stone balustrade giving the illusion of ending in her lap, just under her child's knee. He saw that if her strong hand, holding the child securely, were to open more widely, it could be holding firmly not only her son but also the bottom of the balustrade, which would become an upright beam. Mary would then support on her lap both Jesus and the cross on which He would be crucified. But where was the transverse bar? The boy John, the cousin of Jesus, was playing on top of the steps. If he threw John's plump arm across the balustrade at a right angle, the boy's body and right arm would form the living crossbeam.

Bringing out the figures involved long hours and longer days. The birth of substance could not be hastened. Finally, with the carving of two other children playing above the stairs, his Madonna and Child was finished and he began the

The Madonna of the Stairs

polishing. Bertoldo hammered into him the evils of "overlicking," which made a piece sentimental. He used a rasp on the rough surfaces, then a fine-grain emery stone with water to give his work a tactile quality. Next he used lightweight pumice to expose fresh, sparkling crystals. Slowly the highlights emerged: on the Madonna's face, on the curls, cheek and shoulder of the Child, on the drapery covering the Madonna's leg, on John's back, on the inside of the balustrade. All the rest was in shadow. Now one felt the crisis, the emotion on Mary's face as she felt the tug of her child at her breast and the weight of the cross in her hand.

Lorenzo summoned the Plato Academy scholars to examine the Madonna. They studied it, searching, pondering. Then, one by one, they turned to Michelangelo with pride in their eyes. Lorenzo gave him a purse of gold florins as a completion prize so that he might travel and study other art works, and he rushed home at once, despite the lateness of the hour. Everyone was asleep, but they quickly gathered around him, each carrying a candle, their nightcaps askew. Michelangelo spilled out the golden coins in a dramatic sweep across his father's desk.

"My prize money," he explained.

"It's a lot," exclaimed his uncle. "How much?"

" . . . thirty, forty, fifty," counted his father. "Enough to support the family in ease for half a year. Michelangelo, you must start on another piece immediately." No word of thanks; only joy at the pile of gold pieces shimmering in the candlelight . . . "We'll look for another farm," Lodovico went on. "Land is the only safe investment."

"I'm not sure I can let you do that, Father. *Il Magnifico* gave me the money for travel: to see sculptures."

"Travel to see sculptures!" Lodovico was aghast. "You look, you leave, the money is gone. But with farms . . . "

Buonarroto asked, "Are you really going traveling?"

"No," said Michelangelo. "I want only to work." He turned to Lodovico. "They're yours, Father."

SEVERAL TIMES A WEEK Bertoldo insisted that they go to the churches to draw from the masters. They were sketching in the Brancacci chapel when Torrigiani set his stool so close to Michelangelo that his shoulder pressed against Michelangelo's arm. Michelangelo moved his stool. Torrigiani was offended.

"I can't draw without a free arm," explained Michelangelo.

"What are you so cranky about? We've drawn these frescoes fifty times. What more is there to learn?"

"How to draw like the great Masaccio."

"I want to draw like Torrigiani. That's good enough for me."

Michelangelo barked impatiently, "But not good enough for me."

Torrigiani said with a crooked smile, "I'm surprised the favorite student still has to submit to these schoolboy exercises."

"This is a schoolboy exercise only to a schoolboy mind."

Torrigiani flared up. "Oh, so now your mind is better than mine. Why, you can't do anything but draw. You don't know how little you are alive. It's as they say: little man, little life; big man, big life."

"Big man, big wind."

Torrigiani was furious. "You meant that as an insult!"

He sprang from his stool and yanked Michelangelo to his feet. Michelangelo had barely time to see the grim set of Torrigiani's expression. Then Torrigiani's fist hit the bridge of his nose with the sound of powder exploding. He tasted blood and crushed bone; and then, as from a distance, heard Bertoldo's anguished cry. While the stars burst in a black heaven, he slipped to his knees and lost consciousness.

He awakened in his bed in the palace, his head a mass of pain. Bending over him were Dr. Leoni, Lorenzo's physician, Lorenzo and Bertoldo. He heard someone say: "Torrigiani has fled the city, Excellency."

"Send riders after him. I'll lock him in the stocks."

The doctor began exploring Michelangelo's face with his fingers.

"The bridge of his nose is crushed. The bone splinters may take a year to work their way out. The passage is completely closed now. Later, if he's lucky, he'll be able to breath through it again." He slipped an arm under Michelangelo and pressed a cup to his lips. "Drink. It will put you to sleep. When you wake the pain will be less."

He gulped down the draft painfully. When he woke again he was alone in the room. The pain had localized and he felt the throbbing behind his eyes and nose. He got out of bed, using the side of the wash table to steady himself. Then, summoning courage, he looked in the mirror. He could barely recognize himself; Torrigiani's big fist had thrown his whole face out of focus. He crawled back to bed on hands and knees, sick at heart.

He heard the door open. Unwilling to see anyone, he remained motionless. A hand pulled back the cover from his head, and he gazed up at Contessina.

"Michelangelo *mio.*"

"Contessina."

"I'm sorry it happened."

"I blame myself. I taunted him." He felt hot tears stinging his eyes as he forced himself to say the words: "I'm ugly."

Her face had been close to his as they spoke. Now she placed her lips on the swollen bridge of his nose, and he felt their warmth like a balm. Then she was gone from the room.

THE SWELLING RECEDED, the discoloration faded; but he was still unable to face the world in this mutilated form. He slipped out late at night to walk the silent streets of Florence. Torrigiani had not been caught, and probably never would be.

Poliziano, of the Plato Academy, one of the ugliest of men, came to the apartment one day. His face glowed as he said, "Michelangelo, I have just completed my translation of Ovid's *Metamorphoses.* While I was translating the story of the centaurs I thought what a fine carving you could make of the battle between the centaurs and the Thessalians." He put his manuscript into Michelangelo's hands. "Read it," he said. "I thought of you carving the scenes even while I translated them."

When he left, Michelangelo began reading the translation. He began to see pictures in his mind: of struggles between men and centaurs, of the rescue of women, of the wounded, the dying. But how could one carve this legend? It would require a piece of marble the size of a mountain. Nor could a sculptor show all the weapons used in the mythological battle: torches, spears, javelins, tree trunks. Then he recalled an early line and leafed back through the pages: *Aphareus . . . lifted a sheet of rock ripped from the mountainside. . . .* Here could be the unifying theme! Since one could not portray all weapons he would use only the earliest, most universal: stone.

As he stretched himself out to sleep, he realized that all evening he had not once thought of his nose. He had been thinking only of the Battle of the Centaurs. "Glory be to God," he thought, "I'm cured."

Next day he walked to Settignano. The Topolinos greeted

him casually, pleased that he would spend the night. They did not seem to notice his damaged face.

At dawn, he made his way over the ox road to the quarries, where the stonemasons began work an hour after sunrise. The *pietra serena* cut the afternoon before was a turquoise blue while the older blocks were taking on a beige tone. The quarrymen and masons were already forging and tempering their tools. They greeted Michelangelo jovially. "Come to do an honest day's work, eh? Once a stonemason always a stonemason."

"In this weather?" quipped Michelangelo. "I'm going to sit under a tree and never pick up anything heavier than a stick of charcoal."

It was hot in the quarries, and the masons worked in breechclout, straw hat and leather sandals. Michelangelo sat watching them. Their wiry, sweating bodies shone and glistened like polished marble as they cut and lifted the stone. They were completely unselfconscious as Michelangelo sketched them, seeking the strength that lay buried in their bodies.

When the sun was high overhead several boys appeared, carrying long branches with a row of nails in them; hanging from each nail was a basket with a man's dinner. The masons gathered in their "hall," a cave at the base of the mountain which remained the same temperature the year round, and shared their vegetable soup, boiled meat, bread, cheese and wine with Michelangelo. Then they lay down for an hour's sleep. While they slept he drew them again: sprawled out on the ground, hats over their faces, their bodies quiet, recuperative.

Back in Florence, he found the block of marble he wanted and started working it. Then, one morning as he left the palace, a monk stopped him, handed him a letter, and disappeared as soundlessly as he had appeared. The note was from his brother Lionardo, pleading with him to abandon the pagan theme of the centaurs, which could put his soul in jeopardy. If he must carve graven images, they should be ones sanctified by the Church. "The battle of the centaurs is an evil story," Lionardo concluded, "told to you by a perverted man. Renounce it and return to Christ."

Michelangelo shook his head. How could Lionardo, buried in a monastery, know what he was carving, or about Poliziano? He was a little frightened at how much the monks inside San Marco knew of everyone's business.

He showed the letter to Lorenzo. "If my carving this theme can do you harm," he said with concern, "perhaps I ought to change?"

Lorenzo seemed weary. Bringing Savonarola to Florence had been a mistake. "Savonarola is trying to cow us, to impose his rigid censorship. If we give in now it will be easier for him to win next time. Continue your work."

SATURDAY NIGHTS THE PALACE emptied, as the Medici family began their social rounds. According to rumor, Lorenzo sought pleasure with his group of young bloods, in orgies of drinking and lovemaking. On such evenings Michelangelo had supper with Contessina and sometimes Giuliano, her younger brother. As they ate cold watermelon and chatted, he sketched the Battle of the Centaurs and told Contessina that all twenty figures in the work would represent facets of man's nature, animal and human, each attempting to destroy the other parts.

"I once heard you say that behind a carving there must be worship. What will there be to worship in this Battle?"

"The supreme work of art: the male body."

"I can blackmail you for your pagan worship of the body of man," Contessina said facetiously. "Savonarola would have you burned as a heretic."

"I do not worship man, Contessina. I worship God for creating man."

They laughed, their heads close. Their intimacy permeated the room. Suddenly Contessina's eyes moved to the door and her head came up sharply. He turned and saw Lorenzo, standing silent, his lips compressed.

"We were . . . discussing . . . "

Lorenzo came forward to look at the drawings.

"Giulio reports your meetings to me. Your friendship is

good. It is important that artists have friends. And Medici as well."

A few nights later when the moon was full and the air stirring with wild scents, they sat together in a library window seat.

"Florence is full of magic in the moonlight," Contessina sighed. "I wish I could look down from a height and see it all."

"I know a place," he exclaimed. "Just across the river."

"We could slip out the back garden, separately."

They met and set out for the Arno, crossing it and climbing up to the ancient Belvedere fort to sit on the stone parapet. Michelangelo pointed out the glistening white Baptistery, Duomo and Campanile; the golden, high-towered Signoria; and on their side of the river the moonlit Pitti palace. Caught up in the beauty of the city, their fingers fumbled toward each other on the rough surface of the stone; touched and interlocked.

IT WAS SHORTLY afterward that Lorenzo summoned him to his office. Michelangelo did not need to be told why he had been sent for.

"She was safe, Excellency. By my side the whole time."

"Did you really think you would not be observed?"

Miserable now, Michelangelo replied, "It was indiscreet. But it was so beautiful up there."

"I am not questioning your conduct, Michelangelo, but its wisdom. You know that Florence is a city of wicked tongues."

"They would not speak evil of a young girl."

Lorenzo studied Michelangelo's face a moment. "Contessina is growing up. That is all, Michelangelo, you may return to work."

"Is there anything I can do to make amends?"

Lorenzo put both hands on the boy's trembling shoulders. "You meant no wrong. Now, at dinner, there is someone you should meet."

That night he met Gianfrancesco Aldovrandi of Bologna. He told Michelangelo of Bologna's great sculptors. "It is my hope," he said, "that you will come to Bologna to see their work. A visit there could have a profound influence on you."

Michelangelo wanted to reply that profound influences were precisely what he wished to avoid; but Aldovrandi would prove to be a prophet.

During the ensuing days Michelangelo heard that Piero and Alfonsina had protested against "a commoner being allowed to associate on intimate terms with a Medici." "If some decision is not taken about Contessina," they added, "we may regret it."

Several nights later he learned that Contessina had been sent for a visit to the villa of the Ridolfi family.

His father was concerned about Lionardo, who had been reported ill in the monastery at San Marco. "Couldn't you use your Medici connections to get in to see him?" asked Lodovico. But Michelangelo found that no outsider was allowed in the monks' quarters.

Then he learned that Savonarola would preach in San Marco the following Sunday. He took up a position at the door to the cloister, so that Lionardo would have to pass him; but the monks' cowls were pulled so far forward that their faces were buried.

Savonarola mounted the pulpit, a slight figure under his robe, his head and face deep in his Dominican cowl. Michelangelo could see little but a pair of dark veiled eyes. His voice was commanding as he spoke of the corruption of the priesthood. Most priests were put into the Church by their families for worldly gain; they sought only wealth and power, and were guilty of simony, of nepotism, bribery, selling the relics of the saints. "The adulteries of the Church," he cried, "have filled the world!"

Savonarola pushed back the cowl and revealed his face. His upper lip was thin and ascetic; the lower voluptuous. He had flashing black eyes, high-boned, hollow cheeks and a jutting nose. "O Italy," he cried, "O Rome, O Florence, your villainies are bringing us tribulation! Give up your pomps and shows! O priests! Your worship is to spend your nights with harlots, your days gossiping in the sacristies. 'I will descend on you in . . . your wickedness . . . ' says the Lord. Italy will feel God's wrath.

177

Blood will run in the streets. Unless ye repent! repent! repent!"

The cry of "Repent!" echoed a hundredfold as Savonarola pulled his hood forward, came down the pulpit stairs and went out the cloister door. Michelangelo felt deeply moved, a little sick.

Later he received a note from Lionardo asking him to come to San Marco. He found the cloister beautiful and tranquil; the grass freshly cut, the hedges trimmed.

Lionardo seemed to Michelangelo as cadaverous as Savonarola. "The family has been worried about your health."

Lionardo's head shrank deeper into the cowl. "My family is the family of God." Then he spoke with affection. "I called for you because I know you have not been corrupted by the palace. In the midst of Sodom and Gomorrah, you have lived like an anchorite."

Amused, Michelangelo asked, "How do you know these things?"

"We know everything that goes on in Florence. Fra Savonarola has had a vision. The Medici and all their obscene, godless art works will be destroyed; but you can still save yourself. Forsake them while there is still time. There are to be nineteen sermons, starting on All Saints' Day, through to Epiphany. By the end of them, Florence and the Medici will be in flames."

Michelangelo was shocked into silence.

"You won't save yourself?" implored Lionardo.

"If my soul is to be saved, it can only be through sculpture. That is my faith, and my discipline. You say I live like an anchorite; it is my work that keeps me that way. We both serve God."

Lionardo's eyes burned into Michelangelo's. Then he was gone.

CONTESSINA HAD RETURNED. She came to Michelangelo, who was sketching in the library, her face ashen. He jumped up. "Contessina, are you ill?"

"I have something to tell you." She sank into a chair. "The contracts have been drawn for my marriage to Piero Ridolfi."

After an instant he asked brusquely, "Why should it affect me? Everyone knows Medici daughters are given in political marriages."

"I don't know why it should affect you, Michelangelo, any more than it should affect me."

He met her eyes squarely. "Forgive me," he said. "I was hurt. The marriage . . . when is it?"

"I asked for another year. I am too young."

"Will Ridolfi make you happy? Is he fond of you?"

"We do not discuss such matters. I will do what I must. But my feelings are my own." She rose and went close to him: he saw tears sparkling in her eyes. He reached out his hand, and they locked their fingers together. Then she withdrew, leaving behind only her faint mimosa scent.

SAVONAROLA CONTINUED HIS impassioned sermons against the vices of his time, predicting the downfall of the Medici and of the Pope. Women wept to hear him, and the whole city was soon shaken by religious upheaval.

The first defection in the sculpture garden was a fun-loving apprentice called Baccio. He fell silent for hours on end, then began disappearing for a day or two at a time. Soon he was criticizing the Medici and extolling Savonarola. One day he joined Savonarola's friars.

Savonarola's sermons were now attracting such large crowds that he transferred his activities to the cathedral, where Florentines stood packed together. Because of rigid fasting and penance on his knees, the friar could barely summon the strength to mount the pulpit stairs. He had completely identified himself now with Christ. "I do not speak with my own tongue but that of God. . . . I am His voice on earth."

A cold shiver ran through his listeners. Michelangelo gazed up at the Donatello and Della Robbia carvings of children singing, dancing, laughing in joyous love of life. For Michelangelo, the marble cried out, "People are good!" While Savonarola was thundering, "Humanity is evil!"

The city council invited Savonarola to address them in their great hall. All the Medici and their household were present. When Savonarola first attacked Lorenzo as a tyrant, Michelangelo saw Lorenzo's lips lift in a faint smile. But the smile vanished as Savonarola mounted his attack, and Michelangelo began listening intently. Savonarola charged that Lorenzo had confiscated the Florentine Dower Fund, money paid into the city treasury by poor families as guarantee that they would have the dowry without which no Florentine girl could hope to marry; he had used the money to buy sacrilegious works of art, to stage bacchanals. Lorenzo, the corrupt tyrant, and the city council—the Signoria—itself must go. A new government must be installed to make Florence a City of God. And who would govern Florence? Savonarola. God had ordered it.

Hysteria now began to rise in Florence. Few dared attend the lectures of the Plato Academy. Printers refused to print anything the friar did not approve. Botticelli deserted to Savonarola, declaring his own paintings of nudes to be lewd and lascivious. Michelangelo approved Savonarola's crusade for political and religious reform; he disapproved only of his attacks on Lorenzo and the arts. When his brother Lionardo visited him to urge him again to destroy the Battle of the Centaurs, he put him gently but firmly in the street.

Bertoldo, on the other hand, said querulously that the Battle of the Centaurs showed Savonarola's influence: it was bare, lacked richness.

He had planned to do weeks of polishing. Instead he asked Granacci to help him move the block into the palace at once. They carried it to Lorenzo's sitting room. Lorenzo, who was ill, came into the room, hobbling painfully with a cane. "Ah!" he exclaimed, and dropped into a chair, studying the sculpture silently section by section. Finally he said, "I can feel every body, every crushed bone. It's unlike anything I've seen."

"We've already had an offer for the piece; Savonarola would offer it up to God on a bonfire. I answered that I was not free to give it up. It belonged to Lorenzo de' Medici."

"The marble is yours," Lorenzo said.

"Excellency, I had already offered it to God. The God who created man in His own image of goodness, strength and beauty."

Lorenzo rose abruptly, walked about the room. "Michelangelo, the arts of each age are broken and burned by the next. The Florentines are a fickle people; if they follow Savonarola to the end of his road, the arts in Florence will be wiped out. We will slip back into darkness." He paused, then said, "Come with me. There is something I must show you."

They went to the church of San Lorenzo, where generations of Medici were buried. "The last great work of art I must complete for my family," Lorenzo said, "is a marble façade here, with twenty figures in its niches."

"Twenty figures!" Michelangelo did not know whether he felt joy or dismay. He cried, "I will do it, but I will need time. I still have so much to learn."

When he reached his apartment he found Bertoldo, wrapped in a blanket, crouching over a live-coal brazier. Michelangelo went quickly to his side. "Are you all right, Bertoldo?"

"No! I'm a stupid old man who has outworn his time. Tonight I looked at your Centaurs and remembered the things I said. I was wrong. You must forgive me."

"Let me put you to bed." He settled Bertoldo under a quilt, and went to get him a mug of warm wine. He held the silver cup to Bertoldo's lips. "If the Centaurs is good," he said, "it's because you taught me how to make it good. Tomorrow we will start a new piece, and you will teach me more."

"Yes, tomorrow . . . " sighed Bertoldo. "Are you sure, Michelangelo, there is a tomorrow?" and he dropped off to sleep.

In a few moments, his breathing became heavy, labored. Michelangelo sent for Lorenzo's doctor, but the doctor could do nothing. The boy spent the night holding Bertoldo to let him breathe more easily; he died the next day. After the priest had given him Extreme Unction, he uttered his last words with a little smile. "Michelangelo, you are my heir—as I was Donatello's."

"Yes, Bertoldo. And I am proud."

"I want you to have my estate. . . . It will make you . . . rich . . . famous. My cookbook."

"I shall always treasure it."

Bertoldo smiled again, as though they shared a joke, and closed his eyes for the last time.

Michelangelo had lost his master. There would never be another.

THE DISORGANIZATION OF the garden was now complete. All work stopped, and there were no more meetings with the Plato scholars, for Lorenzo had decided that he must take a cure in his villa at Careggi. There he could lay his plans to fight Savonarola in a battle to the death. All the weapons were in Lorenzo's hands: wealth, power, friends in other great city-states; while Savonarola had nothing but the cloak on his back. Yet Savonarola, dedicated, incorruptible, had already effected reforms in the lives of the clergy and the rich Florentines. He seemed to have the upper hand.

Michelangelo was troubled by Lorenzo's approaching departure, for Piero would now be in command. Meantime, he was invited to see Giovanni invested as cardinal. That night, all Florence was entertained lavishly by the Medici. Two days later Michelangelo bade farewell to the new cardinal and his cousin Giulio, who was accompanying him to Rome, and gaiety left the palace. Lorenzo departed for Careggi.

TWO WEEKS LATER word came that Lorenzo was failing. The doctor had administered pulverized diamonds and pearls, but this hitherto infallible medicine had failed to help. Lorenzo had sent for Pico and Poliziano to read to him to ease his pain, and Piero had already left for Careggi, taking Contessina and Giuliano with him.

Michelangelo paced the corridors in an agony of apprehension. Finally, he mounted a horse and rode the four miles to Lorenzo's beautiful villa. There was a wailing coming from the kitchen as he softly climbed the broad staircase. He stood for an irresolute moment before Lorenzo's bedchamber, then slipped in and hid behind a wall hanging by the door. Peeking out, he saw Lorenzo propped up in his high-bolstered bed; at its foot sat Poliziano, tears streaming down his face, and Pico, reading from a book. Soon Lorenzo's confessor entered and banished everyone from the bedside. He took Lorenzo's confession and gave him absolution; then Pico and Poliziano returned with a servant who fed Lorenzo a hot broth.

Poliziano asked Lorenzo: "How are you relishing your food, *Magnifico?*"

Michelangelo saw a smile light Lorenzo's tired features.

"As a dying man always does," he replied cheerfully.

Piero came in and stood by the bedside, his head bowed.

Lorenzo said: "Piero, my son, you will possess the same authority that I have had. Florence is a republic, and it will not be possible for you to please everyone. Pursue that course of conduct which strict integrity prescribes. Consult the interests of the whole community. If you will do so, you will protect both Florence and the Medici."

Piero kissed his father on the forehead. Then, to Michelangelo's amazement, Savonarola hurried into the room. "You sent for me, Lorenzo de' Medici?"

"I did, Fra Savonarola. I wish to die in charity with all."

"Then I exhort you to hold the faith."

"I have always held it firmly."

"Finally, I urge you to endure death with fortitude."

"Give me your blessing, Father," Lorenzo said hoarsely.

Savonarola lowered his head, recited the prayers for the dying, blessed Lorenzo, and departed.

Next, Lorenzo sent for his servants. He bade them farewell and asked their forgiveness if he had ever offended them. Michelangelo strove with all his might not to run to Lorenzo's side, drop to his knees and cry, "I, too, have loved you! Bid me farewell!" He had not been summoned here. And so he buried his face in the rough undersurface of the velvet hangings, even as Lorenzo fell back on his pillow and the doctor covered his face.

Michelangelo slipped out of the door, and ran down the stairs and into the garden. Lorenzo was dead! And why had he summoned Savonarola, his avowed destroyer?

Michelangelo knew only that he had lost his greatest friend.

BOOK FOUR

The Flight

HE KNEW PIERO did not want him at the palace; he moved back home and shared his former bed with his brother Buonarroto. Granacci wanted him to finish out his apprenticeship to Ghirlandaio. But he knew that he could not go back to painting. He would lose all that he had learned of sculpture over the past three years.

He found that Buonarroto, who kept the account book, was holding enough from his palace savings to buy a piece of marble. "You must back me in a lie to Father," he said. "I shall tell him that I have a commission, and that they are paying a few scudi while I work. I'll give him some of my savings. And I shall say that I have the right to resign the commission, to protect myself if I can't sell the statue."

The single desire of Michelangelo's heart rose out of love and sorrow: to do a memorial to Lorenzo, expressing the courage, knowledge and understanding of this great leader.

Lorenzo had often spoken of Hercules, suggesting that the legends about his twelve "labors" should not be taken literally. Hercules' feats perhaps were symbols for the near-impossible tasks with which each new generation was faced. Had not Lorenzo labored like a Hercules against ignorance and intolerance? His Lorenzo must be heroic, larger than life size. But where to find such a huge marble block?

He went to the stoneyard of the cathedral where a bald, pink-faced foreman, who said his name was Beppe, asked if he could be of service. Michelangelo introduced himself as a former apprentice in the Medici garden. "I need a large marble," he said, "but I have little money. Would the city be willing to sell me something? That big column, for instance?"

"The Board of Works bought that for Duccio to carve a Hercules. It's seventeen feet high. Duccio ordered it blocked out in the quarry. They ruined it."

Michelangelo ran his fingers over the enormous block. "Would the Board of Works sell it?"

"Not possible. They speak of using it one day."

"Then what about this smaller one?" Michelangelo indicated a nine-foot block. "And would you plead price for me?"

The foreman gave him a toothless grin. "Never yet knew a stone carver with tomorrow's pasta money in today's purse. I'll ask them. Come back tomorrow."

Beppe did a good job for him. "I told them it was an ugly piece of meat and we'd be glad of the room. How about five florins?"

Michelangelo counted out the money joyfully.

Now he had to find a workshop. Nostalgia drew him to the Medici garden. It was unused since Lorenzo's death, the summer grass high, the little casino stripped bare. He thought, "Perhaps Piero would let me work in my old shed if I told him what I was carving." But he could not make himself go to Piero.

As he turned to leave, he saw Contessina and Giuliano coming from the Piazza San Marco. Contessina's face was sallow, but under her wide hat her brown eyes were enormously alive. Giuliano said: "Why haven't you come to see us?"

Contessina's voice was reproachful. "You could have called."

"But Piero . . ."

"I too am a Medici. So is Giuliano." She was angry. "The palace is our home. Our friends are welcome."

"I have not been invited."

"I invite you," she cried. "Giovanni has been here, but he must go to Rome. Pope Innocent is dying, and Giovanni must try to protect us against a Borgia being elected Pope." She looked out at the garden. "Giuliano and I have walked over here nearly every day. We thought you would be working."

"I have not permission to work here."

"I shall secure it for you."

For four days he waited patiently in the garden, but she did not come. Then, on the fifth day, she came through the main gate with her old nurse. Her eyes were red. "I have asked Piero a hundred times," she said, "but he remains silent. That is his way. Then it can never be said that he refused."

"I was afraid it would be so, Contessina."

She moved so close that their lips were only inches apart. The nurse turned away. "Piero says the Ridolfi family will be displeased if I see you again; until after my marriage, at least."

Neither of them moved closer, their slight young bodies did not touch; yet he felt himself held and holding in an embrace.

Contessina and the nurse disappeared into the piazza.

BEPPE CAME TO his rescue. "I tell the Board I can use part-time man, that you offer to work for no pay. For free a Tuscan refuses nothing. Set up your shop along the wall."

So Michelangelo set up a forge, and, with chestnut wood and Swedish iron, fashioned a set of chisels and hammers.

Now he was ready to begin. But how could he convey Lorenzo's Herculean accomplishments? He must be shown as the strongest man who ever walked the earth. Where in Tuscany, land of small, lean men, would he find such a model? He scoured Florence, looking at coopers, blacksmiths, stone bevelers, porters. Then he returned to his workshop; sketched, modeled . . . and was dissatisfied. He thought, "I can achieve nothing but surface sculpture, outlines of bones, a few muscles brought into play. What do I know of the vital inner structure of a man?"

He knew what he must do. He must learn anatomy. He must train himself through dissection until he knew the workings of the human body, in every bone, muscle, tendon. But how could he dissect? Become a surgeon? That would take years.

Could he find corpses then? He thought, "Which dead in Florence were unwatched, unwanted? Only the very poor, the wandering beggars who were taken to church hospitals when they were sick." And the church with the largest charity hospital was Santo Spirito, whose prior, Father Nicola Bichiellini, had grown up in Michelangelo's own neighborhood! He had often allowed Michelangelo to read in his library, and had given him a key which unlocked all the outside gates.

Could he ask Prior Bichiellini for his unclaimed corpses? If the prior was caught, he would be excommunicated. But this was a man who, when he thought he was right, knew not fear.

He wandered around and through Santo Spirito, checking entrances, approaches to the room where bodies were kept overnight for morning burial. Then he went to see the prior, who greeted him heartily, his sparkling blue eyes enormous behind magnifying lenses. He had been a great athlete; at fifty his hair was shot with gray, but his body was charged with vitality. He let Michelangelo recite only a part of his proposal.

"Enough!" he said. "You have never brought this subject up. It has vanished like smoke, leaving no trace."

Stunned by this rapid rejection, Michelangelo was about to leave when the prior added, "Michelangelo, I thought of you when we received a new book with figure drawings from the fourth century. Would you like to see it?"

Michelangelo followed Bichiellini across the cloister and into his study. The prior reached into his desk and took out a long key which he laid across the book to keep the leaves spread. Then he said: "*Allora,* I have work to do. Come back again soon."

Michelangelo felt a warm glow: so he had been forgiven, the incident forgotten.

After that, he returned often to the library. Always the prior laid the same bronze key across a book—but never when others were present. Why? "It must mean something," Michelangelo realized finally. "How many doors are there in which I am interested? Only one. The dead-room door." If the key fitted that door . . .

IT WAS MIDNIGHT when he reached the monastery, having left his house noiselessly and taken a circuitous route to the hospital in order to miss the night guards.

He slipped through a little gate beneath a fresco of the

Madonna, skirted the walls of the dark kitchen, his breath coming faster now, and darted down a corridor to the dead room. An oil lamp stood in a niche. He took a candle out of the green canvas bag he carried, lit it and shielded it under his cape.

The bronze key did indeed unlock the door of the dead room. He went in and locked the door behind him. He did not know whether he dared face the task ahead.

The room was small, windowless, with whitewashed walls. Narrow planks, mounted on wooden horses, held a corpse, wrapped from head to foot in a burial sheet. He leaned against the door, breathing hard, the candle shaking in his hand. It was the first time he had been alone with the dead, let alone locked in, and on a sacrilegious errand. Who lay wrapped in that sheet? What had he done that he should now be mutilated?

"What kind of nonsense is this?" he demanded of himself. "What difference could it make to a man already dead? His body does not enter the kingdom of heaven, only his soul."

He put down his bag and set his candle—which would burn only three hours—on the floor. It was important not only for light but as a clock, for he had to be safely out of here before the monks who operated the bakehouse rose to make the day's bread. When the candle began sputtering he would have to leave.

He emptied his bag of its scissors and kitchen knife, took off his cape, for he was already sweating in the cold room, uttered a short prayer and approached the corpse.

The trestle bench was narrow. He wrestled the stiff body, first raising the legs, and pulling the sheet out from under its lower half; then lifting it from the waist and holding it against his chest until he could maneuver the cloth from the torso and head. The winding sheet was long; he had to go through the process five times. He picked up his candle and studied the body. His first feeling was one of pity. His second was fear: *"This is how I shall end!"*

The face was expressionless; the mouth half open. The man had been strongly built and was in mid-life when he had received a stab wound in the chest. The cadaver had sunk to the temperature of this cold room. There was an odor like very old

flowers dying in water. It was not strong, but it remained in his nostrils from then on.

He propped his candle on the trestle, but it was a considerable time before he could pick up the knife, recall what he had read about the human body, the few illustrations he had seen. Swallowing hard, he brought the knife down and made his first incision, studying the layer of fat, then cutting deeper to observe the dark-red fibers of the muscles.

The smell seemed heavier now, and nausea started within him; but his disgust was overcome by excitement. He picked up his knife and began to dissect the chest. Suddenly the candle spluttered. Almost three hours! He could not believe it. He picked up the winding sheet. The wrapping process was a thousandfold more difficult than the unwrapping. Perspiration ran down into his eyes; his heart pounded so loudly he thought it would wake the monastery. He had barely a moment to make sure that the corpse was stretched out upon the planks as he had found it before the candle flickered out.

He took a wandering route home, stopping repeatedly to retch. He washed his hands with lye soap, and got into bed, his body icy. He huddled against his brother, but not even Buonarroto's warmth could help him. He had chills and fever all the next day. Lucrezia made a chicken broth, but he could not hold it down; nothing could remove the smell of death.

About eleven at night he rose, dressed and made his way shakily to Santo Spirito. There was no corpse in the dead room, then or on the following night.

The third night he again found a body on the planked table. The second cadaver was older, with a white beard. This time he used his knife with more authority. Experimentally, he pressed a lung; a hissing noise came out of the corpse's mouth. He dropped the candle in fright. When he regained his calm, he realized that in touching the lung he had forced out the residual air; and for the first time he could see the connection between lungs and mouth.

Moving the lung, he found a dark-red mass; this must be the heart, shaped something like an apple, almost free in the chest. He held it in his hands and, unexpectedly, he was hit by an emotional impact as strong as Hercules' club: now he was holding the most vital organ of the body. His candle began to sputter as he replaced the heart in its cavity. With great difficulty he rewrapped the corpse and ran home, emotionally exhausted.

He crept silently up the stairs of his house to find his father waiting for him. "Where have you been? What is that horrible odor? You smell like death."

Michelangelo mumbled an excuse, brushed past Lodovico to his bedroom. He could not sleep.

HE COULD NOT risk his father's again detecting the odor of death; so next time he found a wineshop open in a workmen's quarter and drank a little Chianti. When the proprietor turned his back, he sprinkled the rest of his glass over his shirt.

Lodovico was outraged when he smelled the wine. "It is not enough that you wander the streets all night no doubt associating with loose women; now you come home smelling like a tavern. What is driving you to these evil ways?"

The only protection he could give his father was to let him believe he was carousing. But as the days passed, and Michelangelo stumbled into the house every morning toward dawn, the family rose in arms. Lucrezia was outraged because he was not eating, Francesco because he was afraid Michelangelo would run into debt, his aunt on moral grounds.

But he persisted, learning slowly, painfully, the function of the facial muscles and how they could move the face in laughter or in tears. He studied the brain, looking at it in wonder and admiration. From this small organ, weighing no more than a couple of pounds, emerged the greatness of the human race: art, science, philosophy, government, all that men had become for good as well as evil.

Spring came, and one afternoon he went to Prior Bichiellini, casually laid the key on the book the prior was reading, and said, "I would like to carve something for the church."

The prior looked pleased, but not surprised. "We have need of a wooden crucifix for the central altar," he said.

Michelangelo had never even whittled, but if the prior wanted a Crucifixion in wood, then wood it must be. He was soon at work in the monastery carpenter shop. The lay brothers there treated him like another carpenter. This suited him; he felt at home in the comfortable, sunny silence framed by the pleasant sounds of saw, plane and hammer.

He started rereading the Gospels of Matthew and Mark. The more he read, the more the terror-laden, agonized Crucifixions to be seen in the chapels of Florence receded from his mind, and into it came the hearty image of Prior Bichiellini: serving all humanity in God's name, with a great mind and noble spirit that gloried in living.

He started sketching those Crucifixions of the thirteenth century carved with the head and knees of Christ turned in the same direction, a design which suggested unquestioning acceptance. But did Christ feel only acceptance between the hour when the Roman soldier drove the first nail through His flesh, and the hour when He died?

As he sketched, he realized his own Christ must be twisted in conflict, torn by inner questioning, yet with a divine inner force strong enough to meet His hour of trial. He turned the head and knees in opposite directions, establishing the intense physical and spiritual conflict of a man pulled two ways.

He carved his figure in walnut, sandpapered it down, and rubbed the surface with oil and wax. His fellow carpenters made no comment, but they stopped by his bench to observe. Nor did the prior discuss the figure's message. He said only: "It is what I envisioned for the altar. Thank you."

A HEAVY SNOWSTORM left Florence a white city. He was in his Duomo workshop, huddled over a brazier, when Piero's groom came to summon him to the palace.

He found the Medici children and grandchildren assembled in Lorenzo's study, a bright fire burning. It was Giuliano's birthday. Cardinal Giovanni, who had returned to Florence when a member of the hostile Borgia family was elected Pope, looked plumper than ever sitting in Lorenzo's chair, hovered over by his cousin Giulio, both in their gayest brocades and jeweled satins. Contessina, gowned in aquamarine and silver, seemed taller, her arms and shoulders filled out. Her eyes, when they met his, sparkled as brightly as the silver threads in her dress.

Piero smiled. "Michelangelo, we welcome you back to the palace. Today we must do everything that pleases Giuliano. The first thing he said this morning was, 'I would like to have the greatest snowman ever made.' And since you were our father's favorite sculptor . . . "

His heart sank; but his crushed hopes seemed less painful when Giuliano cried: "Please do it for *me*, Michelangelo!" and Contessina added, "Do help us, Michelangelo! We'll all serve as your assistants."

Late that afternoon, when the last of the crowds had thronged through the palace grounds to see the hilariously grotesque snowman, Piero sat at his father's desk in the big office. "Why not move back into the palace, Michelangelo?" he said. "You would have the same privileges as when my father was alive."

Michelangelo gulped; he was almost eighteen now. Hardly an age to receive spending money left on his washstand. Yet it was a chance to get out of the drear Buonarroti house.

But at the palace, everything was different. The Plato Academy held its meetings elsewhere; the great ruling families of Italy, the merchant princes, the councilmen no longer filled the dinner table. They were replaced by entertainers and Piero's young sporting friends.

Settled in with his Hercules block, Michelangelo designed a compact figure bursting with power. His heroic block was Seravezza marble, quarried high in the Alps. After he had penetrated its weathered outer skin, its pure milky-white slivers behaved like a lump of sugar under his chisel. Soon the anatomy of the marble began matching the anatomy of his clay model: powerful chest, magnificent arms, a head focusing enormous power. Hammer and chisel in hand, he stood back from the galvanic male figure before him, still faceless, thinking that marble had again yielded to his love. From love came all of life.

MONNA ALESSANDRA WENT to bed feeling tired one night, and never awoke. Lodovico took the loss hard; he was deeply attached to his mother, and had for her a gentleness he showed no one else. For Michelangelo the loss was poignant; since the death of his own mother, she had been the only woman to whom he could turn for love or understanding. Without his grandmother the Buonarroti house seemed gloomier than ever.

The palace by contrast was in an uproar over Contessina's approaching marriage. Piero was preparing to give Florence the greatest celebration in its history. The palace was full of singing, dancing, drinking, revelry; yet Michelangelo was lonely. He spent most of his time in the sculpture garden. Piero was polite but distant. Michelangelo heard him boast that he had two extraordinary people in the palace: Michelangelo, who made great snowmen, and a Spanish footman who could outrun his best horse. He showed no interest in Michelangelo's work, and when the Hercules was finished it was Granacci who sold it to the Strozzi family for their new palace. They offered a hundred gold florins. It was Michelangelo's first sale, and he gave the fee to his father.

Three thousand wedding guests had poured into the city by the morning of May 24. Michelangelo walked with Granacci behind the wedding party as Contessina and Ridolfi paraded through streets decorated with flags, preceded by trumpeters. In front of the palace was a fountain garlanded with fruits, from which red and white wine flowed so abundantly that it ran down the street. On the steps of the cathedral a notary read aloud the marriage contract, with Contessina's huge dowry, to the thousands who jammed the piazza.

Michelangelo went to the church, but slipped out in the middle of the Nuptial Mass. He watched the wedding party emerge from the church, Ridolfi tall in his white satin cloak, jet-black hair framing his thin face; Contessina in an embroidered crimson gown with long train and collar of white ermine.

As soon as she was seated in a bedecked stand the entertainment began: a play depicting "A Fight Between Chastity and Marriage," a tournament in which Piero jousted, and, as the climax, a favorite of the times: a contest of the "Knights of the She-Cat" in which a man, naked to the waist, entered a cage where he had to kill a cat with his teeth, without using his hands.

Later, a seat was reserved for Michelangelo in the banquet hall. Eight hundred barrels of wine, a thousand pounds of meat and game provided the feast. A child was placed in Contessina's arms and a gold florin in her shoe to bring fertility and riches.

After the feast Michelangelo left the palace and walked from piazza to piazza, where Piero had set up prodigal tables of food and wine for all of Florence. But the people seemed glum.

He did not return to the palace to see Contessina taken to the

Ridolfi palace. High in Settignano, he waited and watched at the Topolinos' until the sun lit the roof of the Buonarroti house across the ravine.

AFTER CONTESSINA'S MARRIAGE everything seemed to change: for himself, for Florence. Ghirlandaio had died suddenly. Savonarola demanded that Piero be prosecuted by the council for violation of the city's laws against extravagance; and the Medici cousins began a political campaign against Piero. When they asked Michelangelo to carve a young St. John in white marble as the patron saint of their home, he hesitated. He needed work, but Prior Bichiellini had told him that the aim of the cousins was to drive Lorenzo's family out of Florence, and he still felt a great loyalty to Lorenzo. Finally he declined the commission.

Piero was ignoring the city council, neglecting affairs of state. Prior Bichiellini, his eyes snapping with anger, said to Michelangelo: "His Medici ancestors loved Florence first, themselves second. Piero won't listen to counsel. A weak man at the helm and a power-hungry monk working to replace him—these are sad days for Florence, my son."

"I have heard Savonarola's sermons on the 'coming flood.' Half the people of the city believe Judgment Day is the next rain away. What is his purpose in terrorizing Florence?"

"He wants to become Pope. He has plans to conquer the Near East, then the Orient."

One day Lodovico sent for Michelangelo. When he reached home, his father took him into the boys' bedroom, opened Giovansimone's clothing chest, and scooped out jewelry, gold and silver buckles, medallions. "What does this mean?" he asked. "Has Giovansimone been burglarizing people's homes?"

"No, Father. But I have heard he is a captain in Savonarola's Army of Boys. They strip women in the streets who violate his orders against wearing jewelry in public. If they hear a family is violating the sumptuary laws, they strip the house bare. If they meet opposition, they stone people half to death."

"But is Giovansimone allowed to keep these things?"

"He is supposed to bring them to San Marco. He has

converted his gang of hoodlums into what Savonarola calls his 'White-Shirted Angels.' The Signoria is powerless to stop them."

WITH THE FALL, Florence became embroiled in an international dispute. Charles VIII of France, whose grandfather had built the first standing army since Caesar, was now bringing that army into Italy to conquer the Kingdom of Naples. Piero's cousins had assured the king that Florence awaited his triumphal entry.

But Piero refused Charles safe passage. The citizens of Florence were ready to welcome the French because they would help drive out Piero, and Piero had only one hundred mercenaries to stop Charles's army of over thirty thousand. A dozen times Michelangelo realized he should flee the palace and the city; but he could not bring himself to desert Lorenzo's family.

On September 21 Savonarola preached a sermon in the Duomo. His voice rang out like a clap of doom. The hair of the Florentines stood on end as he protrayed the destruction of Florence and every living creature in it. His faintest whisper pierced the remotest corners of the vast cathedral. People left the Duomo half dead with fright, speechless, their eyes glassy.

The web closed tighter each day: it could be only a few days before the French army entered Florence. One morning Michelangelo rose to find the palace abandoned except for a few old servants. Piero had rushed out to treat with Charles, while the rest of the family sought refuge in a hillside villa. The palace was frightening in its hollow silence, as Michelangelo walked the echoing corridors and looked into the big empty rooms.

Piero offered Charles Florence's vassal cities of Pisa and Leghorn and two hundred thousand florins if he "would continue down the coast and avoid Florence." Outraged at this humiliating capitulation, the Signoria sounded the bell to summon the people and publicly castigated Piero for his cowardice and ineptitude. When Piero returned, the city was wild with rage. Crowds yelled, "Go away!" hissed, and threw stones. Piero drew his sword; the crowds chased him through the streets. He disappeared into the palace and diverted the throngs momentarily by having the remaining servants bring out wine and cake.

Then couriers came down the street crying, "The Signoria has banished the Medici! There is a price of four thousand florins on Piero de' Medici's head!"

Piero managed to escape through the rear garden with his brother, Cardinal Giovanni; but Florence was only a moment behind. Into the courtyard surged the mob. Rioters poured down into the wine cellars, and hundreds of bottles passed from mouth to mouth. Then the mob mounted the stairs to sack the palace.

Michelangelo stood defensively before the Donatello David. The crowd was still pouring through the main gate, jamming the courtyard, faces he had known all his life, quiet, good-natured people, suddenly inflamed with the faceless irresponsibility of the mob. He saw a Donatello statue carried out through the rear garden. Roman portraits and busts were smashed with pikes and poles.

He raced up the main staircase to Lorenzo's study and slammed the door behind him. He looked about at the priceless treasures. How could he protect them? His eyes fell upon the dumbwaiter. He pulled on the ropes and, when the lift was level, began piling in the small objects. The toothless Faun that he had copied for his own first piece of sculpture he stuffed inside his shirt. Then he sent the lift down part way and closed the door. The mob reached the study at that moment and began looting the room. He fought his way to his own apartment, where he hid Bertoldo's models under the beds.

Hundreds of rioters were now sweeping through the palace. In Lorenzo's room Michelangelo watched helplessly as they cut paintings out of their frames, ripped statues off their bases. Some burly porters smashed open the safe: out came a rain of twenty thousand florins which sent the mob into a paroxysm of joy as they fought one another for the gold coins.

He made his way down the rear staircase and cut through back alleys to the Ridolfi palace. There he left Contessina a brief note: *When it is safe, send someone to your father's study to look in the food lift.* He signed it *M.B.* When the city at last slept, he slipped out to the Medici stables. Two grooms had stayed with the horses. They helped him saddle one. There was no guard at the city gate as he left Florence.

BY AFTERNOON OF THE second day he had crossed the Apennines and dropped down into Bologna, with its high-towered orange brick walls. He entered the city through a produce market where old women were sweeping up litter with brooms made of twigs. The narrow, tortuous streets, covered over by the protruding second stories of the houses, were suffocatingly airless. Each house had a tower for protection against its neighbors, a custom that had been abolished in Florence by Cosimo de' Medici, who had obliged the Florentines to saw off their towers at roof height.

He reached a square with a majestic church, and was suddenly surrounded by Bolognese guards. "You are a stranger?"

"Florentine," Michelangelo replied.

"Your thumb, if you please. To see the mark of the red wax."

"I don't carry red wax."

"Then come with us. You are under arrest."

He followed the guards to the customs office, where an officer explained that every stranger coming into Bologna had to register and be thumbprinted. "Ignorance of our law excuses no one," he said. "You are fined fifty Bolognese pounds."

"I don't have that much money."

"Too bad. Fifty days in jail."

Michelangelo stared. Before he could recover his wits a man stepped forward. He said, "Is not your name Buonarroti?"

"Yes, sir."

The Bolognese turned to the officer. "This young man's father has charge of a customs office, as you have. Might not our sister cities offer hospitality to each other's important families?"

Flattered, the officer replied, "Assuredly, Excellency."

As they left the customs house, Michelangelo studied his benefactor. He was a man in his mid-forties, with a strong, pleasant face. "I am Gianfrancesco Aldovrandi," he said. "We met at a dinner of Lorenzo de' Medici's."

"Of course! You told me you had great sculptors in Bologna."

"Now I can show you their work. Won't you give me the pleasure of your company at supper?"

"The pleasure will be mine," Michelangelo said. "I haven't delighted my stomach since I lost sight of the Duomo."

"You have come to the right city," replied Aldovrandi. "Bologna is known as *La Grassa,* The Fat. Here we eat better than anywhere in Europe."

The Aldovrandi palace was a gracefully proportioned building, three stories high. A groom took Michelangelo's horse and Michelangelo went with Aldovrandi to see his library, which Lorenzo de' Medici had helped him assemble.

He told Michelangelo that the fleeing Medici and their party had passed through Bologna the day before. "But why do you not remain here?" Aldovrandi went on. "I may find a sculpture commission for you."

Michelangelo's eyes gleamed. He would find lodgings . . .

"Unthinkable!" replied Aldovrandi. "No friend of Lorenzo de' Medici may live in a Bolognese inn. You will be our guest."

HE HAD BEEN invited into a joyful house, with laughter ringing through it. Aldovrandi had six sons, and Signora Aldovrandi welcomed Michelangelo as though he were a seventh. His host, a retired banker, was free to spend his time as he would. He took Michelangelo for a tour of the city.

They walked under arcades displaying the most delicious foods of Italy: exquisite cheese, the whitest of breads, the rarest of wines; and in every block, of course, the world-famous *salame.* Students from the university studied at little cafés under orange-colored porticoes, or played dice and cards.

"There is one thing I miss, Messer Aldovrandi," Michelangelo said. "I have seen no stone sculpture in Bologna."

"We have no quarries. Our sculpture is usually of terra-cotta."

They soon came upon a young man making terra-cotta busts. He was powerfully built, and his skin was burned the color of Bologna brick. "Vincenzo, this is my friend Buonarroti," Aldovrandi said, "the best young sculptor in Florence."

"Then it is proper that we meet," replied Vincenzo, "for I am Bologna's best young sculptor. I am the great Dell' Arca's successor. I am to finish his Pisano tomb in San Domenico."

"You have received the commission?" asked Aldovrandi sharply.

"Not yet, Excellency, but it must come."

They walked on to the church of San Domenico and Aldovrandi pointed out Dell' Arca's marble carvings. "There are three figures left to be sculptured: an angel, St. Petronius and St. Proculus. These are the marbles that Vincenzo said he was going to carve. Successor to Dell' Arca, indeed! He is the successor to his grandfather and father, who are the finest brickmakers in Bologna. He should stick to their trade."

MICHELANGELO FOUND A NEW kind of excitement in Bologna. At a supper given by his host's nephew, Marco, he met Clarissa Saffi, who acted as Marco's hostess.

She was slender, sensuous, golden-haired, the hair plucked back from the natural hairline of the brow in the fashion of the day. She was unlike any woman he had ever seen, one of those rare creatures whose every breath was made for love. He was aware of her not merely through his eyes, but through the blood pounding in his veins; and Clarissa's welcoming smile for him was embracing, for she liked all men. She had been Marco's mistress for three years, since he had stumbled across her cleaning her father's cobbler shop. He had taught her how to wear rich gowns and jewels, had hired a tutor to teach her to read and write.

After supper, while the men were discussing politics, Michelangelo found himself alone with her in a little French music room. He could not tear his eyes away from her bodice, a golden net which seemed to expose her breasts while keeping them under cover. Clarissa was amused at his gaucherie in staring. "You are an artist, Buonarroti?"

"I am a sculptor."

"Could you carve me in marble?"

"You're already carved," he blurted out. "Flawlessly!"

Color rose in her creamy cheeks. They laughed together, leaning a little toward each other. "Will I see you again?" he asked.

"If Signor Aldovrandi brings you."

"Not otherwise?"

She smiled. "You wish me to pose for you?"

"No. Yes. I don't know. I don't even know what I am saying."

She laughed, her movements tightening the net over her bosom. He thought: "This is *pazzesco,* crazy! What has happened to me?"

His friend Aldovrandi saw the naked longing in his eyes. On the way home, he warned him: "My nephew has the quickest temper and rapier in Bologna."

But a few Sundays later Aldovrandi again took him to Marco's villa, where a group of intimates were playing cards. Michelangelo knew nothing of such games. He sat with Clarissa before a fire in another room, watching her face in the firelight, the features so fragile, yet with such implicit passion.

"It's pleasant to have someone my own age to talk to," Clarissa confided. "All of Marco's friends are older."

"You do not have young friends?"

"Not any more. But I am happy." She put her hand in his, studied his face. "Why do you always seem embarrassed with me? It is good to be desired. Have you ever been in love?"

"In a way," he said.

"It's always 'in a way.' "

"Is love never whole?"

"Not that I know of. It's political; or to get children born and scrubbing done; or for pearls and palaces, as with myself."

"Or for what we feel for each other?"

Her body stirred and he trembled. She said, "We are young people together. Why should we not want each other?"

He thrashed the night through, hearing her words over and over again in the darkness of his room.

IT WAS DURING the Christmas festivities, with the symbolic "good-wish" log burning in the drawing-room fireplace, and the poor children of the town singing carols outside, that Aldovrandi told Michelangelo he had secured for him the commission to complete the San Domenico tomb. Aldovrandi had also arranged for him to use Dell' Arca's workshop, one of the work stalls for maintenance crews in the courtyard of a huge church.

He had been working only a few days at his drawing table when Vincenzo, the terra-cotta sculptor, loomed massively above him. His face was a raw umber from the cold, his eyes intense. "Buonarroti, you stole the commission I been after. You take bread out of the mouths of us native sculptors."

Placatingly, Michelangelo replied, "I understand. I lost a commission last year."

"It's good you understand. Go tell Messer Aldovrandi you decide against doing this. Or I make you sorry you came here."

Michelangelo looked at Vincenzo. He was Michelangelo's own age, about nineteen, but loomed a head taller than he did and probably weighed twice as much as his own one hundred and twenty pounds. He thought of Torrigiani, could see Torrigiani's powerful fist coming through the air. . . .

"What's the matter, Buonarroti? You don't look good. Afraid I make life miserable for you?"

"You already have."

But not so miserable as to relinquish the opportunity to carve three beautiful blocks of white Carrara marble . . .

ONCE A WEEK business associates of Aldovrandi made the trip to Florence and brought back the latest news. Charles VIII had entered the city, raised a hundred and twenty thousand florins from it and won the right to maintain two fortresses there until his war with Naples was over. Now he had taken his army on south. The wheels of the city-state had creaked to a halt; it was torn by factions. But by mid-December news reached Bologna that Savonarola had introduced a democratic system of elected councils and universal suffrage.

With the coming of the New Year, Piero de' Medici set up headquarters in Bologna. One night he dined at the Aldovrandi palace. When they met, Michelangelo exclaimed, "Excellency, I wish this meeting were at the Medici palace."

"We'll be back there soon," Piero growled. "I am assembling

an army." He outlined his plan for the reconquest of Florence, and asked Aldovrandi to contribute two thousand florins.

"Excellency, are you sure this is the best way?" asked Aldovrandi. "When your great-grandfather Cosimo was exiled, he waited until the city found it needed him and called him back."

"Florence wants me back now. It is just Savonarola and my cousins who have schemed against me." He turned to Michelangelo. "You shall enter my army as an engineer."

Michelangelo sat with his head bowed. "But if the city were bombarded, the art treasures could be destroyed," he said.

"We can replace all that paint and marble in a year."

Aldovrandi said, "Excellency, I must decline. Lorenzo would have been the first to stop you, were he alive."

Piero looked at Michelangelo. "And you, Buonarotti?"

"Excellency, I cannot wage war against Florence."

Piero pushed his chair back in a rage and left the room.

MICHELANGELO WAS CARVING a lusty angel with the wings of an eagle for the Domenico tomb when he acquired a neighbor in the stall opposite his workshop. It was Vincenzo, whose father had a contract to make brick and tile for repairs to a cathedral. Vincenzo gave the workmen running entertainment by taunting Michelangelo throughout the day. When he arrived with a wagonload of fresh tiles, he would say: "I made a hundred durable stones yesterday. What did you make? Charcoal scratches on paper?" Encouraged by the laughter of the workmen, he continued, "Why don't you go home and leave Bologna to its natives?"

The sneers of Vincenzo and the workmen made him ill: the forces of destruction always one short step behind creation! Ignoring them, he finished the angel and carved a St. Petronius, patron saint of Bologna, holding the city in his arms.

"Dell' Arca could not have surpassed it," said Aldovrandi when he saw the polished piece.

THE FIRST OF May came, the happiest day in the year for Bologna, when the Countess of Love reigned, people gathered wild flowers for relatives and friends, and each lover placed a leafy tree tied with colored silk ribbons under the window of his beloved while friends serenaded her. A platform was erected, covered with damask and festoons of flowers, where the Countess of Love was crowned, with all Bologna gathered to pay homage.

Michelangelo too wanted to pay homage to love, or whatever it was that had started to boil in his blood in this intoxicating air. But he did not see Clarissa. He saw Marco in the midst of his family, he saw the old woman who accompanied Clarissa on her trips to the city; but no Clarissa. . . . And then his feet were carrying him swiftly up the road to her villa.

The front gate was unbolted. He went to the door, pushed on the clapper, knocked again and again. Just as he began to think that no one was at home, the door opened a crack. There stood Clarissa, in a peignoir, her golden hair hanging loose.

He stepped inside the door. There was no sound in the house. She threw the bolt. Then they were in a passionate embrace, their mouths moist and sweet and drinking deep, their bodies merging. She led him to her bedroom.

AFTER MAY DAY he started to work on a virile St. Proculus, the man who had been martyred before the gates of Bologna in 303, while in the full flower of his youth. Quite unabashedly, he modeled his own portrait: the broken nose, the steadfast eyes, resolved to triumph against the enemies of art, of life.

The hot summer months passed busily. Vincenzo had disappeared, and so had Clarissa. He learned that Marco had taken her to his hunting lodge in the Apennines for the summer. The Aldovrandi family, too, spent the summer in the mountains, but one day Aldovrandi rode in to take care of his affairs. He brought startling news from Florence.

"Fra Savonarola has come out into the open. He has declared war on the Pope!"

Michelangelo was not as shocked as Aldovrandi expected, for Prior Bichiellini had predicted this long ago.

"How has the Pope replied?"

"He summoned Savonarola to Rome, but Savonarola declared, 'It is not the will of God that I should leave this place.' "

BY FALL, ST. PROCULUS was finished. Michelangelo was exhausted, but happy with it; so was Aldovrandi.

With his work done, Michelangelo had grown homesick for Florence, but he could not go without saying good-by to Clarissa. Aldovrandi invited him to a party at a villa in the hills where the wealthy young Bolognese brought their mistresses for feasting and dancing. Michelangelo saw that there would be no chance for even a moment of privacy. They would have to say good-by in a crowded room, and on their faces they would have to wear the bantering Bolognese smile. When he told Clarissa he was leaving, her fixed smile never wavered. "I'm sorry. When will you return?"

"I don't know. Perhaps never."

"Everyone returns to Bologna," she assured him.

THE FAMILY WAS GLAD to have him home. Lodovico was delighted with the twenty-five ducats he brought. Buonarroto had grown a foot; Sigismondo was apprenticed to the Wine Guild; Giovansimone was maintaining himself regally in a flat across the Arno as one of the leaders in Savonarola's Army of Boys.

Granacci, who was working to keep Ghirlandaio's old studio afloat, told Michelangelo that the "Popolano family" wanted him to carve something for them.

"Popolano?" he said. "I don't know any Popolanos."

"Yes, you do." Granacci's voice had an edge to it. "It's the Medici cousins, Lorenzo and Giovanni. They have changed their name to sound like the 'People's Party,' and are helping to rule Florence."

The brothers received him in a drawing room filled with Lorenzo's art treasures. Michelangelo glanced from a Botticelli to a Donatello, stupefied. "We did not steal them," Giovanni said easily; "the city auctioned them off and we bought them." He added that they were still interested in having Michelangelo do a young St. John. If he cared to move into the palace, he would be welcome.

He went at once to the Ridolfi palace. Contessina received him in the drawing room, still attended by her old nurse. She was heavy with child. "Contessina. *Come va?*"

"You said I would bear many sons."

He gazed at her pale cheeks and burning eyes. And he remembered Clarissa: "All love is 'in a way.' "

"I have come to tell you that your cousins have offered me a commission. I could not join Piero's army, but I want no other disloyalty on my conscience."

"You proved your loyalty, Michelangelo, when they first made the offer. If you wish to accept now, do so."

He went to tell the Popolanos he would accept. As he walked the familiar streets of the city he felt an air of hostility and suspicion. Florentines who had lived at peace with one another since Cosimo de' Medici had split into three factions, shouting imprecations at one another. The *Arrabbiati*—the "Maddened Ones"—were men of wealth and experience who hated both Piero and Savonarola. The "Whites," including the Popolanos, disliked Savonarola, but supported him because he was on the side of popular government. Lastly, there were Piero's "Grays," intriguing for his return.

On New Year's Day of 1496 a large group of men from the anti-Savonarola parties converged on his monastery, carrying torches and chanting: "Burn Savonarola's house! Burn San Marco! Burn the dirty friar!"

The San Marco monks came out and stood shoulder to shoulder in a line across the front of the church and monastery, arms linked. The crowd continued to shout imprecations, but the monks held their ground; and after a time the mob began to drift out of the piazza.

MICHELANGELO COULD NOT bring himself to live in the renamed "Popolano palace," but he did set up his workbench in the garden. He saw Beppe in the Duomo workyard and found a good piece of marble at a reasonable price. The rest of the money the Popolanos gave him he turned over to his father. The Popolanos treated him as a friend, frequently inviting him inside to see a new piece of art. Even Lodovico seemed pleased with him. Yet he could find little joy, and no creative surge, although St. John was a sympathetic subject.

He read the story of John in Matthew: *In those days John the Baptist appeared, preaching in the wilderness of Judaea; Repent, he said, the kingdom of heaven is at hand. . . . There is the voice of one crying in the wilderness, Prepare the way of the Lord. . . .*

This boy, first going out to preach, was not the older man who baptized Jesus. So Michelangelo carved a fifteen-year-old, a vital portrait of a youth, and the Medici cousins were well pleased. But despair enveloped Michelangelo. "I have carved six pieces in four years," he said to Granacci. "But only my St. Proculus has something original in it."

On his birthday he walked disconsolately into the workshop in the Popolano garden. He found a block of marble sitting on his workbench. Across it, scrawled in charcoal in Granacci's handwriting, was the greeting: "Try again!"

He did, immediately; an infant, robust, pagan, sleeping with his right arm under his head, carved in the Roman tradition. It was a lark, something simply for fun.

When Lorenzo Popolano saw the piece his face flushed with pleasure. "If you were to treat it so that it seemed to have been buried in the earth, it would pass for an antique Cupid. You could sell it then in Rome for a good price. I have a shrewd dealer there, Baldassare del Milanese."

So Michelangelo rubbed dirt into the statue, stained the outside edges with earth tans and rust, and used a hard bristle brush to rub in the discoloration. He was as amused at the idea of the fraud as he had been at the carving itself.

It was sold to the first customer to whom Baldassare offered it: Cardinal Riario di San Giorgio. Lorenzo handed on thirty gold florins to Michelangelo. Michelangelo had thought an antique Cupid would bring at least a hundred florins in Rome; even so, it was twice what it would have brought in Florence.

JUST BEFORE LENT Michelangelo saw Giovansimone hurrying down the street at the head of a group of white-robed boys, their arms laden with mirrors, paintings, statuary, jewel boxes. Michelangelo grabbed his brother, almost toppling his load of loot. "Giovansimone! I haven't laid eyes on you for four months."

Giovansimone shook his arm loose. "Can't talk now. But come to the Piazza della Signoria tomorrow at dusk."

It would have been impossible for Michelangelo or anyone else in Florence to miss the giant spectacle the following evening. In the four main quarters of Florence the Army of Boys in their white robes were shaped into military formations. Preceded by drummers, pipers and mace bearers, carrying olive branches in their hands and chanting, "Long live Christ, the King of Florence! Long live Mary, the Queen!" they marched on the Piazza della Signoria, where a huge pyramidal scaffold had been erected. The citizens of Florence and the outlying villages poured into the square. The section for the burning was roped off by the monks of San Marco standing arm in arm, with Savonarola in commanding position.

The boys built their pyre. At the base they threw rouge pots, perfumes, mirrors, bolts of silk, earrings, bracelets. Then came all the paraphernalia of gambling: cards, dice, checkerboards. Next, they piled on books, manuscripts, paintings, ancient sculpture. Above them came musical instruments, masks and fancy-dress costumes, and jewels which sparkled as they landed. Michelangelo saw Botticelli run up and throw some of his pictures on the pyre. Monks of the Della Robbia family added their terra-cotta sculptures. It was difficult to tell from the cries of the crowd whether they greeted the sacrifices with fear or ecstasy.

Savonarola raised his arms for silence. The guarding line of monks unlocked their arms and raised them to the heavens. A monk handed a lighted torch to Savonarola, who walked around the pyre, touching it in one place after another until the scaffolding was one huge mass of flames. Then the Army of Boys marched about the pyre chanting, "Long live Christ! Long live

the Virgin!" Great answering shouts went up from the packed mass: "Long live Christ! Long live the Virgin!"

Tears came to Michelangelo's eyes as the flames mounted amid wild singing and crying. With all his heart he wished to go away, far from the sight of the Duomo.

As if in answer to his thoughts, a groom came, a few months later, to ask Michelangelo if he would come to the Popolano palace to meet a Roman nobleman named Leo Baglioni. He had been sent to Florence by Cardinal Riario to find the sculptor of the Cupid. "It was I," Michelangelo confessed. "Baldassare sent me thirty florins for the piece."

"Thirty! But the cardinal paid two hundred."

"Two hundred! Why, that . . . that thief!"

"Precisely what the cardinal said." Leo Baglioni had a mischievous gleam in his eye. "He suspected it was a fraud. Why not return to Rome with me and settle your account with Baldassare? The cardinal wants you to stay with him. He said anyone who could imitate so well should do even better original carvings."

"A few articles from my home, and I shall be ready for the journey."

BOOK FIVE

The City

HE PAUSED ON A rise just north of the city. Rome lay below in its bed of hills, destroyed, as though sacked by vandals. The Romans no longer had any civic pride. The small piazza Michelangelo and Baglioni passed as they entered the city stank from piled garbage. They rode through narrow lanes with broken cobbles underfoot; shops were huddled between ancient palaces that looked as though they would topple at any moment. Neglected, badly governed, the Mother City of Christendom was now a waste heap and a dunghill, where dead animals lay underfoot, and citizens burned ancient marble columns for their lime content.

Baglioni led Michelangelo at last into the Campo dei Fiori, an open-air market with clean and colorful stalls full of cooks and housewives shopping for their dinner. At last Michelangelo was able to smile. "I almost turned my horse and made a run for Florence," he told Baglioni.

"Rome is pitiful. Pope Sixtus IV made an effort to improve it, but under the Borgia family it is decaying again."

Michelangelo was given a temporary room in Baglioni's house, and late that afternoon they strolled to Cardinal Riario's palace. Riario had a long hooked nose that clamped down on a tight-lipped mouth; he greeted Michelangelo perfunctorily and sent him out to see the sculpture of Rome. With Baglioni guiding him, Michelangelo moved half stunned in a forest of sculpture: surely this miserable dirty city must hold the greatest collection of antique art in the world.

"What do you think of the marbles you have seen?" the cardinal asked him later. "Can you do something equally beautiful?"

"Perhaps not as beautiful. But we will see what I can do."

"I like that answer, Buonarroti; it shows humility."

He did not feel humble. All he had meant was that his pieces would be different from anything he had seen.

"We had best start at once," said Riario. "My carriage is outside. It can take us to the Trastevere stoneyards."

In a stoneyard just outside the Vatican wall Michelangelo wandered among the blocks wondering how large a piece he dared select. He stopped before a white Carrara column over seven feet tall and four feet thick. His eyes lighted with excitement. He assured the cardinal that there could be a fine statue contained in it. Cardinal Riario paid thirty-seven ducats from the purse on his belt.

As soon as the marble was delivered to a workshop Baglioni had located, the cardinal sent for Michelangelo, and told him that he was to live in the Riario palace. No word about what he wanted sculptured. Or what the price would be. Or whether he was to have regular payments during his stay. A chamberlain directed him to one of twenty narrow cells at the rear of the ground floor, where he unpacked. At his first meal he found himself relegated to the "third category" dining room, with the cardinal's scriveners and bookkeepers, purchasing agents for his far-flung business enterprises. Michelangelo was to live in the palace as one of a crew of skilled workmen. Nothing more.

EARLY THE NEXT morning he went to see Baldassare, the art dealer, who had been obliged to return Cardinal Riario's two hundred ducats for the Cupid. He was a swarthy fat man with an enormous stomach which he pushed ahead of him as he came forward in his sculpture yard. Michelangelo demanded the return of his Cupid, offering to repay the thirty florins.

"Certainly not!" the dealer cried.

"You defrauded me on the price."

"It is you who are the fraud. You sent me a false antique."

Fuming, Michelangelo left the yard. Then he burst into laughter. "Baldassare is right. It is I who was the cheat."

He heard someone behind him exclaim: "Michelangelo Buonarroti! Do you always talk to yourself?"

He turned, recognized a man who had worked briefly for his Uncle Francesco. They had never become friends in Florence, but here they fell on each other's necks. "Balducci! What are you doing in Rome?"

"Working for Jacopo Gallo's bank. Head bookkeeper. The dumbest Florentine is smarter than the smartest Roman, so I'm moving up fast. How about having dinner together? I'll take you to a Florentine restaurant. When you taste the *tortellini* and beefsteak, you'll think you're back in sight of the Duomo."

After dinner Balducci took him to see a distant cousin of Michelangelo's, the banker Paolo Rucellai, who had a palace in the Ponte district. Here the Florentines in Rome lived close together, with their own markets, their own foods brought down from Tuscany. No Roman could move into this district: the hatred was mutual. The Romans said: "Better a corpse in the house than a Florentine at the door," while the Florentines reinterpreted the S.P.Q.R. of the Roman *Senatus Populus Que Romanus* to read, *"Sono Porci, Questi Romani.* They are pigs, these Romans." In the midst of the chaos and filth of Rome, the Florentines washed their streets every day, kept their houses in repair. There were fines against dumping refuse in the streets. Guards policed the quarter at night; it was the only section where one was sure not to stumble over a corpse on one's front steps at daybreak. Michelangelo was presented to the leading families of this Florentine community, and was accepted at once.

Meantime the cardinal, who gave him no commission, ignored him. Each morning he drew from models: Corsicans from the papal bodyguard, German typographers, French glovemakers, Spanish booksellers, Portuguese trunk makers. The months of dissection had given his drawing an authority, an inner truth. Yet he could not take up his carving tools.

"Exercise extreme care," Leo Baglioni warned him, "not to touch that column until Cardinal Riario gives you permission to do so. He is adamant about his properties."

He was humiliated at being cautioned like a laborer not to manhandle the property of his *padrone*.

He received an invitation from Paolo Rucellai to attend a reception for Piero de' Medici, who was attempting as usual to gather an army, and Cardinal Giovanni de' Medici, who had taken a house in Rome. That morning, as he finished shaving and combing his hair, forming deep curls on his forehead, he heard the sound of trumpets and ran out to see at last the Borgia Pope whom the Medici so feared, and whom Savonarola had picked as his special target. Preceded by red-robed cardinals and followed by purple-cloaked princes, Pope Alexander VI, born Rodrigo Borgia in Spain, white-robed on a white horse, progressed toward the Franciscan convent in Trastevere. He was a big, virile man with a swarthy complexion. As a cardinal he had won the reputation of amassing more beautiful women and vaster wealth than anyone preceding him. He had been reproved by Pope Pius II for "unseemly gallantry," a euphemism that covered six known children by various mothers.

When his colorful procession had passed, Michelangelo walked to the Rucellai palace. In the drawing room he bowed to Piero, who was cool; but Cardinal Giovanni, despised by the Borgia Pope and frozen out of all church activity, seemed genuinely happy to see him. Giulio was frigid.

Thirty Florentines sat down to dinner, eating *cannelloni* stuffed with chopped beef and mushrooms and veal in milk, drinking Brolio wines and talking animatedly. They always referred to their adversary only as "the Borgia," striving to preserve their reverence for the papacy while expressing their contempt for the Spanish adventurer who had seized the Vatican and was ruling on the premise that all the wealth of Christendom belonged to the papacy. The Florentine colony favored Savonarola in his struggle against the Pope, and found Piero's attempt to gather an army embarrassing.

In November Piero finally left with troops to reconquer Florence, but he came back to Rome penniless, and with his army scattered. He proceeded to scandalize Rome by his heavy gambling and a passion for every vice the city offered. Giovanni's paintings, bronzes, tapestries and silver plate were all pledged, at twenty percent interest, to cover Piero's debts. Florentine bankers said: "Every florin the Medici spend costs them eight lire interest." Michelangelo was shocked to see the ravages on Piero's face: his once handsome features were bloated and red.

WEEKS PASSED AND still no commission came from Cardinal Riario. Then one day Michelangelo met a Florentine architect named Giuliano da Sangallo, a friend of Lorenzo. Sangallo listened intently while the younger man spilled out his frustration.

"You are in the service of the wrong cardinal," Sangallo said. "When Cardinal Rovere returns to Rome, I shall introduce you. And tomorrow I will show you the Rome of grandeur, when the world's greatest architects built here; the Rome I shall rebuild once Cardinal Rovere becomes Pope. By tomorrow night, you'll forget sculpture and give yourself over to architecture."

It was a needed diversion. They sketched the great Roman buildings, re-creating them from the ruins and from the descriptions of Plutarch and other writers. By nightfall, Michelangelo was exhausted, Sangallo triumphant. He was the first man to instruct Michelangelo in the art of architecture.

Still more time passed before he could get an appointment with Riario. "What have you been thinking of for me?" the cardinal asked in good humor. "Something vigorously pagan, to match those fine antiques in Cardinal Rovere's garden?"

Michelangelo thought quickly. Who was the most joyous of the Greek gods? Why, Bacchus, god of wine, symbol of fruitfulness. "Yes, Your Grace," he said. "I have. A Bacchus."

But while he was drawing his plans for it, violence broke out in the Florentine quarter, the cobblestones running with blood. It flared up because the Pope had excommunicated Savonarola; and it ended in the grisly murder of the Pope's son, Juan Borgia. His body, hands tied, slashed with knife wounds, was found in the Tiber. The Romans could not conceal their joy, but Riario went into mourning with his Pope. The palace was closed to all but the most compelling business: sculpture was forgotten.

A second blow to Michelangelo was the news of his step-mother Lucrezia's death, in a few broken sentences from his father. *"La Migliore,"* he thought with affection, "The Best." She had given of her best to all the nine Buonarroti. Her stepson shed a tear for her passing.

A few days later his brother Buonarroto arrived in Rome. "How is Father?" Michelangelo asked at once. "How has he taken Lucrezia's death?"

"Badly. Locks himself in his bedroom." He paused, then added, "And he is about to be arrested for a bad debt. Since we have only a few florins left it could mean prison."

"Prison! *Dio mio!* He must sell the villa and farm."

He says he will not deprive us of our last inheritance."

Michelangelo was furious. "Our last inheritance is the Buonarroti name. We've got to protect it."

"But what to do? I earn only a few scudi a month. . . . "

"And I earn nothing. But I will! I'll make Cardinal Riario see the justice of my position."

The cardinal listened, toying with the gold chain around his neck. "Of course, you should not have given all this time for nothing. For your patience, I give you the marble block."

He had only one recourse: the Florentine bankers, Rucellai and Cavalcanti. He explained his plight to Paolo Rucellai.

"A loan from the bank? No; it is too expensive for you at twenty percent interest. From me, yes, as a personal loan without interest. Will twenty-five florins help? You are to forget about it until you have money in your belt."

He ran home, gave Buonarroto the credit slip, and promised he would be responsible for the balance of Lodovico's debt.

"That's what Father wanted, of course," Buonarroto said. "He's not going to earn anything more; nor is Uncle Francesco. We can expect no help from Lionardo or Giovansimone. And Sigismondo . . . the Wine Guild has released him. You now have the support of the whole Buonarroti family on your hands."

Buying a small piece of marble with some of his last florins, Michelangelo carved a Cupid, a lovely child just awakened from sleep and holding up his arms to his mother. Balducci, his Florentine friend, was enchanted with its lighthearted warmth and asked if he might show it to his employer, Jacopo Gallo, the banker.

They found Gallo in his garden. He put down a copy of Aristophanes' *Frogs,* and pulled himself up from his chair. Slowly, he unfolded: six feet, six and a half; surely not seven? The tallest man Michelangelo had ever seen, hunched over at the shoulders from a lifetime of stooping to the short-statured Romans. He placed the Cupid on a pedestal, then settled back to study it. "I feel as though your Cupid had been sitting there since the day I was born," he said finally. "We must set a price; but first, tell me your circumstances."

Michelangelo related the story of his year with Riario.

"So you end up with no pay, and a seven-foot marble block? Shall we say the Cupid is worth fifty ducats? Because I know you need money, I will allow my cupidity to knock the price down to twenty-five ducats. Then, because I detest shrewdness in dealing with artists, I will take the twenty-five ducats I was going to underpay you, and add them to my original estimate. Do you approve my formula?"

Michelangelo's eyes shone. "Messer Gallo, for a year I have thought bad things about Romans. In your name, I apologize to the whole city."

"Now, what could you carve from your big marble block?"

Michelangelo told him about his plans for a Bacchus. Gallo was intrigued. "Would you be willing to move in here, and carve this Bacchus for me? For three hundred ducats?"

WHILE MICHELANGELO WAS carving the Bacchus, using as a model a self-indulgent young nobleman, much addicted to wine, Gallo brought the aged, saintly French Cardinal Groslaye to see it. "But how do you achieve in a half-finished figure this sense of throbbing vitality?" the cardinal asked. "I can feel the blood and muscle under your marble skin." His fading eyes gleamed as he studied the figure. "My son," he said, "I am growing old. I must leave something behind me, to add to the beauties of Rome. I have secured permission from the Pope to dedicate a large sculpture in the Chapel of the Kings of France in St. Peter's. You, I believe, are the best sculptor in Rome."

A sculpture for St. Peter's, the oldest, most sacred basilica in Christendom! He went to St. Peter's the next day to see a niche the cardinal had described to him, and was aghast at the dilapidated condition of the church, which was leaning sharply to the left. In the chapel he measured the niche with his eye, disappointed to find it so deep that a statue would be seen only from the front.

He knew very soon that his theme would be a Pietà: Sorrow. The Madonna and Child was the beginning, the Pietà was the preordained conclusion of everything that Mary had accepted in that fateful hour of decision he had carved in his Madonna of the Stairs. Now, thirty-three years later, her son was again on her lap, having completed His journey.

Gallo took him to Groslaye's palace, where they waited for him to complete the five hours of prayer and offices required daily of a Benedictine. The cardinal was ashen after his long devotions, but when he heard about the Pietà his eyes sparkled. He urged Michelangelo to find the most perfect marble and begin.

Later, Michelangelo said to Gallo, "But first, the Bacchus."

"The Bacchus can wait. The cardinal can't. One day soon God will rest His hand just a trifle more heavily on his shoulder, and Groslaye will go to heaven."

"I cannot stop now," Michelangelo insisted stubbornly. "The Bacchus is completing itself in my mind. It must be perfect."

The following Sunday he went to dine with the Rucellai, eager to hear news of Florence. His Florentine friends told him that Savonarola had again defied the Pope; though he was excommunicated, he had celebrated three Masses in San Marco at Christmas. A vast throng saw him raise the Host in his hand, beseeching God to strike him dead if he deserved excommunication. When God refrained, Savonarola celebrated his vindication with another Burning of the Vanities.

But Florence was turning against Savonarola, tired from seven years of wrangling, and fearing the Pope's threat to put an interdict on the entire population, which could paralyze trade. They elected a new council; it arrested Savonarola and his chief aides, Fra Domenico and Fra Silvestro, and jailed them in the Palazzo della Signoria. Then they appointed a Commission of Seventeen to secure a confession from him that his words were not divinely inspired.

Savonarola refused to recant. The commission tortured him; first, using the rack and the screw; then roping him to a pulley, raising him in the air, and dropping him with a sudden jerk of the rope. Savonarola, delirious, agreed to write a confession, but what he wrote was not satisfactory to the Signoria. He was tortured again, finally signed another confession but rejected it and was tortured a third time. At last, the commission declared Savonarola guilty of heresy and sentenced him to death.

A throng filled the Piazza della Signoria when Savonarola, Fra Domenico and Fra Silvestro were led out onto the Signoria steps, and stripped of their vestments. They mounted the gibbets, praying silently. Ropes and chains were put about their necks. Within an instant, all three were dangling, their necks broken. Then a pyre under the gibbets was lighted. The three bodies were held aloft by the chains after the ropes had burned. The half-consumed corpses were stoned, and the ashes dumped into the Arno.

Savonarola's martyrdom shook Michelangelo profoundly. Filled with pity, he turned to work on his Bacchus: with marble in his hands, the world was good. He worked intensely and by the end of the summer the statue was finished.

Gallo was overjoyed with it. "I feel as though Bacchus is fully alive and will drop his cup at any moment. You have made for me the finest sculpture in all Italy."

The following night Gallo brought home a contract for Michelangelo with Groslaye. In it Michelangelo found himself called *maestro* for the first time. It was agreed that for the sum of four hundred and fifty ducats he would make a marble Pietà to be completed in a year. In addition Gallo had written: *I, Jacopo*

Gallo, do promise that the work will be more beautiful than any work in marble to be seen in Rome today, and such that no master of our own time will be able to produce a better.

Michelangelo gazed at Gallo with affection. "Suppose when I finish, the cardinal says, 'I have seen better marbles in Rome.' What happens then?"

"I give His Grace back his papal ducats."

"And you are left with the statue!"

Gallo's eyes twinkled. "I could endure it."

THOUGH HE FELT DEEP and grateful affection for Gallo, the time had come to establish his own quarters and workshop where he could live quietly. On the Via Sistina, near the Tiber, he found a big corner room with two windows, and a smaller room with a fireplace. Oiled linen on wooden frames served as window coverings; the wooden floor was thin, the ceiling plaster crumbling. He paid a few scudi for two months' rent.

At the Gallos' he found Buonarroto, come to pay him a visit. Michelangelo gazed with pleasure at the stubby features; it had been a year since they had seen each other after Lucrezia's death. "You couldn't have come at a better time," he cried. "I need help with my new place."

They bought wood, plaster and whitewash, and went to the Via Sistina, where they set to work at once patching the broken floor and plastering the ceiling. Balducci knew a secondhand furniture dealer with whom he bargained shrilly for a bed with a rope mattress, a table, two cane chairs, a chest of drawers, a few pots, dishes and knives to furnish the place.

Buonarroto settled Michelangelo in, shopped and cooked the food, cleaned the rooms. The housekeeping went downhill the moment he left. Immersed in his work, growing thin, Michelangelo saw nothing but the huge white block sitting on beams in the center of the floor. His bed was unmade, the dishes unwashed.

Then, late one afternoon, he answered a knock to see a plain-faced, olive-complexioned lad of about thirteen, holding out a letter from Buonarroto. It introduced one Piero Argiento, who wished to become Michelangelo's apprentice. He had made the long trip from Florence to Rome on foot. Michelangelo invited him in, and the boy told of his family and their farm near Ferrara.

"Can you read and write, Argiento?"

"The Jesuit fathers in Ferrara taught me. I want a three-year apprenticeship. With a guild contract."

Michelangelo was impressed by his forthrightness. He gazed into the lad's brown eyes, noted the thin cheeks. "I live simply, Argiento. You can expect no luxury."

"I am of *contadini*. What is to eat, we eat."

"Suppose we try it for a few days?"

"Agreed. *Grazie.*"

"Take this coin, and go to the market for food."

"I make a good soup-of-the-country."

Argiento left the house before dawn for the markets. Michelangelo was touched by the way he painfully kept his accounts: so many denari for vegetables or meat or pasta, every coin accounted for. He was a relentless pursuer of bargains.

They established a routine. After their one-dish midday dinner, Argiento cleaned up and laundered while Michelangelo took a walk along the Tiber, listening to the Sicilians sing as they unloaded the boats. By the time he returned, Argiento was taking his *riposo* on the trundle bed under the wooden sink. Michelangelo had two hours of quiet at his workbench before Argiento woke and came to the worktable for his daily instruction. At dusk Argiento was back in the kitchen. By the time dark settled in he was asleep again on his trundle bed, while Michelangelo lit a lamp and returned to work on his Pietà.

SEARCH AS HE MIGHT, he could find no place where the Bible spoke of a moment when Mary could have been alone with Jesus after the descent from the cross. But in his concept there could be no one else present. Perhaps after the soldiers had laid Him on the ground, when Joseph of Arimathea went to Pontius Pilate to ask for Christ's body, Nicodemus was gathering myrrh and aloes, and the others had gone home to mourn. Then she might have held her child. . . . There would be no halos, no angels; only two human beings whom God had chosen.

But how was Mary to hold Christ on her lap without the relationship seeming ungainly? She would be slender and delicate, yet she must hold this full-grown man securely.

He started by making sketches, walking the streets, watching sweet-faced young nuns. Though this sculpture would show Mary with a grown son, he could not conceive of her as a broken woman in her mid-fifties. His image of the Virgin had always been that of a young woman, like the memory of his mother.

He completed a life-size clay figure, then bought yards of lightweight material, wet the cloth and covered it with moist clay. Each turn of the drapery served organically, to cover the Madonna's slender legs and feet so that they could support Christ's body.

He went into the Jewish quarter in Trastevere, to see how Christ might have looked. The Spanish Inquisition had driven many Jews into Rome. For the most part they were well treated; many were prominent in the Vatican as physicians, musicians, bankers. They did not object to his sketching them at work, but no one would come to his studio to pose.

Finally he was told to ask for Rabbi Melzi. He found the rabbi in his study, a gentle old man with a white beard and luminous gray eyes, reading the Talmud. When Michelangelo explained why he had come, the rabbi replied gravely: "The Bible forbids Jews to make graven images."

"But you don't object to others creating works of art?"

"Not at all. Each religion has its own tenets."

"I am carving a Pietà and I wish to make Jesus a Jew. I am looking for young, strong, intelligent men as models."

Rabbi Melzi smiled at him with old but merry eyes. "Leave me your address. I will send you the best we have to offer."

His first model arrived at dusk. When Michelangelo stretched him over a trestle stand, explaining the pose to him, the man quite plainly thought him crazy; only the instructions from his rabbi kept him from bolting. But when Michelangelo showed him the drawings, with the mother roughed in, holding her son, he helped him to find more models.

Michelangelo spent weeks putting his two figures together: a

Mary who would be young and sensitive, yet strong enough to hold her son on her lap; and a Jesus who was strong even in death.

SOMETIMES MICHELANGELO COULD not figure who was master and who apprentice. Argiento had been trained rigorously by the Jesuits and Michelangelo was unable to change his habits: up before dawn to market and scrub the floors every day; water boiling on the fire for washing laundry, the pots scoured with river sand after each meal. "Argiento, this is senseless," he complained, not liking to work on the wet floor. "Scrub the studio once a week."

"No," said Argiento stolidly. "Every day, before dawn."

The boy soon became acquainted with the farmers who brought produce into Rome. Sundays he would walk out to visit them and see their horses. The one thing he missed from his farm in the Po Valley was the animals.

It took a piece of bad luck to show Michelangelo that the boy was devoted to him. He was crouched over his anvil getting his chisels in trim when a splinter of steel flew into his eye. Argiento put him on the bed, brought a pan of hot water, dipped some clean white linen cloth and applied it to extract the splinter. Though the pain was considerable Michelangelo assumed he could blink the splinter out. But it would not come. Argiento never left his side, applying hot compresses throughout the night.

By the second morning Michelangelo was in a panic: he could see nothing out of the eye. At dawn Argiento went to Gallo. He arrived with his family surgeon, who carried a cage of pigeons. He told Argiento to take a bird out of the cage, cut a vein under its wing, and let the blood gush into the injured eye. At dusk the surgeon came back again and cut the vein of a second pigeon, again washed out the eye. All the next day Michelangelo could feel the splinter moving, pushing. By nightfall it was out.

Argiento had not slept for some seventy hours.

"You're tired," said Michelangelo. "Take a few days off."

Argiento's face lit up. "I go visit the horses."

The next day, hammer and chisel in hand, Michelangelo

broke into his block at the side of the Madonna's head. He turned the block so that the play of light and shadow showed him where he must cast out stone. The weight of the material of the Madonna's head covering, forcing her head downward to the inner hand of Christ that crossed her heart, compelled attention to the body stretched across her lap. Because she was gazing down on her son, all who looked must turn to her face to see the sadness, the compassion for all men's sons. All who saw would feel how heavy was her son's dead body on her lap, how much heavier the burden in her heart. Yet Michelangelo bathed the two figures in tranquillity.

Winter arrived: cold, wet, raw. The roof leaked. They moved the workbench and bed to dry sections of the room, bought a black iron brazier to put under Michelangelo's work stool. When his fingers were blue he tried to carve in woolen mittens. He wore a cap over his head and ears. Argiento fell ill, and Michelangelo spent weeks nursing him. He began to worry that he could not finish his Pietà within the allotted year.

By March the *campagna* was flooded with brittle sunlight; and with the warmer weather came Cardinal Groslaye to see how his Pietà was faring. "Tell me, my son," the cardinal said, "how does the Madonna's face remain young, younger than her son's?"

"Your Grace, it seemed to me that the Virgin Mary would not age. She was pure; she would have kept her freshness of youth."

The answer was satisfactory to the cardinal.

"I hope you will finish in August. It is my dearest wish to hold services in St. Peter's for the installation."

So Michelangelo carved in a fury from first light to dark, then threw himself across his bed, fully clothed. At midnight he got up, nibbled a heel of bread, lit the lamp and tried to throw its light on the area he was carving. The light was too diffused.

He bought some heavy paper, made a hat with a peak, tied a wire around the outside and in the center fashioned a loop big enough to hold a candle. The light, as he held his face a few inches from the marble, was bright and steady. The candles burned quickly, the wax running over the peak of his cap and onto his forehead, but he was delighted with his invention.

One night the door opened to reveal Baglioni and a group of his young friends, holding torches on long poles. "I saw the light," Baglioni said, "and came to see what you were doing at this ungodly hour. What's that stuff all over your eyebrows?"

Michelangelo proudly showed them his cap and candle. Leo and his friends burst into laughter. "At least use goat's tallow," Leo said. "It's harder; you won't be eating it all night." Next day he sent Michelangelo a bundle of candles. He was right; the goat's tallow melted more slowly and remained in a pool where it fell.

He refused all invitations, saw few of his friends now. But one day Paolo Rucellai sent for him. He said, "My cousin writes me that Florence is planning a sculpture competition, *'To bring to perfection the marble column already blocked out by Agostino di Duccio . . .'* "

"The Duccio block!" Michelangelo began to tremble. "I tried to buy it for my Hercules. I can see it this minute."

"Could you make something good of it?"

Michelangelo's eyes shone. *"Dio mio.* Tell me, what must the theme be: political, religious? Is this for Florentines only? Must I be there to compete?"

"Wait!" cried Rucellai. "The theme has not yet been determined. The competition will take place in 1500."

"Only six months from now! And I have so much to do on the Pietà." His face was anguished. "I cannot rush it."

Paolo put an arm about him. "I will keep you informed."

CARDINAL GROSLAYE LOST his race with time: he did not live to see the Pietà completed. Gallo attended the funeral with Michelangelo, standing below a catafalque sixteen feet long. Returning to the Gallo home, Michelangelo said uneasily: "I still have six to eight months of work on my Pietà. Would you send that last hundred ducats to my family?"

Gallo looked at him sharply. "I have sent almost all the cardinal's ducats to Florence. This is a bottomless well."

"I want to invest in a shop for my brothers. Buonarroti cannot seem to find a place for himself. Giovansimone, since Savonarola's death, disappears for days. If I shared in the profits . . . "

"Michelangelo, neither of them is a good businessman; how are they going to make a profit?" Gallo was exasperated. "I can't let you pour your last money down a hole. Eighty percent of it has gone to your family. I ought to know, I'm your banker."

Nevertheless almost all the money was transferred to Florence. Michelangelo and Argiento went on short rations; their clothing became ragged. It took a letter from Lodovico to bring him to his senses: *Dearest Son: Buonarroto tells me that you live in great misery. Misery is bad; it is a vice displeasing to God and to man, and also will hurt the soul and the body. Live moderately and abstain from discomfort. Above all, keep your head warm and never wash yourself.*

He went to Rucellai, borrowed twenty-five florins and took Argiento to an inn for *costata alla fiorentina*. Then he bought them each a new set of clothes.

HE WORKED NOW WITH his head lower than Mary's, his tools angled upward. He had left behind earlier Pietàs, dark, unforgiving, their message of love blotted out by blood. Here was no sign of violence: Jesus slept peacefully in His mother's arms. Michelangelo projected his deep religious faith in the figures; their harmony portrayed the harmony of God's universe.

When the sculpture was finished, Gallo came to the studio and studied it. After a time he said softly, "I have fulfilled my contract with the cardinal: this is the most beautiful marble in Rome."

"Our contract doesn't say that we have the right to put it in St. Peter's," Michelangelo said. "With the cardinal dead . . . "

"We will install it quietly. Once it is in its niche, no one will bother to have it removed. Suppose you hire those stoneyard friends of yours to help you."

Guffatti brought his family: three husky sons and a variety of cousins. They wrapped the Pietà in mangy blankets and carried it, eight strong, to an ancient wagon and roped it in place. With Michelangelo guarding it, they made their way cautiously along the cobbled streets to the foot of the thirty-five steps of marble and porphyry leading up to the basilica. Only the fact that they bore a sacred burden kept them from cursing as they carried it up the long steps, set it down to rest and wipe their brows, then picked it up again to carry it to the church door.

Michelangelo observed that the dilapidated basilica was leaning even more than when he had begun the work. It seemed beyond repair. He swallowed hard at the thought of putting his lovely Pietà in it, but he led the Guffatti to the niche in the Chapel of the Kings of France. They unwrapped their bundle and raised the Pietà reverently to its place. Then the Guffatti bought candles and lit them before the statue.

Pietà; St. Peter's, Vatican City

They refused to take one scudo for their backbreaking labor. "We take our pay in heaven."

It was the best tribute Michelangelo could receive. It was also the only tribute he received.

He returned to St. Peter's day after day. Few of the city's pilgrims bothered to visit the chapel; few in Rome knew the statue had been installed. One afternoon he wandered in and saw a family—from Lombardy, he guessed by their dialect—standing in front of his Pietà. He went to their side to eavesdrop.

"I tell you I recognize the work," cried the mother. "It is by that fellow from Osteno, who makes all the tombstones."

Her husband said, "No, no, it is that Cristoforo Solari from Milan. He has done many of them."

That night Michelangelo entered St. Peter's, took a candle

and put it in the wire loop of his hat; he took up his hammer and chisel, leaned forward, and on the band going across the Virgin's bosom he cut in swift, decorative letters:

MICHAEL·AĜLVS·BONAR⊕VS·FL⊕EN FACEBAT
Michelangelo Buonarroti of Florence made this.

He returned to his rooms, despondent. Then he and Argiento packed up, rented mules and set out for Florence.

BOOK SIX

The Giant

BACK IN FLORENCE with no funds, he was obliged to send Argiento to board at his family's farm and go himself to live with his father. Lucrezia's death had aged Lodovico, his face was thin, his cheeks sunken.

As Gallo had predicted, nothing had come of the business Michelangelo had set up for his brothers. Buonarroto was working in a wool shop, Giovansimone apathetically took jobs, then disappeared after a few weeks. Sigismondo was earning a few scudi as a professional soldier, Lionardo had disappeared.

Michelangelo climbed the Settignano hills to see the Topolinos. There were now five grandchildren. He learned that Contessina and her husband had been banished from Florence; they lived in a peasant's house in Fiesole.

The city had undergone many changes in the almost five years he had been gone. People bowed their heads in shame when they passed the spot where Savonarola's body had been burned; at the same time they were trying to replace what Savonarola had destroyed. Artists who had fled the city had returned; they had organized a club called "The Company of the Cauldron," restricted to twelve members. Each was allowed to bring guests to a monthly dinner in the painter Rustici's studio. Granacci was a member and invited Michelangelo to accompany him. Michelangelo refused, preferring to wait until he had a commission.

He went to the Duomo workshop to talk to Beppe and study the thin, seventeen-foot Duccio column. At night he read in the Old Testament, looking for a heroic theme. He heard that many had favored giving the commission to Leonardo da Vinci; but Leonardo had rejected it on the ground that he despised marble sculpture as an inferior art, good only for stonecutters. Michelangelo, who admired Leonardo's work, was relieved to have him out of the running, but he resented this statement.

One day he went at dawn to the Duomo workshop. The diagonal beams of first sunlight streamed across the marble, projecting his shadow up the full seventeen-foot height of the column, turning him into a giant. He caught his breath. "This is how David must have felt," he told himself, "on that morning when he stepped forth to face Goliath." He had his theme now: a Giant for the symbol of Florence! For days he drew, seeking a David worthy of the Biblical legend. He submitted design after design to Gonfaloniere Piero Soderini, governor of Florence; to the Wool Guild; to the Board of Works of the Duomo. But nothing happened, and he was burning up with marble fever.

Jacopo Gallo was still working for him in Rome. One day a letter arrived from him, telling Michelangelo that Cardinal Piccolomini was giving him a contract for some statues for his family altar in the cathedral of Siena. "I must warn you," Gallo wrote, "that it is not the kind of commission you want or deserve."

Michelangelo's face dropped as he read on to learn that he would have to carve fifteen small figures, all fully clothed, to fit into narrow niches. The pay was five hundred ducats with no advance, and he could take no other contract for three years.

"How do they think you can buy supplies?" Lodovico said, hearing this. "Do they think the money is coming from me?"

"No, Father, I'm sure they know better than that."

"Thanks to God! Gallo must make it part of the contract that they advance you one hundred gold ducats."

Michelangelo ran out the door and hurried to Soderini's office. It was a magnificent room, its ceiling painted with the lilies of Florence, the oaken desk massive. *"Ben venuto,"* Soderini murmured. "What brings you here?"

"Troubles, Gonfaloniere," replied Michelangelo.

"That's why the gonfaloniere sits behind such a capacious desk: so that it can hold all the problems of Florence."

"It is your shoulders that are broad."

Soderini ducked his head deprecatingly. He was not handsome, with his long, pointed chin and hooked nose, but he was an honest man who could induce opposing factions to work together. Michelangelo told him how much he longed to do his Giant, how he disliked the Piccolomini contract.

Soderini said thoughtfully, "This is not a good time to force things. Cesare Borgia is threatening to conquer Florence. Last night, we bought him off—for thirty-six thousand gold florins."

"Blackmail," said Michelangelo.

Soderini's face turned red. "Many kiss the hand they wish to see cut off. The guilds have to provide this money; so the Wool Guild is hardly in a mood to discuss sculpture. Hadn't you better be more receptive to the Piccolomini offer? For Florence, for you as an artist, one law prevails: survival."

But at Santo Spirito, Prior Bichiellini pushed his papers aside, his eyes blazing.

"Survival on what plane? To stay alive as an animal stays alive? For shame! The Michelangelo I knew six years ago could never think, 'Better mediocre work than no work at all.' Don't take the commission. Don't squander these God-given years." Then, as Michelangelo hung his head in shame, he went on quietly, "I moralize only because it is my duty to be concerned with your character."

But in his studio Granacci said, "Without work, Michelangelo, you are the most wretched creature alive. Do as many figures as you have time for. Then, when something better comes along, take it."

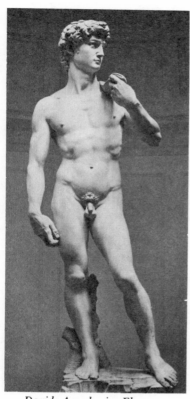

David; Accademia, Florence

He returned to the drawing board, to sketch saints for Cardinal Piccolomini's contract; he finally carved two of the statues, St. Peter and St. Paul, while his sculptor friend Baccio did two more figures for him. This should be enough to earn him a respite. Meanwhile, he could think of nothing but the Duccio column and the Giant David. In I Kings, he read David's answer when Saul questioned the wisdom of his challenging Goliath: *My Lord, I used to feed my father's flock; and if lion or bear came and carried off one of my rams, I would go in pursuit, and get the mastery and snatch the prey from their jaws. . . . Lion or bear, my Lord, I would slay them.* "Lion or bear, I would slay them." What strength and courage! Yet earlier artists had shown such delicate, almost feminine Davids.

At dawn he carried his measuring equipment to the Duomo workyard. Other sculptors had now given up on the block; it had been gouged so deeply, midway on its height, that they said it would break in two. He must try to design a David whose thighs, the shortest distance across the body, could be fitted safely into the narrow section of the marble that was left.

"For fifty years I watch sculptors measure across here," commented Beppe. "Always they say, 'Too bad. No figure will fit.' "

"Look, Beppe. Suppose we were to swivel the hips *away* from this narrow area, and use a strong, outpushing wrist or hand to compensate?"

Beppe scratched his behind.

"Ah," cried Michelangelo, "you think it might work! I can tell how pleased you are by what part of your anatomy you scratch."

Days passed, and a courier from Rome brought the final Piccolomini contract. Jacopo Gallo had secured an advance of a hundred ducats. It contained the crowning indignity: "A figure of St. Francis has already been sculptured by Torrigiani, who left the draperies and head unfinished. Michelangelo will complete the statue in Siena. . . ."

"So Torrigiani went to Siena," Michelangelo cried to Granacci. "Think of the ignominy of my scavenging after him!"

"Let's just say that Torrigiani could not finish even one figure adequately, and so the cardinal had to turn to you. Why don't you go to Siena? You'll feel better."

He left that day.

TORRIGIANI HAD LEFT Siena; Michelangelo finished redesigning his lifeless St. Francis with all the love and skill at his command. Then Soderini sent for him to return at once to Florence: the Wool Guild and the cathedral had finally commissioned his Giant. Soderini told him, "When we realized that our best Florentine carver was bound by a Sienese cardinal, we asked, 'Does Siena suppose that Florence does not appreciate its own artists?' Out of patriotic duty, we ask you to postpone the rest of the Piccolomini contract, and take over the Duccio block."

Fighting down the thought of what the cardinal would think of him, he let joy carry him up the hills to the Topolinos. "Listen," he called out. "The Duccio column—it's mine!"

"We should be able to trust you now with window frames," teased the father.

Michelangelo turned to the mother. *"Madre mia,* how is Contessina?"

"She is frail. People are forbidden to help them." She made the eloquent Tuscan gesture of hopelessness, her hands circling out and down. "The hatred of Piero still poisons."

Michelangelo put wood in the forge, lit it, and fashioned a set of small chisels and hammers. Then, taking a small piece of *pietra serena,* he bade the Topolinos farewell, and rode to Fiesole. He tied his horse to an olive tree on a slope and looked down at the Ridolfi family on the small stone-paved terrace in front of their cottage.

Contessina was sitting on a cane-backed chair, a baby at her breast, a six-year-old playing at her feet. He called softly: "It is I, Michelangelo Buonarroti, come to visit."

Contessina covered her breast. "Michelangelo! Come down, come down. The path is over to the right."

Ridolfi lifted his proud, bitter face in the constrained silence as Michelangelo made his way down the path with the toy chisels, hammers and marble.

"Yesterday I received the Duccio column," he said. "I had to come to tell you. Besides, your oldest son must now be six. It is time he started learning to carve; I shall be his teacher."

Ridolfi's stern mouth twitched with amusement. He said, "You are kind to come to us. You know that we are pariahs."

Ridolfi was short of thirty, but ostracism and bitterness were already ravaging his face. Though he had not been involved in the conspiracy to bring back Piero de' Medici, he was known to despise the Republic.

It was good to be with Contessina again, to gaze into those dark eyes. Had they not loved each other, if only with the love of children? She divined his thoughts; she always had. She turned to her son. "Luigi, would you like to learn to carve?"

"Can I help you with the new statue, Michelangelo?"

"I will teach you as Bertoldo taught me in your grandfather's garden. Now, hammer in one hand, chisel in the other—"

It was midnight when he reached home. His father was awake.

"So! Finally you come to your father with the news. What price will they pay? How long will it take to carve?"

"Six florins a month. Two years."

Lodovico said, "But that adds up to only a hundred and forty-four florins."

"The Board will pay more when I'm finished, if in their conscience they think I deserve it."

"Their conscience! Don't you know that a Tuscan's conscience stops short of his belt? The Piccolomini contract pays more than double this. We cannot afford to make a large charitable contribution to the Wool Guild and the Duomo."

Michelangelo said quietly, "Father, I am going to carve the David."

But Lodovico continued to complain. Later, Buonarroto asked: "Before the argument, how many florins a month were you planning to pay Father?"

"Three. Half for him, half for me."

"And now you have agreed to give him five."

Michelangelo sighed. "What can I do? He looks so old and white. Besides, the Board is paying my costs. Still, you're right about father. I am his quarry."

GRANACCI LAUNCHED A celebration party for Michelangelo at a meeting of the Company of the Cauldron in Rustici's studio. There were chains of sausages, cold beef, suckling pig, demijohns of Chianti. Soggi had contributed an enormous basin of pickled pigs' feet. The entire Ghirlandaio studio was there together with the Medici garden apprentices; all the best-known sculptors and painters, craftsmen, architects, government officials, and the Boards of the Wool Guild and the Duomo. The huge assemblage spilled out of Rustici's studio into the square, where acrobats and wrestlers entertained, musicians and minstrels chanted songs, and young people danced. Everyone wrung Michelangelo's hand, pounded him on the back and insisted upon drinking a toast with him. The party lasted until dawn; and before it ended, two incidents occurred which would affect the pattern of Michelangelo's life.

First, the aged painter, Cosimo Rosselli, announced his resignation from the Company and nominated Michelangelo to succeed him; he was instantly accepted. He had belonged to no group since the Medici sculpture garden. He remembered his lonely childhood, how difficult it had been for him to make friends. Now all the artists of Florence, even those who had long waited to be invited into the Company, were applauding his election.

The second incident was begun, unwittingly, by Leonardo da Vinci. Michelangelo had often seen him around Florence. He carried his head aristocratically, the broad forehead topped by reddish hair worn to his shoulders; and he had a chin carved out of the Carrara marble he despised, a flawless nose, cool blue eyes of a piercing intelligence; and the fair complexion of a country girl. He was always dressed in regal splendor, a rose-colored cloak, lace about his neck and wrists.

When Michelangelo spoke of this to Rustici, Rustici said, "Don't be fooled by his exterior. Leonardo has a magnificent brain. He is a mathematician, an expert on anatomy, a geologist, an engineer and an inventor. Even now he is completing experiments for a machine that will fly through the air as the birds do. He dresses like the nobility to try to make the world forget that he is the illegitimate son of an innkeeper's daughter. Actually, he is the only man in Florence who works as hard and long as you do."

Now, Michelangelo could hear Leonardo's high-pitched voice declaring: "I refused to compete for the Duccio block because sculpture is a mechanical art. It is much less intellectual than painting. Sculpture is for laborers: sculptors end the day as filthy as plasterers."

A rage rose in Michelangelo, not just for himself but for all sculptors. He took a vow: one day he would make Leonardo eat those words.

NEXT MORNING BEPPE gave him a raucous welcome. "So you own the Duccio block. The Board of Works say give him everything he wants: marble, chisels, pretty girls. . . ."

Michelangelo laughed, bringing the artisans running. They welcomed him to the yard, and then with block and tackle and rollers moved the two-thousand-pound column to Michelangelo's own section of the yard, by a private gate.

Now he could finally think out his David. He would be the incarnation of everything Lorenzo had fought for: not a sinful creature living only for salvation in the next life, but a man with faith in his own kind, with a brain and a will. His David would be the most fully realized man the world had yet seen, functioning in a rational and humane world.

When did David become truly a giant? After killing Goliath? Or at the moment he decided that he must try? For Michelangelo, it was David's decision that made him a giant, not his killing of Goliath. This was the David he was seeking, caught at the exultant height of resolution.

He began to model a clay figure, eighteen inches high, and

with astonishing facility he knew where the David lay in his block. Its limitations began to seem assets.

Every now and then he would climb the hill to Fiesole to give Luigi a lesson. He was a bright-faced, handsome child, with Contessina's alert mind. "You are wonderful with Luigi," she remarked. "Sometime you must have your own son."

He shook his head. "Like most artists, I wander: to Rome, Siena, Bologna. That is no life for a family."

"It goes deeper than that," said Contessina in her small, sure voice. "Marble is your marriage. The Bacchus, Pietà, David are your children. But while you are here, Luigi will be your son."

MEANTIME GUILIANO DA SANGALLO had returned to Florence. "Have you heard of any architectural jobs here?" he asked.

"Design me a revolving table strong enough to turn a two-thousand-pound column of marble," said Michelangelo, "so I can control the light on my work. And a fifteen-foot scaffold in which I can change the height and work all around the block."

Sangallo was amused. "Let's get pen and paper. What you need is a series of four towers, with open shelves that take planks from either direction. As for your turntable . . . "

BEPPE'S CREW ROPED the column, attached a block and tackle and slowly raised it to stand upright on Sangallo's turntable. Michelangelo and Argiento then built the scaffold towers.

Now the column cried out to him. His tools tore into it, searching for elbows, thighs, chest. The white crystals that had lain dormant for half a century yielded to every touch, from the subtlest nuance to the driving "Go!" in which his hammer and chisel swept upward from the ankle past the knee and thigh without stopping.

This was his most glorious experience in working marble; he could not bring himself to stop for food or change of clothes. He fed his marble hunger twenty hours a day, the acrid dust coagulating in his nostrils, his hair white with it, the vibrations running from the chisels and hammer through his body long after he had thrown himself across his bed in exultant exhaustion.

At Christmas, he accompanied his family to High Mass at Santa Croce; the New Year he ignored. Argiento turned the table to catch the light, moved the plank platform up and down, forward and back as Michelangelo worked the four sides of the frame simultaneously. The neck was so tremendous he could work it without fear of the head breaking off.

Soderini came into the yard to observe progress. He knew that Michelangelo would have no peace at home until a price was set on the finished David. Toward the middle of February, he suggested that the Boards see the work. They came and were pleased. They gave Michelangelo four hundred florins with the stipulation that he complete the work to perfection within two years. "Now I can forget money," Michelangelo said. "That is paradise."

The figure began to push out of its mass, striving to define itself in space. His own pace matched the drive of the material, so that Soderini, visiting him of a Sunday afternoon, was staggered by his passion. "I've been watching fragments hurled four feet in the air," he said, "until I thought the whole marble would fly to pieces."

The one thorn in Michelangelo's flesh was Leonardo da Vinci's constant belittling of the sculptor's art. But one day he learned that Leonardo, together with Torrigiani and Piero de' Medici, had joined the army of Cesare Borgia, who was helping to incite a rebellion in Tuscany against Florentine rule. Michelangelo was outraged. "He's a traitor," he cried angrily to Rustici.

Rustici shook his head wistfully.

"You two stand like the Apennines above the rest of us, yet you hate each other. It doesn't make sense. Or does it?"

TOWARD THE END OF April, Soderini asked Michelangelo if he would carve the Twelve Apostles in marble for the Duomo.

Michelangelo said, "But it's a lifetime of work!"

"So were Ghiberti's doors. It would make you the official sculptor of Florence. The contract includes a house and studio."

"A house of my own!"

"I thought that would please you. You could do one Apostle a year; each year, you would own another twelfth of your house."

Michelangelo went to Sangallo, who said, "You can't turn down the Florentine government. Take the contract, build your house, carve as many Apostles as you can. When you're through, simply buy the rest of the house in cash."

"Another Piccolomini contract," said Michelangelo mournfully, thinking of all he had already promised to do.

But next day he signed the papers. He returned home to find the Buonarroti excitedly planning their new house. "Get it built quickly," said his father. "The faster we move in, the sooner we stop paying rent here."

Michelangelo spoke without emotion. "This is to be my home. And my workshop. It is not to be the family residence."

There was a stunned silence. Then his father, uncle and aunt all began talking at once. "But your home is our home. We can save rent. Who will cook and clean . . . "

The storm lasted the rest of the day, but Michelangelo was adamant; the least he could get out of the contract was privacy.

THE FIRST FRUIT of his contract to become Florence's official sculptor was a visit from Agnolo Doni, whom he had known as a boy. Doni had made a fortune in the wool business, and risen so high in the social world of Florence that he was now engaged to Maddalena Strozzi. He wanted Michelangelo to do a Holy Family as a wedding present for his bride-to-be.

Michelangelo flushed with pleasure; Maddalena had been brought up with his statue of Hercules in the Strozzi *palazzo*.

"A Holy Family in marble . . . " he mused.

"Who said anything about marble?" Doni said. "That would cost a lot. I want a painting."

"But why come to me? I haven't painted for years."

"Pure loyalty. We are of the same quarter. What do you say? Thirty florins. Ten for each figure. That's generous, isn't it?"

"I don't know how much a painter would charge you, Doni."

"Look, Buonarroti. I want you to paint it. It is well known that to carve marble is to be only a fraction of an artist."

"Enough." Michelangelo was furious at this echoing of Leonardo. "I'll paint it. For one hundred gold florins."

"One hundred!" screamed Doni. "How can you cheat one of your oldest friends? The playmate of your youth!"

They compromised on seventy florins; but by the crafty smile in Doni's shrewd eyes, Michelangelo perceived that Doni had outshouted him and would have paid the hundred.

He had been an idiot to let the man goad him into this; yet his interest was piqued. A Holy Family, he thought, should be earthy, a family of simple people.

He tramped the roads of Tuscany on hot summer days, sketching the farmers in the fields, the country mothers nursing their young. He drew for his Holy Family a strong-limbed young girl, a red-cheeked child, a bearded grandfather, and he arranged them in an affectionate grouping on the grass. To amuse himself, he painted a sea on one side of the family, mountains on the other; then he drew five nude youths, like a Greek frieze behind them.

Doni's face went red when he saw the picture.

"Show me one thing that is holy about this picture of peasants! One sentiment that is religious! You're mocking me! I cannot give this picnic on the grass to my delicate bride."

"Remember, you did not reserve the right of rejection."

Doni's eyes narrowed to slits. He cried in horror: "What are those five naked boys doing in my Holy Family?"

"They've just come out from a swim in the sea," replied Michelangelo calmly. "If I wanted to be greedy I could charge you fifty florins extra for them. But I won't, because we are of the same quarter."

Doni stormed out. The next day his servant arrived with a pouch of thirty-five florins, half the agreed price. Michelangelo sent Argiento back with the pouch and a note: *The Holy Family will now cost you one hundred and forty florins.*

Florence placed bets on who would win, with Michelangelo on the short end of the odds because no one had ever bested Doni. However, he had bragged all over town that he was having Florence's official artist paint a wedding gift for his bride. He came to the Duomo with a purse of seventy florins, crying: "Here's your money, give me my painting."

"Doni, you hate the picture. I'll release you from your agreement."

"Don't try to outwit me. I'll force you to fulfill your contract. You agreed to paint the picture for seventy."

"And you reopened the negotiations by offering me thirty-five florins. My price is now one hundred and forty."

"I'll see you hanged from the Bargello first," screamed Doni.

Michelangelo decided he had had his fun, was about to send the painting to Doni when a boy brought him a note: *Maddalena wants your painting. She has said no wedding present will please her more. Contessina.*

He chuckled, sat down at his workbench, and wrote a note to Doni: *As an old friend, I will release you from any financial embarrassment by giving the Holy Family to another friend.*

Doni came running, and poured the hundred and forty gold pieces onto the worktable. He picked up the painting and left, grumbling, "Artists! Supposed to be impractical. Ha!"

Michelangelo gathered up the coins. He had enjoyed the whole affair. It was as refreshing as a vacation.

THERE WAS REJOICING in August when the Borgia Pope, Alexander VI, died. But when Cardinal Piccolomini was elected to the papacy, Michelangelo was apprehensive. He had done no further work on the Piccolomini statues. One word from the new Pope, and he would have to leave the David until the figures were completed.

For a month he worked in a frenzy. Only David's head remained. Then he was saved. Piccolomini died at the end of one month as Pope Pius III, and Cardinal Rovere was elected Pope Julius II.

Leonardo da Vinci returned from Cesare Borgia's army. At once, he was awarded a commission to create a fresco for the Great Hall of the Signoria. The payment was to be ten thousand florins!

Michelangelo was livid. This was the largest and most important painting commission given by Florence in decades. Ten thousand to Leonardo for a fresco! Four hundred to him for the

Giant David! Leonardo—who would have helped Cesare Borgia conquer Tuscany!

He ran in his rage to Soderini's office. Soderini heard him out; he also allowed a few moments of silence for Michelangelo to hear his angry words echoing off the walls before answering: "Leonardo is the greatest painter in Italy. I have seen his Last Supper in Milan. Frankly, I covet it. If he paints a fresco for Florence, it will enrich us all enormously."

Reproved and dismissed, Michelangelo went back to his David. Winter came on, and in January 1504 he learned that Piero de' Medici had drowned while fighting with the French army against Spain, in the hope of securing French help against Florence. Michelangelo had a moment of pity as he remembered Lorenzo, on his deathbed, telling Piero how to rule Florence. Then he was conscious that Piero's death meant that Contessina was nearer to being released from her exile.

He concentrated on finishing his David, and a committee of artists decided that it should be placed in front of the Signoria. The statue was to be carried upright, in a sling, inside a big wooden frame. Encased in a net of enormous ropes, lifted by grapples, it was moved suspended inside the open cage. The wall behind the workshed was ripped out, the cage raised onto round logs for its mile-long journey through the streets. Forty men dragged the huge crate, moving it but a few feet an hour, with hundreds of people watching the procession. They had maneuvered only as far as a sharp turn into the Via del Proconsolo when darkness fell. Next morning, work started again and went on all day and the next day. It was the evening of the fourth day when the David finally arrived at its destination at the foot of the Signoria steps. There it stood in all its majestic grace, lighting up the Signoria with pure white light. Michelangelo stood below the figure, feeling insignificant, and powerless now that the statue was out of his hands.

Next morning he woke refreshed and returned to the Signoria. A crowd was standing below the David in silence. Fluttering from the statue were pieces of paper stuck to the marble. He had seen this sight in Rome, when people had pasted up verses denouncing the Borgias on the door of the Vatican, or affixed their smoldering complaints to a statue.

He walked through the crowd, trying to read their expressions. When he came to the David, he climbed up on the base and began taking off the papers. His eyes began to mist as he read them: *You have given us back our self-respect. . . . We are proud to be Florentines. . . . How magnificent is man!*

His eye caught a familiar handwriting. He read: *Everything my father hoped to accomplish for Florence is expressed in your David. C.*

Contessina had made her way into the city at night, past the guards. She had taken the risk to join her voice to that of Florence.

He turned to the crowd gazing up at him. There was silence in the square, and yet he felt complete communication, as though they read one another's thoughts. They were a part of him, every Florentine standing below, eyes turned up to him, and he was a part of them.

MEANWHILE, HIS HOUSE was being planned and the Topolinos were soon cutting *pietra serena* according to his specifications. When the blocks were ready the entire family built the house on a corner lot in Florence beside a monastery. Michelangelo painted the interior walls in warm blues, rose and orange, hung his earliest Madonna and Child in his bedroom and installed his Centaurs in the family room.

He worked joyfully now on a St. Matthew for the Duomo, on a new Madonna and Child commissioned by some cloth merchants of Bruges. These smaller, compact figures came almost without effort after the overpowering massiveness of the David.

Prior Bichiellini came to give Michelangelo's new house the traditional blessing. He knelt, spoke a prayer to the Madonna. Then he rose, put both hands on Michelangelo's shoulders. "This Madonna could not have evolved in such tender purity if you were not pure in heart. Bless you and this workshop."

After that came the happiest time he had known. Cesare Borgia, seriously ill, had ceased to be a menace to Florence. There was a spirit of confidence and energy in the air. Trade was

booming; the government under Soderini was stable and secure. Michelangelo's David, called the Giant by most Florentines, was accepted by the city as its new symbol and protector. A few months short of thirty, Michelangelo seemed to have reached the full expression and acceptance for which he had yearned.

But in May Leonardo da Vinci, rebuked by the Signoria for neglecting his fresco, had started to work on the cartoon for it in earnest. The cartoon quickly became the talk of Florence: artists

flocked to it to study, admire, copy. Word went around the city that something wondrous was in the making. Michelangelo began to perceive that he was being superseded. Florence proudly proclaimed Leonardo "the first artist of Tuscany."

This was bitter medicine to Michelangelo. He went to see the Leonardo cartoon for the Battle of Anghiari: it was tremendous! Leonardo, who loved horses, had created a masterpiece of the horse at war, ridden by men in ancient Roman armor, men and horses alike caught up in bloodthirsty conflict.

Michelangelo was forced to admit that Leonardo was a great painter, perhaps the greatest the world had yet seen. Instead of reconciling him, this inflamed him the more. He knew that he himself was the best draftsman in all Italy, but he would have to prove it. Leonardo's fresco was to occupy the right half of the eastern wall of the Great Hall. He would ask Soderini for the left half. Then Florence could say who was the first artist of the time!

When he presented himself at Soderini's office and told him why he had come, Soderini cried, "But that is unreasonable! You've told me yourself that you never liked fresco."

"But I can paint fresco better than Leonardo," he said doggedly. "This would be a great *palio* between us, a race."

Soderini shook his head. "You already have a contract with the Wool Guild and Duomo to carve the Twelve Apostles. That's why we built you that house and studio."

"I'll carve them. But the other half of the wall must be mine. You are a wise and persuasive gonfaloniere who will persuade the city to appropriate another ten thousand florins for my painting."

To persuade the Signoria to spend this sum, and to delight the

Wool and Duomo Boards enough to release him from his contract for a year, he knew he would have to paint a scene of Florentine pride and glory. He remembered a scene from Florence's conquest of Pisa. The Florentine forces had stopped on the bank of the Arno on a hot summer day. A number of soldiers, having shed their heavy armor, were bathing in the river, while others were sunbathing on the grass. Suddenly a guard cried: "We are lost! The Pisans are about to attack!" The Florentines scrambled out of the river to find their armor, their weapons, in time to beat back the Pisan attacks.

He went to the Street of the Stationers, bought the largest squares of paper he could find. Three days later he fitted together on the floor beside Soderini's desk a dozen large sheets with twenty male figures, drawn with bold slashing lines. Soderini studied the drawings in silence. When he looked up, Michelangelo recognized the affectionate regard in which Soderini held him.

"I was wrong to discourage you. This fresco can be as revolutionary as the David. I'm going to get you this commission."

And so he did, for a sum of three thousand florins, less than a third of Leonardo da Vinci's pay.

He set to work at once on the cartoon he called "The Bathers." By New Year's Day, only three months after he had started it, it was completed. Argiento, Granacci and Michelangelo stretched and tacked it to a light frame against the rear wall. It filled the room with desperately challenged men, with fear, terror, hopelessness; but all the manly emotions surging upward to overcome surprise and disaster by swift purposeful action.

Painters came to see the miracle he had wrought. Ghirlandaio's son, Ridolfo, and Andrea del Sarto asked if they might sketch; and one day a young man named Raphael Sanzio appeared. Michelangelo liked Raphael immediately. He had a sensitive and patrician face, yet altogether manly. He said: "This makes painting a different art. I shall have to start over again. What I have learned from Leonardo is no longer sufficient."

He asked if he might move his materials and work before the cartoon. Without willing it, Michelangelo found himself at the head of a school of talented young apprentices.

It was at this moment that a summons to Rome arrived from Pope Julius II. It was a bad time for him to leave, for he wanted to transfer the cartoon to the Signoria wall; he also must carve the Apostle Matthew to start to pay for his house.

He reported the summons to Soderini, who said: "You cannot refuse the Pope. His friendship is important to Florence. We will hold your contracts in abeyance while you are gone. When you start the Apostles again, you shall have your house back."

MICHELANGELO HAD ONLY to enter Rome's Porta del Popolo to see and smell the startling changes. Gaping walls and abandoned houses had been torn down so that the streets could be widened and repaved; the swine market had been cleaned out of the Roman forum. New buildings were under construction.

He found Giuliano da Sangallo, who had been called to Rome several months earlier, living in one of the many palaces belonging to Pope Julius II. A big music room had been converted to a draftsmen's workshop. Here half a dozen young apprentices were working on plans for rebuilding Rome.

Sangallo, now official architect of Rome, appeared twenty years younger than when Michelangelo had last seen him: he had the air of a man fulfilling himself. "I have waited these many months to welcome you to Rome," he said. "The Holy Father is eager to see you."

"I still don't know what the Pope wants me to carve!"

"A tomb. Not just *a* tomb; his own tomb."

"A tomb!" groaned Michelangelo. "Oh no!"

"The Holy Father wants you to carve more than thirty heroic marbles. You'll be the first sculptor to have that many in one place since Phidias did the Parthenon frieze."

Sangallo took him to see Julius II, who was sitting on an emormous purple-backed throne, surrounded by his secretary, two masters of ceremonies, cardinals, bishops and ambassadors, all waiting their turn for a private word.

The sixty-two-year-old pontiff, a member of the great Rovere family, was the first Pope to wear a beard, now streaked with white. He was an honest, blunt, hot-tempered man; Michelangelo felt his enormous energy as he waved them in. They knelt and kissed his ring. "I have seen your Pietà in St. Peter's," the Pope said. "That is where I wish my tomb to be erected."

"Could Your Holiness stipulate where in St. Peter's?"

"In the center," Julius replied coldly.

"Would you speak, Holy Father, about your wishes for the tomb? I must build on the foundation of Your Holiness' desires."

This remark pleased Julius. He began pouring out plans, ideas. "I desire a bronze frieze around all four sides of the tomb. Bronze is best for storytelling; through it you can relate the important episodes of my life."

Michelangelo locked his teeth, wanting to exclaim, "To tell stories is for those who sing ballads." But he said nothing.

Next morning he walked to St. Peter's, overjoyed to see that it was now securely braced. He went to see his Pietà, and ran his fingertips over it; it was warm to his touch. Then he entered the main basilica and gazed at the altar in the center, under which was the tomb of St. Peter. He walked about, wondering where in the central nave there could be a place for Julius' tomb among the ninety-two other Popes buried there.

He rented an apartment at an inn, and set to work designing the tomb, a three-storied affair thirty-six feet long, twenty-three feet wide, thirty feet high.

Moses, the lawgiver, symbolizing the maturity of man, would occupy one corner of the first story; in the opposite corner he would put the Apostle Paul, who had laid the foundations of the Church. These two would dominate the tomb.

On the level above them would be four male Captives, shoulders and heads towering over the columns to which they were bound. There would be figures of Victors too, the uncrushables, struggling, hoping, conquering. The storytelling bronze frieze would be a narrow band. The true frieze would be these magnificent nude figures extending around the four sides of the tomb.

His agent, Jacopo Gallo, was furious at this elaborate concept. "Who is to carve these cherubs below the Victors?" he asked. "And these angels holding up the Pope's sarcophagus? You would have to hire a whole studio full of helpers; then your own good figures will be surrounded by so much mediocrity they will be lost. And these endless chains of decorative sausages . . . "

"They're rows of garlands."

"And why a bronze frieze on a marble tomb?"

"The Pope wanted it."

"And if the Pope wants you to stand on your head in the Piazza Navona, you'll do that too?" Then Gallo's manner softened. He said, *"Caro mio,* how many statues alone are indicated here?"

"About forty."

"How long did you carve on the Pietà?"

"Two years."

"The David?"

"Three."

"Then these forty figures on the tomb will take you between eighty and a hundred years."

"I've learned my craft and can work fast. I'll be all right."

Gallo shot him a piercing look. "Will you? Let's make sure." He reached for a batch of papers. "Here are the contracts I drew for the Pietà, and the Piccolomini altar. We'll write the best clauses from each." He glanced through the contracts. "Now, if I know the Pope, he will want the tomb completed immediately. Hold out for ten years, more if you can. As for price, he drives a hard bargain because he is financing an army. Don't take a scudo less than twenty thousand ducats."

When he next visited the Pope, Michelangelo was taken aback to find Sangallo's rival, the architect Bramante, there. He disliked at first sight the pale-green eyes, snub nose and rosebud mouth; the bullneck and heavy shoulders. He felt uneasy; why should the architect Bramante examine sculpture drawings?

Julius spread the sketches eagerly before him. "It is even more imposing than I had dreamed," he said. "Bramante, will it not be the most beautiful mausoleum in Rome?"

"In all Christendom, Holy Father," replied Bramante.

"Buonarroti, Sangallo says you wish to choose the marbles

yourself in Carrara. Set out immediately. One thousand ducats will be provided to you for the purchase of the stones."

There was a moment of silence. Michelangelo asked respectfully, "And for the sculpturing, Your Holiness?"

"The Papal Treasurer will pay you ten thousand ducats when the tomb is completed."

Michelangelo gulped, heard Gallo's voice . . . but how could he demand double what the Holy Father had offered? The thousand ducats would barely pay for the marble and get it to Rome. But he wanted to carve these marbles!

"Holy Father, may I speak of the time for completion? If I could have a minimum of ten years—"

"Impossible!" thundered Julius. "It is my dearest wish to see the tomb completed. I will grant you five years."

Forty marble carvings in five years! But one could no more bargain with the pontiff over time than over money. He would manage. . . . He had the power of ten ordinary sculptors. He bowed his head. "All will be done, Holy Father, as you say. And now may I presume to ask that a contract be drawn?"

There was a peculiar silence. The Pope glared, then replied only: "You and Sangallo must visit St. Peter's now to determine the proper place for the tomb. Bramante will accompany you, to give you the benefit of his advice."

The three men soon found that there was simply no room in the basilica for so imposing a tomb. They went outside. In the rear were a number of possible buildings, built over the centuries since St. Peter's had first been erected by Constantine in 319. "But for a tomb as original as yours," said Sangallo, "we must have a new building, designed to fit the tomb."

Hope revived in Michelangelo's bosom.

"I will design it," Sangallo continued. "Here on this eminence there is sufficient space if we clear out these wooden structures and decaying shrines. It would be visible from the city below."

To Michelangelo's surprise, Bramante's eyes were sparkling with approval. "You like the idea, Bramante?" he asked.

"He is right. What is needed is a beautiful new church."

Sangallo beamed with pleasure. But when Michelangelo turned to Bramante to thank him, the architect's eyes had gone opaque, and there was a twitching at one corner of his mouth.

BOOK SEVEN

The Pope

HE HAD NO WAY of knowing, during his stay in the mountains of Carrara, that his years of relative peace were over. He returned to Rome at the end of 1505 to find that Jacopo Gallo had died during his absence; how different Rome felt without him!

He desperately missed his friend's counsel now, for a war between himself and the Pope had begun. Bramante had persuaded Julius to abandon the idea of a separate chapel for his tomb; instead a new St. Peter's was to rise on the hill, incorporating the old one, the design to be chosen through public competition. Michelangelo had spent the Pope's entire thousand ducats for marble and shipping, and Julius refused to give him more money until he had seen one of the statues. When Julius provided him with a house, he was told he would have to pay several ducats a month for its use.

"Could I wait until I am paid something by the Holy Father before I pay him rent?" he asked caustically.

The Guffattis came with the family wagon to carry his marble from the docks to the rear portico of the house. Michelangelo paid them out of a loan from Balducci, Gallo's successor as manager-owner of the bank. Sangallo recommended an elderly carpenter named Cosimo as Michelangelo's assistant. His cooking tasted of resin and shavings, but he helped Michelangelo build a wooden model of the first two floors of the tomb. A young muralist named Piero Roselli joined the establishment. Twice a week he went to the market to buy clams, mussels, shrimp, squid and sea bass, cooking *cacciucco,* a spicy fish stew, over the fire.

To buy a forge, Swedish iron and chestnut for his tools, Michelangelo had to ask Balducci for more money. "I don't mind making a second loan," said Balducci. "But when do you expect to put this tomb on a businesslike basis?"

"As soon as I have some carving to show the Pope."

"But that could take months! Be sensible, go to the Pope. From a bad paymaster, get what you can."

But Sangallo did not think it a good time to ask the Pope for money because he was busy judging the plans for St. Peter's. As it turned out, Sangallo lost the commission, which went to Bramante. Bramante bought an old palace close to the Vatican, and rebuilt it with simple elegance. Leo Baglioni took Michelangelo there. The place was already jammed with courtiers from the Vatican, princes of the Church, nobles, artists, merchants, bankers. Bramante held court, his green eyes crackling with triumph.

Baglioni and Michelangelo went to Bramante's workroom to see his drawings for the new St. Peter's. Michelangelo gasped: it was an edifice to dwarf the Duomo, yet of an elegant, lyrical design, noble in conception. By comparison Sangallo's entry in the competition, a dome over a square, seemed ponderous.

That night, as he lay cold and sleepless in his bed, it became obvious to him that the chapel for the Julius tomb would never be built. Bramante had used Sangallo's and Michelangelo's ideas for his own purpose: the building of a new cathedral. St. Peter's would be a glorious abode for the tomb. But would Bramante allow it there?

In spite of his worries, Michelangelo had the Guffatti family set three giant columns upright for the Moses and the Captives. Pope Julius and Bramante would lay the cornerstone of the new St. Peter's on April 18. When workmen began digging the wide hole into which the Pope would descend to bless the laying of the first stone, Michelangelo realized that the sacred old basilica, instead of being incorporated in it, would be demolished to make room for the new church.

He was outspoken in his disapproval: he felt that it was

sacrilege to destroy the earliest temple of Christendom in Rome. Finally, Baglioni warned him that some of Bramante's coterie were saying that unless he stopped attacking their friend his tomb might be built before that of the Pope.

Bills continued to mount, and finally Michelangelo was forced to approach Pope Julius again. His bristling beard protruding from a high ermine collar, Julius sat in his throne room surrounded by courtiers. Beside him was a jeweler, whom he scolded and sent abruptly away. When the gem cutter had retired, Michelangelo made his plea.

"Return Monday," said the Pope curtly.

He had been dimissed like the tradesman! He went to Baglioni, who told him: "Bramante has now convinced the Pope that it is bad luck to build his own tomb, that it could hasten the day when it has to be used."

Michelangelo was breathing hard. "What shall I do?"

"Go back on Monday as though nothing had happened."

He went back on Easter Monday, Tuesday, Wednesday, Thursday. Each time he was received coolly, told to return. On Friday the guard flatly refused him entrance. He walked home, sat at his table and scrawled: *Most Blessed Father, I have been turned out of the palace today by your orders; therefore, if you want me, you must look for me elsewhere than in Rome.* He sent the letter to the Pope.

That night he rented a horse and left for Florence. At the rise north of town where he had caught his first glimpse of Rome, he turned to gaze back at the sleeping city. Into his mind came a Tuscan adage, born of centuries of feuds: *How much the fool who goes to Rome Excels the fool who stays at home. . . .*

The second day he was resting at an inn at Poggibonsi when he heard thunderous hoofs storming up the road. It was Baglioni at the head of a party of five guards. He went to meet him. "Leo! What brings you to Poggibonsi?"

"You! The Holy Father knew we were friends."

"I'm on my way home to Florence," Michelangelo said.

"No, you're not! I bring you a letter from Pope Julius. He commands you to return under penalty of disgrace. If you do, all will be set right. I have the Holy Father's word for it."

"The Holy Father has lapses of memory."

A burly guard asked, "Shall we truss him up, Messer Baglioni?"

"I was not instructed to use force. Michelangelo, you're not the first to be kept waiting by a Pope. If Julius says, 'Wait!' you wait, if it takes a year."

"I'm going back to Florence for good. I will not allow any man to treat me so."

Leo came close, so the guards could not hear. "Bravo, Florentine! You sound like Marzocco, your heraldic lion. But now that you have asserted your independence, come back. Do not put me in a difficult position."

Baglioni was a good friend, but no one should ask another man to surrender his pride. He told Leo so. Baglioni's face became stern. "It is impossible to defy the pontiff. You will see, now or later. And later could be worse. I urge you not to match your will against his."

"If I return now, I lose everything. But if he wishes it, I'll sculpture his tomb under the shadow of the Signoria tower."

HE TOOK OVER his old room in his father's house. The marble for his Apostle Matthew was safe in a Duomo workshed; his cartoon for The Bathers, in the Palazzo della Signoria.

The news of the exchange in the yard of the Poggibonsi inn took only a few hours to make its way over the mountain. When he and Granacci reached Rustici's studio for supper with the Company of the Cauldron, he found himself a hero. But the following morning he learned that the Florentine government did not agree. Soderini's face was grave when he received Michelangelo. "You're the first Florentine to defy a Pope since Savonarola," he said. "I'm afraid your fate will be the same."

"You mean I'll be hanged from a gibbet, and then burned?"

Soderini smiled. "You are not guilty of heresy, only of disobedience. But in the end the Pope will have his way."

"But all I want to do is settle down in Florence. I'll start the St. Matthew tomorrow so that I can have my house back."

"Florence cannot renew your sculpture contract. No one

can employ you now without incurring the Pope's enmity."

"What about The Bathers? Can't I do my fresco?"

Soderini looked at him. "You have not been in the Great Hall? Let us go there at once."

When he saw Leonardo's great fresco, Michelangelo's hand swung to his mouth. "*Dio mio,* no!" Its entire lower half was in ruin, the colors having run downward: horses, men, trees, rocks flowed into one another in an indistinguishable chaos of color.

All the antagonism washed away in Michelangelo. He felt only deep regret for a fellow artist who had created mightily for a whole year of his life, only to have the results wiped out.

"Leonardo was determined to revive ancient encaustic painting," Soderini said, "using colors mixed with wax and then fused by heat. He applied the heat by lighting fires on the floor. He had tried it on a small mural in Santa Maria Novella, and it had worked well. But this mural is twenty-two feet high, and in order for the heat to reach the upper portion, he had to heap on the fuel. The intense heat on the lower half caused the wax to run."

Michelangelo went to offer his condolences to Leonardo and to apologize for his remarks in the past. Leonardo's initial coolness thawed as Michelangelo spoke. "You were provoked by my remarks about marble carvers," he said. "I saw your cartoon for The Bathers. It will become a glory of Florence."

"I've lost all interest in the fresco, now that your Battle of Anghiari cannot be fought beside mine."

Two days later Soderini sent for him to read him a letter from the Pope, demanding that the Signoria return Michelangelo to Rome at once, under pain of pontifical displeasure.

"I had better keep going north," replied Michelangelo mournfully; "maybe to France."

"You can't run away. The Pope's arm reaches all over Europe."

"Why am I so precious to him now?"

"Because, having repudiated his service, you become the most desirable artist in the world. But don't push him too far."

A month later, Soderini summoned him to hear an official message from the Pope: *"Michelangelo, the sculptor, who left us without reason, and in mere caprice, is afraid, as we are informed, of returning, though we for our part are not angry with him, knowing the humors of such men of genius. . . . If he returns to us, he shall be uninjured and unhurt, retaining our apostolic favor in the same measure as he formerly enjoyed it.*" Soderini put the letter down. "Does that satisfy you?"

"No. Last night I met a Florentine merchant who lives in Turkey. He says I could go out there and work for the Sultan."

His brother Lionardo came to see him. "Michelangelo, I want to help you," he said. "Let me first admit that you were right in following your art. Our brothers in Rome speak reverently of your Pietà. You have been worshiping God in your own way. Forgive my trespass against you."

"You are forgiven, Lionardo."

"I must remind you that the Pope is the viceroy of God on earth. When you disobey His Holiness you disobey God."

"Was that true when Savonarola fought Alexander VI?"

Lionardo let the black cowl slip forward to mask his eyes. "Savonarola disobeyed. No matter what we think of a Pope, he is the descendant of St. Peter."

"Popes are men, Lionardo. I have to do what I feel is right. I believe God loves independence more than He does servility."

"You must be right," said Lionardo, "or He would not help you carve such divine marbles."

Sadly, Lionardo said farewell. They were never to meet again.

The only one who was not frightened for him was Contessina. She had seen her family driven out of the city it had helped make the greatest in Europe, her home sacked by fellow townsmen; she herself had been exiled for eight years. She had little respect for officialdom. But her husband wanted to get to Rome; therefore he did not wish to offend the Pope. "It is with reluctance, Buonarroti," he said one day at their villa, "that I must ask you not to come here again. It is too dangerous now to see you."

"Being born into this world is the primary danger," observed Contessina. "Everything after that is a game of cards."

"I will not come again, Messer Ridolfi," said Michelangelo quietly. "You must protect your family. It was thoughtless of me."

IN LATE AUGUST Julius left Rome with an army of five hundred knights and nobles to reconquer Papal Territories in alien hands. He made a bloodless conquest of Perugia, bribed the Cardinal of Rouen to send away eight thousand French troops protecting Bologna by offering cardinals' hats to the cardinal's three nephews, and marched into the city. Meanwhile, he had not forgotten his errant sculptor. At the Palazzo della Signoria, Soderini shouted at Michelangelo: "We do not wish to go to war on your account! The Holy Father wants you in Bologna. Go!"

Michelangelo knew he was beaten. As the Pope's swollen and confident army advanced through Umbria, reconquering it for the Papal State, the people on the streets began turning their heads when Michelangelo passed. Florence had no defense and desperately needed the Pope's friendship. The whole city was determined that Michelangelo be sent back to the Pope. And they were right: Florence came first. He would go to Bologna, make his peace with the Holy Father. Soderini gave him a letter to his brother, the Cardinal of Volterra, who was with the Pope: *We assure Your Lordship that Michelangelo is a good young man, and unique of his art. . . . He is such that, using good words and kind manners, one can obtain everything from him; one must be tender and kind to him, and he will do such things that anyone who sees them will be amazed.*

It was November. The streets of Bologna were crowded with people who had thronged to the court of the Pope. Michelangelo found the pontiff at dinner in a banner-hung hall. When Pope Julius looked up and saw him, the whole hall fell silent. The two men glared at each other, their eyes flashing fire. Michelangelo threw his shoulders back, refusing to kneel. The Pope said: "You have delayed long! We have been obliged to come to meet you!"

This was true: the Pope had traveled a good many more miles than he had. He said stubbornly, "Holy Father, I did not deserve the treatment I received in Rome in Easter week."

A bishop, attempting to intervene in Michelangelo's behalf, stepped forward. "Holiness, one must be indulgent toward artists. They understand nothing outside their trade, and often lack good manners."

Julius rose. He thundered: "How dare you say of this man things that I myself would not say? It is you who lack manners!"

Having received as close to a public apology as a Pope could proffer, Michelangelo knelt and kissed the Pope's ring.

"Come to my camp tomorrow," Julius said. "We will arrange our affairs."

He left the palace to visit his friend Aldovrandi. Aldovrandi could not stop chuckling at the happenings in the dining hall. "You're so much alike," he commented, "you and Julius. You both have a *terribilità*. No wonder he respects you."

"What do you suppose the Holy Father intends to do with me?" Michelangelo asked.

"Put you to work. You'll stay with us, of course?"

Michelangelo accepted with pleasure. "How is your nephew Marco?"

"Quite well. He had a new girl, one he found in Rimini."

"Then where is Clarissa?"

"She lives in the Via di Mezzo di San Martino."

"Would you excuse me?"

"Love and a cough," Aldovrandi said, "cannot be hid."

Half an hour later, Michelangelo stood with her in the doorway of the roof penthouse overlooking the Piazza di San Martino. She was silhouetted against the orange glow of the oil lamps, her face framed in the fur cowl of a woolen robe. His mind went back to the first time he had seen her, when she was nineteen, slender, golden-haired, delicately sensuous. Now she was thirty-one, at a lush peak of ripeness. Again he was aware of her magnificent body. She led him into a small sitting room, then turned to him. He slipped his arms inside her fur-lined robe. Her body was warm. He held her to him, kissed her yielding mouth.

She murmured: "When I first said, 'It is natural for us to want each other,' you blushed like a boy."

"Artists know nothing of love. My friend Granacci describes it as a diversion."

"How would you describe it?"

"What I feel for you? As a torrent that hurtles a man's body down through rocky canyons, sweeps him along at flood tide."

"And then?"

"I can talk no more. . . ."

The robe slipped off her shoulders. She raised her arms, released a few pins and the long braids of hair fell to her waist. There was no voluptuousness in her movements, but rather the quality he remembered of sweetness, as though love were her natural medium.

Later, as they lay in each other's arms, she asked: "You have found love?"

"Not since you."

"There are available women in Rome."

"Seven thousand. My friend Balducci used to count them every Sunday. It is not my kind of love."

"Tomorrow I will go to church to confess my sin, but I do not believe this love to be a sin," she said.

"God invented love. It is beautiful."

"Could the devil be tempting us?"

"The devil is an invention of man."

"There is no evil?"

"Ugliness is evil."

HE REACHED JULIUS' military encampment on the bank of the Reno River, through heavy snows. Julius was reviewing his troops, wrapped in an enormous furred and wadded overcoat, on his head a bulky gray woolen hood. Abusing his officers in coarse language, storming up and down his lines, shouting orders, he looked like an Old Testament prophet.

He led Michelangelo to his tent, hung with warm furs. "Buonarroti, I have been thinking that I would like you to sculpture a bronze statue of me in my robes and triple crown."

"Bronze!" It was an agonized cry. "It is not my trade!"

Julius' face flushed with anger. "You shall do this as a service to your Pope."

"Holy Father, I know nothing of casting, finishing. Let me return to marble."

The Pope's face was livid. "Buonarroti, stop issuing ultima-

tums. You shall create a stupendous bronze statue of me for the space above the main portal of San Petronio."

"Holy Father, if my bronze statue pleases you, will you permit me to resume carving marble?"

"The pontiff does not make bargains!" cried Julius. "Bring me your drawings in one week."

Humiliated, he made his way into town to Clarissa's apartment. She was dressed in a deep pink silk, with low neckline and bucket sleeves, her hair caught up in a garland of jeweled threads. She kissed him. "There is hot water on the fire. Would you like a bath to relax you? You can take it in the kitchen, while I find some food for you. I will wash your back."

"I've never had anyone wash my back for me."

"Apparently there are a lot of things you have never had."

He dropped his clothes on the kitchen floor and stepped

gingerly into the hot water she had poured into a long oval tub. Then he stretched his legs with a sigh of relief.

"Why don't you spend the week here?" said Clarissa. "No one will know where you are, you will be undisturbed."

"A whole week to think only of love! Is that possible? Not one thought of clay or bronze?"

"I am not clay or bronze." Her musical laugh dissipated the last of the day's humiliation. "Here, dry yourself before the fire."

He rubbed his skin hard, then Clarissa wrapped him in a second enormous towel, sat him at a table before a steaming dish of thin sliced veal and *piselli.* He ate ravenously. Content, he pushed his chair back from the table, turned it toward the fire. Clarissa came to sit at his feet. "No other woman has made me want her," he said. "How can it be explained?"

"Love is not to be explained." She got on her knees and wrapped her arms about his neck. "It is to be enjoyed."

"And to be marveled at." He burst into laughter. "The Pope didn't mean to do me a kindness, but he has . . . the first."

ON THE LAST AFTERNOON of the week, filled with a delicious lassitude, he picked up drawing paper and a piece of charcoal. He drew Julius in a formal pose, with the left leg extended, one arm reaching out, perhaps in benediction.

At the appointed hour he appeared before the Pope, who was delighted with his sketch. He said to Messer Carlino, his treasurer, "You are to give Buonarroti whatever he needs."

Carlino, a sallow, thin-lipped man, gave him a hundred ducats. Michelangelo sent a messenger for Argiento and wrote to the Signoria, asking if the Duomo's bronze casters Lapo and Lotti could be sent to help cast the Pope's statue.

He rented a former carriage house on the Street of the Tuscans, with a high ceiling, stone walls and brick floor. There was a garden at the back, and a fireplace for cooking.

Argiento arrived, and, two days later, Lapo and Lotti. Michelangelo put little Lapo in charge of buying supplies: wax, clay, cloth, brick for the casting ovens.

The hundred ducats were soon exhausted and Michelangelo had to ask Carlino for more money. "What did you do with the first hundred ducats?" Carlino asked.

"None of your business."

"Bring me receipted bills for the first hundred, and written estimates of what you want to spend the second hundred for."

"You're like the gardener's dog, that neither eats cabbage himself nor lets anyone else."

There was the ghost of a smile on Carlino's lips. "It is my job to make people hate me. Then they return as seldom as possible."

"I'll be back."

Lapo quieted him. "I remember what I spent. I'll write up the bills."

Michelangelo walked to San Domenico to see his own angel with the wings of an eagle, his St. Petronius and the young St. Proculus. Suddenly he straightened. The St. Proculus had been broken in two places, awkwardly repaired. He felt someone staring at him and whirled around. It was his old enemy, Vincenzo. "Welcome back to Bologna," Vincenzo said.

"It was you who broke my marble!"

"The day it fell I was in the country, making brick. It could happen again, too. There are wicked folk who say your statue of the Pope will be melted down the day his soldiers leave. But me, I am a devout man. I plan to kneel before it."

MICHELANGELO STARTED WORK at white heat. Much as he detested bronze, his own integrity forced him to do the best he could.

Aldovrandi sent him models, spread the word that those men most closely resembling Pope Julius would be paid a special wage. Michelangelo sketched from light to dark, Argiento cooked and cleaned, Lotti built a small brick oven to test the local metals for fusing, Lapo continued to do the buying.

His only joy was Clarissa. He managed to steal a couple of nights a week to spend with her. No matter what hour he arrived there was food by the side of the fire, ready to be heated.

Mail from Florence came irregularly. Michelangelo received

little but requests for money. Lodovico had found another farm: if Michelangelo could send five hundred florins . . . From Buonarroto and Giovansimone, both working at a wool shop, there was rarely a letter without the lines, *You promised us another shop. We are tired of working for someone else. We want to make lots of money.* . . .

Muttering to himself, "So do I," Michelangelo wrapped himself in a blanket while his three assistants slept, and answered: *As soon as I come to Florence, I will set you up in business. I shall try to get money for the farm.*

He spent hours following Julius about, sketching him as he said Mass, walked in procession, shouted in anger, laughed at a courtier's joke, until he knew every bone and sinew of the Pope's body. Then he worked day and night, slowly adding clay to a thirteen-foot-high armature of wood to create the model from which the bronze would be cast. In the third week of January the model was ready for the Pope's inspection.

Julius arrived, accompanied by Messer Carlino. Michelangelo had draped a quilt over his one comfortable chair. Here the Pope sat in silence, studying his portrait.

He was pleased, but he seemed perplexed by the right hand, which was raised in a haughty, almost violent gesture.

"Buonarroti, does this hand intend to bless or curse?"

"The right hand lifted, Holy Father, bids the Bolognese be obedient even though you are in Rome."

"And the left hand. What shall it hold?"

"Perhaps the keys to the new St. Peter's?"

"Bravissimo!"

Glancing at Carlino, Michelangelo added, "I must buy seven to eight hundred pounds of wax to create the model."

The Pope authorized the expenditure and swept out. Michelangelo sent Lapo to shop for the wax. Lapo returned shortly.

"I cannot get it for less than nine florins and forty soldi a hundred. Better buy it at once, it is a bargain."

Michelangelo was disturbed by a strange note in Lapo's voice. He said quietly to Argiento, "Go to the same shop and ask the price."

Argiento returned, whispered, "They are asking eight

and a half florins, and I can get off the brokerage charge."

Michelangelo went to Lapo. "Lapo, you've been taking a profit from me on everything you bought."

"Why not! You pay so little and there isn't enough to eat!"

"You eat what we eat," growled Argiento. "Food's expensive. If you had stolen less there would have been more for all of us."

"There's food in the inns, wine in the wineshops," Lapo said. "And women in the Street of the Bordellos. I would not live the way you live."

"Then return to Florence," said Michelangelo bitterly.

Lapo packed his possessions and Lotti left with him.

HE LOST NOT ONLY Lapo and Lotti but Clarissa as well.

The Pope announced that he would return to Rome for Lent. This gave Michelangelo only a few weeks in which to perfect the wax model and get the Pope's final approval. Without helpers, he had to work with no thought of food or sleep. In those rare hours when he could tear himself away he had no time to sit companionably with Clarissa, to tell her what he was doing. He went only when hunger for her drove him blindly through the streets to possess her, and then to leave at once. Clarissa was sad; she gave less of herself each time he came.

"Clarissa, I'm sorry for the way things are," he said.

She raised, then lowered her hands hopelessly. "A friend has sent a groom from Milan, with a carriage to take me there. . . ."

A few days later the Pope visited the workyard for the last time, approved the model. He gave Michelangelo his benediction and an order on a banker to continue paying his costs.

Desperately needing a bronze caster, Michelangelo wrote again to Florence, asking for Master Bernardino, the best in Tuscany. But it was May before Bernardino arrived. He built a tremendous brick oven in the courtyard. There followed weeks of experimenting with the fires, testing the way the metals fused. Michelangelo was filled with impatience to cast and go home.

"We must not hurry," Bernardino warned him. "One untested step, and all our work will be for nothing."

Aldovrandi came frequently to watch his work. "This bronze of yours is going to make me a rich man," he commented, wiping his brow as the oven turned the workyard into an inferno. "Bologna is betting that your statue is too large to cast. I'm taking all bets."

"It will cast," replied Michelangelo grimly. "I have watched Bernardino step by step. He could make bronze without fire."

But when they finally poured in June, something went wrong. The statue came out well as far as the waist; the rest of the material remained in the furnace. It did not fuse. To take it out the furnace would have to be dismantled. Bernardino was as wretched as Michelangelo. "This has never happened to me before."

"You are a good artisan. He who works, at times fails."

In a flash it was all over town that Michelangelo had failed to cast the pontiff's statue. Crowds started to pour into the courtyard. Aldovrandi arrived and cleared them out. Bernardino's face was green. "What a cruel city this is! They think they have gained a victory because of our failure."

He worked heroically, night and day, rebuilt the furnace, experimented with the metals. Finally, under the blinding heat of the mid-July sun, he poured again. Slowly, the heated metal began to run from the furnace to the mold. With that, Bernardino said: "There's nothing more for me to do now. I leave for Florence at dawn."

Michelangelo was left to discover the results himself. He had to wait for three weeks, until the mold cooled sufficiently for him to tear it down. The two halves of the statue were joined without a serious mark. "A few weeks of filing and polishing," Michelangelo thought, "and I, too, will be on my way."

He had misgauged the task. He and Argiento were seemingly condemned to an eternity of cleaning up the tremendous statue. Finally the bronze was rubbed down to a shiny dark tone. A crew came over to move the statue to the front of San Petronio. Bells rang all over the city as the statue was hoisted into the niche over the portal. When the covering was removed from the statue, the crowd cheered, then fell to its knees and crossed itself. That evening there were fireworks in the square. Michel-angelo, standing in his worn workman's shirt at the far end of the piazza, went unnoticed. Looking up at Julius in his niche, illuminated by shooting rockets, he felt nothing, not even relief. He was dry, barren, used up.

He had exactly four and a half florins left. At dawn he knocked at Aldovrandi's door to bid his friend good-by, and borrowed a horse to go home.

WITHIN A FEW DAYS after he returned to Florence, Michelangelo learned that Soderini had good reason to be satisfied with himself: through his brilliant ambassador, Niccolò Machiavelli, whom he had trained, Florence had concluded a series of trea-ties which should enable the city-state to live in peace.

"Reports from the Vatican tell us that Julius is delighted with your bronze," Soderini told him. "Now I welcome you back to your house and studio. I will charge you eight florins a month rental until you begin carving the Apostles; then the house will become yours."

"This is where I will live and carve all the rest of my life. May God hear my words."

"I do not usually interfere in family life," Soderini said, "but the time has come for you to secure your freedom from your father. I want him to go with you to a notary and sign a legal emancipation. What you give him then will be a gift, not an obligation."

Michelangelo knew his father's failings yet he loved him. He shook his head. "It would do no good. I would have to turn over the money to him anyway."

"I insist. We will call in the notary."

Lodovico was heartbroken at being obliged to appear before the notary, for under Tuscan law an unmarried son became free only at the death of his father. There were tears in his eyes as they walked home. "Michelangelo, you won't abandon us now?" He had aged ten years in the ten-minute legal ceremony; his head was bowed.

"I will always do everything in my power for the family,

Father," he said. "What else have I? My work and my family."

He renewed his friendships at the Company of the Cauldron. He learned that Contessina's lot was improved; with the growing importance of Cardinal Giovanni de' Medici in Rome, the Signoria had permitted the Ridolfi family to move back to their main villa. Giovanni supplied them with funds. However, since Ridolfi was still an avowed enemy of the Republic, the Signoria would not let him move to Rome.

Contessina was permitted now to enter Florence. One day she caught Michelangelo gazing at his David. "You still find pleasure in it?"

He whirled at the sound of her voice, found himself gazing into the brown eyes that had always been able to stab through his thoughts. She had high color in her cheeks from the walk in the brisk air. "Contessina! How well you look. It is good to see you."

"How was Bologna?"

"Dante's *Inferno.*"

"All of it?"

Though her question was innocently asked, he flushed.

"What was her name?"

"Clarissa. But she left me."

"Then you have known love, some portion of it?"

"In full measure."

"Permit me to envy you," she whispered, and was gone.

He had just started work on his St. Matthew when Soderini summoned him. "We have received a message from Pope Julius," he said. "He wants you in Rome. He has good news for you."

ONCE AGAIN IN THE large throne room, he bowed to Cardinal Giovanni de' Medici, nodded to Cardinal Riario. Pope Julius cried triumphantly, "You see, Buonarroti, you had no confidence in yourself. When I asked for a bronze figure, you cried out, 'It is not my trade!' " The Pope's mimicking of Michelangelo's slightly hoarse voice brought laughter from the court. "Now you see how you have made it your trade, by creating a fine bronze."

"You are generous, Holy Father," murmured Michelangelo.

"I intend to continue being generous. I am going to favor you above all the painting masters of Italy. I am commissioning you to paint the ceiling of the Sistine Chapel."

There was a light patter of applause. Michelangelo was stunned. The Sistine Chapel was known as the ugliest, most clumsy piece of architecture in Italy. He cried passionately: "I am a sculptor, not a painter!"

Julius said icily: "I had less trouble conquering Perugia and Bologna than I have in subduing you!"

"Holy Father, marble is my profession. Let me carve the Moses, Victors, Captives for your tomb. Many would come to see the statues, offering thanks to Your Holiness for making them possible."

"In short," snapped Julius, "I need your sculptures to assure my place in history?"

"They could help, Holy Father."

There was a gasp from those around the throne. The Pope loosened the collar of his cape, took a deep breath and started again. "Buonarroti, my informants in Florence describe your cartoon for The Bathers as 'the school of the world.'"

"Holiness," said Michelangelo, cursing himself for his envy of Leonardo that had led him into this trap. "It was a diversion."

"*Bene.* Make such a diversion for the Sistine." A wisp of a smile drifted across the pontiff's face, was reflected in an amber sparkle in Michelangelo's eyes. Then the Pope said, in the tone of an exasperated but fond father: "Buonarroti, for painting the Sistine ceiling and decorating the vault we will pay you three thousand ducats. We shall also pay the wages of five assistants. When the chapel is completed, you have my promise that you shall return to your marble. My son, you are dismissed."

What could he say? Where could he flee? The Pope's power reached everywhere. There was nothing to do but submit.

He went to the chapel. Sunlight was streaming in from three tall windows, lighting the glorious frescoes of Botticelli and Cosimo Rosselli, shooting strong beams of light across the variegated marble floor. The side walls were one hundred and thirty-three feet long; the barrel vault rose sixty-eight feet above him. Taking a deep breath, he craned his neck and looked up at the ceiling, painted a light blue and studded with golden stars, the enormous area he was to fill with decorations. The motive for the commission now became crushingly clear to him. It was not to put magnificent paintings on the ceiling, but rather to mask the ugly structural supports which made a harsh transition from the top third of the wall into the vault. As an artist he had become merely an obliterator of other men's clumsiness.

He wrote to Argiento, to Granacci; to the Topolinos, asking them to send him assistants. A groom arrived from the Pope, informing him that the house where his marble for the tomb had lain these two years was still available to him.

He signed the contract for the Sistine Chapel and was given five hundred ducats. He paid his long-overdue debts, and then summoned up the courage to return to the Sistine. He found Bramante there, directing the hanging of a scaffolding from the ceiling by means of poles driven through the vault. "There's a scaffolding that will hold you securely for the rest of your life," Bramante said.

"Just what do you intend to do with the holes in the ceiling after the poles come out?"

"Fill them."

"How do we get up there to fill them after the scaffolding is down? Ride on an eagle's back?"

"I hadn't thought of that."

Michelangelo went to the Pope and got permission to build his own scaffold. With the carpenters, he build a scaffold resting on a projecting cornice and solidly wedged against the thick, strong walls. When it was finished, Michelangelo and the carpenters tested it: the more weight on the trestle, the more strongly it pressed against the walls. He was jubilant. It was a tiny victory, but it provided the impetus to begin the detested chore.

Argiento could not leave his brother's farm until the crops had been harvested. Granacci, in Florence, was trying to assemble a crew of assistants for Michelangelo from the old Ghirlandaio studio. Summer clamped down, and miasmic vapors rose from the marshes. Michelangelo climbed the ladder to his scaffold at dawn, drawing scale models and cutting out paper silhouettes of spaces he would have to fill. By midmorning the vault was like a furnace, and he was gasping for breath. He slept as though drugged through the heat of the afternoon, then worked at night in the back garden, evolving designs for the nearly six thousand square feet of sky and stars that had to be frescoed.

In September Granacci arrived with a full workshop crew. The former apprentices had aged: Jacopo was still slim and wiry, but with deeply etched laugh wrinkles; Tedesco, who sported a bushy beard, had become thickset. Bugiardini, still moonfaced, showed a patch of baldness like a tonsure. Giuliano's nephew, Sebastiano da Sangallo, and Donnino were newcomers; there was also Michi, a stonecutter from Settignano.

The studio set to work in earnest. To each of his six assistants Michelangelo assigned a division of the vault for decoration: rosettes, circles and rectangles, trees and flowers. He felt certain he could cover the whole ceiling in seven months.

The group worked well together, Michi mixing the plaster on the scaffold after hauling the sacks up the ladder, Jacopo copying the cartoon colors into the designs that Bugiardini outlined. In October Argiento arrived, and was delighted to keep house for six companions.

After a seventh of the vault had been completed, Michelangelo returned alone to study the result. The Pope's objective would be accomplished; no one would be disturbed any more by a broken-up vault with monotonous circles of stars. The Apostles on their thrones, the thousands of square feet of brightly colored designs would conceal and divert.

But what about the quality of the work? He had never compromised with quality; his integrity as an artist was the rock on which his life was built. And he could not deny that this work was mediocre. His assistants were only ten days away from blowing up the next cartoons to full size. He would have to decide quickly what to do.

Christmas came, and Cardinal Giovanni invited Michelangelo to dinner. A groom with Florentine lilies embroidered on his livery admitted him to the palace. He passed through the spacious entrance hall and music room, then stopped abruptly at the entrance to a small drawing room. There, sitting before a log fire, her hands extended to the flames, sat Contessina. She looked up. "Michelangelo. *Come va?*"

"*Non c'è male.* I don't have to ask how you are. You look beautiful."

Color rose in her cheeks. "You've never said that before."

"But I've always thought it. You are a deep part of me. From the days when my life began, in the sculpture garden." He became aware of others in the room, changed his tone. "Your family is with you?"

"My children, but not my husband. He is still too openly committed to the downfall of the Republic." She smiled at him, wistfully. "Now I want to speak of you," she said. "Is your work going well?"

"Not yet."

"It will."

"Are you sure?"

"I'll put my hand in fire."

She held her hand out as though toward flames. He longed to take it in his own. Then she threw back her head in laughter at the drastic Tuscan phrase she had used. Their laughter joined together. This too was a kind of possessing; rare, beautiful and sacred.

THE ROMAN COUNTRYSIDE was not Tuscany; it did not fill him with an all-absolving grace. But it had power, and history: the flat, fertile plains rolling for miles, traversed by the remains of Roman aqueducts; Hadrian's villa, where Michelangelo watched excavators unearth ancient marbles; Tivoli, with its majestic waterfalls; Tusculum, high in the volcanic hills, with the ruins of Cicero's villa. Seeking a solution for the problem that nagged him, he walked deeper and deeper into the past, stopping each night at a tiny inn or knocking on the door of a peasant's hut to buy his supper and space on a bed to rest. Gradually the decision he must make became clear: his helpers would have to go. He did not have the nature of a Ghirlandaio, able to do the main figures and allow his studio to do the rest. He had to work alone.

On New Year's morning, 1509, he climbed a sheep trail to the summit of a mountain. The air was sharp, clear and cold. As he stood on the peak the sun came up behind him. In the distance stood Rome, sparklingly clear. Beyond and to the south lay the Tyrrhenian Sea, pastel green under a brittle blue winter sky. The whole landscape was flooded with luminosity: forests, the descending range of hills, the fertile plains, the somnolent farms, the stone-pile villages, the roads leading to Rome. He thought, "What a magnificent artist was God when He created the universe." He remembered the lines from Genesis: *God, at the beginning of time, created heaven and earth. Earth was still an empty waste, and darkness hung over the deep. . . . Then God said, Let there be light. . . . God said too, Let a solid vault arise amid the waters . . . a vault by which God would separate the waters which were beneath it from the waters above it. . . . This vault God called the Sky. . . . And God said, Let us make man, wearing our own image and likeness. . . . So God made man in His own image. . . .*

Suddenly he knew that nothing would suffice for his vault but Genesis itself: God's creating the sun and moon, the water and the earth, man and woman. There was a theme to conquer that vault, to overwhelm it with the glory of God's architecture!

He told the Pope about his new plan.

"You are a strange one, Buonarroti," the Pope said. "You screamed in rage that fresco was not your profession. Yet now you come back with a plan that will entail five or six times as much labor as the original plan. Well, paint your ceiling as you will. We cannot pay you five or six times the original three thousand ducats, but we will double it."

He told Granacci that the assistants would have to go home. "I will keep Michi to grind the colors," he said, "and I will have Rosselli lay the plaster. The rest I must do by myself."

"Working alone on top of that scaffolding to re-create the story of Genesis will take you forty years!" Granacci said.

"No, closer to four."

Granacci put his arms about his friend's shoulders. "You have David's courage."

He was determined to get a teeming humanity up on the Sistine ceiling, as well as the God who created it; mankind portrayed in its breathless beauty, its weaknesses, its indestructible strengths: God in His ability to make all things possible. The center space, running the full length of the vault, he would use for his major works: Dividing the Waters from the Earth; God Creating the Sun, the Moon; God Creating Adam and Eve; Expelling Adam and Eve from the Garden; the legend of Noah and the Deluge. Ideas now came tumbling over one another tumultuously. On the ends and sides he would show Prophets and Sibyls, each sitting on a marble throne. Connecting the thrones would be a cornice painted like marble.

While Piero Rosselli used a claw hammer to tear out the plaster already frescoed, Argiento came to Michelangelo with tears in his eyes. His brother had died, and he would have to work the family farm. "My brother left little children," he said. "I'll be a farmer, marry my brother's wife, raise the children."

He paid Argiento's back wages with almost the last of his funds. He had received no money from the Pope for months. He could not ask for more funds until he had an important section of the ceiling finished. He ate his supper in his quiet house, thinking how noisy and gay it had been, with Jacopo telling stories, Bugiardini singing love songs. It would be lonely too, on the scaffolding in the barren chapel.

HE BEGAN WITH THE Deluge. By March he had the cartoon ready to be transferred to the ceiling. Michi carried the sacks of lime, sand and volcanic tufa dust up the steep ladders to the top of the scaffolding. Here he made his mix. Then he and Michelangelo climbed a series of three receding platforms to lay an area of *intonaco*. Michi held the cartoon while Michelangelo outlined the figures; then Michi descended to grind colors below. Michelangelo was now on his top platform, sixty feet above the floor. As always on a scaffolding, he suffered vertigo. He turned from his view of the marble floor and picked up a brush, remembering that so many years ago Mainardi had told him always to keep his colors liquid this early in the morning. . . .

He painted with his head and shoulders pulled back, his eyes staring straight up. Paint dripped onto his face, the wet plaster dripped in his eyes. His arms and back tired quickly from the strain of the unnatural position. During the first week he allowed Michi to lay only modest areas of *intonaco*, proceeding cautiously, experimenting with figures and colors.

He felt more alone than ever when he learned that Sangallo must travel the long road of defeat back to Florence. He had no further commissions from the Pope; his apprentices had joined Bramante, who had taken his place as he had schemed to. When Sangallo and his family left, their departure went unnoticed by the Vatican.

The Deluge took thirty-two days of painting. During the last weeks Michelangelo was completely out of funds. How was it that only he did not prosper from his papal connections? Young Raphael Sanzio, recently brought to Rome by Bramante, had been commissioned by the Pope to fresco his new apartment. Paid a generous retainer, he had rented a luxurious villa, installed a beautiful mistress and a staff of servants. The Pope included him in his hunting parties and dinners. He was seen everywhere, petted, loved, plied with commissions.

Michelangelo buried his hunger and loneliness in work, sketching the next fresco, the Sacrifice of Noah. As the figures came alive under his swiftly moving fingers, his sense of isolation receded. He felt secure only in this world of his own creating. And he sighed, for he knew himself to be a victim of his own character. . . .

Pope Julius came to see the first fresco. He climbed the ladder, joined Michelangelo on the scaffolding, studied the fifty-five men, women and children in the scene. He said: "The rest of the ceiling will be as good?"

"It should be better, Holy Father, for I am still learning about perspective at this height."

"I am pleased with you, my son. I shall order the treasurer to pay you five hundred ducats."

At last he was able to send money home, to buy food and supplies.

Now, while painting the Prophet Zacharias, he had an odd feeling that someone was coming in at night and mounting his ladder to the frescoes. As far as he knew, no one but he and the papal chamberlain, Accursio, had a key to the Sistine. He had insisted upon this, so that no one could spy on his work. Michi hid in a doorway, brought back word that it was Bramante and Raphael. Bramante had a key; they came in after midnight. Michelangelo was furious: before he could get his vault completed, his new techniques would be on the walls of the rooms Raphael was painting. He spoke to the Pope and the key was taken away from Bramante.

Shortly after this, Cardinal Giovanni summoned him to the Medici palace. "Michelangelo," he said, "every day Bramante makes you new enemies. I want you to become an intimate of this house, come to dinner here, be at my side during my hunting parties, ride in my processions. I want Rome to know you are under my protection. This will silence your detractors."

But how could he paint for a few hours, walk to Giovanni's house, talk charmingly to thirty guests, eat a delicious dinner over several hours? When he explained why he was unable to accept, Cardinal Giovanni said: "Raphael does work of high quality, yet he dines out every day. Why can't you?"

"Your Grace, for Raphael, the creating of a work of art is a bright spring day in the country; for me, it is an Alpine wind howling down the valley from the mountaintops. When I have finished a day of work I am empty. I have nothing to give."

"Not even when it is to your best interest?"

"My best interest can only be my best work."

FOR THIRTY DAYS he painted from light to darkness, completing the Sacrifice of Noah, the four titanic male nudes surrounding it, the Erythraean Sibyl on her throne, and the Prophet Isaiah opposite. For thirty days he slept in his clothes; and when, at the completion of this section, utterly spent, he had Michi pull his boots off, bits of skin came away with them.

He grew dizzy from painting standing with his neck arched so that he could peer straight upward; he had learned to blink his eyes with each brush stroke, but they still blurred from the dripping paint. He had Rosselli make him a still higher platform on top of the scaffolding. He painted sitting down, his thighs drawn up tight against his belly for balance, his eyes a few inches from the ceiling, until the unpadded bones of his buttocks became so bruised and sore he could no longer endure the agony. Then he lay flat on his back, his knees in the air, doubled over as tightly as possible against his chest to steady his painting arm. His beard became a catchall for the constant drip of paint. No matter which way he leaned, crouched, lay or knelt, he was always in strain.

Then he thought he was going blind. A letter arrived from Buonarroto. He could not decipher a word. He threw himself on his bed. What was he doing to himself? Sleepless, racked with pain, homesick, lonely, he rose in the inky blackness, lit a candle, and on the back of an old sketch tried to lighten his mood by pouring out his woes:

> *My beard turns up to heaven; my nape falls in,*
> *fixed on my spine: my breastbone visibly*
> *grows like a harp: a rich embroidery*
> *bedews my face from brush drops thick and thin.*
> *. . . foul I fare and painting is my shame.*

When he walked from his house to the chapel and back he did so almost blinded by paint, his head lowered, seeing no one. Passers-by often thought him crazy.

He forced himself to see his only reality: the life and the people on his ceiling. His intimates were Adam and Eve in the Garden of Eden. He portrayed them not as timid, delicate creatures, but powerful, handsome, accepting temptation in calm strength rather than weak stupidity. This was the mother and father of man, created by God, and he, Michelangelo Buonarroti, brought them to life in noble mien and proportion.

In June 1510, a year and a few weeks after he had shown Julius the first frescoes, half of the vault was completed. He had not told anyone, but the Pope knew at once. He sent word to Michelangelo that he would be in the Sistine at midafternoon.

Michelangelo helped him up the last rungs of the ladder, and explained the various scenes to him. Julius at once demanded that the scaffold be taken down so that the world could see how great a thing was being executed.

"It is not yet time to take the scaffold down, Holy Father. There is much still to be done."

"When will it be ready?" insisted the Pope.

Michelangelo was irritated. "When it is ready!"

Julius went red in the face, raised his staff in a fury and brought it down across Michelangelo's shoulder.

There was a silence while the two antagonists glared at each other. Michelangelo went cold all over, he bowed, said formally: "It shall be as Your Holiness desires. The scaffolding will be down by tomorrow, the chapel ready to be shown." He stepped back, leaving space for the Pope to descend the ladder.

"It is not for you, Buonarroti, to dismiss your pontiff!" cried Julius. "You are dismissed."

Michelangelo backed down the ladder, left the chapel. So this was the end! A bitter end, to be beaten like a peasant. He stumbled blindly along unfamiliar streets. He had re-created the world. He had tried to be God! Well, Pope Julius II had put him in his place. *"Foul I fare and painting is my shame."* He made his way home. Michi was already there, owl-eyed.

"Pack your things, Michi," he said. "Get a head start on me. If the Pope orders my arrest, I don't want them taking you too."

"He had no right to hit you."

"He can put me to death if he wants to. Only he'll have to catch me first."

He filled one canvas bag with his drawings, another with his personal things. Just as he finished there was a knock on the door. He opened it, and there was Chamberlain Accursio.

"Have you come to arrest me?"

"My good friend," said Accursio gently, "do you think the pontiff would bother to strike anyone he was not deeply fond of? The Pope loves you, as a gifted, albeit unruly son." He took a purse from his belt. "The pontiff asked me to bring you

these five hundred ducats and to convey his apologies. He did not want this to happen."

"Who knows that the Pope sent you to beg my pardon?"

"Is that important?"

"Since Rome will know the pontiff struck me, I can only go on living here if people also know that he apologized."

Accursio rolled his shoulders. "Who has ever been able to conceal anything in this city?"

Julius chose the week of the Feast of the Assumption to unveil the first half of the vault, but he sent no word to Michelangelo, who spent the intervening weeks at home, drawing. It was an uneasy truce. The first he knew of the gathering in the

Sistine was when Raphael came to his workroom. The younger man's face had aged, the flesh a little flaccid. Only twenty-seven, he looked ten years older. Even as Michelangelo's hard, grueling labor had taken its toll of him, so Raphael's fine looks were dissolving in food, drink, women.

"Messer Buonarroti, your chapel staggers me," said Raphael. "I came to apologize for my bad manners in the past."

Michelangelo remembered his own apology to Leonardo. "Artists must forgive each other their sins," he said.

No one else came to congratulate him. He was as solitary as though he were dead. The painting on the Sistine ceiling was outside the pale of Rome's life, a private duel between Michelangelo, God and Julius II.

And, suddenly, Pope Julius was deep in war. He again left Rome at the head of his army to drive the French out of northern Italy and to solidify the Papal State. Michelangelo was left stranded; the Pope's chamberlain had not brought him permission to put back the scaffolding and commence work on the altar half of the vault. Julius had waited for him to appear at the Vatican; he had waited for Julius to summon him. The Pope might be gone for months. What did he do in the meanwhile?

IT WAS NOT UNTIL after New Year's, 1511, that he was able to start painting again. The Pope sent money for the work he had completed, and permission to do the second half of the chapel. Now Michelangelo could come to grips with the themes of God Creating Adam, Creating the Sun and Moon, Dividing the Waters from the Earth, Separating Light and Darkness. These four panels were the heart of the ceiling.

He had always loved God: now he must make Him manifest. He had only to set down in drawings the image he had carried with him since childhood, of God as the most beautiful, powerful, intelligent and loving force in the universe; in Adam, true creature of his Father, God would be reflected.

While Michelangelo remained high in the heavens painting, Julius plunged into the special inferno reserved for warriors who suffer a rout. He failed in his siege of Ferrara, failed in his efforts to break the alliance between the Holy Roman Empire and France; when the French and Ferrarese recaptured Bologna, Julius lost his armies, artillery, baggage. Crushed, almost bankrupt, crippled with gout, he made his way back to Rome.

Julius' defeat was a defeat for Michelangelo also, for the Bolognese tore his bronze statue of Julius from its niche. The Duke of Ferrara melted it down and recast it into a cannon, which he named *Julius.* . . . fifteen months of his time, energy, talent were gone.

During the warm, light days of May and June he spent seventeen hours a day on the scaffold, taking food and a chamber pot up with him, painting like a man possessed, striving desperately to complete his Genesis before the collapse of its protector.

Julius had returned to Rome the most hated man in Italy, his resources so exhausted that he had to borrow money on the jewels in the papal tiara. Even the Roman nobles were in league against him. Understanding defeat, Michelangelo now felt that he must call on his Pope.

Julius' face was ravaged by frustration and illness, but his voice was friendly as he said: "Your ceiling, it moves along?"

"Holiness, I think you will be gratified."

"If I am, you will be the first to bring me gratification for a long time. I will come to the Sistine with you."

He could hardly climb the ladder: Michelangelo had to haul him up the last few rungs. At the top he stood panting; and then, as he saw God above him, about to impart the gift of life to Adam, a smile came to his lips. "Do you truly believe that God is so benign?"

"Yes, Holy Father."

"I most ardently hope so, since I am going to be standing before Him before long. If He is as you have painted Him, then I shall be forgiven my sins." He turned toward Michelangelo, his expression radiant. "I am pleased with you, my son."

Basking in the rays of the hot sun and the Pope's hearty acceptance of his labors, Michelangelo wanted to hold its warmth for a little while longer; he crossed the piazza to where the piers and walls of the new St. Peter's were beginning to rise.

God Creating the Sun and Moon; Sistine Chapel

He was surprised to find that Bramante was not building of solid stone and concrete, but was erecting hollow concrete forms and filling them with rubble. The bulky mass would give the appearance of being solid, but was it not a dangerous way to support so heavy a structure? And as he watched the men preparing the concrete, he saw that they were not following the sound engineering precept of one portion of cement to three or four of sand, but were using ten and twelve portions of sand to one of cement. This mix could be fatal under the best of circumstances; but to hold the vast St. Peter's with uncompacted debris between its piers—it could be catastrophic.

He made straight for Bramante's palace, was admitted by a liveried footman. Bramante was working in his library.

"Bramante, I will pay you the compliment of believing that you do not know what is going on," he began without preamble. "However, when the walls of St. Peter's crumble, it will make little difference whether you were stupid or merely negligent. Your walls will crack."

"Who are you, a ceiling decorator, to tell the greatest architect in Europe how to build piers?"

"The same one who showed you how to build a scaffold. Someone is cheating you by putting in the mix considerably less cement than the minimum requirements. Watch your foreman."

Bramante went purple with rage. He rose, clenched both fists. "Buonarroti, if you run to the Pope with this scandalmongering I swear I'll strangle you with my bare hands."

Michelangelo remained calm. "I shall watch your cement mix for two days. At the end of that time, if you are not using safe proportions, I shall report it to the Pope and to everyone else who will listen to me."

"No one will listen to you. You command no respect in Rome. Now get out of my house."

Bramante did nothing to change his materials. Michelangelo went to Julius, who listened for a time, then interrupted. "My son, Bramante has already warned me of your attack on him. Are you as good an architect as he is?"

"No, Holy Father."

"Then paint your ceiling and let Bramante build his church."

Michelangelo knelt abruptly, kissed the Pope's ring, left. He was sorely puzzled. Bramante was too good an architect to put his most important creation in danger. There must be an explanation. Leo Baglioni knew everything; he knocked on his door.

"It's not hard to explain," replied Leo. "Bramante is living beyond his means, spending hundreds of thousands of ducats. He has to have more money; now the piers of St. Peter's are paying his debts."

Aghast, Michelangelo cried, "Have you told the Pope this?"

"Assuredly not. You told the Pope. What did it get you?"

Julius paid Michelangelo another five hundred ducats, and kept insisting that he complete his ceiling quickly, quickly! One day he climbed the ladder unannounced.

"When will it be finished?"

"When I have satisfied myself."

"You have already taken four years."

"It will be done, Holy Father, when it will be done."

"Do you want to be thrown down from this scaffolding?"

Michelangelo gazed at the marble floor below.

"On All Saints' Day I shall celebrate Mass here," declared the Pope.

Michelangelo had wanted to touch up some of the draperies

and skies in gold and ultramarines, but there would be no time now. He had Michi take down the scaffold.

On All Saints' Day official Rome dressed itself in its finest robes for the Pope's dedication of the Sistine Chapel. Michelangelo rose early, but he did not go to the Sistine. Instead he walked out under the portico of his house, pulled back the tarpaulin, stood ruminatively before the marble columns he had waited these seven long years to carve. He took up his hammer and chisel. Fatigue, bitterness and pain fell away. Sunlight caught the first shafts of marble dust that floated upward.

BOOK EIGHT

The Medici

POPE JULIUS II survived the completion of the Sistine vault by only a few months. Giovanni de' Medici, first Florentine to be elected to the papacy, was the new Pope.

Michelangelo waited in the Piazza San Pietro among the Florentine nobles who were determined to make this the most lavish procession ever to be seen in Rome. Ahead of him were two hundred spearmen, the captains of the thirteen regions of Rome with their banners flying, the five standard-bearers of the Church carrying flags with the papal arms. Twelve milk-white horses from the papal stables were flanked by a hundred young nobles in fringed red silk and ermine. Behind him were a hundred Roman barons accompanied by their armed escorts, the Swiss guards in uniforms of white, yellow and green. The new Pope, called Leo X, mounted on a white Arabian stallion, was shaded from the warm April sun by a canopy of embroidered silk: he was nevertheless perspiring from the weight of the triple tiara and heavily jeweled cope.

The trumpeters sounded for the beginning of the march

across the city from St. Peter's, where Leo had been crowned. Riding beside his cousin, Paolo Rucellai, Michelangelo watched Pope Leo raising his pearl-encrusted gloved hand in benediction, his chamberlains beside him throwing gold coins to the crowds.

It was late when Michelangelo returned to his new home, on the Macello dei Corvi near Trajan's column. Just before his death Pope Julius had paid for the Sistine ceiling, and when this house with its cluster of wooden sheds, stable, tower and garden had come on the market at a reasonable price, he had bought it.

Half the house had been turned into a large workshop, where he had six young assistants. He lived better than before, felt easy about his future. Had not Pope Leo X told his courtiers: "Buonarroti and I were educated together under my father's roof"?

He was carving three heroic columns for Julius' tomb. One was the Moses who had just received from God the carved tablets of the Ten Commandments. The fierceness of soul which would burn outward through the cavernous depths of his eyes was his passionate resolve that his people must not destroy themselves, that they must obey the Commandments and endure.

Balducci, the banker, whom Michelangelo had first met on the streets of Rome eighteen years before, was advising him on the revision of the tomb contract, and Pope Leo was using his good offices to persuade Julius' heirs, the Roveres, to allow Michelangelo more time and more money. Under the new contract, he would have seven years to complete the work. He set to work vigorously on an eight-foot-tall Moses, the Lord's servant on earth, the voice of his conscience.

Meantime the Sistine ceiling had produced an effect equal to the unveiling of his David. Artists had flocked to Rome from all over Europe to help Leo celebrate his elevation to the papacy, and Michelangelo had rewon the title first earned by his Bathers fresco: "Master of the World." Bramante was no longer art emperor of Rome. Cracks of such dimension had shown in his piers of St. Peter's that all work had been stopped and studies undertaken to see if the foundations could be saved. Not long after, he died, and Raphael became the architect of St. Peter's.

Moses: Pope Julius' Tomb
San Pietro in Vincoli, Rome

Michelangelo had heard Leo remark immediately after his coronation: "Since God has seen fit to give us the papacy, let us enjoy it." Money was now pouring out of the Vatican at an unprecedented rate; Leo needed more millions of ducats for pleasures and the arts than Julius had needed for war. The world of Italy was now the world of the Medici. Leo had legitimized his cousin Giulio and made him a cardinal; Leo's brother Giuliano was governing Florence.

In September Michelangelo was invited to the ceremony in which Giuliano was made a Baron of Rome. He sat with the Medici family: Contessina and Ridolfi—in Rome at last—with their sons, and Contessina's older sisters with their families. Leo had had an open-air theater built over the ancient Capitoline. There were speeches, masques, satires, a bawdy comedy; then a six-hour banquet with a profusion of dishes not seen in Rome since the days of Nero.

Contessina was determined to become Leo's official hostess. She had changed since his election to the papacy. Now, brooking no interference from her sisters, she fought for papal appointments, benefices for the Ridolfi family. More and more the laity, wanting favors and appointments, were coming to Contessina. This wielding of power was understandable, Michelangelo thought, after the years of poverty and exile; but the change in Contessina left him uncomfortable.

Over the mild winter he secured a reprieve from her receptions by bringing her to the workshop to see his three figures of

Moses and two Captives, now emerging from the marble. His only associates during the long productive weeks were his assistants.

Only once did he go into society: when Giuliano urged him to attend a reception for Leonardo da Vinci, whom he had installed in the Belvedere, one of the Vatican palaces. When he entered the Belvedere, Giuliano took him through a series of workrooms renovated for Leonardo's purposes. "Look at these concave mirrors," Giuliano exclaimed, "this metal screw-cutting machine. When I took him out on the Pontine marshes he located several extinct volcanoes, and sketched plans for draining the fever-laden area. He's completing his mathematical studies for the squaring of curved surfaces. His work on optics, his formulations of the laws of botany—amazing! Leonardo feels he will be able to tell the age of trees by counting the rings on the trunk. Imagine!"

"I would rather imagine him painting beautiful frescoes."

Leonardo met them dressed in an elaborate red costume with lacy sleeves. He looked tired and old, his magnificent beard and shoulder-length hair now white. The two men, who understood each other not at all, expressed pleasure at the reunion.

Other guests began to arrive. Soon there was a hubbub in the rooms. Michelangelo stood alone at a side window, neglected, not knowing whether he was perplexed or hurt. Leonardo was astonishing the guests with his new contrivances: animals filled with air which sailed over everyone's head; a live lizard to which he had attached wings filled with quicksilver, and whose head he had decorated with artificial eyes, horns and a beard.

"The mechanical lion I made in Milan could walk several steps," he announced to the guests. "And when you pressed a button his breast fell open, exposing a bunch of lilies."

To himself Michelangelo muttered, *"Questo è il colmo!* This is the limit!" and rushed home.

CONTESSINA'S HEALTH WAS failing. In the spring Michelangelo received an urgent note from her. He hurried to the palace and was taken upstairs to her bedroom. Though the weather was warm, she was covered by several quilts, her pale face lying exhausted on the pillows.

She beckoned him to her bed, patted a place for him to sit. He took her hand, white and fragile, in his own. There were tears in her warm brown eyes. "Michelangelo, I remember the first time we met. In the sculpture garden. I asked, 'Doesn't such furious work exhaust you?' "

"And I answered, 'Cutting stone does not take strength out of you, it puts it back in.' "

"Everyone thought I was soon to die, as my mother and sister had. . . . You put strength in me, *caro.*"

"You said, 'When I am near you, I feel strong.' "

"And you answered, 'When I am near you, I feel confused.' " She smiled. "Giovanni said you frightened him. You never frightened me. I saw how tender you were, under the surface."

They stared at each other. Contessina whispered: "We have never spoken of our feelings."

He touched her cheek gently. "I loved you, Contessina."

"I loved you, Michelangelo. I have always felt your presence in the world." Her eyes lighted for a brief instant. "My sons will be your friends."

She was seized with a coughing spell that shook the big bed. She turned her head away, raising a handkerchief to her lips. He waited, trying to control his tears. She did not turn back to him. He whispered, *"Addio, mia cara,"* and left the room.

CONTESSINA'S DEATH SHOOK him deeply. He turned to his Moses, intense, expressive, and to his two Captives, one resisting death, one yielding, pouring into them his own grief and loss.

Pope Leo had been determined to reign without war, but that did not mean he could avoid his neighbors' incessant attempts to conquer the rich country. He went north to make a treaty with the French; while in Florence, he named the Buonarroti family Counts Palatine, and granted them the right to display the Medici crest of six balls. On his return to Rome he summoned Michelangelo to the Vatican. He was sitting at a table in his library with Giulio when Michelangelo was admitted.

"Holy Father," he said, "you were most generous to my family. I am grateful."

"Good," said Leo, "because we do not want you, a Medici sculptor, to spend your time creating statues for a Rovere. You must leave your work for the Rovere heirs of Julius to undertake the greatest art commission of our age—a façade for our family church, San Lorenzo."

"But, Holy Father, I must finish the tomb for Pope Julius or the Roveres will prosecute me!"

"A Medici artist should serve the Medici," Leo repeated. His face was flushed with anger. "You will enter our service at once. We will protect you against the Roveres, secure a new contract to give you more time. When you have completed the façade for San Lorenzo you can return to Julius' mausoleum."

"Holy Father, I have lived with this tomb for ten years. We are ready to construct the front wall, cast the bronzes, mount my Moses and Captives." He was shouting now. "You must not stop me. If I have to dismiss my trained workmen, leave the marble lying about . . . Holiness, on the love I bore your noble father, I implore you not to do this to me." He knelt, bowed his head. "Give me time to finish this work. I will create a great façade for San Lorenzo, but I must not be tormented."

"Or is it," asked Giulio, "that you do not wish to create the San Lorenzo façade for the Medici?"

"I do, Your Grace. But it is a huge undertaking. . . ."

"You are right!" cried Leo. "You must leave for Carrara at once to choose the blocks. I will send you a thousand florins."

Michelangelo departed with tears streaming down his face.

CARRARA WAS A one-crop town: marble. Each day the Carrarino lifted his eyes to the white slashes in the hills that resembled snow, and thanked God. The life of the quarriers was communal: when one prospered, all prospered; when one starved, all starved. Their life in the quarries was so dangerous that when they parted they did not say "Good-by" but *"Fa a modi,* go carefully."

Michelangelo liked the masons of Carrara. They were more like him than his own brothers; small, wiry, tireless, taciturn, with the primordial power of men who work stubborn stone. They spoke in clipped monosyllabic hammer strokes, the compact Carrarino language Michelangelo had had to learn, for their dialect broke off words the way chips were chiseled off a block, *mama* becoming *ma; brasa,* embers, becoming *bra.*

One morning he joined a stream of quarriers on their way to the Polvaccio quarry, where he had found his best marble for Julius' tomb eleven years before. The owner of the quarry, called The Barrel from his enormous round torso, greeted him heartily. "Ah, Buonarroti, today we have your great block."

"Permit me to hope."

The Barrel grasped his arm, led him to the area where water-soaked wooden pegs had been driven into a V-shaped incision and, in the natural course of swelling, had forced an opening in the solid marble cliff which the quarriers were now attacking with levers and sledge hammers, driving the pegs deeper to dislodge the marble from its bed. The foreman cried, "Fall below!" and the workmen sawing blocks fled to the edge of the flat working area. The topmost block ripped from its hold with the sound of a falling tree, landed with tremendous impact in the level work space below, splitting according to its cracks.

When Michelangelo studied the huge jagged block he was disappointed.

"A beautiful piece of meat, no?" The Barrel said.

"It is good. But it is veined."

"The cut is near perfect."

"I must have perfect," Michelangelo replied.

The Barrel lost his temper. "A month we quarry for you, and not one ducat do we see."

"I will pay you much money . . . for white statuary marble."

"God makes marble. Complain to Him."

"Not until I am convinced that there are not whiter blocks behind these."

"You want me to cut down my whole peak?"

"I will have thousands of ducats to spend for the façade of San Lorenzo. You will have your share."

The Barrel turned away, a scowl on his face, grumbling something which sounded as though he were calling him "Big Noise."

Michelangelo picked up his jacket and dinner, struck out for Ravaccione, using an old goat trail that gave him but a few inches of security as he moved down the cliff. He reached the quarry at ten o'clock. There he was disappointed for a second time that morning; a new cut of marble showed soft fissures.

"A beautiful block," said the owner, hovering near. "You buy?"

"Perhaps. I will see."

The owner's face set in a grim expression. Michelangelo was about to move on to the next quarry when he heard the sound of the horn echoing up and down the valleys. The quarriers froze: one of their members had been hurt, perhaps killed. No further work would be done until the following morning, and none then, if there should be a funeral to attend.

Michelangelo circled to the bottom of the town, entered the Market of the Pigs, admitted himself to his two-room apartment at the rear of apothecary Pelliccia's house. He learned from Signora Pelliccia that her husband had gone to attend the injured man. There was a doctor in Carrara but few of the quarriers used him, saying, "Nature cures and the doctors collect."

Signora Pelliccia had saved Michelangelo some of their midday dinner. He was finishing the *minestrone* when a groom arrived with a note from the Marquis of Carrara, requesting that Michelangelo come at once to his castle, the Rocca Malaspina.

The Rocca was a fortress bastion built in the twelfth century. It had crenelated defense towers, a moat and thick stone walls. Lately it had been converted to an elegantly decorated palace.

The marquis was waiting at the head of a majestic flight of stairs. He was tall, courtly, commanding, with a long thin face and a luxuriant beard. "It was kind of you to come, Maestro Buonarroti," he said, leading Michelangelo to his paneled library. "There is some unpleasantness, I fear. Do you remember a name that a quarry owner called you?"

"I thought I heard one of them call me 'Big Noise.' "

"In Carrarino that means to be a complainer, not to accept anything. The owners say you don't know your own mind."

"They're partly right. Pope Leo promised me a thousand ducats to buy marble, but nothing has arrived."

"May I make a suggestion? Sign two or three modest contracts for marble to be delivered in the future. The quarry owners will be reassured. A number who have quarried blocks for you fear they have cut too much and may have to idle the men. Only a few weeks' beans and flour separate these people from hunger. Threaten this thin margin and you become their enemy."

Michelangelo agreed to do as he suggested, and within the next weeks he signed two contracts. Tension in the area vanished; but he could not dissipate his own tension. Although the Rovere heirs had buckled under to the Pope's demands, writing a third contract which further cut down the size of the tomb and extended the time limit to nine years, Michelangelo knew that they were outraged. Pope Leo had blandly assured the Roveres that Michelangelo could continue to carve their tomb marbles while he did those for the Medici; but no one, least of all Michelangelo, was fooled by this promise.

News from Florence was joyless. Giuliano had died. Young Lorenzo de' Medici, son of Piero, now ruled Florence. His smallest act was dictated by Alfonsina, his Roman mother, and by Cardinal Giulio. The Republic had come to an end, the elected councils banished, the constitution outlawed.

Buonarroto's shop was operating at a loss. He needed more money. He had brought his wife, Bartolommea, into the family house to live. He kept expressing the hope that Michelangelo would like her. She was a good woman, with a quiet sweetness.

Michelangelo wrote his brother, "Let us pray that she will produce sons to continue the Buonarroti name."

When the quarries ceased work in the heavy autumn rains, he returned to Rome and a hearty reception at the Vatican. As he knelt to kiss the Pope's ring he noted that Leo's double chin was cascading over the collar of his ermine robe, the fleshy cheeks almost hiding the small sickly mouth.

Michelangelo spread his plans for San Lorenzo on a desk. The Pope was pleased, and agreed to pay twenty-five thousand ducats for the façade. "But one thing must be changed," Giulio added quietly. "The marble must come from Pietrasanta. They have the finest statuary marble in the world."

"Yes, Your Grace, I have heard. But there is no road. The Roman engineers tried to open one and failed."

"They did not try hard enough."

Michelangelo surmised that more than marble was involved.

"The Carraresi are a rebellious lot," the Pope explained, "while the people of Pietrasanta and Seravezza are loyal Tuscans. They have signed over their quarries to Florence. Thus we shall secure the purest marble for only the cost of labor."

"I don't believe it is humanly possible to quarry in Pietrasanta, Holiness," protested Michelangelo. "The blocks would have to come out of stone precipices a mile high."

"You will make the trip to Monte Altissimo and report on it."

HE RETURNED TO Carrara and, when the Pope's thousand ducats for marble purchases arrived at last, he put out of his mind any worry about the Pietrasanta quarry and began buying marble almost in a fever. But he received a stinging letter from the Vatican: the Pope wanted Pietrasanta marble. He told no one of his destination, but arranged to have a horse take him down the coast road to the quarry. The Pietrasantans' houses were built around a square with a superb view of the Tyrrhenian Sea. Above, towered impregnable Monte Altissimo.

There was a narrow wagon road between Pietrasanta and the hill town of Seravezza. At Seravezza everything was unrelieved stone, the houses interlocked around a cobbled piazza. He found a room for the night, and a guide in a husky boy called Antò.

They left Seravezza in the pitch dark before dawn. Where the trail into the hills ended they had to cut through thickets of underbrush. They climbed straight up dark stone ranges, rock formations that looked as though they had been made as steps for the gods. They descended into dark clammy gorges, then climbed on hands and knees up the next range. By midmorning they emerged at the top of a shrub-covered promontory. Between Michelangelo and Monte Altissimo was only a sharp hogback and beyond this a canyon out of which rose the fearsome Alps. Michelangelo sat on a boulder looking upward. "With the help of God, and the whole French army, one might get a road built to this point. But how could anyone build a road up that perpendicular wall? Well, let's get on, Antò. I want to see how good the marbles are that we can't bring down."

The marbles were perfect: outcroppings of purest white statuary. He found a *poggio* where the Romans had dug, fragments of a marble block they had excavated. After the struggle to keep their footing up the rocky ravines and gorges until they had passed the snow line, it was clear to Michelangelo why the emperors had used Carrara marble to build Rome. Yet he ached to set hammer and chisel to this shining stone, the purest he had ever seen.

It was dusk by the time he came on down to Carrara. He noticed that the farmers in the fields did not appear to see him, and when he entered the Porta Ghibellina the townspeople in front of their shops suddenly became busy. He walked into the apothecary's shop where Pelliccia, the apothecary, was grinding medications on a slab of marble. "What has happened? I left yesterday morning a trusted Carrarino. I return tonight a Tuscan."

"It's your trip up Monte Altissimo. The opening of quarries in Pietrasanta could destroy us."

"I shall report to His Holiness that no marble can be brought down from Monte Altissimo."

He made a contract for another fifty cartloads of Carrara marble and wrote his report to Rome. The Pope answered: "His Holiness wills that all work be done with marble from Pietrasanta and no other."

He looked for a house to rent in Pietrasanta. Within an hour of his return to Carrara a crowd, seven hundred strong, began to gather in the piazza beneath the apothecary's windows. Michelangelo stood behind the curtained doors listening to the murmur grow. Then someone spied him, and the quarriers began shouting: "Big Noise! Big Noise!"

Michelangelo threw open the window and held his arms out. "This is not my doing. You must believe me."

"*Bastardo!* You have sold us!"

"Have I not bought your marble? I will suffer more from this than you."

"You will not suffer in the belly!" A hundred arms were raised and stones filled the air like hail, shattering the windows. A large stone struck him on the forehead. Blood began to trickle down his face. He made no move to stanch the flow. The crowd saw what had happened and within minutes the piazza was deserted, with only the stones and broken glass to tell what had happened.

He rented a house in Pietrasanta. But his attempts to recruit quarriers in Carrara were coldly rebuffed. The Carrarinos would not ship the marble he had already contracted and paid for. In desperation he made the journey back to Settignano, to the Topolino family. He explained his plight. They, too, had contracts to fill, but the family decided that Gilberto, the youngest, should accompany Michelangelo.

Over the next days he assembled a crew of twelve stonecutters. Not one quarrier in the lot! How could he tackle a savage mountain with this inexperienced crew? But on his way home to Florence, he came across Donato Benti, an unemployed sculptor willing to work for him as a quarrier.

Then, in Florence, he learned that the Pope had decreed he must also supply marble for repairs to the Duomo. In exchange, the Duomo and the Wool Guild agreed to pay the salary of an accountant named Vieri who would act as commissary, to arrange supplies and keep the accounts. They would, in addition, finance his road since they were eager to develop the resources of Tuscany.

He had a happy visit at home, for his sister-in-law Bartolommea, who had already borne a daughter, Cecca, was delivered of a healthy boy. At long last the Buonarroti-Simoni name was safe for the future.

THE ACCOUNTANT, VIERI, Gilberto Topolino and Benti moved into the Pietrasanta house with him. Michelangelo found a house in Seravezza for the remaining workers. He marked out the most promising route to the quarry area, set the men to

work to cut a safe ledge for passage. A forge was set up to build iron-supported wagons for transporting the marble columns to the sea.

Just one crag below the summit Michelangelo unearthed a formation of pure statuary marble, crystalline white, flawless. He had the men carve a level area on the peak from which they could quarry. The marble ran straight back in a solid white sheet, an entire cliff. "All we have to do," he exclaimed exultantly, "is strip out great blocks that have been here since Genesis."

"And get them off this mountain," added Benti, gazing downward the five or six miles to the sea.

The first weeks of quarrying were a total waste. Michelangelo tried to show the men how the Carrarinos quarried. Marble was temperamental, easily shattered because of its delicacy, and the Settignano stonemasons were not experienced quarrymen. At the end of the month Michelangelo had not yet quarried one ducat's worth of usable marble.

A road builder arrived from Florence: Bocca, the Mouth, hairy from his skull to his toes, an illiterate laborer on the roads in his youth, who had learned to draw maps and boss road crews. He had a reputation for pushing through roads in record time. Within ten days he had mapped the simplest possible route to the base of Monte Altissimo. The only trouble was that the road was not directed toward those places where the marble was to be found.

Michelangelo took Bocca with him to the quarries. "You see, Bocca, I could never get my blocks to your road. The road must reach the quarries!"

"This is where I build. I'm road. You're marble."

It was a warm night. Michelangelo walked for miles while he wrestled with his problem. He could complain to Pope Leo, have another road builder sent. But what assurance would he have that it wouldn't be another Bocca? He groaned. He must get rid of Bocca and build the road himself!

He mapped the road, laid out stakes. At two points he chose to tunnel through solid rock rather than try to push the road up and down a hogback. For a terminus he chose a spot at the base of the two ravines down which he planned to lower the blocks. By the end of June, Vieri said sternly: "You'll have to stop building now. There's no more money."

"I can't stop. Draw on my own eight hundred ducats."

"But you may never get the money back."

"Spend it. Until I get the marble out, the Holy Father won't let me be a sculptor."

From sunrise to dark he was up and down the mountains on a mule, watching progress. By mid-September the road was passable and he had managed to quarry an enormous column; he started to move it down the ravine. It was roped half a dozen times around its width and its length, crowbarred onto wooden rollers. Down the slide, on either side, stakes had been driven into the ground, angling outward. The ropes from the column, tied to these stakes, were the only hold the crews had on the marble.

Down it went, held by some thirty men. Michelangelo directed the men handling the rollers to pick up the one at the rear, when the end of the marble had passed, and run to put it under the front; the men at the stakes held the ropes with all their might until the column had slid past them, then ran down the trail to the next stakes to tie up their ropes and apply the brake. Hours passed, the sun rose high, the men sweated and strained.

Down the long steep ravine the column slid, the crew exerting all its strength to slow its movement. By late afternoon they were only thirty-five yards from the road. Michelangelo was jubilant; very soon now they would slide the column onto the loading platform, from which it would be moved onto a wagon drawn by a team of thirty-two oxen.

He never quite knew how the accident happened. An agile young Pisan named Gino knelt to put another roller under the front of the column. Suddenly something snapped, and the column started to move on its own.

There were shouts: "Gino! Get out! Quick!"

But it was too late. The column rolled over Gino, swerved

toward Michelangelo. He threw himself over the side of a ledge, rolling a number of feet before he could break his fall.

The men stood paralyzed as the flawless column picked up speed, smashed its way downward, hit the loading platform and broke into a hundred pieces.

Gilberto and Michelangelo knelt over Gino. "His neck is broken," said Gilberto. "Killed instantly."

In his mind Michelangelo heard the mournful sound of a horn echoing from peak to peak. He picked up the boy's body, stumbled blindly down the rest of the descent. He mounted his mule, still holding Gino, while the others led the way into Seravezza.

TORRENTIAL RAINS INUNDATED the piazza and all work was shut down. The crews returned home. Michelangelo's accounting showed that he had spent thirty ducats beyond the eight hundred advanced to him at the beginning of the year. He had loaded not a single block. The lone consolation was the attendance of a group of Carrarini quarriers at Gino's burial. Apothecary Pelliccia linked his arm through Michelangelo's as they left the cemetery. "This death brought us to our senses, Michelangelo. We treated you badly. But we have suffered from the loss of contracts from agents and sculptors waiting to buy from the Pope's quarries at Pietrasanta."

Now the Carrarini boatmen would transport his blocks, still on the beach, to the docks in Florence.

He put his few personal possessions in a saddlebag and made his way home to Florence. He was still too shaken to attempt carving, and so he started to build a studio on the Via Mozza.

By February, his workshop completed, he brought half a dozen of his nine-foot Carrara blocks for Julius' tomb from the Arno storehouse. He had only to return to Pietrasanta, excavate the columns he needed for San Lorenzo; then he could settle down on the Via Mozza for years of work for the Roveres and Medici.

He built a model of the façade of San Lorenzo, making wax

figures to represent his sculptures. Pope Leo signed a contract for forty thousand ducats, payable over eight years.

He did not ask Gilberto Topolino to go back to the quarries; that would have been unfair; but most of the others agreed to join him. Rather than being frightened by Pietrasanta, the masons felt that with the road completed and the quarries open the hardest work was already done. Still disturbed by the accident that had killed Gino, he evolved a system of iron rings which could be driven into the surface of the block, giving the crews a surer grip on the marble as it was brought down the ravine.

The Pope had been rightly informed: there was enough magnificent marble here to supply the world for a thousand years, and now the crystalline cliffs yielded superbly. There were no more accidents. In a few weeks five superb blocks were loaded on wagons and taken to barges on the beach.

The work was progressing satisfactorily when, suddenly, Michelangelo was recalled to Florence. He reported at once to Cardinal Giulio in the Medici palace.

"Your Grace, am I recalled? In a few months I would have had nine giant columns on the beach of Pietrasanta."

"There is enough marble now. We are abandoning the façade for San Lorenzo." Michelangelo was unnerved by the hostility in the cardinal's voice as Giulio continued: "The floor of the Duomo needs repaving. Since the Duomo and Wool Guild Boards paid the cost of the road, they are entitled to the marble you have excavated."

"You would pave the Duomo floor with the finest statuary marbles ever quarried? Why do you humiliate me in this way?"

Giulio replied icily, "The cathedral needs paving."

Michelangelo clenched his fists to stop his trembling. "It is nearly three years now since His Holiness took me off the Rovere tomb. In all that time I have not been able to carve one inch of marble. Of the twenty-three hundred ducats you have sent me, I have spent eighteen hundred on marble, quarries and roads. I do not reckon the years I have wasted, the insults put upon me. I do not reckon my house in Rome, which I left, my marble and blocked-out statues. I only want one thing now: to be free!"

Cardinal Giulio had listened carefully to Michelangelo's complaints. His thin, smooth face grew dark.

"The Holy Father will review your case. You are dismissed."

Michelangelo stumbled down the long hallway, his feet carrying him to what had been *Il Magnifico*'s study. He cried aloud to the long-departed spirit of Lorenzo: "I am ruined!"

BOOK NINE

The War

 WHERE DID A MAN go when he had been destroyed? Where else but to work, bolting the door of his studio, standing his blocks of marble around the walls as though they were soldiers guarding his privacy. The studio had ceilings thirty-five feet high, tall windows to the north, spacious enough to allow him to carve several tomb figures at the same time. This was where a sculptor belonged, in his workshop.

But the tighter he bolted his studio door against the intrusion of the outside world, the more evident it became that trouble was man's natural state. News reached him that Leonardo da Vinci, who had fled to France to escape the Pope's displeasure several years before, had died there, unwanted and unhonored by his countrymen. A letter from Rome told him that Raphael was ill, obliged to turn more and more of his work over to apprentices. Pope Leo's political judgment had proved unsound in backing Francis I of France against Charles V, the Holy Roman Emperor. In Germany, Martin Luther was challenging papal supremacy, crying: "I don't know if the Christian faith can endure any other head of the Universal Church on earth save Christ."

As the months passed he broke into four nine-foot blocks; these were to be four huge Captive figures for Julius' tomb: a somnolent Young Giant, trying to free himself from his imprisonment in the stone of time; an Awakening Giant, bursting forth from his mountain chrysalis; an Atlas, holding God's earth on his shoulders; and a Bearded Giant, old and tired. By spring the four Captive-Giants had become visible under his driving power.

Then Pope Leo and Cardinal Giulio decided to build a sacristy onto San Lorenzo to house a large Medici tomb. Unembarrassed by the fact that he had canceled his contract for the façade, Pope Leo sent his brother-in-law Salviati to Michelangelo asking him to make sculptures for the new chapel and to design the sacristy.

"I am no longer a Medici sculptor," cried Michelangelo. "Another two years and I can complete Julius' tomb. The Rovere family will owe me eighty-five hundred ducats."

"You need the good will of the Medici," Salviati said.

"I also need money."

But Salviati was right: he could not afford the Medici's disfavor. Either he worked for them, or he might not work at all.

MICHELANGELO DESIGNED AN austere sarcophagus for either side of the new chapel, each holding two reclining allegorical figures: Night and Day on one, Dawn and Dusk on the other; two male, two female; great brooding figures, which would represent man's cycle. This plan was accepted.

Then in November Pope Leo caught a chill. By December 1, 1521, he was dead. At the Requiem Mass Michelangelo joined in the prayer for Leo's soul. Later, he whispered to Granacci: "Do you suppose heaven can offer any part of the entertainment Leo provided himself at the Vatican?"

"I doubt it. God would not spend that much money."

With Leo dead, the project of the Medici chapel became as

cold and bleak as the Tuscan winter. The College of Cardinals elected sixty-two-year-old Adrian of Utrecht, a practical-minded Fleming. Cardinal Giulio fled to Florence, for Pope Adrian was a highly moral churchman who had disapproved of the Medici pontificate. The Pope listened sympathetically to the Rovere family, headed by the Duke of Urbino, agreeing that they should file suit against Michelangelo for failure to fulfill his contract on the Julius tomb. The suit was a punitive one, exaggerating the amount he had been paid, taking no account of the other work Julius had forced him to do. With the Pope's backing, it was a disaster.

He asked Granacci: "How could so much have happened to me when I have been simply so full of love for marble, so consumed to carve? I have talent, energy, enthusiasm, singleness of purpose. What am I missing? *Fortuna,* luck?"

"Last out the bad times, *caro.* There is more work to do."

"But what if the Pope won't let me work?"

Fortunately for Michelangelo, God soon gathered Pope Adrian to his everlasting reward. This time Giulio de' Medici garnered·enough votes in the College of Cardinals to get himself elected Pope. As Pope Clement VII he sent word immediately after his coronation: Michelangelo must resume work on the chapel.

He was like a man who has barely escaped death. Pope Clement put him on a lifetime pension of fifty ducats a month, gave him a new workshop by San Lorenzo. The Rovere heirs were persuaded to drop their suit.

He went one evening to the Rucellai palace to hear Machiavelli read the first chapter of his history of Florence. The Plato Academy, bitter against Pope Clement, was at the center of a plot to restore the Republic. Michelangelo heard stories that Clement, called by his enemies "the dregs of the Medici," was making fatal errors of judgment. He rejected the overtures of the Holy Roman Emperor, and in the incessant wars among the surrounding nations he consistently backed the wrong side; though truth to tell, Clement changed sides so often that no one could keep up with his intrigues. In Germany and Holland thousands of Catholics were abandoning their religion for the reformation which Clement refused to carry out within the Church.

A cardinal appointed by the Pope, Passerini of Cortona, ruled Florence autocratically and Clement rejected all appeals to replace this man whom the Florentines found crude, greedy,

Night; Medici Chapel, Florence

contemptuous of their Signoria. The Florentines were waiting only for an advantageous moment to rise, seize arms and once again drive out the Medici.

Their opportunity came when Florence was caught in the wars between the papacy and the Holy Roman Empire. Armies from both sides were threatening the city. But Cardinal Passerini refused to defend it. The citizens rose in revolt and civil war began.

Michelangelo joined the Republican forces defending the Palazzo della Signoria just before pro-Medici forces attacked the doors with pikes. From the windows and the parapet above, desks, tables and chairs rained down on the soldiers. A heavy wooden bench hurtled straight for the David. "Look out!" Michelangelo cried, as though the statue might dodge. But the bench struck. The left arm snapped off below the elbow and fell to the piazza, broken.

The crowd drew back. The soldiers turned to stare. He felt himself moving toward the sculpture. The crowd opened, murmuring: "It is Michelangelo. Let him pass."

He stood below the David, gazing up into the pensive, resolute, beautiful face. Goliath had not scratched him; but civil war had come within inches of destroying him completely. Though

Michelangelo could not know it, it would be years before the statue was repaired.

Meanwhile, the Emperor's army swept south to Rome, breached the walls, and forced Pope Clement to flee to the fortress of Sant' Angelo. He remained a prisoner there while mercenaries looted and burned Rome, destroying works of art, smashing altars, lighting fires on the marble floors of the Vatican, putting out the eyes in paintings. Heartsick, Michelangelo thought of his Pietà and the Sistine ceiling, the Moses and the two Captives.

With Clement a prisoner, the Republic was again proclaimed in Florence. The city-state adopted Machiavelli's new plan for a citizens' militia, trained to defend the Republic against invaders. The Signoria was aided by a Council of Eighty, chosen from the old families. Trade was active again, the city people happy. Few cared what happened to Pope Clement; but Michelangelo was vitally interested. He had put years of loving work into the Medici tombs.

At the end of 1527 the tide turned again. A virulent plague decimated the Holy Roman Emperor's armies, and they were also threatened by a French army financed by the Pope. A few months later, the plague struck Florence. People came down with crushing headaches, pain in the limbs, fever. In three days they were dead. If people dropped in the streets they were left there; if they died in their homes their families fled. Thousands perished. The city became a morgue.

Buonarroto died in Michelangelo's arms. While he mourned, he drew up a paper paying back to Buonarroto's wife the dowry she had brought with her; she would need it to get a second husband. He arranged for his eleven-year-old niece, Cecca, to be educated in a convent, set aside assets to pay for the education of his nephew, Lionardo. He did not greatly care whether he fell victim now. "Perhaps Buonarroto is the fortunate one," he thought.

He escaped, and the plague abated. People filtered down from the hills; the government returned to the city. But Pope Clement now made an alliance with the Holy Roman Emperor, and sent an army to wipe out the Republic and once again restore the Medici to power. Michelangelo was summoned before the current gonfaloniere.

"Since you work stone, Buonarroti," he said, "you can surely design what Florence needs now: walls that cannot be breached."

Dutifully he explored the several miles of city wall, noting that neither the walls nor the defense towers were in good repair. More towers for cannon were needed. The anchor of the defense line would have to be the campanile of San Miniato, from whose height the defenders could command most of the ground over which the enemy troops would have to charge.

He reported these requirements to the gonfaloniere, and work went ahead at full speed, for the Pope's army was reported moving on Florence from several directions. Michelangelo and a hundred peasants built bastions, high walls of brick made of pounded earth mixed with tow fibers and cattle dung. Michelangelo was officially made Governor General of the Fortifications. There was no further thought of sculpture. Nor could he cry, "War is not my trade." Florence had called on him in its time of crisis.

He began a series of deep ditches outside the wall, using the excavated earth to form barricades. He secured permission to level all buildings between the defense walls and the encircling foothills a mile to the south; farmers helped to knock down houses that had been in their families for hundreds of years.

General Malatesta had been brought from Perugia to serve as one of the defense commanders. He quarreled with Michelangelo's plans. "You have thrown up too many walls. Take your peasants away, and let my soldiers defend Florence."

General Malatesta seemed cold, devious, and that night Michelangelo, roaming the base of his ramparts, came upon the eight artillery pieces that had been given to Malatesta to defend the San Miniato wall. They were lying outside the walls, unguarded. Michelangelo went immediately to awaken the sleeping general. "Why are you exposing your artillery pieces?"

"Are you the commander of this army?" Malatesta was livid.

"Just of the defense walls."

"Then go make your cow-dung brick, and don't tell a soldier how to fight."

Everywhere he went he heard stories against Malatesta: he had yielded Perugia without a battle; his men would not fight the Pope's troops at Arezzo; when the armies reached Florence, Malatesta would surrender the city. . . .

The papal armies were now camped thirty thousand strong on the hills beyond his southern defense walls. From the tower of San Miniato, Michelangelo gazed at the hundreds of enemy tents set up a mile away.

He was awakened at dawn by artillery fire, concentrated against the tower of San Miniato. If it could be knocked down, the Pope's forces would pour into the city. One hundred and fifty pieces of papal artillery fired steadily. Whole sections of brick and stone were blasted out by the exploding cannonballs. The attack lasted for two hours. When it was finished Michelangelo let himself out by a tunnel and stood at the base of the bell tower, surveying the damage.

He asked for volunteers to refit the shattered stone into the walls, sent out runners to collect crews of masons and quarriers, at dusk set them to rebuilding the tower. They worked all night: but it would take time for the cement to harden. If the enemy artillery opened fire too soon, his defense would be leveled. He gazed up at the campanile, its crenelated cornice wider by four feet than the shaft of the tower. If there were a way to hang something from those parapets that would absorb the impact of the iron and stone cannonballs before they could strike the tower itself . . .

By first light the militia were beating on the doors of the wool shops and the warehouses. Next they hunted the city for mattress covers. By the time the sun was up dozens of stout covers were stuffed with wool and suspended by ropes across the face of the tower. When the Pope's officers turned their artillery on the campanile, their cannon balls struck the heavy paddings which hung four feet out from the wet stone walls and fell harmlessly into the ditch below. At noon the enemy abandoned the attack.

Heavy rains began to fall. The open mile of cleared fields between his walls and the enemy became a bog. There could be no attack now.

Michelangelo spent the days on the parapets; at night he slipped into the sacristy where his statues for the tombs now stood, and carved by candlelight. The chapel was cold, full of shadows; but he was not alone. His figures were familiar friends: the Dawn, the Dusk; telling him of art as a means of conquering death.

In the spring the war was resumed, but none of the battles except the one against starvation took place in Florence. The papal army had cut off supplies from the sea. Meat vanished first, then oil, greens, flour, wine. People began eating asses, dogs, cats. Summer heat baked the stones, the water supply failed, the Arno dried up, the plague struck again. By mid-July five thousand were dead within the city.

Florence had only one chance to survive, through its heroic general, Francesco Ferrucci, whose army was near Pisa. Plans were laid for him to attack and lift the siege. But Malatesta betrayed the Republic to the Pope's generals. Ferrucci was defeated and killed; Florence capitulated. Malatesta's troops opened the gates and Pope Clement's representatives entered the city to take control. Those members of the government who could, fled; others were hanged. All heads of the militia were condemned.

"You'd better get out of the city this very night," Michelangelo was warned. "The Pope will show no mercy."

He made his way by back passages to the Arno, crossed the river and slipped into the bell tower of San Niccolò, first knocking at the house next door, which belonged to the sons of old Beppe, to let them know he was taking refuge until Malatesta left Florence. He spent the night staring down on the terrain he had leveled to protect the city-state. A one-armed David now stood as a symbol of the vanquished Republic. Lorenzo had said that the forces of destruction were everywhere. That was all Michelangelo had known since the days of Savonarola: conflict. And now here he was cowering in an ancient bell tower.

Before cockcrow each morning he descended to find food and water and hear the news of the day. He learned that Florence knew where he was hiding, but the hatred for Pope Clement was so intense that he not only was safe but had become a hero. Lodovico, whom Michelangelo had sent to Pisa during the siege, had returned safely.

In mid-November he learned through an intermediary that Pope Clement had pardoned him for his part in the warfare. His pension was to be restored, and he was to return to work in the sacristy of San Lorenzo.

His studio in the Via Mozza had been thoroughly ransacked by the papal troops; but none of his marble had been disturbed. After three years of war he could begin to carve again. Sitting among his folio of drawings, he turned over a drawing sheet and with deep emotion wrote a poem ending:

> *. . . If I was made for art, from childhood given*
> *A prey for burning beauty to devour,*
> *I blame the mistress I was born to serve.*

Clement's son, known as Alessandro the Moor because of his swarthy skin and thick lips, was made sovereign of the city-state of Florence. He was a dissolute, ugly youth of low intelligence and rapacious appetites. With his father's troops on hand to enforce his slightest wish, he murdered his opponents, debauched the youth of the city, wiped out its last semblances of freedom, and quickly brought it to a state of anarchy.

Equally quickly, Michelangelo fought with Alessandro. When Alessandro asked him to design a new fort, Michelangelo declined. When Alessandro wished to show the Medici sacristy to the Viceroy of Naples, Michelangelo locked it.

Giovanni Spina, appointed by the Pope to handle his Florentine art projects, cautioned him: "Your conduct is dangerous."

"I'm safe until I complete the tomb. The Pope has made that clear to his thick-skulled son . . . or I would have been dead long ago." He wiped the marble dust from his face, and exclaimed with gratification: "This chapel will outlive Alessandro, even if I don't. With a hammer and chisel in my hands I feel that I am compensating for the spiritual degradation of Florence."

By September he had finished Dawn and Night, Day and Dusk. He was emaciated and racked by a cough as he picked up hammer and chisel to begin the last figures. "It won't do, you know," Granacci reproved him. "Death from overindulgence is a form of suicide, whether it's from work or wine."

"If I don't work twenty hours a day I'll never finish."

He fell ill of a high fever. When it passed he was so weak his legs could barely hold him.

The Pope sent a carriage and driver to Florence, ordering Michelangelo to come to Rome to recuperate in the southern sun, and to hear about an exciting new project he had envisaged. Clement invited Michelangelo's friends in the Florentine colony for dinner at the Vatican to amuse him. His solicitude for Michelangelo's health was genuine, almost like that of a beloved brother. Then he revealed his desire: Would Michelangelo paint a Last Judgment on the altar wall of the Sistine Chapel?

At the dinner that night Michelangelo met a young man of singular beauty, like that of the youths he had painted behind the Doni Holy Family. He had eyes of a luminous gray-blue, a classical nose and mouth, a high, rounded forehead, chestnut hair, the rose-bronzed skin of the youths who competed in the stadia of ancient Greece.

Tommaso de' Cavalieri, twenty-two, well educated, serious, was the heir of a patrician Roman family. Ambitious to become a painter, he asked eagerly if he might become Michelangelo's apprentice. Michelangelo replied that he must return to Florence to finish the Medici chapel before doing his Last Judgment; but they could draw together when he returned to Rome. Meantime he would send drawings which Tommaso could study.

309

LODOVICO'S NINETIETH BIRTHDAY fell on an exhilarating day in June 1534. Florence glistened like a precious stone in its prong of mountains. Michelangelo gathered the Buonarroti family to dinner. Lodovico, so feeble that he had to be propped with pillows, ate only a few spoonfuls of soup, then fell back. Michelangelo picked his father up in his arms. He weighed no more than a bundle of sticks. He put him in bed, tucked a blanket around him. The old man turned his head slightly so that he could see his desk with its neatly stacked account books. A smile came over his ash-gray lips.

"Michelagnolo." The pet name. Lodovico had not used it for years. "I wanted . . . to live to be ninety."

"And so you have."

"But now . . . I'm tired. . . ."

"Rest. I'll close the door."

"Michelagnolo . . . you will take care of . . . the boys?"

Michelangelo thought, "The boys! In their middle fifties!" Aloud he replied, "Our family is all I have, Father."

"You'll give my grandson . . . Lionardo . . . a wool shop?"

"Yes, Father."

"Then all is well. I have kept my family . . . together. We gained back . . . the money . . . my father lost."

Lionardo brought the priest. Lodovico died quietly. Michelangelo had loved his father, just as in his flinty Tuscan way Lodovico had loved his son. The world would seem empty without him. It had not been Lodovico's fault that only one of his five sons had been an earner. That was why he had had to work Michelangelo so hard, to make up for the others. Michelangelo was proud that he had been able to fulfill Lodovico's ambition.

Later, he stood alone in the sacristy under the dome he had designed and built. Standing between his exquisitely carved sarcophagi, each to hold its two giant figures, he felt that *Il Magnifico* would have been gratified. He wrote instructions for his apprentices to mount Day and Night on their sarcophagus, Dusk and Dawn opposite; then he packed his saddlebags. He mounted and crossed Florence, leaving it by the Porta Romana.

At the top of the rise he turned to look back at the exquisite city of stone nestled under its red tile roofs. It was hard to take leave of one's city; hard to feel that, close to sixty, he could not count on returning.

Resolutely he turned his horse south toward Rome.

BOOK TEN

Love

ROME, AFTER ITS LATEST warfare, seemed in a worse state of ruin than when he had first seen it in 1496. He had hired a new, twenty-year-old apprentice and steward, a steady young man named Urbino. With Urbino he walked through his own dilapidated premises on the Macello dei Corvi. Most of the furniture had been stolen, and some of the blocks for Julius' tomb. The Moses and the two Captives had not been injured.

Two days after Michelangelo reached Rome, Pope Clement VII died, and the city poured into the streets in a paroxysm of joy. At the Medici palace Michelangelo found the Florentine exiles jubilant. Clement's son Alessandro, ruler of Florence, could now be replaced by Ippolito, son of the beloved Giuliano.

Twenty-five-year-old Cardinal Ippolito greeted him with an affectionate smile. A dozen of his old friends thronged about him. They had plotted to get rid of Alessandro; now they could act openly. "You'll help us, Michelangelo?" asked Cardinal Giovanni Salviati, son of Lorenzo's daughter Lucrezia.

"Most certainly. Alessandro is a wild beast."

Contessina's son, Cardinal Niccolò Ridolfi, said, "There is only one obstacle: Charles V. If the Emperor were on our side, we could march on Florence. There have been reports, Michelangelo, that he has expressed interest in your work. Would you carve or paint for him if it would help our cause?"

Michelangelo assured them that he would.

Back at home, he asked himself over and over again whether he was relieved to have the crushing burden of the Last Judgment off his shoulders. The altar wall of the Sistine would have required a minimum of five years to paint; yet as his ducats poured out for refurbishing his house he saw that he would soon be in need of money.

Balducci, as wide as he was tall, but of hard flesh and red cheeks, now raising grandchildren in profusion, exploded: "Of course you're in trouble! Spending all those years in Florence without my financial wizardry. But you're in safe hands now. I'll invest all the money you earn."

Early the next morning the Duke of Urbino came to call, followed by a servant with a box containing the contracts for Julius' tomb. The duke was a ferocious-looking man, with a trench-lined battlefield for a face. He informed Michelangelo that the wall had been prepared for the tomb; then he took from the leather box the latest agreement and flung it at Michelangelo's feet. "There will be no more Medici to protect you. If you do not complete this contract by May of next year, I shall force you to fulfill the 1516 contract: twenty-five statues, larger than life."

The duke stormed out. But in the matter of the Rovere tomb the fates were as much against the Duke of Urbino as against Michelangelo. On October 11, 1534, the College of Cardinals elected Alessandro Farnese to the papacy; he became Pope Paul III. He had been educated by Lorenzo, and had acquired a lifelong love of art and learning. At once he sent a courier to the house on the Macello dei Corvi: would Michelangelo Buonarroti come to the Vatican palace?

It was the old story. The Pope demanded that he work on the Last Judgment, put the contract with the Duke of Urbino out of his mind. "Is the Holy See to be intimidated by a war lord?" he asked. "I am determined to have you serve me."

Michelangelo kissed the Pope's ring, backed out of the throne

room. Returning to his house, he sank into an old leather chair. Almost immediately a sharp knock on the door straightened him up from his collapsed position. His assistant, Urbino, admitted two Swiss guards, tall blond giants in identical yellow and green costumes, sent to announce that Michelangelo Buonarroti would receive, the following midmorning, a visit from His Holiness Paul III. "What refreshment does one serve the Holy

Father and his train?" asked Urbino. "I have never seen a Pope, except in procession."

"I wish that was the only place I had ever seen one," grumbled Michelangelo. "Buy raisin wine and cookies."

The Pope arrived with his cardinals and attendants. Paul smiled benignly on Michelangelo, went quickly to the Moses. The cardinals surrounded the figure in a field of red cassocks. Ercole Gonzaga, Cardinal of Mantua, the art authority of the Vatican, declared: "This Moses alone is sufficient to do honor to Pope Julius. No man could want a more glorious monument."

Pope Paul said, "My son, paint the Last Judgment for me. I will arrange for the Duke of Urbino to settle for the Moses and two Captives."

Michelangelo had not lived through four pontificates without learning when he was outmaneuvered. But how to summon at sixty the cyclonic powers he had enjoyed at thirty-three?

Next day he walked slowly to St. Peter's. Sangallo's nephew, Antonio, was now its architect, but as far as Michelangelo could tell, little had been accomplished in the eighteen years since he had left Rome except the repair of the giant piers and the building of the lowest foundation walls. Two hundred thousand ducats from all over Christendom had been poured into the concrete; but mostly, Michelangelo had learned, into the pockets of the contractors who were erecting St. Peter's as slowly as was humanly possible.

Without knowing that he had so directed his steps, he found himself before the residence of the Cavalieri family. As he dropped the heavy clapper on the door he wondered why it had taken him so long to call on Tommaso de' Cavalieri, who had expressed himself eager to work with him.

A servant opened the door, led Michelangelo into a high-ceilinged salon which contained one of the best collections of antique sculpture in Rome. He heard footsteps behind him, turned, and gasped. In the two years since he had seen him, Tommaso had changed from an attractive youth to the most magnificent man Michelangelo had ever seen; even more beautiful than the Greek discus thrower in the salon.

"You've come at last," said Tommaso in his grave and courtly voice.

"I had not wished to bring you my troubles."

"Friends can share troubles."

They gripped each other's arms in a welcoming salute. A warm smile spread over Michelangelo's features. "You know I am to do the Last Judgment for Pope Paul. Up to this moment I had not thought I could summon the courage. Now I am less heavy-hearted."

They climbed a broad flight of stairs to Tommaso's workshop. Tommaso spent half of his day working for the tax commission and as curator of public works, and the other half drawing. On the wall above the table were the drawings Michelangelo had sent from Florence. Spread out over the planks were dozens of sketches. Michelangelo studied them, exclaimed: "You have a fine talent. I shall serve as your master, and in return you shall help me enlarge my drawings."

They became inseparable. Each morning, by the time the sun hit the top of Trajan's Column, Tommaso had come with a packet of freshly baked rolls for his midmorning refreshment. They sketched on the Capitoline or in the Forum on Sundays, had supper in each other's homes, spent the evenings in drawing and conversation.

How did he define his feeling for Tommaso? It was different from his dependent love for his family, from the reverence he felt for *Il Magnifico,* his enduring love for Contessina, the unforgotten passion for Clarissa, his friendly love for Granacci. Perhaps this love, coming so late in his life, was undefinable.

HE STOOD ALONE in the Sistine Chapel, the tumultuous array from Genesis overhead. The fifty-five-by-forty-foot wall on which he was to work had painted tapestries in the bottom zone; above the altar were two Perugino frescoes; then two tall windows; next, portraits of the first two Popes; and in the topmost compartment, two of the lunettes he himself had painted. The wall was fire-blackened, pitted and broken; there was spoilage from damp, and an overall soiling of dust, grime and smoke from candles. He disliked destroying the Perugino frescoes, but since he was also obliterating two of his own paintings no one could think him ruthless. He would seal up the two windows, build a new brick wall slanted outward a foot from ceiling to floor so that dust, dirt and smoke would not adhere.

Pope Paul gave his consent to Michelangelo's plans. Michelangelo found himself liking this Pope more and more. Paul was a Latin and Greek scholar, a fine speaker and writer. He also was blessed with a sense of humor.

Michelangelo was happy during these months of steady drawing in his studio. Every man, woman and child was to stand out in full human dignity; for each was an individual and had worth. This was the key to the rebirth of learning and freedom that had been sired in Florence, after the darkness of a thousand years. Never would he, Michelangelo, reduce man to an indistinguishable part of an inchoate mass, not even en route to heaven or hell!

One day Tommaso and Cardinal Niccolò Ridolfi arrived at his house. "The Emperor Charles V is coming through Rome," Tommaso said. "He will visit Vittoria Colonna, the Marchesa di Pescara. He is a long-time friend of her husband's family."

"I do not know the marchesa."

"But I do," replied Tommaso. "I have asked her to invite you to her gathering this Sunday afternoon."

Niccolò, who had Contessina's somber brown eyes, said, "It would mean a great deal to Florence if you became friends with the marchesa and could be introduced by her to the Emperor when he comes to Rome."

Tommaso said, "I have long wanted you to meet Vittoria Colonna. She has become the first lady of Rome. She is a rare poet. She is beautiful. She is also a saint."

"Are you in love with the lady?" asked Michelangelo.

Tommaso laughed good-naturedly. "Oh no, she is a woman

of forty-five, and has been widowed for the past ten years. Most of the time she stays at a convent. She prefers the austere life."

Vittoria Colonna, daughter of one of the most powerful families in Italy, had married the Neapolitan Marchese di Pescara when each had been nineteen. The honeymoon was short-lived, for the marchese was a general in the service of the Holy Roman Emperor. In the sixteen years of their marriage Vittoria had seldom seen her husband. He had been killed at the Battle of Pavia after heroic action on the field. The lonely Vittoria had spent the long years of separation in study, and had become one of the leading scholars of Italy. She had spent the last ten years giving her service and fortune to the poor.

Late Sunday afternoon Tommaso called for him and they walked to the gardens of the convent of San Silvestro al Quirinale, where there were laurels for shade, and old stone benches against walls covered with green ivy.

Vittoria Colonna, sitting in the midst of half a dozen men, rose to greet Michelangelo. He had expected to meet an aging lady in black. Instead he found himself gazing into the deep green eyes of the the most vitally lovely woman he had ever seen. She had a regal bearing. Beneath her simple robe he envisaged a ripe figure to complement the large expressive eyes, the long braids of honey-gold hair looped low on her neck, the full red lips. He could not take his eyes from her. Her beauty was like the noonday sun, blinding him with its light. She said, "I welcome you as an old friend, Michelangelo Buonarroti, for your works have spoken to me for many years."

"My works were more fortunate than I, Marchesa."

Vittoria's green eyes clouded.

"I had heard that you were a blunt man who knew no flattery."

"You heard correctly," replied Michelangelo.

She continued: "I have been told that you heard Fra Savonarola preach. It is too bad the words did not strike Rome. Then we would have had our reforms inside the Mother Church."

"You admired Fra Savonarola?"

"He died a martyr to our cause."

Michelangelo realized that he was in the midst of a revolutionary group, highly critical of the practices of the Church and seeking reformation of the clergy. The Inquisition had taken thousands of lives on charges far less serious. He admired the marchesa's courage.

The conversation became general. They spoke of Flemish art, then of the origins of the concept of the Last Judgment. Michelangelo quoted from Matthew 25:31–33: *"When the son of man comes in his glory, and all the angels with him, he will sit down upon the throne of his glory, and all nations will be gathered in his presence, where he will divide men one from the other, as the shepherd divides the sheep from the goats; he will set the sheep on his right, and the goats on his left."*

It was many years since a woman's presence had so completely taken possession of him. When they left, Michelangelo asked: "Tommaso, when can we see her again?"

"When she invites us. She goes nowhere."

Two weeks later the marchesa's servant, Foao, arrived with an invitation from the marchesa to come to the chapel of San Silvestro al Quirinale.

His hopes to be alone with her were in vain; as she came to greet him, he saw that the chapel was filled. He recognized illustrious members of the Vatican court and the university faculty. The men began speaking of the art of their own city-states. Michelangelo only half listened, for he was watching Vittoria, sitting beneath a stained-glass window which threw a sheen of variegated color over her flawless skin.

Suddenly he became aware of a silence in the chapel. All eyes were turned on him as Vittoria Colonna said: "Michelangelo Buonarroti, I have long thought that you have a divine gift and were chosen by God for your great tasks."

He searched his mind for an answer but no words came.

"His Holiness has done me the favor of allowing me to build a nunnery at the foot of Monte Cavallo," she continued. "The site I have chosen is near a temple where it is said that Nero watched Rome burning. I would like to see the footprints of such a wicked man wiped out by those of holy women. I do not know, Michelangelo, what shape or proportion to give the house. . . ."

"If you would care to descend to the site, *signora,* we could study the ruins."

He had hoped that they could go alone but Vittoria invited the group to accompany them. Michelangelo walked by her side in an emotional cloud. "Marchesa," he said when they reached the site, "I think this broken portico might be converted into a campanile. I shall make you some drawings."

The warmth of her gratitude reached out to him like embracing arms. "I did not dare to ask for so much."

"When may I bring the sketches to you?"

"Perhaps in a week or two?"

He returned to his studio in a fury. What kind of game was

this woman playing? Shunting him off for another two weeks! Was she paying him compliments merely to bring him to her feet? Could she not tell how completely he was taken by her?

"She is dedicated to the memory of her husband," Tommaso told Michelangelo. "Since his death, she has loved only Jesus."

"If the love of Christ prevented a woman from loving mortal man, the Italian people would have died out long ago."

"I have brought you some of her poems. Perhaps you will learn more about her from them."

When Tommaso had departed, Michelangelo read from a poem written to her husband:

> Thou knowest, Love, I never sought to flee
> From thy sweet prison, nor impatient threw
> Thy dear yoke from my neck . . .

He was puzzled. Why had Vittoria described her love as a prison, a yoke? He had to have the answer: for he knew now that he loved her.

"There are ways of getting information," Leo Baglioni assured him, "particularly among the Neapolitans in Rome who fought alongside the marchese."

Five days later, he came to the studio.

"This was no lyrical love affair," he said. "The marchese never loved his wife, and fled from her a few days after the wedding. He wenched the whole way from Naples to Milan. He used every excuse known to inventive husbands never to be in the same city with her. Further, he committed one of the most dastardly double treasons in history, betraying both his Emperor and his fellow conspirators. He died by poison, a long way from a battlefield."

Into Michelangelo's mind there flashed the thought: "That is why she refuses to love again. Not because the first love was so beautiful, but because it was ugly!" Then he sensed something else. "Her husband never consummated that marriage. She is as virginal as the young girls in her nunneries."

He ached with compassion for her. He would have to persuade this desirable woman that he had a love to offer that could be as beautiful as the one she had invented.

THE OVERALL DESIGN for the Sistine wall was now complete: a tumultuous horde of human beings surrounding Christ in inner intimate circles and outer remote ones; vertical shafts of bodies rising upward on one side, descending on the other. On the bottom to the left was the yawning cave of hell.

The Last Day had been said to coincide with the end of the world. But could that be? Could God have created the world only to abandon it? Would not God sustain the world forever in spite

Last Judgment; Sistine Chapel

of wickedness and evil? Since every man judged himself before death, could not the Last Judgment be man's agonizing appraisal of himself—with no evasions, deceits? Each individual was responsible for his conduct on earth; there was a judge within, an awful suffering.

By fall his cartoon was ready to be blown up to wall size. Pope Paul, wishing to give him security, issued a *breve* which declared Michelangelo Buonarroti to be the Sculptor, Painter and Architect of the Vatican, with a lifetime pension of a hundred ducats a month. This caused a breach between Michelangelo and the architect Antonio da Sangallo which would last for many years.

Antonio had been Bramante's apprentice and was part of the Bramante-Raphael clique that had always been hostile to Michelangelo. His supremacy as architect of St. Peter's and of

Rome had not been challenged for fifteen years; but Michelangelo was aghast at the bad taste with which he was cluttering Bramante's design. The Pope's *breve* infuriated Sangallo. He appeared one night at Michelangelo's house, his fists clenched. "Get your bashed-in nose out of St. Peter's," he cried. "You've meddled in other people's affairs all your life. If you value your life: *St. Peter's is mine!*"

Michelangelo replied coldly: "I am only concerned that St. Peter's remain pure, serene, spiritual, as in Bramante's plan."

By day he locked himself in with his Last Judgment, with only Urbino by his side on the high scaffold. At night he read the Bible, Dante, and Savonarola's sermons sent to him by Vittoria Colonna; all fitted together as parts of a whole.

On the outside, it seemed that Judgment Day had arrived for Pope Paul. Charles V, the Holy Roman Emperor, was traveling north from Naples with the army that had already sacked Rome. Pope Paul had no army. He decided to fight with a display of peace and grandeur. He received the Emperor on the steps before St. Peter's, surrounded by the hierarchy of the Church in their splendid robes, and three thousand valiant young Romans. Charles graciously accepted the Pope's spiritual authority. The following day he called on Vittoria Colonna, who summoned Michelangelo for the meeting so he might speak for Florence.

The Holy Roman Emperor acknowledged Vittoria's introduction with considerable warmth. Michelangelo pleaded with him for the removal of the tyrant Alessandro. The Emperor said: "I can only promise you that when I go to Florence I shall pay a visit to your new sacristy. I have heard it declared one of the marvels of the world."

"Excellence," Michelangelo went on, risking the Emperor's displeasure, "Florence can continue to create noble works of art only if you rescue her from Alessandro."

Charles said: "If your Medici chapel sculptures are all that I have heard, something shall be done."

Charles V kept his word; he was so deeply stirred by his visit to the new sacristy that he ordered the wedding ceremonies of his daughter Margaret to Alessandro to be held in Michelangelo's chapel. The prospect made Michelangelo ill. But the marriage proved to be short-lived; Alessandro was murdered by a Popolano cousin and Florence was freed of its tyrant. Alessandro's body was dumped into the sarcophagus under Dawn and Dusk.

"All Florentines are rid of Alessandro except me," Michelangelo said to Urbino morosely. "Now you see what I am good for: to provide tombs for tyrants."

He was comforted to learn that seventeen-year-old Cosimo de' Medici, a Popolano descendant, was now in the Medici palace in Florence, and that many of the exiles were returning home. But Cosimo, too, soon developed into a tyrant, reducing the newly elected councils to impotence. Civil war broke out again. Hundreds of the finest minds and spirits of Tuscany were executed, including a dozen of the young exiles whom Michelangelo had known in Rome.

"What kind of jungle do we live in," Michelangelo cried, "that such senseless crime can be committed with impunity?"

How right he had been to put up on that wall a terrifying Judgment Day for struggling humanity.

Vittoria Colonna too had come into troubled times. Cardinal Caraffa, a religious fanatic, began his efforts to bring the Inquisition into Italy to wipe out the heretics who were working to oblige the Church to reform itself. Though the group Michelangelo had heard praising Savonarola numbered no more than eight or nine, Caraffa made it plain that he considered it dangerous.

"What will it mean to you if Caraffa gains control?" Michelangelo asked Vittoria anxiously.

"Exile."

Michelangelo turned pale. "Should you not be careful?"

"I might issue the same warning to you. Caraffa does not like what you are painting in the Sistine."

"How could he know? I keep it locked."

"The same way he knows what we say here."

Caraffa was not the only one who knew what he was putting on the wall. A strange letter came from Pietro Aretino, whom Michelangelo knew by reputation as a witty writer and unscrupulous blackmailer, obtaining the most astounding favors and sums of money, even from princes and cardinals, by threatening to flood Europe with evil letters about them. He was at the moment a man of great importance in Venice.

The purpose of Aretino's first letter was to tell Michelangelo how he should paint the Last Judgment, and he wrote often to ask for drawings, cartoons, models. Michelangelo answered evasively, then grew bored and ignored Aretino completely.

It was an error: Aretino saved his venom until the Last Judgment was completed, then struck.

NOW TIME AND SPACE became identical. Each morning Urbino laid the field of *intonaco;* by nightfall Michelangelo had filled it with a body tumbling downward toward hell. At noon a servant brought hot food which was reheated on a brazier on the scaffold.

During the long winter nights he made drawings for Vittoria: a Holy Family, a Pietà; while she presented him with a first copy of her published poems, *Rime.* For Michelangelo, desiring to pour out the whole of his passion, it was an incomplete relationship, yet his love for her, and his conviction that she felt deeply for him, kept his creative powers at the flood.

By the end of 1540, when Michelangelo had completed the upper two thirds of the fresco, Pope Paul arrived at the locked Sistine door unannounced. Urbino could not refuse to admit him. Michelangelo came down from the scaffold and greeted Pope Paul and his Master of Ceremonies, Biagio da Cesena, cordially. The Pope stood facing the Last Judgment, walked toward the wall, and when he reached the altar sank to his knees and prayed. He rose with tears on his cheeks, made the sign of the cross over Michelangelo and then the Last Judgment. "My son, you have created a glory for my reign."

But Biagio had been glaring at the fresco. *"Scandaloso!"* he spat out. "Totally immoral! I cannot tell the saints from the sinners. There are hundreds of nudes! In the Pope's chapel! Shameful!"

"On Judgment Day we shall all stand naked before the Lord," replied Paul. "My son, how do I express my gratitude?"

Biagio da Cesena said roughly: "One day this sacrilegious wall will be annihilated."

"I will excommunicate anyone who dares touch this masterpiece!" cried Pope Paul.

They left the chapel. Michelangelo asked Urbino to lay some *intonaco* on the blank spot on the lower right-hand corner of the wall. There, he painted a caricature of Biagio da Cesena, representing him as the judge of the shades of Hades, with the ears of an ass, and a monstrous snake coiled around the lower part of the torso: a lethal likeness, the pointed nose, lips drawn back over buckteeth.

Word soon leaked out and Biagio da Cesena demanded a second meeting before the fresco.

"You see, Holy Father," he cried. "The report was true. Buonarroti has painted me with a repulsive serpent."

"It's a covering," replied Michelangelo. "I knew you would not want to be portrayed naked."

"A remarkable likeness," observed the Pope, his eyes twinkling. "Michelangelo, I thought you told me that you could not do portraiture?"

"I was inspired, Holiness."

Biagio hopped up and down as though he were standing over the fires of hell. "Holiness, make him take me out of there!"

"Out of hell?" The Pope turned surprised eyes on the man. "Had he placed you in purgatory, I should have done everything in my power to release you. But from hell there is no redemption."

Vittoria Colonna sent a message that she was about to be driven into exile by Cardinal Caraffa. Could Michelangelo come at once? She wished to say farewell.

It was an intoxicating April day, the buds bursting forth in the Colonna gardens, the wild scents of spring enclosed within the walls. The garden was full of people. She greeted him with a somber smile, a black mantilla over her golden hair. "It was good of you to come, Michelangelo."

"Let us not waste time on formalities. Where are you going?"

"To Viterbo, to the convent of St. Catherine."

They stood in silence, probing deep into each other's eyes.

"I'm sorry that I shall not see your Last Judgment."

"You will see it. When do you leave?"

"In the morning. You will write to me?"

"I will write, and send you drawings."

"I will answer, and send you poems."

He turned abruptly and left the garden; locked himself in his studio, bereft. It was dark by the time he roused himself from his torpor and asked Urbino to light his way to the Sistine.

In the flickering half-world of the chapel the Last Judgment sprang cyclonically to life. Judgment Day became Judgment Night. The three hundred men, women, children, saints, angels and demons, many of whom had been submerged in the full light of day, pressed forward to be recognized and to play out their portentous drama. Then, looking up to the vault, he saw his frescoes of God creating the universe. Lines from Genesis came into his mind: *And God saw all that he had made, and found it very good.*

Michelangelo turned back to his painting on the altar wall. He saw all that he had made, and found it good.

BOOK ELEVEN

The Dome

ON ALL SAINTS' EVE, exactly twenty-nine years after Pope Julius had consecrated the Sistine ceiling, Pope Paul said High Mass to celebrate the completion of the Last Judgment.

On Christmas Day, 1541, the chapel was thrown open to the public. Rome streamed through the Sistine, terrified, shocked, awe-stricken. The studio in the Macello dei Corvi was thronged with Florentines, cardinals, artists and apprentices. When the last of the guests had disappeared Michelangelo realized that two groups had not been represented: Antonio da Sangallo and the artists and architects who centered around him; and Cardinal Caraffa and his followers.

Very soon war was declared. An unfrocked monk, Bernardino Ochino, censured Pope Paul by demanding: "How can Your Holiness allow such an obscene painting as that of Michelangelo's to remain in a chapel where the divine office is sung?"

But the Pope was firm in his support; he asked Michelangelo to fresco two large walls of a chapel named after him, the Pauline. He wanted a Conversion of Paul on one wall, a Crucifixion of Peter on the opposite one.

Though he had the constant companionship of Tommaso, who was now one of his chief assistants, Michelangelo sorely missed Vittoria. He wrote her long letters, frequently sending a sonnet or a drawing, but she answered less and less frequently. To his anguished cry of "Why?" she replied: *If you and I were to go on writing without intermission, according to my obligation and your courtesy, I should have to neglect the chapel of St. Catherine here . . . while you would have to leave the chapel of St. Paul. . . . Thus we should both of us fail in our duty.*

He felt crushed, chagrined, as though he were a small boy who had been reproved. He was depleted and tired; he spent his days with hammer and chisel while thinking through the imagery of St. Paul's conversion. He completed the figures for Pope Julius' tomb, added a Virgin, Prophet and Sibyl to be carved from his sketches by Raffaelo da Montelupo, who had carved a statue for his Medici chapel.

Cardinal Caraffa's burning zeal for the dogma of the Church was making him the most feared and influential leader of the College of Cardinals, and when Vittoria Colonna returned to Rome to enter the convent of San Silvestro, Michelangelo feared for her safety. He pressed for a meeting. Vittoria refused. He accused her of cruelty; she replied that it was a kindness. Finally, from sheer persistence, he gained her assent, only to find that illness and the pressure of the accusations against her had aged her twenty years. Her strength and beauty were ravaged. He found her sitting alone in the convent garden, her hands folded. He was overcome. "I tried to save you from this," she said.

327

"You think my love so shallow?"

"Even in your kindness there is a cruel revelation."

"Life is cruel, never love."

"Love is the cruelest of all. I know. . . ."

"You know only a fragment," he interrupted. "Why have you kept us apart? And why have you returned to such danger?"

"I must make my peace with the Church, find forgiveness for my sins. I have indulged my own vain opinions against the divine doctrine, harbored dissenters. My last desire is to die in the state of grace," Vittoria said.

"Your illness has done this to you," he cried. "The Inquisition has tortured you."

"I have tortured myself. Michelangelo, I worship you as God-given among men. But you too will have to seek salvation."

He listened to the noise of the bees as they buzzed in the cups of the flowers. His heart ached for her despair. He said: "My feelings for you, which you would never allow me to express, have not changed. Did you think I was a young boy who had fallen in love with a pretty *contadina?* Do you not know how great a place you occupy in my mind?"

Tears flooded her eyes. "Thank you, *caro,*" she whispered. "You have healed wounds that go very far back." Then she was gone into the convent, leaving him in a cold garden.

WHEN ANTONIO DA SANGALLO began pouring foundations for the ring of chapels on the south side of the tribune of St. Peter's, his long-smoldering feud with Michelangelo became full-blown. According to Michelangelo's measurements, building the corresponding wing to the north would necessitate tearing down the Pauline chapel and part of the Sistine.

"I simply cannot believe my eyes," cried Pope Paul when Michelangelo drew him a plan of what was going on. "How much of the Sistine would his chapels replace?"

"Approximately the area covered by the Deluge, Noah, the Delphic Sibyl and Zacharias. God would survive."

"How fortunate for Him," murmured Paul.

The Pope suspended work on St. Peter's on the grounds that

there was insufficient money to continue. But Sangallo knew that Michelangelo was the cause. He had his assistant begin an attack on the Last Judgment, saying it gave comfort to the enemies of the Church and caused converts to Luther. Yet travelers coming into the Sistine fell on their knees before the fresco, even as Paul III had, repenting of their sins.

Then a letter arrived from Aretino. It began with an attack on the Last Judgment, then went on to call Michelangelo a fraud and a thief for having taken "the heaps of gold which Pope Julius bequeathed you," and given the Roveres nothing in return. Michelangelo then read: *It would certainly have been well if you had fulfilled your promise with due care, had it been only to silence the evil tongues who assert that only a Tommaso knows how to allure favors from you!*

Michelangelo was swept by a cold chill. What evil tongues? What favors? He began to feel ill. In his seventy years he had been accused of many things, of being cantankerous, arrogant, snobbishly unwilling to associate with any but those who had the greatest talent and intellect. But never had such an insinuation been made as this one. Tommaso de' Cavalieri was as noble a soul as there was in Italy! For fifty-odd years, Michelangelo had taken apprentices and assistants into his home; at least thirty young men had lived and worked with him in this traditional relationship. Never in these associations had there been a word breathed against the propriety of his conduct. This false imputation seemed as devastating a blow as he had received in all his stormy years.

It did not take long for Aretino's poison to seep into Rome. A few days later Tommaso arrived, his face pale.

"I heard last night," he said, "about Aretino's letter."

"I'm sorry, Tommaso," Michelangelo said hoarsely. "I never meant to cause you embarrassment."

"It is you I am worried about, Michelangelo. My family and companions will scoff at this canard and ignore it. But you, my dear friend, are revered all over Europe. It is you that Aretino means to hurt. The last thing in the world I want is to hurt you."

"You could never hurt me, Tommaso. With Marchesa Vittoria ill, yours is the only love I can count on to sustain me. I will ignore Aretino, as one should all blackmailers. Let us continue with our lives and our work. That is the proper answer to scandalmongers."

HE WAS PUTTING the final touches on the last of his sketches for the wall of the Pauline chapel when news came that Antonio da Sangallo had died of malaria. Pope Paul gave Sangallo a spectacular funeral. In church, Michelangelo stood with Tommaso and Urbino listening to the eulogizing of Sangallo as one of the greatest architects since the ancients who had built Rome. Walking home, Michelangelo commented: "That eulogy is word for word the one I heard for Bramante; yet Pope Leo had stopped all of Bramante's work before he died, just as Pope Paul had halted Sangallo's on St. Peter's. . . ."

Tommaso stopped, turned to look sharply at Michelangelo. "Do you think. . . ?"

"Oh no, Tommaso!"

But shortly after the funeral, Michelangelo was summoned to the Vatican. "My son," the Pope said, "I am herewith appointing you architect of St. Peter's."

"Holiness, I cannot assume the post."

There was a twinkle in Paul's discerning eyes.

"Are you going to tell me that architecture is not your trade?"

Michelangelo flushed. "Holy Father, I have the Pauline chapel to complete. I am over seventy years old. Where will I find the vital force to build the mightiest church in Christendom? I am not Abraham, Holy Father, who lived one hundred and seventy-five years. . . ."

Pope Paul was unaffected. "You are but a youth. When you reach my august age of seventy-eight you will be allowed to speak of your years. By that time St. Peter's will be well on its way."

At sunset Michelangelo went to St. Peter's. The workmen had gone home. He inspected Sangallo's foundations, and realized that many were inadequate and would have to be leveled. His tour of inspection ended as night closed down. Finding himself in front of the chapel where his Pietà now was, he went in and stood in the dark before it. He was torn by conflict. He knew the dimension of the task, the opposition he would meet, the grueling labor that would make the end of his life harder than any of the years that had gone before.

An old woman came into the chapel, placed a lighted taper before the Madonna. Michelangelo reached into the basket of candles, selected one, lighted it. Of course he must build St. Peter's! Was not life to be worked, and suffered, right to the end?

But he refused to be paid for his services as architect. He painted from first light until dinnertime in the Pauline chapel, then walked to St. Peter's to watch the leveling. The disclosure of the weakness of the piers infuriated the superintendent and contractors who had worked under Sangallo. They put so many obstacles in his path that Pope Paul had to issue a decree declaring Michelangelo superintendent as well as architect.

The fabric of the great basilica began to grow with a momentum that amazed Rome. A committee of Roman Conservators, impressed, came to ask if he would rescue the Capitoline hill and the Campidoglio, which had been the seat of religion and government of the Roman Empire. This glorious spot was a shambles, the old temples reduced to piles of stone.

"Would I?" Michelangelo cried to Tommaso, who was becoming an excellent architect. "You shall help me, Tomao. I know you have always dreamed of rebuilding Rome."

When Michelangelo visited Vittoria at the convent on Sunday afternoons he brought sketches with him, trying to interest her in the works he had projected; but she came alive only when he spoke of the dome for St. Peter's. She knew of his abiding love for the domed Pantheon, and the Duomo of Florence.

"It is pure sculpture," he often said.

"And what of St. Peter's dome? Will that be only a top to keep out the rain?"

"Vittoria, it is good to see you smile, and to hear you tease me."

"You must not think me unhappy, Michelangelo. I await with trembling joy my reunion with God."

"*Cara,* why are you so eager to die, when there are those of us who love you dearly? Is it not selfish of you?"

She took his hand between hers: he could feel how sharp her bones were beneath the skin. Her eyes burned as she whispered: "Forgive me for failing you. I can forgive myself only because I know you have no real need of me. You created majestically before you met me, and you will create majestically after I am gone."

Before there was time for another Sunday meeting he was summoned to the palace of a cousin of Vittoria's where she had been moved. The doctor met him at the gate.

"She will not see the sunrise," he said.

He paced the garden while the heavens moved in their cycle. At the seventeenth hour she died. He was admitted to the palace. In death Vittoria's expression was one of sublimity. She looked as young and beautiful as the first time he had met her.

Speaking in a low voice, the abbess of the convent ordered in the coffin. It was coated with tar. Michelangelo cried: "What is the meaning of this tar-covered coffin? The marchesa has not died of the plague."

"To protect the coffin. We fear reprisals, *signore,*" the abbess murmured. "We must get the marchesa back to the convent and buried before her enemies can claim the body."

Michelangelo trudged wearily homeward, chewing on the bitter herb of irony: the marchese, who had fled his wife during his married life, would now have her by his side for all eternity. And he, Michelangelo, who had found Vittoria the crowning love of his life, had never been permitted to fulfill it.

IN THE EYES OF the world he was now truly the "Master." Duke Cosimo urged him to return to Florence to create sculptures for the city. The King of France deposited money in a Roman bank in his name against the day when he would carve or paint for him. The Sultan of Turkey offered to send a party to escort him to Constantinople to work there.

He spent the better part of the day in the Pauline, painting. When he tired, he returned home to pick up hammer and chisel.

He was carving a Descent from the Cross for his own tomb.

He began to suffer intermittent spells of illness during which he would grow cranky with his friends. When he recovered he would cry to Tommaso: "Why do I behave so cantankerously? Because my seventies are fleeing so fast?"

"Granacci said you were already crusty at twelve."

"Bless his memory."

Granacci, his oldest friend, had died; so had Balducci, Leo Baglioni, and his brother Giovansimone. Tommaso de' Cavalieri married the daughter of a noble Roman family, and within a year she presented her husband with a son.

Then Pope Paul died and the people of the city showed genuine grief. The Florentine colony believed it was the turn of Cardinal Niccolò Ridolfi, Contessina's son, to become Pope. He had no enemies in Italy except Duke Cosimo of Florence. During the conclave in the Sistine Chapel, with the election all but settled in favor of Niccolò, he became suddenly and violently ill. By morning he was dead. Michelangelo's doctor performed an autopsy. Afterward he came to Michelangelo, who looked up with dazed eyes.

"Murder?"

"Beyond any doubt. One of Duke Cosimo's agents may have had the opportunity to administer the poison."

Giammaria Ciocchi del Monte became Pope Julius III. His main interest in life was pleasure. He spent money on such a lavish scale that he used up the funds stipulated for St. Peter's. All work was shut down.

ONE DAY URBINO said to Michelangelo: "*Messere,* I do not like to bring you further problems, but I must leave you. Ten years ago I chose a girl in my village. She is eighteen today. It is time for us to marry."

"Bring your wife here. We'll fix up an apartment for you."

Urbino's eyes were round. "Are you sure, *Messere?* For I am forty now, and I should have children as quickly as possible."

"This is your home. Your sons will be my grandsons."

He gave Urbino two thousand ducats in cash so that he could

be independent, then an additional sum to fix up a room for his bride. In a few days Urbino returned with his wife, a sympathetic girl who took over the management of the household. She gave Michelangelo the affection she would have brought to her husband's father. Nine months later they named their first son Michelangelo.

To Michelangelo's delight, his nephew, Lionardo, at last decided to carry on the Buonarroti name. He married Cassandra Ridolfi, and Michelangelo was so delighted that he sent Cassandra two rings, one diamond and the other ruby. They named their first-born son Buonarroto. The next son they named Michelangelo, but he died, and Michelangelo grieved.

Work proceeded on the restoration of the Campidoglio. Michelangelo took the ancient Roman salt-tax office and converted it into a regal palace with lyrical flights of steps rising from either end to a center entrance. He then planned two palaces, identical in design, for either side of the square. He leveled the piazza, paved it with patterned stones, searched his mind for a work of art for the middle of the square. He thought of the bronze equestrian statue of the Emperor Marcus Aurelius which had stood unharmed in front of St. John in Lateran all through the centuries because Christians believed it to be Constantine, the first Christian emperor. He placed the glorious statue on such a low platform that Marcus Aurelius seemed to have just come down the Senatorial steps and mounted his horse to ride across Rome.

In 1555, Pope Julius III died and was succeeded by Cardinal Cerveni, Marcellus II, who died after a three-week reign. Then the fanatic and disagreeable Cardinal Caraffa became Pope Paul IV. Knowing how much he was hated, he said: "I do not know why they elected me Pope, so I am bound to conclude that it is not the cardinals but God who makes the Popes."

It was his ambition to wipe out heresy in Italy, and his Board of Inquisition tortured and condemned accused people without trial, locked them in dungeons in the cellars, burned them in the Campo dei Fiori. Michelangelo considered himself fit fuel for the fires, but he made no attempt to flee.

334

Finally Pope Paul IV sent for him, and received him in a small monastic room with whitewashed walls. His expression was as severe as his robe. "Buonarroti, it is the will of the Council of Trent that heretical frescoes such as your altar will be destroyed."

"The Last Judgment?" He stood before the Pope's wooden chair, staring blindly at the whitewashed wall.

"Many say that you have blasphemed; they are confirmed by an article written by Aretino of Venice . . . "

"A blackmailer!"

"A friend of Titian, of Charles V, Benvenuto Cellini, the late Francis I of France. . . . Here is one of the copies passing from hand to hand in Rome."

Michelangelo took the paper from the Pope, began to read: *Is it possible that you can have represented in the sacred temple of God . . . in the greatest chapel in the world . . . angels and saints without a remnant of modesty and denuded of all celestial ornament!*

He jerked his head up.

"Holiness, this attack was written when I refused to send Aretino some of my drawings. It was his way of striking at me."

"Decent people are shocked by the nakedness of saints and martyrs. They find it evil."

"My fresco is not evil. It is permeated with a love of God."

"Very well, I shall not demand that the wall be torn down. I shall have it whitewashed. Then you can paint something over it, something simple and devout."

He was too crushed to fight back. Not so, Rome. His friends, including a number of cardinals led by Ercole Gonzaga, began a campaign to save the wall. The painter Daniele da Volterra, one of Michelangelo's most enthusiastic followers, came to the studio one day with high color in his cheeks. "Master, the Last Judgment is saved. There will be no coat of whitewash."

Michelangelo collapsed on his chair, breathing hard.

"I must thank every last person who helped me."

"Master," said Daniele, with eyes averted, "we have had to

335

pay a price. The Pope agreed not to destroy the wall providing breeches and petticoats were put on everybody's nakedness. All must be clothed from the hips to the knees, particularly those whose bottoms are facing the chapel."

"If in my earlier years I had given myself to make sulphur matches," swore Michelangelo, "I should now suffer less."

"Master, let us try to be sensible. The Pope was going to call in a court painter, but I persuaded him to let me do the job. I will injure the wall as little as possible. Don't be angry with me."

"You are right, Daniele. We must offer up these private parts to the Inquisition. I have spent a lifetime portraying the beauty of man. Now he has become shameful again, to be burned in a new bonfire of vanities. We are returning to the darkest, most ignorant centuries of the past."

"I will use so thin a paint," said Daniele placatingly, "that the next Pope can have all the breeches and robes removed without harming anything."

"Go then, and wrap their winding sheets about them."

SIGISMONDO DIED IN Settignano, the last of his brothers. Michelangelo had outlived his generation. Equally sad was the final illness of Urbino, who had been with him for twenty-six years. The nobility of Urbino's spirit shone forth when he whispered to Michelangelo: "Even more than dying, it grieves me to leave you alone in this treacherous world."

Urbino's wife, Cornelia, gave birth to her second son at the moment her husband was being buried. Michelangelo was named guardian of the two boys; when their mother left with them for her parents' home, the house seemed desolate. He busied himself by carving a new Pietà; began searching for worthy poor whom he could help for the salvation of his soul.

The eighties, he decided, were not the most pleasant decade in the span of man. When he left Florence at sixty he had feared that his life might be over; but love had made him young again, and the sixties had flown by. During his seventies he had been so deeply immersed in the Pauline chapel frescoes, his new architectural career, and St. Peter's that no day had been long enough to accomplish his tasks. But now, as he moved toward eighty-two, the hours were like hornets, each stinging as it passed. His step was not as firm as it had been. His stamina was giving way to a series of minor disturbances, sapping his strength, interfering with his drive to create a glorious dome for St. Peter's.

Then he went down with a severe attack of kidney stones. Dr. Colombo pulled him through with the aid of Tommaso's untiring care; but he was confined to his bed for several months and was obliged to turn over the designs for one of the chapels to a new superintendent. When he recovered he found that the new man had misread his plans, making serious errors. He was overcome with remorse; this was his first failure in years of building.

He called on the Pope at once; but Baccio Bigio, representing the old Sangallo faction, had been there before him.

"So the chapel will have to be pulled down," Pope Paul said. "I am saddened. How could such a thing happen?"

"I have been ill, Holy Father."

"Bigio claims you are too old to carry such a heavy responsibility. He feels that you should be relieved of the burden."

"His solicitude touches me. He and his associates have been trying to get this 'burden' off my shoulders and into their own hands for years. Can you believe that Bigio is better on his good days than I am on my bad?"

"No one is questioning your ability."

"Holiness, for thirty years I watched architects futilely pouring foundations for St. Peter's. In the ten years I have been the architect, the church has risen upward like an eagle. If you dismiss me now, it will be the ruin of the edifice."

The Pope's lips twitched. "Michelangelo, as long as you have the strength to fight back, you shall remain the architect of St. Peter's."

That night there was a meeting in the house on the Macello dei Corvi. Because he had so nearly died, Tommaso and a group of his oldest friends insisted that he build a complete model of the dome. Up to now he had made only fragmentary sketches.

"I have heard you say," Tommaso said, "that you wanted the work to progress so far that no one could change its design after your death."

"That is my hope. But I have not yet conceived the final dome. I shall have to find it. Then we shall build a wooden model."

Everyone left. Michelangelo walked to his drawing table, pulled up a chair. A dome was not a mere roof. It was a vault of man, created in the image of the vault of heaven. It was the most natural of all architectural forms, and the most celestial.

Some people said the earth was round; for a man like himself whose travels had been limited, that was hard to prove. At school he had been taught that the earth was flat, ending where the dome of heaven came down to its circular boundaries. Yet he had always observed a peculiar phenomenon of that supposedly anchored-down horizon: as he walked or rode to reach it, it receded at an equal pace.

Just so, his dome. It must not be finite. A man standing beneath it must feel that he could never reach its boundaries. He wanted his dome to be of a mystical beauty that would reassure man of God's presence. Under his dome a man's soul must soar upward to God even as it would in the moment of its final release from his body.

His mind and fingers were moving with clarity and force.

He laid aside his charcoal and drawing pens, started modeling. Over the months he made a dozen models and destroyed them. At last it came, after eleven years of thinking, drawing, praying, experimenting and rejecting: soaring heavenward, constructed of gossamer which carried effortlessly and musically upward its three-hundred-and-thirty-five-foot height.

He hired a carpenter to build the scaled-down model. The giant dome would rest on the piers and on the arches that the piers supported, and on a circular drum. The drum would be built of brick with a sheathing of travertine; the external ribs of the dome would be of travertine, the buttresses held to the drum by a framework of wrought iron. Eight ramps along the lower drum would afford a means of carrying materials on the backs of donkeys up to the dome walls. The plans took months to draw.

Pope Paul IV died suddenly. Rome burst into the most violent insurrection Michelangelo had yet seen at the death of any pontiff. The crowd knocked down a statue of him, dragged its head through the streets, then threw it into the Tiber before storming the headquarters of the Inquisition to release all prisoners and destroy the documents convicting the accused of heresy.

The College of Cardinals elected sixty-year-old Giovanni Angelo Medici from a Lombardy branch of the Medici family. Pope Pius IV had been trained as a lawyer. He was a brilliant negotiator and a man of integrity. The Inquisition, foreign to the Italian character, was ended. Through a series of conferences and contracts the Pope brought peace to Italy and the surrounding nations, and to the Lutherans as well. The Church reunited Catholicism in Europe and achieved peace for itself.

Pope Pius IV reconfirmed Michelangelo's position as architect of St. Peter's, provided him with funds to build the dome. He also commissioned him to design a gate for the city walls, to be called Porta Pia.

It was clearly a race against time. He thought it would take ten to twelve years to complete the dome; this would bring him to a round century mark. Nobody lived that long; but despite his attacks of the stone, disorders of the stomach, aches in the back, bouts of dizziness, he did not feel any true diminishing of his power. There was still good color in his face. His eyes were clear and penetrating. He would get the dome built.

WHILE THE CATHEDRAL structure rose, Michelangelo resumed carving his Pietà. One day while he was working, darkness flooded over him. After a lapse of time he regained consciousness; but he was confused. Had he dropped off to sleep? Why did he feel a numbness and weakness in the left arm and leg? Why did the muscles on one side of his face feel as though they were sagging?

He called his servant. When he asked her to summon Tommaso, he noticed that his speech was slurred. The elderly woman helped him into bed, then put on a shawl to go through the streets. She returned with Tommaso and his doctor, who gave him a warm drink, stirring in a foul-tasting medicine.

"Rest cures everything," said the doctor.

"Except old age."

"I have been hearing about your old age too long now to take it seriously," replied Tommaso. "I'll stay here until you sleep."

He awakened to find deep night outside his window. He lifted himself gingerly. The headache was gone, and he could see clearly the work that was still required on his Pietà. He rose, put a candle in his cap, returned to his carving. It was good to have the feel of marble at his fingertips.

At dawn Tommaso opened the street door cautiously, burst into laughter.

"You rogue! I left you at midnight, deep asleep. I come back a few hours later, and find a snowstorm of marble chips."

"When the white dust cakes inside my nostrils, that's when I breathe the best."

"The doctor says you need rest."

"In the next world, *caro*."

He worked all day, had supper with Tommaso, then threw himself on the bed for a few hours of sleep before rising to fix another candle in his cap and begin polishing.

Two days later, as he stood before his marble, he was struck again. He stumbled to the bed. When he awakened the room was full of people: Tommaso, doctors, friends. Facing him was his statue, which throbbed with a life all its own. He thought: "Man passes. Only works of art are immortal."

He insisted on sitting in a chair before the fire. Once when he was left alone he slipped a robe over his shoulders and started walking in the rain in the direction of St. Peter's. One of his newer apprentices met him in the street, asked: "Master, do you think it right to be about in such weather?"

He allowed the man to take him home, but the next afternoon he dressed and tried to mount his horse. His legs were too weak.

Rome came to bid him farewell. Those who could not be admitted left flowers and gifts on the doorstep. The doctor tried to keep him in bed.

"Don't hurry me," he said. "My father lived to his ninetieth birthday, so I still have two weeks to enjoy life."

"As long as you're feeling so intrepid," commented Tommaso, "what about a carriage ride in the morning? To celebrate your ninetieth birthday, they're going to start the first ring of the dome."

"*Grazie a Dio.* No one will ever be able to change it now. But all the same, it's sad to have to die."

That night, as he lay sleepless in bed, he thought, "Life has been good. God did not create me to abandon me. I have loved marble, yes, and paint too. I have loved architecture, and poetry, too. I have loved my family and my friends. I have loved God, the forms of the earth and the heavens, and people too. I have loved life to the full, and now I love death as its natural termination. *Il Magnifico* would be happy: for me, the forces of destruction never overcame creativity."

He was swept by a massive wave of darkness. When he next opened his eyes Tommaso was sitting on the edge of the bed. He put an arm under Michelangelo and raised him up.

"Tomao . . ."

"I am here, *caro.*"

"I want to be buried in Santa Croce with my family."

"The Pope wants you buried in your own church, St. Peter's."

"It is not . . . home. Promise you will take me back to Florence." His strength was ebbing. "I commit my soul into the hands of God, my body to the earth, and my substance to my family . . . the Buonarroti. . . ."

"It will all be done. I shall finish the Campidoglio, exactly as you planned. With St. Peter's at one end, and the Capitol at the other, Rome will forevermore be Michelangelo's."

"Thank you, Tommaso. . . . I am tired. . . ."

Tommaso kissed Michelangelo on the brow, withdrew weeping.

Dusk was falling. Alone in the room, Michelangelo began to review the images of all the beautiful works he had created. He saw them, one by one, as clearly as the day he had made them, the sculptures, paintings and architecture succeeding one another as swiftly as had the years of his life:

The Madonna of the Stairs and the Battle of the Centaurs he had carved for Bertoldo and *Il Magnifico;* St. Proculus and St. Petronius that he had made for Aldovrandi in Bologna; the wooden Crucifix for Prior Bichiellini; the Sleeping Cupid with which he had tried to fool the dealer in Rome; the Bacchus he had carved in Jacopo Gallo's orchard; the Pietà for St. Peter's; the Giant David; the Holy Family teased out of him by Agnolo Doni; the cartoon called The Bathers; the ill-fated bronze statue of Pope Julius II; Genesis on the vault of the Sistine; the Last Judgment to complete the chapel; the Moses for Julius' tomb; his four unfinished Captive-Giants in Florence; the Medici chapel; the Paul and Peter for the Pauline chapel; the Campidoglio, Porta Pia, the Pietàs sculptured for his own pleasure . . . and, as the pictures came to a stop in his mind's eye, St. Peter's.

St. Peter's . . . He entered the church through its front portal, walked in the strong Roman sunshine down the wide nave, stood below the center of the dome, just over the tomb of St. Peter. He felt his soul leave his body, rise upward into the dome, becoming part of it: part of space, of time, of heaven and of God.

THE
LIFE AND
WORK
OF
SIGMUND
FREUD

A CONDENSATION OF

THE
LIFE AND
WORK
OF
SIGMUND
FREUD

by
ERNEST
JONES

AS EDITED AND ABRIDGED
BY LIONEL TRILLING
AND STEVEN MARCUS

ILLUSTRATED BY
MICHAEL McINNERNEY

His purpose in life, Sigmund Freud once said, was to understand and to liberate human nature. To that end he devoted all his energies, whether in his laboratory or in his consulting office. But Freud was not only a determined scientist. He was also a valiant young suitor, ardent and jealous by turns; a serious researcher ever in need of funds; a devoted husband and father in the bosom of a loving family.

By the end of his life, Sigmund Freud had indeed illuminated the shadowy, uncharted regions of the mind. And even now, more than fifty years after his death, we still find in our society the influence of that brilliant doctor—the first great explorer of the "far country" that is the human mind.

CHAPTER ONE

SIGMUND FREUD was born at 6:30 p.m. on the sixth of May, 1856, at 117 Schlossergasse, Freiberg, in Moravia. Freiberg, a quiet little town 150 miles northeast of Vienna, was dominated by the two-hundred-foot steeple of St. Mary's Church, which boasted the best chimes of the province. The population, which at the time of Freud's birth was about five thousand, was almost all Roman Catholic, only two percent being Protestants and an equal number Jews. A child such as Sigmund, born to Jewish parents, would soon observe that the church chimes rang out not brother love but hostility to the little circle of nonbelievers.

From his father Freud inherited his sense of humor, his shrewd skepticism about the vicissitudes of life, his custom of pointing a moral by quoting a Jewish anecdote, his liberalism, and perhaps his uxoriousness. From his mother came, according to him, his "sentimentality," which should probably be taken to mean his temperament, with the passionate emotions of which he was capable. His intellect was his own.

Freud's father, Jakob Freud, a wool merchant, had married twice. Of the first marriage, contracted at the age of seventeen, there were two sons, Emmanuel and Philipp. In 1855, when

Jakob was forty, he had married nineteen-year-old Amalie Nathansohn in Vienna. Jakob's elder son, Emmanuel, who lived nearby, was by then himself the father of a one-year-old son. The little Sigmund, therefore, was born an uncle, one of the many paradoxes his young mind had to grapple with. Although Freud had five uncles, the only one he refers to by name is Josef. This was a name that often played a part in his life. Above all, the biblical Joseph as the famous interpreter of dreams was the figure behind which Freud often disguised himself in his own dreams.

Of Jakob Freud one knows he bore a resemblance to Garibaldi, and was of a gentle disposition, well loved by all in his family. Freud described his father in rather Micawber-like terms as being "always hopefully expecting something to turn up." Of Amalie Freud's lively personality the present writer has many recollections, both from Vienna and from Ischl, where she used to spend every summer—and to enjoy card parties at an hour when most old ladies would be in bed. When she was ninety Freud's mother declined the gift of a beautiful shawl, saying it would "make her look too old." When she was ninety-five, six weeks before she died, her photograph appeared in the newspaper; her comment was: "A bad reproduction; it makes me look a hundred." She retained to the last her gaiety and sharp-witted intelligence. At her marriage she was slender and pretty. She bore Sigmund at the age of twenty-one, and subsequently Julius, who died at the age of eight months; Anna, born when Freud was two and a half years old, Rosa, Marie (Mitzi), Adolfine (Dolfi), Paula, Alexander—the last-named being just ten years younger than Sigmund.

At birth the baby Sigmund had such an abundance of black ruffled hair that his young mother nicknamed him her "little blackamoor." He was born in a caul, an event which was believed to ensure him future happiness and fame. One day an old woman whom the young mother encountered by chance in a pastry shop fortified this by informing her that she had brought a great man into the world. The proud and happy mother believed firmly in the prediction, but Freud later wrote: "Such prophecies must be made very often; there are so many happy and expectant mothers, and so many old ... women who turn their eyes toward the future; and the prophetess is not likely to suffer for her prophecies."

Nevertheless, the mother's pride and love for her firstborn left an indelible impression on the growing boy. As he explained it: "A man who has been the indisputable favorite of his mother keeps for life the feeling of a conqueror, that confidence of success that often induces real success." This self-confidence,

Freud's early home in Freiberg, Moravia.

which was one of Freud's prominent characteristics, was only rarely impaired, and he was doubtless right in tracing it to the security of his mother's love. It is worth mentioning that, as one would expect, he was fed at the breast.

In the household there was also a nannie, old and ugly, with the nurse's normal mixture of affection for children and severity toward their transgressions; she was capable and efficient. Freud several times refers in his writings to what he called "that prehistoric old woman." He was fond of her and used to give her all his pennies, and he refers to the memory of the latter fact as a screen memory (an unimportant memory that is recalled in place of an important one associated with it); perhaps it got connected with her dismissal for theft later on when he was two and a half years old. She was a Czech and a Catholic and used to take the young boy to attend the church services. She implanted in him the ideas of Heaven and Hell, and probably also those of salvation and resurrection. After returning from church the boy used to preach a sermon at home and expound God's doings.

Freud had only a few conscious memories of his first years. Among them are several, banal enough in themselves, which are of interest only in standing out in the sea of amnesia. One was of penetrating into his parents' bedroom out of (sexual) curiosity and being ordered out by an irate father.

At the age of two he would still wet his bed and it was his father, not his indulgent mother, who reproved him. He recollected saying on one occasion: "Don't worry, Papa. I will buy you a beautiful new red bed. . . ." From such experiences was born his conviction that, typically, the father represented the principles of denial, restraint, and authority. There is no reason to think, however, that his own father was sterner than fathers usually are; all the evidence points to his having been affectionate and tolerant, though just and objective.

An incident which he could not recollect was of slipping from a stool when he was two years old and receiving a violent blow on the lower jaw from the edge of the table he was exploring for some delicacy. It was a severe cut which necessitated sewing up, and it bled profusely; he retained the scar throughout life.

A more important occurrence was his young brother's death when Freud was nineteen months old and the little Julius only eight months. Before the newcomer's birth the infant Freud had had sole access to his mother's love, and he had to learn from the experience how strong the jealousy of a young child can be. In a letter of 1897 written when Freud, through self-analysis, was recovering a great many of his important childhood memories, he admits the evil wishes he had against his rival and adds that their fulfillment in Julius's death had aroused self-reproaches, a tendency which had remained ever since.

The problem of the family relationships came to a head again with the birth of the first sister, Anna, when he was just two and a half years old. How and why had this new usurper appeared, with whom he would have once again to share his mother's warm and previously exclusive love? The changes in her figure told the observant child the source of the baby, but not how it had all come about. So we see that the infant Freud was early assailed by the great problems of birth, love, and death.

There is every reason to think that the most important person in Freud's early childhood was, next to his parents, his nephew John, a boy only a year older than himself. "Until the end of my third year we [were] inseparable; we . . . loved each other and fought each other." On Sigmund's side the feelings aroused were much more intense than is usual. John was naturally the stronger of the two, but little Sigmund, who was endowed with a fair amount of pugnacity, gave as good as he got. When Freud came to review his childhood he repeatedly indicated how his ambivalence toward John had conditioned the development of his character. "An intimate friend and a hated enemy have always been indispensable to my emotional life; I have always been able to create them anew, and not infrequently . . . friend and enemy have coincided in the same person; but not simultaneously, as was the case in my early childhood."

Freud soon learned that this companion, of nearly his own age, was his nephew, and that he addressed father Jakob as grandfather. The older boy should surely have been the uncle. The complexity of the family relationships and their significance to the growing child's mind is worth stressing. From earliest days he was called upon to solve puzzling problems of the greatest import to him emotionally. A powerful incentive to his budding intelligence, to his curiosity and interest.

FOR THE MAN RESPONSIBLE for the welfare of this little family group the times were anxious. Jakob Freud was a wool merchant and, as elsewhere in Central Europe, the introduction of machines had increasingly threatened handwork. In the 1840's the new northern railway from Vienna had bypassed Freiberg, dislocating trade there and leading to considerable unemployment. There were still more sinister portents to add to Jakob's anxiety. One result of the 1848–1849 revolution had been to establish Czech nationalism. Czech hatred against the German-Austrians, the ruling class in Moravia, easily turned against the hereditary scapegoats, the Jews, who were German in language and education. In Freiberg the grumbling clothmakers, Czech to a man, began to hold the Jewish textile merchants responsible for their plight. Moreover, the educational facilities in a decaying town did not hold much prospect of the peasant woman's prediction of young Sigmund's future greatness being fulfilled.

In previous centuries Jakob Freud's ancestors had fled anti-Semitic persecutions in the Rhineland and in Lithuania before settling in Moravia. In 1859, when Sigmund was three, the ancient march of the family was resumed, as he himself would have to resume it once more nearly eighty years later.

Freud has taught us that the essential foundations of character are laid down by the age of three and that later events can modify but not alter the traits then established. This then was the age when he was taken away from the happy home of his early childhood. From this

Freud as a boy of eight, with his father.

journey dated the beginning of a "phobia" of traveling by train, from which he suffered a good deal before he was able to dispel it by analysis. It turned out to be connected with the fear of losing his home.

The family settled in Leipzig for a year before moving on to Vienna. Meanwhile, Emmanuel, with his wife and two children and his brother Philipp, went to Manchester, England, where his knowledge of cloth manufacture brought him some success. In later years Sigmund never ceased to envy Emmanuel for this migration to a land where he could bring up his children far from the daily persecutions Jews were subject to in Austria.

THE FREUD FAMILY'S EARLY YEARS in Vienna were evidently very unpleasant. Freud said later: "They were hard times and not worth remembering."

From Freud's mother and sister one gets a picture of him as having been a "good" boy. He was the eldest child, at least of his mother. This fact may give a child a special sense of importance and responsibility. There is no doubt that this was true in Freud's case; responsibility for all his relatives and friends became a central feature of his character. So he possessed the self-confidence that told him he would achieve something worthwhile in life, and the ambition to do so.

One of his few recollections of his years between three and seven was of his mother assuring him at the age of six that we were made of earth and therefore must return to earth. For the first time he captured some sense of the inevitable. As he put it: "I slowly acquiesced in the idea I was later to hear expressed in the words 'Thou owest nature a death.'"

The family's flat in Vienna during these years was in the Pfeffergasse, a small street in the quarter (largely Jewish) called the Leopoldstadt. It consisted of a living room, a dining room, three bedrooms, and a long, narrow room called the *"cabinet."* There was no bathroom, but once a fortnight a couple of strong carriers brought a large wooden tub, with several kegs of hot and cold water, into the kitchen and fetched them away the next day. When the children were old enough, however, their mother would take them to one of the many public baths.

The *cabinet*, separated from the rest of the flat, with a window looking onto the street, was allotted to Sigmund; it contained a bed, chairs, shelf, and writing desk. All through the years of his school and university life the only thing that changed in it was an increasing number of crowded bookcases. In his teens he would even eat his evening meal there so as to lose no time from his studies. He had an oil lamp to himself, while the other bedrooms had only candles. When his sister was eight their mother got her to practice on the piano. The sound disturbed the young student; he insisted on the piano being removed, and removed it was—an illustration of the esteem in which he and his studies were held in the family.

After the first lessons with his mother, Freud's father took charge of his education. Jakob Freud was above the average in intelligence and outlook, though self-taught. The good progress of the boy would be evidence of the satisfactory relationship between him and his father. When Sigmund was nine years old he passed an examination that enabled him to attend high school (Sperl Gymnasium) a year earlier than the normal age.

Jakob was not at all the strict paternal type then so common, and he used to consult the children over various decisions to be made, in what was called the "family council." An example was the choice of a name for the younger son. It was Sigmund's vote for the name of Alexander that was accepted, his selection being based on admiration for Alexander the Great. To support his choice he recited the whole story of the Macedonian's triumphs.

From the age of twelve Sigmund used to accompany his father on walks in the neighborhood of Vienna. The only difference between father and son seems to have occurred when Freud, at seventeen, indulged his propensity for buying books to such an extent that he was unable to pay for them.

Freud at the age of sixteen, with his mother.

Of Freud's religious background not a great deal is known. His father must have been brought up as an orthodox Jew, and Freud himself was certainly conversant with all Jewish customs and festivals. But Jakob Freud was a man of progressive views and it is not likely that he kept up orthodox Jewish customs after migrating to Vienna. When Freud spoke of having been greatly influenced by his early reading of the Bible he can only have meant in an ethical sense. He does not appear ever to have felt the need of belief in a God or immortality, and his emotional needs found expression in an earnest adherence to the principles of science.

At the Sperl Gymnasium young Sigmund had a brilliant career. For the last six of the eight years he stood at the head of his class. He repaid his father's instruction by helping his sisters with their studies. He even exercised some censorship over their reading; when his sister Anna was fifteen, for instance, she was warned off Balzac and Dumas. He was altogether the big brother.

Reading and studying filled the greater part of his life. Friends who visited him were at once closeted in the *cabinet* for the purpose of serious discussion, much to the pique of his sisters who had to watch the youths pass them by. He read widely outside the studies proper, and had a very considerable gift for languages. Besides being completely at home in Latin and Greek, he acquired a thorough knowledge of French and English; in addition he taught himself Italian and Spanish. He had of course been taught Hebrew.

He was especially fond of English and he told me once that for ten years he read nothing but English books. Shakespeare, whom he started reading at the age of eight, he read over and over again, admiring his superb understanding of human nature.

His main exercise was that of walking, especially on mountains, and he was a good swimmer.

During his development Freud went through a militaristic phase. He pasted onto the backs of his wooden soldiers little labels bearing the names of Napoleon's marshals. His favorite one was André Masséna, later governor of Paris. The Franco-Prussian War, which aroused his keen interest, broke out when he was fourteen. He followed the campaign on a large map by means of small flags. His dreams of becoming a great general himself, however, gradually faded.

The anti-Semitism that pervaded Vienna eventually put an end to the phase of German nationalistic enthusiasm through which Freud passed in early years. His father never regained the place he had held in his esteem after he told his twelve-year-old boy how a Gentile had knocked off his new fur cap into the mud and shouted at him: "Jew, get off the pavement." To the indignant boy's question: "And what did you do?" Jakob Freud replied: "I stepped into the gutter and picked up my cap."

This lack of heroism on the part of his model man shocked the youngster, who at once contrasted it in his mind with the behavior of Hamilcar when he made his son Hannibal swear on the household altar to take vengeance on the Romans. Freud evidently identified himself with Hannibal, for he said that ever since then Hannibal had a place in his fantasies.

Freud's first love experience was at the age of sixteen when he revisited Freiberg, his birthplace. He stayed there with the Fluss family, who were friends of his parents. With their daughter, Gisela, a year or two younger than himself, a companion of his early childhood, he fell in love on the spot. He was too shy to even address a single word to her, and she went away to her school after a few days.

The emotion of love would not touch him again till ten years later. The disconsolate youth had to content himself with wandering in the woods with the fantasy of how pleasant his life would have been could he have grown up a stout country lad, like Gisela's brothers, and married the maiden. Had this fantasy been reality, much might have been different in our world.

WHEN, AT THE AGE OF SEVENTEEN, Freud was graduated *summa cum laude*, his father rewarded him with a promise of a visit to England, which was to be fulfilled two years later. Meanwhile, he had to face the problem of choosing a career. His father had left him entirely free in the matter. For a Viennese Jew the choice lay between business, law, and medicine. Here is Freud's own account of his choice:

> Neither at that time, nor indeed in my later life, did I feel any particular predilection for the career of a physician. I was moved, rather, by a sort of curiosity, which was, however, directed more toward human concerns than toward natural objects. . . . At the same time, the theories of Darwin, which were then of topical interest, strongly attracted me, for they held out hopes of an extraordinary advance in our understanding of the world; and it was hearing Goethe's beautiful essay on Nature read aloud at a popular lecture just before I left school that decided me to become a medical student.

Goethe's essay is a romantic picture of Nature as a beautiful and bountiful mother who allows her favorite children the privilege of exploring her secrets. At this critical period of Freud's life he perceived that the ultimate secret of power was not force, but understanding. To understand man's behavior it was necessary, so he thought, to learn something about nature, man's place in nature, and man's physical constitution.

I told him once the story of a surgeon who said that if he ever reached the Eternal Throne he would come armed with a cancerous bone and ask the Almighty what He had to say about it. Freud's reply was: "If I were to find myself in a similar situation, my chief reproach to the Almighty would be that He had not given me a better brain." It was the remark of a man who had set himself a lofty goal and had great expectations.

CHAPTER TWO

FREUD ENTERED THE UNIVERSITY OF VIENNA in the autumn of 1873, at the early age of seventeen. Not surprisingly, since he had chosen medical studies for such unorthodox reasons, he pursued in only a negligent fashion the studies obligatory to the medical career itself and seized every opportunity to dally in those neighboring fields that interested him. In his first semester he signed up for twelve lectures a week in anatomy and six in chemistry, with practical work in both. During his first summer semester he spent twenty-eight hours weekly in anatomy, botany, chemistry, microscopy, and mineralogy. He also followed courses on biology and Darwinism and one by Ernst von Brücke, the famous Prussian physiologist, on the physiology of voice and speech. In following semesters, in addition to his medical studies, he attended reading seminars in philosophy, added a course on Aristotle's logic and lectures on zoology proper, not those on "zoology for medical students." Thus Freud's medical studies took, in the end, three years longer than necessary. In later years he talked of having been twitted over his dilatoriness, as if he were a backward student.

In the summer of 1875, when he was nineteen, Freud finally

visited the land of his dreams, England. There he renewed his relationship with his older half brother, Emmanuel, who soon wrote their father an extremely enthusiastic letter, lauding young Sigmund's development and character.

Back in Vienna, Freud continued to live at home. The family had moved to a larger flat in the Kaiser Josefstrasse. He was still dependent on his father's generous support. Jakob Freud, now in his sixties, had lost his small capital in the financial crash of 1873 and had to be helped out by loans from his wife's family. But he was without doubt proud of his son's achievements, content that Freud should continue on the path he had chosen, and glad to be able to make it possible as long as he could. Sigmund's needs were very modest. Apart from peace and quiet for reading, and the company of like-minded friends, he wanted little else than books.

IN THE AUTUMN OF 1876 Freud was accepted in Brücke's Physiological Institute at the age of twenty as what was called a *famulus*, a sort of research scholar. Freud later wrote: "During my first three years at the University I . . . [made] the discovery that the peculiarities and limitations of my gifts denied me all success in many of the departments of science into which my youthful eagerness had plunged me. Thus is learned the truth of Mephistopheles' warning: 'It is in vain that you range round from science to science; each man learns only what he can.' In Ernst Brücke's physiology laboratory I found rest and satisfaction— and men, too, whom I could take as my models; the great Brücke himself and his assistants Sigmund Exner and Ernst von Fleischl-Marxow."

Brücke was the disciplined scientist that Freud felt he should aim at becoming—uncompromising, idealistic, almost ascetic in outlook. He was a small man with "terrifying blue eyes," rather shy, but stern. Throughout Freud's life the image of those steel-blue eyes would appear at any moment when he might be tempted to any remissness in duty.

A student who in one of his papers had written: "Superficial observation reveals . . ." had his paper returned with the objectionable line violently crossed out and Brücke's comment on the margin: "One is not to observe superficially." General opinion had labeled him an indefatigable worker, a cold, purely rational man. But it is said that no pupil or friend ever became unfaithful to him. To the student who proved his ability he was a benevolent father, extending counsel and protection far beyond scientific matters. He respected the student's own ideas, and sponsored talents even if they deviated considerably from his own opinions.

The famous Brücke Physiological Institute was miserably housed in the ground floor and basement of a dark and smelly old gun factory. It consisted of a large room where the students kept their microscopes and listened to lectures, and two smaller ones, one of which was Brücke's sanctum. There were also on both floors a few small cubicles that served as chemical, electrophysiological, and optical laboratories. There was no electricity or gas. All heating had to be done over a spirit lamp, and the water was brought up from a well in the yard where a shed housed the animals experimented on. Nevertheless this institute was the pride of the medical school on account of the distinction of its foreign visitors and students.

Ernst von Brücke.

Brücke set Freud behind the microscope to study nerve cells in the spinal cord of the Ammocoetes (Petromyzon), a primitive genus of fish.

The question of whether the nervous system of the higher animals is composed of elements different from those of the lower animals was highly controversial at that time, when the excitement caused by Darwin's work was at its height in every country in Europe. Brücke believed the living organism was a part of the physical universe and the world of organisms itself one family, to include plants, animals, as well as man, and that in this evolution of life, no spirits, no ultimate purposes were at work.

Freud, after devising an improvement in the technique of preparing the nervous tissue for examination, established definitely, by precise observation and genetic interpretation, that the cells of the nervous system of lower animals showed a continuity with those of higher animals. Any zoologist would have been proud to have made this discovery.

Freud had early grasped the fact that further progress in knowledge requires new or improved methods. Then come the new facts thus discovered, followed by the organization of the new and old knowledge in a theory of them. The theory may then lead to speculation, a glancing and guessing at questions and answers beyond existing means of observation. It is extremely rare for one and the same man to be equally successful in all these phases of development. Freud's work in psychoanalysis was to prove an example of this rarest case. He devised the instrument, used it to discover a great number of new facts, provided the organizing theory, and ventured on stimulating speculations beyond the actually known. It can be shown that the principles on which Freud later constructed his psychological theories were those he had acquired as a medical student under Brucke's influence.

One notable feature in Freud's neurological researches was his adherence to anatomy. The microscope was his one and only tool. Physiology seemed to mean examination to him, and not experimentation. This might at first sight seem strange in a man of Freud's active mind and revolutionary tendencies, but reflection shows that this preference of the eye over the hand, of passively seeing over actively doing, corresponded to something highly significant in his nature. When later on it fell to his lot to treat neurotic patients he soon abandoned the customary method—recently revived in another form—of stimulating them by electricity. And it was not long before he gave up hypnosis, which he found "a coarsely interfering method." He chose to look and listen, confident that if he could perceive the structure of a neurosis he would truly understand and have power over the forces that had brought it about.

IN THE AUTUMN OF 1879 Freud was called up for his year's military service. That was far less strenuous in those days. Medical students continued to live at home and had no duties except to stand about in the hospitals. Freud coped with the terrible boredom by translating a book by John Stuart Mill. He was specially gifted as a translator. This was the only work he ever published that had no connection with his scientific interests. His main motive was undoubtedly to kill time and, incidentally, to earn a little money.

The translation gave rise to a revealing account of his views on women. He wrote:

> [Mill] lacked in many matters the sense of the absurd; for example, in that of female emancipation. . . . We surely agree that the management of a house, the care of children, demand the whole of a human being. . . . It never emerges that women are different from men. . . . It is possible that changes in up-bringing may suppress all a woman's tender attributes, needful of protection and yet so victorious, and that she can then earn a livelihood like men. It is also possible that in such an event one would not be justified in mourning the passing away of the most delightful thing the world can offer us—our ideal of woman-hood. I believe that all reforming action would break down in front of the fact that Nature has determined woman's destiny through beauty, charm, and sweetness.

Freud regarded women as finer and ethically nobler than men; there are indications that he wished to absorb some of these qualities from them.

There is little doubt that Freud found the psychology of women more enigmatic than that of men. He said later: "The great question that has never been answered and which I have not yet been able to answer, despite my thirty years of research into the feminine soul, is 'What does a woman want?'"

THE YEARS FREUD WAS SPENDING in Brücke's laboratory were doing nothing to advance him toward a future livelihood. But he pushed this staring fact aside as long as he could, not only because of his aversion to the practice of medicine, but also because of his great liking for his laboratory work. To discover something new and add to our stock of knowledge was perhaps the strongest motive in his nature. The only lectures he found at all interesting were Dr. Theodor Meynert's on psychiatry.

Freud passed his final medical examinations with the grade "excellent." This result, according to Freud, was due only to the photographic memory that he had enjoyed all through his childhood and adolescence, although it was gradually becoming unreliable. "In the tension before the final examination I must have made use of the remnant of this ability, for in certain subjects I gave the examiners apparently automatic answers which proved to be exact reproductions of the textbook which I had skimmed through but once, and then in greatest haste." The graduation ceremonies took place in the beautiful assembly hall of the baroque building of the old university, and Freud's family were all present.

THE OBTAINING OF HIS MEDICAL QUALIFICATION appeared outwardly to make no difference in Freud's life. For about a year he went on working in Brücke's institute. He was soon promoted to the position of demonstrator, one with some teaching responsibility. In the natural course of events this would lead to a position as assistant, then assistant professor, and finally professor of physiology.

Yet his prospects in Brücke's laboratory were in fact dark, and he later termed 1882 "the gloomiest and least successful year of my professional life." Both the assistants, Fleischl and Exner, were only ten years older than Freud himself and so would not be likely to vacate such a position for him for years to come. Furthermore, the salaries were so meager that, although his needs were modest, he could hardly support himself without private means and there were times when he had to borrow money from friends.

About this time Freud found a philanthropic patron in the person of Dr. Josef Breuer, who was to play so important a part in his subsequent career. Breuer, one of the most highly thought of physicians in Vienna, was the family doctor to Brücke, Exner, and others of high standing. Freud had first met him at the Physiological Institute, and they had soon found they shared the same scientific interests and outlook. They became friends, and for a considerable period Breuer used to lend, or give, Freud, a certain sum every month.

A sensitive nature like Freud's could not help feeling some painfulness in the situation. "Breuer seems to regard these loans as a regular institution, but I always mind them." His longing for independence, economic and otherwise, was vehement. But the debt went on increasing.

From his subsequent account one could get the impression that it was only Brücke's intervention that suddenly woke Freud out of a dream of serving the cause of science irrespective of mundane considerations. "In 1882," he wrote, "my teacher, for whom I had the highest possible esteem, corrected my father's generous improvidence by strongly advising me, in view of my bad financial position, to abandon my theoretical career."

Martha Bernays.

But what had brought the matter to a head at this particular moment, had triggered the decision to earn his livelihood as a physician and resign his position in Brücke's institute, was something quite new in his life.

He had fallen head over ears in love!

MARTHA BERNAYS, born on July 26, 1861, and therefore five years younger than Freud, came of a family distinguished in Jewish culture. Her grandfather Isaac Bernays had been chief rabbi of Hamburg. In 1869, when Martha was eight, her father, Berman Bernays, a merchant, had brought his family from Hamburg to Vienna, where he became secretary to a well-known Viennese economist. Ten years later, on a cold December night in 1879, Berman Bernays had been stricken with heart failure and had died in the street. Since his death his son Eli, Martha's older brother, who edited a journal on economics and was a shrewd businessman, had entirely supported his mother and two sisters.

Now, on an evening in April 1882, Martha Bernays and probably her younger sister Minna were visiting the Freud family. On returning from work Freud usually rushed straight to his room to resume his studies, irrespective of visitors. But on this occasion he was arrested by the sight of a merry maiden peeling an apple and chatting gaily at the family table; to the general surprise he joined the family.

That very first glimpse was a fatal one. For several weeks, however, Freud found it easier to present an unsociable and rather eccentric exterior than to court Martha Bernays straightforwardly, but as soon as he apprehended the seriousness of his feelings he hurried to bind her to himself.

No man's inner life can be comprehended without some knowledge of his attitude toward the basic emotion of love. This was a side of his nature that Freud kept strictly reserved for his private life. Of his emotional experiences with his wife—or future wife—he never spoke or wrote. As an old lady Martha Bernays Freud herself, when the early days of their engagement were mentioned, would respond with a beatific smile that recalled her great happiness, but any information she would vouchsafe was naturally factual rather than emotional. Her lover had been in her eyes quite perfect; that was the essence of what she had to convey. Only after her death, at the end of 1951, was it possible to inspect the love letters she had preserved.

Freud wrote more than nine hundred letters to his betrothed. In the four and a quarter years of their engagement they were separated for fully three years. Their custom was to write daily, and there were very many occasions when two or even three letters had to be composed on the same day. In this correspondence we are confronted with all the passions of which Freud's intense nature was capable.

Martha Bernays was almost twenty-one when she and her future husband met. She was well educated and intelligent,

though she would not be called an intellectual. In later years
the affairs of everyday life were rich enough to absorb her
attention. She was slim, pale, rather petite. That her winning
ways made her attractive to men is evident from the many
jealous allusions in the correspondence to the ardor of her
admirers and suitors.

A few weeks after they met Freud began sending Martha a
red rose each day; each flower was accompanied by a visiting
card with a motto, in Latin, Spanish, English, or German. His
first compliment was to liken her to the fairy princess from
whose lips fell roses and pearls. From this came his favorite
name for her, "Princess."

On the last day of May they had their first private talk together as they walked down from the Kahlenberg arm in arm.
In his diary that day he wondered whether he could mean
remotely as much to her as she did to him.

On June 8 he found her making a portfolio for a certain
cousin of hers in Hamburg, a musician named Max Mayer, and
concluded he had come on the scene too late. But only two days
later in a garden in Mödling they came across a double almond,
which the Viennese called a *Vielliebchen*, and which exacts a
forfeit from each in the form of a present. Now for the first
time Freud dared to hope. The next day she sent him a cake of
her own baking for him to "dissect," signing the note "Martha
Bernays." Before she sent it off, however, a copy of *David
Copperfield* arrived from him; so she added a few warm lines
of thanks, signed "Martha."

It was on June 12 that Freud informed Brücke he was leaving
the laboratory to earn a living by private practice.

The following day Martha was dining with his family, and
he took possession of her name card as a souvenir; in appreciation
of the gesture she pressed his hand under the table. It was not
unobserved by his sisters. The next day she again wrote him a
few lines, and on the following day they went for a stroll accompanied by her brother and she told him she had plucked for
him in Baden a sprig of lime blossom. Emboldened by this
news, Freud, who already had permission to call her by her
first name, sought to extend it to the intimacy of *"du."* So he

went home and wrote his first letter to her, shy, hesitant, and elaborate, asking for this privilege.

Martha's response to the letter was to present him with a ring of her father's which her mother had given her. Freud wore it on his little finger. It was December 1883 before Freud could afford to give her an engagement ring, a plain one with a garnet.

Until Freud had a private practice the engagement had to remain a terrible secret. When Martha, her mother, and her sister left a few days later for their customary vacation at Wandsbek, near Hamburg, her letters to him were sent to the laboratory assistant at Brücke's institute, and he sent his letters to her in envelopes addressed by one of her old friends.

These letters reveal the happiness and misery being felt by Freud. The day after their parting Freud was afraid to wake from what had perhaps been a deceptive dream of bliss. Never had he imagined such happiness.

Freud's characteristic aversion to compromises, to evasions, and palliations of the full truth displayed itself to the full in this greatest emotional experience of his life. Their relationship must be quite perfect; the slightest blur was not to be tolerated. At times it seemed as if his goal was fusion rather than union. This aim was humanly impossible. Only a week after the parting there was the first faint hint of his intention, never to be fulfilled, to mold her into his perfect image. Rebuking him for sending her an extravagant present she said firmly: "You musn't do that." This brought an immediate reproof.

A week later trouble descended. His jealousy was fed by one of his sisters telling him how enthusiastic Martha had been over some songs Max Mayer had composed and sung to her. Freud wrote Martha of his feelings, then felt ashamed. "Can there be anything crazier, I said to myself. You have won the dearest girl quite without any merit of your own, and you know no better than only a week later to torment her with jealousy. . . . When a girl like Martha is fond of me how can I fear a legion of Max Mayers? . . . The feeling I had came from a distrust of myself, not of you." This clear wisdom, however, got clouded over again and again.

To reestablish harmony Freud decided to borrow enough money to travel to Wandsbek. He stayed ten days, his first of half a dozen visits there over the years of their betrothal. In Wandsbek itself, where he put up at the Post Hotel, there was the problem of meeting Martha without her relatives finding out he was there. Days of despair passed before Martha managed to arrange a rendezvous, in the marketplace in Hamburg. As he said, "Women are much cleverer at such things than men." The few meetings were very happy, and on his return to Vienna he wrote that he was refreshed for a hundred years.

The restored happiness, however, did not last long. In lucid moments he knew that his distrust in Martha's love sprang from a distrust of his own lovableness. He had none of the magic for women that a musician such as Max had. "I think there is a general enmity between artists and those engaged in the details of scientific work. We know that they possess in their art a master key to open with ease all female hearts." It was a penance to expiate for his indifference to women in his youth.

Freud was evidently looking for trouble, and he found it or made it. Eli Bernays, a year older than his sister, was an open-hearted friend of Freud's, of a generous nature. Freud cherished the copy of the American Declaration of Independence he gave him and later hung it up over his bed in the hospital. But Freud had remarked, only a fortnight after the engagement, that Eli was going to be his "most dangerous rival": soon Eli had become "unbearable" to him.

Martha's mother, Emmeline Bernays, was a well-educated woman: her family had come from Scandinavia and she could still speak Swedish. Like her husband she adhered to the strict rules of orthodox Judaism, and her children were brought up to do the same. This was in itself a serious source of friction, since Freud despised what to him was pure superstition. Out of consideration for her mother's feelings Martha would on the Sabbath, when writing was forbidden, compose a letter in pencil in the garden rather than use the pen and ink in her mother's presence. That sort of thing greatly annoyed Freud and he would call her "weak" for not standing up to her mother.

Martha's own attitude to her mother was one of devotion and

strict obedience; her mother's resolute will was to her not selfishness but something to be admired, and not questioned. Her sister Minna, on the other hand, was quite frank in her criticisms of her mother; it was the first bond between her and Freud. He neatly characterized the contrast with psychological acumen: "You don't love her very much and are as considerate as possible to her; Minna loves her, but doesn't spare her."

It was of paramount importance to Freud that there was to be no one other than himself in Martha's life, or at all events in her affection. He was experiencing in his own person the full force of the terrible power of love with all its raptures, fears, and torments. If ever a fiery apprenticeship qualified a man to discourse authoritatively on love, that man was Freud.

CHAPTER THREE

THE DECISION TO LEAVE Brücke's institute for private practice had been a painful one, but in admitting to Martha what a wrench the "separation from science" had been, Freud cheerfully added "perhaps it is not a final one."

On July 31, 1882, soon after his return from Wandsbek, he inscribed himself in the Vienna General Hospital. In those days medical students on the Continent learned through lectures and demonstrations, and Freud had no experience in personal care of patients. So he hoped to spend at least two years living and studying in the hospital, although he was not to move there until 1883. Meanwhile, he chose to begin his studies with surgery. He found the work physically tiring and remained only a little over two months in the surgical wards.

From his correspondence one receives two outstanding impressions of Freud's life in this period: his poverty, and the high quality of his friends. Freud's attitude toward money seems always to have been unusually normal and objective. It had no interest in itself; it was there to be used, and he was always very generous whenever he had the opportunity. There were two distinct groups of personal friends: those he got to know in his medical work, mostly older than himself; and a little group of about his own age, fifteen or twenty in number, who called themselves the *Bund* (Union). They used to gather regularly once a week in the Café Kurzweil for conversation and games of cards and chess.

Soon after his engagement Freud had put himself "under *Kuratel*" [in trusteeship] because of his extravagance, by making his betrothed his banker. He sent Martha all the money he could spare and she took charge of the common fund; from this he borrowed and paid back according to his financial situation. There were times when Martha seemed shy at accepting the money, but he rallied her by asking her whether she wished to return to the relationship of Fraülein and Herr Doktor.

After he entered the general hospital he sent her a weekly account of his expenses. From the first one, in the middle of September 1882, soon after her return to Vienna, we learn that the only two meals he took in the day cost him 1 gulden 11 kreuzers altogether. Twenty-six kreuzers went for cigars, on which he comments, "a scandalous amount." One day 10 kreuzers went in chocolate, but the excuse is added, "I was so hungry in the street as I was going to Breuer's." A dream of his that never came true was to be able to give Martha a gold snake bangle—a distinguishing mark of docents' wives.

Something may now be said about Freud's state of health in these years. All his life he was subject to incapacitating spells of migraine, quite refractory to any treatment. But he said, "It was as if all the pain was external; I was not identified with the disease, and stood above it." This complaint, however, caused him far less suffering than those of psychological origin. We do not know when what he then called his "neurasthenia" began. It must have been exacerbated by the conflicting emotions that surrounded his love passion, although, curiously enough, it seems to have reached its acme some years after his marriage.

The symptoms that troubled him were severe indigestion, and moodiness in a pronounced degree. But he notes that all his troubles vanished as soon as he was in the company of his betrothed. At such times he felt that he had all that mattered and that his troubles would cease were he only to choose a modest and contented life. So everything would be all right as soon as they got married, a prediction which was not fulfilled.

One evening young people were dancing at Breuer's. "You can imagine how furious so much youth, beauty . . . and merriment made me, after my painful headache and our long hard separation," he wrote. "I am ashamed to say that on such occasions I am very envious . . . really disagreeable and unable to enjoy anything. The occasion itself was very pleasant: there were mostly girls of from fifteen to eighteen, and some very pretty ones. I fitted in no better than the cholera would have."

When things went well his moods could be markedly euphoric. "The work is going splendidly and is most promising. Martha, I am altogether so passionate, everything in me is at present so intense, my thoughts so sharp and clear, that it is wonderful how I manage to keep calm when I am in company." But the moods could rapidly change. On March 21, 1885, we read, "I can't stand it much longer."

The bad moods cannot be called true depressions in a psychiatric sense, for what is remarkable throughout is that there is never any sign of pessimism or hopelessness. Over and over again we come across the note of absolute confidence in ultimate success and happiness. "Nothing can really touch us; we shall come together at the end and will love each other the more since we have so thoroughly savored privation. No obstruction, no bad luck, can prevent my final success, merely delay it, so long as we stay well and I know that you are cheerful and love me."

We may now turn to more external interests. Freud was still a great reader despite his preoccupations, and he did all he could to share the interest with Martha. At first he hoped to arouse her interest in the direction of his work, and he went so far as to write a general introduction to philosophy, which he called a "Philosophical A.B.C.," for her benefit. Then followed Thomas Huxley's *Introductory Science Primer*, which probably had no greater success. Nor could he persuade her to master English, though he often pressed her to it at a time when English literature was his chief relaxation. On the other hand, Martha enjoyed discussing good novels with him.

The two books that made the deepest impression on Freud, at least in these years, were *Don Quixote* by Cervantes and *The Temptation of St. Anthony* by Flaubert. He had read the former in boyhood. He sent a copy to Martha, and wrote, "Don't you find it very touching to read how a great person, himself an idealist, makes fun of his ideals?"

The Temptation evoked more serious reflections. "I was deeply moved by . . . this book which in the most condensed fashion and with unsurpassable vividness throws at one's head the whole trashy world: for it calls up . . . the real riddles of life, all the conflicts of feelings and impulses; and it confirms the awareness of our perplexity in the mysteriousness that reigns everywhere. These questions, it is true, are always there, and one should always be thinking of them. What one does, however, is confine oneself to a narrow aim every hour and every day and get used to the idea that to concern oneself with these enigmas is the task of a special hour, in the belief that they exist only in those special hours. Then they suddenly assail one in the morning and rob one of one's composure and one's spirits."

Freud could not have been a Viennese without frequenting the theater a good deal; in Vienna it often came before food. There was Hugo's *Hernani*. All seats were gone except at six francs. Freud walked away, but returned in an extravagant mood, and declared he had never spent six francs so well.

On October 12, 1882, Freud transferred to a new department at the hospital, entering the division of internal medicine as an *Aspirant*, roughly the position of our clinical assistant, until he could be appointed a *Sekundararzt*, a combination of our (resident) house physician and registrar. Theodor Meynert, his former professor in psychiatry, spoke in his favor.

The division of internal medicine was headed by Dr. Carl Nothnagel, a great physician who had just come to Vienna from Germany. Freud admired him, but found no more interest in treating the sick patients in the wards than in studying their diseases. By now he must have been doubly convinced that he was not born to be a doctor.

Meanwhile, though Sigmund's and Martha's engagement was still secret, there had been other romantic developments. Eli,

Martha's brother, had been courting Anna, the eldest sister in the Freud family, and sometime during the Christmas holidays in 1882 they became engaged. The holiday family atmosphere was perhaps the reason why Freud and Martha decided to divulge their secret to Martha's Mamma on December 26. There are indications that it was long before Frau Bernays reconciled herself to Martha's choice of a suitor with neither means nor prospects, and one obviously out of sympathy with her religious views.

In January 1883 the lovers started writing an account of their engagement—to be read in far-off days—in what they termed a *geheime Chronik* (secret record). Being in the same town, there would be few letters to remind them in the future of those exciting days. They wrote alternately; it was a combination of diary and self-confession. Freud's first entry contained the following: "There is some courage and boldness locked up in me that is not easily . . . extinguished. When I examine myself strictly, more strictly than my loved one would, I perceive that Nature has . . . endowed me with a dauntless love of truth, the keen eye of an investigator, a rightful sense of the values of life, and the gift of working hard and finding pleasure in doing so. Enough of the best attributes for me to find endurable my beggarliness in other respects. . . . We will hold together through this life, so easily apprehensible in its immediate aims but so incomprehensible in its final purpose."

ON MAY 1, 1883, FREUD TRANSFERRED again, this time to Meynert's psychiatric clinic, where he was at once appointed *Sekundararzt*. He now moved into the hospital, the first time he had left home except for short holidays. He was twenty-seven years old and never again slept at his parents' home. He was given a room and fire with the hospital allowance, the same pittance as the lamplighter. Afterward this rose to 30 gulden a month, which was less than his meals cost him. For long his midday meal consisted of a plate of veal, which cost 60 kreuzers, the evening one of corned beef and cheese for 36 kreuzers; sweets could be dispensed with. At one time he tried to save time and money by cooking for himself, or rather, not cooking.

He bought a coffee machine, together with a store of cold ham, cheese, and bread.

Freud served in Meynert's clinic for five months, two months in the male wards and then three in the female. This constituted his main purely psychiatric experience. It was hard work, and the seven hours daily in the wards were barely sufficient to cover the ground. He was determined to master the subject and read assiduously in it; he remarked how little psychiatrists seemed to understand it.

Freud had made many good friends among the resident physicians, and when the united *Sekundarärzte* made a protest to the authorities about their accommodations, it was Freud they chose to be their spokesman. He was evidently already beginning to stand out among the rest.

In the meantime, however, Freud was about to be separated from Martha again, for a quite unforeseeable future. Frau Bernays had decided to move permanently with her daughters to her beloved Wandsbek. Eli encouraged his mother's idea, doubtless thinking he would have more peace in her absence. Martha objected, but her protests were not so vigorous as Freud wished.

The total separation affected Freud severely. He had not started on any research work that might further his professional and marriage prospects, and as Jakob's earning powers waned, his family cares were crushing. And now he was even deprived of the only consolation—sharing his troubles in talks with Martha—that had sustained him. His antipathy toward Martha's brother became so intense that Freud did not go to the wedding when Eli married his sister Anna in October 1883, though this was partly because of his dislike of formal occasions. It was a full-dress affair and accompanied by ceremonies which Freud described as "simply loathsome"; he did not think then that his time would come to submit to the same ceremonies.

In the meantime, as the result of this rupture, Freud no longer cared to visit Martha's home, and for two months they met in the street or in the crowded flat of the Freud family. These circumstances changed only when he had a room of his own in the hospital, from May 1, where she used then to visit him.

Freud's resentment toward Martha's family even included Martha at first, because she had not fought harder against their separation. The month following her departure from Vienna was filled with bitterness on his side, bewilderment on hers. In one letter after another he accused her of choosing easy paths instead of bravely facing painful situations. Martha, in very sweet and patient replies, made it clear she did not propose to join him in an assault on her family. With all her sweetness and tact, Martha was not a pattern of yielding docility, and was, indeed, a steadfast personality.

After several painful weeks Martha's letters had the desired effect, and matters were quieter. "I do not need a comrade-in-arms, such as I hoped to make you into; I am strong enough to fight alone. You shall not hear another harsh word. . . . I have asked of you what is not in your nature."

Resignation, however, never suited Freud. Time and again, in the three years that were still to elapse before their union became permanent, his letters would reveal how mighty were the passions that animated him, and how unlike he was in reality to the calm scientist he is often depicted. Freud was beyond doubt someone whose instincts were far more powerful than those of the average man, but whose repressions were even more potent. The combination brought about an inner intensity of a degree that is perhaps the essential feature of any genius.

IN THE MIDDLE OF SEPTEMBER 1883, just before his period of work in Meynert's psychiatric clinic came to an end, Freud called on Dr. Josef Breuer to seek advice.

Of Freud's older friends, Breuer, the only Jew among them, was the most sympathetic personality. Freud's letters are full of his high appreciation of Breuer's wisdom and, above all, his delicate understanding. To talk with Breuer was "like sitting in the sun." Freud was also very fond of Breuer's young and pretty wife, and would one day name his own eldest daughter Mathilde after her.

On this occasion Freud wanted to discuss with Breuer the possibility of specializing in neurology. The question was raised because of the recent death of a young colleague of

Freud's at the hospital, one who had been regarded as the coming neurologist in Vienna. Freud expounded the situation. If he confined himself to neurology he would be tied to Vienna and might have to keep his future bride waiting an indefinitely long time, whereas if he had an all-round medical training, could help in childbirth, pull out a tooth, and mend a broken leg he would surely be able to make a living, and would be free to go "to the country, to England, to America, or to the moon."

Freud always had a profoundly ambivalent attitude toward Vienna. Consciously he loathed it—"Must we stay here, Martha? . . . let us seek a home where human worth is more represented." But unconsciously something held him there. During this period he and Martha were writing of the possibility of sailing from Hamburg after their marriage, directly to America, where many German scientists were finding a home. And Emmanuel, Freud's older half brother in England, whose opinion he had recently asked, wanted him to come to Manchester.

Martha's younger sister, Minna, also made a suggestion: that he stay in Austria until his fame reached America, when so many American patients would flock to him that he would be saved the trouble of emigrating. A prediction that came true, even if it took another thirty years to do so.

On this September day in 1883 Breuer gave the sage advice to choose a middle way, to continue as he was doing and keep an eye on both possibilities. So the next day Freud asked the director of the hospital to enter his name on the list waiting for a vacancy in the department for diseases of the nervous system and liver (!) and in the meantime to transfer him to the ward for syphilitic patients. Freud wanted experience there because of the important connection between syphilis and various diseases of the nervous system.

It was very light work, the ward visits finishing at ten in the morning and taking place only twice a week. Freud thus had plenty of time for the laboratory, and undertook some important research, beginning the brain-anatomy studies that would continue for the next two years. Under Brücke he had investigated the cells of the spinal cord, the part of the nervous system that then held his chief interest, but in order to become an all-round neuropathologist it was necessary to proceed higher. So he now turned to the next proximate part of the central nervous system, the medulla oblongata.

The structure of this extremely complicated little organ, into which is condensed a great variety of nervous tracts, was at that time very imperfectly known. To trace the fibers passing through it to their connections elsewhere required great dex-

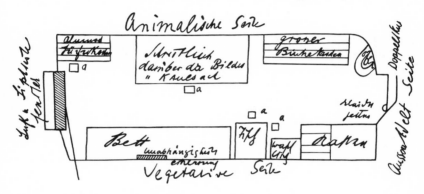

Facsimile of a diagram by Freud of his room in the Vienna General Hospital, drawn for Martha Bernays.

terity, patience, and precision. Many years later, in commenting on medical attempts to explain morbid anxiety as a disorder of that organ, Freud wrote, one might say laughingly: "The medulla oblongata is a very serious and beautiful thing. I remember very well how much time and trouble I devoted to the study of it years ago. Today, however, I must say I do not know of anything that seems to me more irrelevant for the psychological understanding of anxiety than a knowledge of the nervous paths its excitations follow."

As I have said, before she had moved to Wandsbek Martha used to visit Freud in his hospital lodging. In October, after leaving Meynert's service, he had to move to a different room, and in order to keep Martha in touch with the details of his daily life he described the new room and drew a diagram of it.

377

ON JANUARY 1, 1884, FREUD ENTERED on his longest spell of work in the hospital. He was now transferred to the department of nervous diseases, where he would spend the next fourteen months. The superintendent, Dr. Franz Scholz, seems to have been interested in nothing but keeping down the costs; the patients went hungry and new drugs could not be tested since they were expensive. Freud was revolted by the condition of the wards. They were not kept clean, so that the occasional sweeping meant an intolerable cloud of dust. No gaslights were installed anywhere in the hospital, and after dusk the patients had to lie in complete darkness. The doctors would make their rounds, and even perform any urgent operations, with the aid of a lantern.

Freud worked on steadily for the next six months, spending two hours a day, between ward visits, in the laboratory. In a letter of April 1, 1884, he wrote: "I am gradually marking myself off as a neuropathologist to my Chief in the hopes of its furthering my prospects."

Freud referred later to Dr. Scholz as being at that time "a fossil and feeble-minded." But, although there was little to be learned from him, his senile indolence had at least the advantage that he gave the younger doctors under him a very free hand. Freud also had the opportunity of doing some more or less unofficial teaching.

This is what he says about it in his usual candid manner: "I gradually became familiar with the ground; I was able to localize the site of a lesion in the medulla oblongata so accurately that the pathological anatomist had no further information to add; I was the first person in Vienna to send a case for autopsy with a diagnosis of polyneuritis acuta. The fame of my diagnoses ... brought me an influx of American physicians, to whom I lectured upon the patients in my department in a sort of pidgin English. I understood nothing about the neuroses. On one occasion I introduced to my audience a neurotic suffering from a persistent headache as a case of chronic localized meningitis; they quite rightly rose in revolt against me, and my premature activities as a teacher came to an end. By way of excuse I may add that this happened at a time when greater authorities than myself in Vienna were in the habit of diagnosing neurasthenia as cerebral tumor."

Freud had arranged to spend his month's holiday that year with Martha in Wandsbek. But in July, three days before he was to leave, news came that the Montenegrin government had sent an urgent request for some Austrian doctors to help them control the frontier across which an epidemic of cholera was threatening to spread. To Freud's dismay both of the other *Sekundarärzte* volunteered for this adventure, and he was left alone, the only doctor in the department. His chief, Scholz, had already left on his two months' holiday. Freud's first impulse was to resign altogether from the hospital, proceed to Wandsbek, and then take his chance as a general practitioner somewhere. But cooler reflections, aided by the calming influence of his friends Fleischl and Breuer, prevailed, and he consented to stay.

Two new junior doctors were placed under him, and Freud himself had the responsibility of superintendent, a jump of two grades in rank. When Martha asked him to explain its significance, he tersely replied: "It means the Hospital Director invites you to sit down in his presence."

During the six weeks Freud occupied his new position, he had full charge of 106 patients, with ten nurses, two *Sekundarärzte*, and one *Aspirant* under him. Freud enjoyed the experience. "In these weeks I have really become a doctor."

Freud had assured Martha that anatomy of the brain was the only serious rival she was ever likely to have. Now, on September 1, he left for a well-earned holiday in Wandsbek. The month he spent there seems to have been one of unalloyed happiness. Martha met him at the station at six in the morning, and he greeted her "as in a dream." Freud for the first time got on good terms with Mamma, which from then on were permanent. Evidently Martha had at last persuaded him that he came first in her love. And a couple of months later he observed that their relationship was far lovelier than before the reunion. From now on, except for rare relapses in mood, his resentment at their separation changed into longing, which grew more and more intense as the hope of fulfillment grew nearer.

THROUGHOUT HIS THREE HOSPITAL YEARS Freud was constantly trying to make a name for himself by discovering something important in either clinical or pathological medicine. He was seeking to attain as soon as possible the position of privatdocent. In Austria and Germany a privatdocent receives no salary, but he is permitted to hold a certain number of classes. The position enjoys high prestige since it is an assurance of special competence. Few such positions are granted, the small group is an elite. Success would yield enough prospect of private practice to justify an early marriage.

By 1884 it began to seem probable that the detailed researches Freud was then carrying out on the anatomy of the medulla might win him the desired prize. But he continued his search for other new ideas. One effort was his interest in the clinical use of cocaine. The first mention of cocaine had come in the spring of 1884, some weeks before the idyllic reunion in Wandsbek; he had reported to Martha news of "a therapeutic project and a hope."

"I have been reading about cocaine, the essential constituent of coca leaves which some Indian tribes chew to enable them to resist privations. . . . A German [Army doctor] has . . . reported that it increases [soldiers'] capacity to endure. I . . . will try it with cases of heart disease and also of nervous exhaustion, particularly in the miserable condition after the withdrawal of morphium. . . . We do not need more than one such lucky hit to be able to think of setting up house."

He ordered some cocaine from Merck of Darmstadt, and he tried the effect of a twentieth of a gram on himself. He found it turned the bad mood he was in into cheerfulness "so that there is nothing at all one need bother about," but without robbing him of any energy for exercise or work. Then, in a decision he would bitterly regret in years to come, Freud decided to offer the drug to Brücke's assistant Fleischl, whose friendship meant much to him.

Ernst von Fleischl-Marxow was young, handsome, a brilliant speaker. He had the charming manners of old Viennese society, ever ready to discuss scientific and literary problems with a flow of challenging ideas. But this wonderful man, at twenty-five, while conducting research in pathological anatomy, had contracted an infection. An amputation of the right thumb had saved him from death, but continued growth of neuromas [amputation tumors] required repeated operations. His life became an unending torture of pain and of slowly approaching death. This mutilated hand nevertheless performed experimental work of technical perfection. His sleepless nights he used for studying physics and mathematics and, later, Sanskrit.

In a letter to Martha, Freud once wrote: "I admire and love him with an intellectual passion, if you will allow such a phrase. His destruction will move me as the destruction of a sacred and famous temple would have affected an ancient Greek."

The unbearable nerve pain gradually wore Fleischl down. He took large doses of morphine, with the usual consequences: he became addicted to it.

Freud now proposed that Fleischl substitute cocaine for morphine. Fleischl clutched at the new drug "like a drowning man." Within a few days he was taking it continually, and was completely weaned from morphine.

Freud was now becoming more and more enthusiastic. He had a dazzling success with a case of gastric catarrh, where it immediately put an end to the pain. "I will write an essay on it and I expect it will win its place in therapeutics, by the side of morphia and superior to it. . . . I take very small doses of it regularly against depression and against indigestion, and with the most brilliant success." He sent some to Martha "to make her strong and give her cheeks a red color," he pressed it on his colleagues, both for themselves and for their patients, and he gave it to his sisters.

In short, looked at from the vantage point of our present knowledge, he was rapidly becoming a public menace. But when he said he could detect no signs of craving for it in himself, he was telling the strict truth: as we know now, it needs a special disposition to develop a drug addiction, and fortunately Freud did not possess that.

Freud's essay on cocaine in a July 1884 medical journal might well be ranked higher as a literary production than as a scientific contribution. It was couched in Freud's best style, with his characteristic liveliness, simplicity, and distinction. There is, moreover, in this essay a tone that never recurred in Freud's writings, a personal warmth as if he were in love with the content itself. He used expressions uncommon in a scientific paper, such as "the most gorgeous excitement" that animals display after an injection of cocaine, and administering an "offering" of it rather than a "dose." Breuer, with his characteristic caution, was one of those who was not impressed.

For many years Freud suffered from periodic depressions and fatigue or apathy—neurotic symptoms which were later to be dispelled by his own analysis. Due to the turmoil of his love affair, with its lengthy privation, in the summer of 1884 in particular he was in a state of great agitation. Cocaine calmed the agitation and dispelled the depression; a really normal person does not need the fillip.

In his essay Freud narrated a number of self-observations in which he had studied the effects on hunger, sleep, and fatigue. The total value of the drug was summed up as applicable in "those functional states comprised under the name of neurasthenia," in the treatment of indigestion, and during the withdrawal of morphine.

In his final paragraph, written hurriedly, he noted that the capacity of cocaine "to anesthetize cutaneous and mucous membranes suggests ... some additional uses ... are likely to be developed in the near future." This is the aspect that he would reproach himself with not pursuing, for within a couple of months a young colleague of Freud's, Carl Koller, an intern in the department of ophthalmology, was to attain world fame by inaugurating the use of cocaine for local anthesesia, and thereby revolutionizing eye surgery.

And within two years Freud would be condemned for having through his indiscriminate advocacy of a "harmless" drug introduced what his detractors called the "third scourge of humanity" (the other two being alcohol and morphine). He had forsaken the straight and narrow path of sober "scientific" work on brain anatomy and seized a surreptitious shortcut: one that was to bring him suffering instead of success. He would reproach himself for having inculcated in a dear friend a severe cocaine addiction, for Fleischl's state was worse than ever. By this time he was taking enormous doses of cocaine; the huge doses needed led to a chronic intoxication, and finally to a delirium tremens with white snakes creeping over his skin.

On the evening of June 4, 1885, Freud found Fleischl in such a state that he went to fetch Breuer and then spent the night there. It was the most frightful night he had ever spent.

Although Freud thought Fleischl could not go on for more than another six months, he would, in fact, live six painful years longer. And Freud, too, was far from having done with the episode. In the summer of 1885 the first pointed criticisms of cocaine and Freud would appear. By 1886 cases of cocaine addiction and intoxication would be reported from all over the world, causing a general alarm. Freud, the man who had tried to create a reputation by curing "neurasthenia," would find himself accused of unleashing evil on the world, or, at least, regarded as a man of reckless judgment.

CHAPTER FOUR

FREUD'S POVERTY, his worries about his family, had been constant all through this period of concern for Fleischl and separation from Martha. Every expense had to be thought over; he would discuss beforehand with Martha the desirability of using some of their small capital for a new suit; on one occasion Martha presented him with a new necktie, so at last he had two good ties. Freud all his life set store on a neat appearance, and pointed out its close connection with self-respect. Once he had commented, "The good opinion of my tailor matters to me as much as that of my professor." Now there were times when he could not go out of doors because of the holes in his coat: he twice mentions having to borrow a coat from Fleischl in order to call on a respectable friend. His father, now nigh on seventy, was relapsing into a state of fatalistic helplessness, and it is hard to say what the family lived on.

Freud's mother suffered from a serious tuberculosis of the lung. It was Freud's care to see to it that she left Vienna in its hot season for the country. In 1884 he wrote that they were all trying to keep her alive a little longer; he would have been relieved, and very surprised, to know that she was to survive for nearly a half century longer into a hale old age. Often he had to admit he had nothing at all to send to his mother or to the family. At such times he could not bring himself to visit his home and witness their miserable condition. Once, when he was invited out to lunch, he related how hard he found it to eat roast meat with the knowledge of how hungry his sisters were.

Freud's own income, aside from his hospital allowance, was uncertain. Throughout his years of hospital life Freud had private patients, which in those days was allowed. In the first couple of years they were sent by friends, mostly by Breuer, but in 1884 he proudly announced that he had seen the first patient come to him from outside, someone who had heard of his cocaine discovery.

Despite worries and hardships, 1885 was a far happier year than the preceding ones. Freud's confidence that he had succeeded in completely winning Martha's love made the world seem enchanted.

Freud was always very anxious about the health and safety of his precious betrothed. In that summer there was news that she was not quite well. "I really get quite beside myself when I am disturbed about you. I lose at once all sense of values, and at moments a frightful dread comes over me lest you fall ill." The next day, after getting a card from her, he wrote: "So I was quite wrong in imagining you to be ill. I was very crazy. . . . One is very crazy when one is in love." Thirty years later Freud was to discuss the pathological nature of the state of being in love, and he had some personal experience to instruct him.

When Martha was on a holiday in Lübeck and played with a fantasy of being drowned while bathing, he replied: "There must be a point of view from which even the loss of the loved one would seem a trivial occurrence in the thousands of years of human history. But I confess I take the extreme opposite one in which the event would be absolutely equivalent to the end of the world."

We may now descend from these heights and relax the tension by relating a less serious story. That winter when Martha asked his permission to skate Freud sternly refused, not as one might suppose from fear of her breaking her leg but because it might necessitate her being arm in arm with a man other than himself. Three days later he granted permission, but on condition that she was to skate unaccompanied.

Freud partook in much of the prudishness of his time, when allusions to lower limbs were improper. He wrote: "You don't seem to know how observant I am. Do you remember how in our walk with Minna along the *Beethovengang* you kept going aside to pull up your stockings? It is bold of me to mention it, but I hope you don't mind." In the middle of 1885 Martha announced her wish to stay with an old friend, recently married, who, as she delicately put it, "had married before her wedding." Contact with such a source of moral contamination, however, was sternly forbidden.

Eighteen eighty-five was also a year of professional success. Freud finished his important researches on the medulla and then, with the backing of his former professors Meynert, Nothnagel, and Brücke, was at last appointed to the rank of privatdocent in neuropathology, after having passed an oral examination, delivered a trial lecture, and reported to the police headquarters to ascertain if his character was worthy of the honor. The invitation to attend the oral examinations, however, had created a minor financial crisis since it brought up the anxious matter of costume. A silk hat and white gloves were bought, but it was hard to know whether to borrow the full evening suit that was expected or get one made with no prospect of being able to pay for it; Freud decided on the latter.

Earlier that spring Freud had applied for the postgraduate *Stipendium* (scholarship) offered to the successful candidate among the junior *Sekundarärtze*. He had resolved, should he win the grant, to visit Paris and become a pupil of the great Dr. Jean Martin Charcot, who was at the zenith of his fame. His Salpêtrière clinic was the Mecca of neurologists; Charcot had stalked through the old wards of that infirmary for chronic cases, marking off and giving names to a number of diseases of the nervous system in a most Adamlike fashion. But knowing the cardinal part played by favoritism in Vienna, Freud had referred to his application as "an empty hope," for one of the other applicants was the nephew of an influential professor.

And yet, on June 19 he learned that he had won his way to Charcot. He was told that what had brought his success had been "Brücke's passionate intercession, which had caused a general sensation" when the faculty voted on the award. The day after his selection, he wrote to Martha: "Oh, how wonderful it is going to be. I am coming with money and am staying a long while with you and am bringing something lovely for you and shall then go to Paris and become a great *savant* and return to Vienna with a great, great nimbus. Then we will marry soon and I will cure all the incurable nervous patients and you will keep me well and I will kiss you till you are merry and happy— and they lived happily ever after."

On the last day of August 1885 Freud left the Vienna General Hospital for good, after having lived and worked there for just a month over three years. It was nearly the end of his general medical experience. To have become a good general practitioner Freud would have needed more experience in midwifery and surgery, but on the medical side he was fully equipped. He was twenty-nine years old. After six weeks in Wandsbek with Martha, he would be on his way to Charcot and Paris, where he could present himself as a privatdocent in neuropathology.

FOR THE FIRST SIX WEEKS of his life in Paris in the winter of 1885–1886 Freud lived at the Hôtel de la Paix in the Latin Quarter. All told it cost him three hundred francs a month to live, including books and what he sent to his mother.

On the first day in Paris he felt so lonely in the throng that were it not that he had a long beard, a silk hat, and gloves he could have broken down and cried in the street. Loneliness and longing ran through his letters. "I am here as if marooned . . . you are my whole world." After a time, however, he found the town "magnificent and charming," spoke of its "magic," and even began to develop a "local patriotism for Paris." He sent Martha a long account of its geography and sights, illustrated by an excellent sketch. In the Louvre he first visited the Egyptian and Assyrian antiques; he does not mention ever having got to the pictures. The building that most impressed him was the Cathedral of Notre Dame. It was the first time in his life that he had the feeling of being inside a church. The tower became his favorite resort.

His impression of the French people was less favorable. "Arrogant" and "inaccessible" are words that recur in the

Dr. Charcot lecturing to his students.

letters. The tradespeople "cheat one with a cool smiling shamelessness." "Everyone is polite but hostile." Even the womenfolk did not redeem them. "The ugliness of Paris women can hardly be exaggerated: not a decent pretty face."

But Charcot made up for everything. When they first met, on October 20, 1885, Freud described him thus: "M. Charcot came in at ten o'clock, a tall man of fifty-eight, a silk hat on his head, with dark and curiously mild eyes . . . long hair held back by his ears . . . like a worldly priest, of whom one expects much wit and that he understands how to live well."

Freud had brought a letter of introduction, and Charcot received him politely. Freud was invited to his first soirée. Evening dress had to be worn, an unwonted experience. Freud gave up in anger the attempt to tie the white tie he had bought and fell back on a ready-made black one. Before Freud left Paris Charcot would consent to the translation of his lectures into German by Freud. In the meantime in the ward visits through the extraordinary, indeed unique, wealth of clinical material reposing

The Salpêtrière clinic in Paris, where Freud studied.

in the Salpêtrière, illuminated by Charcot's pregnant utterances, Freud must have learned much neurology. He contrasted Charcot's warm and keen interest in the patients with the "serene superficiality" of the Viennese physicians. And as a teacher in the classroom, "Charcot was perfectly fascinating; each of his lectures was a little masterpiece in composition . . . and so impressive that the words spoken echoed in one's ears for the rest of the day."

The abiding impressions left on Freud were of Charcot's revolutionary views on hysteria. Before that time hysteria was regarded either as a matter of simulation and "imagination," on which no reputable physician would waste his time, or else a peculiar disorder of the womb. Now, thanks to Charcot's systematic study, it became a respectable disease of the nervous system.

Charcot showed that many affections otherwise attributed were really of an hysterical nature. He also laid stress on the existence of the complaint in the male sex, which, since it was now classified among nervous diseases, was not to be wondered at. Above all Charcot demonstrated that in suitable subjects he could by the use of hypnotism elicit hysterical symptoms, paralysis, tremors, anesthesias, etc., that were identical with those of the spontaneous hysteria as seen in his other patients.

All this meant that, whatever the unknown neurological basis of hysteria might be, the symptoms themselves could be both treated and abolished by ideas alone. They had a psychogenic origin. This opened the door to a medical motive for investigating the psychology of patients, and put psychology itself on a totally different footing from its previous academic one. It made possible discoveries concerning the deeper layers of the mind that could not have been made in any other way, and with all the ramifying results that the past half century have shown.

Charcot's role in generating a more scientific attitude toward hysteria in French medical circles, and—most important—with Freud himself, was undoubtedly decisive. When Freud went to Paris his anatomical researches were still more in his mind than any clinical interests. But now he wrote: "I believe I am changing a great deal. Charcot . . . simply demolishes my views and aims. Many a time after a lecture I go out as from Notre Dame. . . . Whether the seed will ever bring forth fruit I do not know; but what I certainly know is that no other human being has ever affected me in such a way." To Charcot, therefore, must be ascribed the most important influence in turning Freud from a neurologist into a psychopathologist.

On February 23, 1886, Freud took his leave of Charcot, whom he never saw again, and left Paris. Announcing this decision to Martha, he wrote: "I have overcome my love for science insofar as it came between us." On his way home he spent a few weeks in Berlin, in order to learn at Dr. Adolf Baginsky's clinic something about the general diseases of children. He had no prospect, probably for "racial" reasons, of obtaining a position in the university psychiatric-neurological clinic in Vienna, and in fact never did; whereas the pediatrician Max Kassowitz had offered him before he left for Paris the post of director of a neurological department that was being opened in the modernization of the old Institute for Children's Diseases in Vienna.

Freud was disappointed in the Berlin neurologists. He reported to Martha how one neurologist had expressed regret that Charcot had turned his attention to such a difficult and unreliable theme as hysteria. "Do you understand why one should regret that the most powerful mind should tackle the most difficult problems? I don't."

Freud brought back from Paris a lithograph in which Charcot is depicted impressively holding forth to his assistants and students. The patient whose case he is demonstrating is languishing in a semiconscious state supported by an assistant's arm around her waist. Freud's eldest daughter writes about it: "It held a strange attraction for me in my childhood and I often asked my father what was wrong with the patient. The answer I always got was that she was 'too tightly laced,' with a moral of the foolishness of being so. The look he would give the picture made me feel then even as a very young child that it evoked happy or important memories in him and was dear to his heart."

FREUD HAD ONCE SUGGESTED June 17, 1887, five years to a day from the moment of their engagement, as a good wedding date. As soon as he got back to Vienna in April 1886 and knew that his post at the Kassowitz institute was assured, he advanced the date to autumn of that year. But Freud had first to establish himself in Vienna. He got his mother to find him a room two doors from where the family now lived, and spent a week looking for a place where he could start practice.

There were many visits to pay after such a long absence. Meynert greeted him warmly, and invited him and any pupils he might have to work in his laboratory. Nothnagel was noncommittal and could not promise much. Breuer embraced him warmly, but expressed himself pessimistically about Freud's professional chances. Freud concluded he would have to emigrate, but Breuer thought there was no hope in that either unless he went as a waiter. After a day or two, however, Freud got over his discouragement.

Freud observed that all these men had a certain characteristic "manner," so that he had better decide to adopt one also. He chose to exploit his native tendency to uprightness and honesty: he would make a "mannerism" of that, and the various people would have to get used to it. If it didn't succeed, at least he would not have lowered himself.

On April 15, he moved to a suite he had taken a 7 Rathausstrasse, just behind the magnificent town hall, the best professional quarter in Vienna. He paid 80 gulden a month for it with service included. It had a hall and two large rooms. One of them was divided by a curtain, so that the far half could be used as a bedroom. The flat was elegantly furnished, and all he had to buy was a medical couch; books and bookcases he already had. There was a glass professional plate, with gold letters on a black background, for the street, and a porcelain one for his door.

Freud made known his start in private practice by the following announcement in the daily newspapers and medical periodicals: "Dr. Sigmund Freud, Docent in Neuropathology in the University of Vienna, has returned from spending six months in Paris and now resides at Rathausstrasse 7." He also sent out two hundred cards to various doctors. The date of this fateful venture was Easter Sunday, April 25, 1886, a curious day to choose, since everything in Vienna was suspended on that holy day. When Freud's first consultation fee came it went at once to Wandsbek, to buy a feather for Martha and some wine to be merry on. For the next few months patients came from Breuer. In July Nothnagel sent him the Portuguese ambassador. On the whole his success was greater than he had expected; once his waiting room was full from twelve to three. In the month of June alone he earned 387 gulden, a very satisfactory sum for a beginner.

Freud, however, complained of his sense of inadequacy when dealing with patients. After all, sole responsibility in private practice was different from the communal work in a hospital. His confidence was further impaired when things went wrong. Once he performed a slight operation on a well-known actor, Hugo Thimig, but unsuccessfully. Freud returned the fee he had sent him. He wrote to his bride-to-be that he needed a good sense of humor to save him from getting "ashamed of his ignorance, embarrassment, and helplessness." Besides his own practice and his laboratory work he spent several hours three times a week in the Kassowitz institute.

A startling episode had taken place in June of that year, three months before the wedding. To understand it we have to picture Freud's state of mind at the time. The possibility of some new obstacle to his wedding appearing at the last minute must have haunted him, since he still had not been able to solve the financial arrangements on which everything depended.

It would have taken several years to save from his practice enough to make marriage possible; thus it depended almost entirely on the money Martha had, and she had entrusted half of her dowry to her brother Eli. Freud's idea of such a trust was that the notes would be locked up in a safe. He does not seem to have been able to distinguish between investment and speculation, and in fact never invested a penny of his money until late in life. To a businessman like Eli, on the other hand, the idea of "idle money" was completely abhorrent, so he invested Martha's money. He had heavy commitments and, at that juncture, some investments not having proved successful, he was not finding it easy to lay his hand on ready money. Freud, hearing that Eli was having difficulties, put the worst construction on the news and told Martha to ask for her money back. After a fortnight there came an evasive postcard which aroused Freud's darkest suspicions and reanimated all his old mistrust and hostility. He sent a number of frantic letters to Martha, insisting that she use the strongest pressure on Eli to release the money. He told Martha of his suspicions that Eli had used the money for himself, which she denounced as a calumny. She was quite sure Eli would pay, he had never let her down in his life, and her loyalty to her brother to whom she owed so much made her resent the strong language Freud was using about him.

Then the old emotions that had long lain dormant and which seemed to have been dissipated burst forth with a greater violence than ever before. His loved one was siding, not with him, but with his hated rival, the villain who was thwarting the union with her. It was truly unbelievable that the confidence he had at last come to repose in her love should after all prove to be misplaced. They were face to face with an irreparable rupture.

Freud addressed an ultimatum to Martha with four points, the first of which was that she was to write an angry letter to her brother calling him a scoundrel. Martha got no further than that point. Freud himself wrote a forcible letter to Eli and got Moritz, a future brother-in-law, to deliver it by hand and explain how serious the situation was. Eli got the money together somehow and sent it to Martha the next day. And he deplored the "brutal" manners of her future husband. Martha rebuked Freud for his unmannerly behavior and expressed her amazement that he should be so wrought up over "a few shabby gulden." He explained to her that it was not the money as such that mattered, but that their hope of married happiness had been at stake. She was not to write to him again until she promised to break off all relations with Eli. They were by now on the edge of an abyss.

But Martha's tact and firmness again won. She knew his tenderness would in the last resort overcome everything else. But she was utterly exhausted. Freud, on the other hand, although he said he had nearly perished, was rather triumphant at having defeated his enemy singlehandedly without any help from her, and the hurricane blew itself out.

Freud had been torn by love and hate before, and was to be again more than once, but this was the only time in his life—when such emotions centered on a woman—that the volcano within was near to erupting with destructive force.

By July Freud felt confident that he could find a living in Vienna. At this moment another blow fell on the sorely tried couple. Freud was called up for army maneuvers, something he had not expected until the following year. This meant the loss of a whole month's earnings on which they had counted. Freud faced the situation stoically and was resolved not to allow it to interfere with their plans. Frau Bernays was horrified at the idea of going forward in such circumstances, and wrote him a letter which ended:

> I beg and implore you not to do it . . . wait quietly until you have a settled means of existence. . . . At the moment you are like a spoilt *child* who . . . cries, in the belief that in that way he can get everything. . . . Take to heart these truly well-meant words and don't think badly of
>
> Your faithful
Mother

We do not know whether Freud answered this pronunciamento, but it did not affect his decision to go ahead with the preparations. All that remained was to find a suitable home to bring his bride to, one which would include living quarters as well as a suite where Freud could practice, and to furnish it. A telegram early in July from Martha conveyed joyful news: HURRAH, 1250 GULDEN LÖWBEER! This was a wedding present, a generous one, from her Aunt Lea Löwbeer in Brünn. So now the cost of furniture was covered and they could go ahead with the preparations. Despite all his efforts and advertising, however, Freud found that acceptable flats were extremely scarce. He finally rented a large four-room apartment at 5 Maria Theresienstrasse.

All along Freud had comforted himself with the thought that since he would marry in Germany, where a civil ceremony was all that was necessary, he would be spared the pain of going through the complicated religious ceremonies of a Jewish wedding, which he abhorred. Now, early in July, Martha had to inform him that Austria would not recognize a civil marriage, so that on reaching Vienna they would find themselves unmarried. There was nothing for it but to go through a Jewish ceremony. But she would make this as easy as possible for him, arranging for it to take place on a weekday in her mother's home. Thus very few friends could attend, and a silk hat and frock coat could replace the more formal evening dress.

THE MILITARY MANEUVERS lasted from August 9 to September 10, and were held at Olmütz, a small town in Moravia. Freud was attached as a senior army surgeon to the Landwehr. It was a strenuous performance. Rising at half-past three in the morning, they marched and marched until after noon, after which the medical work itself had to be attended to. Like a true woman, Martha advised him not to do any marching when it was very hot. That the experience did not increase Freud's admiration for the profession of arms is graphically depicted in a letter he wrote to Breuer.

> Here I am tied fast in this filthy hole. . . . I play at being an army doctor, dealing out chits on which ghastly wounds are noted. . . . There is fake ammunition as well as fake leadership, but yesterday the General rode past and called out, "Reserves, where would you be if they had used live ammunition? Not one of you would have escaped."
>
> The only bearable thing in Olmütz is a first-class café. . . . Like everything else the service there is affected by the military system. When two or three generals—I can't help it, but they always remind me of parakeets, for mammals don't usually dress in such colors (save for the back parts of baboons)—sit down together, the whole troop of waiters surround them and nobody else exists for them. Once in despair . . . I grabbed one of them by the coattails and shouted, "Look here, I might be a general sometime, so fetch me a glass of water." That worked.

Freud returned to Vienna to change from his uniform before leaving for Wandsbek on September 11. The military pay had been only one half of what he had expected; he had to write privately to his future sister-in-law, Minna Bernays, who, like Martha, had received a generous gift from their Aunt Lea, to borrow money for the fare to Wandsbek. He had managed, however, to buy a wedding present for his bride, a beautiful gold watch.

THE CIVIL MARRIAGE took place on September 13, 1886, in the town hall of Wandsbek. Sixty-five years later the bride still vividly recollected how the official at the ceremony had commented on her signing her new name in the marriage register without the least hesitation. Freud spent the two nights before the fourteenth at the house of Martha's uncle Elias Philipp, who was charged with the task of coaching him in the Hebrew prayers he would have to recite at the wedding proper that would take place on that day.

Freud probably bit his lip when he stepped under the *chuppah* (the canopy, representing the Temple, under which a Jewish couple stands during the wedding ceremony), but everything went off well. The bride was then just twenty-five and her husband thirty. They must have been a good-looking couple.

Freud was a handsome man, slender but sturdy, with his well-shaped head, regular features, and dark flashing eyes. His wife later was fond of extolling the beautiful tan with which he had returned from his military exercises. Only eight relatives were present besides the immediate family, and the couple then departed for Lübeck.

From Lübeck they wrote a joint letter to Mamma in Wandsbek, in alternating sentences. Freud's concluding one was: "Given at our present residence at Lübeck on the first day of what we hope will prove a Thirty Years' War be-

Freud and Martha in 1885, the year before their marriage.

tween Sigmund and Martha." The only sign of "war" recorded in all the ensuing fifty-three years was a difference of opinion over the weighty question whether mushrooms should be cooked with or without their stalks.

After a couple of days they moved on to Travemünde on the Baltic, where the main part of the honeymoon was spent. They returned to Vienna on October 1. Here the bride was warmly welcomed by Freud's friends.

October was a fine month and all the doctors complained that people preferred to enjoy the warm weather rather than come for any treatment. Freud wrote to Minna that he had already pawned the gold watch Emmanuel had given him, and now his wedding present to Martha, her gold watch, had to go too unless Minna would help them—which of course she did. But in the next month the tide began to turn.

Freud had at last reached the haven of happiness he had yearned for. "All we need is two or three little rooms where we can live and eat and receive a guest, and a hearth where the fire for cooking does not go out. . . . Tables and chairs, beds, a mirror, a clock to remind the happy ones of the passage of time, an armchair for an hour of agreeable daydreaming, carpets so that the *Hausfrau* can easily keep the floor clean, linen tied up in fancy ribbons . . . clothes of the newest cut and hats with artificial flowers, pictures on the wall, glasses for the daily water and for wine on festive occasions, plates, and dishes . . . a large bunch of keys which must rattle noisily. There is so much we can enjoy: the bookcase and the sewing basket and the friendly lamp. And everything must be kept in good order, else the *Hausfrau*, who has divided up her heart in little bits, one for each piece of furniture, will object. . . . All of it a little world of happiness, of silent friends and emblems of honorable humanity," he had written Martha.

Children do not come into this picture; Freud's great fondness for children had not yet become manifest. Later he would write: "It is a happy time for our love now. I always think that once one is married one no longer—in most cases—lives for each other as one used to. One lives rather with each other for some third thing, and for the husband dangerous rivals soon appear: household and nursery. Then, despite all love and unity, the help each person had found in the other ceases. The husband looks again for friends, frequents an inn, finds general outside interests. But that need not be so."

For the next five years Freud would be absorbed in family, professional work, and translations of Charcot's lectures. There can have been few more successful marriages. Martha made an excellent wife and presently, when children arrived to complete their happiness, an excellent mother. She was an admirable manager—the rare kind of woman who could keep servants indefinitely—but she was never the kind of *Hausfrau* who put things before people. Her husband's comfort and convenience always ranked first. In the early years he used to discuss his cases with her in the evening, but later on it was not to be expected that she should follow the roaming flights of his imagination any more than most of the world could.

CHAPTER FIVE

AFTER NINETEEN WEEKS with Charcot, Freud had gone back to Vienna in the spring of 1886 agog with revelations. But when on October 15, 1886, Freud read his paper entitled "On Male Hysteria" before the *Gesellschaft der Ärzte* [medical society] the occasion caused him much distress. In this paper he challenged the prevailing conception of hysteria as a vague malingering, and reported that, according to Charcot, there was no connection between the disease and the genital organs, or any difference between its manifestations in male and female. Freud described a case of traumatic hysteria which had followed a fall from a scaffold, a case he himself had observed at the Salpêtrière, and mentioned Charcot's suggestion that some cases of "railway spine" after accidents might be hysterical. This was not diplomatic, since neurologists had rather a vested interest in injuries to the nervous system which often led to court cases.

Meynert later wrote that hypnotism "degrades a human being to a creature without will or reason and only hastens his nervous and mental degeneration." Now he challenged Freud to produce for them a case of male hysteria with the typical Charcot symptoms. But when Freud found suitable cases in the general hospital the senior physicians of the departments refused to allow him to make any such use of their material. One of the surgeons asked if he did not know that the very word "hysteria" came from *hysteron* (*sic*), the Greek for womb, a fact that by definition excluded the male sex. However, Freud succeeded in finding such a patient elsewhere, a young metalworker, who after a quarrel with his brother developed a classical hemianesthesia [loss of sensation in either lateral half of the body], with typical disturbance in the field of vision and color sense. The case was demonstrated before the medical society on November 26, 1886, at a meeting chaired by Freud's old friend and colleague from Brücke institute days, Sigmund Exner.

Referring to the incident nearly forty years later, Freud still displayed some bitterness. "This time I was applauded, but no further interest was taken in me. The impression that the high authorities had rejected my innovations remained unshaken, and . . . I found myself forced into the opposition. As I was soon afterward excluded from the laboratory [Meynert's] of cerebral anatomy . . . I withdrew from academic life. . . . It is a whole generation since I have visited the *Gesellschaft der Ärzte*."

The conflict with Meynert did not cease. But Meynert had passed his prime; he died a few years later, in 1892, in the same year as Brücke. Freud visited him during his last illness, and Meynert, who was known to be a very erratic and neurotic person and a heavy drinker, confessed to Freud at that time that he had himself been a classical case of male hysteria, but had always managed to conceal the fact.

Meanwhile, Freud's practice naturally consisted mainly of neurotic patients. In the early months of private practice, when he was complaining about his sense of inadequacy, he was attempting to use the orthodox electrotherapy as described in Erb's textbook, then one of the leading works on the subject. "I was soon driven to see that following these instructions was of no help whatever. . . . The realization that the work of the greatest name in German neuropathology had no more relation to reality than some 'Egyptian' dreambook, such as is sold in cheap bookshops . . . helped to rid me of another shred of the innocent faith in authority from which I was not yet free."

He had had ample experience with hypnotism at Charcot's clinic and in December 1887 he turned to hypnotic suggestion for his own patients. This often brought gratifying successes but he found that he was not always able to induce hypnosis, either at all or deeply enough for his needs. A few years later he expressed his dissatisfaction with the method: "Neither the doctor nor the patient can tolerate indefinitely the contradiction between the decisive denial of the disorder in suggestion and the necessary recognition of it away from suggestion."

He felt sure there were many secrets hidden behind the manifest symptoms, and his restless imagination burned to penetrate them. At this point Freud decided to try a psychotherapeutic method that had once been used with some success by his friend Breuer—a method Breuer had called "catharsis," and one which had impressed Freud greatly some years earlier when, while still a young hospital doctor, he had first heard of the case.

FROM DECEMBER 1880 TO JUNE 1882 Breuer had treated what has become recognized as a classic case of hysteria, that of Fraülein Anna O. The patient was an un-usually intelligent and extremely attractive girl of twenty-one, who developed a museum of symptoms in connection with her father's fatal illness. Among them were paralysis of three limbs, complicated disturbances of sight and speech, inability to take food, and a distressing nervous cough which was the occasion of Breuer being called in. More interesting, however, was the presence of two distinct states of consciousness: one a fairly normal one, the other that of a naughty and troublesome child. It was a case of double personality. The transition from one to the other was marked by a phase of self-induced hypnosis from which she would awake mentally normal. This phase happened by luck to be the time when Breuer visited her, and she soon got into the habit of relating to him the disagreeable events of the day, including terrifying hallucinations, after which she felt relief.

Josef Breuer.

On one occasion she related the details of the first appearance of a symptom and, to Breuer's great astonishment, this resulted in its complete disappearance. Perceiving the value of doing so, the patient herself continued in later sessions with one symptom after another, terming the procedure "the talking cure."

After a while Breuer supplemented this evening proceeding by inducing an artificial hypnosis every morning, since the mass of material was becoming overwhelming. At that time, to devote hours every day for more than a year to a single patient, and an hysteric at that, signified very special qualities of patience, interest, and insight. This psychotherapeutic method, catharsis, is still used extensively and is still associated with his name. But peculiar circumstances surrounded the end of this treatment.

It would seem that Breuer had developed what we should nowadays call a strong countertransference to his interesting patient. At all events he was so engrossed that his wife became jealous. This provoked a violent reaction in Breuer, perhaps compounded of love and guilt, and he decided to bring the treatment to an end. He announced this to Anna O., who was by now much better, and bade her good-by. But that evening he was fetched back to find her in a greatly excited state. The patient, who according to him had appeared to be an asexual being and had never made any allusion to such a forbidden topic, was now in the throes of an hysterical childbirth, the logical termination, of a phantom pregnancy that had been developing in response to Breuer's ministrations. Though profoundly shocked, he managed to calm her down by hypnotizing her, and then fled the house in a cold sweat. The next day he and his wife left for Venice to spend a second honeymoon.

The poor patient did not fare so well. Relapses took place, and she was removed to an institution. She did, however, improve later and eventually became a social worker in Germany.

THE CASE OF ANNA O. had made a deep impression on Freud, and he would discuss the details of it with Breuer over and over again. Now, in the spring of 1889, he began to use hypnosis not only for therapeutic suggestion but also for tracing back the history of symptoms.

The first case in which he employed the cathartic method was that of Frau Emmy v. N., whose treatment he began on May 1, 1889, eighteen months after he had started using hypnotism. In his first attempts, however, using deep somnambulism, no very penetrating explorations took place. He seems to have still relied on therapeutic suggestion, combined with massage, baths, and rest. Freud learned in this case that the reason why so many beneficial effects of hypnotic suggestion are transitory is that they are brought about by the patient in order to please the physician, and hence are apt to fade when contact is withdrawn. One notes that Freud was still completely under the influence of Charcot's teaching about the importance of traumas in the symptomatology of hysteria. If the patient's brother had thrown a

19 Berggasse, Vienna, where Freud lived from 1891 to 1938.

toad at her in childhood, that would apparently suffice to account for the permanent phobia of such creatures. The idea of personal thoughts (wishes) of an unacceptable nature would be recorded for the first time only three years later.

"WE LIVE PRETTY HAPPILY in steadily increasing unassumingness. When we hear the baby laugh we imagine it is the loveliest thing that can happen to us," Freud wrote in a letter to a friend in 1888. "I am not ambitious and do not work very hard."

At their domicile at 5 Maria Theresienstrasse the Freuds' first child, a daughter named Mathilde, had been born in October 1887. Two sons followed, in 1889 and 1891, and were named Jean Martin after Charcot, and Oliver after Cromwell, Freud's early hero, whom he may have admired for his reintroduction of the Jews into England. More room was needed for the growing family, so in August 1891 they moved to the well-known address of 19 Berggasse. A year later Freud rented a professional flat on the ground floor.

The Berggasse slopes steeply down from a main street and consisted of massive eighteenth-century houses, typically Viennese. The entrance to the main house was very wide, so that a horse and carriage could drive straight through into the garden and stable behind. The ground floor of No. 19 also had a butcher's shop. The butcher's first name was Sigmund and his plate affixed on one side of the large entrance doors contrasted curiously with that of Prof. Dr. Sigm. Freud on the opposite side.

A flight of half-a-dozen steps led to Freud's professional flat, which had three rooms, used as patients' waiting room, consulting room, and study. The windows of these rooms gave onto the garden behind. A noble flight of low stone steps then led to the next floor, called the mezzanine, and that is where Freud and his growing family lived for forty-seven years.

Three more children were born there, a son in 1892, named Ernst after Brücke, and two daughters, Sophie, born in 1893, and Anna, the youngest, born in 1895. Freud was a loving, indulgent father, and remarked in one letter that his life was spent in either his consulting room or the nursery upstairs. Giving presents to the children was one of Freud's great delights. Despite his wife's protests, a birthday present to a child always reached its destination on the evening before. His letters are full of the children's remarkable sayings and deeds. They all grew up to be sturdy, healthy people, but childhood diseases were much more dangerous then than now, and when Freud's eldest daughter was five or six years old she nearly died of diphtheria. At the crisis the distracted father asked her what she would like best in the world and got the answer "a strawberry." They were out of season, but a renowned shop produced some. The first attempt to swallow one induced a fit of coughing that completely removed the obstructive membrane, and Mathilde's life was saved by a strawberry—and a loving father.

Freud was very much a family man, interested in all that concerned his many relatives. Moreover, in addition to maintaining his own full household, he had to contribute to the support of his parents and sisters.

From his correspondence and from other sources we know much concerning Freud's mode of life during this period. He

The study of Freud's house in Vienna. The couch at center was used by his patients during psychoanalysis.

paid a daily visit to his barber—indicating, for a fully bearded man, an unusual care of his person; he loathed fowl and cauliflower so much that he avoided taking a meal with a family where they were apt to be provided. He had a telephone installed as early as 1895. He played a certain amount of chess, but gave it up when he found it demanded too much concentration, which he preferred to devote elsewhere. Now and then he would attend the theater, opera, or a public lecture; he greatly enjoyed listening to Mark Twain, an old favorite of his. He had one extravagance, his passion for antiquities.

Reading with enjoyment Jakob Burckhardt's *A Cultural History of Greece* years later, he noted parallels to his psychoanalytic findings: "My fondness for the prehistoric in all human manifestations remains the same." When he made himself a present of Schliemann's *Ilios*, he was especially interested in the account of his childhood the author gives in his preface, and the early ideas that later resulted in the discovery of the buried Troy. "The man was happy when he found the treasure of Priam, since the only happiness is the satisfaction of a childhood wish." In an earlier letter he had said: "That is why wealth brings so little happiness: .... money was not a wish in childhood."

On account of heat schools closed in Vienna at the end of June, and it was customary for families to spend two or three months in the country even if the men could join them only at intervals. It was Freud's habit in those days to send his family away in June, or even May, and to continue working alone in Vienna until well into July. Then he would join them and not return to work until the middle of September. At first they remained pretty much in the environs of Vienna. But Freud would often set out on more distant travels, accompanied by his wife, his brother Alexander, or, on one occasion, by his sister-in-law. He found early, as all other analysts have since, the strain of the work to be such that without an ample period of recuperation its quality would surely deteriorate.

Holidays meant a very different life for Freud. His requirements were very specific: a comfortable house with a suitable room in which he could write, a certain altitude with sun and good air, pine forests for walks, glorious scenery. Before the war Freud would sport a Tyrolese costume with visible braces, shorts, and a green hat with a little chamois brush at its side. A stout walking stick and in wet weather a shaggy Alpine cape completed the outfit. The most characteristic feature of Freud's holiday pursuits was his passion for finding mushrooms. On an expedition he would often leave the children and they would be sure to hear soon a cry of success from him. He would creep silently up to it and suddenly pounce to capture the fungus with his hat as though it were a butterfly. There was the endless detection of rare wild flowers, with a careful identifying at leisure. Freud could never find his way in the country and would start back for home in an absurdly wrong direction. Railway timetables were beyond his comprehension.

His son Martin tells me of an incident of one of Freud's mountain holidays which is worth recording. On returning from a walk they found their way home barricaded by a noisy crowd who were shouting anti-Semitic slogans at them. Swinging his walking stick, Freud unhesitatingly charged into them with an expression on his face that made them give way before him.

CHAPTER SIX

THE ORTHODOX WAY for a genius to make an important discovery or invention is by a lightninglike flash of intuition, and the history of science abounds in dramatic accounts of such happenings. But although Freud's swift intuition functioned freely in his mature years, when one piece of insight followed another in rapid succession, between 1875 and 1892, the years we have so far been considering, he made characteristically painful progress through arduous work and hard thinking. He had been impressed by Charcot's description of his way of working—to stare at the facts over and over again until they spoke to him; it corresponded with something in Freud's own attitude.

We come now to Freud's all-important transition from the cathartic method to the "free association" method, from which psychoanalysis dates. The devising of this new method was one of the two great deeds of his scientific life. It enabled him to penetrate into the previously unknown realm of the unconscious and make the profound discoveries with which his name is imperishably associated. His other great feat, his self-analysis, through which he learned to explore the child's early sexual life, including the famous Oedipus complex, we shall examine shortly.

The free association method evolved very gradually between 1892 and 1895, becoming steadily refined and purified. By 1892 Freud had had considerable experience with the cathartic method. His growing insight into the nature of hypnotism had taught him that therapeutic improvement often disappeared when the personal relationship between patient and physician was dissolved. One day a patient suddenly flung her arms around his neck, an unexpected contretemps fortunately remedied by the entrance of a servant. Unlike the scared Breuer on a similar occasion, Freud regarded the problem as one of general scientific interest. From then on he understood that the peculiar relationship so effective therapeutically had an erotic basis, whether

Freud fishing with his son Ernst.

concealed or overt. Now he was all the more desirous of freeing himself from the mask of hypnotism. He explained years later how this conceals the important phenomena of resistance* and transference,** which had by then become the essential features of psychoanalytical practice and theory.

---

*The action of the ego resisting the return to consciousness of unpleasant experiences. (Editors' note)
**The transfer of emotions associated with forgotten experiences of early life from the original object to another, and in the case of the mentally ill, usually to the psychoanalyst. (Editors' note)

When Freud undertook the treatment of Fraülein Elisabeth von R. in the autumn of 1892 and found he was unable to hypnotize her, he was determined to proceed. What encouraged him was his knowledge that things experienced in hypnosis were only apparently forgotten afterward; they could at any time be brought into recollection if the physician insisted forcibly enough that the patient knew them. Freud divined that this should equally be true for the forgotten memories in hysteria. He therefore tried what he called a "concentration" technique.

Fraülein Elisabeth, lying down with closed eyes, was asked to concentrate her attention on a particular symptom and try to recall any memories that might throw light on its origin. When no progress was being made Freud would press her forehead with his hand and assure her that some memories would indubitably come to her. Perhaps on the fourth attempt the patient would bring out what had occurred to her mind, but with the comment: "I could have told you that the first time, but I didn't think it was what you wanted." Such experiences confirmed his confidence in the device. He gave the patient a strict injunction to express every thought even if she considered it to be irrelevant or too unpleasant.

When Freud put his trust in the validity of free associations, he said he was "following an obscure intuition." We have a clue to the source of this interesting intuition. It happens that an author, Ludwig Börne by name, had in 1823 written an essay with the arresting title, "The Art of Becoming an Original Writer in Three Days." It concludes with the words: "Here follows the practical prescription I promised. Take a few sheets of paper and for three days in succession write down, without any falsification or hypocrisy, everything that comes into your head. Write what you think of yourself, of your women, of the Turkish war, of Goethe . . . of the Last Judgment, of those senior to you in authority—and when the three days are over you will be amazed at what novel and startling thoughts have welled up in you. That is the art of becoming an original writer in three days."

Freud relates that Börne had been a favorite author of his. When he was fourteen years old he had been given his collected

works, and they were the only books he preserved from his adolescent years. We may be sure that Börne's startling proposal had sunk into Freud's mind and played a part twenty years later in stimulating him to give his patients' thoughts free play. Freud was still given to urging, pressing, and questioning, which he felt to be hard but necessary work. On one historic occasion, however, Fraülein Elisabeth reproved him for interrupting her flow of thought. He took the hint, and thus made another step toward free association. This was another example of a patient's furthering the physician's work.

Once started, the free association method went on becoming freer, but only by degrees. Freud did not finally renounce hypnotism in certain stages of the treatment until four years after he had proved the possibility of doing so. He acquired confidence in the belief that relaxing conscious censoring would inevitably lead to the important memories, and urging was therefore given up; so was pressing on the forehead. Closing the eyes was still advocated until 1904, when he stated that this also was not necessary. The only relic of the old hypnosis period that remained was the patient's reclining on the couch.

At first sight this transition to the free association method might seem a curious step to have taken; it meant displacing a systematic and purposeful search with a known aim in view by an apparently blind and uncontrolled meandering. But Freud felt intuitively that there must be some definite agency guiding and determining the course of those wandering associations.

Early in his practice he had detected his patients' unwillingness to disclose memories that were painful. This opposition he termed "resistance," and connected it with the "repression" that had led to certain memories being replaced by symptoms. Perhaps the roundabout meanderings were an attempt to postpone the emergence of the significant memory, and yet they followed a route ultimately connected with it. This would justify his patience in following the trains of thought with the closest attention and in the greatest detail.

In his endeavor to trace back the patient's memories, Freud observed that they did not stop at the starting point of the symptom, or even at the unpleasant "traumatic event" which would seem to be its cause, but instead insisted on going back and back, into childhood itself. A traumatic event unmistakably concerned in the origin of a symptom, but seemingly quite banal in itself, was found to produce its effects only if it had become associated with some such earlier mental experience (or attitude) which was neither emotionally wounding nor pathogenic. This manner of reacting he termed "regression," and it was at once clear to him that it was a noteworthy discovery.

He gradually noticed also that a remarkable number of the significant memories concerned sexual experiences. This fact astonished him. Some intuition told Freud that he had lighted on an important theme. He began to make deliberate inquiries into the sexual life of his patients, a habit which, as he soon found, had a harmful effect on his practice.

FREUD WAS NOW FINDING HIMSELF in increasing opposition to his "respectable" colleagues. There was the serious way in which he regarded all hysteria, followed by the growing interest in the still more suspect topic of hypnotism, and before long his appreciation of sexual factors in the neuroses. He felt he was leading a crusade against the accepted conventions of medicine in Vienna.

There was still enough left of the youthful need of support, however, to make him welcome the possibility of joining forces with some colleague in a more stable position than his own.

Freud started trying to induce Breuer to give the world the discovery his patient, Fraülein Anna O., had made. It gradually dawned on him that Breuer's reluctance was connected with his disturbing experience with her. So Freud told him of his own experience of a female patient suddenly flinging her arms round his neck in a transport of affection. Freud's tale evidently made a deep impression, for Breuer said later, "I believe [the transference phenomenon] is the most important thing we both have to make known to the world." At all events Freud secured his cooperation, it being understood that the theme of sexuality was to be kept in the background.

They first published together in the *Neurologisches Zentralblatt*, in January 1893, a paper entitled "On the Psychical Mechanism of Hysterical Phenomena." This is where their well-known dictum occurs that "hysterical patients suffer mainly from reminiscences." The joint paper was followed two years later by the book, *Studies on Hysteria*, from which it is customary to date the beginnings of psychoanalysis. It consists of a reprint of the joint paper, then five case histories, including those of Fraülein Anna O. and Fraülein Elisabeth, an essay by Breuer, and a chapter on psychotherapy by Freud, which is generally regarded as the inception of the psychoanalytic method. However, he still called his method "Breuer's cathartic method," though he often talked of the "psychical analysis." The term "psychoanalysis" was first employed in a paper published in French on March 30, 1896.

Studies on Hysteria was not well received in the medical world. Eight hundred copies of the *Studies* were printed, and at the end of thirteen years 626 of them had been sold.

IT WAS NOT THE DISCOURAGING RECEPTION of their work that led to the separation of the two co-workers at that point, but Breuer's unwillingness to follow Freud in the far-reaching conclusions he was drawing from his investigation of his patients' sexual life. That disturbances in the sexual life were the *essential* factors in the origins of both neuroses [nervous disorders] and psychoneuroses [emotional conflicts] was a doctrine Breuer could not easily stomach.

Still Breuer wrote, in a letter to a friend: "Freud's intellect is soaring at its highest. I gaze after him as a hen at a hawk."

Scientific differences alone cannot account for the bitterness which Freud later felt toward Breuer. When he was most in need of a companion with understanding sympathy, the one man who had the intellectual knowledge for the purpose and who had been the one to start him on his path withdrew from the fight. And in all this sad story one has to remember Freud's confessed need for periodic experiences of intense love and hate, one which his self-analysis had not yet softened.

On May 2, 1896, Freud disclosed his seduction theory of hysteria in an address to the Society of Psychiatry and Neurology in Vienna. Referring to the proposition that at the bottom of every case of hysteria will be found one or more premature sexual experiences, belonging to the first years of childhood, he was evidently full of confidence, and added: "I believe this to be a momentous revelation." But the paper, entitled "The Etiology of Hysteria," met with an icy reception. Dr. Richard von Krafft-Ebing, who was in the chair, contented himself with saying: "It sounds like a scientific fairy tale." Freud read only one other paper in Vienna, eight years later. That month his consulting room remained empty for the first time, and he saw no new patient for some weeks.

Perhaps Freud's own attitude on sexuality throws light on his fundamental interests and the motives that still urged him forward in his researches. His descriptions of sexual activities are so matter-of-fact that many readers have found them almost dry. From all I know of him I should say that he displayed less than the average *personal* interest in what is often an absorbing topic. There was never any gusto or even savor in mentioning a sexual topic. He would have been out of place in the usual clubroom, for he seldom related sexual jokes and then only when they had a special point illustrating a general theme. He always gave the impression of being an unusually chaste person—the word "puritanical" would not be out of place. This must be the explanation of his almost naïve surprise when his announcement of discoveries in this field met with such a cold reception. He later wrote: "The void which formed itself about me, the insinuations that found their way to me, caused me gradually to realize that . . . from now onward I belonged to those who have 'troubled the sleep of the world,' as Hebbel says. . . . I made up my mind . . . to accept that fate."

HOWEVER UNPALATABLE THE IDEA may be to hero-worshippers, the truth is that Freud did not always possess the serenity and inner sureness so characteristic of him in the years when he was well known. For ten years or so—roughly comprising the nineties—he suffered from a very considerable psychoneurosis. That Freud was able, in the end, to achieve self-mastery by use of psychoanalysis, the unique instrument he himself forged, is remarkable. In doing so he followed a path hitherto untrodden by any human being, and explored his own unconscious mind.

Freud never ceased to function, even in the worst times. He continued with his daily work and with his scientific investigations, his care and love for his wife and children remained unimpaired, and in all probability he gave little sign of neurotic manifestations. Nevertheless, his sufferings were very intense.

Freud would later have classified his neurosis as an anxiety hysteria. It consisted essentially in alternations of mood between periods of elation, excitement, and self-confidence on the one hand and periods of severe depression, doubt, and inhibition on the other. The only respects in which the anxiety got localized were occasional attacks of dread of dying and anxiety about traveling by rail. He retained in later life relics of the latter anxiety in being so anxious not to miss a train that he would arrive at a station a long while—even an hour—beforehand.

In the depressed moods he would spend leisure hours of extreme boredom, cutting open books, looking at maps of Pompeii, playing patience or chess, but being unable to continue at anything for long—a state of restless paralysis. Sometimes there were spells where consciousness would be greatly narrowed: states with a veil that produced almost a twilight condition of mind.

Yet it was just in the years when the neurosis was at its height, from 1897 to 1900, that Freud did his most original work. The neurotic symptoms must have been one of the ways in which the unconscious material was indirectly trying to emerge.

Thanks to the survival of some remarkable correspondence with a young Berlin physician named Wilhelm Fliess, we know a good deal about Freud's struggles and difficulties during this period. The two men had first met when Fliess, a specialist in affections of the nose and throat, came to Vienna for postgraduate study and attended some of Freud's lectures. Their friendship gradually ripened into a close one and after Fliess returned to Berlin they corresponded regularly. Freud badly needed approval and encouragement after his "scientific intercourse with Breuer" had ceased, and he sent Fliess, two years younger, reports of his findings, details of his patients, and, most valuable of all, periodical manuscripts containing his ideas of the moment.

These letters reveal that Freud burned with a passionate desire to discover the secrets of human life, yet he still feared to set free the demon of curiosity. Fliess, far from balking at sexual problems as Breuer had done, made them the center of his studies. He had attempted to link some cases of what he called a "nasal reflex neurosis" to disturbances of sexual origin.

The two men met fairly often in Vienna, and occasionally in Berlin. But whenever possible they would meet for two or three days elsewhere, at Dresden, or Salzburg, or Innsbruck, away from their work, when they could concentrate on the development of their ideas. These special meetings Freud half jocularly, half sadly, called "congresses." Fliess was, as he put it, his sole public. And this was literally so.

In their correspondence Freud was very given to complaining to Fliess about his distressing moods. It is surprising to learn this. Freud had much to endure later on: misfortune, grief, and severe physical suffering, but he faced it all with the utmost stoicism. How often have I seen him in agony from the cancer that was eating away his life, and on only one single occasion did a word of complaint escape him. To be precise, it was two words: *"höchst überflüssig"* (most uncalled-for).

There were also complaints to Fliess about physical ill-health: migraine, nasal infections, irregular disturbance of the heart's action. "The maddest racing and irregularity, constant cardiac tension, oppression, burning, hot pain down the left arm . . . all that in two or three attacks a day and continuing. And with it images of dying and farewell scenes."

The attack was attributed to nicotine poisoning. Freud was a heavy smoker—twenty cigars a day was his usual allowance—and he tolerated abstinence with the greatest difficulty.

Looking back one would come to the conclusion that all these troubles were in the main special aspects of his psychoneurosis. There was assuredly no myocarditis. In those years he was proving it, for a man of forty-three who can climb a mountain in three and a half hours could not have had much wrong with his heart.

Evidently there was something in leaving the safe field of neurology for the unexplored one of psychology which had some supreme inner meaning for Freud. It is as if he divined that the path he was treading would sooner or later lead to terrible secrets, the revealing of which he dreaded but on which he was nevertheless as determined as Oedipus himself.

In the long history of humanity, philosophers and writers, from Solon to Montaigne, from Juvenal to Schopenhauer, had attempted to follow the advice of the Delphic oracle, "Know thyself," but the words of Heraclitus still stood: "The soul of man is a far country, which cannot be approached or explored." The realm of the unconscious remained dark. Now Freud was to be the first to explore those depths.

FREUD'S DECISION, sometime in the summer of 1897, to undertake the psychoanalysis of his own unconscious was hardly one of conscious will, but of a growing intuition of its necessity. Two important parts of Freud's researches are intimately connected with his self-analysis: the interpretation of dreams, and his growing appreciation of infantile sexuality.

Freud once told me: "It seems to be my fate to discover only the obvious: that children have sexual feelings, which every nursemaid knows; and that night dreams are just as much a wish fulfillment as day dreams."

Freud's interest in dreams went back very far: he was always a good dreamer and even in early life not only observed but also recorded them. In following his patients' free associations he had observed that they often interpolated in them an account of a dream, to which of course they would in turn produce associations. The first dream analysis of which we have any published record (March 4, 1895) is that of Breuer's nephew, a medical student, who, to save himself the trouble of getting up, dreamed he was already at work in the hospital. It is the first indication of the theory that the fulfillment of a hidden wish is the essence of a dream.

It was, however, observing and investigating his own dreams, the most readily available material for study, that gave Freud the idea, in conscious terms, of pursuing his own psychoanalysis to its logical end. Therefore its earliest inception might be referred to that historic occasion in July 1895 when his wish-fulfillment theory was further confirmed by the first complete analysis he made of one of his own dreams.

Freud once took me to the Schloss Bellevue restaurant, and we occupied the table at the northeast corner of the terrace where the great event had taken place. When I made the obvious remark about a tablet I did not know that Freud had once half-jokingly asked Fliess if he thought there would ever be a marble tablet on the spot bearing the inscription: "Here the secret of dreams was revealed to Dr. Sigm. Freud on July 24, 1895." Two years later those casual analyses of his own dreams became a regular procedure with a definite purpose. He had already perceived the similarity in the structure of dreams and neuroses. "Dreams contain the psychology of the neuroses in a nutshell," he wrote.

Why was the decision taken just at that time? We probably have to do here with Freud's changing views on sexuality and childhood. In 1893 he had first recorded the idea that the sexual seduction of an innocent child on the part of some adult, most often the father, was an essential cause of hysteria. Three years later this "momentous revelation" had startled his colleagues in Vienna when he had addressed them in May 1896. He had held firmly to his belief in the reality of these childhood traumas—the seductions his patients had revealed—even though being increasingly surprised at the frequency of the supposed occurrence. It began to look as if a large proportion of fathers carried out these assaults. By the spring of 1897 doubts had begun to creep in.

In the previous October of 1896 Freud's father had died. Thanking Fliess for his condolence he wrote: "My father's death has affected me profoundly. . . . With his peculiar mixture of deep wisdom and fantastic lightness he had meant very much in my life . . . inside me the occasion of his death has reawakened all my early feelings."

Freud has told us that it was this experience that led him to write *The Interpretation of Dreams*, in which he records many of the details of his self-analysis. After finishing the book he wrote, "It revealed itself to me . . . as my reaction to my father's death . . . the most poignant loss in a man's life."

In the February after his father's death Freud mentioned in a letter to Fliess that according to his own theory he must infer from the existence of some hysterical symptoms in his brother and several sisters (not himself, however) that even his own father would be incriminated in acts of seduction; he immediately added that the frequency of such occurrences had raised his suspicions.

Just after the self-analysis was begun we have the poignant letter of July 7, 1897, "What has been going on inside me I still do not know. Something from the deepest depths of my own neurosis has been obstructing any progress in the understanding of neuroses. . . . I believe I am in a cocoon, and God knows what kind of beast will creep out of it."

WE COME HERE to one of the great dividing lines in Freud's story. Quite suddenly, on September 21, 1897, he decided to confide in Fliess "the great secret of something that in the past few months has gradually dawned on me." It was the awful truth that most—not all—of the seductions in childhood which his patients had revealed, and about which he had built his whole theory of hysteria, had never occurred. The first two months of his self-analysis had disclosed to Freud the truth of the matter: that irrespective of incest wishes, or even occasional acts of incest of parents toward their children, what he had to concern himself with was the general occurrence of incest wishes of children toward their parents, characteristically toward the parent of the opposite sex.* These emotions conceived in all innocence were afterward transformed by the socializing process into repressions which might later be behind many neuroses.

It was a turning point in his scientific career, and it tested his integrity, courage, and psychological insight to the full. Now he had to prove whether his psychological method on which he had founded everything was trustworthy or not. It was at this moment that Freud rose to his full stature.

---

*Even then Freud had not really arrived at the concept of infantile sexuality as it was later to be understood. The incest wishes and fantasies were later products, probably between the ages of eight and twelve, which were thrown back onto the screen of early childhood. They did not originate there.

In the letter in which he made this announcement to Fliess he gave several reasons for his doubts. First, his numerous disappointments in the results of his analyses, both scientifically and therapeutically. Second, his astonishment at being asked to believe that all his patients' fathers were given to sexual perversions. Third, his clear perception that in the unconscious there is no criterion of reality, so that truth cannot be distinguished from emotional fiction. Fourth, the consideration that such memories never emerge in the deliriums of even the most severe psychoses (profound mental derangements).

He ruefully reflects that, now that he has to renounce his key to the secrets of hysteria, he can no longer feel sure of being able to cure neuroses, on which his livelihood depends. "The expectation of lasting fame, the certainty of wealth . . . the thought of travel, of sparing my children the heavy cares that robbed me of my own youth: it was such a fair prospect. All that depended on the problems of hysteria being resolved."

Many years later, in 1914, Freud described his situation when his seduction theory broke down under its own improbability:

> The result at first was helpless bewilderment. . . . At last came the reflection that . . . if hysterics trace back their symptoms to fictitious traumas, this new fact signifies that they create such scenes in phantasy, and psychical reality requires to be taken into account alongside actual reality.

In the famous letter of September 21, 1897, he confesses with surprise that he is not at all ashamed of his far-reaching blunder: "Between you and me I have the feeling of a victory rather than of a defeat." Well might he be elated, for with the insight he had now gained he was on the verge of exploring the whole range of what has ever since been known as infantile sexuality and of completing his theory of dream psychology—his two mightiest achievements.

FREUD HAD ONCE WRITTEN: "I always find it uncanny when I can't understand someone in terms of myself." He had evidently taken to heart Terence's saying: *Humani nihil a me alienum puto* (Nothing human is alien to me).

Ultimately Freud came to discover his deeply buried hostility to his own father, and he now recognized that his father was innocent. He had projected onto him ideas of his own. Memories had come back of sexual wishes about his mother. We get an account of his childhood jealousy and quarrels, and in a letter to Fliess written in October 1897 Freud related how he inquired of his mother about his early childhood. He in this way got objective confirmation about the truth of his analytic findings.

In this letter Freud announced the two elements of the Oedipus complex: love for the parent of the opposite sex and hostility toward the other. He had discovered in himself the passion for his mother and jealousy of his father; he felt sure that this was a general human characteristic and that from it one could understand the powerful effect of the Oedipus legend. He even added a corresponding interpretation of the Hamlet tragedy. Evidently his mind was now working at full speed, and we may even speak of swift intuitions.

The overcoming of his own resistances now gave Freud a clearer insight into those of his patients, and he could understand their changes of mood far better. "Everything that I experience with patients I find here: days when I slink about oppressed because I have not been able to understand anything of my dreams, my phantasies, and the moods of the day, and then again days in which a flash illuminates the connections and enables one to comprehend what has gone before as a preparation for today's vision."

Naturally Freud's analysis, like all others, produced no magical results at once. And for three or four years his neurotic suffering actually increased in intensity. In the later letters there are characteristic accounts of variations in the progress: optimism alternating with pessimism, exacerbations of symptoms, and the like. His moods were also influenced by the amount of work in his practice, and the varying anxiety over his economic situation after the collapse of his seduction theory of hysteria in the autumn of 1897. In October of that year, shortly after his self-analysis got underway, he had only two gratis patients besides himself: "that makes three, but they bring in nothing." For a whole year he could not leave Vienna: he could not afford to miss a single day's work. But Freud's determination to win through never faltered and ultimately conquered. There came at last the emergence of the serene and benign Freud, henceforth free to pursue his work in imperturbable composure.

In later years he told me he had never ceased to analyze himself, devoting the last half hour of his day to that purpose. One more example of his flawless integrity.

BY GENERAL CONSENSUS *The Interpretation of Dreams*, the book which was so integral a part of his analysis, is Freud's major work. Freud wrote in his preface to the third English edition: "Insight such as this falls to one's lot but once in a lifetime." The main conclusions in it were entirely novel. It affords a secure basis for the theory of the unconscious in man and provides one of the best modes of approach to this dark region. The book's main topic, the investigation of dream life, was carried out with such thoroughness that the conclusions have experienced only a minimum of modification in the half century since the book was published. It took Freud the best part of two years to write the book, and the work got under way sometime in the autumn of 1897.

In March 1898 Freud wrote: "It seems to me that biologically the dream life proceeds altogether from the relics of the prehistoric period (age one to three) . . . the period for which there is normally an amnesia analogous to that of hysteria. I surmise the formula: what was *seen* in that prehistoric period gives rise to dreams; what was *heard*, to phantasies; what was *sexually experienced*, to psychoneuroses. . . . A recent wish can bring about a dream only when it can become connected with material from the prehistoric period." This passage shows the restless penetration of Freud's mind. At one point, partly because of the book's intimate allusions, Freud felt disinclined to publish it.

Freud's mode of working was far removed from purely intellectual activity such as takes place in mathematics and physics. His own descriptions make it plain that he was being moved forward almost entirely by unconscious forces and was at the mercy of them. "The new ideas that came to me during my state of euphoria have gone; they no longer please me, and

I am waiting for them to be born afresh. Thoughts throng my mind that . . . seem to unify the normal and the pathological . . . and then they vanish. . . . On days like yesterday and today everything is quiet inside me, and I feel terribly lonely. . . . I must wait till something stirs in me and I can feel it. So I often dream whole days away." Later, when he was very depressed over his clinical work, he said: "Every single patient is a torturing spirit when I am not myself and cheerful. I really believed I should have to succumb. I helped myself by renouncing all conscious mental effort so as to grope my way into the riddles. Since then I have been doing the work perhaps more skillfully than ever, but I hardly know what I am really doing."

By October 1898 Freud's practice picked up; he was hard at it with eleven hours of psychoanalysis a day. When he had ten patients a day he remarked that it was perhaps one too many, but, "I get on best when there is a great deal of work." The significant point is that happiness and well-being were not conducive to the best work. "I have been very idle because the moderate amount of misery necessary for intensive work has not set in."

In 1899 the Freud family spent the first of many summer holidays in a large farmhouse near Berchtesgaden in Bavaria. The formidable final chapter of *The Interpretation of Dreams* was composed in an arbor in the garden. It is the most difficult and abstract of all Freud's writings, but he wrote it "as in a dream." Ernst Freud in later years remembered how his father used to come to meals, from the arbor where he had been writing, "as if he were sleepwalking." The last of the manuscript was dispatched to the press by the middle of September. Six hundred copies of the book were printed, and it took eight years to sell them. Freud was paid 522.40 gulden for it.

Seldom has an important book produced no echo whatever, but *The Interpretation of Dreams* was simply ignored. In Vienna a Professor Raimann, an assistant at the psychiatric clinic, gave a lecture on hysteria and concluded: "You see that these sick people have the inclination to unburden their minds. A colleague in this town has used this circumstance to construct a theory about this simple fact so that he can fill his pockets."

None of this seems to have at all depressed Freud. In 1900, after the book's publication, he made a half-serious but very interesting description of himself: "I am not really a man of science, not an observer, not an experimenter, and not a thinker. I am nothing but by temperament a *conquistador*—an adventurer, if you want to translate the word—with the curiosity, the boldness, and the tenacity that belong to that type of being."

I doubt very much if Freud ever thought of himself as a great man. Marie Bonaparte once told him she thought he was a mixture of Pasteur and Kant. He replied: "That is very complimentary, but I can't share your opinion. Not because I am modest, not at all. I have a high opinion of what I have discovered, but not of myself. Great discoverers are not necessarily great men. Who changed the world more than Columbus? What was he? An adventurer. He had character, it is true, but he was not a great man. So you see that one may find great things without its meaning that one is really great."

He often voiced the opinion that "none of the undiscovered provinces of mental life which I was the first mortal to enter will bear my name or follow the laws I have formulated."

CHAPTER SEVEN

WHEN FREUD SPOKE LATER of ten years of "splendid isolation" he referred purely to his scientific, not his social, life. In 1895 he had sought congenial company in the B'nai B'rith Society, to which he belonged for the rest of his life. And during the summer months, when he was alone as a grass widower in Vienna, almost every day there was an invitation to spend the evening with friends.

He also enjoyed the warm contact of his family which, by 1896, numbered six children. Late that year his sister-in-law Minna Bernays had joined the family, and would remain with them until her death in 1941. *Tante* Minna was witty and interesting, and had a pungent tongue that contributed to a store of family epigrams. She had once been engaged to Ignaz Schönberg, a Sanskrit scholar who was a good friend of Freud's during his university days. Then, after Schönberg's death from pulmonary tuberculosis early in 1886, Minna had been a lady's companion, an occupation she never found congenial. As a girl she had gone about her housework with a duster in one hand and a book in the other, so it is not surprising that intellectual, and particularly literary, interests absorbed her life.

Tante Minna and Freud got on excellently together. She was a stimulating companion and he had found he could, to some extent, discuss his novel scientific findings with her. But Minna never helped Freud in his literary work, for instance by learning shorthand and typing. He evidently thought best when he had his pen in his hand. Occasionally Minna would make short holiday excursions with him when Martha was unable to go. All this had given rise to the malicious and entirely untrue legend that Minna replaced her sister in Freud's affections.

Freud always welcomed the society of intellectual and rather masculine women, of whom there was a series in his acquaintanceship. But he was quite peculiarly monogamous. Of few men can it be said that they go through the whole of life without being erotically moved in any serious fashion by any woman beyond the one and only one. Men are fortunate indeed if all goes well with the great choice. This really seems to have been true of Freud.

Undoubtedly he exercised a remarkable attraction on members of both sexes, and this assuredly cannot be attributed to charm of manner or gallantry only. Women often found irresistible his peculiar combination of confident strength with unfailing considerateness and tenderness; here was a man that could be trusted. They were also impressed by his evident interest in their own personality. Men were struck by the air he gave of authoritative finality, a true father image, by his transcendent knowledge, and by his kindly tolerance; he was plainly a person they could look up to and perhaps take as a model.

What was Freud's most distinctive characteristic? I once put that question to Anna Freud, the person who knew him most intimately in the last twenty or thirty years of his life. She unhesitatingly answered, "His simplicity." Freud disliked anything that complicated life. It was a feature that extended to the smallest details of every day, the most personal matters. Thus he would own no more than three suits of clothes, three pairs of shoes, and three sets of underclothing. Packing, even for a long holiday, was a very simple matter.

Freud always held very strongly that only he had the right to decide how much of his personality he would reveal to others: he would resent any intimate questioning. On the other hand, oddly enough, Freud was not a man who found it easy to keep someone else's secrets.

On one occasion I sent Freud some private information I thought he should have about a patient of mine he was treating—it was a question of surreptitious use of morphine—and told him it was important that the patient should not know of my communication. He wrote back assuring me he would keep the knowledge to himself, but it was not long before I received a furious letter from the patient complaining of my action.

No one knew better than Freud what a composite mixture of good and bad qualities goes to make up a human being. Yet they were for him mostly divided into good and bad—or, perhaps more accurately, into liked and disliked. Still stranger with such a supreme psychologist was the fact that he was also a poor judge of men. Perhaps one should not call it strange, since the two characteristics go together.

Freud had more than once something to say on the subject of the people at large (*das Volk*). One was a train of thought that occurred to him during a performance of *Carmen*, and it was deeply revealing.

The mob give vent to their impulses, and we deprive ourselves. We do so in order to maintain our integrity. We economize with our health, our capacity for enjoyment, our forces: we save up for something, not knowing ourselves for what. And this habit of constant suppression of natural instincts gives us the character of refinement. We also feel more deeply and therefore dare not demand much of ourselves. Why do we not get drunk? Because the discomfort and shame of the hangover gives us more "unpleasure" than the pleasure of getting drunk gives us. Why don't we fall in love over again every month?

Because with every parting something of our heart is torn away. Why don't we make a friend of everyone? Because the loss of him or any misfortune happening to him would bitterly affect us. Thus our striving is more concerned with avoiding pain than with creating enjoyment.

WHEN DID THE TEN YEARS of splendid isolation come to an end? Like most happenings in Freud's life, it was a gradual process. More and more abstracts of his writings appeared in psychiatric periodicals, and this was soon to turn into a flood of lengthy reviews, sometimes hundreds of pages long. Freud's practice, meantime, increased, though few patients came, either then or later, from Vienna. The majority came from eastern Europe: Russia, Hungary, Poland, Romania.

In the late summer of 1901 there took place an event which Freud called "the high-point of my life." It was his first visit to Rome, yearned for since his boyhood, yet evidently always opposed by some mysterious taboo. He had tried to rationalize his inhibition by saying that the climate of Rome in the summer made it impossible, but all the time he knew there was something deeper holding him back. There was Freud's ancient and passionate identification of himself with Hannibal. Hannibal's attempt to gain possession of Rome, the "Mother of Cities," was thwarted by some nameless inhibition when he was on the point of success. Freud's extensive travels in northern and central Italy had up to this time brought him little nearer to Rome than Lake Trasimene, the place where Hannibal finally halted. Thus far and no farther had said the inner voice, just as it had spoken to Hannibal at that spot two thousand years ago. To Freud, Rome meant two things. There was ancient Rome, whose culture and history gave birth to European civilization. This appealed powerfully to Freud's interest in origins and beginnings. Then there was the Christian Rome that destroyed and supplanted the older one. This could only be an enemy to him, the source of all the persecutions Freud's people had endured throughout the ages. Freud had no compunction in admitting his love for the first Rome and his dislike of the second.

In September 1901, after four years of self-analysis, Freud at last conquered his resistances. Accompanied by his brother

Alexander he spent twelve unforgettable days in Rome. It was the first of seven visits he was to pay to the Holy City. The morning after he arrived he started at half-past seven by visiting St. Peter's and the Vatican Museum, where he found the Raphaels "a rare enjoyment." "And to think that for years I was afraid to come to Rome." On the following day he rode in a fiacre, from three to seven, getting a general impression, and the next day he caught his first glimpse of Michelangelo's statue of Moses. He was still in an exalted mood. The Palatine became his favorite corner. A day was spent in the Alban hills and the children must be told that he rode for two hours on a donkey.

One sign of the heightened self-confidence that Freud's entering Rome betokened was his willingness, upon his return to Vienna, to take appropriate steps to circumvent the clerical anti-Semitic authorities who had for so many years denied his well-earned entry into the ranks of university professors.

IN VIENNA THE WHOLE COMMUNITY was permeated by a kind of snobbishness not equaled anywhere else. Reputation and capacity were quite subordinate to the simple matter of title, and the cream of medical practice went to those doctors with the envied title of professor.

After Freud had been a privatdocent for the unusually long period of twelve years, his former teacher, Nothnagel, told him that he, Krafft-Ebing, and another colleague were proposing him to the ministry of public instruction for the position of associate professor. The anti-Semitic attitude in official quarters could have been decisive in itself, but Freud's reputation in sexual matters did not further his chances. Against this his European standing as a neurologist counted for nothing. In the annual ratification in September, he and his group were ignored in 1897, 1898, and 1899. In 1900 all the names proposed had been ratified with the sole exception of Freud's.

Four years had passed during which Freud took no steps. Then came the great visit to Rome, after which Freud says his pleasure in life had increased and his pleasure in martyrdom diminished. Then one of Freud's patients, a Frau Marie Ferstel, wife of a diplomat, heard of the situation and did not rest till she had got to know the minister of public instruction personally and struck a bargain with him. He was eager to get hold of a certain picture by Böcklin for the newly established Modern Gallery, and her aunt owned it. It took three months to get it out of the possession of the old lady, but at the end the minister graciously announced to Frau Ferstel at a dinner party that she was the first to hear he had sent the necessary document to the Emperor to sign. The next day she burst into Freud's room with the cry: *"Ich hab's gemacht"* ("I've done it").

This absurd story had the expected results. Acquaintances when passing him now bowed, his children's school friends voiced their envy, and—the only thing that mattered—his practice took a permanent turn for the better. He had become, if not respectable, at least respected. Followers began to gather around him, to whom he would always be known simply as "Herr Professor," and before long the outer world would be taking serious notice of his psychological work.

FREUD AVAILED HIMSELF freely of his right to give lectures at the university up to the time of the First World War. He was a fascinating lecturer. He always used a low voice, but spoke with the utmost distinctness. He never used any notes. I remember once while accompanying him to a lecture asking him what the subject was going to be that evening and his answer was, "If I only knew! I must leave it to my unconscious." His lectures were always enlightened by his peculiar ironic humor.

He liked to gather his audience close to him. The audience was assumed to consist of highly intelligent people to whom he wished to communicate some of his recent experiences. As his work became better known there was a risk of this pleasant intimacy being disturbed by numbers. On one occasion a large batch of students flocked in. Freud, divining their motives, announced, "If, ladies and gentlemen, you have come here in such numbers expecting to hear something sensational or even lewd, rest assured I will see to it that your efforts were not worth the trouble." In later years Freud controlled the situation by admitting no one without a card which he granted only after a personal interview.

AMONG THOSE WHO LISTENED to Freud's early university lectures on the psychology of the neuroses there were two doctors whose interest persisted: Max Kahane and Rudolf Reitler. They, along with two other Viennese physicians, Wilhelm Stekel and Alfred Adler, were the earliest followers of Freud. In the autumn of 1902 Freud addressed a postcard to these four men suggesting that they meet at his residence for discussion of his work. From then on they formed the habit of meeting every Wednesday evening in Freud's waiting room, which was suitably furnished for the purpose with an oblong table. The meetings were given the modest title of the "Psychological Wednesday Society." In the next few years others would join the circle, often only temporarily. Not until 1908 would it acquire a more formal designation: the "Vienna Psychoanalytical Society," the mother of so many subsequent ones.

Meanwhile, the early years of the century were relatively happy ones. In August 1904 Freud and Alexander set out for Greece. On September 3 they were in Athens. The following morning they spent two hours on the Acropolis, for which visit Freud had prepared himself by putting on his best shirt. More than twenty years later he said that the amber-colored columns of the Acropolis were the most beautiful things he had ever seen in his life. When standing there he had a curious psychological experience, a disbelief in the reality of what was before his eyes. He puzzled his brother by asking him if it was true that they really were on the Acropolis. Freud traced this sense of disbelief to the incredulity with which he would have greeted in his impoverished student years the idea that he should ever be in a position to visit such a wonderful place, and he compared the mechanism at work with that he had described as operative in the people who cannot tolerate success.

In Vienna the even tenor of Freud's life passed between professional work, including literary work, and private relaxations. There was the weekly game of cards on Saturday, his favorite tarok; after giving his university lecture from seven to nine he would hire a cab at the hospital and drive to his friend Königstein's house for the game.

Freud acquired an ever increasing mastery of the psychoanalytic method. *The Psychopathology of Everyday Life*, published in 1904, is perhaps the best known of Freud's books among the general public. In 1905 appeared *Jokes and Their Relation to the Unconscious*, which dealt with the psychological significance of humor. It contains some of Freud's most delicate writing. Another book was *Three Essays on the Theory of Sexuality*, one of the two most important books Freud ever wrote, ranking next only to *The Interpretation of Dreams*. There for the first time Freud put together, from what he had learned by analyses of patients and other sources, all he knew about the development of the sexual instinct from its earliest beginnings in childhood. The book certainly brought down on him more odium than any other of his writings. The main opprobrium fell on his now taken-for-granted assertion that children are born with sexual urges, which undergo a complicated development before they attain the familiar adult form, and that their first sexual objects are their parents.

At about the same time Freud filled his cup of turpitude in the eyes of the medical profession by deciding to publish a case history generally referred to as the "Dora analysis," a fascinating application of dream analysis to the elucidation of an obscure case of hysteria. His colleagues could not forgive publication of such intimate details of a patient without her permission.

After the *Three Essays on the Theory of Sexuality* and the Dora analysis appeared, Freud's critics took a more active line. If his ideas would not die by themselves, they had to be killed. Freud evidently was relieved at this open opposition. "It was a confession that they had to deal with a serious opponent."

In 1906, on the occasion of his fiftieth birthday, the little group of adherents in Vienna presented Freud with a medallion designed by a well-known sculptor, Karl Maria Schwerdtner, having on the obverse his profile in bas-relief and on the reverse a Greek design of Oedipus answering the Sphinx. Around it is a line from Sophocles' *Oedipus Tyrannus: Who divined the famed riddle and was a man most mighty.*

When Freud read the inscription he became pale and in a strangled voice demanded to know who had thought of it. He disclosed that as a student at the University of Vienna he used to stroll around the great arcaded court inspecting the busts of former famous professors of the institution. He then had the fantasy of seeing his own bust there in the future, inscribed with the *identical* words he now saw on the medallion.

Not long ago I presented to the University of Vienna, for erection in the court, the bust of Freud made by the sculptor Königsberger in 1921, and the line from Sophocles was added. It is a very rare example of such a daydream of adolescence coming true in every detail, even if it took eighty years to do so.

IN THE AUTUMN OF 1904 Freud had heard from Eugen Bleuler, the professor of psychiatry in Zurich, that he and his staff had for a couple of years been finding various applications for psychoanalysis. The main inspiration was coming from Bleuler's chief assistant, Carl Gustav Jung. Jung had read *The Interpretation of Dreams* and had devised some ingenious association tests which confirmed Freud's conclusions about the way in which emotional factors may interfere with recollection. The news that his researches of the past thirteen years, so scorned and despised elsewhere, were finding enthusiastic acceptance in a famous psychiatric clinic abroad warmed Freud's heart.

Jung's first visit to Freud took place in February 1907. That year Jung published a book that made history in psychiatry: *The Psychology of Dementia Praecox*, which extended many of Freud's ideas beyond the classical types of psychoneurosis and other forms of neurotic troubles into the realm of the psychoses proper. Jung regarded his encounter with Freud as the high point of his life. He had very much to tell Freud and poured forth in a spate for three whole hours. Then the patient, absorbed listener interrupted him with the suggestion that they conduct their discussion more systematically. To Jung's astonishment Freud proceeded to group the contents of the harangue under several precise headings that enabled them to spend the further hours in a more profitable give-and-take.

That July, at the International Congress of Psychiatry and Neurology in Amsterdam, Jung made a strong defense of psychoanalytic methods against critics who were denouncing psychoanalysis as dangerous, immoral, and evil. Freud wrote to

Jung about it: "I hate gladiator fights in front of the noble mob and find it hard to agree to an unconcerned crowd voting on my experiences." Nevertheless he had some misgiving at the thought of how he would enjoy a pleasant holiday when someone was fighting on his behalf. So just before the congress he wrote to Jung: "If you needed any encouragement I could tell you about my long years of honorable, but painful, loneliness that began for me as soon as I got the first glimpse into the new world . . . and of the calm certainty I finally compassed which bade me wait until a voice from beyond my ken would respond. It was yours!"

Freud was very attracted by Jung's vitality, liveliness and, above all, his unrestrained imagination. He soon decided that Jung was to be his successor and at times called him his "son and heir." Jung was to be the Joshua destined to explore the promised land of psychiatry which Freud, like Moses, was permitted to view only from afar. Incidentally, this remark is of interest as indicating Freud's self-identification with Moses, one which in later years became very evident.

Jung's quality of imagination echoed something of great significance in Freud's own personality, over which his highly developed capacity for self-criticism had to exercise the strictest control.

Before this memorable year was over a Berlin psychoanalyst visited Freud, Karl Abraham. The two men soon cemented what was to be an unbroken friendship. The next foreign visitor, Sandor Ferenczi, of Budapest, was to become Freud's closest friend and collaborator. He was a general practitioner who had experimented with hypnotism. He called on Freud on Sunday, February 2, 1908. The impression he made was such that he was invited to spend a fortnight in August with the Freud family, with whom he soon became a special favorite, on their holiday in Berchtesgaden.

Freud was early attracted by Ferenczi's lively speculative turn of mind. They spent many holidays together, and between 1908 and 1933 exchanged more than a thousand letters. The two men in their talks and correspondence evolved several important conclusions in psychoanalysis between them.

AT THE END OF NOVEMBER 1907 I spent a week in Zurich with Jung, where I met, among others working there, Abraham Arden Brill of New York, the man who would, in time, do the first English translations of Freud's works and help introduce his methods in America.

A little "Freud Group" had just been started in Zurich, which included among others Jung's chief, Professor Bleuler, and a relative of Jung's called Franz Riklin. I now suggested to Jung the desirability of arranging a general gathering of those interested in Freud's work, and he organized the International Congress of Psychoanalysis in Salzburg for the following April.

It was the first public recognition of Freud's work. We assembled in the Hotel Bristol. There were forty-two present, half of whom were or became practicing analysts. Nine papers were read: four from Austria, two from Switzerland, and one each from England, Germany, and Hungary.

Jung had begged Freud to relate a case history as his paper, so he described the analysis of an obsessional case, "The Man with the Rats." He sat at the end of a long table along the sides of which we were gathered and spoke in his usual conversational tone. He began at the Continental hour of eight in the morning and we listened with rapt attention. At eleven he broke off, suggesting that we had had enough. But we were so absorbed that we insisted on his continuing, which he did until nearly one o'clock.

Among the ideas he put forward were the alternation of love and hate in respect to the same person, the early separation of the two attitudes usually resulting in repression of the hate. When the two attitudes are of equal strength there results a paralysis of thought. Obsessive tendencies, the great characteristic of this neurosis, signify a violent effort to overcome the paralysis by the utmost insistence.

This was my first meeting with Freud. At the age of fifty-two he was only beginning to show slight signs of grayness. He had a strikingly well-shaped head, adorned with thick, dark, well-groomed hair, a handsome mustache, and a full pointed beard. He was about five feet eight inches tall, somewhat rotund, and he bore the marks of a sedentary profession. He had a lively and

perhaps somewhat restless or even anxious manner, with quick darting eyes that gave a penetrating effect.

At a small gathering after the papers, it was decided to issue the first periodical to be devoted to psychoanalysis. It was to be directed by Bleuler and Freud and edited by Jung. Freud could now afford to laugh at his opponents. The Viennese, however, were offended at being ignored in the production of the new periodical, and their resentment would grow and come to open expression two years later.

AFTER THE SALZBURG CONGRESS I went on to Vienna. There I experienced the delightful hospitality of the Freud family. Freud's favorite sister, Frau Rosa Graf, had vacated her flat opposite his, and Freud had obtained more accommodation by taking it over, giving up the little flat on the ground floor where he had seen his patients for some fifteen years. He now occupied the whole of the first floor of No. 19 Berggasse. An opening was made so that he could pass from the new to the old flat without having to open the front door, and he regularly took advantage of this in the few minutes between patients. Another alteration was made to enable a patient to leave at the end of the hour without returning to the waiting room, so that two patients seldom encountered each other.

Freud's waiting room was decorated with various antiquities from his collection. Between this and the adjoining consulting room he had had double doors fitted, lined with baize and overhung on both sides with heavy curtains as well; this ensured complete privacy. With the analytical couch at his side, Freud sat upright in a not too comfortable chair facing the window which gave on to the little garden. The consulting room led into his inner sanctum. This was lined with books, but there was room for cabinets of still more antiquities. To dust the desk at which he wrote must have been a trial, because it was replete with little statues, mostly Egyptian, which Freud used to replace from time to time by others from his cabinets.

In Vienna Freud's life consisted of little besides work. It would begin with the first patient at eight in the morning. It was never easy to get him up so early, since his hard work and late hours combined made him yearn for more rest than was allotted. However, a cold shower refreshed him. Freud's apparel was invariably correct, though not fashionable. There was a hurried breakfast and a glance at the *Neue Freie Presse*. Each patient was given precisely fifty-five minutes, so that there was an interval of five minutes between each to clear his mind for fresh impressions. Lunch was the only time when the whole family would be together; the evening meal was often so late that the younger members had already retired. It was the chief meal of the day, and was a substantial one of soup, meat, cheese, etc., and a sweet. Freud enjoyed his food and would concentrate on it. He was very taciturn during meals, a source of embarrassment to visitors who had to carry on a conversation alone with the family. Freud, however, never missed a word of the family intercourse and daily news. If a child should be missing for a meal, Freud would point at the vacant chair and look inquiringly to his wife at the other end of the table. She would explain, whereupon Freud, his curiosity satisfied, would nod and silently proceed with his meal. In Vienna Freud never took any wine; he wanted always to be clear-minded.

Unless he was exceptionally busy, Freud was free from one to three, so after a few minutes' rest he would proceed on his constitutional walk through the neighboring streets. His headgear was the broad black hat then customarily worn in Vienna; silk hats were for ceremonial occasions, which Freud was mostly successful in avoiding. The walk was an opportunity for minor shopping, perhaps a visit to the tobacconist's shop near St. Michael's Church to replenish his stock of cigars.

Three o'clock was the hour for consultations, for which purpose Freud would don his frock coat. Nine was the hour for supper. Steady therapeutic work till nine without food seems a long run, but it was only after he was sixty-five that Freud allowed himself the luxury of a cup of coffee at five o'clock.

Freud would relax with his family more readily at the evening meal. Afterward he would take another walk, this time with his wife, his sister-in-law, later on with a daughter or with a visiting colleague. I remember the swift pace and rapid spate of speech on such walks. It was at times breathtaking for a companion who would have preferred to pause and digest Freud's thoughts. Sometimes on these occasions they would go to a café.

When his daughters went to the theater, Freud would meet them at a particular lamppost near the theater and escort them home. One of them, Mathilde, tells a story of Freud's courtesy toward his family. When she was fourteen she was invited to walk on the right-hand side of her father during their strolls. A school friend observed that one's father should always be on the right-hand side. But the daughter proudly replied: "With *my* father I am always the lady."

On returning home Freud would retire at once to his study to concentrate on his correspondence. Indicative of the vein of impatience in Freud's ardent nature, he not only greatly enjoyed getting letters but also was apt to be impatient with his friends if they were not so swift in answering correspondence as he himself was. Letter writing done, he worked on whatever paper he was composing. There was the grind of preparing new editions and correcting proofs of his own writings and of the periodicals of which he was editor. He was never in bed before one and often much later.

On Sunday morning Freud always paid a visit to his mother. One or more sisters might be there too, and there would be much family gossip. On Sunday evening his mother and all his sisters would come for a family meal, but Freud would get away to his room as soon as it was over. If anyone wanted a private word with him, she would have to pursue him there. Sunday was also the day when Freud did most of his writing.

It is desirable to say something about Freud's married life; Martha always came first before all other mortals. While it is likely that the more passionate side of married life subsided with him earlier than it does with many men—indeed we know this in so many words—it was replaced by an unshakable devotion and a perfect harmony of understanding. Martha was a cultivated lady to whom the graces of life meant a great deal. Her evening was given up to keeping abreast of current literature to the end of her long life. It was a special pleasure to her when the great Thomas Mann, one of her favorite authors, was a guest.

Pictures have been drawn of a patriarchal severity in which

awe of their father and obedience to his slightest whim constituted the basis of the upbringing of Freud's children. There comes to my mind the memory of a daughter, then a big school-girl, cuddling on his lap in a manner that showed no doubt at all of his affection or his readiness to show it. It is perhaps possible to criticize Freud's education of his children on one point only—it was unusually lenient. To allow a child's personality to develop freely with the minimum of restraint or reprimand was in those days a very rare occurrence, and Freud may even have gone to the extreme in that direction—with, however, the happiest results in their later development.

Life in the Berggasse was full of jokes and there might also be a slight amount of good-natured mutual teasing. But none of the children can remember anything like a quarrel among themselves, still less with either parent. The whole atmosphere was free, friendly, and well balanced. Freud himself was not the sort of man who would think of kissing his wife in front of strangers, but the deep fount of affection that radiated from him inspired the entire family.

Freud used to say that there were three things one should never economize on: health, education, and travel. He also remarked that it was important for children's self-respect that they should always be given good clothes. Freud was determined that his children should not experience any of the anxiety about money which had so marred his own early life.

On the other hand, Freud's considerateness and sense of fairness would take into account the financial circumstances of any friend. His eldest son Martin's chief friend happened to be a youth who was badly off. When the two wanted to start off together on some mountain tour, Freud would first make his son inquire how much money his friend was taking with him and then give him precisely the same, so that the friend would not be embarrassed.

IN THE SUMMER OF 1908 Freud again visited his half brother Emmanuel in Manchester. On the return journey he stopped in Zurich as Jung's guest in Burghölzli. Back in Vienna a domestic event took place that gave Freud great pleasure. Mathilde, his eldest daughter, got engaged to a young Viennese, Robert Hollitscher. Thanking Ferenczi for his congratulations on Mathilde's wedding, Freud confessed he had wished that Ferenczi had been the lucky man.

Meantime Freud's personality and work were about to be introduced to a far wider and more distant circle. Stanley Hall, the president of Clark University, Worcester, Massachusetts, had invited him to give a course of lectures. Freud said he felt very worked up at the prospect. He invited Ferenczi to accompany him, and Ferenczi started to learn English and ordered books on America. Freud could not bring himself to read them. All he wanted to see of America, he said, was Niagara Falls.

In the middle of June Freud heard that Jung had also received an invitation. They at once arranged to travel together, sailing from Bremen on the Norddeutscher Lloyd ship, the *George Washington*, on August 21, 1909. Ferenczi was concerned over whether he should bring a silk hat. Freud told him that his plan was to buy one there and heave it into the sea on the way back.

During the voyage the three companions analyzed each other's dreams—the first example of group analysis—and Jung told me afterward that Freud's dreams seemed to be mostly concerned with cares for the future of his family and of his work. Freud told me he had found his cabin steward reading *The Psychopathology of Everyday Life*, an incident that gave him the first idea that he might be famous. They arrived in New York on August 27.

Ashore Freud called on his sister and brother-in-law, Anna and Eli Bernays, who had settled with their children in New York in the early 1890's. Freud's former antipathy to Eli had long since lost all its intensity. But the Bernays family was on holiday, so A. A. Brill showed the travelers around Central Park and then drove them through Chinatown and the Jewish section of the Lower East Side. The afternoon was spent in Coney Island, the next morning at the Metropolitan Museum with its Grecian antiquities.

I joined the party on the following day and we all dined together in Hammerstein's Roof Garden, afterward going on to see one of those primitive films with plenty of wild chasing.

Freud was only quietly amused; it was the first film he had seen. On the evening of September 4 we all left for Worcester.

Freud's arrival was awaited with a good deal of eagerness. He had felt that Americans might regard the subject of dreams as frivolous. So he decided to give a more general account of psychoanalysis. Each lecture he composed in half an hour's walk beforehand in Ferenczi's company—an illustration of how harmoniously flowing his thoughts must have been.

Freud during his visit to America. Top row, left to right, are Brill, Jones, and Ferenczi. Bottom row, Freud, Hall, and Jung.

Freud delivered his five lectures in German, without any notes, in a serious conversational tone that made a deep impression. A lady in the audience was very eager to hear him talk on sexual subjects, and begged me to ask him to do so. When I passed on her request, he replied: *"In Bezug auf die Sexualität lasse ich mich weder ab- noch zubringen."* That goes better in German. It meant that he was not to be driven *to* the subject any more than *away from* it.

When Freud stood up to thank the university for the doctorate that was conferred on him, he was visibly moved: "This is the first official recognition of our endeavors."

I shall never forget the parting words of William James, the American philosopher, then fatally ill: "The future of psychology belongs to your work."

Leaving Worcester, the three friends visited Niagara Falls, which Freud found even grander than he had expected. But in the Cave of the Winds he had his feelings hurt by the guide's pushing the other visitors back and calling out: "Let the old fellow go first." After all he was then only fifty-three.

Despite his gratitude for his friendly reception Freud did not go away with a very favorable impression of America. A personal reason for his disgruntlement was his difficulty with the language. I recollect an occasion when one American asked another to repeat a remark he had not quite caught. Freud turned to Jung with the acid comment: "These people cannot even understand each other." He also found it hard to adapt himself to the free and easy manners of the New World. He said to me afterward in his terse way: "America is a mistake; a gigantic mistake, it is true, but none the less a mistake."

By now Freud was in a position where he could look forward to a career of recognition and fame on which he had never counted in his lifetime. From now on he might meet with opposition, but he could no longer be ignored. He was at the height of his powers and eager to employ them to the full.

CHAPTER EIGHT

"IT RAINS ABUSE FROM GERMANY," Freud remarked toward the end of 1910. He was referring to the storm of opposition that he had to endure, particularly in the years just before the First World War, but to some extent for the rest of his life. His name had by now become a byword of notoriety to psychiatrists and neurologists, and his theories were having a profoundly disturbing effect on their peace of mind. Freud and his followers were regarded not only as sexual perverts but also as either obsessional or paranoic psychopaths. Freud's theories were inter-

preted as direct incitements to reverting to a state of primitive license and savagery. No less than civilization itself was at stake.

At a congress of German neurologists and psychiatrists that took place in Hamburg in 1910, Professor Wilhelm Weygandt banged his fist on the table when Freud's theories were mentioned, and shouted: "This is not a topic for discussion at a scientific meeting; it is a matter for the police." A psychiatrist, Ernst Trömner, made the original criticism that there could be no sexual factors in hysteria since most hysterics were frigid. At the annual meeting of the American Neurological Association, a New York neurologist urged the association to "crush out Christian Science, Freudism and all that bosh, rot and nonsense." In far-off Australia a Presbyterian clergyman, Donald Fraser, had to leave the ministry because of his sympathy with Freud's work. The only reply Freud ever deigned to make to the flood of criticism was the same as Darwin's: he merely published more evidence in support of his theories. Yet with all Freud's iron self-control, sometimes criticisms moved him deeply, or infuriated him.

FAR MORE DISTURBING to Freud than all the opposition was evidence of growing dissension among his valued adherents, in particular those divergencies instituted first by Alfred Adler, and then by C. G. Jung.

The trouble began in the spring of 1910. Freud had for some time had the idea of bringing together analysts in a closer bond, and had charged Ferenczi with working out necessary plans. At the Nuremberg congress of psychoanalysts that spring, Ferenczi proposed that an international psychoanalytical association be formed, with headquarters in Zurich. Psychoanalytical groups already existing in various countries were to enroll themselves as branch societies and new groups would join as they were formed.

That Jung, with his commanding presence, his psychiatric position, and his devotion to the work, should be designated by Freud to be president seemed only natural. But the Viennese, and especially Freud's oldest followers, Adler and Wilhelm Stekel, angrily opposed the nomination, feeling their faithful services were being ignored. The discussion was so acrimonious that it had to be postponed to the next day. Freud, hearing that several of the Viennese were holding a protest meeting in Stekel's hotel room, went up to join them, hoping to convince them of the advantages of establishing a broader basis for the work than could be provided in Vienna, where all his adherents were Jewish. Freud had often pointed out that Jung's adherence was very valuable because it removed from psychoanalysis the danger of becoming an entirely Jewish affair. "We Jews," he had once written, "if we want to cooperate with other people, have to develop a little masochism and ... endure a certain amount of injustice."

Now Freud made an impassioned appeal to his Viennese colleagues. Seeking for more practical measures for appeasing the two leaders of the revolt, he announced his retirement from the presidency of the Vienna society, in which he would be replaced by Adler. He also agreed that, partly so as to counterbalance Jung's editorship of the *Jahrbuch*, a new periodical be founded, the monthly *Zentralblatt für Psychoanalyse*, which would be edited jointly by Adler and Stekel. They calmed down, and Jung was made president of the association. Freud's endeavor to appease the disgruntled Viennese was only temporarily successful. Adler's theory of the neuroses had a very narrow basis, and his scientific differences with Freud were so fundamental that I can only wonder at Freud's patience in managing to work with him for so long. Adler had two good ideas, in terms of which, however, he interpreted everything else: a tendency to compensate for feelings of inferiority, the spur to do so being reinforced by an innate aggressiveness. Even sexual intercourse itself was not impelled by sexual desire so much as by pure aggressiveness. The concepts of repression, infantile sexuality, and even that of the unconscious itself were discarded, so that little was left of psychoanalysis. Thus he interpreted everything in terms of Nietzche's will to power.

When the Vienna society, early in 1911, arranged a full-dress debate on the subject, Freud was unsparing in his criticism of Adler's insistence that the Oedipus complex was a fabrication. Other members of the society were even more vehement in their denunciation of Adler's theories. Adler and Stekel resigned their positions as president and vice-president and gave up their editorial duties. Eventually Adler formed his own group, the Society for Free Psychoanalytic Research.

Freud's response to the separation from Adler and Stekel was purely one of relief from unpleasantnesses. A couple of years later Freud heard that Stanley Hall had invited Adler to lecture in America and said: "Presumably the object is to save the world from sexuality and base it on aggression."

FROM 1906 TO 1910 Jung had given the appearance of being a most enthusiastic adherent of Freud's work and theories. Only a very keen eye could have perceived any signs of the future rift. On the Worcester visit in 1909 Jung had startled me by saying he found it unnecessary to go into details of unsavory topics with his patients; it was disagreeable when one met them at dinner socially later on. It was enough to hint at such matters and the patients would understand without plain language being used. Later we heard that this idea of not going into details had become a regular part of Jung's teaching. By 1912 Freud was forced to see that Jung was moving in a direction that might well end in both a personal and a scientific separation.

For the past two years the recriminations against Freud's sexual theories had been permeating Switzerland. Riklin told Freud that the campaign had had a disastrous effect on their private practice, even on Jung's, and begged him to send them some patients. There are few parts of the civilized world where it is harder for an individual to stand apart from the prevailing moral standards of the community than in Switzerland.

In September 1912 Jung gave a course of lectures in New York. Reports soon were coming in that Freud was being represented as an out-of-date person whose errors Jung was now able to dispose. All this created a most awkward situation. Jung was still president of the International Psychoanalytical Association and editor of the *Jahrbuch*. He still had the function of holding the various societies together. By the spring of 1913 there was uncertainty about whether the international association would survive the split.

At Munich, where another congress met that September, we made a point of staying in the same hotel as the Swiss so as to avoid the appearance of strained relations. There were eighty-seven members and guests at the congress, but the scientific level of the papers was mediocre. One of the Swiss papers was so tedious that Freud remarked to me: "All sorts of criticisms have been brought against psychoanalysis, but this is the first time anyone could have called it boring."

When Jung's name came up for reelection as president, two-fifths of the audience expressed disapproval by abstaining. After that only formalities remained. In October Jung resigned his editorship of the *Jahrbuch* and announced that no further cooperation with Freud was possible. In April 1914 he resigned his position as president. We decided that Karl Abraham should act as interim president until the next congress. By then most of Europe was at war.

Just before the outbreak of war Jung announced his withdrawal from the international association, and practically all of the Swiss joined him. Freud was under no illusion about the harm Jung's defection would do to psychoanalysis. In a letter to me he wrote: "It may be that we overrate Jung. . . . Anyone who promises to mankind liberation from the hardship of sex will be hailed as a hero, let him talk whatever nonsense he chooses."

Freud has been proved right. As early as January 1914 Jung's conversion was hailed in the *British Medical Journal* as "a return to a saner view of life." To this day in certain quarters one hears of Jung as the man who purged Freud's doctrines of their obscene preoccupation with sexual topics. Then the general psychologists and others gladly proclaimed that since there were three schools of psychoanalysis—Freud, Adler, and Jung—who could not agree among themselves over their own data, there was no need for anyone else to take the subject seriously; it was compounded of uncertainties.

FREUD HAD SHOWN no special interest in politics. His brother Alexander was vehemently opposed to socialism, but Freud used merely to listen to his tirades with a quiet smile. Then on June

28, 1914, the world was startled by the news that the heir to the throne, Archduke Franz Ferdinand, had been assassinated. The Austrian ultimatum to Serbia came on July 23. Freud's first response was one of youthful enthusiasm, a reawakening of the military ardors of his boyhood. He said that for the first time in thirty years he felt himself to be an Austrian. After Germany had handed round her three declarations of war he wrote: "I should be with it with all my heart if only I could think England would not be on the wrong side." He was quite carried away, could not think of any work, and spent his time discussing the events of the day with his brother Alexander. He was excited, and made slips of the tongue all day long.

This mood, however, lasted little more than a fortnight and then Freud came to himself. Curiously enough, what brought about the reversal of Freud's feelings was a loathing for the incompetence of the Austrian campaign against the Serbians. After the crushing Austrian defeats in Galicia Freud commented, "Germany has already saved us." In the first two or three years of the war Freud sympathized completely with the Central Powers, the countries for whom his sons were fighting. It was only late in the war that he became doubtful about the moral issues involved.

In the second week of the war Freud's eldest son Martin volunteered for the army, became a gunner, and was sent to be trained in Innsbruck, where his father soon paid him a visit. Freud's daughter Anna, who it had seemed might be marooned in England, got home safely via Gibraltar and Genoa in the care of the Austrian ambassador.

This was the first August Freud had spent in Vienna for thirty years, and he spent the time minutely examining and describing his collection of antiquities, while Otto Rank, one of his early Viennese followers who often helped him with editorial tasks, made a catalog of his library. Rank would have made an ideal private secretary, and indeed he functioned in this way to Freud in many respects. He had a special analytic flair for interpreting dreams, myths, and legends. And yet the two men never really came near to each other. Rank lacked the charm which seemed to mean much to Freud.

On September 16 Freud left Vienna for a visit to his daughter Sophie. The previous year Sophie had married Max Halberstadt of Hamburg, and they had presented Freud with his first grandson, the first of six he was to have. That grandson later became a psychoanalyst. From Hamburg he wrote that for the first time he did not feel he was in a foreign city; he could talk of "our" battles, "our" victories, and so on.

In November, after his return to Vienna, Freud received news of his beloved brother Emmanuel's death in a railway accident. Freud's spirits were not improved by an offer of asylum from an analyst in Baltimore, which, as he wrote to me, "shows what the Americans think of our chances." To Ferenczi, who had been called up to serve as a doctor in the Hungarian Hussars, he wrote: "Now I am more isolated from the world than ever."

As I have said, there was often some intellectual woman, usually a patient or student, in Freud's life whose company he specially enjoyed. At this time it was Lou Andreas-Salomé, who had studied with him before the war, and had been a member of the Weimar congress in 1911. It was said of her that she had attached herself to the greatest men of the nineteenth and twentieth centuries: Nietzsche and Freud respectively. Freud greatly admired her lofty and serene character as something far above his own.

In this depressing autumn he wrote to Lou: "I do not doubt that mankind will surmount even this war, but I know for certain that I and my contemporaries will never again see a joyous world. . . . And the saddest thing about it is that it has come out just as from our psychoanalytical expectations we should have imagined man and his behavior. . . . My secret conclusion: since we can only regard the highest civilization of the present as disfigured by a gigantic hypocrisy, it follows that we are organically unfitted for it. . . . The Great Unknown, He or It, lurking behind Fate, will sometime repeat such an experiment with another race."

Freud's productivity, however, was at its height, as often happened when he felt in low spirits. Inner concentration was taking the place of interest in the dismal happenings in the outer world. Work of some sort was daily bread to Freud. "I secretly pray: no infirmity, no paralysis of one's powers through bodily distress. We'll die with harness on, as King Macbeth said."

To me, in his last letter of the year 1914, Freud wrote:

> The flowering time of our science has been violently disrupted. ... What Jung and Adler have left of the movement is being ruined by the strife of nations. Our Association can as little be kept together as anything else that calls itself International. ... Hold fast till we meet again.

AS 1915 BEGAN there was considerable anxiety about the two sons who were fighting: Martin, the eldest, in Galicia and Russia; Ernst, the youngest, against Italy after her entry into the war that April. Martin had already won a decoration for special gallantry. Oliver, the other son, was engaged in engineering work throughout the war, constructing tunnels, barracks, and so on; he had qualified as an engineer the same day Freud's youngest daughter, Anna, qualified as a schoolteacher. Freud had several dreams about calamities to his sons, which he interpreted as envy of their youth.

The Vienna society ceased meeting when war broke out, but meetings were resumed in the winter and took place every three weeks. Practice, of course, was meager. Early in the year there were only two or three patients, all Hungarian aristocrats.

In 1915 Freud mentioned the matter of the Nobel Prize. "The granting of the Nobel Prize to Bárány, whom I refused to take as a pupil some years ago because he seemed to be too abnormal, has aroused sad thoughts about how helpless an individual is about gaining the respect of the crowd. ... But it would be ridiculous to expect a sign of recognition when one has seven-eighths of the world against one."

Freud was now in his sixtieth year, and moaned that he was on the threshold of old age. Throughout his life Freud was much preoccupied with thoughts about death. There were reflections on its significance, fears of it, and later on the wish for it. He had even adopted a superstitious belief—that he had to die in February 1918. When that date passed quietly Freud made the characteristically dry comment: "That shows what little trust one can place in the supernatural."

Among the papers Freud published in 1915 was a pair of essays, "Thoughts for the Times on War and Death." And he decided not to give his annual university lectures after the winter session of 1916–1917. Everything seemed to be closing down.

FREUD'S CHIEF PREOCCUPATION for the remaining years of the war was somehow or other to keep the psychoanalytical periodicals going, all that was left of the psychoanalytical movement. By filling the journals himself with papers written specially for that purpose, by reducing the size of the periodicals, and—when it came to the worst—by letting them appear less frequently, Freud succeeded in part.

Ferenczi had urged that the word "International" be omitted from the title of the *Internationale Zeitschrift*, a journal Freud had founded in Vienna in 1912, but I begged that this should not happen and my own name remained as co-editor. At the end of the war Freud was proud to think that this was the only scientific periodical that had kept the international flag flying despite the frightful bitterness between the nations in those days.

On New Year's Day of 1916 Freud sent greetings to his long-time follower, analyst Max Eitingon, and added that his eldest son had been made a lieutenant and the youngest one a cadet; both were now fighting on the Italian front. Oliver was constructing a tunnel in the Carpathians and had taken a bride with him there. A month later Freud told Ferenczi he was reading four newspapers a day.

The food shortage was already making it hard to arrange any holidays in Austria, and the closing of the frontier excluded both Freud's beloved Berchtesgaden and also any further visits to his daughter Sophie in Hamburg. In 1917 came the first Russian revolution. "How much one would have entered into this tremendous change if our first consideration were not the matter of peace."

Freud soon lost all sympathy for Germany. Writing to Abraham in Berlin he said, "The only cheerful news is the capture of Jerusalem by the English and the experiment they propose about a home for the Jews."

The population behind the front was now suffering severely, especially in Austria, and the year had started badly without a single patient. From time to time Ferenczi managed to smuggle flour, bread, and occasionally a few luxuries from Hungary by various complicated maneuvers. Freud wrote: "Curiously enough . . . my spirits are unshaken. It is a proof of how little justification in reality one needs for inner well-being."

Freud would, in time, be lucky to have the inner resources he hinted at. Near the end of the year something happened which our later knowledge might be tempted to call sinister. "Yesterday I smoked my last cigar and since then have been bad-tempered and tired. Palpitation appeared and a worsening of a painful swelling in the palate which I have noticed since the straitened days [cancer?]. Then a patient brought me fifty cigars, I lit one, became cheerful, and the affection of the palate rapidly went down. I should not have believed it had it not been so striking."

That was six years before the real cancer attacked him there. The connection with smoking is unmistakable.

At the beginning of 1917 Freud had written a paper under the title of "A Difficulty in the Path of Psychoanalysis." It described the three great blows man's pride had suffered at the hands of science: his displacement from the center of the universe, then from a unique position in the animal world, and lastly the discovery that he was not master of his own mind. At intervals throughout that year one important theme occupied Freud's thoughts. It was a study that he and Ferenczi were jointly undertaking on the bearing of Lamarckism on psychoanalysis.

Freud sent Abraham the following summary: "Our intention is to . . . show that [Lamarck's] 'need' which creates and transforms organs is nothing other than the power of unconscious ideas over the body, of which we see relics in Hysteria: in short, the 'omnipotence of thoughts.' Purpose and usefulness would then be explained psychoanalytically; it would be the completion of psychoanalysis. Two great principles of change or progress would emerge: one through (autoplastic) adaptation of one's own body, and a later (heteroplastic) one through transmuting the outer world." This train of thought ran through much of Freud's more speculative period.

I now propose to make the daring attempt of approaching as near as I can to the secret of Freud's genius. When I first got to know Freud I could not fail to observe such manifest qualities as his directness, absolute honesty, tolerance, ease of approach, and his essential kindliness. But I also soon noticed another feature which was more peculiar to him. Once his will was really set he would not be driven or even guided in any particular direction. In his old age he would repeat the words *"nein, nein, nein,"* to the accompaniment of a vigorous shaking of the head.

Freud had inherently a plastic and mobile mind, one given to the freest speculations and open to new and even highly improbable ideas. But it worked this way only on condition that the ideas came from himself; to those from outside he could be very resistant, and they had little power in getting him to change his mind. I would come across instance after instance where he was believing statements which I knew to be certainly untrue and also, incidentally, refusing to believe things that were as certainly true. An English patient complained bitterly of monstrous, and indeed fantastic, ill-treatment she had suffered at the hands of an English analyst in Ipswich—of all places. Freud was deeply shocked at such scandalous behavior. Shortly afterward he received a letter from Abraham saying he had recommended an English lady to consult him, a wild paranoiac with a fondness for inventing incredible stories about doctors. So poor Abraham had been the wicked analyst in Ipswich!

But when I commented to my friend James Strachey on Freud's strain of credulity, he very sagely remarked: "It was lucky for us that he had it." Freud was willing to believe in the improbable and the unexpected—the only way, as Heraclitus pointed out centuries ago, to discover new truths.

It is an interesting thought that very possibly this trait may be not a weakness but an indispensable tool of genius. In the last twenty years of his life Freud gave his speculative daemon a freer rein than ever before, with the bewildering results that are as yet far from adequately appraised.

In February 1918 a patient he had cured left Freud ten thousand kronen in his will. He "played the rich man," distributing it among his children and relatives.

Later that year Freud wrote, "My Mother will be eighty-three this year and is no longer very strong. I sometimes think I shall feel a little freer when she dies, for the idea that she might have to be told that I have died is a terrifying thought."

There were two experiences that summer that raised Freud's hopes for the future. First his friend Anton von Freund, a wealthy Budapest brewer, decided to devote his vast fortune to the furtherance of psychoanalysis. Freud had conceived the idea of founding an independent publishing firm of his own to give him control of psychoanalytic publications. Now, with this financial backing, arrangements were getting under way.

The other cheering event was the Fifth International Congress of Psychoanalysis in Budapest on September 28 and 29, 1918. It was the first congress at which official representatives of the Austrian, German, and Hungarian governments were present. The reason for their attendance was the increasing appreciation of the part played by "war neuroses" in military calculations. The excellent practical work in this field by Abraham, Ferenczi, and others had made an impression on the high-ranking army medical officers. There was even talk of erecting psychoanalytical clinics for the treatment of war neuroses.

The mayor and magistrates of Budapest placed a special steamer on the Danube at the disposal of the participants in the congress, and various receptions and dinners were given. Although he kept aloof as far as possible from the formal ceremonies, Freud could not fail to be moved by the bright prospects unexpectedly opening for the extension of his work.

Then came the downfall, with the breakup of the Austro-Hungarian empire. Freud could not suppress his gratification. "I shall not weep a single tear for the fate of Austria or Germany." For many weeks, however, Freud had one personal anxiety; there was no news whatever of his son Martin. It was not until December 3 that a postcard came to Vienna baldly announcing Martin's presence in an Italian hospital. At the end of the following August he was released. Despite many hazardous adventures, Ernst also came safely through the war.

FOLLOWING THE ARMISTICE everything had come to a stand-still in Vienna and life there was scarcely bearable. The monot-onous diet of thin vegetable soup was far from adequate, and the pangs of hunger were continuous. The winters were the worst of all, with their unheated rooms and feeble illumination. Freud treated patients for hour after hour in that deadly cold, equipped with an overcoat and thick gloves. The publishing house which was to play a large part in Freud's life from then on, the *Internationaler Psychoanalytischer Verlag*, was founded in Vienna in the middle of January 1919.

In the early months of that year Martha contracted influenzal pneumonia and had to go to a sanatorium near Salzburg to con-valesce. Moreover, Freud was concerned about his sons' chances of finding work and he had to help other members of his family and various friends. His practice had by now revived and he was treating nine or ten patients a day. But the thousand kronen they brought in were worth only a tenth of their previous value, and he was forced to live on his savings.

THE BRITISH PSYCHOANALYTICAL SOCIETY had been reorganized that February with twenty members. Freud and I were equally anxious to resume personal contact. At the end of the summer I managed to get to Vienna. It did not take long to confirm Freud's hints of the desolation of his country. The starved and ragged officials were evidence enough, nor shall I forget the vain efforts of the emaciated dogs to stagger to the food I threw to them. We were the first foreign civilians to reach the city.

I found Freud somewhat grayer and a good deal thinner than before the war, but his mind had lost nothing of its alertness. He was as cheerful and warmly friendly as ever. We had not been together long before Ferenczi burst into the room and effusively kissed us both on the cheeks. We had endless news to exchange about the vast changes in the European situation. Freud had recently had an interview with an ardent Communist, who had informed him that the advent of Bolshevism would result in some years of misery and chaos, and that these would be followed by universal peace, prosperity, and happiness. Freud said: "I told him I believed the first half."

He had hard things to say about President Wilson, whose vision of a friendly Europe based on justice was rapidly becoming illusory. When I pointed out how complex were the forces at work in arranging the peace settlement, he replied: "Then he should not have made all those promises."

It was evident to Freud that what he called "the center of gravity of psychoanalysis" would have to be moved westward. So he proposed to Ferenczi that he transfer to me the acting presidency of the international association to which the Budapest congress had voted him during the war. Also discussed was the newly founded *Verlag*, which was already bringing Freud enormous personal labor, but also profound satisfaction. The *Verlag* would eventually, in its twenty years of existence, publish some one hundred and fifty books, including Freud's *Collected Works*, besides maintaining five psychoanalytical periodicals. Otto Rank had been installed as managing director, and what is certain is that the *Verlag* could not have survived for a day without the truly astounding capacity and energy with which Rank threw himself into his editorial and managerial tasks. Paper and type had to be scrounged from odd corners; he had to make up the parcels of books to be dispatched, and carry them himself to the post office. The five years in which Rank continued at this furious tempo must have been a factor in his subsequent mental breakdown.

Von Freund was dying of cancer. And so it was agreed I should take his place as a director of the *Verlag*, joining Freud, Ferenczi, and Rank. Von Freund had set up a sum—the equivalent of $500,000—to support the *Verlag* and other psychoanalytic undertakings. But with the Red Terror in Budapest followed by the White Terror and its strong wave of anti-Semitism, something less than a quarter of the total had been transferred to Vienna. Now it was decided to keep half of this and transfer the other half to London. Thus it was that when Eric Hiller and I left Vienna we undertook to smuggle a quarter of a million kronen out of the country and into England. This feat, however, met with no reward, since in another year or two the notes were hardly worth the paper they were printed on. No one believed then that a national currency could entirely disappear.

Soon Freud had lost all his savings, amounting to 150,000 kronen (then worth $29,000). His chief anxiety concerned his wife's future, on the expectation that she would survive him— as she did. He had insured his life on her behalf for 100,000 kronen ($19,500). Through the inflation this was soon not enough to pay a cab fare.

It was plain that the only hope of keeping his head above water lay in the possibility of acquiring American or English patients who would pay in their relatively unimpaired currency. Early in October 1919 a London physician, Dr. David Forsyth, came for seven weeks to learn something of psychoanalysis. Then in that November I induced an American dentist who had sought my help to brave the rigors of life in Vienna. He was to pay the low fee of $5.00, but Freud commented it was right he should pay only half fees since he was only half American; the other half was a Hungarian Jew. In the following March I was able to send him an Englishman who paid a guinea fee. Freud asked Ferenczi: "What would happen to me if Jones were not able to send me any more patients?" At the end of that year the flow became continuous. Budding analysts from England and America came to learn his technique. Freud did not find it easy to understand the differing accents and after six hours' effort to follow such patients he would be completely exhausted.

He had been toying with the idea of England as a last resort: "My two brothers already rest in English soil; perhaps I shall also find room there." But to my urging him to come to England, he gave the answer, as he was to later in 1938: "I will stay at my post as long as I reasonably can."

IN THE FIRST MONTH OF 1920 fate dealt Freud a grievous blow. On January 23 came news of the serious illness of Freud's beautiful daughter Sophie, the one they called their "Sunday child," at her home in Hamburg; it was the influenzal pneumonia. There were no trains leaving Vienna for Germany, and so no possibility of her parents' reaching her. Two days later a telegram announced her death. She was only twenty-six, had been in perfect health and happiness, and left two small children.

Ferenczi was deeply concerned about Freud. Freud reassured him in these pathetic lines:

> Since I am profoundly irreligious there is no one I can accuse.... "The unvarying circle of a soldier's duties" and the "sweet habit of existence" will see to it that things go on as before. Quite deep down I can trace the feeling of a deep narcissistic hurt that is not to be healed.

In the summer Freud returned to contemplation of new ideas that had been fermenting for some time. In March 1919 he had written: "I have just finished a paper, 26-pages long, on the genesis of masochism, the title of which will be 'A Child Is Being Beaten.' I am beginning a second one with the mysterious caption 'Beyond the Pleasure Principle.' I don't know whether it is the cold spring or the vegetarian diet that has suddenly made me so productive."

Freud anticipated some speculation that the startling ideas put forward in *Beyond the Pleasure Principle*, on the relation of life to death, had been influenced by his depression over losing his daughter. He asked analyst Max Eitingon of Berlin, with whom he had been corresponding about the work, to bear witness that it had been half ready at a time when his daughter Sophie was in the best of health.

Freud seemed to have landed in the position of Schopenhauer, who taught that "death is the goal of life." But Freud dexterously extricated himself by pointing out that sexual instincts thwarted the aim and indefinitely postponed the final goal of the death instinct through creating ever new life. He termed the two opposing forces in the mind "life instincts" and "death instincts," the former being entitled *Eros*. Of equal validity and status, they were in constant struggle with each other. He had often admitted having a fantastic side to his nature. Now he was allowing his thoughts to soar to far distant regions. He said: "Many people will shake their heads over it."

Freud first announced these ideas as purely tentative, a private train of thought, so to speak, that amused him but of the validity of which he was far from convinced. Within a couple of years, in his book *The Ego and the Id*, he came to accept them fully.

As he once said to me, he could no longer see his way without them, they had become indispensable to him.

Most students of Freud have been struck by what has been called his obstinate dualism. Running all through his work there is what Heinz Hartmann has called "a very characteristic kind of dialectical thinking that tends to base theories on the interaction of two opposite powers." This was of course most pronounced in his basic classifications: love–hunger; ego–sexuality; auto-erotism–heteroerotism; life–death, and so on. It is as if Freud had a difficulty in contemplating any topic unless he could divide it into two opposites, and never more than two.

Freud and two of his grandchildren, Ernst and Heinerle.

One is naturally tempted to cor-relate this tendency with its mani-festations in Freud's own person-ality. There was the fight between scientific discipline and philosoph-ical speculation; his passionate love urge and his great sexual repression; his vigorous masculinity, which shines through all his writings, and his feminine needs; his desire to create everything himself and his longing to receive stimulation from another; his love of independence and his needs of dependence. But such thoughts assuredly bring the risk of falsification from the lure of simplistic solutions.

From this time onward Freud took fewer patients, there being so many pupils, mainly from America and England, who wished to learn his technique. His books were eagerly sought and were being translated into various languages. In Germany new so-cieties were being founded in Dresden, Leipzig, and Munich. In December 1921 Freud was gratified at being made an honor-ary member of the Dutch Society of Psychiatrists and Neurolo-gists. It marked the beginning of a change in the professional estimate of his work. Two thousand copies of the Russian trans-lation of the *Introductory Lectures on Psychoanalysis* were sold in

Moscow in a single month. In Vienna Freud had been asked to give lectures by the *Medizinische Doktoren-Kollegium* [college of physicians], and even by the highest police authorities (!).

It would have been affectation, of which Freud was never capable, to deny that he was glad of the increasing signs of recognition.

About the time of Freud's sixty-fifth birthday in May 1921 his constant complaints about getting old had taken a sudden turn: "On March 13 of this year I quite suddenly took a step into real old age. Since then the thought of death has not left me, and sometimes I have the impression that seven of my internal organs are fighting to have the honor of bringing my life to an end. . . . Still I have not succumbed to this hypochondria, but view it quite coolly, rather as I do the speculations in *Beyond the Pleasure Principle*."

In July Freud went to Badgastein with his sister-in-law Minna, who also needed treatment there. On August 14 they met his wife and daughter at a village nearly four thousand feet high in the north Tyrol. Freud was still complaining of cardiac symptoms, but he soon recovered in the mountain air.

Then, in September, Freud went to Berlin to meet a small group of us—firm friends and trustworthy analysts—known informally as the Committee. Otto Rank, Hanns Sachs, Max Eitingon, Sandor Ferenczi, Karl Abraham, and myself, had formed an unofficial "Old Guard" around Freud before the war to give him support in the event of further dissension such as the Jung and Adler embroilments. Freud liked the idea of a group that would "defend the cause . . . when I am no more."

We had planned a ten days' holiday tour of the Harz region. Every day there were walking expeditions, and we were all impressed with Freud's swift and tireless capacities in this pursuit. There was of course ample time for extensive discussions among us on various scientific topics of common interest. Freud read to us two papers he had specially written for the occasion.

There were many pleasant events in these years. In June 1922 Freud's youngest daughter, Anna, who had recently read her first analytical paper before the Vienna society, was made a member of the society. That same month the *Ambulatorium*, a psychoanalytical clinic similar to one which had opened in Berlin in 1920, was opened in Vienna. Three more grandsons had arrived, and Freud complained at having five grandsons but no granddaughter.

CHAPTER NINE

ONE OF THE CRITICAL YEARS in Freud's life was 1923, which brought the first signs of the mortal disease that was to cause untold suffering before it attained its final goal. The first I heard about it was in a letter dated April 25. "I detected two months ago a leucoplastic growth on my jaw and palate right side, which I had removed on the 20th." It was not Freud's custom to discuss his health so I half wondered whether he was making light of something serious.

What had happened was this. In the third week of April Freud consulted a leading rhinologist, Marcus Hajek, an old acquaintance of his. Hajek said the trouble was a leukoplakia due to smoking. He advised "a very slight operation" and asked Freud to come to his outpatient clinic one morning. Freud quietly turned up at Hajek's clinic without saying a word at home. Presently the family were surprised by getting a telephone message from the clinic requesting them to bring a few necessities for him to stay the night. Wife and daughter Anna hurried there to find Freud sitting on a kitchen chair in the outpatient department with blood all over his clothes. There was no available bed, but one was rigged up in a small room already occupied by a cretinous dwarf who was under treatment.

The ward sister sent the two ladies home at lunchtime. When they returned an hour or two later they learned that Freud had had an attack of profuse bleeding. The friendly dwarf had rushed for help; perhaps his action saved Freud's life. Anna refused to leave again and spent the night sitting by her father. The next morning Hajek demonstrated the case to a crowd of students, and later in the day Freud was allowed to go home.

So ended the first of thirty-three operations Freud underwent before he ultimately found release.

The excised growth was examined and found to be cancerous, but Freud was not told of this. Many years later, the deception still rankled. With blazing eyes he asked me: *"Mit welchem Recht?"* ("By what right?")

The surgeon had not taken precautions against the shrinking of the scar, so considerable contraction took place, which reduced the opening of the mouth and thereby caused great hardship ever after. Two X-ray treatments followed. Then came a series of drastic treatments with radium capsules, administered by an assistant of Hajek's. Freud suffered greatly from the toxic effects. Four months later he wrote saying he had not had an hour free from pain since the treatment ceased.

IN THE SAME MONTH of April 1923 something happened that had a profound effect on Freud's spirits for the rest of his life. His grandchild, Heinerle (Heinz Rudolf), Sophie's second child, had been spending several months in Vienna with his aunt Mathilde. Freud was extremely fond of the boy, whom he called the most intelligent child he had ever encountered. He had had his tonsils removed, and when the two patients first met after their experiences he asked his grandfather with great interest: "I can already eat crusts. Can you too?" Unfortunately the child was very delicate, having contracted tuberculosis the previous year. He died, aged four and a half, on June 19.

Freud found the blow much more unbearable than his own cancer. It was the only occasion in his life when he was known to shed tears. Three years later, on condoling with a Swiss analyst whose eldest son had died, he said that Heinerle had stood to him for all children and grandchildren. Since his death he had not been able to enjoy life; he added: "It is the secret of my indifference—people call it courage—toward the danger to my own life."

Hajek raised no objection to Freud's going away for his usual three months' summer holiday. But in Badgastein the general discomfort was so great that, on Anna's insistence, Freud asked Felix Deutsch, another physician friend, to visit him at Lavarone in the Dolomites, where he was to spend most of the holiday with his family. Deutsch at once perceived a recurrence of the growth. So Deutsch and Anna came down to San Cristoforo, where the members of the Committee had gathered to hold a meeting. To our consternation we were informed of the seriousness of the situation. During supper Freud's name was of course mentioned, whereupon Rank broke out in a fit of uncontrollable hysterical laughter. It was only a couple of years later that the events related to Rank's failing mental integration made this outburst intelligible.

Thinking to himself that it might be his last opportunity, Freud now decided to carry out a long-cherished plan of showing Rome to his daughter.

During Freud's absence in Rome Deutsch persuaded Professor Hans Pichler, the distinguished oral surgeon, to take charge of Freud's case. He also made all the arrangements for the probable operation.

On September 26, following Freud's return, Pichler and Hajek examined him and found a malignant ulcer in the hard palate which invaded the upper part of the lower jaw and even the cheek. Pichler decided at once that a radical operation was necessary, and performed it, in two stages, on October 4 and 11. The surgeon removed the upper jaw and palate on the affected side, which threw the nasal cavity and mouth into one.

These frightful operations were performed under local anesthesia! Freud wrote to Abraham, who had sent him one of his most cheerful letters: "Dear Incorrigible Optimist. . . . Out of bed. What is left of me put into clothes."

Now began sixteen years of pain, interrupted only by further operations. A huge prosthesis, a sort of magnified denture, designed to shut off the mouth from the nasal cavity, was fitted and was labeled "the monster." It was very difficult to take out or replace because it was impossible for him to open his mouth at all widely. If it were left out for more than a few hours the tissues would shrink, and the denture could no longer be replaced without being altered.

From now on Freud's speech was nasal and thick, rather like that of someone with a cleft palate. Eating also was a trial, and he seldom cared to do so in company. Furthermore he became almost entirely deaf on the right side. It was the side next to his patients, so the position of his couch and chair had to be reversed.

From the onset of this illness to the end of his life Freud refused to have any other nurse than his daughter Anna. He made a pact with her at the beginning that all that was necessary had to be performed in a cool, matter-of-fact fashion, with the absence of emotion characteristic of a surgeon. This attitude, her courage and firmness, enabled her to adhere to the pact even in the most agonizing situations.

FREUD RESUMED his professional work with six patients on January 2, 1924, but the difficulty he had in talking made this effort very tiring. Smoking was allowed him, but to get a cigar between his teeth he had to force the bite open with the help of a clothespin. In April I went to Vienna to visit Freud. It was a considerable shock to observe his altered appearance; one had to get used to his habit of keeping his prosthesis in its place with his thumb; this, however, after a time produced rather the impression of philosophical concentration. But it was plain that Freud was as keen mentally as he had ever been.

Freud was already becoming somewhat of a lion. Romain Rolland visited him on May 14. Stefan Zweig brought him and acted as an interpreter; with his defective speech Freud found French was beyond him. A couple of years later when Freud was visiting Yvette Guilbert, the famous French diseuse, he turned to her husband with the pathetic remark, "My prosthesis doesn't speak French."

George Seldes kindly sent me details of the following incident belonging to that time. Two youths, Leopold and Loeb, had carried out in Chicago what they described as "the perfect murder." They were nevertheless detected, and the long trial that ensued provided a first-class sensation in America. Their wealthy relatives and friends made every effort to save them from capital punishment, an aim they ultimately achieved.

Seldes, on the staff of the Chicago *Tribune*, received the following telegram from his publisher, Colonel Robert McCormick: OFFER FREUD 25,000 DOLLARS OR ANYTHING HE NAME COME CHICAGO PSYCHOANALYZE [he meant the murderers]. Freud wrote to Seldes:

> I cannot be supposed to be prepared to provide an expert opinion about persons and a deed when I have only newspaper reports to go on and have no opportunity to make a personal examination. An invitation from the Hearst Press to come . . . for the duration of the trial I have had to decline for reasons of health.

The last sentence refers to another invitation, from William Randolph Hearst, for Freud to come to America to "psychoanalyze" the two murderers, and presumably to demonstrate that they should not be executed. He offered Freud any sum he cared to name and, having heard that he was ill, was prepared to charter a special liner so that Freud could travel quite undisturbed by other company.

The year brought Freud three more grandchildren: his sixth and last grandson and two granddaughters.

This year also brought Freud a growing rift with Otto Rank. Rank's newly formulated theories on the trauma of birth as the cause of all subsequent mental conflicts seemed to contradict Freud's theories on the Oedipus complex, even though Freud had long thought that the painful experience of being born was a prototype of all later attacks of fear (*Angst*). Rank's book on the subject, however, was written like the announcement of a new religious gospel: All neuroses concerned the relation of the child to its mother, and what might appear to be conflicts with the father were but a mask for the essential ones concerning birth. Freud's reaction when the book was first published was a shock of alarm—lest the whole of his life's work on the causes of the neuroses be dissolved. Soon, however, his interest turned to the problem of how Rank's contribution was to be woven into the previous fabric of psychoanalysis.

Then, in the spring of 1924, Rank went to America for six months at the invitation of the New York Psychoanalytic Society. Disturbing accounts of his teachings there began to reach Europe. "Old" psychoanalysis had been quite superseded by his discoveries and an analysis could now be completed in three or four months. Rank's pupils gleefully related that it was no longer necessary to analyze dreams, and they were relieved also from going into the unpleasant topic of sexuality.

The whole episode of Rank's curious behavior in America was very reminiscent of Jung's visit there in 1912.

Then dissension even affected the harmony of the Committee, for Ferenczi and, to a lesser degree, Sachs were more sympathetic to Rank's innovations than were the rest of us. Freud could not conceal his distress: "I have survived the Committee that was to have been my successor. . . . It is to be hoped that psychoanalysis will survive me."

One of the rare allusions to Rank that Freud made later was written in 1937. "It cannot be denied that Rank's train of thought was bold and ingenious, but . . . it was designed to accelerate the tempo of analytic therapy to suit the rush of American life."

In 1925 came Freud's *Autobiography*, an account of his scientific career. Death and thoughts of death continued to be his companions. On June 20 Josef Breuer died, at the age of eighty-four. Karl Abraham was dying of cancer of the lung.

ON FEBRUARY 19, 1926, Freud suffered in the street a mild attack of angina pectoris. He found himself only a few steps from the house of a friend, Dr. Ludwig Braun. Braun advised a fortnight's treatment in a sanatorium. Freud moved to the Cottage Sanatorium on March 5, where he continued to treat his patients. His daughter Anna slept in the adjoining room and acted as nurse for half the day, his wife and sister-in-law taking turns for the other half. He returned home on April 2.

At the time Freud wrote Max Eitingon in Berlin:

> I cannot be out of humor with my heart, since the affection of the heart opens up a prospect of a not too delayed and not too miserable exit. . . . Were it not for the one trouble of possibly not being able to work I should deem myself a man to be envied. To grow so old; to find so much warm love in family and friends; so much expectation of success in such a venturesome undertaking . . . who else has attained so much?

Freud continued a semi-invalid existence after returning to Vienna, and he used to take a drive in the morning to the green suburbs before beginning work. That gave him the opportunity of discovering how beautiful the early spring can be—lilac time in Vienna! "What a pity that one had to grow old and ill before being able to make this discovery."

He decided to take only five patients instead of his previous six, but since he then raised his fees from $20 to $25 he did not lose financially by the reduction in his work.

Freud and his wife traveled to Berlin at Christmas to see their two sons and four grandchildren. They stayed with their son Ernst, and Albert Einstein and his wife paid Freud a visit. They chatted for two hours together, after which Freud wrote: "He is cheerful, sure of himself and agreeable. He understands as much about psychology as I do about physics, so we had a very pleasant talk."

FREUD'S MAIN administrative preoccupation in these later years was the problem of lay analysis. He recognized that his discoveries, leading to a more profound understanding of the motives and emotions of mankind, had an extremely wide bearing outside the field of psychopathology. Anthropology, mythology; the historical evolution of mankind; the upbringing and education of children; the significance of artistic endeavor; the various social institutions, such as marriage, law, religion, and perhaps even government—psychoanalysis should be in a position to make crucial contributions to such fields.

So in Freud's opinion it was a matter of indifference whether candidates for psychoanalytic training held a medical qualification or not. However, Freud insisted that lay analysts were never to function as consultants; the first person to examine the patient must be a doctor, who would then refer suitable cases to the analyst. But there were some countries, such as Austria and France, and some states of the United States, where the law forbade any therapeutic measures being carried out by anyone not possessing a medical qualification. Then in May of 1927 the New York Psychoanalytic Society passed a resolution condemning lay analysis outright, a precipitate action which did not improve the atmosphere. By the spring of 1928 Freud would comment to Ferenczi that "psychoanalysis is everywhere . . . contrary to my intentions . . . becoming a pure medical specialty, and I regard this as fateful for the future of analysis."

FREUD'S HEALTH IN THE NEXT TWO YEARS continued to grow worse. "I find living *for* one's health unbearable," he said. From April 1927 on he took only three patients. He did, however, in that year publish a book, *The Future of an Illusion*, which concerned religion; it started many acrimonious controversies which still continue. And he wrote an extensive essay, "Dostoevsky and Parricide," Freud's last and most brilliant contribution to the psychology of literature. He said: "*The Brothers Karamazov* is the greatest novel that has ever been written, and the episode of the Grand Inquisitor one of the highest achievements of the world's literature." Freud thought far less of Dostoevsky as a man. "That," he wrote a friend, "is because my patience with pathological natures is drained away in actual analyses. In art and in life I am intolerant of them."

When Freud left for his summer vacation on June 16, 1928, he had the company of his first chow, Lun Yu. The following year the dog broke loose in a railroad station and was found run over on the line. Freud remarked that the pain they all felt resembled in quality, though not in intensity, that experienced after the loss of a child. She was replaced by another, Jo-fi, who was a constant companion for seven years.

That spring the discomfort and pain in Freud's mouth had been almost unbearable. His son Ernst had for a year been begging him to consult a famous oral surgeon in Berlin. Freud left on August 30 with Anna as his companion, and they stayed for the first time at the Tegel sanatorium. When he returned to Vienna at the beginning of November his new prosthesis was proving a distinct advance on the previous one, so that life was once more tolerable.

In a year so full of bodily suffering Freud seems to have written nothing at all; it was a quarter of a century since such a statement could have been made.

EARLY IN 1929 the *Verlag* was passing through one of its periodic crises and Freud was greatly relieved when Marie Bonaparte volunteered to save it from bankruptcy. She was a princess of Greece and Denmark, who had come from France to study with Freud, and was another of the several intellectual women who played a part in his life. She had been pressing Freud to engage a regular medical attendant who could watch daily over his general health and also be in contact with the surgeons. She recommended Dr. Max Schur, an excellent internist who had the advantage of being analytically trained as well. Freud gladly agreed. At their first interview Freud laid down the basic rule that Schur should never keep the truth from him, however painful it might be. They shook hands on it. He added, "I can stand a great deal of pain and I hate sedatives, but I trust you will not let me suffer unnecessarily." The time was to come when Freud had to call on Schur to fulfill this request.

Schur and Anna made an ideal pair of guardians to watch over the suffering man and to alleviate his manifold discomforts. Moreover, the two became in time highly competent experts at evaluating the slightest change in the local condition. Their watchful care undoubtedly prolonged Freud's life by years.

Freud was touchingly grateful for any relief. A favorite expression was, "It is no use quarreling with fate." His gracious politeness toward his doctor never wavered.

That summer Freud resumed his literary activity and finished the first draft of a new book, *Civilization and Its Discontents*. In a year's time the edition of twelve thousand was sold out. Freud himself, however, was very dissatisfied with the book. He wrote to Lou Andreas-Salomé: "In writing this work I have discovered afresh the most banal truths."

The main point of the book may be expressed in Freud's words as his "intention to . . . convey that the price of progress in civilization is paid by forfeiting happiness through the heightening of the sense of guilt."

Freud went to Berlin on May 4, 1930, for a new prosthesis to be made. It was during this stay that the American ambassador, W. C. Bullitt, persuaded Freud to cooperate with him in writing a psychoanalytic study of President Wilson's life.

Ambassador Bullitt told me of a remark Freud made to him which shows how hopeful he then was of the Germans' being able to contain the Nazi movement: "A nation that produced Goethe could not possibly go to the bad." It was not long before he was forced to revise this judgment radically.

At the end of July Freud received "a quite charming letter" announcing that the Goethe prize for literature for that year had been awarded to him. Freud had been rated a master of German prose. He had an enormously rich vocabulary. It seemed impossible for him to write even simple sentences without infusing them with something of his originality, elegance, and dignity. The same was true of his conversation; banality, even in the tritest matter, was alien to him, and every remark would be

Freud and his daughter Anna.

trenchant, well turned, and distinctive. Freud's composing had the erratic quality of a poet. He might go for months without feeling that he had anything he wished to write. Then would come some urge of creation, and an important essay would appear in a few weeks, with Freud snatching at high pressure the very few hours he could spare at the end of a day of toil.

The amount of the prize was ten thousand marks, which just covered the expenses of Freud's long stay in Berlin. In Freud's opinion, the association with Goethe made it a specially worthy honor.

Freud had to compose an address for the ceremony, and in it depicted in masterly lines the relation of psychoanalysis to the study of Goethe. He made a convincing plea justifying his intimate psychological studies of great men such as Leonardo and Goethe, "so that if his spirit reproaches me in the next world for adopting the same attitude toward him likewise I shall simply quote his own words in defense." Anna Freud read this at the dignified ceremony that took place at the Goethe House in Frankfort on August 28.

In the same eventful month of 1930 Freud's mother was in a dangerous state from gangrene of the leg, the pain of which necessitated the constant use of morphine. She died in Vienna on September 12, aged ninety-five. Freud described to two of us his response to the event. "No pain, no grief . . . a feeling of liberation, of release. . . . I was not allowed to die as long as she was alive, and now I may. Somehow the values of life have notably changed in the deeper layers."

FREUD USED OFTEN TO EXPRESS in a half-jocular tone his intense dislike of ceremonies. "When someone abuses me I can defend myself, but against praise I am defenseless," he once said in explanation of his failure to attend a festival in his honor. By January 1931 his seventy-fifth birthday was already casting its shadow ahead. Freud had unwillingly consented to a fund being collected for the occasion, his motive being the acute need of money for the *Verlag*.

On April 24 another operation was carried out on a suspicious spot and a pretty large piece excised, "at the twelfth hour," on the point of becoming definitely malignant.

For eight years the hope had been entertained that the first radical jaw operation had led to a permanent cure. Now that hope had vanished. Freud had to face a future that was to endure still another eight years, and could only consist of watching for further recurrences and combatting them as early as possible. He never left Vienna again until his flight from the Nazis in 1938.

Freud returned from the sanatorium on May 4, so to the family's relief he was able to spend his birthday at home. But there was no seventy-fifth birthday celebration in Vienna.

We had collected a fund of fifty thousand marks, and Eitingon sent Freud a check for twenty thousand marks to repay *Verlag* debts. The rest he proposed to give to Freud himself as part payment for the royalties long due to him. From the beginning Freud had refused to accept any royalties whatever from the *Verlag* for the sale of his books, and by now they had amounted to 76,500 marks. Freud, however, sternly refused to touch a penny of this sum.

Naturally there was a mass of congratulatory letters and telegrams, including one from Einstein. Not to mention "a forest of splendid flowers." Thanking Marie Bonaparte for the Grecian vase she had sent he added, "it is a pity one cannot take it into one's grave"; a wish that was strangely fulfilled, since his ashes now repose in that vase.

In October the town council of Freiberg honored Freud by placing a bronze tablet on the house in which he was born. The streets were beflagged for the ceremony. But Freud said, "The world has changed its treatment of me into an unwilling recognition, but only to show me how little that really matters. What a contrast a bearable prosthesis would be."

CHAPTER TEN

WE COME NOW to a period when external events began to press on Freud's life and on the psychoanalytical movement in general. The world economic crisis was in full swing in 1931, and in every country analysts were feeling the pinch badly in their practices. Since only a handful could afford to attend the congress due to take place that autumn, we decided to postpone it for another year. Far more serious was the real crisis in the affairs of the *Verlag*. Martin Freud had resigned his position in a bank in order to take over its management. Now it cost all his efforts to come to a compromise with one creditor after the other; but by the end of the year he had accomplished this difficult task.

The year 1933, however, brought still more serious crises. In March, after the fateful Reichstag fire in Berlin had proved to be a prelude to the assumption of dictatorial powers by Adolf

Hitler, and the signal for widespread persecutions by the Nazis, Freud wrote to Marie Bonaparte in France: "I have even been advised to flee . . . to Switzerland or France. . . . I am firmly resolved to await [danger] here. If they kill me—good. It is one kind of death like another. But probably that is only cheap boasting."

The first signal of how psychoanalysis would be affected came on April 17, 1933, when the German analyst Felix Boehm visited Freud in Vienna to tell him of the new order that no Jews were to serve on any scientific council. Freud was of the opinion that it would be wise not to give the government the pretext of forbidding psychoanalysis in Germany by refraining from making the change, and he agreed that Boehm, who was not Jewish, replace Max Eitingon on the council.

One of those advising Freud to flee was his old friend Sandor Ferenczi, writing from Budapest. For several months Ferenczi had been suffering from pernicious anemia; in March the disease attacked the spinal cord and brain. Ferenczi now was unable to stand. In Freud's last letter to his old friend he wrote:

> As to the flight motif, I am not thinking of leaving Vienna. I am . . . too dependent on my treatment. . . . Probably, however, I should stay even if I were in full health and youth. In my opinion flight would only be justified by direct danger to life. . . .
>
> Only a few hours ago Ernstl [Freud's grandson] arrived from Berlin after disagreeable experiences in Dresden and on the frontier. He is German and so cannot go back; after today no German Jew will be allowed to leave the country. . . . I hope you will remain undisturbed in Budapest and soon send me good news of your condition.

Ferenczi now had delusions about Freud's supposed hostility. Toward the end, as if to remind us all once more how terrible can be the power of the lurking demons within, came violent paranoiac and even homicidal outbursts, which were followed by a sudden death on May 24.

That was the tragic end of a brilliant, lovable personality who had for a quarter of a century been Freud's closest friend.

Freud replied to my letter of condolence: "Ferenczi takes with him a part of the old time. . . . Fate. Resignation. That is all."

On Freud's birthday Schur as usual examined his condition. Schur's wife was expecting a baby which was nine days overdue. Freud urged him to hasten back to his wife, and on parting said in a meditative tone, "You are going from a man who doesn't want to leave the world to a child who doesn't want to come into it."

With his great fondness for children Freud always took a special interest in the news of a fresh arrival. I told him about this same time that we were expecting another baby, and when I notified him of the event, these were his reflections: "I no longer feel anxious about the future of psychoanalysis. It is assured, and I know it to be in good hands. But the future of my children and grandchildren is endangered and my own helplessness is distressing."

THE TIDE OF JEWISH EMIGRATION from Germany was soon in full flood. Some emigrant psychoanalysts would find a resting place, for a year or two, in Copenhagen, Oslo, Stockholm, Strasbourg, and Zurich, but the majority ultimately reached America. Among them were Karen Horney, going to New York, and Hanns Sachs, who had already settled in Boston. But Freud reported: "One can be sure that the Hitler movement will extend to Austria . . . but it is very improbable that it signifies the same kind of danger as in Germany."

Nor did the Nazi bonfire of his books in Berlin, which took place at the end of May, much perturb him. His smiling comment was: "What progress we are making. In the Middle Ages they would have burnt me; nowadays they are content with burning my books." He was never to know that even that was only an illusory progress, that ten years later they would have burned his body as well.

Then in June 1933 the German Society for Psychotherapy came under Nazi control. Reichsfuhrer Dr. Hermann Göring explained that all members were expected to make a thorough study of Hitler's *Mein Kampf*, which was to serve as the basis for their work. Ernst Kretschmer, who two years earlier had paid

Freud a birthday tribute, promptly resigned as president. His place was as promptly taken by Freud's onetime disciple, C. G. Jung. Jung also became editor of the official organ, the *Zentralblatt für Psychotherapie.* His chief function was to discriminate between Aryan psychology and Jewish psychology, and to emphasize the value of the former. Afterward Jung would be severely criticized in many quarters for his departure from the neutrality of science.

In November 1933 official Nazi psychotherapists announced that the only chance of psychoanalysis being allowed to continue lay in the exclusion of all Jewish members from the German society. The various branches of science were being "nationalized" and brought under a central control.

By the end of 1933, then, Karl Abraham and Sandor Ferenczi were dead, Rank had left us, Sachs was in Boston, and Eitingon was in Palestine. I was the only remaining member in Europe of the little group who for so long had been defending Freud's theories. And Freud himself was commenting: "The world is turning into an enormous prison. . . . [It] seems to me to have lost its vitality and to be doomed to perdition."

THE YEAR 1934 saw the "liquidation" of psychoanalysis in Germany. Twenty years afterward the knowledge of Freud and his works there would still be at a lower level than, for instance, in Brazil or Japan. It was in this year that Freud conceived, and for the most part wrote, his ideas on Moses and religion, ideas that were to engross him for the rest of his life.

In January 1935 he wrote to Lou Andreas-Salomé a full account, several pages long, of his ideas about Moses and religion. They culminated in a formula to the effect that religion owes its strength not to any real literal truth, but to an historical truth it contains. He concluded: "One cannot publish this formula, which has quite fascinated me, in Austria today without running the risk of the Catholic authorities officially forbidding the practice of analysis. And only this Catholicism protects us against Naziism. . . . So I remain silent. It is enough that I myself can believe in the solution of the problem. It has pursued me through my whole life."

THE AMERICAN PUBLISHERS of his *Autobiographical Study*, Brentano, asked him that summer to write a supplement to it. In it he expressed his regret at having ever published details of his private life and advised his friends never to do the same.

Freud was to celebrate his eightieth birthday in the year 1936. He wrote to me: "What is the secret meaning of this celebrating the big round numbers of one's life? Surely a measure of triumph over the transitoriness of life, which, as we never forget, is ready to devour us."

When the day arrived Freud's rooms turned into a flower shop of bouquets. One of the many callers asked Freud how he felt and received the answer: "How a man of eighty feels is not a topic for conversation." At the same time Freud was made an honorary member of the American Psychoanalytic Association, the French Psychoanalytical Society, the New York Neurological Society, and the Royal Medico-Psychological Association. Above all there was the highest recognition he ever received and the one he most treasured: he was made a corresponding member of the Royal Society.

That summer Freud underwent two exceptionally painful operations, and for the first time since the original one in 1923 unmistakable cancer was found to be present. For the last five years the doctors had been warding it off by removing precancerous tissue, but now they knew they were face-to-face with the enemy itself and must expect constant recurrences of the malignancy.

On September 13 Freud's golden wedding anniversary was quietly celebrated. Four of his surviving children were present. He commented in a characteristically succinct understatement: "It was really not a bad solution of the marriage problem, and she is still today tender, healthy and active."

And at the end of the year Anna detected another suspicious spot. Freud wrote: "Pichler told me he was obliged to burn [it] . . . the reaction was frightful. . . . I carry on with my analyses by changing a hot water bottle every half hour to hold by my cheek. I get slight relief from short wave therapy. . . . I wish you could have seen what sympathy Jo-fi [the chow] shows me in my suffering, just as if she understood everything."

The operation was the only occasion in the long travail when Freud cried out, "I can't go on any longer." But Pichler's iron nerve enabled him to complete the operation.

In January 1937 Jo-fi died. Freud, feeling he could not get on without a dog, took back from Dorothy Burlingham, a close family friend, another chow called Lün which he had had to transfer to her four years before on account of Jo-fi's jealousy.

THE NAZI INVASION OF AUSTRIA, which took place on March 12, 1938, was the signal for Freud to follow the road his ancestors had so often wearily trod, and leave his home for a foreign land. But something deep in his nature had always striven against such a decision and at this final and critical moment he was still unwilling to contemplate it. I decided to make a final effort to persuade Freud to change his mind.

There were no airplanes flying to Vienna just then, but I got one on March 15 as far as Prague and there found a small monoplane that completed the journey. The airfield was stacked with German military planes and the air was full of them assiduously intimidating the Viennese. The streets were crowded with roaring tanks and also with roaring people shouting "Heil Hitler," but it was easy to see that most of these were Germans from the trainloads Hitler had sent in for the purpose.

After calling at my sister-in-law's, where Anna Freud got in touch with me, I went first, on her advice, to the premises of the *Verlag,* where we hoped that my asserting its international character might be of use. The stairs and rooms were occupied by villainous-looking youths armed with daggers and pistols, Martin Freud was sitting in a corner under arrest, and the Nazi "authorities" were engaged in counting the petty cash in a drawer. As soon as I spoke I was also put under arrest, and their remarks when I asked to be allowed to communicate with the British Embassy showed me how low my country's prestige had fallen after Hitler's successes. After an hour, however, I was released and then made my way down the street to Freud's residence.

A curious scene had been taking place there. It had been invaded by a similar gang, and two or three of them had forced their way into the dining room. Mrs. Freud, as people do in an emergency, had responded with the essence of her personality. In her most hospitable manner she invited the sentry at the door to be seated; as she said afterward, she found it unpleasant to see a stranger standing up in her home. This caused some embarrassment, which was heightened by her next move. Fetching the household money she placed it on the table with the words, so familiar to her at the dinner table, "Won't the gentlemen help themselves?" Anna Freud then escorted them to the safe in another room and opened it. The loot amounted to six thousand Austrian schillings.

Just then a frail and gaunt figure appeared in the doorway. It was Freud, aroused by the disturbance. He had a way of frowning with blazing eyes that any Old Testament prophet might have envied, and the effect produced by his lowering mien completed the visitors' discomfiture. They hastily took their departure.

Immediately after this I had a heart-to-heart talk with Freud. To my first plea, that he was not alone in the world and that his life was dear to many people, he replied with a sigh: "Alone. Ah, if I were only alone I should long ago have done with life." But he had to admit the force of what I had said and then proceeded to argue that he was too weak to climb up to a compartment, as one has to with Continental trains. This not being accepted, he pointed out that no country would allow him to enter. There was certainly force in this argument; it is hardly possible nowadays for people to understand how ferociously inhospitable every country was to would-be immigrants, so strong was the feeling about unemployment.

I could only ask Freud to allow me on my return to England to see if an exception could not possibly be made in his case. Then came his last declaration. He could not leave his native land; it would be like a soldier deserting his post. I successfully countered this attitude by quoting the analogy of Lightoller, the second officer of the *Titanic* who never left his ship but whom his ship left; and this won his final acceptance.

That was the first hurdle, and possibly the hardest. The second one, that of obtaining permission to live in England, I felt pretty hopeful about. The third one, persuading the Nazis to release Freud, I could do nothing about, but great men often have more friends, even in high places, than they know of.

W. C. Bullitt, then American ambassador in France, was a personal friend of President Roosevelt, and he immediately cabled to him asking him to intervene. Roosevelt got his Secretary of State to send instructions to his chargé d'affaires in Vienna, Mr. Wiley, to do all he could in the matter. Mr. Wiley called on Freud on the evening of the first Nazi raid described above, and from then on kept a watchful eye on what was happening. In

Paris, Bullitt called on Graf von Welczeck, the German ambassador to France, and let him know in no uncertain terms what a world scandal would ensue if the Nazis ill-treated Freud. Welczeck, being a man of culture and a humanitarian, needed no persuading, and at once took steps to bring the matter before the highest Nazi authorities. Edoardo Weiss, who was at the time in close contact with the Duce, tells me that Mussolini also made a *démarche*, either directly to Hitler or to his ambassador in Vienna. This was at the moment

Freud at eighty-two.

when Hitler was feeling genuine gratitude toward Mussolini for the free hand he had been given in the seizure of Austria.

So between one thing and another the Nazis would eventually decide they dared not risk refusing Freud an exit permit, though they were determined to exact their pound of flesh first.

The few days I could spend in Vienna were hectic ones. A Nazi commissar arrived from Berlin with the purpose of liquidating the psychoanalytical situation. A meeting of the board of the Vienna society had decided that everyone should flee the country if possible, and that the seat of the society should be wherever Freud would settle.

So there was nothing for the Germans to take over and they

had to be content with seizing the library of the society, not to mention the whole property of the *Verlag*.

On March 17 Marie Bonaparte arrived from Paris and I felt easier about leaving Vienna for the urgent task of seeking permits in England. My first act on reaching London was to obtain a letter of introduction to Sir William Bragg, the famous physicist who was then the president of the Royal Society. I saw him the next day and he at once gave me a letter to Sir Samuel Hoare, the Home Secretary. Sir Samuel Hoare without hesitation gave me carte blanche to fill in permits, including permission to work, for Freud, his family, his servants, his personal doctors, and a certain number of his pupils with their families.

There remained the greater difficulty of obtaining permission from the Nazis to leave. In Vienna the Gestapo had come again to Freud's home and made a thorough search of the rooms, allegedly seeking for political anti-Nazi documents; significantly enough, they did not enter Freud's own rooms. When they departed the Gestapo took Anna Freud away with them.

It was certainly the blackest day in Freud's life. There had grown up in these years a deep silent understanding between father and daughter, a communication almost telepathic in quality. The daughter's devotion was as absolute as the father's appreciation of it and the gratitude it evoked. The thought that this most precious being in the world, on whom he so depended, might be in danger of being tortured and deported to a concentration camp was not to be borne. Freud spent the whole day pacing up and down and smoking an endless series of cigars. When Anna returned at seven o'clock that evening—the American chargé d'affaires, Mr. Wiley, having intervened by telephone with some success—Freud's emotions were no longer to be restrained.

Nearly three months of anxious waiting followed. The Nazi authorities demanded large sums of money under imaginary captions of income tax, *Reichsfluchtsteuer* (fugitive tax), and so on. Marie Bonaparte advanced some Austrian schillings for the purpose. The inquisition proceeded in great detail. When, for instance, the Nazis found that Martin Freud had for safety been keeping a store of Freud's *Collected Works* in a neutral country,

Switzerland, they insisted that his father issue instructions for them to be brought back to Vienna, to be ceremoniously burned. Of course Freud's bank account was confiscated.

There were many ways of killing the weary time of waiting. Freud went through his books and read guidebooks about London; and there was still correspondence. He wrote: "I also work for an hour a day at my Moses, which torments me like a 'ghost not laid.' "

In May the chances of obtaining an exit permit were getting more hopeful. Freud wrote to his son Ernst in London: "I sometimes compare myself with the old Jacob whom in his old age his children brought to Egypt. It is to be hoped that the result will not be the same, an exodus from Egypt. It is time for Ahasverus [the wandering Jew] to come to rest somewhere."

The first member of the family to be allowed to travel was Minna Bernays, whom Dorothy Burlingham escorted to London; they left Vienna on May 5. Freud's eldest son, Martin (whose wife and children were already in Paris), and daughter, Mathilde Hollitscher (with her husband), both managed to get away before their parents.

Freud retained his ironic attitude toward the complicated formalities that had to be gone through. One of the conditions for being granted an exit visa was that he sign a document that ran as follows: "I Prof. Freud, hereby confirm that after the Anschluss . . . I have been treated by the German authorities and particularly by the Gestapo with all the respect and consideration due to my scientific reputation." When the Nazi commissar brought it along Freud asked if he might add a sentence, which was: "I can heartily recommend the Gestapo to anyone."

At last on June 4, armed with the exit permits, Freud, with his wife and daughter and two maidservants, took a final leave of the city where he had dwelt for seventy-nine years.

AT THREE O'CLOCK the next morning they crossed the frontier into France on the Orient Express. They were met in Paris by Marie Bonaparte, Ambassador Bullitt, and Ernst Freud, who was to accompany them on the last stage of their journey. They spent twelve wonderful hours in Marie Bonaparte's beautiful home, then crossed the English Channel by night on the ferry-boat to Dover.

In London we made a quick getaway in my car, and I drove past Buckingham Palace to Piccadilly Circus and up Regent Street, Freud eagerly pointing out each landmark to his wife. The first stop was at 39, Elsworthy Road, where Ernst Freud had rented a house while he was searching for a permanent home. The garden abutted on Primrose Hill with Regent's Park beyond and a distant view of the city.

Freud's heart had stood the journey better than he expected, though it had needed several doses of nitroglycerine and strychnine to carry him through. On his first stroll into the garden he threw up his arms and made the famous remark to me: "I am almost tempted to cry out 'Heil Hitler.' "

The change from his long confinement to his flat in Vienna cheered him enormously, and he had moments of great happiness. This was added to by the welcome with which he was received in England. The newspapers were for a few days full of friendly accounts of Freud's arrival. There were gifts of valuable antiques from people who evidently shared Freud's uncertainty about getting his collection sent from Vienna. Freud wrote two days after his arrival: "Numerous letters from strangers who only wish to say how happy they are that . . . we are in safety and peace. Really as if our concern were theirs as well."

The medical journals published leading articles expressing welcome. One such, the *Lancet*, wrote: "His teachings have in their time aroused controversy more acute and antagonism more bitter than any since the days of Darwin. Now, in his old age, there are few psychologists of any school who do not admit their debt to him. Some of the conceptions he formulated clearly for the first time have crept into current philosophy against the stream of wilful incredulity which he himself recognised as man's natural reaction to unbearable truth."

It was not entirely unmixed happiness. Not having any prospect of maintaining them in London, Freud had had to leave his four old sisters, Rosa Graf, Dolfi Freud, Marie Freud, and Paula Winternitz, in Vienna. Fortunately Freud never knew of their fate; they were incinerated some five years later.

THE FAMILY COULD NOT STAY LONG in the house they had rented temporarily. Freud and his wife and daughter went to the Esplanade Hotel in Warrington Crescent on September 3. But a new suspicious spot had been discovered in the scar, and Freud was transferred to a surgical clinic. Pichler was fetched from Vienna and he performed the operation, which lasted two and a quarter hours: the most severe operation since the original radical one in 1923. Freud never really fully recovered, and became more and more frail.

Mrs. Freud and Paula Fichtl, one of the maids who had come with them from Vienna, were installed in a permanent home at 20, Maresfield Gardens on September 16. Freud and Anna joined them, and he was highly pleased with it. There was a roomy garden behind the house, its beds and borders well stocked with flowers and shrubs; rows of high trees secluded it from neighboring houses. Freud spent as much time as possible here, in a comfortable swing couch shaded by a canopy. All his furniture, books, and antiquities had arrived safely in London, and his large consulting room, now filled with his loved possessions, opened through French windows directly into the garden. Paula's memory enabled her to replace the various objects on Freud's desk in their precise order.

Among Freud's callers in the early days were H. G. Wells; Professor Abraham Yahuda, the learned Jewish historian, who begged Freud not to publish his Moses book; and Chaim Weizmann, the famous Zionist leader, whom Freud held in the highest esteem.

Stefan Zweig brought Salvador Dali to visit, and the famous painter made a sketch of him on the spot, maintaining that surrealistically Freud's cranium was reminiscent of a snail! On the following day Freud wrote to Stefan Zweig: "Until now I have been inclined to regard the surrealists, who apparently have adopted me as their patron saint, as complete fools. . . . That young Spaniard, with his candid fanatical eyes and his undeniable technical mastery, has changed my estimate. It would indeed be very interesting to investigate analytically how he came to create that picture."

By the end of the year Freud had so far recovered as to be

able to conduct four analyses daily. He had managed to add the finishing touches to the third part of his Moses book before his operation, and it was printed in Amsterdam by August; that German edition sold some two thousand copies by the following summer. He wrote: "The Moses is not an unworthy leave-taking."

WE APPROACH THE END. At Christmas 1938 a swelling appeared and gradually took on an increasingly ominous look. A biopsy had disclosed an unmistakable malignant recurrence, but the surgeons decided it was inaccessible and that no further operation was feasible.

So the case bore now the fatal title "inoperable, incurable cancer." Daily administration of Roentgen rays gave Freud a few more weeks of life during which he could continue his analytic sessions.

Marie Bonaparte got the last letter she was ever to receive from him: "My world is again what it was before—a little island of pain floating on a sea of indifference." By July 1939 his condition was much worse. There was a cancerous ulceration attacking the cheek and the base of the eye cavity. Even his best friend, his sound sleep which had sustained him so long, was now deserting him.

Freud, like all good doctors, was averse to taking drugs. As he put it once: "I prefer to think in torment than not to be able to think clearly." Now, however, he consented to take an occasional dose of aspirin. And he managed somehow to continue with his analytic work until the end of July. In August everything went downhill rapidly. A distressing symptom was an unpleasant odor from the wound, so that Lün, his favorite chow, shrank into a far corner of the room, a heartrending experience which revealed to the sick man the pass he had reached. He was getting very weak and spent his time in a sick bay in his study from which he could gaze at the flowers in the garden.

He followed world events to the end. As the Second World War approached he was confident it would mean the end of Hitler. But when a broadcast announced that this was to be the last war, and Dr. Schur asked him if he believed that, he could only reply: "Anyhow it is my last war."

The cancer ate its way through the cheek to the outside. The exhaustion was extreme and the misery indescribable. On September 19 I was sent for to say good-by to him and called him by name as he dozed. He opened his eyes, recognized me, and waved his hand, then dropped it with a highly expressive gesture that said as plainly as possible: The rest is silence. In a second he fell asleep again.

On September 21 Freud said to his doctor: "My dear Schur, you remember our first talk. You promised me then you would help me when I could no longer carry on. It is only torture now and it has no longer any sense." Schur pressed his hand and promised he would give him adequate sedation. Freud thanked him, adding after a moment of hesitation: "Tell Anna about our talk." There was no emotionalism or self-pity, only reality.

The next morning Schur gave Freud a third of a grain of morphine. For someone at such a point of exhaustion as Freud then was, and so complete a stranger to opiates, that small dose sufficed. He sighed with relief and sank into a peaceful sleep. He died just before midnight the next day, September 23, 1939. His long and arduous life was at an end and his sufferings over.

Freud's body was cremated at Golder's Green on the morning of September 26 in the presence of a large number of mourners. The family asked me to deliver the funeral oration. Stefan Zweig then made a long speech in German which was doubtless more eloquent than mine but which could not have been more deeply felt.

GOOD NIGHT,
SWEET PRINCE

A CONDENSATION OF

GOOD NIGHT, SWEET PRINCE

The Life and Times of John Barrymore

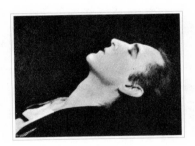

by
GENE FOWLER

Called the greatest actor of this century, John
Barrymore lived life on a huge scale.
Publicly, he was a colorful centerpiece for
America's Gilded Age—handsome, witty, flamboyant,
unpredictable. In private, he was a spendthrift
playboy, four times married, who often fell prey to
immoderate passions.

Yet behind the quixotic exterior was a
good-hearted, appealing man, and once on stage
he could turn in electrifying performances. By
the end of his life, tragic though it sometimes was,
both theater and films had been vastly enriched
by his presence.

PROLOGUE

I WAS A REPORTER for the New York *American* when I first met my friend John Barrymore. A sports writer on temporary loan to the theatrical department, I had been sent to get an interview with the actor who was then starring in the Tolstoy play *Redemption*.

I found him in his dressing room at the Plymouth Theatre after a matinee performance. He was perspiring and swearing eloquently, while molting a false beard. I never had seen him before, on or off stage, and when he rose to put on his somewhat seedy coat, I noticed that he was athletic, had an extraordinary sense of balance, and moved on the balls of his feet like a boxer.

He was on his way to see the Baron. "The Baron," he explained, "is my only true friend."

The star of *Redemption* now put on a fedora, a vintage number in every respect. It might once have been forest green. But as he adjusted the crown, giving it certain deft tugs and pats, it suddenly took on a quality of magnificence.

"The only reason why a man should pay the least attention to a hat," he said, as we went outside the theater, "is that it is something one tips to a lady."

It was twilight as we walked into the West Forties, and the last of the matineegoers, stragglers from other playhouses, were turning to look at the eminent actor. In that decent era, shortly after the end of World War I, autograph seekers had not yet begun to pounce like gadflies upon their celebrities. Barrymore caught the attention of the Broadway pedestrians but did not take much notice of them. Vanity was not among his vices.

"You'll love the Baron," he said. "He is a savant, a philosopher, the seventh son of a seventh son, and one of the greatest alchemists since Trismegistus. The Baron is seeking the philosophers' stone."

The Baron, I discovered in due time, was making gin.

Soon after we arrived at the Baron's boardinghouse lodgings, where we were greeted warmly by our host and his elderly pug dog, I found myself standing with Barrymore in the dark hall outside a tiny bathroom, watching the celebrated alchemist at his labors over an ancient zinc bathtub.

"Prohibition enforcement will not find me napping," announced the Baron, a small balding fellow of perhaps seventy. He was busy diluting some alcohol with juniper essence.

Barrymore and I, meanwhile, were speaking of pug dogs. The affection the Baron's dog had displayed for the actor was evidently mutual. And I was interested because this was the first pug I had seen since my own had gone mad and been chloroformed when I was a child.

"I don't think you'll find many pug dogs left in this whole world," Barrymore said.

"I had one," I replied.

He now looked at me with genuine interest. His bantering manner fell like a bullfighter's cape. "You really owned one? Tell me about him."

"There's not much to tell," I said. "I was living with my grandmother . . ."

"You *were?*" he asked, with such emphasis that I hesitated a moment.

"Is there anything remarkable about having lived with one's grandmother?"

"Yes," he said quietly. "Yes, there is." There was no mistaking his sincerity. "The only bringing up I ever had was by my grandmother, Mrs. Drew. . . ."

He seemed to catch himself being sentimental. He called to the Baron, "Are you dissolving a pearl?"

"All in good time," the Baron replied gently.

I found Barrymore studying me in the half-light from the bathroom door. "I interrupted you," he said. "The pug dog?"

"He went mad," I replied. "I couldn't understand why they had put him under a wooden washtub, then placed a rag soaked with something beneath the tub, and my uncle standing there like an elephant hunter being photographed after the kill."

"What did you do?" he asked slowly.

"I yelled my head off. And told my grandmother I'd never forgive my uncle. She was a religious woman. She told me what a sin it was not to forgive—anything. She said that Jesus always had forgiven everybody. I remember how terribly shocked she was when I blurted out, 'Yes, but He never had a dog.' "

Until now we had not shaken hands, nor had Barrymore even asked my name. He put out his hand, and said, "Hello!"

The Baron, carrying a filled jug, emerged from the bathroom, an aura of ecclesiastical peace upon him.

We followed him back to his quarters and sampled his experimental nectar, drinking from cracked china cups with no handles. Then we helped ourselves to another portion.

Suddenly Barrymore remembered he was due at the theater.

"Good God!" he said. "Time to smear on the paint and pretend I'm somebody else."

It wasn't until we were on our way back to the theater that I remembered I had been sent to get an interview.

CHAPTER I

A GLASSED-IN CARRIAGE with an Irish coachman drew up at the entrance of the old Chestnut Street wharf in Philadelphia on a cold, rainy Saint Valentine's Day, 1882. Sitting upright in this smart brougham, looking rather like the Queen Victoria of calendar chromos, was a smallish lady, caped with a dolman of embossed black velvet, who did not seem her sixty-two years. There was authority in the way she sat on the broadcloth cushions, a regal fire in the large, bright blue eyes. Even the dullest beer guzzler among the passing rivermen could sense that she was a personage.

This was Louisa Lane Drew, manager of the Arch Street Theatre; widow of John Drew, a fine actor who had died young; and herself in her fifty-seventh season of footlights and grease-paint, having recently returned home after thirteen weeks as the famous Mrs. Malaprop in Sheridan's *The Rivals*. Mrs. Drew was presently awaiting the arrival of one Dr. J. Nicholas Mitchell on the steamboat from Wilmington. She had summoned the family doctor home from his emergency labors in Delaware, fighting cholera, because her actress daughter, Georgianna Drew, wife of actor Maurice Barrymore, was momentarily expecting a third child.

She *was* history, this woman. Born the same year in which King George III had died, 1820, her parents, players of provincial reputation, had brought her at the age of seven from England to Philadelphia. Here, at nine, when she had played all five roles in *Twelve Precisely*, a Revolutionary War veteran had come backstage to hold her on his knee. She had listened to the Liberty Bell tolling in 1834 for the death of Lafayette; and a year afterward heard its last note, as the great bell cracked while sounding the requiem for Chief Justice John Marshall. A block to the east of her Arch Street Theatre lay the wise bones of Benjamin Franklin, and a square beyond his grave the Betsy Ross house.

Now a whistle sounded. "She's a-dockin'!" the coachman announced. Soon the doctor came ashore, carrying a battered clinical valise and an umbrella, and he and the expectant grandmother were at once driven through the rain to a three-story brick house at Number 2008 Columbia Avenue.

This was not so fine a home as might have been expected of the successful manager of a famous theater, one who maintained a coachman and brougham, a cook and maids; still, it was not commonplace. Mrs. Drew was prospering at this time. An adroit actress-manager, she had persuaded Edwin Booth, Joseph Jefferson, and others of public favor to appear before her footlights, and her own achievements as an actress enlarged her personal income. Yet, underneath the armor plate of her dignity was a warm generosity. Always she shared her purse and herself; her several successive homes sheltered her children and theirs, and an assortment of poor relations. Perhaps she regarded the saving of money too lightly, a quirk that became manifest in her talented descendants.

As she and the doctor entered the hallway, a maid helped her remove the dolman, and informed her that an actor who was appearing at the theater in a new comedy that night was in the parlor. "He's excited," the maid reported.

Mrs. Drew removed her plumed turban. "Never mind him. How's Georgie?"

"She's havin' pains."

Mrs. Drew turned to the doctor, gesturing toward the stairs with a long hatpin. "I think you know the way, Doctor," she said, and followed him up, ignoring the distraught actor who emerged from the parlor to call after them, "It's about the scenery. My cliff has been lost." But Mrs. Drew had disappeared.

As the actor turned to go back to the parlor, Mrs. Drew's favorite son, Sidney Drew, appeared in the hallway carrying his sister Georgianna's three-year-old Ethel, and followed by four-year-old Lionel, burbling happily.

"I've lost my cliff," said the actor, solemnly eyeing the Barrymore children while addressing himself to Sidney. "Your mother pays no attention whatsoever."

In her daughter's bedroom, Mrs. Drew was paying attention to the new baby boy she held in her arms. "He looks like a pretty little lad in a storybook," said his grandmother.

John Sidney Blythe Barrymore had arrived.

JOHN BARRYMORE'S FATHER, Maurice, a much-loved, sometimes envied man of wit, charm, and outstanding physical endowments, had first come to America some seven years before the birth of his younger son, having crossed to New York from Liverpool in the spring of 1875. At that time, Maurice Barrymore's fellow passengers, mostly of English stock themselves, had accounted their twenty-eight-year-old shipmate an amiable dandy, and were uncritical of the tall silk hat and monocle he wore. But when he went ashore he attracted considerable attention.

As soon as he had cleared the customs at Castle Garden, Maurice, deciding not to ride the horsecar, started walking confidently up Broadway as if on a familiar round. Soon he entered the famed Hoffman House Bar, where he ordered a whiskey and soda, without ice, his speech as neatly clipped as the hedges of Oxford University. The bartender pretended not to notice the eyeglass, the silk hat, or the un-American request for no ice, but not the guests in this best of all possible bars. They stared, nudged their companions, and several were not satisfied to let Mr. Barrymore mind his own thirst.

Their leader, a locally renowned social light and all-around athlete, placed a silver dollar in his eye, leaned toward Mr. Barrymore, and drawled, "I say, Percy, I suppose this is the *English* way? Wot?"

"Oh, no," replied the actor, removing his monocle and settling the silk hat to his head. "Allow me to show you." His fist traveled a short, jolting arc. "*This* is the English way!"

The spectators sucked in their breaths. Their leader lay like a dissected frog on the tiles, while the Barrymore hat remained as solidly on his head as a cornice. Lifted to his feet and informed where he was, the vanquished sportsman blinked, then put out his hand to Barrymore. He was delighted to learn, in the friendly conversation that ensued, that his conqueror, during student days at Oxford, had been amateur lightweight champion of England.

During this and other evenings at the Hoffman House, Maurice Barrymore's new friends learned many other things about him. He had been born in India, in 1847, as Herbert Blythe, son of an army officer. Sent to England for his formal education, he finally matriculated at Lincoln College, Oxford, where he occupied the rooms of John Wesley. Upon leaving there, his family had decided that he should read for the law, which he proceeded to do.

Yet Herbert Blythe really wished to be an actor, an ambition that horrified his elders. When he obtained his first acting role, therefore, he had assumed the stage name Maurice Barrymore,

Maurice Barrymore, and, at right, his wife, Georgianna Drew with Ethel, Lionel and John.

Above, Maurice and Georgie together; at left, Maurice's mother, Mrs. John Drew.

a name he had once seen on an old playbill hanging in the foyer of London's Haymarket Theatre. Then, forsaking the law forever, he had toured the provinces until, after a series of family harangues against theatricals, he had finally left for America.

During those first several months in New York, Maurice Barrymore lived rather scantily. But, in the autumn of 1875, he became a member of the famous stock company founded by Augustin Daly. There he met the twenty-two-year-old John Drew, Jr., himself destined to become one of the most accomplished actors on the American stage, but now only a short time away from Louisa Lane Drew's apron strings, having made his debut in a minor role in his mother's Philadelphia theater. Together Drew and Maurice appeared in support of Edwin Booth's eighty-fourth appearance as Hamlet. Maurice was Laertes, and Drew was Rosencrantz.

At the close of the *Hamlet* engagement, John Drew said to Maurice, "I'm going home for the weekend. Like to come along?" Barrymore accompanied his friend to Philadelphia, there to meet John's younger sister, Georgianna, herself a talented actress, and, after a swift courtship, to marry her.

Mrs. Drew did not bless the merger. She not only had little respect for any actor whose family, unlike her own, had not been professionals for at least fifty years, but she also believed no one good enough for her daughter, particularly an irresponsible dreamer like this new son-in-law. She consistently addressed him as "you," nor did he feel safe to address her as other than "Ma'am." He may have been amateur lightweight champion of England, but in her house *she* was the champion.

CHAPTER 2

GEORGIANNA, after her marriage to Maurice Barrymore, appeared with her husband and her brother as well as far better known players like Edwin Booth and Mme. Helena Modjeska. She also became a Catholic, for Mme. Modjeska converted her from the Episcopal faith of her upbringing. Mrs. Drew was well pleased by her daughter's choice of career, and, being a believer in freedom of religion, neither opposed nor approved her change of creed. As for Maurice, it made no difference to him so long as Georgie was satisfied.

Georgianna won the favor of critics and public, and was best known as a skilled comedienne. Her daughter, Ethel Barrymore, later said of her: "My mother was blond, fair, and gay. She was a natural actress, so restrained in word and action that many persons could not appreciate her. She was twenty-five years ahead of her time."

The Drew household in Philadelphia readily expanded to include Maurice and Georgie Barrymore, whenever they were not on tour, and, eventually, their children too. Mrs. Drew was a burden bearer. No matter how many relatives thronged her home, she never complained. Whenever the increase strained domestic comfort, she would promptly move to more commodious quarters. Of these successive residences which they shared with their grandmother, Lionel, Ethel, and John remembered best the house at Number 140 North Twelfth Street, near the Arch Street Theatre. It was a three-story building with cavernous halls, a nursery known as "The Annex," and two attics. The boys slept in one of the attics. Across the street was a tombstone carver, samples of whose handiwork occupied the sidewalk in front of his establishment, and Georgie named their house the "Tomb of the Capulets."

Some overnight actor guests thought the place well named, for the faint tinklings of a little bell could be heard at all hours of the night, like something from the Great Beyond. Not daring to ask—people of the theater have an absorbing respect for the supernatural—the guests seldom learned that the ghostly sound came from the bedroom of the aged, bedridden Eliza Lane Kinloch, Mrs. Drew's mother and great-grandmother to the Barrymore children, who had been a sweet singer of ballads in England, where she was born in 1799. She would tinkle a little bell, like that used by Punch in the old puppet shows, whenever she needed attention or was lonesome—which was often, and could be anytime, for Great-grandmother Kinloch kept later hours even than Maurice Barrymore.

Whenever Lionel and little Jack sought a pretext for staying up beyond their prescribed curfew, they would visit Great-grandmother's room and, after the customary good-night kiss, begin questioning her about her memories of performers of the past. "Isn't it time to say your little prayers?" the dear old lady would say. She was, however, easily sidetracked, and would happily lapse into reminiscences of Joseph Grimaldi, greatest of the clowns, and others long gone.

Then, at last, when further delay was impossible, the Barrymore boys would kneel to say the prayer their father had been at solemn pains to teach them.

"God bless Mother, and Papa, and Grandmother, and Great-grandmother, and Uncle Sidney; and please, God, make Uncle Jack a good actor."

The Twelfth Street house has long since been razed. So has the Arch Street Theatre with which it was, for the Barrymore children, linked in memory. But one can vicariously relive the days when Charles Dickens visited the theater during his second American tour, and, in imagination, see Walt Whitman, who often crossed over from Camden as a welcome though non-paying patron of the storied playhouse. President Lincoln, too, had visited the theater.

The Barrymore children's uncle, John Drew, used to tell them of the day he ran home from the Episcopal Academy where he attended school to inform his mother of the death of Abraham Lincoln. Mrs. Drew was greatly shocked. For a long time she sat wordlessly at her desk. Then she took from a drawer a letter Lincoln had written in 1862, thanking her for providing the presidential party with seats at the Arch Street Theatre.

"Who did such a monstrously wicked thing?" she said, still gazing at the letter.

"Mr. Booth's brother," said John.

"No!" she exclaimed. The gentle, talented kinsman of the slayer had been a star at her playhouse and often a guest in her home. "It is unthinkable! . . . Will our profession ever atone?"

WHENEVER MAURICE PLAYED the Arch Street Theatre the three little Barrymores behaved as if their grandmother had done them a personal favor. Although the iron-encased businesswoman was really only booking the best available attractions, and if such an attraction happened to be Modjeska, and Maurice Barrymore tagged along as her leading man, well, we must take the bitter with the sweet. But to the children their father's Philadelphia engagements meant that Papa had come home for a season.

What a gay companion he was! If not otherwise occupied after the night performance, he would pay surreptitious visits to the attic, smuggling food for late suppers in violation of Mrs. Drew's strictest orders against waking the children. Recalling his own boyhood, he would tell them stories of India, or act out the Sepoy Mutiny, playing the parts of both armies. It was perhaps the only military action in all history to be dramatized on tiptoe and in whispers.

And Papa was never grouchy, even when the boys came shouting into his room of a morning. He refused to wear night-shirts, but reposed in a kind of rowing-club jersey. As he rose from tousled sleep, he would gulp some water, shudder, snort, as if returning to mortality, then stride up and down the room like a Roman senator in half a toga. Pointing a long finger at his sons, he would recite excerpts from the Bard.

All three children inherited his theatrical presence and charm, and also partook in varying degrees of his offstage attributes and deficits. In appearance, Ethel and Lionel resembled their mother, while Jack possessed his father's physique, quicksilver humor, and voice, along with many of his epic frailties—such as moods of self-centered arrogance, deafness to others' opinions, and a constant tragic restlessness.

Maurice loved his wife and family in his own will-o'-the-wisp fashion. When among his children, he seemed a doting and contented parent, elaborately suggesting what he and his young ones would do on a tomorrow that was to find him gone. If his waywardness seemed inexcusable to the Broadway moralists, his family (other than the stern Mrs. Drew) conceded that Papa was not a homing pigeon. His wife, as beautiful as any of his admirers, seemed serenely confident that no matter how far or for how long he might wander, he would always come back to her.

On one of these belated homecomings, a Sunday morning, Maurice approached the Tomb of the Capulets as Georgie and the little ones were descending the marble steps.

"Why, hello, darling!" he called, with the overdone cordiality of the two-faced male. "I was delayed getting in from New York. Up all night with Wilton Lackaye."

"Until now," said Georgie, "I had always thought Wilton Lackaye to be a *man*."

Maurice sought to change the subject. "Where are you going, darling?"

"I'm going to Mass," said Georgie, leading the children away, "and you can go to hell!"

BY NOW Maurice was an acknowledged figure in the theater, although not eulogized by everyone. American critics deplored his English accent. In London, when he returned for an engagement, they scoffed at his Yankee nasalities.

"Great God!" he groaned. "Must I be condemned for the rest of my life to giving recitations on ocean liners?"

Maurice also had difficulty in learning and remembering a part—a trait that offered an odd contrast to the retentiveness of other members of the family. His children became remarkably quick studies, as all the Drews had been.

Such flaws as could be found in his portrayals did not lessen the ardor of his partisans, however. Maurice Barrymore had an arresting personality, and the foremost actresses of that day, notably Olga Nethersole and Minnie Maddern Fiske, as well as Mme. Modjeska, regarded him as first choice among their leading men.

One weekend Maurice appeared at the Drew home in Philadelphia to announce that he would take his wife and ten-year-old Lionel on a tour with Mme. Modjeska, during which he would present a play he had written especially for the Polish star. The work was named *Nadjezda*, and it incorporated much coquetry, terror, and some retributory bloodletting to parade her talents. In fact, Maurice went on, he might become a playwright exclusively. He had grown a little tired of taking orders—as if he ever had!

The children rejoiced over Papa's becoming a playwright. They saw in him a magnificent success. But their grandmother continued to sit complacently at her desk, her back turned. "Mme. Modjeska," she said over her shoulder, "is deserving, after all she has suffered, of the cream of the gentleman's efforts in her behalf."

Perhaps Mrs. Drew was remembering how Modjeska, even though she regarded Maurice as a splendid necessity in her company, still complained about his failure to memorize his lines, and his occasional amazing excursions from the text. Indeed, one evening, after he had slipped away from the scene at hand into an entirely different play, Mme. Modjeska had rebuked him. "Now look, Mr. Barrymore, you must not be so careless. Please remember who made it possible for you to rise to such fame as you may think you own."

This was no way to address a Barrymore. "Madam, I was quite well known to the American public at a time when they thought Modjeska the name of a toothwash."

ON THE NIGHT they went to Philadelphia's Reading Station to see their parents and Lionel off on the train for the great American tour which, Papa had now revealed, would extend all the way to San Francisco, little Jack and Ethel Barrymore huddled in the background watching their older brother's actions with wide appraising eyes. They marveled as he moved about like a world traveler, conferring with the man at the ticket gate, advising the porter about the luggage. A windfall of grandeur blessed him.

Then came the call of "All aboard!" There was a last embrace by Mamma, then Ethel and Jack watched the lucky ones disappear through the ticket gate. Outside, Mrs. Drew's coachman was waiting to drive them home.

Ethel took Jack's hand and they walked slowly, like Hansel and Gretel, to the brougham. The coachman helped Ethel into the carriage where she sat upright and regal, as her grandmother always did. Jack climbed onto the box beside the driver and from time to time, when the roadway became clear of traffic, held the reins.

CHAPTER 3

WHEN, IN 1889, shortly after returning from the successful western tour, Papa decided to move Georgie and the children to New York, their grandmother showed no tears. Mrs. Drew knew the family had outgrown the Tomb of the Capulets. Her home already had lost some of its familiar members. The tinkle of Great-grandmother Kinloch's bell was heard no longer, and both of the children's uncles, Sidney, now married, and John Drew, had become residents of New York.

And, too, Mrs. Drew's Philadelphia fortunes had begun to fade, for the city was moving away from the Arch Street Theatre. Yet the courageous little manager would not leave the historic neighborhood, and the older actors still answered her calls when rheumatism and ague permitted. On occasional weekends, after the move, Mrs. Drew would travel to New York, however, to see her grandchildren.

Lionel was then eleven years old, Ethel ten, and Jack seven, and New York a city of almost one million four hundred thousand population. It was the Horatio Alger time of luck and pluck, of rags and riches, and there was so much to be seen and heard in this Manhattan of adventurous growth!

Each afternoon a parade of great names moved along Broadway, where the Barrymore children often strolled, for their first Manhattan home was a brownstone house at 1564 Broadway, afterward the site of the Palace Theatre, shrine of vaudevillians. Papa would sometimes introduce them to his friends, such as John L. Sullivan, the heavyweight champion, but the Barrymore children were timid with strangers.

Indeed, an inward shyness possessed them during their subsequent private lives, notwithstanding their ease on the stage. To protect his mental privacy, each child set up his own kind of barrier. Lionel might either punch a well-meaning dullard in the nose, or retreat into an ossified cocoon. Ethel could become a bundle of claws when approached clumsily. Jack, after adolescence, concealed from the world his sensitivity by cock-o'-the-walk mannerisms and prussic-acid humor, too often closing the door on those who otherwise might have come to know his surpassing inner decencies, his starlit charm.

On Indian summer days Papa took the children to the Central Park Zoo. He knew a great deal about animals because of his experiences in India. His lectures enchanted other zoo visitors, and a crowd would soon be following them from cage to cage. "The llama," he would explain, "is a domesticated variety of guanaco, and spits in your eye if he doesn't like you. The first dramatic critic was a llama. Llama meat is not good for the dinner table. Tastes like a forgotten sponge."

In Philadelphia the children had attended Catholic day schools, but now the elder Barrymores, because of their frequent theatrical tours, decided to send Ethel to a convent school and to place the boys in Catholic boarding schools. Jack went to Georgetown's elementary school near Washington, and Lionel to Seton Hall at South Orange, New Jersey.

Jack did not stay long at Georgetown. His preceptors soon notified Papa that Jack had been cast out for a "serious breach of conduct," a circumstance which caused Maurice to inquire of the lad, "What did they catch you doing? Selling French postcards to congressmen?"

It was agreed that Jack should join Lionel at Seton Hall. Maurice accompanied his younger son to South Orange. There they toured the campus with the head of the school, Father Marshall, and Lionel.

Father Marshall had a serene personality, and the face of an ascetic Spanish nobleman. In the gymnasium he indicated the parallel bars. "Have you ever exercised on the horizontal bars, my son?"

"Yes, Father," Jack replied.

"Then get up on the bars and try the giant swing, my son."

While Father Marshall, Papa, and Lionel looked on, Jack stood on his hands on the bars. Suddenly from his pockets there showered a razor, a pistol, a pack of playing cards, and a pair of dice.

Father Marshall picked up the contraband, saying matter-of-factly, "I don't think you will need these articles *here*, my son."

THE YOUNG STUDENTS OF SETON HALL found the locker room of the gymnasium a comparatively safe place for their smoking exercises. One afternoon after baseball practice they opened a box of Sweet Caporals, a brand of lung-foggers that had as a premium in every package a colored picture of some famous athlete or actor.

To the astonishment of the Barrymore boys, the card in today's cigarette box contained a bright miniature portrait of Georgie Drew in an evening gown.

"It's Mamma!" Jack shouted. "Look, everybody!"

"It's Mamma, all right," Lionel said. "What an honor!"

One of the baseball players, a boy of such severe moral restraints as never to countenance the locker-room vice, said, "I think it's disgusting."

Lionel stared incredulously. Then he knocked the boy down. The lad lay quite still. "Even if he dies," Lionel blurted out, "he never should have said my mother was disgusting."

On another occasion an assistant instructor at the seminary reprimanded Jack for reading *Buffalo Bill's Adventures* behind an opened textbook. During this rebuke he placed a hand on Barrymore's head.

That night Jack composed a letter to his grandmother in Philadelphia:

> I was attacked by this huge fellow and without cause. I tried to placate him; but he struck me, and as I reeled beneath the cruel blow the world went black before my eyes. . . .

When Mrs. Drew read this curdling document, she hastened to New York. She displayed the letter to Sidney, commanding him to find Maurice. "Here's something, for once, that he can take care of."

Sidney commissioned his brother-in-law, in Mrs. Drew's name, to punish the brute of Seton Hall. When Jack got wind of his father's coming visit, he ballyhooed the event to his schoolmates: "My father's on his way to beat seven kinds of hell out of the entire faculty. Blood will flow from here to Newark."

Jack and a gallery of expectant fellows waited in the shrubbery to witness the arrival of the fierce avenger. Finally a carriage drew up and a sturdy yet seemingly carefree Mr. Barrymore entered the building where Father Marshall had an office.

The boys listened for the beginning of the battle. "It's mighty quiet in there," said one of them. "Mighty quiet."

"Just wait," Jack advised. "My father is studying the situation. In a minute priests will sail out of doors and windows, their ears torn loose."

But silence, except for laughter, continued over this scene. Peering through a window, Jack saw his father seated opposite Father Marshall, engaged in amiable discussion. After their talk, Mr. Barrymore and the head of the school walked arm in arm out of the building, past the group of gaping schoolboys to Maurice's carriage.

Papa was so delighted by his visit with Father Marshall, of whom he afterward said: "A priest so honest that Diogenes would have put away his lantern," that he failed to see Jack and his friends. And Jack was so let down by the collapse of his own advertisement of the decimation of the faculty that he had no voice left to call out to his father as he drove off.

IN 1892, WHEN JACK WAS TEN, his mother went to Philadelphia to keep an engagement at the Arch Street Theatre. She caught cold, but insisted on taking her place at the opening performance, and became quite ill. Back in New York, Georgie's health faded rapidly, and physicians decided she must take a rest. But when she returned from a long cruise to the Bahamas, the doctors diagnosed her condition as advanced tuberculosis. They then advised sending her to California.

Since the family was now widely scattered—Mrs. Drew, having at last given up the Arch Street Theatre, was playing an engagement in Boston, Uncle John Drew was abroad, and Papa was with a stock company out West—the theatrical tradition of never missing a curtain left no one but Ethel, barely fourteen, available to accompany her mother on the eight-day train trip, and to stay with her in Santa Barbara. It was a shock for a girl to exchange the cloistered serenity of the convent for the shove-about rudeness of railway stations, but Ethel managed everything.

"All my children," said Georgie, "have Drew eyes and Drew hair—" then she added, as if to herself "—and Drew courage."

The Barrymores' old friend, Mme. Modjeska, between Shakespearean tours with Edwin Booth, was now residing in California at Anaheim, not far from Santa Barbara. Sometimes she visited her friend Georgie at the sanitarium, and saw that she undoubtedly was gravely ill. The great actress tried gently to prepare Ethel for the coming shock. Death came to Georgie Barrymore one morning in July 1893, just as Ethel was returning from Mass. Now the young girl was faced with the responsibility for returning her mother's body to Philadelphia. Papa had not been heard from for weeks, and his young daughter spent almost her last dollar on a telegram to her uncle Sidney. He would know how to break the terrible news to the family. Perhaps he could even find Papa.

Once more Ethel sat for eight days and nights in a day coach, wearing a long black dress to make herself look older. She would never be a child again. And from this time on she would be the successor to Mrs. Drew as family burden bearer, a willing, dependable, uncomplaining refuge for madcap relatives in their hours of bewilderment.

CHAPTER 4

It was at Madame Bourquin's, a theatrical boardinghouse on Staten Island, the summer after their mother's death, that the young Barrymores appeared in their first dramatic effort. Mrs. Drew, now seventy-three years old, had undertaken the temporary care of her grandchildren, pending a tour in *The Rivals* under the management of her son, Sidney. The Barrymore boys had said good-by to Seton Hall, and they, along with Ethel, their grandmother, and their uncle Sidney and his family, were living at Madame Bourquin's, where Barrymore and Drew credit always was good. Their hostess knew she would get her money eventually, with Mrs. Drew at the family helm.

There, one afternoon, for an audience of neighborhood children, relatives, and out-of-work Hamlets, they performed

Camille. Ethel played the name role, coughing most convincingly. Lionel, after much coaxing (he always detested love scenes), undertook the part of Armand, and Jack that of the Count de Varville, with a swirling black mustache. Actually, none of them had a compulsion toward acting, despite the century of stage tradition on the Drew side of their house, and the mimicry bequeathed them by their handsome father.

"We became actors," Ethel once said, "not because we wanted to, but because it was the thing we could do best."

Meanwhile old Mrs. Drew, gallantly preparing once again to lift the plumes and corset stays of Mrs. Malaprop from the mothballs, still regarded her son-in-law Maurice as an untrustworthy guardian. Though he had at first seemed unable to believe his wife had died, he was now often seen in bright spirits at The Lambs bar, or in company of beautiful young women. He could hardly be depended on to look after the children while she was away. So, once more, the family's living arrangements were revised.

Lionel, it was decided, would tour with his grandmother. He made his professional debut in the small part of a coachman in *The Rivals* when they opened in Kansas City, and survived, despite the fact that, at age fifteen, his voice was still changing. Later he recalled that the experience was "like trying to play a French horn while standing on my head." Jack, meanwhile, went to live with his uncle John Drew, who had returned from London and now welcomed his favorite nephew to his rooms at the Marlborough Hotel.

Jack had always drawn pictures. He said he wanted to be an artist and his aunt Dodo, Uncle John's wife, permitted him to sketch on anything other than walls or table linen. His uncle also patronized his passion for the drawing board, yet adroitly sought to keep him on the path of family tradition. Drew now graced the Standard Theatre under the management of Charles Frohman, and before long would move into the newly built Empire Theatre, there to rule the greenroom as the first gentleman of the American stage. He saw himself and his family as a theatrical dynasty, with no allowances made for abdication.

Jack had great respect for his uncle, and would eventually

take on many of his stately mannerisms, but he did not now choose to be reminded of his duty to the profession of acting. At this formative period he was both shy and confused. Lionel might begin to heed the call of tradition. And soon Ethel, too, would make her debut, appearing in a minor role when Louisa Lane Drew and an all-star cast brought *The Rivals* to New York. But their younger brother was still daydreaming, sketching, or strolling about New York, unmindful of the crowds.

JOHN BARRYMORE spent the summer of his fifteenth year with his grandmother at the old Bevan House in Larchmont, New York. The boy seldom left her, for the seventy-seven-year-old actress was afflicted with dropsy, her first and last devastating illness.

"I saw you come into this world," she said to her grandson, "and now you are seeing me out of it. A fair exchange."

It was an early, hot summer, notwithstanding the cool, blue reaches of Long Island Sound. Each afternoon Jack would help his grandmother Drew get settled in her rocking chair on a veranda overlooking the sound. He would sit beside her, sketching seascapes, and listening to her reminiscences when she would sometimes put aside the book she was reading.

"Waves and actors," said the old lady, "are much alike. They come for a little time, rise to separate heights, and travel with varying speed and force—and then they are gone, unremembered. Our good friend Joseph Jefferson has correctly observed, 'Nothing is as dead as a dead actor.'"

The family once again had become widely scattered. Papa was in Kansas City, John Drew was on tour with Maude Adams, Ethel, who had been soaring high by means of both talent and beauty, was in London, where she had appeared in *Secret Service*, a play starring William H. Gillette, one of the great matinee idols of the day. Word reached Larchmont that she had become the most talked of young beauty in England.

Lionel was in New York preparing to play in a new comedy, *Uncle Dick*, and when he came to visit them in Larchmont he was saddened to find his grandmother in constant pain. Her doctor confided to him that she could not live much longer.

After the physician had left, Mrs. Drew said to Lionel, "Whatever that learned calomel merchant has been telling you, pay no attention. I shall appear for rehearsals next season as has been my custom for seventy-two years. And I shall send you a large red apple on your opening night."

The red apple was a traditional gift. Back in the days when John Drew was at boarding school, his schoolmaster used to say: "If you learn your lesson well, you shall have a nice red apple." After he became a star, Drew began to send red apples to his relatives on the first nights of their respective bows as actors, or whenever one of them appeared in a new play. Among the Drews and Barrymores it had become a signal of interfamily regard and a good-luck token as well.

Mrs. Drew now turned to Jack. "We must be sure to send one to Ethel, too. Can one cable an apple?"

That night she fell asleep, never to awaken.

Of his grandmother, Jack said in afteryears, "If such a thing be possible, I know that at Heaven's gate she was given not a red apple but one of purest gold."

AFTER THE PASSING OF his grandmother, Jack entered upon a bouncing behaviorism, together with spontaneous alliances, such as novelists call romantic and physicians diagnose as glandular. It was during his fifteenth year (according to him) that he had his first complete relationship with an ardent and experienced young woman; what is more, a woman currently the loved one of Maurice Barrymore, his father.

Although Jack's was not a nature to harbor feelings of guilt of moral wrongs, it seemed from his own manner of referring to this cyclonic premiere that he felt he had let his father down. And it may well be that his later stage interpretation of Hamlet's problem rested somewhat on the circumstances of this initiation of the adolescent dreamer. In any case, it appeared that the inconstancy of this woman fixed in Jack's mind the idea that all beautiful women might be the same.

When Ethel returned briefly from London to find her younger brother doing nothing with, yet doing everything *to*, his life, she decided to take him back to England with her. Perhaps he would improve himself when meeting some worthwhile per-

Sketch of Dolores Costello, and, below, a fantasy entitled "Fear."

John Barrymore as artist. Above, self-portrait as King Lear; below, a theatrical poster.

E.H. SOTHERN

MANAGEMENT DANIEL FROHMAN

IF I WERE KING

sons. No sooner had they arrived than he fell in love with an actress of magnificent face and figure. She had a husband of mellow years, but he suddenly became less mellow and threatened a suit for divorce, until friends pointed out to him how ridiculous it would seem for a man of years to name a "sapling" as corespondent.

Ethel played upon Jack's desire to be a painter, and for a time managed to shunt him from the romantic track and into the Slade School of Fine Art, where he was greatly influenced by the macabre Aubrey Beardsley, although they never met. Perhaps we should discuss John Barrymore's easel abilities now and have done with it. He had an abiding passion for art, a driving imagination, and a compelling sense of color, but he himself once summed up his artistic talents, saying, "I might have been, but wasn't."

When Jack returned to America he still wanted no part of the stage, although his uncle Jack Drew kept reminding him of his "birthright." Newspaper life and newspapermen always enchanted him, and he was now determined to combine his art with journalism.

He obtained a fleeting job on the *Morning Telegraph*, then went to work for Arthur Brisbane, the dome-browed savant who edited Hearst's *Evening Journal*. Mr. Brisbane had such a high regard for Ethel that he waived his usual practicality and assigned Jack to the task of illustrating weekly editorials and occasional court stories.

Jack, however, did not seem to realize that newspapers had to be published on time. He was consistently late with his copy. He also disregarded the text of articles he was supposed to emblazon. Then one day he created a picture that miraculously satisfied Mr. Brisbane. It showed mankind in the chains of dope and liquor habits. But after the first edition reached Park Row newsstands, the picture was found to be published upside down!

Although Jack could in no wise be held accountable for this mishap, Mr. Brisbane's magnificent forehead wrinkled with outrage.

"I believe," he said to Jack, "that all your family were, or are actors?"

"Yes, sir," Jack replied.

"Then shall we allow the Fourth Estate, or anything else, to spoil that splendid record?"

"I AM NOT a constant reader of the calendar," John Barrymore said to Lionel one day, "but Uncle Jack informs me that I am twenty-one years old."

"What do you propose to do about it? Vote?"

"It begins to look as though I'll have to succumb to the family curse, acting," Jack replied sadly.

Lionel was properly sympathetic. "I know how you feel. There is no escape. We are in the cul-de-sac of tradition. Did Uncle Jack finally influence you?"

"Partly, but also my stomach. It abhors a vacuum." They were sitting in the Café Boulevard on Second Avenue, which they patronized for three reasons: Hungarian food, gypsy music, and twin sisters from Budapest, whom they never saw anywhere else. The romance carried over from one visit to the next. It seemed an ideal poetic arrangement.

"Well," Jack went on, "if I do stumble onto the stage, I'll not be any good. Then I'll *have* to come back to painting."

"You'll certainly fail, unless you try. But if you do try—" Lionel paused "—you're hooked forever."

CHAPTER 5

THE FIRST GREAT bell-beat of tragedy sounded for John Barrymore in 1903, the year that saw him at last on the New York stage. The sudden, evil occurrence was the collapse of his father's once brilliant, gay mind. The bleak overtone of this breaking of his parent's reason never quite died away in Jack's thoughts, and toward the end of his own life provoked the only discernible fear in an otherwise exceptionally brave character.

It was Maurice Barrymore's sardonic lot to reach his topmost place in the theater just before the world went dark for him. He had magnificently enacted the part of Rawdon Crawley in support of Mrs. Fiske's Becky Sharp. The irony was that the actor was not entirely simulating the frenzies of this stage role, but giving to it the agonies of his own mental disintegration.

One afternoon in late autumn, as one of John Barrymore's newspaper friends, a police reporter named Jack Francis, was leaving the doorway of the West Thirtieth Street station house, he observed Maurice Barrymore sitting on the cast-iron steps, staring fixedly at a sign across the street advertising a Negro mission. The sign read:

ALL YE THAT ENTER HERE,
LEAVE SIN AND CARE BEHIND.

"May I take you home, Mr. Barrymore?" Francis asked. "You look kind of sick."

Maurice glanced up. "Home?" he asked. "Is there such a place?" He rose slowly, then lurched. Francis caught his arm before he could fall, and hailed a cab.

But when the cab reached the place where Maurice was living, the actor refused to get out, and the worried Francis instructed the cabbie to drive to Bellevue Hospital instead. Barrymore didn't appear to mind. Perhaps he had forgotten where he had wished to be taken. He was for the most part incoherent, but would return abruptly to his usual bright manner for a minute or so. Among other things, he recalled that his friend Wilton Lackaye recently had posted a notice on the bulletin board of The Lambs: LOST: ONE CUFF LINK. WILL BUY OR SELL.

At last the cab arrived at the hospital, where the examining physician told Francis it would be best for the stricken man to remain for observation in the psychopathic ward. It was so arranged, though Ethel and Lionel were out of the city and Francis was unable to locate Jack.

After several days some of Maurice's friends procured his release. Yet they soon conceded that the actor, now in his fifty-sixth year, was deranged. It was recommended that he enter a private sanitarium.

And now the family burden bearer, Ethel, arrived home to take her father to a place in Amityville, Long Island. As in the death of her mother, this, too, became a grievous journey for the beautiful young woman. Yet again she did not shirk her

duty. She assumed all the expenses and made all the arrangements for her father's care.

Maurice remained in the sanitarium until his death in 1905,
although occasionally when friends visited him, he conversed
with such sustained animation that they hoped he might someday be released. But then he would plunge back into the darkness of his malady.

Among these longtime comrades was Frank Case, proprietor
of the Hotel Algonquin. On his last visit to the sanitarium he
found the actor in comparatively high spirits. Many sheets of
manuscript lay on a table in his room.

"I have written a new play," he told Case. He handed the
pages to his visitor. "Run your eye over this."

There was but one sentence written on the many pages, repeated again and again: "It was a lovely day in June." Case
finally was able to say, "I think it is fine, Barry, perfectly fine."

LONG BEFORE his father's illness had run its course, John Barrymore was on the stage. Yet he had revealed little evidence of the
powers locked inside himself. His first appearance (for a single
night) had come when he substituted for an absent actor at the
Philadelphia tryout of *Captain Jinks of the Horse Marines*. The
hastily rehearsed Jack blew up in his lines. His sister Ethel, a
principal in *Captain Jinks*, went into a hysterical state which
Jack described as "a cross between hilarity and strangulation."
As if that were not enough, the mischievous actor took a curtain
call by himself.

The play failed to impress Philadelphia. It moved gloomily
to New York (with Jack out of the cast!) and stayed on for a
triumphant seven months, firmly establishing Ethel Barrymore as a star of the first magnitude.

That summer, while waiting for a second role, Jack enjoyed
the hospitality of Frank Case. Members of the Drew-Barrymore
family often stayed at the Algonquin. And Uncle John Drew
was a resident of that hotel for nineteen winters.

By now Jack had assumed many of the courtly mannerisms
of his uncle John, and much of his wardrobe as well, for he
was entering upon a "dressy" period. But if his uncle hap-

pened to be out of town, Jack levied upon Frank Case for linen. Case was a much larger man, but Barrymore had a talent for pinning up sleeves and making collars fit by adjusting borrowed neckties.

One day a friend asked Jack what kind of man Case was.

"There are no adjectives available. He's . . . he's . . ." Jack resorted to a Broadway phrase: "Why, he's the sort of man who'd give you his . . ." He paused, then pointed to his own bosom and exclaimed, "My God! This *is* his shirt!"

Case became concerned about Jack's drinking, a matter subsequently pondered by a multitude of men and women. Barrymore appeared one morning in the Algonquin restaurant, somewhat earlier than his usual noon, to request, "Waiter, will you create for me an absinthe frappé? On second thought, prepare two."

Case whispered to the waiter to delay the service of absinthe, then invited Barrymore to his own table. "Have a cup of coffee," Case said. "It takes time to mix a real frappé."

Barrymore had three cups of coffee with Case; then, after the absinthe frappé arrived, found his stomach out of humor for wormwood distillations.

"What a great idea, Frank," he said.

"What idea?" Case asked.

"Coffee for breakfast!"

Like numerous other famous Algonquin guests, Barrymore did not pay his bills on the barrelhead. Case was passing through the main dining room one evening when Jack was entertaining an eye-arresting young lady—one of the fabled Floradora show girls—with hearts of artichoke. Case leaned over Barrymore's shoulder to whisper, "Couldn't you have selected something less costly?"

Jack seethed. He insisted that the young lady go with him at once to a restaurant that didn't quibble with guests, and he even went so far as to check out of the Algonquin. No one at the desk brought to his attention a long-standing bill.

It happened that delegates to a political convention had taken all hotel space in the White Light district. Barrymore and his girl drove about mid-Manhattan for hours. Late that night he returned alone to the Algonquin, and, having no money with which to pay the hack driver, matter-of-factly signed Frank Case's name to a tab.

SUCCESSFUL MEN tend to stay silent in regard to benefactors who gave them a leg up, but John Barrymore acknowledged that his career often had been accommodated by timely help. One early monitor of Jack's professional course was the comedian Willie Collier, who had been a friend of the Drews and Barrymores since 1882, the year that he had quit school to enlist as a call boy at Augustin Daly's Theatre, and the year in which Jack had been born.

Collier had left Daly's to become a comedy favorite with Weber and Fields. And by the time Jack began to nibble at his theatrical inheritance, Collier was a star for Charles Frohman. John Drew, Ethel, and Lionel also were Frohman actors, so young Jack's availability was often brought to the attention of the dubious impresario.

Frohman had seen Jack the night he took the curtain call by himself in Philadelphia and admitted that the youngest Barrymore "might" have some hidden talent for comedy. Still, he wasn't too sanguine. So, when Collier was preparing, early in 1904, to open in Richard Harding Davis's new play, *The Dictator*, and suggested Jack for a secondary role, the part of a wireless operator, Frohman hesitated.

"Why overlook a horse of such good bloodlines?" Collier asked.

Then Ethel appeared next day to make a Portian plea, and Mr. Frohman surrendered, becoming one of the first of many theatrical believers in "always taking a chance on a Barrymore."

Collier's new protégé gave him little rest for the better part of the next four years. But for Jack the four years of training under Collier became a solid education as well as a boisterously gay odyssey. It began on the night of *The Dictator*'s out-of-town tryout in New Haven, when Jack met some convivial friends who, later, had to carry him into the theater. Yet, once onstage, Barrymore managed his part well. Fortunately the wireless operator was characterized as a profound bottle man.

But Jack's tardiness and general misbehavior continued through a long season with *The Dictator* in New York and then on the road. His abuse of stage costumes galled Collier. Jack would slip away from the theater in the white tropical pants of the wireless operator, and often would sleep in them. Or he would stand, barefoot, on his makeup towel, then rub his hands on his white trousers instead of the towel. In Bangor, Maine, he didn't materialize for the matinee on Washington's Birthday. When asked if he didn't know that a holiday always meant a matinee, Jack said, "I never knew until this instant that Washington's Birthday was a holiday!"

Such experiences at last caused Collier to telegraph Mr. Frohman that he was about to dismiss Jack from the company.

"Don't fire him, Willie," Frohman wired back. "It would break Ethel's heart."

"If I keep him, it will break mine," Collier replied.

But he never fired Jack. "The trouble," he said, "was that I liked him too much to discipline him. He assimilated direction easily, especially in the art of timing. His memory was wonderful, yet no one ever caught him studying a part. I thought that he would be a fine comedian, which indeed he did become. But I didn't then realize that he was to become a really great actor."

The Dictator proved so popular in America that in 1905 Mr. Frohman sent the company to London. On the opening night, with much at stake for Collier, two of his actors put him in a fine predicament. Jack, of course, was the worse offender.

At the rise of the curtain, Collier, playing the role of a character called Travers, is in desperate need of a new name to cover his identity as a fugitive from the law. Another character enters to sell him his name, Bowie, for twenty-five thousand dollars. That night when Collier asked, "By the way, what is your name, the one I am to purchase?" the actor refused with alcoholic hauteur to tell it. In fact he exited, leaving the first-nighters still ignorant of his identity.

"Of course I know his name," Collier improvised. "Happened to meet his wife. It's 'Bowie.'"

Then Jack, as the wireless operator, arrived onstage. He was to give Collier a dispatch written on two long sheets of paper which the star would read aloud. It was important, for it advised the audience of the why, when, and wherefore of the action. Jack appeared on cue, but in his hand was only a small fragment torn from a menu card. He offered this tiny absurdity to the astounded Collier. "Here, Chief, is the dispatch."

"Where is the longer one?" Collier ad-libbed.

Jack also improvised, "Here it is, sir. Or have your eyes gone back on you again?"

Knowing the long, plot-point speech he was supposed to deliver could hardly be accepted as being read from the menu fragment, Collier said, "Someone is trying to double-cross us. Look again. I'm sure you will find the genuine message."

Jack went offstage, then reappeared with exactly the same bit of paper. "Sir, I have had this authenticated. It was written by the fellow who engraves the Lord's Prayer on the heads of pins." There was no other course for Collier than to take the miserable paper, hurriedly edit down his regular lines, and hope for the best.

CHAPTER 6

THE ONLY LETTER of introduction John Barrymore ever bothered to deliver was handed to drama critic Ashton Stevens, of the San Francisco *Examiner*, late one April night in 1906. Collier had brought *The Dictator* west for a San Francisco season, to be followed by a long Australian tour, and Ethel had written Stevens to keep an eye on her twenty-four-year-old brother, and eventually see that he got aboard ship for Australia.

Mr. Stevens was a brilliant critic who brought a gay creativeness to his job. He never coddled an inferior performance, but he smeared no poison on his critical darts, and thus was celebrated in San Francisco, Chicago, and New York as "the mercy killer." He grew up in friendly intimacy with successive Drews and Barrymores, and he later recalled that, when Jack first visited the *Examiner* office, at one o'clock on an April morning, the young actor was faultlessly attired in evening clothes. How he had managed to acquire this finery is still a mystery.

"The youngest of the Barrymores pulled himself out of a big overcoat," Stevens said, "and sprawled, a picture, in the nearest chair. His supper coat was double-breasted; mine was the same old single; his shirt buttons were three; mine the same old two. And where I wore shoestrings, he wore bows. Even our cigarettes were of different shades. Nevertheless, he treated me as an equal."

Jack sniffed the atmosphere of the newspaper office. Then, Stevens recalled, he smiled and said, "I used to work in a shop like this, drawing cartoons. I liked it—still like it—gives me nostalgia. This acting is a new game. But I don't have to tell a critic that I'm new on the stage."

Stevens told him that under any other name he might fool the best of them.

"Still," Jack said, "don't overlook my good fortune in being the nephew of John Drew and the brother of Ethel and Lionel. It helps, fabulously."

He rose and looked around the room again. "Great, isn't it? I'd like to be back at it. But acting comes easy," he said, "and it pays well. That's the narcotic."

On April 18 and 19, 1906, shortly after this meeting, San Francisco was devastated by its great earthquake and fire. Three days later when Jack finally managed to locate him in the *Examiner*'s temporary offices in Oakland, Ashton Stevens said, in reference to that disaster, "When God does such things, He has style."

In early press reports, Barrymore's name was erroneously listed among the missing in the disaster. Regular telegraph facilities were lacking; Jack didn't think his family would worry about him, but Ashton Stevens prevailed upon his editor to permit Jack to tag onto the close of a news-service bulletin to New York a message to Ethel. The actor wrote as dramatically as possible within the space allotted him an imaginative and completely fabricated account of how he had been thrown out of bed, had wandered dazedly to the street, where an army sergeant put a shovel in his hand and made him work for twenty-four hours among the ruins of the city.

When Ethel asked her uncle John whether he believed this, he replied, "Every word. It took an act of God to get him out of bed, and the United States Army to put him to work."

Because of the San Francisco fire, *The Dictator* company sailed for Australia minus scenery, wardrobe, trunks, and prompt-books. Aboard the ship Willie Collier rewrote the play from memory and had Jack draw designs for new sets to be built in Melbourne.

Neither Barrymore nor Collier enjoyed Australia. They found the nights too quiet. One day, after Jack had been late for rehearsal, Collier said to him, "I've been crying wolf long enough. The next time you are late or miss a performance, I'm going to abandon you in Australia. Maybe your sister will send you the boat fare. But I warn you, it will be awful to be marooned among the kangaroos." From then until the close of the Australian tour, Barrymore appeared on time at the theater.

A day or two before the voyage home, Collier pointed out in a "fatherly talk" to Jack that he had been with him for almost four years, but instead of having a dime to show for this he owed the company five hundred dollars.

"I'll write off the debt," Collier continued, "and I'll show you how to make a stake during the five and a half weeks we are at sea. Get some art materials, do some sketches on the ship; then, after you arrive in New York, you can sell them. See?"

Jack promised, and labored over a dozen or so. Weeks afterward, in New York, Collier found him at The Lambs. He said he was broke.

"But what happened to those sketches?" Collier asked.

"Good God!" Jack shouted. "I left them on the ship!"

BARRYMORE SPENT the hot New York summer of 1909 rehearsing a leading part in Winchell Smith's play, *The Fortune Hunter*. And it was during this time that he confided to his sister that he was in love with Nora Bayes, singing star of musical comedies. This time, however, he had fallen in love at long range, a singular departure from his customary behavior.

"But you've never met her," said Ethel.

"Did Dante meet Beatrice?" asked Jack.

"Besides, she's the romantic ideal of W. C. Fields."

"And who is he?"

"Mr. Fields," Ethel informed him, "happens to be the star comedian of the *Ziegfeld Follies*. You should at least know about the *Follies*. They were named after you."

"Will you accompany me to the theater where this trivial mugger is performing? I shall study him for future reference."

After seeing Mr. Fields juggle Indian clubs and otherwise display his remarkable talents, Ethel turned to Jack. "Well, what do you think?"

"Ethel," said Jack, "he's one of the greatest artists of all time. I'm not in love with Miss Bayes now. Hell! I'm in love with W. C. Fields!"

LIONEL RETURNED from Paris in time to witness his brother's debut in *The Fortune Hunter*. He sent a red apple, as did Ethel and Uncle Jack, and that night he saw his brother become a star in a faultless, vital performance. From now on the theater would be enriched by his electric presence, and his fame would endure for as long as his own volatile desires permitted.

Backstage, Lionel found a swarm of first-nighters crowding Jack's dressing room. "Well, Jake," he said, after the room was cleared out, "it looks like you are hooked for good."

"I'm scared stiff. Why didn't I give a stinking performance?"

"Because you couldn't."

"For God's sake!" said Jack. "In all the other arts, poor bastards starve, freeze, and strip their souls year after year. In this stage paradox, so-called success comes overnight. I'll tell you why I'm so scared. I heard thunder in the applause. A sign of storms to come."

CHAPTER 7

ONE NIGHT in 1910, after the curtain had fallen on the final scene of *The Fortune Hunter*, John Barrymore changed to evening clothes and left the Gaiety Theatre to attend a debutante's ball for Katherine Corri Harris, a taffy-haired beauty with blue mirrors for eyes. Her parents occupied a comfortable place in the *Social Register,* and certainly didn't anticipate that a theatrical weasel would spring the golden trap they had baited for ermine, but a few months later the nineteen-year-old girl married the twenty-eight-year-old actor.

"This event," Jack said, "was the first of my four marriages—all of them bus accidents."

The bridegroom announced blandly, after the wedding breakfast, that he had to go on the road with *The Fortune Hunter.* "It will only be for a year," he told his wife. "We'll be seeing each other at propitious moments."

The bride stayed with one of the few family members who cared to receive her as Mrs. Barrymore, and upon Jack's return, the couple moved into an apartment on the east side of Gramercy Park. Kathy tried hard not to quarrel with her husband, but none of his wives could exist happily with him for long. The bottle may have been the chief cause of each domestic furor. But Barrymore always sought the impossible, according to one of his associates, demanding that a mate consist of, all in one, "saint, siren, mother, wife, and friend." Other elements, too, increased the discord of this first marriage. Katherine, young and blossoming, wished to exhibit her husband in public, where everyone might view her handsome prize. Jack wanted no self-display after theater hours.

Between engagements, or on Sundays, in old clothes and with a beard stubble, he would slouch about Gramercy Park feeding the pigeons, or take solitary strolls. He stayed up all night with newspapermen, and sometimes forgot his marriage vows. He failed to advise Katherine as to where he was going or where he had been. He was not a man of explanations, nor a man to be explained. He simply *was.*

Sometimes, however, Katherine would be hopefully gay, as when Jack bought a small automobile, one of the open models then in fashion. One day he parked her and the car outside Tiffany's and went into that Fifth Avenue establishment to buy her a present.

He saw Geraldine Farrar examining some jewels and shyly introduced himself to the Metropolitan Opera beauty.

"If you will do me a favor, Miss Farrar," Jack said, "I'll rear a stained-glass window to you in any cathedral of your choice. Of course you don't know me . . ."

"But I do know you, Mr. Barrymore," Miss Farrar interrupted graciously. "And what is your favor?"

"My wife is outside waiting for me. If you'll only let me introduce you . . . She adores you."

Katherine was indeed impressed. Barrymore got into the car, preened his mustache, then drove off, completely forgetting to buy the present.

Barrymore's first marriage always seemed vague in his own memory, as if he merely had dreamed it. It endured, actually, for seven years. Concerning this and his other alliances, Barrymore once said: "They always ran about seven years, like a certain kind of skin rash."

THE NINE successive roles that Barrymore portrayed following his success in *The Fortune Hunter* found his talents marking time. His popularity increased, largely because of the Villonesque legends that attached themselves to his personality, but he smelled more of alcohol than of fame.

Perhaps it was because of his personal charm that managers put up with his idiosyncrasies. Perhaps it was because the impresarios had loved the Barrymores and the Drews. But during these years Jack survived demerits that, for any other actor, would have meant expulsion from the stage.

When in the spring of 1914, at the age of thirty-two, he undertook a Byronic flight to Italy, certain intimates attributed it to domestic miseries. Others thought his uninspiring roles had become intolerable. Whatever the cause, the effect of that Italian journey, both upon John Barrymore himself and upon the theater, would eventually be expressed in terms of meteors. For it was then that the wise words of a friend combined with the stimulating Italian environment to arouse in his artistic consciousness the powers long hidden beneath superficial charms and headlong actions.

Several years earlier Barrymore had become friends with a young playwright named Edward Brewster Sheldon who was well on his own way to professional eminence. Like Barrymore,

Above, a scene from "Justice"; at right, Barrymore as he looked in 1903, the year of his stage debut.

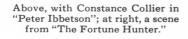

Above, with Constance Collier in "Peter Ibbetson"; at right, a scene from "The Fortune Hunter."

Sheldon had uncommon physical presence, was courageous and generous; unlike Barrymore, he had consistent professional purpose. *Salvation Nell*, written for Mrs. Fiske while Sheldon was still an undergraduate at Harvard, had brought him immediate recognition. His more recent drama, *Romance*, had achieved equal success, and he was enjoying a holiday in Italy when Barrymore bobbed up at his Venetian quarters that April.

The men were mutually delighted by their reunion. They strolled at night among the deserted squares and across the bridges. They listened to music, and studied architectural classics, sculptures, mosaics, and paintings. They had long serious talks. And some of Jack's confusions of mind began to fall away.

As long ago as *The Fortune Hunter*, Sheldon had advised Barrymore to undertake the playing of serious roles and therewith find recognition comparable to his powers. Now, in Italy, with reminders of man's artistic upsurge to be seen everywhere, this Harvard master of arts judiciously revived his suggestion, and this time Barrymore listened. Though he always blithely ignored friendly counsels regarding matters of the heart, Jack was receptive to artistic recommendations he found valid. They would be pigeonholed in his mind, seemingly forgotten, for he was by birth and by habit a procrastinator, but then they would pop out, vital and fresh. And when creative urgings finally stirred his will to action, he would rise to prodigious labors, undergo drudgeries even, to achieve perfection in his art. Edward Sheldon divined this slumbering quality in his friend, and awakened Barrymore to his mission. He unbound Prometheus.

When Barrymore expressed a desire to see Rome and Florence, the young dramatist didn't hesitate to interrupt his own plans. In Florence, one morning, they watched a sunrise from their hotel roof. They had found a trapdoor and climbed out in their pajamas to negotiate the steep slates seven stories above the ground. They sat there until the sun came up to reveal the Arno, the Ponte Vecchio, Santa Maria del Fiore, the Uffizi Gallery, and Santa Croce, in which was entombed the dust of Michelangelo, Galileo, Machiavelli. . . . Under the blue sky, holy bells and morning songs of peasants began to echo against the surrounding hills.

Barrymore, standing in his pajamas, said, "All this seems highly improbable."

In Rome they visited churches and galleries, the little cemetery where Keats's body and the heart of Shelley are buried, and in the moonlight re-created for themselves the Roman Empire from the shadows of ancient stones.

One night in an outlying village they heard singing, and left their carriage to enter a candle-lighted cellar that proved to be an inn. Mouths of wine caves could be seen dimly in the background, and a hunchback with a great key slung from a chain at his wrist moved about in this medieval scene. Jack *was* medieval. He became a part of the setting as naturally as if, on cue, he had entered into one of his own dreams.

The peasants at the tables were momentarily startled by the advent of the strangers, yet, after Jack had sat with charming familiarity among them, they ate and drank with him as if he were an old, beloved friend. A little girl got up on the table to sing "Tripoli," with what Sheldon recalls as "a voice like a slate pencil." Yet the song seemed entirely right and beautiful.

In a letter to Sheldon, twenty years afterward, Jack wrote:

Dear Ned:

I spent several days in Rome, where I attempted to make a pious pilgrimage to that marvelous inn where that charming child sang "Tripoli" to us. I found various other *albergi*, but regret to say not that particular one. Perhaps after all it was the walled garden with the little green door that one finds only once. . . .

CHAPTER 8

BARRYMORE RETURNED to America in the early summer of 1914, resolved to find a role that might place him solidly among the serious artists of the theater. Perhaps the gravity of war's announcement in July accentuated his purpose. Such a play was found, Galsworthy's *Justice*, in which Barrymore starred as William Falder, a tragedy-marked bank clerk. The amazement of the critics at his immediate triumph is understandable. They were unprepared for his sudden "size." *Justice* had a memorable season on Broadway, then went on tour.

It was during this time that Katherine Harris Barrymore established residence in Santa Barbara to sue for divorce on the grounds of incompatibility. Jack's unhappiness in this marriage lacked any bitterness, or lasting rancor. And in subsequent marital rifts even the pauperizing drains of alimony brought no martyr's whines.

"A man properly must pay the fiddler," he once said. "In my case it so happened that a whole symphony orchestra often had to be subsidized."

Upon his return to New York after the tour of *Justice*, Jack undertook, somewhat reluctantly, his first straight romantic role. It was only at the urging of Edward Sheldon that he agreed to play the title part in *Peter Ibbetson*, a dramatization of the George du Maurier novel. The English actress Constance Collier was his leading lady, and his brother, Lionel, played the wicked Colonel Ibbetson.

Jack never became convinced he was a romantic figure, nor did he wish to be one and become known as a "pretty boy." In this case, he also had some doubts about the virility of the character he was to play. He interrupted the rehearsal of one love scene with a howl: "This is nauseating! How can I bring myself to say such angel-cake speeches?"

However, the Broadway premiere of *Peter Ibbetson* was a night of excitement. The audience was alive and sympathetic from the moment the curtain rose; even the ushers were affected by the spiritual and emotional appeal of the play. Jack and Constance seemed the greatest lovers since Romeo and Juliet, and the story so poignantly real that even an exasperating mishap failed to spoil the illusion.

At the beginning of the third act a forest is supposed to dissolve before the dripping eyes of the spectators, and a magical opera house is conjured up in response to the romantic pair's wish to hear a song from the opera *Mignon*. Jack and Constance were walking hand in hand toward the opera house when it toppled, enveloping them with canvas and dust. The curtain was lowered, the scene rehung, and the beginning of the act repeated. Despite this intrusion, the audience sat like lotus-eaters, happy and anesthetized.

The play was a great success and it made John Barrymore a legendary romanticist. Love letters and sentimental gifts came in with the tide. But he never read the letters, and each Sunday afternoon consigned the previous week's accumulation to the furnace along with unopened bills and duns. Flowers were sent to city hospitals.

Lionel, with his Colonel Ibbetson role, also took a great step forward in public esteem. The scenes between Jack and Lionel were gritty actorial duels. The brothers often revealed sibling envy of each other's abilities, and with reason. Both men were strikingly honest in private life, but when trying to steal scenes from each other they surpassed the rogueries of purse snatchers.

During the *Peter Ibbetson* run Jack suddenly stopped drinking, his creative urge superseding for a time his self-destructiveness. The period of sobriety lasted two years, his longest dry spell. But as the eventual road tour lengthened, his irritability and restiveness began to increase, possibly because of the lack of alcoholic escape.

Jack began to snarl at those nearest him. He was genuinely fond of Constance Collier, and admired her as an artist, yet he frequently provoked quarrels with her.

He had always detested coughing by an audience during a stage performance. Now he began to do something about it. He would interrupt the play to reprimand the offenders, suggest picturesque clinical procedures, show an ironical concern for the ill health of the stricken ones, or else join in their hackings with thorough sarcasm.

He was tiring of the part. That was his destiny, to tire of parts. To relieve the dullness of one-night stands in the smaller towns, Jack began to collect cookery gadgets purchased at the five-and-ten-cent stores. He set up a portable kitchen in his dressing room, disregarding the fact that the curtain soon would rise on a romantic play, and that fumes of onions, garlic, and sizzling meat would spread over the place. He was entirely serious about his cooking, as he was about anything—for a time.

Then finally, in Chicago, he told Constance that he was physically and mentally tired, and could not continue. It was a blow. *Peter Ibbetson* could have gone on for weeks to capacity business. Yet she understood.

In later years Constance Collier said she considered John Barrymore the greatest of all the actors she had known—and she had known most of the great ones.

IN OCTOBER of 1917 Barrymore found a sanctuary on the attic floor of a century-old house off Washington Square. He began at once to transform it into a studio which he called "the Alchemist's Corner." During his first two years of residence he admitted no women callers, and entertained few men other than his brother Lionel and Edward Sheldon. He embraced this off-stage loneliness, it seems, as an opportunity for self-evaluation. That he did possess a deep spiritual consciousness was apparent to those who had access to his confidence.

He was also capable of platonic friendships with women, and one of his deepest friendships of this nature was for his landlady, Mrs. Juliette S. Nicholls. She had been slow to accept him as a tenant, having heard of his bohemian antics. But the agent who had discovered the attic in response to Jack's request for a quiet hideaway "that would please a nun's grandfather" had assured her the actor would behave.

When Barrymore asked her permission to fix up the place, at his expense, she agreed, little knowing the extremes to which he was planning to go. The walls of the bedroom were covered with pink-striped paper; baseboard and moldings were painted black. Square glass mirrors, framed in black, formed the doors. The window drapes were pale mauve taffeta edged with white bead fringe. A French fireplace of white marble faced the foot of a bed which Barrymore specified should be narrow and hard. "A bed that implies celibacy for a change," he said.

He fashioned a bay window on the north side of the studio, stretched saffron chiffon over the wide skylight, from which hung an elaborate lantern. A cover of embroidered gold brocade was flung over the baby grand piano. A tall candlestand, an old Venetian mirror, a large antique globe, and a Lombardian chair completed this music corner. After he had surfaced the walls with Chinese gold, he spent hours smoke-smudging them. It was this "aging" of his retreat that caused him to refer to it as the Alchemist's Corner.

Now he turned his attention to the roof. Mrs. Nicholls was out of the city at the time, so Barrymore wrote to her:

> You have been so lenient in permitting me to exercise my fancy on the studio. Would you mind very much if I did a few ornamental things to the roof, at my own expense, of course? I'd like to build a little stairway to it, and place a few plants there, with perhaps a small pavilion in which I could sit when the locust blossoms come to the courtyards of Greenwich Village. It would be like living in Paris in the twelfth century.
>
> Yours entreatingly,
Top Floor

Mrs. Nicholls again consented. Barrymore hired a carpenter to build a crooked, steep staircase to the roof, and a small structure near the skylight, which he said was the first penthouse in New York. He put ships' models in the little house, a Franklin stove, and outside it the wheel from a wrecked schooner and a ship's bell.

Now, with customary disregard for consequences to the old beams, or a thought for proper drainage, he had thirty-five tons of topsoil hoisted onto the roof and planted cedars eight feet tall, as a hedge on the street side of the roof. He also installed wisterias, arborvitae, cherry trees, and grapevines, and a fountain, the overflow of which eventually seeped into the bedroom and streaked the Chinese gold walls of the studio.

Mrs. Nicholls returned from a trip to Europe to find a horticultural frenzy atop her house. She was somewhat amazed, but did not complain. She could not, she said, for there was a startling yet weird beauty to Barrymore's creation, and the man himself seemed so childishly content as he fed the birds on his "estate."

Even later, after he had moved away and a subsequent tenant one morning found himself in bed with water from a spring rain pouring down upon him and the ceiling beams sagging dangerously, this remarkably fine woman did not resent what Barrymore had done. It cost fifteen hundred dollars to remove the topsoil and reinforce the beams with steel girders, for which she never billed him. She knew him more objectively than most other women. When asked later what she thought of him, she said: "I think he was a confused child."

IT WAS A SIGNIFICANT MOMENT for me when, during the writing of this book, I sat in Arthur Hopkins's managerial office at the Plymouth Theatre in New York examining old pictures of Jack and inquiring into his promptbooks. Never far from my thoughts was that long-ago afternoon when I had come as a young reporter to a dressing room of this same theater to get an interview with the star of *Redemption*, an actor I had never met or seen.

Now I was seeking the recollections of one who had worked with John Barrymore during that period when he was at his apogee. Arthur Hopkins produced four of the actor's most noteworthy plays, including two by the Bard—*Richard III* and, eventually, *Hamlet*. But that afternoon as we sat talking, Hopkins, too, was remembering *Redemption*. It had been their first venture together, and during rehearsals for that production he came to know Barrymore's deep earnestness about his work.

"He was tireless in preparation," the producer told me, "never burdened by vanity or the need of impressing others. It was less humility than concentration. Rehearsals for him were a ceaseless quest. He created out of his own texture. He borrowed nothing. He copied nothing. His whole search was within himself."

Later Arthur and I went out into the theater, and from the balcony looked down upon the stage where Barrymore had played *Redemption* so many years before. Here, also, he had appeared with his brother Lionel in *The Jest*, another great success. And from this balcony audiences had seen John Barrymore's brilliant playing of *Richard III*.

The pilot light shone small in the down-distance, making the theater seem darkly huge. The stage, the back walls were bare, the seats empty—yet were they? The clear small light, standing like a votive lamp among cathedral shadows, exercised an almost hypnotic power. Illusion was everywhere about the old playhouse. One traveled back to the time when the slim, springing figure of the great young actor dominated this stage, and the voice we knew so well sounded with rhythmic majesty.

Each man carries within his own memory a golden age. Here in the still theater, with the star-gleam of the distant stage light, the halo of dust about it, the smell that is the theater and like no other smell, the slow, chill updraft of air that comes from the great mouth of the proscenium arch, here one dreamed of days that were great with youth and circumstance.

"A man is not old," Barrymore once said, "until regrets take the place of dreams."

CHAPTER 9

A BLITHE AND HANDSOME poetess, whose quill name was Michael Strange, became Barrymore's second wife. She had the face of a Romney portrait and the spirit of a U.S. Marine. Numerous heart experts have written about this striking alliance. The principals themselves, Michael Strange in a memoir, *Who Tells Me True*, and Barrymore in his poppings off to the recording angels of Park Row, alternately evidenced their ardor and their disillusionment.

They dressed alike for a time, a symbol of their unity. Even so they indulged in unreasonable jealousies, trumped-up quarrels, mutual threats of suicide, unpredictable separations and wild reunions, for both were stubborn, egotistical, and intense.

The poetess, born Blanche Oelrichs of Newport's social caste, had first met Barrymore when he was playing in *Justice*. He had already left his first wife and, according to Miss Strange, "looked elfin and forsaken." This courtship—three years of it— leaves confusing echoes, like a voice loosed in a rain barrel. The poetess mentions family opposition to her alliance with the actor, but gives no account of any personality clashes during the wooing period. Barrymore occasionally referred to prenuptial battles, but he was unreliable chronologically and may have had in mind the strife after the wedding aisle had been turned into a warpath.

John Barrymore's movie roles, clockwise: as Mr. Hyde, the alter ego of Dr. Jekyll; as Louis XV in "Marie Antoinette"; in "Twentieth Century"; as the Duke of Gloucester in "Show of Shows."

Michael Strange, it seems, became the only one of his admirers to breach the walls of his sanctuary, the Alchemist's Corner. Jack maintained that she accomplished this by sending him potted plants instead of cut flowers.

"I never cared to see flowers imprisoned in pots," he said. "It offended my own sense of freedom. Consequently, when potted plants arrived at the house, I would free them, like pigeons, on my roof. I began to notice that Blanche had exquisite taste in flowers, a taste that precisely suited my own predilections. I read into this the existence of other congenial qualities."

She also sent him notes, and he made an exception to his rule against opening mail to read these gracefully worded missives. The barrage of plants and notes had a siegelike quality, and may have stimulated Barrymore's remark, years later: "I never married any of my wives. They married me."

He was in a taut state of nerves before and for a long time after the marriage in August 1920. His theatrical labors taxed him and he also had done a few silent motion pictures, among which was *Dr. Jekyll and Mr. Hyde*. Besides, it was at this time that he was hurling himself with unprecedented intensity into preparations to play the role of Gloucester in *Richard III*.

"We had been planning *Richard* for a year," Arthur Hopkins said. "This was the great challenge. If we could successfully open the door to Shakespeare, then we might someday master *Hamlet*, the crowning dream."

For his role in *Richard*, Barrymore insisted on authenticity of costume, and hired an old armorer who did repair work for museums to fashion actual suits of heavy plate armor, making some forty trips to the armorer's forge in Newark for metallic fittings. This was not the customary tinny plate of wardrobe warehouses. Whenever Barrymore fell encased in it, he suffered skull shocks and body bruises.

In playing the deformed and lamed Gloucester, Barrymore glided across the stage like some unearthly spider. Once he was asked how he managed such a "swift limp," and how he prevented the efforts of contortion from intruding upon his difficult speeches. He replied:

"I merely turned my right foot inward, pointing it toward

the instep of my left foot. Then I forgot all about it. I did not try to walk badly. I walked as *well* as I could. You will find, I think, that a cripple does not try to walk with a worse gait than he has to employ. He endeavors to walk as *well* as he can."

Finally he undertook the task of reforming his voice to meet the classic demands of Shakespearean projection. In spite of the rare quality of his voice, it was of short range and rather furry, due to a complete lack of breath control.

He had met Margaret Carrington, a retired opera singer, who had made a long study of voice production and the relation of words to meaning. She found it difficult to believe that the most popular actor in America was asking her to help him, especially as *Richard III* was announced to open in six weeks. Never before had a voice been "built" in six weeks. With Mrs. Carrington, he now worked incessantly and successfully to gain the control necessary to sustain the long unbroken phrases of Shakespeare's verse, a veritable tour de force in the use of his will.

The production opened on time, but as Arthur Hopkins later said, "With the intensity required by *Richard*, a long run would have been possible only if Jack had saved himself otherwise; but in his frantic pursuit of a new marriage he gave himself completely. The crash occurred. After four weeks he was obliged to close, and thus came an abrupt ending to his great triumph."

It is said that after the evening performance he would take the train to Atlantic City where Michael Strange was temporarily residing, go without sleep, quarrel with his beloved, and get back just in time for the rise of curtain. For him this emotional depletion was catastrophic. As for Miss Strange, being married to Barrymore seemed to have been like setting up light housekeeping inside the crater of Vesuvius.

UNHAPPILY, Jack sublet the Alchemist's Corner, rightly divining that his new wife would not be content in this sequestered, cobwebbed setting. And he went to live with her on Sixty-seventh Street. "It was delightful," Michael Strange said in her memoir, "to have someone in the 'home' at last whom the servants considered more temperamental than myself."

He seemed to have given up the theater during the first year of this marriage. Then when Michael, who was expecting a baby, wrote a play during her pregnancy, her twofold productivity enchanted Jack. He volunteered to appear in it. His producer, Arthur Hopkins, could not share his enthusiasm for the play, *Clair de Lune*, a work suggested by Hugo's novel *The Man Who Laughs*, and its production was undertaken by Alf Hayman of the Frohman offices. Jack played the role of the clown, Gwymplane, and persuaded Ethel to appear as Queen Anne.

The critics set fire to his wife's theatrical monument. As Barrymore's good friend Alexander Woollcott of the New York *Times* later recalled, all the critics "privately thought that the play would scarcely have been produced had it not been for the somewhat irrelevant circumstance of Michael Strange having married Barrymore." One critic elaborated on this conjecture in print, summing up *Clair de Lune* thusly: "For the love of Mike."

In any case, the reviews so irked Barrymore that he went into a three-alarm rage and had to be dissuaded forcibly from making a speech about critics on the second night.

Not long after *Clair de Lune* closed, Michael Strange gave birth to a girl who was christened Joan Strange Barrymore, but afterward officially called Diana. For a time Jack forgot his troubles, private or public. He really had wished for a boy, but said, "I'm glad it's a girl. If she were a boy, she'd inherit all my habits, and I wouldn't know how to combat them: I'd have such sympathy with them."

He had been planning to appear in a dramatization of *Monsieur Beaucaire*, by his friend Booth Tarkington, but now he thought he would postpone it, perhaps retire altogether from the stage. He eventually took Michael abroad, a trip punctuated by the usual quarrels, threats of suicide, noisy accusations of extramarital romance. Barrymore afterward admitted to a major share of the provocations, recalling one of them had been his drinking the alcoholic fuel in Michael's curling-iron heater. Why he should have preferred such a low grade of beverage in Paris, a city of wine, might have perplexed any woman.

One day in June 1922, after months of storms and rages both in Europe and back in New York, Jack appeared at Ethel's home in Mamaroneck. He seemed gaunt and stricken, not because of any specific physical ailment, but from long harassment of mind. "I don't know what the hell to do," he said to his sister. "I feel like a soufflé that has been out of the oven too long. Guess you'd better take me in."

Ethel, of course, "took him in." The next morning she put into his hand a small, inexpensive edition of *Hamlet*. "Jake," she said, "read the two soliloquies. You may enjoy them." He reappeared to announce that he had done so. Then he added slowly: "I think I'll run over to see my friend Margaret Carrington."

"That's the last I saw of him for two months," Ethel said.

CHAPTER 10

HAMLET'S SOLILOQUIES possessed him. His irresolution fled. He would climb the highest of the magic mountains, the last great peak he was to scale in the fabulous domain of the theater.

"Do you really believe," I asked Lionel one day, years later, "that Jack was on the level when he said that Hamlet was the easiest role he ever played?"

"Of course he was," Lionel replied. "You must take into account that when the Bard wrote *Hamlet* he had Jack in mind."

It did not, however, happen quite that simply. Mrs. Carrington agreed to coach Jack only on the condition that there be no date fixed for the *Hamlet* premiere until she felt that he was professionally and psychologically ready for the assignment. Producer Arthur Hopkins readily consented. On the first day Jack appeared at her Connecticut farm, where he was to stay with her, he brought with him an armload of works having to do with the character and the motivations of Hamlet, which she suggested be put away where the silverfish might chew on them. She chose for their only text the small Temple edition of *Hamlet* which sister Ethel had given Jack. It contained not many footnotes, which Jack detested anyway. "Reading footnotes is like having to run downstairs to answer the doorbell during the first night of a honeymoon," he said.

By throwing out all previously conceived Hamlets, Mrs.

Carrington brought immediate response from Barrymore's creative nature. He worked six to eight hours a day, and underwent night sessions of painstaking analysis and evaluation, having agreed not to attempt to memorize the role until he had explored its every shade of meaning.

Wearing tights, as was demanded by the Hamlet role, had always been one of Barrymore's chief antipathies, notwithstanding his superb physique.

"When I first got into these skin-fitting jollities," Barrymore said of his tights, "I felt as if I had put on the intimate wear of Peg Woffington. Good God! What an ass a grown male can become on occasion! Then at last I decided to conquer these counterfeits of nudity or be conquered. I spent at least three hours before a pier glass. True, I had to take a few drinks to brace myself. Then I began to stare at the asinine fellow in the mirror. I sneered at him, I reviled him, I questioned his authenticity in matters of romance. I walked, I turned this way and that, never taking my eyes from him. Finally I got so tired of surveying myself, so sick, so fed up with tights that I no longer gave a damn how they looked on me or anyone else. I had 'em licked."

When the *Hamlet* rehearsals finally began in September, Hopkins followed the directorial plan that had been so rewarding in *Richard*. "Previous interpretations were ignored. We made ourselves servants of the play, untempted by any beckoning to leave our personal imprint on it. The result? The unfolding pattern had the unbelievable authenticity of a witnessed miracle. The unseen and unheard were being communicated. The theater has known few moments so startling as Jack's opening-night reading of his first soliloquy. The new prince was entering his kingdom."

Press and public acclaimed Barrymore as "the first Hamlet of our generation."

Of what did this man himself think during the hour of laurels? With the audience wildly applauding and the curtain lowering, then rising again and again, were we to believe him when he afterward said, "Fear was leaking out of every pore"? Had he again "heard thunder in the applause"?

Whatever his emotions, he allowed no one inside his dressing room following the performance that night, except a few immediate friends and relatives, whom he soon sent away with promises to join them at a supper party in his honor. He picked up the red apple sent by Uncle John Drew.

"I sat there for a long time thinking about Uncle Jack. He was getting old, about seventy, and he had arthritis. His liquor and he were beginning to quarrel with each other. . . . Not long before I had been up with him all night at The Lambs. He was meticulously dressed in evening clothes, but his jaw would drop down, and my job was to tuck it back in place from time to time. He was always so spruce and neat, you know, and would have been shocked to learn that his jaw ever drooped in public. . . ."

Barrymore, now in his street clothes, telephoned his old friend Frank Case at the Algonquin Hotel. "Is the kitchen still open, Frank?" he said. "I'm coming over."

When he arrived, he ordered a glass of milk and some finnan haddie. "We talked until morning," Case said, "and never once, even remotely, did Jack refer to *Hamlet* or to theatrical matters. It was as if the night of his greatest triumph had never been."

ONE THING THAT ENCHANTED Jack with the Hamlet role was the physical leeway it permitted the actor. "You can play it standing, sitting, lying down, or, if you insist, kneeling," he once said. "You can have a hangover. You can be cold sober. You can be hungry, overfed, or have just fought with your wife. It makes no difference as regards your stance or your mood. There are, within the precincts of this great role, a thousand Hamlets, any one of which will keep in step with your whim of the evening."

And yet it wasn't long before Jack was tiring of *Hamlet*, as he invariably wearied of all theatrical iteration, at about the sixtieth performance. He began to talk to Hopkins of "quitting this damned nonsense."

Nevertheless, he played the role of Hamlet on Broadway one hundred and one times, one more than had Edwin Booth. Then he toured as the Dane for a brief season of nine weeks the following year. Concerning this campaign, Hopkins said somewhat sadly: "The largest theaters were inadequate. In Cleveland his last classical appearance in America was made, and there passed from us the theater's richest gift."

It was during this tour, in Boston, that he met the aging portraitist, John Singer Sargent. Sargent had once sketched Ethel, and Jack hoped he might perhaps paint his portrait. Sargent, however, had put away his brushes for all time, but did do a crayon sketch of Barrymore's head and face. "You would be a difficult subject for any artist," Sargent said. "Your features are too regular. There is, you know, a bit of caricature in every great portrait."

The sketch, presented by Sargent to Jack, bears out the artist's contention. Although highly prized by Jack, it lacks distinction, having a pretty-boy aura. A sheriff impounded it many years later in behalf of Barrymore's greathearted persecutors during his dark days, and it now hangs in the San Diego Museum.

AFTER SEVERAL ATTEMPTS to mend his domestic life, Jack went to Europe, where he and Michael Strange were alternately together and apart. He was unhappy with her or away from her.

He finally decided to put on *Hamlet* himself in London. Constance Collier, forever grateful to him for *Peter Ibbetson*, agreed to play Hamlet's mother and offered to try to interest London managers, but it required many months of diplomatic persistence before a six-week lease was signed for the Haymarket Theatre, in the foyer of which, on an old playbill, his father long ago had found the stage name Maurice Barrymore.

Attending Jack's London debut as Hamlet was an old friend and confirmed fan of the Barrymores, Winston Churchill. Also in that critical audience was playwright George Bernard Shaw, who took exception to the shortened version being presented and next day sent Barrymore a letter attacking him not as an actor but as a person who dared to alter Shakespeare's play as written.

Shaw or no Shaw, the production was an incredible success. "Our six weeks were soon over," Constance Collier said afterward, "with standing room only for every performance." Then,

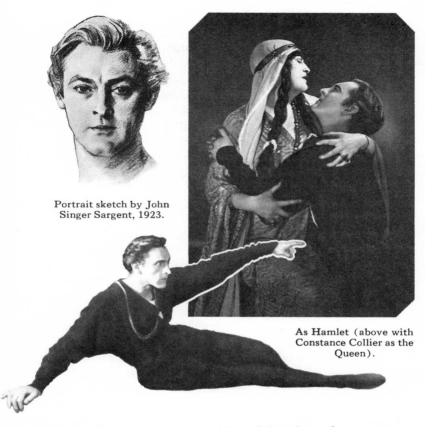

Portrait sketch by John Singer Sargent, 1923.

As Hamlet (above with Constance Collier as the Queen).

to continue for six more weeks, Jack paid the salaries for an entire cast of another play which had been scheduled to open at the Haymarket and was standing by.

At the close of this London run, offers came to Barrymore to take the *Hamlet* company to Berlin and to Paris, but he declined.

"By this time," Miss Collier said, "that strange resentment of any part Jack played too long had overtaken him. He hated the very sight of the stage and the sound of his lines. He gave so much of himself to every performance that each one seemed a chip off his life."

After the London *Hamlet* closed, Jack arrived home in America with a valet, Blaney, a small white-nosed monkey named Clementine, the gift of actress Gladys Cooper, and the announced intention of leaving the theater for good, a decision which many persons deplored.

Alexander Woollcott was not among them. "Why in hell shouldn't he have quit? Must the monstrous demand be heeded that a delicate instrument do *Hamlet* every night, merely because there is a public for it? After all, he couldn't show *Hamlet* to all the population that keeps pouring from the human assembly line if he kept on playing it for fifty years, and in a hundred Yale Bowls at a time."

CHAPTER 11

IN THE SPRING of 1925 Barrymore obtained a legal separation from his second wife. Similar agreements had been drawn previously, but the Barrymores had become "reconciled" before the notarial seals were dry. Jack had, however, renounced the guardianship of his daughter, Diana, in June 1921, a mere month after her birth, implying that he wished to assure his wife he would never interpose himself between mother and child, no matter what might arise to plague the parents.

Suddenly, now that their separation had the aspect of finality, there was no more bitterness between Barrymore and Michael Strange. With their egos no longer competing, the emotional causes of torment vanished, and their occasional correspondence was polite and calm, as if each were more interested in the other's success now than when in wedlock.

The separation agreement provided an annual payment of $18,000 for the maintenance of his wife and daughter, and the premiums on a large life-insurance policy, with Diana as the beneficiary. In regard to alimony—and he paid several hundreds of thousands of dollars of it—Jack once said: "Alimony is the most exorbitant of all stud fees, and the worst feature of it is that you pay it retroactively."

That same spring Jack also signed a contract with Warner Brothers to go to California to appear in three "super" motion pictures. He had made one picture for Warner Brothers, *Beau*

Brummel, the year before his London *Hamlet*. Like his other early cinematic experiments, it had contributed little to his own prosperity or the public's cultural advancement. His new contract, however, was extraordinary. He was to work only seven weeks on each photoplay, and receive $76,250 a picture. Overtime would be $7,625 a week. He was granted the then unusual privilege of approving or disapproving the stories, and of being the only starring actor, unless he himself approved a co-star. Publicity was to be in keeping with his "reputation and prestige." An examination of the first draft of this document discloses that Jack had penciled in numerous shrewd amendments and notations, an indication that he could focus his mind intently and analytically upon matters of moment when he wished to do so.

He was in a high-sky mood all the way to California, accompanied by Blaney and Clementine, perhaps the best loved of the multitude of pets he eventually had. Jack amazed Blaney by holding grave conversations with Clementine, warning her against the pitfalls of Hollywood. Blaney, a short, staid man of much dignity, did not like Clementine at all. His former employer, Sir Herbert Tree, had had several eccentricities, but he never had requested his man to superintend a monkey's business in the WC.

Jack, Blaney, and Clementine took up quarters in a detached bungalow of the Ambassador Hotel. It had a large living room, two bedrooms, and another room which Barrymore used as a combination "museum" and office, and in which he installed a cage for Clementine. During the day she was tied by a long leash to an outdoor balcony.

His initial commitment was *The Sea Beast*, a story based on Herman Melville's *Moby Dick*. Jack himself had chosen that story, although the studio had hoped that he would first make *Don Juan*.

During the formulation of his earlier pictures Barrymore entered into each production with the same great care and industry that had possessed him during his best theatrical days, taking advantage of the terms of his contract to see to it that his stories were superior to the child-mind tales sometimes regarded as proper amusement for motion-picture patrons. He even participated in the supervision of sets and costumes, and refused to have doubles, or stunt actors, take his place in action scenes. He eventually had several deep scars and evidences of old fractures because of this adventurous quirk.

For *The Sea Beast*, Jack was permitted, among other things, to choose his leading lady. There was, to be sure, no lady in the novel *Moby Dick*, not even a woman. However, the studio, somewhat alarmed about the box-office aspects of a picture that had, as its principals, Mr. Barrymore and a whale, devised a scenario that would include a love story. One evening Jack announced to his script writer that he had found a leading lady for *The Sea Beast*.

"She's the most preposterously lovely creature in all the world. She walked into the studio like a charming child. Slender and shy and golden-haired. I shall not eat nor sleep till I see her again." He paused reverently, then said, "But I'll have just one short drink to tide me over till tomorrow."

Barrymore's new star and, as was soon apparent, his new love, was Dolores Costello, the daughter of actor Maurice Costello. She had recently been screen-tested by Warner Brothers and signed to play the part of a maid in another picture. "Maid, hell!" Jack said. "Can you imagine them casting an angel to wear a cap and apron? I suppose they'd hire Lord Nelson to run a coal barge." Thus a little-known girl was about to become a Cinderella because of Barrymore's having chanced to see her. Still, such things did happen in Hollywood.

He looked young, yet Jack was forty-three years old and Dolores in her twenties when they met. She seemed to fill his need for expressing paternal as well as romantic love, and he was incredibly happy with her; but he was annoyed by the fact that he was expected to be secretive about the romance. There was the technical obstacle of Michael Strange, from whom he was legally separated but not divorced, and the studio was on guard against any scandalous implications touching the eminent actor and the young actress.

In the Costello household, to complicate things further, Jack was regarded as an unwelcome suitor. He slyly insisted, therefore, that his on-set love scenes with Dolores be repeated more than was necessary, although he had always maintained that actors in love usually gave unconvincing performances.

"The trouble is," he said, "that their pale faces and throbbing temples can cause an audience to believe that ptomaine poisoning has just set in."

His lovemaking in *The Sea Beast* refuted his own theories. As for Dolores, though her part was a minor one, her actual love for Jack was so like the bright spring that the role seemed important. They won each other, and *The Sea Beast* won the love of the world.

MARY ASTOR had been approved by Jack as leading lady for his second picture, *Don Juan*, before he had met Dolores. Early that October, at Miss Astor's home, he met Mr. and Mrs. Henry Hotchener, two persons who were to become closely associated with him during the ten best years of his Hollywood career.

Mrs. Hotchener had as a girl attracted the attention of the famous Adelina Patti, who recommended she study for the opera. In Europe she sang leading roles, sometimes with composer Puccini conducting the orchestra, then suddenly renounced her operatic career and turned to the study of theosophy and abnormal psychic phenomena. In India she met Annie Besant, president of the Theosophical Society, who called her "Helios," because of her brilliant, sunlike character. Her husband, Henry, was a calm-mannered, experienced businessman whose pleasant exterior, when scratched too rudely, disclosed steel beneath the surface. He would introduce a new word into the Barrymore lexicon, the word "no."

Both Hotcheners had lived much in India, which could explain why Barrymore, upon meeting them at Mary Astor's home, was at once drawn to them. Because his father had been born there, he had always been interested in that land of ancient culture; also, deep within his own nature lay a poetic mysticism. However, on his mind that night besides India—and Dolores—was a materialistic problem. "Hotchener," he said, "do you know anything about the damned income tax?"

Hotchener knew a great deal about the income tax and volunteered to examine Jack's return, which government sleuths had regarded without humor. At lunch next day, at Jack's Ambassador bungalow, Henry found taxes the least garbled of the actor's business affairs. His huge paychecks were sent directly to his New York attorney, who paid alimony and other fixed obligations out of this account, but Barrymore hadn't the slightest idea how much money he had left, for he never kept bank statements. When Hotchener finally had the papers sent to California some weeks later, he discovered that Jack had more than a hundred thousand dollars in his checking account, on which he was receiving no interest.

"Hank, for the love of God," Barrymore cried, "take over! Manage me."

MEANWHILE, JACK WAS FEELING the need to reexamine his life. He wanted to decide how best to ward off the antagonism of Dolores's parents. More than that, though, he sensed that even if he were free to marry Dolores their love might languish. He believed that for him a dark spell lay upon any marriage.

Now, with no Alchemist's Corner in which he might immure himself, he turned to the sea as a place for meditation. He was an excellent sailor. And for the first time in his life he was enjoying financial elbowroom. So he chartered an eighty-foot cabin cruiser, *The Gypsy*, along with its captain and crew, and sailed away upon what he termed "a quest for myself."

His coastwise course to the tip of the Mexican peninsula of Lower California took three weeks, during which he drank no hard liquor. His log, which he subsequently entrusted to Hotchener as his literary executor, expressed the rapture of being alone at sea, and frequently mentioned sleeping well, as if this were a phenomenon. But its overall mood was one of ecstatic yearning, and contained constant references to Dolores, for whom he had various nicknames: "Wink," "Small Cat," "Egg."

He fished, read, lay in the sun, observed with delight herons, curlews, flocks of ducks, and once a school of whales. Remembering his duel with a whale in *The Sea Beast*, he even tried to harpoon one. He went ashore in the little seaside villages of Mexico and made sketches of them. "Perhaps in time," he wrote, "I will again become a human being, the person I *was* fourteen or fifteen years ago."

He returned from his voyage with a dream. He would buy a yacht in which Dolores and he together would sail away from a conventional world. The fact that his grandiose projects hatched out as infrequently as porcelain eggs never occurred to him, nor that until the watchful Mrs. Costello heard the word "marriage" for her daughter she would visa no passports.

Eventually he found a ninety-three-foot schooner, *The Mariner*, sleek and white, and the winner of a San Francisco-to-Tahiti race in record time. Although Jack preferred sail, he wanted the boat both comfortable and safe for Dolores, so he installed a diesel engine.

But, having spent $110,000 on *The Mariner* and her alterations, he had still not asked Mrs. Costello whether Dolores could sail with him to far places, or even near ones. She now informed the pained dreamer that her daughter might not even step aboard without a chaperon: herself, Mrs. Costello.

In early June of 1926, therefore, *The Mariner* left San Pedro harbor and headed for Catalina and adjacent ports, carrying Dolores and her mother. Under full spread of canvas, the yacht heeled over beautifully in a bouncing groundswell which presently caused Mrs. Costello to retire to her cabin.

She became more seasick with each chime of the ship's bell, and after three days, Dolores insisted they put back to San Pedro. Jack said, yielding, "I shall never again celebrate Mother's Day."

CHAPTER 12

SOMETIME EARLIER, attracted by the prestige of United Artists, a company graced by Mary Pickford, Douglas Fairbanks, and Charlie Chaplin, Jack had agreed that upon completion of his Warner Brothers' contract he would make two pictures for them and share in the profits. This was before Henry Hotchener became Barrymore's manager and would, in time, prove why he needed advice in such matters. There was no time clause in this United Artists' contract and it would take two years to complete two pictures. After fixed studio charges and expenses had been subtracted, there would be no profits for Jack other than his original price of $100,000 for each picture. This meant that he would earn less than $2,000 for each workweek, as against the more than $10,000 a workweek he was making at Warner Brothers, who also paid all his hotel and transportation bills, whether he worked or not. When Henry Hotchener officially took over Jack's affairs, however, United Artists signed the actor for a third picture at $150,000, with a time limit and many other concessions.

Meantime, Jack was still under contract to complete another picture for Warner Brothers, a camera version of *Manon Lescaut* entitled *When a Man Loves*. Dolores was again his leading lady.

Between "shots" Jack spent his time (Dolores in a canvas-back chair beside him) designing silverware for *The Mariner*, selecting linens, curtains, and other decorations. Onstage, in his desire to make Dolores an acknowledged actress, he "threw" many scenes to her. Ethel Barrymore, visiting her brother on the set, was amazed at the spectacle of an accomplished artist deliberately "tossing away" his scenes. She expected "a Barrymore to live up to tradition in regard to art."

He was not only immune to her criticism but also wired his future employer, Joseph M. Schenck, the head of United Artists, that he was going to advise Dolores to quit Warner Brothers, and recommended that Schenck help Dolores "jump the league." United Artists handled the message as if it were a bomb, Hollywood having recently appointed Will Hays, former postmaster general, to keep a super-eye on censorship, morals, and the industry's codes of competitive business practice.

When the Hays office telephoned Jack, advising him to confine himself to acting, he could not understand why he was in trouble.

"I simply wanted Dolores to work beside me," he told Hotchener, who vainly tried to explain the sanctity of contracts.

By the end of the year Jack had completed his first picture for United Artists, a scenario based on the life of François Villon called *The Beloved Rogue*. That Christmas he bought jewelry for Dolores, but he himself left aboard *The Mariner* for another

John Barrymore,
with the white-
nosed monkey
Clementine, in
the Warner
Brothers film
"The Sea Beast."

long cruise in Mexican waters. He was again undergoing emotional conflict over the wisdom of entering for a third time into matrimony. He was also in doubt as to his ability to quit drinking, although he had tried, since meeting Dolores, to do so, not wanting to hurt the one person he said he loved more than he had ever loved anyone else. During these dry intervals he was in excellent health, and would vow never to drink again; then some bottle companion would come along, or some worry arise, and he would lapse into old habits. Each "fall" made him morose and desperate.

Sometimes he was haunted by the fear that his mind was doomed to impairment. Once a visitor to his dressing room had the bad taste to inquire: "Mr. Barrymore, is it true that your father died at an institution for the insane?" Jack rose, his face pale, his eyes turning green. In a slow, agonized tone, he said: "I am now going to kill you, you miserable, stupid son of a bitch!"

The visitor was most fortunate in reaching the door.

On this winter cruise, Jack took along a calendar on which he had asked Helios Hotchener to mark any days of special import to him: she had studied astrology in India and he regarded her as a woman of profound intuition. She circled one date with red crayon, warning him against accidents, and when he returned the Hotcheners asked him if anything of moment had happened that red-crayoned day.

"Happened?" he said. "I damned near lost my life; that's what happened." He then told how, while moored off the Mexican coast, he had reversed his decision to stay in his bunk all day, and had gone ashore alone to hunt game birds. Suddenly he found himself sinking waist-deep in some kind of quagmire. Only with great effort had he managed to draw an overhanging branch within reach of his fingers, and, after five desperate minutes of struggle, free himself.

From that time on Jack would not begin a motion picture, or even an important scene, without first conferring with Helios, who, in turn, consulted the stars. His director would have to accelerate or delay the shooting of various portions of the script, as the heavens might recommend. Barrymore wanted all battle scenes photographed under the sign of Mars, love scenes under the zodiacal influence of Venus.

IN SEPTEMBER 1927 Dolores's parents were divorced, and Barrymore began to visit her more frequently than when her father had been on the premises. Mr. Costello had not regarded him as the village paragon. Dolores also leased a new home which revived his longing for a place of his own, even though it did not resolve his uncertainty about matrimony. One morning he telephoned Hotchener: "Clementine told me last night that she wants a home in the country."

"A bachelor's house?"

"A house for two, meaning myself and Clementine, who has persuaded me that a reconnaissance in Beverly Hills is indicated. All the swells live there."

Hotchener, talking things over at Jack's hotel, suggested that property owners might raise the price when it became known that Barrymore was house hunting. "We'll fix that," the actor said, opening a chest of drawers. Hotchener thought he was looking for a bottle until he wheeled suddenly, to present a horrible face. Fangs protruded from his lips, and talonlike nails curled from his fingers—all part of the makeup he had used in *Dr. Jekyll and Mr. Hyde*. He drew on a wig and a battered hat. "I doubt the real-estate harpies will mistake me for a man of means," he said, tucking Clementine under his arm.

Barrymore eventually bought a hilltop home which had belonged to King Vidor, the Hollywood director. It was a five-room Spanish-type dwelling located on a private drive off Tower Road. "That's the place," he said when he saw it. "Buy it instantly!"

Jack now divided his interests among Dolores, *Tempest* (a film story of the Russian revolution, for United Artists), and his new home, for which he immediately hired a Japanese gardener, who enchanted him with horticultural marvels such as bushes on which red and white roses bloomed simultaneously.

During March of 1928 Dolores and her mother left for a holiday in Havana. Jack was lonesome and still worried about his drinking. He thought that if he could undertake some big theatrical enterprise, such as giving *Hamlet* in the huge open-air Hollywood Bowl, it might help him. With Hotchener he went there very late one evening and, standing in the moonlight on the bare stage, he began the "O, what a rogue and peasant slave am I!" soliloquy.

His voice, clear and resonant in the night air, reached the farthest row of empty seats where Henry sat. The next day he reserved the Bowl for a week in September and said he also intended to do *Hamlet* at the Greek Theatre of the University of California at Berkeley.

After Dolores's return Jack decided to confer with Helios about his romance. He asked her what the stars foretold for Dolores and himself.

"You will marry her," Helios said.

"But Blanche will never divorce me."

"Why not go East to ask her?"

Jack began again to drink, the idea of seeing Michael Strange seeming much on his mind. Finally he went to New York in April and stayed nearly a month. Upon his return he admitted that he had not directly broached the matter of a divorce. "Blanche was so friendly that I couldn't," he said. "We had a really happy visit together. How could I tell her I wanted to marry someone else?"

"So you went on a six-thousand-mile errand for nothing," Henry Hotchener said. "I advise you *right now* to telephone and ask her for a divorce."

Jack winced. "I'll wait for a propitious moment."

A few days later a Hollywood gossip column ran an exposé of his romance, which infuriated him.

"It seems the propitious moment has arrived," he said grimly, and was amazed to find that Michael Strange was quite willing to divorce him. This was to take several months, however, because of the legal technicalities.

During this time Jack finished his third and last photoplay for United Artists. He waived all plans for playing *Hamlet* in the Hollywood Bowl and concentrated on the enlargement of his Tower Road estate. He was adding to the original Vidor hacienda a structure of six rooms which he called the "Marriage House." The older house was "Liberty Hall," and the two were connected by a cloisterlike pergola. Jack rose early each day to watch the builders at work.

"This place is beginning to look like Angkor Wat," he said.

But no one foresaw then that this establishment one day would comprise sixteen separate structures, fifty-five rooms, storerooms, dressing rooms, a projection room, a large aviary, a rathskeller, six pools, a bowling green, a skeet range, several fountains, and a totem pole.

Meanwhile plans for the wedding got under way. *The Mariner* was showing signs of dry rot in her hull, but was pronounced safe for a honeymoon cruise. A Unitarian minister agreed to conduct the marriage service, and the prospective groom settled on thirty-seven as the age to put on the license instead of his actual forty-six.

On November 24, 1928, he and Dolores were married in her mother's house on Schuyler Road.

As they set off on their long-delayed voyage without a chaperon, and the weeping Mrs. Costello was saying good-by to

Away from it all: John Barrymore and the crew of "The Mariner," his 106-ft. racing schooner.

Below, the yacht "Infanta," carrying Barrymore, Dolores Costello and their two children, at anchor in Shoal Bay, British Columbia; inset, the skipper.

her daughter, Jack said, "Don't worry, Mamma. I'll cable you every day, and I'll take good care of Dolores, always."

But the honeymooners' cruise into South American waters was forty-three days old before Barrymore remembered to cable his mother-in-law: DOLORES IS WONDERFUL.

CHAPTER 13

WORK WAS STILL in progress at the Tower Road estate when, in March 1929, its master returned from the wedding cruise. Crews were bringing hundreds of tons of topsoil to the rocky slopes, planting numerous trees and shrubs, among them a dwarf Japanese cedar that cost eleven hundred dollars, and an olive tree from Palestine, said to be a hundred years old. New water mains were being laid, and power lines brought from considerable distance. Jack was reluctant to turn his thoughts from his unfinished home long enough to confer with producers about *General Crack*, his first talking picture, which he was making under a new contract with Warner Brothers.

He was getting $30,000 a week (including a profit-sharing bonus) for this picture at a time when other stars were quaking in their buskins because voice had come to the screen. Already the thin voice of Douglas Fairbanks, Sr., was disillusioning a public that somehow had associated his athletic virilities with the larynx of a Cossack basso profundo. And the hitherto enormously popular John Gilbert, Greta Garbo's co-star, was suddenly deserted to sit out his fabulous contract, partly because of the chickadee sound recordings of his voice.

"From Garbo to Limbo," Barrymore observed.

"But," a producer inquired, "do you consider your first attempt at the talkies of secondary importance?"

"Not secondary," said Jack. *"Tertiary."*

He had brought back from his cruise a cargo of skins of fishes and reptiles, which now were mounted and placed in the trophy room. He also had become interested in tropical birds. At Balboa, Canal Zone, he had ordered ten pairs of them and had sent a cable costing over a hundred dollars to his business manager in California with detailed instructions as to the immediate construction of an aviary at Tower Road. But this was just the beginning. Now he obtained feathered rarities from many dealers: Australian green parakeets, broadtailed whydahs, redbilled Chinese magpies, bleeding-heart doves, pearl-necked doves, gallinules, black-headed nuns, white-headed nuns, and strawberry, saffron, and fire finches. Six birds of paradise cost him $1,900.

By day he supervised every decorative detail of the aviary, and by night he pored over the available authorities on birdlife. He set artificial as well as stunted live trees inside the aviary, installed birdbaths, and devised cotes for nesting. Instead of gravel, the floor was planted with tough Korean grass, which could be raked without being uprooted.

Ordinarily he was a heavy smoker, but he never smoked when in his aviary, where he often stayed for hours. It was amazing to see his birds yield to whatever power he seemed so definitely to possess over dumb creatures. Perhaps it was his patience with them. Strange dogs singled him out wherever he went. Unlike most persons, he permitted them to lick his face. And now he allowed his birds to peck mealworms from his mouth. He didn't mind when they lime-streaked his clothes or hair.

Strolling near the aviary one day, he heard servants' voices.

"This worm business ain't safe. The way Mr. Barrymore holds them in his mouth for the birds."

"You mean it ain't safe for Mr. Barrymore?"

"Hell no! I mean safe for the birds. It's the booze on Mr. Barrymore's breath. The worms get drunk when he holds them on his lip. Then the birds eat the drunk worms. Get me?"

"By God, you're right! I noticed how some of the birds flies sideways after he feeds 'em off of his lip."

Barrymore promptly went on the wagon—for twenty-four hours.

A king vulture named Maloney occupied an especially high place in Jack's affection. This goose-sized bird would preen Barrymore's mustache lovingly, and even caress his hair and eyebrows with his rapacious beak. This sort of thing drove Lionel out of his wits.

557

Lionel, Ethel and John
Barrymore in the film
"Rasputin."

With Katharine Hepburn in
"A Bill of Divorcement."

Above, with Mary Astor in "Beau
Brummel"; at left, as Captain Ahab
in "Moby Dick."

"God Almighty!" Lionel would say. "Get rid of that stinking bird!"

"Vultures are most tidy about their persons," Jack said. "They wash and preen their plumage, and take hours at their toilets!"

"Toilets is right," said Lionel. "They *are* toilets!"

To find enough aged meat to satisfy the ever hungry Maloney, Jack frequently picked up tidbits from trash cans. One evening when the $30,000-a-week actor was strolling in town, dressed rather shabbily, having spent the afternoon in his aviary, he saw a trash can near the curb and began exploring its contents with a stick.

Just then a well-groomed stranger passed by, halted, and reached into his pocket.

"Here, my man," said the generous stranger, gingerly holding out a ten-cent piece. "But be sure to spend it only for food."

Jack looked up, took the dime, and touched the brim of his hat in a kind of salute.

"God bless you, sir!" he said throatily.

THE YEAR 1929 found him with an income of $430,000 and no debts, which seems amazing when one considers that he was putting a quarter of a million dollars into his estate. Furthermore, *The Mariner* had at last succumbed to dry rot, representing a dead loss of more than $110,000.

He should have been happy in his new marriage, and in general he was, although he had quarreled with Dolores as early as May, when she suggested that he do less drinking. His first severe illness also occurred in May, when he was treated for a duodenal ulcer. Then his throat began to bother him. A doctor recommended a tonsillectomy, but another medical man made a sounder diagnosis: "Your throat merely is raw from bad booze," he said. "I advise you to switch to better liquor. No operation necessary."

Ethel arrived in Hollywood in July. Concerned about Jack's drinking, she asked Hotchener, "Why is he doing it so heavily?" to which Barrymore's manager replied, "Is there always a reason?"

For a time Jack became happily occupied in planning a new

yacht, called the *Infanta*, a name suggested by Dolores, who was expecting her first child. The steel diesel cruiser was to be 120 feet in length overall, powered by two engines, and would cost $225,000. Barrymore suggested a mint bed aft the main deckhouse for juleps.

In August he made a Technicolor sequence of *Henry VI* for the Warner Brothers *Show of Shows*—the first time that Shakespeare came to the sound screen. This part of the production was beautifully done and demonstrated that the actor had lost none of his powers.

In September Winston Churchill called at the Warner studio to watch Jack make some scenes for *The Man from Blankley's*. The two men were photographed together and Barrymore sent a copy to his old friend, Max Beerbohm, in London. In an accompanying letter the actor revealed that he had had a recurrence of his ulcer but added that he in no wise blamed Mr. Churchill's visit for this condition.

He went on the bland Sippy diet, and stayed at home for two weeks, occupying himself by painting on navigational charts scenes illustrating his real or fancied adventures, in the style of fifteenth-century cartographers, a hobby he had begun as early as 1913, after a fishing expedition to the Bahamas.

When he returned to the studio he still was not well. His blood pressure was very low. He also began to lose interest in his yacht, partly because he could not associate a shell of metal with the sea. *The Mariner* had been different: born of blue water, descended from a long line of Gloucester boats that made history. A steel hull seems to one who has been under sail as a barnyard hen compared to a bird of paradise.

He did show an interest, however, in one item of the *Infanta*'s equipment, the galley stove. Specifications called for a five-burner range, fueled by diesel oil, but his cook said that he could do better work with an eight-burner.

"Give him eighty burners if he insists," Jack said. "The most important man on a ship, next to the skipper, is the cook. Anyone who thinks that food is merely something to eat is the kind of moron who would make penwipers of the Sistine tapestries or hang a First Folio in an outhouse."

The Honorable
Winston Churchill
visits John Barrymore
on the set of
"The Man from Blankley's"
in Hollywood (1929).

A FEW DAYS AFTER his first wedding anniversary, Jack said to his manager, "Dolores is harping on my drinking, and says I ought to go on the wagon."

"That doesn't seem unreasonable."

"No, but I've noticed it isn't so easy to stop drinking as it used to be."

"Well," his manager replied, "you're getting older, and the habit stronger. The question is, do you really *want* to stop?"

Barrymore looked Hotchener directly in the eye. "I'm not sure that I do. Drinking helps me not to worry too much about the future."

It was the time of his greatest wealth, and of his finest screen portrayals. He was forty-seven, and still vital, but the next five years would be for him a dress rehearsal for personal disaster. The wild winds frequently had blown across his heavens, but soon he would know the gale, and then the hurricane. He hurled himself against these years with fist-shakings and scornful cries. His prodigious follies, quixotic deeds, intense bursts of labor, together with his disregard of repose, would have felled a god.

He strove now, in his own fashion, to keep alive the love that he so gloriously had dreamed. He fleetingly inspired new hopes in Dolores that things again might be as they had been, but soon his good intentions strayed like soap bubbles, bursting to nothingness in the air.

In March of 1930 he began work on *Moby Dick*, the talking-picture version of *The Sea Beast*. By the end of the month the *Infanta* had been launched and taken for a shakedown cruise to Ensenada, but without Jack or Dolores; he was busy, and she expecting their first child. His daughter Dolores Ethel Mae was born the morning of April 8. "I'm sorry for your sake that it's a girl," his wife said.

"Doesn't my whole life prove that I get along better with girls?" he replied.

He was especially restless that autumn and decided to go on a long cruise, taking Dolores and the infant, revisiting the places described with passionate earnestness in his diary nearly five years before when aboard *The Gypsy*. He employed a woman doctor as well as a nurse to look after the baby's health aboard the *Infanta*, and the family sailed from Long Beach bound for Cape San Lucas, Mazatlán. He could not, however, as the voyage progressed, rouse the nodding gods of romance who, in the days of yearning aboard *The Gypsy*, had seemed to promise him a lifelong blessing.

In fact, he was miserable. He had no "freedom," as he interpreted the word. Everywhere he moved about the boat, some shadow of restriction fell: a nurse, a doctor, no sails to hoist in fair winds or shorten when storms might be ridden out adventurously.

About two months after this southward sailing, he suffered a severe gastric hemorrhage. Dolores summoned a doctor in Guatemala. The bleeding was controlled, the doctor given a thousand-dollar fee, then the *Infanta* made for home, her owner stretched out on his bed. When she reached port, Barrymore dressed fully and disembarked to meet reporters and press photographers. Public word of his illness was being withheld. Someone wanted a picture of him holding a sea turtle he had captured, weighing more than a hundred pounds. Dolores started to protest but Barrymore stooped, seized the armature of the turtle, then held it in a pose.

He stayed in bed for the next month. He now suffered headaches on the right side of his head, forerunners of neuralgic attacks that recurred periodically.

IN THE FALL of 1931, since Dolores was expecting a second child the next year, her husband decided to build an addition to the Marriage House, a nursery known as the "Children's Wing." Other additions were undertaken, including a rathskeller with a wine cupboard, the door to which had a combination lock, because he lost keys so often. Then he mislaid the paper with the combination. After a legal safecracker had twice reopened the door, Jack wrote down the numbers on the wall, where anyone might read them—and did.

The rathskeller had in it an old bar which had once been in a Virginia City saloon patronized by Mark Twain. Barrymore decorated this bar with cigarette premium cards and cigar bands of other days, including one which he prized most of all—a John Drew Cigar band with his dapper uncle's picture on it. Often, while sitting in this retreat, Jack would hold his daughter on his lap and improvise stories for her entertainment, fabulous recitals of the deeds of a mysterious people called the "Magoozalums."

From a financial standpoint 1931 had been the best in Barrymore's career, with an income of $460,000, although he spent money almost as rapidly as he made it. The next year also was one of professional activity, beginning with the all-star production *Grand Hotel*, in which he appeared with his brother, Lionel, and Wallace Beery, Joan Crawford, and Greta Garbo.

When he was introduced to Miss Garbo, Jack kissed her hand in the John Drew tradition, then said with Victorian politeness: "My wife and I think you the loveliest woman in the world." He behaved toward this shy, sensitive artist as with a timid bird in his aviary. They became good friends, and once, after completing a particularly difficult scene together, Miss Garbo electrified the director, the camera crew, *and* Barrymore by impulsively kissing him.

In later years she said, "Barrymore was one of the very few

who had that divine madness without which a great artist cannot work or live."

Jack's son was born on the afternoon of June 4, 1932. The expectant father had been pacing the hall in the presence of a considerable audience of nurses and hospital attendants, swearing that if it were a boy he would quit drinking. Yet when he had seen the child who he thought resembled his own father, he said he was going out for a few minutes.

For a few minutes . . .

He stayed away for hours, then returned to the hospital room next to that of Dolores, to sink into a deep sleep with his clothes on. Dolores was heartsick.

"I swore that if God would give me a son, I would never drink again," Jack said some days afterward. "What happens to a man who makes a sacred oath, then breaks it?"

CHAPTER 14

BARRYMORE made five pictures at a fast tempo during 1932. Playing the part of the half-crazed father in *A Bill of Divorcement*, a motion picture that made a star of the dynamic young actress, Katharine Hepburn, he gave a portrayal that was one of the finest of his film career. Indeed, producer David O. Selznick later held it to be the finest all-time performance in the history of the screen.

Immediately after completion of *A Bill of Divorcement*, Jack appeared in *Rasputin and the Empress*, with his brother and sister as co-stars. Playwright Charles MacArthur wrote the *Rasputin* scenario, working on it from hour to hour to tailor it to the measurements of three mighty individualists, and one of his main jobs was assuring the Barrymore brothers that he was not favoring one against the other in the dialogue.

After a summer of hard work in 1933, during which his drinking increased—as did domestic uncertainties, jealousies, and quarrels—Jack began *Counsellor-at-Law* for Universal Studios. This role required the fastest and most sustained delivery of lines of any part he had so far undertaken. He finished it successfully, then completed *Long Lost Father* for RKO. Then he was recalled by Director William Wyler to Universal for the remaking of a single scene opposite actor John Qualen for *Counsellor-at-Law*.

He was tired on that October evening, but definitely not drunk, having had only one or two glasses of beer during recent days. He seemed wearily confident as he began the scene, but suddenly he stumbled over one brief speech. He made a comic face and everyone laughed.

The scene was undertaken again and Barrymore "blew up" in his lines at almost the same place as before. A third take was ordered, and Jack failed at it. He was not making jokes now. He was angry.

He continued to falter during several successive trials, and a recess was ordered to give him an opportunity to consult the scenario. But when the actors at length resumed their places before the camera, Jack again failed to remember the lines he had newly reviewed. Director Wyler and his cameraman exchanged perplexed glances, and Jack's manager, Henry Hotchener, stood in sad amazement on the sidelines as the actor stubbornly persisted and repeatedly flunked out. At the fiftieth attempt he still was fighting gamely to conquer the scene, his face drawn, his jaw set. Finally, at Hotchener's suggestion, the retake was put over until the next morning.

Barrymore looked straight ahead as he walked off the stage. During the drive home he did not speak, and Hotchener left him at about one a.m. with a "get some sleep now; everything will come out all right."

Jack merely nodded. Then he went into his library. What he thought to himself during the next hour, what fears he had of an approaching shadow, we cannot know. But we do know that a knock sounded on his door at two o'clock in the morning, an hour after his manager had left him.

The man who knocked was Noll Gurney, the manager of several of Hollywood's foremost actors, and a trusted friend of Barrymore's neighbor, John Gilbert.

"Jack Gilbert is in a bit of trouble," Gurney explained when Barrymore greeted him at the door in bathrobe and slippers.

Above, a family group (with "Tatters").

Family matters. Top, the house in Beverly Hills; above, on vacation with Dolores and John, Jr.; at right, "The Royal Family" together: Lionel and his wife; Ethel in the center, flanked by her daughter and two sons; the John Barrymores at right.

Gurney, of course, was unaware at this time of Barrymore's own travail. "Trouble?" asked Jack. "Never heard of the word. What can I do for Gilbert?"

"Would you mind coming over right away?" Gurney said. "He's very depressed. His Filipino servant is keeping an eye on him while I'm here."

"I see," Barrymore said. "Threatens to do away with himself. Is that it? Well, I'll get dressed. We have plenty of time, Noll. No actor would kill himself without an audience."

Was Gilbert drinking heavily? Jack asked Gurney as they walked across the lawns. Yes. Having woman trouble? Yes, his third wife, Virginia Bruce, was threatening to leave him. And his first and only sound picture had been hissed at its Palo Alto premiere.

"What the hell!" Jack snorted. "Even Caruso was once hissed in Naples."

"But so many slurs have been made about Gilbert's voice," Gurney said, "that he's convinced the public thinks him some kind of a softie."

"Well," Barrymore said, "my friend Jack Dempsey has a voice like a constipated sparrow, but I'd hesitate to suggest he was anything but a lethal bull."

Gilbert was surprised to see Barrymore, but greeted him with a hollow cordiality: "Great to see you. We'll make a night of it. Drinks for everybody," he said.

"There will be no more drinks tonight for anybody," Barrymore said quietly, then added, "I hear you've been making a damned fool of yourself, all because someone says this or that. Why do actors read the papers anyway? Christ! Do you think the world turns on the importance or the unimportance of a ham? Well, it doesn't!"

Gilbert stared at the floor, stunned.

"Why should you give a damn about your voice?" Barrymore went on. "You can dig ditches, can't you? Or work for Western Union. How old are you? Shut up! Gurney here tells me you're thirty-three or thirty-four. My grandmother went broke for the tenth time when she was seventy-two. Did she bump herself off? No. She had guts, God bless her! She went out and got a job."

He paused. Gilbert was sitting openmouthed, his hands clenched. He flushed.

"You've got a baby daughter. Never entered your head, did it, that you owe the *child* something? No. The ham always thinks only of himself. Get up! Where is she?"

"In the nursery," said Gilbert meekly.

"Lead the way," Jack commanded. "It'll do us all good to look at something decent in this sinkhole of culture."

In the nursery he directed Gilbert to take the child in his arms. "Just hold her close," he said. "Isn't she more important than newspaper gossip?" Gilbert was crying, and after a minute Barrymore took the baby from him and held her for a moment himself. Then he kissed her head and gently placed her back in the crib.

"You go on home, Noll," Barrymore said. "I'll stay here for a while."

At seven o'clock he left his neighbor asleep and went home to dress for the remaking of the *Counsellor-at-Law* scene.

This time, notwithstanding the experiences of the night, his own galling failure of memory, his lack of sleep, Barrymore worked expertly, unfalteringly, before the camera. He made the scene without a break, at the first trial.

Here was a champion.

IT WAS only some six weeks after Barrymore's *Counsellor-at-Law* ordeal that tests began for a screen portrayal of *Hamlet* in Technicolor. This undertaking promised an enhancement of his artistic fame as well as a significant broadening of motion-picture dimensions. Barrymore's brilliant teacher, Margaret Carrington, and her husband, Robert Edmond Jones, who was to direct the enterprise, arrived in Hollywood. John Hay ("Jock") Whitney, the young multimillionaire, had arranged to finance the project if the tests warranted the production.

The afternoon of the test found Jack ably reciting the "rogue and peasant slave" soliloquy. That evening, after dinner, he invited friends to see him do the ghost scene. He began the speech from Act I, Scene V, in which Hamlet is confronted by the specter of his dead father:

> *"O, all you host of heaven! O earth! What else?*
> *And shall I couple hell? O fie! Hold, hold, my heart;*
> *And you, my sinews, grow not instant old,*
> *But bear me stiffly up! Remember thee?*
> *Yea, from the table of my memory . . ."*

Suddenly he broke off and put his hand to his head. He could not proceed. The reference to "memory" seemed a psychological deadlock. Mrs. Carrington prompted him but it was of no use. He tried again and again, then left the stage to sit beside Helios Hotchener, who was present.

"Are you ill?" she asked.

"No," he replied, "not ill of *body*." After a pause he said, "I've been frightened for some time by my lapses of memory. God knows I've said those lines onstage hundreds of times. Am I to be struck down as was my father? He, too, developed headaches and memory lapses onstage. I've had headaches . . ." He paused again. "But I don't want to see a doctor. I want to beat back whatever it is myself. And, by God! I will!"

Robert Jones and his wife sadly canceled their plans for *Hamlet* and went back to New York.

BARRYMORE's homelife by now was straining at the seams. He was beset by domestic annoyances, whether real or imaginary, such as that his daughter's companionship was being denied him, and that he was unwelcome in the nursery of his young son.

When rehearsals began, in May 1934, of *Hat, Coat, and Glove*, for producer Kenneth Macgowan at RKO, he seemed listless and low in vitality, and on the first day of filming, although he had not been drinking for several days, he swayed into the scene, knew none of his lines, and kept walking in the wrong direction. When work was halted for the remainder of the day, Jack seemed unaware of what had happened.

In the morning he failed again. Macgowan, a discerning man, called Henry Hotchener aside and said: "I know he isn't drunk. His trouble is more serious than that. Please make him take a long rest. We must regretfully cancel the contract."

Dolores now advised her husband to enter the Good Samaritan Hospital, a suggestion Jack yielded to almost indifferently.

There laboratory and other tests determined beyond question that he was not a paretic, and the existence of a brain tumor as a possible cause of his memory defect was also ruled out. His doctors said, as others had before, that drink was the basic cause of his trouble, and added that he had a Korsakoff's syndrome. This is a loss of memory of recent events, presumably caused by a toxemia with a specific affinity for brain tissue, and not, in a strictly scientific sense, regarded as insanity.

In the opinion of authorities I have interviewed, Jack could have been cured of his loss of memory at this point if he could have gone on the wagon once and for all. But this was not to be. Toward the end of his life Barrymore frequently experienced a disorientation of time and place. He sometimes would forget, halfway through a recital, what subject he was discussing. Then he would enlist his great inherent dramatic art. His "ad libs" would arrest the interest of his listeners until he regained the traffic lane of his narrative. It was as if he had skidded off the road, then struggled back again to the solid pavement. He could not always get back. Then it would seem that the roadbed of memory itself had been sabotaged.

When acting in pictures, after 1934, it became necessary for him to read his speeches from a blackboard held by an athletic fellow, who dashed about the set, out of range of the camera, but always within eyeshot of the unretentive Barrymore. Jack did not even always know the story of the play; but he could give the blackboard lines such rich interpretation and inflection as to make up for their dramatic dependency upon what preceded or what followed.

CHAPTER 15

IN JUNE 1934, soon after Jack left the hospital, it was agreed that he might benefit by a nonalcoholic cruise in northern Pacific waters off the Canadian coast with his wife and children. But once aboard the *Infanta*, with alcohol denied him, Barrymore drank Dolores's perfume, downed all the mouthwash available, and even partook of a bottle of spirits of camphor.

Late in August Henry Hotchener received a telegram sent by Jack from Vancouver, stating that something serious had happened on the boat, that his family was motoring to Seattle, where they would board the train to Los Angeles, and that he would arrive alone on his yacht at Long Beach on August 24.

What actually happened the day of the "trouble" aboard the *Infanta* is not clear, but the children's nurse received a broken nose, threatened suit for damages, and sometime later was given $3,000 out of court. Meanwhile Dolores, when Hotchener discussed the matter with her, said that a "serious attack" had been made upon the nurse and herself; that Jack was far from normal, and she feared that matters were growing worse.

On the Sunday after his return from this ill-fated cruise, Barrymore, obviously disturbed, telephoned Hotchener. He asked him to come at once to the Tower Road estate and try to slip unseen into the office over the garage for a secret conference.

"I am not drinking," the actor greeted him. "There are times when a man does not *dare* drink. This is one of them."

He alleged that he had overheard on his telephone extension a conversation between Dolores and her physician, arranging for a group of specialists to examine him. This meant, in Jack's opinion, that he might be judged mentally incompetent. "It once happened to a close friend of mine," Jack said. "He was privately examined by physicians, then a few days later a petition was signed by his wife and he was put into an institution. He never came out of it."

Then he said, "I would be a damned fool not to get out of California and the jurisdiction of its courts as quickly as possible. We must get away without letting Dolores have any idea we are leaving. She'll be furious anyway, for no woman likes a man to walk out on her."

They left the Glendale Airport on Tuesday evening, traveling under fictitious names. Jack had not even packed a handbag, but he took the precaution before his departure to indicate legally that he was not "deserting" his wife. In a wire to his doctor and in a phone conversation with Dolores, he stressed that he was leaving to get radio work in order to continue supporting her and the children.

Called "The
Great Lover"
of the screen,
John Barrymore,
right, about
to embrace
Carole Lombard
in the film
"Twentieth Century."

Below, with Greta Garbo
in "Grand Hotel."

Below, with Gladys Swarthout
in "Romance in the Dark."

Both Dolores and the physician maintained that at no time was it planned to place Jack in an institution for the mentally unfit. Nor was any medical conference discussed "behind Jack's back." But his fears were terrifyingly real to him. It is understandable that Dolores was deeply concerned over recent events; and it is understandable that a sinister river of doubt overflowed the dikes of Jack's brilliant mind.

In New York his attorney advised that he be examined by a recognized authority on nervous and mental disorders as a precaution against possible extradition procedure. The examination was made by neurologist Dr. Lewis Stevenson, member of the faculty of the Cornell University Medical School, whose written report stated, in part, that John Barrymore's "mental status is in every way normal except that there is some slight impairment of memory for recent events, which in my opinion, is due to fatigue. . . ."

But Barrymore still felt unsafe. He announced that he would go abroad at once. "I want to put a lot of water between myself and my worries," he said. "I need a moat for my castle. The Atlantic is just the right size." Aboard the *Berengaria* he promptly locked the doors of his suite. "I'll not rest easy," he said to Hotchener, "until this damned ship passes the Statue of Liberty."

IN LONDON Barrymore signed a contract to do a picture for London Film: $60,000 for a six-week term before the English cameras. Jack suggested that his friends Ben Hecht and Charles MacArthur write the scenario. They had written the recent screen version of their own zany stage play, *Twentieth Century*, in which Barrymore's talents as a comedian had flared brilliantly. But a transatlantic telephone call to the playwrights established that they were up to their mighty chins in a dozen enterprises of their own concoction.

One evening, during a conference in Barrymore's hotel suite, Director Alexander Korda asked, "Why not film *Hamlet?*"

Barrymore agreed readily. He was pleased.

Then, after Korda's departure, he turned to Hotchener. "I wonder if I'm up to doing *Hamlet?* Thousands here remember me in it ten years ago." He examined his features in a mirror.

"Well, it would be a vintage Hamlet, but a good cameraman might be able to counteract the furrows and the dewlaps of fifty-two years."

Now he looked at his ankles. They were swollen. "That is bad for the wearing of tights," he said. "The swelling goes down when I lay off drinks. But the way I feel now . . ."

"Do you suppose you could recall the *Hamlet* lines now?" asked Hotchener.

"Sure," Jack said. He did both soliloquies without trouble, then began the ghost scene. But now Barrymore faltered at precisely the same place as during the test in Hollywood a year ago.

The actor quietly sat down near a window, stared into the night over Hyde Park, then said, "It looks as if *Hamlet* is out. What do we tell Korda?"

"If we tell him the real reason," said Hotchener, "he'll doubt your ability to do *any* picture for him. Let's think it out."

A week later Jack announced that he had "found a way out, maybe." He confided to the Hotcheners—Helios having arrived in London to join them—that he would like to go to India.

"I've just come from a luncheon with a remarkable Hindu woman," he said buoyantly, "who told me of an ancient cure for an ailing memory. Besides, she knows several maharajahs. Claims they would lend me their palaces, retinues, elephants, and other properties if I decide to make pictures in India." Then he asked Helios, "Is there such a cure?"

"Yes," she replied. "The Ayurvedic treatment."

"Do you think they'd take me on? Whom do we ask?"

"Dr. Srinivasa Murti, president of the Ayurvedic Conference. He is also a regular physician, but unless you are in earnest . . ."

A few days later Hotchener told London Film the actor wished to take a holiday in India, and *Hamlet* was postponed until the next spring.

THEY FIRST WENT to Italy, so Jack could revisit the places he had been with Edward Sheldon twenty years ago. During much of this journey he suffered from headaches and drowsiness, seemed feverishly restless, and ate hardly at all. His uncertainty was accentuated by the fact that he had heard nothing from Dolores as yet, although a letter from his caretaker was waiting at Naples and indicated much unrest at Tower Road. This put Jack into a rage, and he wrote the caretaker authorizing him to see a lawyer if necessary.

Aboard the Italian Line's *Victoria*, bound for Bombay, Jack stayed up nights, remaining most of the day in his stateroom, occasionally appearing for tea or for dinner wearing a cerise cummerbund and a smart dinner jacket. He spent his "loose" moments at the bar in the company of a Eurasian salesman from Calcutta, a person of great alcoholic capacity.

As the vessel neared Bombay, Jack frequently mentioned his father, and spoke of the times when Maurice Barrymore had described India's mysteries and beauties. He expressed a fear that he would never rejoin his wife and children on Tower Road, that he might not even return alive to the Western world.

This visit to India, Jack felt, was his "last chance"; in this time-old land of secrets he might find the miracle that would rid him of his weaknesses.

At Madras he received an undated letter from Dolores, saying his plans seemed "so indefinite" that it would be best for her to await his return to England before deciding what was "the best thing to do." She closed by saying that "the children send you their love." Jack made no reply to this letter.

He now turned his mind to the "cure."

To his surprise Dr. Srinivasa Murti was no patriarchal apostle with white beard and robes. He was a middle-aged gentleman of brisk military manner, who wore a turban, but otherwise dressed in occidental fashion. When Jack offered him a drink, he declined, but didn't seem to mind when Barrymore mixed two drinks for himself.

Then Dr. Murti explained the treatment, to last six weeks, which consisted of certain spiritual factors, internal and external medication, and a simple vegetable diet. During the first three weeks the patient would feel debilitated, but no hospitalization was required; Dr. Murti did, however, advise Barrymore to move to a quieter hotel.

"Because there is no bar there?" asked Jack.

"Not at all," replied the doctor. "There are bars almost everywhere in India. You must decide for yourself whether or not you can stay away from them."

"I've made up my mind to try," Jack said.

Tests were made in accord with modern medical practice. Then an Ayurvedic specialist and four assistants, all of whom held medical degrees, began the treatments in a room adjoining Barrymore's sleeping quarters at the hotel. They brought with them a small brass altar in which receptacles filled with sacred oils were lighted, and incense burned in a brazier.

Barrymore was asked to seat himself before the altar, and to keep in mind a desire that health be restored him. The five physicians also seated themselves near him and began to intone ancient Sanskrit chants, explaining that the purpose of the ceremony was purely psychological, intended to dissipate thoughts of ill health or depression and turn the mind into invigorating channels.

Barrymore was then undressed and placed on a broad slab of highly polished wood. Now began manipulations, each physician being assigned to a certain area of the body. The massage continued for about an hour, after which he was bathed in a brew of leaves simmered for several hours, then cooled to body temperature. Finally he was put to bed, where he lapsed at once into a deep sleep.

Massages, baths, periods of relaxation, together with herbal medication, continued for three weeks. Barrymore's memory improved. His ankles no longer were swollen, he lost his headaches and his indifference to food. He enjoyed rides around the city and along the beach of the Bay of Bengal. He asked for reading matter, listened to records of his favorite operas, and spoke infrequently of past griefs. He surely would do *Hamlet* for Korda when spring came.

But Dr. Murti admonished him not to construe his physical and mental well-being as a sign that he could return to former indulgences.

By the middle of December he seemed almost restored to good health, and he planned to tour India in a private railway car as soon as possible, staying some time in Agra, the birthplace of his father.

Then one day, while he was supposed to be napping in his room, he disappeared. The Eurasian, the Calcutta salesman who had been Jack's bar companion on shipboard, had called him at the hotel and soon afterward they left to go to a Madras club, where they had several drinks. Then they visited a bagnio, at which place Barrymore promised the madam a twelve-hundred-dollar fee to close her doors to her usual clientele.

When he returned to his hotel a week later, the doctor arrived to discuss with him the consequences of his activities. The actor apologized, and the treatments were resumed. Then two days afterward he again disappeared for several days. It now became apparent to the doctor as well as to Jack that it was futile to continue with the treatment.

Plans to visit Agra vanished; Barrymore decided to return to England to fulfill his contract for *Hamlet*. With the Hotcheners, he sailed from Bombay early in January 1935. He picked up some bar companions, a few days out of Bombay, and his headaches returned, his ankles again became swollen. By the time the ship reached Naples, he was seriously ill.

"What shall we do about *Hamlet?*" asked his manager.

"Hamlet is dead, very dead. Cable Korda that urgent business calls me to America." Then, with a smile, Jack added: "Of course, there is always King Lear . . ."

CHAPTER 16

Now BEGAN the seven last years of a lifetime. At an ailing fifty-three Barrymore began to pay at the usurious rates demanded of a man of public name when he does not conform to the gospels of exemplary behavior. He forfeited his material belongings. He lost his health. But his spirit remained essentially young and unconquered.

He had come to Hollywood ten years before with no assets other than his talent and his fame. During the following decade he earned $2,634,500, although in 1934, the year of the flight, his gross income had shrunk to $74,264.42: the combined proceeds from one picture, *Twentieth Century*, two radio broadcasts, and the yield from bonds, but he had spent $288,497.76, and kept on spending at a maharajah's pace.

His financial position on January 31, 1935, was as follows: he had physical assets (his Tower Road home, his yacht, and a lot in Beverly Hills) in the amount of half a million dollars. He possessed negotiable securities in excess of $140,500. He had no outstanding debts. He had ready cash to pay February bills amounting to $15,108.14.

We are now about to see how a fortune melts under the high temperature of a man's caprices.

WHILE STILL in New York after his return from India, Barrymore's already depleted physical condition began further to deteriorate. News reaching him from California, where Dolores had moved the children and most of the furniture from Tower Road to a new residence in the Wilshire district, merely stimulated his reckless nature to headlong indiscretions.

Toward the end of February Jack collapsed in his hotel and was sent to New York Hospital, where he stayed until late March. It was during this time that a stagestruck young student at Hunter College, Miss Elaine Jacobs, one day entered Jack's suite, and what was left of his life. When the doctor protested his patient's reception of a stranger, Jack announced that she was his protégée, and that he was going to help her become an actress. She soon announced her new name, Elaine Barrie, and the subsequent publicity did not restore any laurel leaves to the actor's molting crown. As usual he paid no attention to the furor of print, and Miss Barrie did not seem to try to avoid public mention. She was nineteen years old, an age when a sudden emergence from prosaic privacy sometimes creates the illusion that notoriety is fame.

Jack, who seldom spent wisely, now began to spend wildly. His yacht and its crew remained idle at an East River mooring at an average expense of $3,000 a month. His bill at Saks Fifth Avenue for a month was $4,811.15. On one day he purchased gowns and coats at Milgrim's costing $1,051.31. Yet between April and September he earned only $5,000 for two radio broadcasts, an average income of $33 a day, while his expendi-

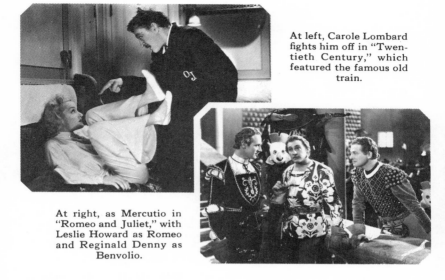

At left, Carole Lombard fights him off in "Twentieth Century," which featured the famous old train.

At right, as Mercutio in "Romeo and Juliet," with Leslie Howard as Romeo and Reginald Denny as Benvolio.

tures were at the rate of $827 a day, forcing him to sell about $125,000 in bonds.

Meantime his affairs steadily grew more muddled. Dolores's attorneys and his were conferring about divorce terms and a property settlement. The flood of publicity regarding Jack's young protégée had not put his wife in a mood to make any concessions to her hopscotching spouse, who by now was staying with Elaine and her mother at their apartment. But Jack had informed Hotchener that he was "willing to settle with Dolores on her *own* terms," as he felt he no longer could tolerate this legal obstacle to a marriage with Miss Barrie.

In early September, however, he had "a serious quarrel with Elaine," and moved to Essex House. The next day a lawyer representing Miss Barrie and Mrs. Jacobs made demands for reparations for properties Jack allegedly had brought to, then taken from the Jacobs' apartment, including a $1,800 canary diamond he had bought Elaine. The actor then moved what was left of his ready assets to a New Jersey bank, and moored his yacht beyond the reach of possible attachment.

On September 16 he received for his signature the property

agreement in his wife's suit against him, which gave custody of the children, certain stocks and bonds, and support payments to Dolores, and allowed Barrymore to retain title to the Tower Road house and the *Infanta*.

It seems incredible that on the day he received this agreement, and in the midst of his confusion, Jack, chancing to be reminded that the morrow was his wife's birthday, composed the following telegram to her:

DEAR WINKIE, HAPPY BIRTHDAY AND LOVE TO THE CHILDREN. I WOULD LOVE TO THINK THAT YOU ARE AS LONESOME AS I AM, BUT THAT IS AS IT MAY BE. ANYWAY, MY LOVE TO YOU AND THE BABIES. YOU MUST ALWAYS REMEMBER THAT ONCE WE HAD LOTS OF FUN AND DON'T LET ANYTHING EVER MAKE YOU FORGET IT. PLEASE BELIEVE I MEAN THIS, BABY, AND WE WILL BOTH FEEL BETTER. MUCH LOVE.   JACK

More incredible developments were to come. With his divorce terms agreed upon and arrangements made for an out-of-court settlement of the reparations demanded by Miss Barrie and her mother, Barrymore was now free to leave New York and return to California without danger of colliding with bailiffs or psychiatrists.

He arrived in Beverly Hills on September 25, and his brother Lionel gave him sanctuary. But that same night, after Barrymore had assured his brother, as well as a delegation from the press, that his giddy interlude of young romance was done, he telephoned Miss Barrie in New York.

Dolores Barrymore obtained an uncontested divorce on October 9, 1935, and Miss Barrie and her mother soon thereafter arrived in California. Their lawyer, Aaron Sapiro, now became Jack's attorney-manager, the Hotcheners having returned to India.

New brooms began to function. The caretaker was dismissed from Tower Road; the captain was ousted from the *Infanta*, after having served for ten years as Barrymore's skipper. Some months later a mortgage of $40,000 was placed on the yacht.

During this period Jack seldom saw anyone in private other than his new mentors, although his longtime friends Ben Hecht and Charles MacArthur were trying to keep friendly eyes upon him whenever he took recess from his preoccupations with Miss Barrie. I joined them in this endeavor after returning to Los Angeles from a trip abroad early in 1936 and receiving from them a firsthand report on my friend, whom I had not seen for more than a year. The playwrights told me at this time that Barrymore, when informed by them that his romance could be seen almost daily in the headlines, seemed amazed, then splendidly detached about the whole business.

Canceled checks indicate that spending, meanwhile, continued at the rate of a Mississippi flood. Let us take, for example, the actor's bank statement for April 1936, captioned JOHN BARRYMORE (AARON SAPIRO, POWER OF ATTORNEY). It shows that on April 1 he had $22,629.17 in cash on hand, and that $17,312.84 of this sum was disbursed during the month. He or his agencies were spending his money at the average rate of $577 a day. His telephone bill was $1,691.07. Checks made out to cash, bearing the endorsement Elaine Barrie, amounted to $950. Checks drawn to and endorsed by Aaron Sapiro amounted to $4,222.27.

In India, at about this time, the Hotcheners learned that Sapiro was bringing suits against both Warner Brothers and Henry for an accounting of Barrymore's funds. The ex-manager returned to California, and, unable to get in touch with the actor, who was ill, Hotchener immediately transferred all his own financial records of Barrymore's business to his attorney, who voluntarily placed them in the custody of the court. When the case came to trial, Hotchener's testimony caused the judge to order the suit dismissed.

BARRYMORE often asked, in these later years, "What has become of all the money I've made?" He thought it strange that yammerings so often rose concerning his lack of funds. He had made $2,600,000 during his first ten years in Hollywood. He would earn another half-million dollars, $3,100,000 in all, sometimes working when half dead, with only his stout spirit to sustain him on the motion-picture set, the stage, or at the radio microphone. While he had invested in a few great luxuries, such as his yachts, his house, his hobbies, he spent comparatively little on himself. He cared nothing for clothes. He didn't own a watch. He entertained infrequently, much preferring eating in the kitchen, or in some friend's kitchen, to sitting at a costly restaurant table.

He had drunk much in his time, but he was not a connoisseur of wines. Indeed, he had a beachcomber's taste for the cheaper grades of liquor, and his tolerance for alcohol had become so slight that he drank far less than was believed of him. Many times he was accounted drunk when the fact was that he was genuinely ill.

Aside from his almost fierce desire to see that his bills were paid, he did not appear to bother much about money. He seldom had much pocket money even when affluent, and now he carried even less.

In May of 1936 he had obtained the part of Mercutio in the M-G-M production of *Romeo and Juliet*, supporting Norma Shearer as Juliet and Leslie Howard as Romeo. Returning to the screen after a year and eight months' absence, he permitted himself to be placed in residence in the private West Los Angeles sanitarium of Mrs. Louise Simar Kelley, whose husband, Jim, became Barrymore's "guard."

Jim Kelley accompanied his charge to the motion-picture sets, and watched over him during occasional social expeditions. Possibly Jack was not given money lest he wander off from the Kelley sanitarium to spend it on something more fiery than the single can of beer permitted him each day.

Jack did "wander off" frequently, to the worriment of Jim Kelley, who even became afraid to bathe, for each time that he stripped himself for the tub, the resourceful actor would flee the premises and the nude Kelley could not very well pursue him into the street. Then Hecht, MacArthur, or myself would receive the news from Kelley over the telephone: "The Monster has broke loose again!"

We had come to call Jack "The Monster." If anyone is so dull as to think this was not said with affection, and is not being recorded here with affection, then . . . but why should one explain such things?

CHAPTER 17

IN NOVEMBER 1936 Jack suddenly decided to elope with Miss Barrie. Charlie MacArthur and Ben Hecht sought to dissuade him from this enterprise with a long list of reasons why he should not, at fifty-four, again draw on the beekeeper's veil of matrimony. He remained calm and amiable as the two playwrights harangued him, then said with finality: "Gentlemen, you are talking to a man who is about to go over Niagara Falls in a barrel!"

The next day he flew with Miss Barrie and Attorney Sapiro to Yuma, Arizona, to be married by a justice of the peace.

A separation occurred one month and twenty-three days later, after a public skirmish between husband and wife on New Year's Eve at the Trocadero, rendezvous of Hollywood's elite. There Barrymore's name-callings, directed at his young mate, rose above the happier sounds made by celebrants of the arriving year of 1937. And Elaine then went alone to the rented home in Benedict Canyon where they were residing with her mother and three servants.

Five hours after this set-to Barrymore telephoned Henry Huntington, attorney for Mrs. Kelley, in whose sanitarium he had sought temporary refuge, and asked that he come there "instantly" for a conference: his wife was contemplating filing a divorce complaint. Reluctantly the attorney, who was but slightly acquainted with Barrymore and was not, at this time, one of his admirers, went at dawn to the Kelley establishment, there to learn that Jack knew nothing of his recent business affairs, and that Aaron Sapiro still had the actor's power of attorney.

On January 2, 1937, Huntington appeared early at the courthouse to file a revocation of Sapiro's power of attorney. Things commenced to happen. Creditors began to hound for immediate payment of debts amounting to $161,503.82, including the mortgage of $40,000 on the *Infanta*. Bills for the seven weeks of Barrymore's fourth marriage added up to $10,108.90, of which $511.83 appeared to have been spent on himself. He could have undertaken ordinary bankruptcy proceedings, but he preferred to do otherwise.

"I want to owe no one," he told Huntington. "We'll pay up."

The attorney then filed a petition, under Section 74 of the Bankruptcy Act, indicating that all Barrymore sought of his creditors was time for a proper liquidation of his assets.

It was almost two years before these claims eventually reached settlement, and the bankruptcy court honorably discharged the debtor (who, in accord with his philosophy, would promptly go into debt again). At times it seemed that he could not survive the travail of ill health and harassment.

But he was never forced, now or later, to "liquidate" Tower Road. It remained a symbol to him, as the Alchemist's Corner had been, as his yachts had been. And it is important, when all else is lost, that a man of great imagination be permitted to keep the relics associated with his dreamworld.

Once, early in 1937, I called upon Jack at Kelleys' to suggest that we visit Tower Road. He brightened at once. Miss Barrie, following their marriage, had not chosen to reside at the now deserted estate, and Jack had not been there for some time.

As we walked slowly up the hill, he spoke happily of the "old days." Each landmark reminded him of some adventure: the totem pole, the aviary, the now stilled fountains, the drained pools. But Tower Road, like its master, had come to a run-down condition. He said little of the lack of life about the place, the stillness of the stripped rooms, the cobwebs in the rathskeller.

One thing, however, did disturb him. Someone had removed the John Drew Cigar band from its place of honor among other cigar bands pasted on the façade of the old Wild West bar.

"That," he said, "was worth more to me than all the rest of the things put together."

MISS BARRIE'S REPRESENTATIVES served a divorce summons the middle of February 1937, and also a temporary restraining order tying up her husband's property and possible funds. She asked for $2,500 a month alimony, listing her necessary expenses at their rented Benedict Canyon home at $2,225 a month. But Barrymore's faulty memory, unpredictable health, and un-

Visiting the set of "The Scoundrel," in which Noel Coward (right) made his film debut. With them are Martha Sleeper (left) and Julie Haydon of the cast, authors Ben Hecht (standing) and Charles MacArthur.

Above, two great hams (W. C. Fields on the left) strike a pose for posterity; above left, Clark Gable and Barrymore on the firing range; at left, in Beverly Hills with his German shepherd.

toward publicity caused producers to hesitate to employ him. How was he to meet these demands?

A number of his friends actively assisted Attorney Huntington, now a fierce admirer of the never whimpering actor, in trying to untangle his affairs. He still seemed to them a great man.

Ben Hecht made a fine effort that year to write into the scenario of *Nothing Sacred* a part for Jack, to which David O. Selznick, the producer, agreed if he would memorize but one speech of twenty lines. With only his single can of beer a day, and after a week of painstaking rehearsals at the sanitarium, Jack went to the studio. He failed this test.

"Jack didn't know a word of the speech," Hecht told me, "but he got off one of his own, ten times as good as mine; then he read like Coleridge from the script. Still David couldn't take the risk."

Trips to the desert near La Quinta were prescribed for the actor, and Kelley took him there, using a trailer he had attached to his car. A remote house was found. These holidays among the dunes seemed to benefit Jack.

Soon Edmund Goulding, who had directed him in *Grand Hotel*, agreed to give him a part in his forthcoming picture, urged to do so by Warners' executive Gordon Hollingshead, who had worked as an assistant director on many of Jack's early pictures. Here was a chance to make at least $30,000 for two weeks' work.

However, other studio officials demanded that he take a screen test before being assigned the role. Arrangements were made for such a test, and Jack now returned to the sanitarium to await the appointed day.

When he finally appeared at the studio, Goulding was reluctant, for Barrymore's own sake, to begin the test. But Hollingshead, who had recommended the part for his old friend, said, "Don't humiliate him by refusing to go through with it. And *don't* have any film in the camera to record a flop."

Goulding never let Jack know the real reason the test failed. He merely announced to one and all: "He was fine. Really fine. But he made the star a bit nervous, and the studio, you know, has to consider her wishes."

WHEN ATTORNEY HUNTINGTON took Barrymore as a client, he did so with the proviso that whenever Miss Barrie reentered the actor's life in a positive fashion, the relations between lawyer and client would automatically cease. Early in August of 1937 Jack received a telegram from Miss Barrie. She was arriving at the Glendale railway station from the East. Would he meet her?

He did meet her, with flowers. Then on August 9, 1937, the interlocutory decree of divorce was dismissed. Exit Attorney Huntington.

CHAPTER 18

AT THIS POINT the only means available to the now fifty-six-year-old man to pay his debts was the out-and-out commercialization of a great family name. Apparently no one with access at this time to the actor and his affairs reverenced the century and a half of shining tradition which had been passed on to him, and by him briefly but brilliantly enhanced. Now he permitted himself to be exploited in an array of claptrap motion pictures and a series of raffish broadcasts, which made him seem a buffoon to a new generation.

And yet, even now the man stayed peculiarly and definitely himself. Drama critic Richard Watts, Jr., a good friend of Jack's, once wrote: "In some paradoxical fashion the very manner in which Barrymore seemed almost to revel in his disintegration convinced people who had never seen him in *Hamlet* and *The Jest* that he must have been among the giants. For even when he showed signs of physical and spiritual collapse he did not enter into any kind of ordinary decline. Everything he did was in an epic way, and, even when he appeared to be making an embarrassing clown of himself, he did so on a grand and wholesale scale, coming apart with boisterous gargantuan humor and a sardonic air of self-criticism."

Or as another old friend, Ashton Stevens, once put it, when commenting on the last years of Barrymore's career: "No one can run downhill as fast as a thoroughbred."

Late in 1938 it was decided that John Barrymore would return

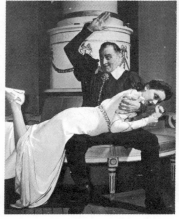

At right, Barrymore rehearses a radio
script with his daughter, Diana; at left,
a vigorous scene with Elaine Barrie in
"My Dear Children."

to the stage with Elaine Barrie as his leading lady in a play called
My Dear Children. His role in this crude comedy practically
amounted to an autobiography of the Barrymore of first-page
fiction, gossip columns, and radio self-caricature. And in playing
it the shorn Samson performed a last theatrical feat, the pulling
down of the pillars of the house of his art.

The play opened at the McCarter Theatre, Princeton, New
Jersey, on March 24, 1939, after which a road tour began. The
theatrical firm of Aldrich & Meyers produced this comic valentine and Otto L. Preminger directed it.

When the show reached St. Louis, Miss Barrie left the company after a quarrel with Barrymore. A few weeks later she
notified him that she was again suing him for divorce.

"Soon I shall be unable to count these things on my fingers,"
Jack said. "I must rent an adding machine."

He had meanwhile telephoned Henry Hotchener in Hollywood who, in response to the actor's suggestions that they "get
together on the same basis as before," flew to join him at Omaha.
It had been more than three years since they had seen each other.

"This time it is final," Jack said of his troubles with his wife. "I shall never see her again."

Hotchener found Barrymore hazy about his business affairs, as always, and concerned about a home he had bought on Bellagio Road in Bel Air after his fourth marriage. He telephoned his Los Angeles lawyer, who informed Jack that the property was neither in his name nor his wife's, but in the name of a third person. After some incendiary language on Barrymore's part, there was another telephone call. The attorney now told the actor that the Bellagio Road house was in Mrs. Elaine Barrymore's name. Confused, Jack said to Hotchener: "Can't you do something about all these things?"

Hotchener asked for a statement of the play's weekly expenses and ventured an opinion that they seemed rather large. Then he learned that $500 of the weekly overhead was being paid to Mrs. Elaine Barrymore, that her contract provided for this stipend whether or not she stayed on with the troupe, and that Jack himself had approved the arrangement. Barrymore loudly denied this, but when the document was shown him, he found to his amazement that he *had* signed it.

There was an air of defeat as the company reached Des Moines on May 4. Audiences had not been large but Jack was determined to prove he could make a success of the play, particularly since Elaine had left the cast. He predicted that business would pick up in Chicago, adding, "That is a Barrymore stronghold."

When the play opened in Chicago, Jack was playing always and ever for the laugh. According to Ashton Stevens, now dean of the Chicago drama critics, he fiddled and faddled his hands, hemmed and hawed his lines, and blurted ad libs to the hoarse delight of the opening-night audience. "But what was left of the most fascinating actor of his day still held some of the old magnetism," Stevens added.

It seemed certain the show would run, so Henry Hotchener left for California three days after the Chicago opening. It was his understanding that the actor desired a restoration of their longtime business and personal relationship. But this was not to be. Whether or not Jack was influenced against Hotchener after the former manager's departure is a matter of conjecture, but the briefly renewed relationship came to a cool termination.

My Dear Children remained in Chicago for thirty-four weeks. All during that successful run of the play Ashton Stevens watched over the man who first had come to him, late on an April night in 1906, in San Francisco, with a letter of introduction from Ethel. Jack was sometimes ill, visibly and audibly, and there was a period when the show had to be temporarily closed. But Stevens said that the last performance of *My Dear Children* was the saddest of the Chicago engagement. The show was shortly to move on to New York, which meant, for Barrymore, a return to Broadway after an absence of more than fifteen years. He had been worrying about the New York critics, most of whom had been in knee pants when their predecessors acclaimed his *Hamlet*. To these brilliant young gentlemen, he would be a stranger—or worse, a picture actor, and a decayed one at that.

"Anyhow," Stevens said, "he fortified himself beyond his limited capacity, and the simple, friendly curtain speech he had intended fled his memory. He forgot this was a 'farewell'; forgot the loyal 'repeaters' out front; forgot everything but the presence in a near row of a pair of youthful nightclub performers with whom he had consorted the previous after-night. To these unknown small-timers, the grand old-timer addressed his spattering speech.

"I couldn't stay. I had grown more or less hardened to the caricatures he visited on himself—but this wasn't Jack Barrymore at all. I went out with great, gawky, sentimental tears salting my face."

BARRYMORE ARRIVED in New York in late January 1940, a few days before the play was to open at the Belasco Theatre. Ethel Barrymore stayed with her brother at Bayside, Long Island, in a place "remote from the gang," watching over him until his opening night.

The premiere proved a disappointment to the New York audience that turned out, ready for anything.

"I'm certain that the majority expected the curtain to rise on Jack removing his trousers while tossing off Oscar Wilde epigrams," wrote Spencer Merriam Berger, a longtime admirer of Barrymore. "What followed was an unbelievably baleful performance. The final curtain brought the first spontaneous reaction of the evening. Relieved that the show was over, the audience gave him a thunderous ovation, to which he responded with bows and tears."

Backstage, after the performance, Mrs. Elaine Barrymore appeared, and, ignoring his friends' protests against this reunion, Jack retired to her apartment in Fifty-ninth Street. "After all," he said, "I am not committing a statutory offense. She is still my wife."

After the third New York performance of *My Dear Children*, Barrymore's nervous depletion sent him to Mount Sinai Hospital. When he resumed his appearance in the play some days later, Miss Barrie was once again his leading lady, supplanting Miss Doris Dudley.

The play ran for four months, with its chief actor vacillating between poor health and worse. It closed toward summer, this play in which he had achieved the greatest anticlimax of his career, having earned $666,519.06. Barrymore, after long months of work, had left as his share of these proceeds $5,000. It was a check, not payable to him, but to his Japanese gardener, Nishi. Jack had thought it advisable for Nishi secretly to hold this "nest egg," so that no one might get it away from him.

"I remind myself of Grantland Rice's destitute ballplayer friend," Jack said. "That wastrel veteran of the diamond told Rice that he had enough money to last him the rest of his life— provided he drop dead on the spot!"

CHAPTER 19

SOMEHOW, BETWEEN THE TIME of his honorable discharge by the bankruptcy court in November 1939 and that summer of 1940, Barrymore had incurred another $110,000 in debts. This amount did not include the neglected payment of alimonies and child support, arrears estimated variously in court recitals at between $50,000 and $100,000.

Now in Hollywood once again, the debtor shook his head like a tired bison, then voluntarily undertook the payment of these newer liabilities. He entered, for a second time, the serfdom of a bankruptcy arrangement. And although he subsequently was to earn $241,085.18 by means of picture work and radio broadcasts, he still would be adjudged a bankrupt *after* his death.

During June and July of 1940 he made a motion picture at Twentieth Century-Fox, a celluloid delicacy instigated by his own latter-day legend. He pretended, when on public view, to be undisturbed by this cartoon, or by the radio caricatures he weekly draped about his person. But when away from all this, he sometimes seemed wilted and deeply hurt by the horseplay demands of his work. Even a tricky memory did not altogether shut out from his ears the echoes of yesterday's empty laughter.

Lionel once told me of one of his last conversations with Jack. It was on the night they did their final radio broadcast together, and Jack was near the end of everything.

"No matter what has happened of recent years," Lionel told him, "you really did climb up among the stars. You were one of the great ones."

Jack looked at him for a while, grinned, then said, "This is a hell of a time to tell me!"

THE TWO LAST YEARS of his life, notwithstanding many illnesses and the squabblings of the law, became for Barrymore a reunion with several companions who represented the gay days. The private meeting ground for these Barrymore cronies was, more often than not, the studio home of John Decker, the artist, in Bundy Drive. Actors Thomas Mitchell, Roland Young, John Carradine, Fannie Brice, and Tony Quinn were among the habitués of Decker's studio.

Decker, in his own youth, had been an art student at the Slade School in London, where Barrymore had been enrolled, and had painted scenes for Sir Herbert Tree's His Majesty's Theatre. Later, in New York, he had been the theatrical caricaturist for the *Evening World*, and as such, made Barrymore's acquaintance at the time of *The Jest*. Now the artist and his wife made Jack welcome at the studio, where his drinks would be cut

Barrymore's first wife,
Katherine Harris.

Above, with Michael Strange,
his second wife; below, with
Elaine Barrie.

With Dolores Costello on their
wedding day, 1928.

to a small alcoholic content and he could relive his own time as a painter, sniffing the turpentine happily and watching Decker work.

"Aside from Decker's art, which I admire no end, I find him enchanting," Jack once said, "because he dislikes sunsets and his mother."

One evening early in September 1940 Decker and I received word that Barrymore was becoming increasingly unhappy at the Bellagio Road home where he was living with Elaine. We drove out there. A maid answered; then Jack, in an old bathrobe and slippers, came downstairs. His nurse, Karl Stuevers, followed him.

Jack pointed to the ceiling, then whispered, "Get me the hell out of here, quick!"

"Collect your things, Jack," I said. "We're on our way."

"I don't think I'd better go upstairs myself." Then he looked at his nurse. "Would you be so kind?"

Karl assembled an outfit, including a Tyrolean hat with a jaunty brush in the crown band, and Jack dressed hurriedly. He insisted, before we left, on inspecting the ancient olive tree from Tower Road which Nishi had transplanted to the grounds of the Bellagio place.

"Let us take this noble plant with us," Jack said. "Did you gentlemen bring derricks and spades?"

He was dissuaded from this nocturnal uprooting, but took a sprig from it for his hatband, saying that it was "an emblem of peace."

And a few hours later he was back where he belonged, at Tower Road, inspecting the grounds by flashlight and announcing plans to install a pool table in the deserted aviary. "I've wanted a pool table all my life," he said.

Jack never returned to the partner of his fourth bus accident. A divorce was granted to Mrs. Elaine Barrymore in late November 1940.

KARL STUEVERS stayed on for some months with Jack at Tower Road, and Decker and his friends in Bundy Drive also kept in close touch with Jack.

But one night, while I was visiting him, he confided that he still feared being "put out of circulation."

"What? Again? Don't be ridiculous."

"It's constantly on my mind," he said, "and besides, the creditors are planning to take Tower Road away from me for keeps."

"I think both these hurdles can be cleared," I said. "Have you known of anyone ever being committed when regularly earning big money?"

"They're always claiming people are incompetent to handle their own fortunes."

"That's an entirely different situation," I said. "If Aunt Bessie retires with a full sock and no longer earns money, she is a cinch to be put away. But never if she is making money each week. I am informed that you are making, at the moment, six thousand dollars a week—"

"Then where in hell is it?" he interrupted.

"Keep on the beam," I said. "It goes, most of it, to your creditors, though they let you have some occasionally for pin money. Now, if you keep on working, no judge is going to rule that a person smart enough to earn a thousand dollars a day is nuts. The judge himself would seem nuts to make such a ruling."

"By God!" he said. "You're right. I'll just keep on working."

"As for Tower Road, you threaten the creditors to quit work entirely . . ."

"You're reversing yourself," he said. "I must keep working to stay away from the chicken wire."

"Just a moment. You won't actually quit. You'll merely threaten to, and the creditors will be so upset at the prospect of losing a huge sum each week that they will let the golden goose stay on its nest."

"I shall burn a candle to you," Jack said, "in some great cathedral. I shall, of course, burn it at both ends."

Such creditors as had objected to maintaining Jack in the Tower Road house were persuaded by his attorney that the actor should be permitted to stay, unmolested, so that he could continue his work.

The making of the life mask, and, right, the result.

Three scenes from "The Great Profile" (1940), in which Barrymore parodied himself. The girl is Mary Beth Hughes.

BARRYMORE NOW ENTERED his final year of markedly failing health, but gamely got to his feet again and again. Nor did he complain of being ill. He *acted* the part of a well man, not the least effective of his many roles.

It became apparent to his doctor that he had cirrhosis of the liver and a kidney involvement. He caught cold frequently. He had chronic chills. But he held his chin high. Ben Hecht, at whose Hollywood house Jack spent a night, said of him:

"People are mistaken when they pity Jack. He doesn't remember his aches and pains at all the next day. Think how fine it would be for all invalids, mooning over yesterday's attacks and dreading tomorrow's, if they too could be stripped of this overshadowing fear. Jack will never die of fear. Perhaps he will never die at all."

Jack seemed equally optimistic for, when a Pennsylvania innkeeper wrote to ask if he would sell him his bed for a collection of couches of historic lovers now being assembled at the inn, he promptly answered, in part:

> I was charmed by your letter, and am devastated to have to inform you that the bed is still in use—and will continue to be, I most sincerely trust—for some years to come. When I have no further use for it, I should be most happy to consider your offer, although it is practically committed to the Smithsonian Institution. I feel sure, however, that some *blanket* arrangement might be made with them to transport the bed to your hostelry during whatever is your mating season.

CHAPTER 20

BY 1942 JACK'S MEMORY of recent events became still more loosely seated than before. He had experienced another illness, with an internal hemorrhage so severe as to warrant blood transfusions. But he stayed on at his radio work, and even appeared in a motion picture.

On the afternoon of May 19, 1942, he prepared to leave Tower Road late in the afternoon to go to the rehearsal of his weekly radio program. He dressed himself slowly, then called out for Nishi. There was no response to his summons, for now, after Pearl Harbor, Nishi no longer was at Tower Road. He had been sent weeks before to a camp for enemy aliens at Manzanar. But Jack had forgotten all about that. He had forgotten the day of leave-taking when the belongings of the gardener and his large family were piled high at the doorway. He had forgotten how he had protested when it was explained to him that, with America at war with Japan, Nishi must be interned.

Now he went out to look for his gardener in the Victory garden which Nishi himself had urged planting. When Nishi had inquired what vegetables Barrymore wished him to plant, he had replied, "Horseradish!" The obedient and literal-minded gardener had therefore planted whole beds of horseradish, and nothing else, and this pungent herb grew luxuriantly and uselessly on the estate.

Barrymore's secretary-attendant now reminded him that it was time for him to go. He settled himself in the seat of the motor car, shivering inside his camel's-hair overcoat, although the late afternoon air was not chill. He had had a bad head cold since March, but when he arrived at the broadcasting studio he said that he was fit. He had not been drinking for the last two or three days.

After the rehearsal he lost his way to his own dressing room and entered the first door that yielded to his hand, a room that had been assigned to John Carradine, who was broadcasting elsewhere in the building.

It was a curious happening, for this young actor, only two weeks before, had sought Barrymore's advice on how to play the character Louis XI in a revival of *If I Were King*. Carradine had opened in it only the night before, in Los Angeles, and now was amazed upon entering his room to find someone lying on the couch, and still further astonished to see Jack Barrymore himself slowly sit up.

"How are you, old man?" Jack asked.

"Why, hello, Jack," said Carradine. "Are you all right?"

"Never better," he said, but Carradine saw that he was gray with illness and had difficulty in breathing. Carradine was too confused for the moment to do other than mutter something about having "opened in the play last night," to which Jack said, "Of course; and I take it that you received splendid notices."

"I haven't read them yet," said the younger actor.

"Good," Jack said. "Actors should never read them. If you don't believe the bad ones, why should you pay attention to the good ones?"

Jack broke off then, dreadfully weak, and gasping. The doctor was called and Jack was half carried to his car and driven to Hollywood Hospital, where it was learned that he had bronchial pneumonia in the right lower lung. He lost consciousness.

News of his illness was withheld for a time. Lionel took his brother's place on the next radio program. Ethel, touring New England with *The Corn is Green*, kept in touch with the hospital by long-distance telephone.

The primary cause of Jack's collapse was cirrhosis of the liver. There were secondary conditions, such as the failure of kidney function, chronic gastritis, ulceration of the esophagus, which hemorrhaged, and hardening of the arteries. The pneumonia, however, was the terminal event. Still, his heart somehow beat on against all these odds for ten more days.

On the seventh day he was seemingly unconscious when I went into his room, but after I had sat there for several minutes he said, without opening his eyes, "I thought you were closer." Believing he was talking in a haze, I did not reply, but sat looking at his pale face. . . . What superb bone structure that face still owned, no matter the years or the illness.

Now he called me by name, his eyes still closed. I went and stood beside him. He opened his eyes, which seemed almost to sparkle as of other days.

"Lean over me," he said quite clearly. "I want to ask you something."

Unprepared for anything but some last request from a dying man, I did so. I should have foreseen that this mighty fellow would not surrender with a sentimental statement.

"Tell me," he asked, "is it true that you are the illegitimate son of Buffalo Bill?"

I was so jolted out of my sorrow that I laughed. That had been his purpose, I am sure, for he never wanted his friends to grieve.

"Yes," I replied, "I am told that Colonel Cody was my natural father, but we mustn't let anyone else know it."

He smiled, then said, "I have always thought so," and promptly became unconscious again. Those were the last words he ever said to me.

THREE DAYS LATER, at ten twenty o'clock the night of May 29, 1942, John Sidney Blythe Barrymore died. Shortly afterward, Dr. Hugo Kersten, his physician, made the following statement:

"That Mr. Barrymore survived this attack for more than a few hours is more of a tribute to the patient's amazing vitality than to any medical science practiced in his behalf. Perhaps this unexplained vitality had something in common with the several other matchless qualities of this talented artist. As his physician, I became acquainted intimately with the man himself, his fine mind, his philosophies. His great personal strength and courage, even his foolhardiness, cloaked the gentlest sort of soul, tolerant, generous, without conceit, and almost childlike in honesty of thought. It is not for a medical practitioner to say that these qualities have any bearing whatsoever on a man's physical fortitude at the threshold of death. Yet, who knows?"

In writing this book, I have seen again, in rich recollection, the face of my friend; I have heard his gay, brave voice once more. I sought to fashion a green wreath, with few false leaves, and now I place it beside the crypt upon which his brother carved the words:

Good Night, Sweet Prince

ACKNOWLEDGMENTS

The condensations in this volume have been created by The
Reader's Digest Association, Inc., and are used by permission of
and special arrangement with the publishers and the holders of
the respective copyrights.

CAPTAIN BLIGH AND MR. CHRISTIAN: THE MEN AND THE
MUTINY, copyright © 1972 by Richard Hough, is reprinted by
permission of Richard Hough and Viking Penguin Inc.

THE AGONY AND THE ECSTASY, copyright © 1961 by
Doubleday, is reprinted by permission of Doubleday and William
Collins Sons & Co. Ltd.

THE LIFE AND WORK OF SIGMUND FREUD, by Ernest Jones,
edited and abridged by Lionel Trilling and Steven Marcus, copyright ©
1961 by Basic Books, Inc., is reprinted by permission of Basic Books,
Inc., Publishers and The Hog.

GOOD NIGHT, SWEET PRINCE (The Life and Times of John
Barrymore), copyright © 1943, 1944 by Gene Fowler, renewed © 1970,
1971 by A. Fowler, G. Fowler, Jr., J.F. Morrison and W. Fowler, is
reprinted by permission of the heirs of Gene Fowler.